Fundamentals of
Operations Management

SECOND CANADIAN EDITION

MARK M. DAVIS
Bentley College

JANELLE HEINEKE
Boston University

JAYDEEP BALAKRISHNAN
University of Calgary

**McGraw-Hill
Ryerson**

Toronto   Montréal   Boston   Burr Ridge, IL   Dubuque, IA   Madison, WI   New York
San Francisco   St. Louis   Bangkok   Bogotá   Caracas   Kuala Lumpur   Lisbon   London
Madrid   Mexico City   Milan   New Delhi   Santiago   Seoul   Singapore   Sydney   Taipei

Fundamentals of Operations Management
Second Canadian Edition

ISBN-13: 978-0-07-096539-3
ISBN-10: 0-07-096539-0

1 2 3 4 5 6 7 8 9 10 VH 0 9 8 7

Printed and bound in the United States

Care has been taken to trace ownership of copyright material contained in this text; however, the publisher will welcome any information that enables them to rectify any reference or credit for subsequent editions.

Editorial Director: *Joanna Cotton*
Publisher: *Lynn Fisher*
Sponsoring Editor: *Rhondda McNabb*
Developmental Editor: *Jennifer Bastarache*
Editorial Associate: *Stephanie Hess*
Supervising Editor: *Graeme Powell*
Copy Editor: *Jim Zimmerman*
Senior Production Coordinator: *Paula Brown*
Cover Design: *Dianna Little*
Cover Image: © *Dugald Bremner/Firstlight*
Interior Design: *Dianna Little*
Page Layout: *S R Nova Pvt Ltd., Bangalore, India*
Printer: *VonHoffman Press, Inc.*

Library and Archives Canada Cataloguing in Publication

Davis, Mark M., 1944–
    Fundamentals of operations management / Mark M. Davis, Janelle Heineke, Jaydeep Balakrishnan. — 2nd Canadian ed.

Includes bibliographical references and index.
ISBN-13: 978-0-07-096539-3
ISBN-10: 0-07-096539-0

1. Production management—Textbooks. I. Heineke, Janelle N. II. Balakrishnan, Jaydeep III. Title. IV. Title: Operations management.

TS155.D2485 2007   658.5   C2006-905553-X

To my wife Cookie and my two sons,
Andy and Alex

—Mark Davis

To my students—and in particular to two long-term
students, my sons, Pat and Doug. I hope I have
been able to help you to learn some things that will
help you in your careers and your lives. I know you
have done that for me!

—Janelle Heineke

To my wife Vineetha, my two sons
Rohil and Aneesh, and my parents

—Jaydeep Balakrishnan

About the Authors

Mark M. Davis Dr. Davis is professor of Operations Management at Bentley College in Waltham, MA. He received his BS degree in Electrical Engineering from Tufts University and his MBA and DBA degrees from Boston University's School of Management. He worked as a manufacturing engineer for the General Electric Company and is a graduate of its Manufacturing Management Program. He was also a programs manager for the U.S. Army Natick Research Laboratories.

Dr. Davis's primary research interest is service operations management with a focus on customer waiting time issues. He has published articles in this area in several journals, including *The Journal of Operations Management*, *Decision Sciences*, *The Journal of Services Marketing*, *The Journal of Business Forecasting*, *OM Review*, *The International Journal of Production and Operations Management*, and *The International Journal of Service Industry Management*.

Dr. Davis is currently vice president of the Decision Sciences Institute and is a past president of the Northeast Decision Sciences Institute. In 2000, he was named a Fellow in the Decision Sciences Institute. In 1998, Dr. Davis received Bentley College's Scholar of the Year Award. He was appointed to the 1996 Board of Examiners for the Malcolm Baldrige National Quality Award. Dr. Davis currently serves on the editorial review board of *The International Journal of Service Industry Management*.

Janelle Heineke Dr. Heineke, joining the book with this edition, is associate professor and chair of the Operations and Technology Department at Boston University. She holds a DBA degree from Boston University, an MBA degree from Babson College, an MSN degree from Boston College, and a BSN degree from Marquette University. Dr. Heineke worked in health care both as a clinician and a manager and, while practicing, held positions as a lecturer and clinical preceptor at Harvard Medical School, Boston College Graduate School of Nursing, and Northeastern University's Physician Assistant program.

Dr. Heineke's research focuses on service operations and quality management. She has published in several journals, including *The Journal of Operations Management*, *California Management Review*, *Quality Management Journal*, *The Services Industries Journal*, *The International Journal of Production and Operations Management*, *The International Journal of Service Industry Management*, *Business Horizons*, *Operations Management Review*, and *Decision Sciences*. She is co-author of three other books, *The Physician-Manager Alliance: Building the Healthy Health Care Organization* (with Stephen Davidson and Marion McCollom), *Games and Exercises for Operations Management: Hands-on Learning Activities for Basic Concepts and Tools* (with Larry Meile), and *Managing Services: Using Technology to Create Value* (with Mark M. Davis) and has contributed chapters and cases to several other books. Dr. Heineke is an associate editor for *The Journal of Operations Management* and is a regular reviewer for several other journals.

Jaydeep Balakrishnan Dr. Balakrishnan is currently an Associate Professor of Operations Management at the Haskayne School of Business, University of Calgary. Dr. Balakrishnan received his doctorate in Operations Management from Indiana University. Prior to this he obtained an MBA at the University of Georgia and an undergraduate degree in Mechanical Engineering from Nagpur University, India.

He has worked for Ashok Leyland Limited, a truck and bus manufacturer in India. He has been a visiting professor in Engineering Management at the Chinese University of Hong Kong, and at the National University of Singapore Business School and has also taught in Warsaw, Vienna and Tehran. Dr. Balakrishnan has served as the President of the Calgary Chapter of the Canadian Operational Research Society and the Calgary chapter of APICS—The Association for Operations Management.

His research interests include facility layout and supply chain management. He has presented papers at various international conferences and his work has been published in reputed journals such as *Management Science*, *Journal of Operations Management*, *European Journal of Operational Research*, *IIE Transactions*, *International Journal of Production Research*, and the *International Journal of Operations and Production Management*. He has also provided seminars to professionals and academics internationally. Dr. Balakrishnan has been a recipient of Natural Sciences and Engineering Research Council (NSERC) grants. He is listed in the *Who's Who in Canadian Business* published by the University of Toronto Press and is also a volunteer soccer coach.

Brief Contents

Bonus Chapters available in PDF format on our Web site at www.mcgrawhill.ca/olc/davis

Contents

Bonus Chapters available in PDF format on our Web site at www.mcgrawhill.ca/olc/davis

WS10 Waiting Line Management
WS17 Human Resource Issues in Operations Management

Preface

Operations management continues to be an evolving discipline. Just as the economies of Canada and other developed countries of the world were once largely dependent on manufacturing for growth, operations management initially focused almost exclusively on manufacturing-related issues. In the last 20 years, however, the field of operations management has changed dramatically. The reasons are many, including: (*a*) the emergence of a truly global economy, (*b*) significant advances in technology, specifically the information economy, and (*c*) the continued growth of services in all of the world's economies, to the point where services now represent a major portion of the economies in the more highly developed countries.

For these same reasons, the fundamentals of managing a business in Canada, in general, have also changed. No longer are the functional areas within a firm seen as being independent from each other; instead they are viewed as being interrelated. As a consequence, operations management cannot be studied in isolation from marketing and finance. Equally important, the study of operations management is no longer confined to manufacturing. Today, operations management also includes services. In addition to the growing importance of services in today's economies, manufacturers are also recognizing the need to provide their customers with high-quality service, which can provide them with a significant advantage in today's highly competitive environment.

A major goal of this second Canadian edition of *Fundamentals of Operations Management* is to reflect the changes that have taken place in business by emphasizing services and the need for manufacturing and services to become more fully integrated to better meet customer requirements. To reinforce this emphasis on services, examples from a wide variety of service organizations have been liberally included to provide students with a link between theory and practice as well as a contemporary view of operations management.

Another goal has been to acknowledge the significant impact of technology on the practice of operations management. Technology, especially information technology, continues to change the ways in which companies do business. And we are seeing only the tip of the iceberg. Technology will continue to advance in the form of faster and more accurate transmission lines, more powerful computers, and larger electronic data storage equipment. At the same time, unit costs in all of these areas will continue to decrease.

In addition, barriers to trade across national borders continue to be lowered with the creation of regional free trade zones such as the European Union (EU), the North American Free Trade Agreement (NAFTA), World Trade Organization (WTO) agreements and the possible creation of a Free Trade Agreement of the Americas (FTAA).

The combination of advances in technology and lower trade barriers has facilitated the world's economies to continue their trend toward a single global village or global landscape. Both customers and suppliers now exist in every corner of the world, with no company being immune to international competition. In such a hypercompetitive environment, it is imperative that managers continue to develop innovative applications for these new technologies as they become available. This ever-changing environment has a significant impact on the operations management function in terms of how goods and services are produced and delivered.

To address these changes, as well as to link theory with practice, this text provides:

- Emphasis on several topics in operations management that are currently high-priority issues with both business and operations managers. These include: new product and service development and the role of technology in operations management (Chapter 3 and S3). Supply chain management (Chapter 12), which addresses both the changing role of the supplier and the fact that supply chains are becoming longer as firms now look to the four corners of the world for suppliers; and yield management (Chapters 14 and 15), which focuses on maximizing capacity utilization and profits in service operations.

- An emphasis on how Canadian companies are successfully applying operations management. The chapter opening vignettes, Operations Management in Practice (OMP) boxes, and other examples are derived from a variety of Canadian businesses to demonstrate that the practice of operations management in Canada is not restricted to certain industries or situations, but is universally applied.

- A pedagogical feature, entitled "Managerial Issues," begins the text in most chapters to provide students with a managerial framework for the topic as well as an understanding of how the topic contributes to the success of the organization.

- Recognition that the operations function in every organization involves individuals and that their role is changing as are the organizations themselves. As part of these changes, there is an increasing emphasis on teamwork (Chapters 4 and W17), and (Supplement 5), and personnel scheduling (Chapter 11).

- Demonstration of how operations management needs to be fully integrated with the other functional areas within an organization, and that many of the operations management tools are being applied in these other functional areas, such as marketing, engineering, and finance. For example, business process analysis can show engineering managers how to accelerate the development and introduction of new products (Chapter 3), and just-in-time (JIT) concepts (Chapter 13) are used to market mass-customized products that can be delivered to customers with minimal delays. These tools and techniques from operations management are also now used in a wide variety of new applications that go far beyond the walls of the traditional factory. As an illustration, quality management tools (Supplement 6) such as statistical process control are now used to predict impending medical problems for patients with asthma or congestive heart failure.

- Some topics that are of importance to operations management, but not widely used in introductory OM courses have been included as downloadable chapters (in PDF) on the book's online learning centre (www.mcgrawhill.ca/olc/davis). Thus, the topic Waiting Line Management, is included as a Web Supplement to Chapter 10. Similarly, Human Resource Issues in Operations Management has been included as stand alone Web Chapter 17.

Our goal is to present these concepts in a brief and interesting way, focusing on core concepts and utilizing quantitative techniques only where necessary, while making the mathematics intuitive and less formal.

Based on the feedback from reviewers and our own thoughts, we have made valuable revisions in this second Canadian edition. First, we have improved and streamlined the text wherever it was felt necessary, naturally with a focus on Canada.

- **Opening Vignettes**—Many of the opening vignettes have been updated. As introductions to each chapter, these are excellent vehicles to discuss important managerial issues that OM can help address.

- **Detailed Solutions**—Recognizing that students (as well as instructors) greatly appreciate detailed explanations of the process for solving quantitative problems, we have revised and expanded the sections on the different problem solution methods.

The solution process is now explained in more detail in a step-by-step procedure, using spreadsheets where necessary. Examples include PERT/CPM diagrams in Chapter 4, designing process layouts in Chapter 8 and ABC analysis in Chapter 15.

- **New and Updated Cases**—To help students apply concepts, more cases have been added and some existing cases have been revised.
- **Updated Exhibits**—Many of the tables, figures, and photos have been updated in the new edition of the text to highlight important concepts visually.
- **Focus on Canada**—Further emphasis has been placed on discussing practical application of OM methods with a focus on Canada with the use of new headings, Operations Management in Practice boxes, and within the text. Specific chapter by chapter changes are as follows:

Chapter	Important Changes/Additions
1	<ul><li>Opening vignette has been revised to discuss the role of OM in aircraft boarding—a service that many students will have had an experience with.</li><li>Revised OMP example emphasizing the use of manufacturing principles in service firms.</li><li>The material on the development of OM in Canada has been revised.</li></ul>
2	<ul><li>The strategy process has been updated with an improved exhibit and more detailed explanation.</li><li>More material has been added on globalization and on the environment.</li></ul>
3	<ul><li>Opening vignette has been revised.</li><li>Material on modularization is introduced in Chapter 3 rather than Chapter 5 since it is a design issue.</li><li>Emphasis is placed on the need for understanding the customer and using human factors in product design through added OMP boxes and text.</li><li>The discussion of Quality Function Deployment (QFD) has been enhanced.</li></ul>
4	<ul><li>PERT/CPM procedure explained in more detail using additional diagrams.</li><li>The short building constriction case has been replaced by a longer and more realistic case on building recreational facilities.</li><li>New text has been added to look at project management within the concept of class projects so that all students can relate.</li><li>Discussion of work breakdown structure (WBS) has been enhanced.</li><li>A section on PERT/CPM in Practice replaces Criticisms of PERT/CPM.</li></ul>
5	<ul><li>Opening vignette has been revised.</li><li>Concept of Value Stream Mapping has been introduced.</li><li>Chapter material has been reorganized for better flow.</li></ul>
6	<ul><li>Material on the dimensions of quality and Six Sigma have been revised.</li></ul>
7	<ul><li>Opening vignette has been revised. It now discusses Toyota's decision to locate in Woodstock, Ontario.</li><li>Sections reorganized for better flow.</li></ul>

Chapter	Important Changes/Additions
8	• Diagrams and photographs that illustrate different types of layouts have been moved to this chapter from Chapter 13 for better flow. • Process layout example is explained in more detail. • A new case on layout based on a real Canadian company has been added. This case also links layout design to product and process design issues discussed in Chapter 3.
9	• Opening vignette has been revised to discuss forecasting at Krispy Kreme.
10	• Opening vignette has been replaced with one on analyzing queues at Vancouver International Airport • New case on queuing in a port has been added as a good example in services. • New case added in Chapter 10 web supplement.
11	• Material has been added on the importance of scheduling in health care. • Johnson's Rule example has been revised to demonstrate its use in practice.
12	• Opening vignette has been revised • Expanded discussion of the evolution of supply chain management added • A more detailed explanation of the importance of the bullwhip effect in supply chain management is included. • Corporate responsibility (environment fair trade purchasing, and counterfeiting) and product design aspects of supply chain management are emphasized.
13	• The chapter material has been reorganized and revised for better flow. • Additional diagrams and OMP included to explain concepts better. • A discussion of the 5S concept has been added.
14	• A new section Aggregate Planning in Practice has been added. • Expanded discussion of the costs of chase plans is included.
15	• The chapter material has been reorganized and revised for better flow. • Additional material on uncertainty and safety stock with new exhibits has been included. • The ABC analysis procedure is explained in more detail using Excel screen shots. • A new case based on a real Canadian company has been added.
16	• The BOM concept is explained using new exhibits. • A new case that extends the case in Chapter 15 to MRP has been added. • A new exhibit has been included to explain DRP.

Specific Objectives of This Book

Most students do not major in operations management. In fact, some Canadian business schools do not even offer a major in operations management. Nevertheless, it is important for you to understand how the operations management function contributes to the overall success of an organization. The reasons are twofold. First, understanding how the different elements within the OM function fit into the overall organizational structure will provide you with a broader perspective that, in turn, will allow you to do your own job better. In addition, as we stated above, the concepts developed initially within the OM function have application in all of the other functional areas within an organization. Understanding and applying these tools and concepts can improve your ability to be both effective and efficient in the way you do your work.

Many students don't appreciate the importance of operations management until after they graduate and begin work. For example, consider the employment area of information technology (IT). Specialists in IT really should have a working knowledge of the best practices in process management, forecasting, quality control, and project planning to correctly apply many of the software tools that they will encounter on the job.

For these reasons, the specific objectives of this book are to:

1. Introduce the various elements that comprise the field of operations management, and some of the new and evolving concepts within OM with an emphasis on their application in Canada.

2. Identify some of the OM tools and concepts that can be applied to a wide variety of situations, including non-OM-related areas.

3. Develop an appreciation of the need for interaction between operations management and the other management functions within an organization.

4. Explain the role of technology in operations management and its impact on the different OM elements.

5. Describe the growing trend toward globalization among firms and how it affects operations management.

6. Demonstrate that manufacturing and services are becoming more integrated within companies.

7. Provide an integrated framework for understanding the field of OM as a whole and its role in an organization.

With respect to the last objective, our goal is to demonstrate that operations management is not just a loosely knit aggregation of tools, but rather a synthesis of concepts and techniques that relate directly to operating systems and enhance their management. This point is important because OM is frequently confused with operations research (OR), management science (MS), and industrial engineering (IE). The critical difference between OM and these fields is this: OM is a field of management, whereas OR and MS are branches of applied mathematics and IE is an engineering discipline. Thus, while operations managers use the tools of OR and MS in decision making, and are concerned with many of the same issues as IE, OM has a distinct business management role that differentiates it from OR, MS, and IE.

Special Features of the Book

In an attempt to facilitate the learning process, we have incorporated several pedagogical features, including

- ***Chapter objectives.*** At the beginning of each chapter, a list of objectives is presented to highlight the important concepts upon which the chapter focuses.

Chapter Objectives

- Illustrate the importance of the development of new products and services to a firm's competitiveness.

- Identify the various types of new products that are developed by companies.

- Introduce the new product design process and the concept of a product's life cycle.

- Demonstrate the necessity of concurrent product and process design as a new product or service is developed.

- Present a framework for understanding how new services are developed and introduced into the marketplace.

- ***Vignettes.*** Each chapter begins with a short vignette that shows how the chapter topic is actually applied in a real-world (most often Canadian) setting, to create student interest for the chapter material.

Strategic Facility Decisions: Location and Capacity

Toyota Chooses Woodstock, Ontario, for its New Assembly Plant

October 11, 2005: Toyota President, Katsuaki Watanabe and Canadian Prime Minister Paul Martin attend the sod-turning ceremony for Toyota's latest planned North American plant in Woodstock, a small town located between Toronto and London. When completed the plant will employ 2000 workers and churn out 200 000 automobiles per year.

What made Woodstock attractive to Toyota? Location and aggregate capacity are major decisions and thus are made on the basis of multiple factors, not cost alone. In the case of Toyota, one factor would have been that Ontario is now the number one jurisdiction for assembling automobiles in North America (a distinction it wrested from Michigan in 2004), with a very strong auto parts industry as well. Besides, southwestern Ontario, along with the geographically proximal U.S. Midwest, traditionally forms the heart of the North American auto indus-

Ontario. As Toyota gears up to attempt to overtake General Motors and become the world's biggest automaker, it will have to rely on its existing plants to train new employees in the new plants in its JIT system which focuses on waste elimination. So having Cambridge nearby was a plus.

Also rural locations close to big cities are ideal since the cost of land is lower than in the city, yet highways make it easy to get parts in and vehicles out to cities such as Toronto, a road, rail, air, and sea transportation hub. In addition, the major North American markets of central Canada and the midwestern, eastern, and south-eastern U.S. are nearby.

It helped that the Ontario government contributed $70 million in incentives to help land the deal and that the federal government chipped in another $55 million. Lobbying by top ministers in Ontario and the federal government (including the Prime Minister) probably helped also.

Another advantage of Woodstock is the many universities and technical institutions nearby from which Toyota can recruit skilled employees. Canada's socialized health system is also a plus since Toyota won't be burdened as much by employee health care costs as it would be in the United States. Furthermore, general liberalization of trade rules means that Toyota can take advantage of a good location in Canada and

Application of OM concepts. Examples of how many of the OM concepts presented in this text are applied in actual business situations are provided throughout the text. The use of real-world examples reinforces the critical role of operations management, showing how it contributes to the overall success of an organization. These applications take several forms, including the opening vignette to each chapter and the Operations Management in Practice boxes, as well as the numerous examples that are included throughout the text itself. Again we emphasize the application of these concepts within a Canadian setting.

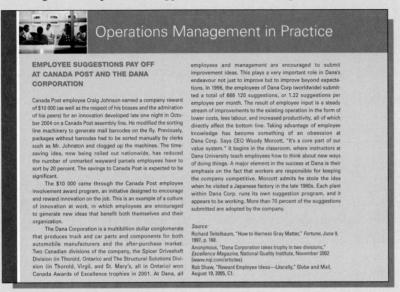

Operations Management in Practice

EMPLOYEE SUGGESTIONS PAY OFF AT CANADA POST AND THE DANA CORPORATION

Canada Post employee Craig Johnson earned a company reward of $10 000 (as well as the respect of his bosses and the admiration of his peers) for an innovation developed late one night in October 2004 on a Canada Post assembly line. He modified the sorting line machinery to generate mail barcodes on the fly. Previously, packages without barcodes had to be sorted manually by clerks such as Mr. Johnston and clogged up the machines. The time-saving idea, now being rolled out nationwide, has reduced the number of unmarked wayward parcels employees have to sort by 20 percent. The savings to Canada Post is expected to be significant.

The $10 000 came through the Canada Post employee involvement award program, an initiative designed to encourage and reward innovation on the job. This is an example of a culture of innovation at work, in which employees are encouraged to generate new ideas that benefit both themselves and their organization.

The Dana Corporation is a multibillion dollar conglomerate that produces truck and car parts and components for both automobile manufacturers and the after-purchase market. Two Canadian divisions of the company, the Spicer Driveshaft Division (in Thorold, Ontario) and The Structural Solutions Division (in Thorold, Virgil, and St. Mary's, all in Ontario) won Canada Awards of Excellence trophies in 2001. At Dana, all employees and management are encouraged to submit improvement ideas. This plays a very important role in Dana's endeavour not just to improve but to improve beyond expectations. In 1996, the employees of Dana Corp (worldwide) submitted a total of 666 120 suggestions, or 1.22 suggestions per employee per month. The result of employee input is a steady stream of improvements to the existing operation in the form of lower costs, less labour, and increased productivity, all of which directly affect the bottom line. Taking advantage of employee knowledge has become something of an obsession at Dana Corp. Says CEO Woody Morcott, "It's a core part of our value system." It begins in the classroom, where instructors at Dana University teach employees how to think about new ways of doing things. A major element in the success at Dana is their emphasis on the fact that workers are responsible for keeping the company competitive. Morcott admits he stole the idea when he visited a Japanese factory in the late 1980s. Each plant within Dana Corp. runs its own suggestion program, and it appears to be working. More than 70 percent of the suggestions submitted are adopted by the company.

Source:
Richard Teitelbaum, "How to Harness Gray Matter," *Fortune*, June 9, 1997, p. 168.
Anonymous, "Dana Corporation takes trophy in two divisions," *Excellence Magazine*, National Quality Institute, November 2002 (www.nqi.com/articles).
Rob Shaw, "Reward Employee Ideas—Literally," Globe and Mail, August 19, 2005, C1.

Internet exercises. The Internet continues to be a powerful tool for obtaining and disseminating information, and this information is constantly changing. Where appropriate, an Internet exercise is provided at the end of a chapter to encourage students to obtain the latest information on a particular topic. From the *Fundamentals of Operations Management* Web site, www.mcgrawhill.ca/olc/davis, students will find direct links to the Web sites included in these exercises.

Application of Microsoft® Excel® spreadsheets. Again, where appropriate, examples are provided using Microsoft® Excel® spreadsheets that encourage the student to explore alternative solutions.

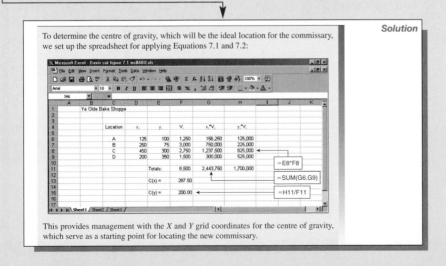

Solution

To determine the centre of gravity, which will be the ideal location for the commissary, we set up the spreadsheet for applying Equations 7.1 and 7.2:

This provides management with the *X* and *Y* grid coordinates for the centre of gravity, which serve as a starting point for locating the new commissary.

Managerial Issues. This feature provides students with a managerial framework for the topic as well as an understanding of how the topic contributes to the success of the organization.

Managerial Issues

In Chapter 15 we discussed the inventory management of items that are considered to have independent demand, generally end items such as appliances or automobiles. In this chapter we discuss the inventory management of components that go into the manufacturing of these end items. Although some of the models used in Chapter 15 can be used for managing some components, others cannot. This chapter introduces new methods for managing the inventory and production schedule of components and subassemblies. Furthermore, because each end item may have thousands of components, the use of a computerized system is necessary. Thus, not only do we have inventory management issues, we also have data processing and system implementation and management issues.

Highlighting links with other functional areas. Ideas and processes flow seamlessly across traditional functional boundaries in successful organizations, often to the point where it is practically impossible to determine where one function leaves off and another begins. To emphasize this integration within organizations, icons are used throughout the text to highlight examples of how OM is linked to other functional areas.

Global perspective. Another feature of the book is its emphasis on the global impact of operations today; where appropriate, we show how the concepts apply in a global context. Special icons are used in the book to highlight this area.

Margin definitions. Key terms are in boldface when first defined and definitions added in the margin. At the end of the chapter these key terms are listed with page numbers for quick student reference.

Examples with solutions. Examples follow quantitative topics and demonstrate specific procedures and techniques. These are clearly set off from the text and help students understand the computations.

Example

Find the economic order quantity and the reorder point, given the following data:

$$\text{Annual demand } (D) = 1000 \text{ units}$$
$$\text{Order preparation cost } (S) = \$5.00 \text{ per order}$$
$$\text{Holding cost } (H) = \$1.25 \text{ per unit per year}$$
$$\text{Cost per unit } (C) = \$12.50$$
$$\text{Lead time } (\bar{L}) = 5 \text{ days (constant)}$$
$$\text{Daily demand } (\bar{d}) = 1000/365 \text{ (constant)}$$

What quantity should be ordered, and when?

Solution

The optimal order quantity is

$$\text{EOQ} = \sqrt{\frac{2DS}{H}} = \sqrt{\frac{2(1000)5}{1.25}} = \sqrt{8000} = 89.4 \text{ units}$$

The reorder point is

$$R = \bar{d}\bar{L} = \frac{1000}{365}(5) = 13.7 \text{ units}$$

Rounding to the nearest unit, the inventory policy is as follows: When the number of units in inventory drops to 14, place an order for 89 more units.

The total annual cost will be

$$TC = DC + \frac{D}{Q}S + \frac{Q}{2}H$$

$$= 1000(12.50) + \frac{1000}{89}(5) + \frac{89}{2}(1.25)$$

$$= \$12611.81$$

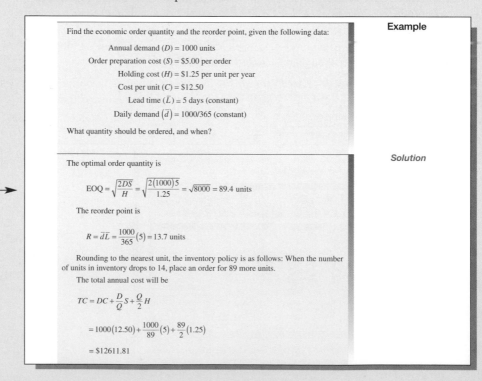

- **_Formula review._** Key formulas and equations are numbered within each of the more quantitative chapters and are repeated in summary form at the end of those chapters for easy student review.

- **_Solved problems._** Representative example problems are included at the end of appropriate chapters. Each includes a detailed, worked-out solution and provides another level of support for students before they try homework problems on their own.

- **_Review and discussion questions._** These questions allow students to review the chapter concepts before attempting the problems and provide a basis for classroom discussion.

- **_Problems._** A wide range of problem material follows each chapter, asking students to solve realistic, interesting problems.

- **_Cases._** Located at the end of most chapters, short cases allow students to think critically about issues discussed in the chapter. These also can provide good classroom discussions or provide a capstone problem for the chapter. We've included both long and short cases.

 Merdeka Gas Grills: Inventory and Supply Chain Management

Merdeka manufactures premium gas grills for the North American market. Its gas grills require over 30 separate components, ranging from the relatively expensive bowl, lid, and burner (unit costs greater than $50), down to the many low unit cost (less than $1) items such as grill clips and screws. All Merdeka models use common low unit cost components which can be purchased from any industrial supply company.

Merdeka uses an integrated business system (ERP) software package to manage its purchasing, sales, inventory and production management, and accounting functions. Excited by the information and control the software can provide, Merdeka entered into the computer system as an item every single component required for its gas grills. Furthermore, by having shop floor staff enter into the system the quantity consumed of every component used during the assembly process, the computer system keeps constant track of on-hand inventory of every component. Purchasing staff then print inventory reordering reports each morning and compare on-hand inventory to previously calculated reorder points to determine if a purchase order needs to be prepared.

In an effort to keep material costs down, Merdeka's purchasing department has identified multiple suppliers for each component. When an order for a component is required, a buyer contacts potential suppliers requesting a quotes, then orders from the supplier that quotes the lowest unit cost. By using various suppliers for each component, with each supplier having various delivery lead times, Merdeka maintains a significant safety stock on each component to buffer this delivery variability.

Once a year, production shuts down for a two-day inventory count of all components. After the year-end count is entered, discrepancies between the actual physical inventory and the on-hand quantity in the computer system are corrected (they typically range from a 10% to 15% quantity loss for each individual component). Recognizing this

Superior Service

Service takes on a whole new meaning with McGraw-Hill Ryerson and *Fundamentals of Operations Management*. More than just bringing you the textbook, we have consistently raised the bar in terms of innovation and educational research. These investments in learning and the academic community have helped us understand the needs of students and educators across the country and allowed us to foster the growth of truly innovative, integrated learning.

Integrated Learning

Your Integrated Learning Sales Specialist is a McGraw-Hill Ryerson representative who has the experience, product knowledge, training, and support to help you assess and integrate any of our products, technology, and services into your course for optimum teaching and learning performance. Whether it is using our test bank software, helping your students improve their grades, or putting your entire course online, your *i*Learning Sales Specialist is there to help you do it. Contact your local *i*Learning Sales Specialist today to learn how to maximize all of McGraw-Hill Ryerson's resources!

iLearning Services

McGraw-Hill Ryerson offers a unique *i*Services package designed for Canadian faculty. Our mission is to equip providers of higher education with superior tools and resources required for excellence in teaching. For additional information, visit www.mcgrawhill.ca/highereducation/iservices.

Teaching, Technology & Learning Conference Series

The educational environment has changed tremendously in recent years, and McGraw-Hill Ryerson continues to be committed to helping you acquire the skills you need to succeed in this new milieu. Our innovative Teaching, Technology & Learning Conference Series brings faculty together from across Canada with 3M Teaching Excellence award winners to share teaching and learning best practices in a collaborative and stimulating environment. Pre-conference workshops on general topics, such as teaching large classes and technology integration, are also offered. We will also work with you at your own institution to customize workshops that best suit the needs of your faculty at your institution.

Research Reports on Technology and Student Success in Higher Education

These landmark reports, undertaken in conjunction with academic and private sector advisory boards, are the result of research studies into the challenges professors face in helping students succeed and the opportunities that new technology presents to impact teaching and learning.

Comprehensive Teaching and Learning Package

We have developed a number of supplements for both teaching and learning to accompany this text:

Student Online Learning Centre (OLC)

The Online Learning Centre, prepared by Jackie Shemko of Durham College, at www.mcgrawhill.ca/olc/davis, offers online quizzes, Microsoft® Excel® templates, chapter objectives, a searchable glossary, interactive OM Exercises, short video clips, access to the OM Centre, and other robust aids for student learning and exploration.

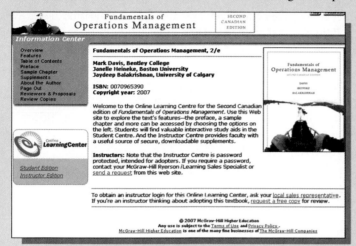

Operations Management Centre (OMC)

This site supports students and faculty in search of resources related to all aspects of operations management. The site covers OM resources by topic, contains links to the "top 50" company tours, offers Internet-published articles and business news, and lists OM publications and organizations. The site also contains selected articles from *Business Week* that are available exclusively to users of the site, as well as links to many other McGraw-Hill operations management resources. To explore, link to the OMC from the Online Learning Centre at www.mcgrawhill.ca/olc/davis.

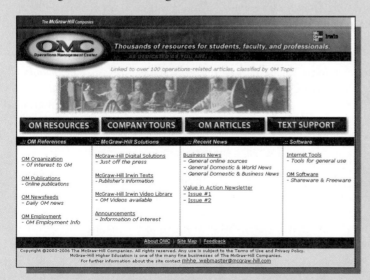

Instructor's Online Learning Centre (OLC)

The Online Learning Centre, at www.mcgrawhill.ca/olc/davis includes a password-protected Web site for instructors and offers downloadable supplements and access to PageOut, the McGraw-Hill Ryerson Web site development centre, as well as a host of tools for students and instructors alike to use in the classroom or at home.

Instructor's Resource CD-ROM

Instructor's Resource CD-ROM is an all-in-one resource offered to adopters of the text. It contains the Instructor's Manual, Computerized Test Bank, and Microsoft® PowerPoint® slides (described below), as well as video clips, all text exhibits, and Excel® templates.

- *Instructor's Manual*, prepared by the authors includes answers to discussion and review questions and solutions to text problems. There is a useful reference grid showing which problems correspond to specific topics in the chapters for ease in assignment.

- *Computerized Test Bank*, prepared by Rob Shepherd, Niagara College, provides true/false, multiple/choice, and narrative problems for each chapter. A computerized testing package is available, allowing instructors to generate, add, and edit questions; save and reload tests; and select questions based on type or level of difficulty.

- *Microsoft® PowerPoint® Presentation Slides*, prepared by Carl Persaud, Algonquin College, provide lecture outlines plus graphic material from the text to complement and customize lectures.

Video Library

The McGraw-Hill OM Video Series includes professionally developed videotapes showing students real applications of key manufacturing and service topics. Each tape or DVD contains plant tours to help students see how companies are using operations management concepts and techniques to be productive and competitive. For full descriptions of all 12 volumes, visit www.mcgrawhill.ca/olc/davis.

Course Management

PageOut

McGraw-Hill Ryerson's course management system, PageOut, is the easiest way to create a Web site for your *Operations Management* course. There is no need for HTML coding, graphic design, or a thick how-to book. Just fill in a series of boxes in plain English and click on one of our professional designs. In no time, your course is online!

For the integrated instructor, we offer *Fundamentals of Operations Management* content for complete online courses. Whatever your needs, you can customize the *Fundamentals of Operations Management* Online Learning Centre content and author your own online course materials. It is entirely up to you. You can offer online discussion and message boards that will complement your office hours, and reduce the lines outside your door. Content cartridges are also available for course management systems, such as **WebCT** and **Blackboard**. Ask your *i*Learning Sales Specialist for details.

We also have tried to practise what we preach. In applying the quality concept of continuous improvement, we have attempted to incorporate many of the suggestions made by our reviewers.

There is an old Chinese proverb that states, "May you live in interesting times." Like it or not, from an operations management perspective, those "times" are now and we should take full advantage of the opportunity—and enjoy it while doing so!

Acknowledgments

Although only three names appear on the cover of this book, a project of this magnitude could not be successfully completed without the assistance and co-operation of many individuals. Specifically, we would like to thank the reviewers for their contribution to the second Canadian edition and for their manuscript reviews. We thank them for their suggestions and comments. They include:

Todd Boyle, St. Francis Xavier University

Lloyd Clive, Fleming College

Liming Dai, University of Regina

Mary Drane, Seneca College

Cyril Foropon, University of Manitoba

Jim Kealey, Seneca College

Sam Lampropoulos, George Brown College

Marcel Lopez, University of New Brunswick

Ron McLachlin, University of Manitoba

Les Miscampbell, Centennial College

Mahesh Nagarajan, University of British Columbia

Ragu Nayak, Centennial College

Carl Persaud, Algonquin College

Rob Shepherd, Niagara College

The authors are thankful to Giovani da Silveira, Janice Bodnarchuk, Brent Snider, Tim Sweet, Todd Bowman, and Rob Isaac of the Haskayne School of Business for their help with reviewing some of the chapters and concepts in the second Canadian edition. The support of Bonnie Walter and Bonnie Ressler Administrative Assistants in Operations Management, the Haskayne School of Business, colleagues, and the National Sciences and Engineering Research Council of Canada (NSERC) is also gratefully acknowledged. Jaydeep Balakrishnan would also like to thank the National University of Singapore Business School where he was on sabbatical during the revision of this textbook.

Finally we wish to thank the staff at McGraw-Hill Ryerson for their support, encouragement, and assistance: Lynn Fisher, Publisher; Rhondda McNabb, Sponsoring Editor; Jennifer Bastarache, Developmental Editor; Graeme Powell, Supervising Editor; Jim Zimmerman, Copy Editor; and Joy Armitage Taylor, Marketing Manager.

Mark M. Davis
Janelle Heineke
Jaydeep Balakrishnan

1

Introduction to Operations Management

Chapter Objectives

- Introduce and define operations management (OM) in terms of its contribution to an organization and the activities it involves.

- Describe how operations management contributes to the overall betterment of society.

- Present operations management as a function that addresses issues in both manufacturing and services.

- Show how operations management is gaining more recognition both internally and externally to an organization.

- Demonstrate how the operations management function interacts with the other functional areas within an organization.

- Present a brief history of operations management internationally and in Canada and its evolution to its current role in an organization.

Operations Help You Get Seated on Your Flight More Smoothly

You have probably experienced waiting in line at the gate to board an airplane. You may also recall that the gate attendant, after first boarding passengers with special needs, probably boarded passengers depending on their seat numbers. Those passengers seated at the back of the plane are boarded first so they will not get in the way of others. Have you ever wondered whether there is a better way?

There definitely is a better way, according to Clive Beddoe, CEO of Calgary-based WestJet Airlines Ltd. After trying different methods, he was convinced that the best way to board passengers is to do so randomly. The reason, according to Mr. Beddoe, is that even when boarding is done by rows it doesn't account for passengers with complications such as a big overcoat or big bag blocking others. Interestingly, WestJet hit upon this method when a boarding gate attendant as a joke decided to board passengers by the colour of their socks. This created a random order which WestJet discovered to be the most effective.

Air Canada, however still feels that the best way to ensure smooth boarding is to give priority to passengers at the back of the plane. United Airlines boards passengers seated at window seats first, then those

Source: www.bigfoto.com.

seated in the middle, and finally passengers seated at the aisle. United feels that this method reduces boarding times on average by four to five minutes and save US$1 million annually. America West uses what it calls a "reverse pyramid" whereby passengers with window seats in the middle and rear of the plane are boarded first and those with aisle seats in the front are boarded last.

Every business, whether in manufacturing or services, uses processes or operations to take inputs and create outputs that satisfy customers. In the case of an airline, the boarding process is just one of the many processes it uses. Some processes, such as boarding, are used frequently; others, such as route scheduling and fleet planning, are used less frequently. Managing all these operations effectively can be the difference between success and failure for a business. Herein lies the importance of operations management. As the boarding example above shows, there often are different ways of doing things. One way may be more appropriate to one situation; another way may be better in a different situation. Operations management allows the decision maker to analyze processes and improve them by selecting appropriate strategies and methods.

Like other functions, operations management also involves evaluating trade-offs. For example, at Vancouver International Airport, WestJet is able to load passengers through front and back doors at the same time. This requires an additional jetway to the plane. Managers have to evaluate whether this additional investment is justified by improved efficiencies and increased customer satisfaction from quicker aircraft turnarounds.

Sources:

Brent Jang, "Best boarding rules are no rules, Beddoe says," *The Globe and Mail*, November 4, 2005, B1.

Nicholas Zamiska, "Plane geometry: Scientists help speed boarding of aircraft; America West saves minutes with 'reverse pyramid'; Link to Relativity Theory," *The Wall Street Journal*, November 2, 2005, A21.

Managerial Issues

Today's operations managers, those responsible for producing and delivering the goods and services that we use every day, face a wide variety of challenges in the twenty-first century. The highly competitive business environment that currently exists, caused in large part by the globalization of the world's economies in conjunction with the growth in e-commerce, has shifted the balance of power from the producers to the consumers. As a result, consumers are now demanding increased value for their money. To put it simply, they want more for less.

From an operations management perspective this means providing continuously higher-quality products with shorter delivery times and better customer service while simultaneously reducing labour and material costs and increasing the utilization of existing facilities—all of which translates into higher productivity.

To accomplish all of this, operations managers are turning to a wide variety of technologies. These include the use of robotics on assembly lines and automation, which can take the form of ATMs and vending machine purchases with cell phones. In the forefront is the increasing use of information technology, driven by an improved telecommunications infrastructure, which also is providing faster service at lower costs. Examples here include the Internet and customer support centres, which now can be located in any corner of the world.

Firms that ignore the important role of operations management within an organization pay a price: failure, as evidenced by the many dot-com bankruptcies that have occurred in recent years. Many of these firms were virtual in every sense. All they had were Web sites with no operational infrastructure to support them. (This can be compared to putting up wallpaper without having a wall behind it!) Stories abound of Christmas shoppers who could not get deliveries on time (and couldn't even speak to someone about the problem) and virtual banks that were incapable of providing customers with something as simple as deposit slips. In every case, these customers took their business elsewhere as a result of their bad experience, never to return.

What Is Operations Management?

An Organizational Perspective

operations management

Management of the conversion process that transforms inputs such as raw material and labour into outputs in the form of finished goods and services.

Operations are what must be done internally in order to deliver value to the customer, whether in goods or services.[1] Thus, from an organizational perspective, **operations management** may be defined as the management of direct resources that are required to produce and deliver value via the organization's goods and services. Every function in the organization—whether marketing, finance and accounting, production, purchasing, or human resources—adds value to the customer. Keep in mind as you read through this textbook that operations management concepts can be used productively in every function of the organization.

Operations management, just as every functional area within an organization, can be defined from several perspectives: one with respect to its overall role and contribution within an organization; another focusing more on the day-to-day activities that fall within its area of responsibility.

Within the operations function, management decisions can be divided into three broad areas:

- Strategic (long-range) decisions
- Tactical (medium-range) decisions
- Operational planning and control (short-range) decisions

These three areas can be viewed as a top-down (hierarchical) approach to operations management, with the decisions made at the lower level(s) depending on those made at the higher level(s).

---

[1] Robert S. Kaplan and David P. Norton. *Strategy Maps* (Boston: Harvard Business School Press, 2004).

LETTERS FROM TWO MBA STUDENTS AT THE UNIVERSITY OF CALGARY

... the ever-increasing cost of delivering health care along with government funding constraints has resulted in challenges in managing the tension between those administering care to patients i.e., doctors and nurses, and the managers running hospitals as organizations.

Among the many facets of health care delivery that requires [*sic*] a critical re-evaluation, the processes used to deliver care certainly come to mind. Why do some patients wait for up to 3–4 hours before seeing a doctor with whom they had an appointment? Why do some patients get laboratory or imaging results a week after the test is performed, when the results often are available the same day? Why do hospitals work full throttle from Monday to Friday, 8 a.m. to 5 p.m., and continue at half speed (if that) after 5 p.m. or on the weekend?

It would be too easy (and erroneous by the way) to blame the doctors and nurses for these inexplicable shortcomings. The challenge in how health care is delivered is a more fundamental one, doctors and nurses just work the best they can in the systems they are provided with. Operations management provides the tools to start analyzing and subsequently optimizing the fundamental structures upon which health care delivery is build. Concepts such as process selection, total quality management, statistical quality control, capacity planning, facility layout, and scheduling, just to name a few, have the potential to modernize health care delivery in a manner that will allow health care providers to provide true medical excellence, as expected by the public.

Max J. Coppes, MD, PhD

I thought my management accounting background would be all I needed when I became a business analyst, but within weeks I found myself re-reading my old operations management textbook.

In order to understand how the business operated, I was forced to learn about the information system the business used. I was initially shocked at how much operations management stuff was in the software, and that it actually was being extensively used.

Working now as a business consultant, an understanding of operations management has proven invaluable in working with various product and service organizations. It seems that regardless of the type or size of business, some form of operations management is always a part of it.

Please share this with your current students—effort put into an operations management course will pay off regardless of what role they will eventually play in an organization. At the very least, it will prevent them from having to re-read their textbook like I did.

Brent Snider, BComm, CMA

The strategic issues usually are very broad in nature, addressing such questions as:

- How will we make the product?
- Where should we locate the facility or facilities?
- How much capacity do we need?
- When should we add more capacity?

Consequently, by necessity, the time frame for strategic decisions typically is very long, usually several years or more, depending on the specific industry.

Operations management decisions at the strategic level impact the long-range effectiveness of the company in terms of how well it can address the needs of its customers. Thus, for the firm to succeed, these decisions must be closely aligned with the corporate strategy. Decisions made at the strategic level then define the fixed conditions or constraints under which the firm must operate in both the intermediate and short term. For example, a decision made at the strategic level to increase capacity by building a new plant becomes a capacity constraint with respect to tactical and operational decisions.

At the next level in the decision-making process, tactical planning primarily addresses the issue of how to efficiently schedule material and labour over a specific time horizon and within the constraints of the strategic decisions that were previously made. Thus, some of the OM issues at this level are:

- How many workers do we need?
- When do we need them?

Exhibit 1.1

**Hierarchy of
Operations
Decisions and
Operations
Management
Topics**

Type of Planning	Typical Issues (and related chapters in this textbook)
Strategic	Facility location and capacity (Chapter 7), process selection (Chapter 3), supply chain structure (Chapter 12)
Tactical	Aggregate planning (Chapter 14), quality and process improvement (Chapters 5, 6, and 13), material requirements (Chapter 16), layout (Chapter 8)
Operational	Daily scheduling of employees and machines (Chapter 11), inventory control (Chapter 15), quality control (Chapter 6)

- Should we work overtime or put on a second shift?
- When should we have material delivered?
- Should we have a finished goods inventory?

These tactical decisions, in turn, define the operating constraints under which the operational planning and control decisions are made.

Management decisions with respect to operational planning and control are very narrow and short term, by comparison. For example, issues at this level include:

- Which jobs do we work on today or this week?
- To whom do we assign which tasks?
- Which jobs have priority?

Exhibit 1.1 relates some of the topics covered in the textbook relating to the hierarchy of operations decisions. Not all topics are exclusive to one category. For example, Chapter 15 discusses inventory management. Although the decision to have a finished goods inventory is a tactical one, the decision to place an order to replenish finished good stock when the stock is low is a operational one.

Exhibit 14.1 in Chapter 14 gives an overview of the different operations planning activities.

An Operational Perspective

The day-to-day activities within the operations management function focus on adding value to the organization through a **transformation process** (as illustrated in Exhibit 1.2), sometimes referred to as the *technical core,* especially in manufacturing organizations. Some examples of the different types of transformations are:

**transformation
process**

Actual conversion of
inputs into outputs.

- Physical, as in manufacturing
- Locational, as in transportation
- Exchange, as in retailing

Exhibit 1.2

**The
Transformation
Process
within OM**

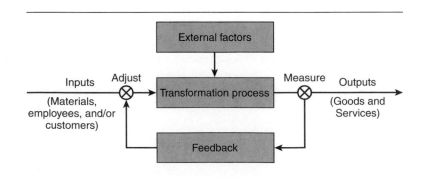

Exhibit 1.3

Input–Transformation–Output Relationships for Typical Systems			
System	**Inputs**	**Primary Transformation Function(s)**	**Typical Desired Output**
Hospital	Patients, medical supplies, MDs, nurses, equipment	Health care (physiological)	Healthy individuals
Restaurant	Hungry customers, food, chef, waitstaff, environment	Well-prepared food, well served; agreeable environment (physical and exchange)	Satisfied customers
Automobile factory	Sheet steel, engine parts, tools, equipment, workers	Fabrication and assembly of cars (physical)	High-quality cars
College or university	High school graduates, books, teachers, classrooms	Imparting knowledge and skills (informational)	Educated individuals
Department store	Shoppers, stock of goods, displays, salesclerks	Attract shoppers, promote products, fill orders (exchange)	Sales to satisfied customers
Distribution centre	Stockkeeping units (SKU), storage bins, stockpickers	Storage and redistribution	Fast delivery, availability of SKUs

- Storage, as in warehousing
- Physiological, as in health care
- Informational, as in telecommunications

The inputs are customers and/or materials which undergo the transformation. Also part of the transformation process are a variety of components supplied by the organization, such as labour, equipment, and facilities, which convert the inputs into outputs. Every transformation process is affected by external factors, which are outside the control of management. External factors include random, unexpected events such as natural disasters, economic cycles, changes in government policies and laws, as well as changes in consumer preferences and tastes. These external factors can also include anticipated changes, such as seasonality, over which management has little or no control.

Another important role of the operations management function is the measurement and control of the transformation process. This consists of monitoring the outputs in various ways, including quality and quantity, and then using this information as feedback to make the necessary adjustments that will improve the process.

The various transformations that take place are not mutually exclusive. For example, a department store can (a) allow shoppers to compare prices and quality (informational), (b) hold items in inventory until needed (storage), and (c) sell goods (exchange). Exhibit 1.3 presents sample input–transformation–output relationships for a wide variety of processes. Note that only the direct components are listed; a more complete system description would also include managerial and support functions.

Operations Management's Contributions to Society

Operations management plays an important, although not always obvious, role in the societies in which we live. It is responsible for the food we eat and even the table on which we eat it; it provides us with the clothing we wear and with transportation, whether in the form of an automobile, train, or airplane, as well as being responsible for making these vehicles themselves. In other words, operations management affects nearly all aspects of our day-to-day activities.

Exhibit 1.4

International Manufacturing Productivity (1980–2000)

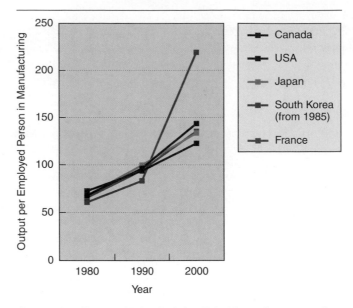

Source: News (Bureau of Labor Statistics, United States Department of Labor, February 26, 2003).

Higher Standard of Living

A major factor in raising the standard of living in a society is the ability to increase its productivity. (Productivity, which can be broadly defined as how efficiently inputs are converted into outputs, is discussed in greater detail in Chapter 5.) Higher productivity is the result of increased efficiency in operations, which in turn translates into lower-cost goods and services. Thus, higher productivity provides consumers with more discretionary income, which contributes to their higher standard of living. As seen in Exhibit 1.4, Canada was a leader in manufacturing output per employee, a measure of productivity, in 1980. However, in the past two decades we have slipped relative to our competitors, so that by 2000 we lagged behind the others. This has implications for our competitiveness relative to other countries and can lead to loss of jobs and a decline in our standard of living.

Better Quality Goods and Services

One of the many consumer benefits of increased competition is the higher-quality products that are available today. Quality standards are continuously increasing. Many companies today, as we will learn in Chapter 6, have established six-sigma quality standards (pioneered by Motorola in the late 1980s), which means no more than 3.4 defects per million opportunities. Such high-quality standards were once considered not only prohibitively expensive, but also virtually impossible to achieve even if cost wasn't a consideration. Today we know that such high-quality standards not only are possible, but they also result in lower costs, because firms no longer have large amounts of waste and rework to deal with.

One example of increasing quality is the focus on safety in automobiles. Honda Motor Co. voluntarily displays crash-test scores on the window stickers of its 2006 models. The company sees its product safety ratings as giving it an edge in the competitive auto industry.

Not only is operations management important in producing better quality goods and services, it also plays a vital role in ensuring that products and services (such as the Apple IPod or Dell computers) are designed and delivered, and if necessary customized, to customer specifications, in a timely manner.

Excellent quality is not limited to goods. Many Canadian for-profit companies, such as Telus in telecommunications and Amex Canada in financial services, as well as not-for-profit organizations such as government departments and educational institutions, have won national awards for the quality of their services (these are discussed further in Chapter 6).

Concern for the Environment

Many companies today are taking up the challenge to produce environmentally friendly products with environmentally friendly processes, all of which falls under the purview of operations management.

Even Canadian companies in industries that have traditionally been considered unfriendly to the environment have committed themselves to being environmentally friendly. Edmonton-based EPCOR is the first utility in Canada to have all its generating plants meet the internationally recognized standard for Environmental Management Systems—ISO 14001 (ISO standards are discussed further in Chapter 6)—and is currently in the process of certifying its distribution and transmission operations as well.[2] Forestry companies across the country, such as Vancouver's Canfor[3] and Montreal's Domtar,[4] are already ISO certified or are moving in that direction, with regards to forest lands and mills. Many companies are also taking steps toward energy efficiency and water conservation. Canada reiterated its commitment as a country to reducing greenhouse gases when it ratified the Kyoto Protocol in 2002.

Ford's new River Rouge manufacturing plant in Detroit provides another good example. No longer will raw waste be dumped into the waterways or the air be polluted with smoke from its operations. Vegetation will be used to clean up contaminated land, and the River Rouge will be restored so that fish will have access to the upper part of the river.[5] Given the location of this plant near Windsor, Ontario, the cleanup will have a beneficial effect for southwestern Ontario also.

Improved Working Conditions

Managers recognize the benefits of providing workers with better working conditions. This includes not only the work environment, but also the design of the jobs themselves. Workers are now encouraged to participate in improving operations by making suggestions. After all, who would know better how to do a particular operation than the person who does it every day? Managers have also learned that there is a very clear relationship between satisfied workers and satisfied customers, especially in service operations.

Organizations also are recognizing the importance of corporate responsibility in their supply chains, especially with regard to suppliers in developing countries. This ensures that employees in supplier companies have acceptable working conditions and human rights.

---

[2]Epcor, www.epcor.com.
[3]Canfor Corporation, www.canfor.com.
[4]Domtar Inc., www.domtar.com.
[5]John Holusha, "Ford Thinks Green for Historic River Rouge Plant," *The New York Times*, November 26, 2000, p. 11.7.

The Emergence of Operations Management

Operations management has been gaining increased recognition in recent years for several reasons, including (*a*) the application of OM concepts in service operations, (*b*) an expanded definition of quality, (*c*) the introduction of OM concepts to other functional areas such as marketing and human resources, and (*d*) the realization that the OM function can add value to the end product.

Application of OM to Service Operations

Initially, the application of operations management concepts was narrowly focused, concentrating almost entirely on manufacturing. However, as shown in Exhibit 1.5, as countries become more developed, services represent a larger percentage of their respective Gross Domestic Products (GDPs). Henri De Castries, CEO of French insurance giant AXA, illustrated how important operations management has become in services when he said, "We have to increase productivity in our factories. The first to understand that financial services are an industrial business will be the winners."[6] (Also see OM in Practice box on service providers, p. 11).

The growth in services over time (see Exhibit 1.6) combined with the increased recognition that services could learn much from manufacturing and vice versa, expanded the application of operations management to also address related issues in services.

Theodore Levitt of Harvard Business School, in his article, "Production-Line Approach to Service,"[7] was one of the first to recognize that many of the concepts that previously had been developed for manufacturing could actually be applied to service operations. He observed that operations concepts can be seen readily at McDonald's fast-food outlets (where hamburgers are cooked in batches of 12 at a time) or at the Shouldice Hospital (see case at the end of Chapter 7) where patients are batched into groups of thirty to increase efficiency.

Exhibit 1.5

Services as a Percentage of Gross Domestic Product (GDP) for Different Countries

Country	Services as a Percentage of GDP
Industrialized Countries:	
United States	80%
United Kingdom	73%
France	70%
Canada	66%
Japan	63%
Lesser Developed Countries:	
Brazil	50%
Thailand	49%
Peru	45%
India	45%
Ghana	30%

Source: The World Factbook 2000, Central Intelligence Agency, Washington, DC.

---

[6]Charles Fleming and Thomas Kamm, "AXA's CEO Set to Push Synergies," *The Wall Street Journal,* May 3, 2000, p. A21.

[7]Theodore Levitt, "Production-Line Approach to Service," *Harvard Business Review* 50, no. 5 (September–October 1972), pp. 41–52.

SERVICE PROVIDERS INCREASE OPERATIONS EFFECTIVENESS AND PROFITABILITY BY ADOPTING PRINCIPLES FROM MANUFACTURING

According to McKinsey, one of the leading global consulting companies, many executives in service companies are looking to adopt methods and tools used by manufacturers to increase the effectiveness of operations. One of these companies is AXA, the well-known French insurance giant. The insurance industry that traditionally relied on investments for profitability is realizing in these days of lower market returns that effective operations management is key in maintaining profitability.

Some of the manufacturing-originated tools that AXA uses include six sigma in quality and productivity improvement, benchmarking to compare processes against others within the company, and cost modelling. Cost modelling includes improving costing by identifying fixed and variable costs with the goal of reducing some of them. Just as in manufacturing, the goal is for employees to understand what a process is, how to analyze it,

and improve it. As in manufacturing, this includes reducing the time required to develop a new insurance or financial product and launch it before AXA's competitors in order to gain an advantage. So far AXA has seen encouraging results from the implementation of these tools.

Service managers are also realizing that the concept of a bottleneck, a key consideration in managing manufacturing operations, is equally applicable to services. For example, Dr. Plaxton, chief of critical care medicine at Grand River Hospital in Kitchener, Ontario, calls the ER wait time "the most visible barometer of any hospital's inner machinery." But he also understands that this wait time depends on the slowest (bottleneck) part of the process relied upon by ER doctors to decide whom to admit and treat, transfer, or send home.

Sources:

Eric Monnoyer and Stefan Spang, "Manufacturing lessons for service industries: An interview with AXA's Claude Brunet," *The McKinsey Quarterly*, May 2005, www.mckinseyquarterly.com.

Blatchford, Christine, "Doctor's note reveals system's sad reality," *The Globe and Mail*, March 30, 2005, A12.

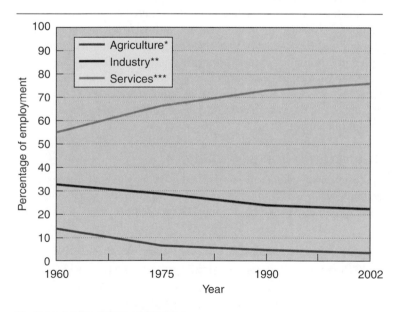

Exhibit 1.6

Growth in Services in Canada

*Includes farming, fishing, and hunting.
**Includes manufacturing, mining, and construction.
***Includes transportation, communication, public utilities, trade, finance, public administration, private household services, and miscellaneous services.

Source: Comparative Civilian Labor Force, Statistics—Ten Countries 1959–2002, Bureau of Labor Statistics U.S. Department of Labor, April 14, 2003, http://stats.bls.gov/fls/home.htm.

Goods	Services
Tangible	Intangible
Can be inventoried	Cannot be inventoried
No interaction between customer and process	Direct interaction between customer and process

Exhibit 1.7 lists some of the major differences between goods and services. Goods are tangible, something "you can drop on your foot," whereas services, being acts rather than objects, are considered to be intangible. Another difference between goods and services is that goods can be inventoried, whereas services cannot. For example, you can buy a good, such as a book, or even food, and use it sometime in the future. This is not possible with services, because they are acts associated with a specific point in time. The revenue from a hotel room that remains vacant for a given night, or an airline seat that is not sold on a scheduled flight, or a rental car that is not leased on a given day is lost forever. (Wouldn't it be great if the airlines could save in inventory all the empty seats they have during the year to use at peak holiday periods?) The third distinguishing characteristic between goods and services is that the customer does not have to be present when the good is actually produced, but must be present for the performance of a service. For example, you do not have to go to an automobile assembly plant to buy a car, but it would be difficult to have your hair cut without actually being at the barbershop or beauty salon, or to undergo a series of tests in a hospital without being physically present.

However, it is becoming more difficult to differentiate between services and manufacturing. Consequently, instead of looking at operations from two perspectives (that is, manufacturing and services), today's approach suggests that the vast majority of products consist of both a goods component and a service component, as suggested in Exhibit 1.8, and that both elements need to be addressed as a whole for a firm to be successful. (Note: Throughout this book, *product* will refer to the combination or "bundle" of goods and services being provided, whereas *goods* will refer to the tangible output, and *services* will refer to the intangible output.)

An Expanded Definition of Quality

Another key component in operations management is quality. Successful firms now acknowledge that quality is no longer limited to the operations management function, but is important in all the functional areas throughout an organization. For example, quality is

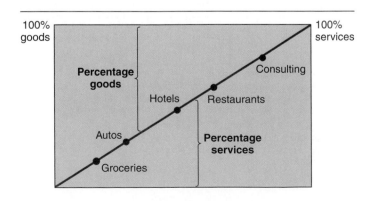

important in accounting: The bill for the items purchased must be properly prepared to reflect any special terms of payment and appropriate discounts, and then sent to the customer at the correct address.

The integration of manufacturing and services also has expanded the definition of quality. Quality is no longer limited to the technical requirements of the goods being produced on the manufacturing floor. Service quality (that is, how we deal with our customers on a wide variety of issues) is equally important. How companies integrate all of these aspects of quality to properly meet the needs of their customers is a major challenge to today's managers. The customer service department of a car dealership, for example, must know how to resolve customers' complaints so they will continue to do business with the dealership in the future. For these reasons, today's managers are recognizing that improving quality in all areas of their businesses improves customer satisfaction and increases customer loyalty.

Expansion of OM Concepts into Other Functions

Successful companies are also recognizing that, in addition to quality, many of the tools and concepts now widely used within the operations function also have application to other functional areas of an organization such as marketing, finance, and accounting. For example (as we shall see in Chapter 5), process analysis is a major tool that provides insight into how inputs are converted into outputs, and can be applied to every type of process regardless of where it exists in an organization. As an illustration, the hiring of personnel in human resources is a process, as is the design of a new product in engineering or the rolling out of a new product by marketing. In accounts receivable, the preparing and mailing of an invoice to a customer is also a process.

A New Paradigm for OM

For many years following World War II, the United States was the obvious world leader in manufacturing. U.S. dominance was the result of several factors, including (*a*) available capacity built to support the war effort, (*b*) pent-up demand for consumer goods during the war, and (*c*) the virtually total destruction of most of the production capabilities of the other leading industrialized nations of the world. As Tom Peters said, "You couldn't screw up an American Fortune 500 company between 1946 and 1973 if you tried."[8] With demand significantly exceeding capacity during this period of time, emphasis was placed on output, and the operations function typically reacted to situations only when they occurred. Corporate managers during this period usually told operations managers to focus only on controlling production costs.

As we shall see in Chapter 2, in the early 1970s, Wickam Skinner at Harvard Business School introduced the notion of operations strategy. He proposed that the operations function,

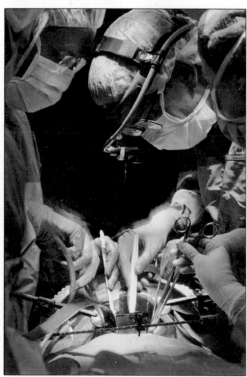

Service industries, such as health care, continue to provide growing opportunities in operations management. Many of the lessons learned in manufacturing with respect to process improvement, quality, and efficiency are now being applied in the service sector (see OMP box on services, p. 11).

---

[8]Tom Peters and KQED Golden Gate Productions, *The Power of Excellence: The Forgotten Customer* (Jack Hilton Productions, Video Publishing House, Inc., 1987).

rather than being only reactive, could take a proactive role in developing the overall strategy for an organization. In other words, Skinner suggested that the operations function could actually add value to the products a company manufactured (that is, adding value in terms of what a customer is willing to pay for the products). In developing this concept of operations strategy, he suggested that a firm could compete on dimensions other than cost to increase profit margins. These dimensions included *quality, speed of delivery,* and *process flexibility*. Each of these dimensions, in their own way, adds value to the end product. Skinner's notion of an operations strategy resulted in a new paradigm for the operations function.

The Ever-Changing World of Operations Management

Operations management is continuously changing to meet the new and exciting challenges of today's business world. This ever-changing world is characterized by increasing global competition and advances in technology. Emphasis is also shifting within the operations function to link it more closely with both customers and suppliers.

Increased Global Competition

global economy, global village, global landscape

Terms used to describe how the world is becoming smaller and countries are becoming more dependent on each other.

The world is rapidly transforming itself into a single **global economy**, which is also referred to as a **global village** or **global landscape**. Markets once dominated by local or national companies are now vulnerable to competition from literally all corners of the world. For example, IBM's computer manufacturing business was recently bought out by Lenovo, a Chinese company. Montreal-based Bombardier Aerospace competes primarily with Embraer, a Brazilian company. According to World Steel Dynamics, a U.S.-based steel information provider, in 2001, a company from India called the Tata Iron and Steel Company was the best steel company in the world. Thus, competition for Canadian companies comes not only from North American, European, and Japanese companies, but from other, developing countries as well.

The creation of international trade through agreements such as the North American Free Trade Agreement (NAFTA), World Trade Organization (WTO), and the proposed Free Trade Agreement of the Americas (FTAA) greatly affect how business is done in Canada. As explained in the Operations Management in Practice Box in Chapter 7, the reduction of tariffs means that the world-class Canadian companies will have new global markets, will be able to invest in foreign countries more easily and prosper (see the Operations Management in Practice box in this chapter for a description of Canadian companies that have gone global). At the same time Canadian markets are no longer protected, and many companies may not be able to compete against foreign competition, which may lead to job losses. The reduction in tariffs also means that Canadian companies will be have to be innovative when developing products and services to compete against standardized, mass-produced goods from low-labour-cost countries, which would have been restricted by tariffs many years ago.

Although these agreements protect Canadian companies against unjust tariffs imposed by other countries, Canada has to ensure that these agreements do not impede its ability to protect its environment, to ensure the welfare of its citizens, to ensure the quality and safety of products and services that it allows into the country, and to prevent unfair business practices by other countries.[9]

---

[9]Julie Demers, "NAFTA: Free Trade or Trade Dispute," *The New Canadian Magazine* (May/June 2003), pp. 37–41.

Consequently, as companies expand their businesses to include foreign markets, so too must the operations management function take a broader, more global perspective for companies to remain competitive. To survive and prosper in such a global marketplace, companies must excel in more than one competitive dimension, which previously was the norm. With the rise of the global economy, companies are no longer limited as to where they can make or buy their products and components. This means that supply chain management (SCM) is more complex, and critical SCM decisions have to be made more carefully. As seen in Exhibit 1.9, the Boeing 777 is assembled in the U.S. from parts sourced from all over the world. The number of countries actually involved in building the Boeing 777 may be many more than those listed in the exhibit since it does not include those that may be supplying parts to Boeing suppliers. This trend toward globalization has placed increased emphasis on the logistics of where to locate facilities and the issues associated with moving material long distances, issues which are addressed in Chapter 7 and Chapter 12 respectively.

Advances in Technology

Advances in technology in recent years also have had a significant impact on the operations management function. The increased use of information technology, automation, and robotics has also permitted us to improve the quality of the goods that are being provided.

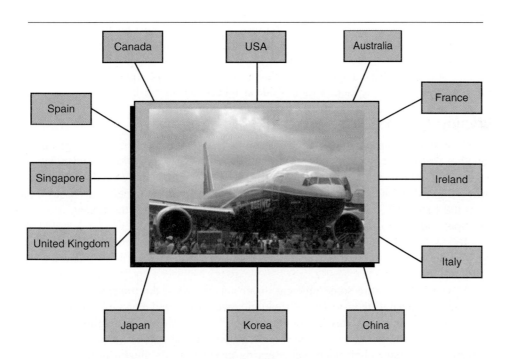

Exhibit 1.9

Boeing's Global Network to Support the Manufacture of the 777

Boeing's Global Supplier Network to Support the Manufacture of the 777.

Source: 21st Century Jet, VHS (London, UK: Channel 4 Television, 1993); www.boeing.com, Jay Heizer and Barry Render, *Operations Management* (Upper Saddle River, NJ: Prentice Hall, 1999), p. 54.

Photo: Copyright © deagel.com, used with permission.

A worker assembles doors on Passat cars at a production line in Shanghai Volkswagen Automotive Company.

However, advances in technology place new requirements on the workforce and even on customers, especially in service operations. (For example, customers now must have computer skills to access companies that advertise on the Internet or the World Wide Web.) Consequently, skilled workers are replacing unskilled workers in all types of operations. As we shall see in Web Chapter 17, an organization's workforce should be considered its most valuable asset, only increasing in value as it becomes more educated.

Linking OM to Customers and Suppliers

In the past, most manufacturing organizations viewed operations strictly as an internal function that had to be buffered from the external environment by other organizational functions. Orders were generated by the marketing function; supplies and raw materials were obtained through the purchasing function; capital for equipment purchases came from the finance function; the labour force was obtained through the human resources function; and the product was delivered by the distribution function.

It was felt that buffering would prevent external influences (from both within and outside the organization) from having a disruptive influence on the efficiency of the operations function.

However, there were some inherent disadvantages when the transformation process was totally isolated. One was that information lagged between the process and the boundary functions, which inevitably led to inflexibility. Another was that for high-tech products in particular, communications between the shop floor and the customer could be extremely valuable in solving technical problems during production. As shown in the OMP box, Foxboro Company's Customer Friend Program provides a good example of how manufacturing is now directly interacting with customers.

More and more firms are recognizing the competitive advantage achieved when the transformation process is not isolated, as when customers are invited to view their

LOCAL CANADIAN COMPANIES GO GLOBAL

Fortis Inc. was established as the parent company of Newfoundland Power in 1987 to pursue growth through diversification. Newfoundland Power and its predecessor companies have been distributors of electricity in Newfoundland since 1885. Fortis is the principal supplier of electricity in the provinces of Prince Edward Island and Newfoundland and Labrador. At the same time it has also expanded beyond its traditional markets and is a good example of a company that has recognized global opportunities in an industry that historically was very local.

Fortis expertise is in the management of small hydroelectric facilities. It has managed to maintain this focus and at the same time go global. As a result it now holds interests in companies that supply power to Ontario and New York State from small hydroelectric facilities. It also purchased majority stakes in hydroelectric and distribution facilities in Belize in Central America and holds almost a 40 percent interest in Caribbean Utilities Company Ltd., the sole provider of electricity to the island of Grand Cayman, Cayman Islands.

Potash Corp. was created as a Crown corporation by the Province of Saskatchewan in 1975 and became a publicly traded company in 1989. Currently it is the world's largest integrated producer of nitrogen, phosphate, and potash for agricultural production. Since 1989 it has also made the transition from being a local company to one that has seven phosphate operations in Canada and one potassium nitrate plant in Chile. It has seven phosphate operations in the United States and one in Brazil, four nitrogen plants in the United States, a large complex in Trinidad, and a 26 percent interest in a potash producer in Jordan.

Finning International Inc. is a Vancouver-based international corporation that sells, rents, finances, and provides customer support services for Caterpillar equipment and engines and complementary equipment on three continents around the world. In the 1980s, to combat the domestic recession, it transformed itself from a company that only served British Columbia, Alberta, Yukon, and the Northwest Territories to an international company. Currently, there are Finning dealerships in the United Kingdom, Argentina, Bolivia, Chile, and Uruguay. It also owns Hewden Stuart, the U.K. leader in equipment rental and associated services.

Sources:

Fortis Inc., www.fortis.ca.

Potash Corp., www.potashcorp.com.

Finning International Inc., www.finning.com.

"Fortis Buys Belize Stake," *The Globe and Mail*, January 29, 2001, B13.

"Potash Corp Acquires 26% of Arab Potash," *The Globe and Mail*, October 17, 2003, B16.

operating facilities firsthand. For example, Green Giant, a unit of Minneapolis-based Pillsbury, believes that the tours of their production facilities that they provided to Japanese distributors were a major factor in their ability to penetrate that market with their Green Giant food products.[10]

In a like manner, companies are working more closely with suppliers. Firms such as Toyota, for example, have suppliers deliver product directly to the factory floor, eliminating any need for a stockroom. Wal-Mart and Proctor and Gamble (P&G) partake in a program called Vendor Managed Inventory (VMI), whereby the supplier, P&G, manages the inventory of its products stocked by Wal-Mart. Canadian home improvement firm RONA allows suppliers to access RONA's inventory system so that the supplier can decide when to replenish. RONA's competitor, Home Depot, has a similar arrangement with suppliers.

As more and more companies outsource manufacturing to focus on core competencies, the *make* versus *buy* decision is becoming more important. In addition, in a *buy* decision, when comparing suppliers, companies are also looking at the "total cost of ownership" rather than only at initial price. (These issues are discussed more in Chapter 12.)

This trend toward having the transformation process work more closely with both suppliers and customers alike is often referred to as a product's **value chain**. We can define

value chain
Steps an organization requires to produce a good or a service regardless of where they are performed.

---

[10]J. Ammeson, "When in Rome," *Northwest Airlines World Traveler*, March 1993.

THE CUSTOMER FRIEND PROGRAM AT FOXBORO'S SYSTEMS MANUFACTURING OPERATION

The Foxboro Company's systems manufacturing operation, which produces control systems for process industries such as refineries, chemical plants, and breweries, has a Customer Friend Program that directly links its customers to manufacturing. This program is offered free of charge and provides each customer with a contact person or "friend" in manufacturing who is responsible for helping the customer resolve any and all product- and service-related problems. Since its inception in 1992, more than 40 individuals from manufacturing have taken part in the Customer Friend Program involving more than 300 customer systems, both large and small.

The benefits of this program to manufacturing are to (a) identify more closely with the customer's needs, (b) feel the customer's pain when a problem does occur, (c) gain a better understanding of how manufacturing can improve its support to its customers, and (d) obtain direct feedback from "where the rubber meets the road" in terms of how manufacturing can improve its processes and products.

The program benefits the customer by (a) identifying more closely the customer's needs, (b) passing the pain directly to the source when a problem does occur, (c) having a dedicated individual within manufacturing who has a personal commitment to customer satisfaction, (d) having direct contact with manufacturing to analyze product failures, and (e) acting as a conduit for new and improved ideas.

Foxboro's Customer Friend Program is proactive rather than reactive. Depending on the needs and desires of the customer, the Foxboro friend will call his assigned customer every one to four weeks just to make sure everything is running smoothly. Many of these customer–friend relationships are long standing. Ray Webb, the employee involvement manager at Foxboro's Systems Manufacturing Operation, for example, has had a five-year association with Ergon Refining of Mississippi.

Source: Special thanks to Ray Webb, Systems Manufacturing Operation, The Foxboro Company.

a value chain as consisting of all those steps that actually add value to the product without distinguishing where they are added. This concept attempts to eliminate all nonvalue-added steps (such as inspections and inventory), and consequently results in a higher degree of dependence among the value-added functions within the chain. The relationship between the transformation process, its support functions, and the other value-added functions is shown in Exhibit 1.10.

virtual enterprise

Company whose boundaries are not clearly defined due to the integration of customers and suppliers.

This integration of both suppliers and customers into the transformation process begins to blur the boundaries between what were previously totally independent organizations. What appears to be emerging now is a concept known as the **virtual enterprise**, which is a fully integrated and interlocked network of *inter*dependent organizations. With this new approach, it is often difficult to determine where one organization leaves off and the next one begins. (See the Bose JIT II example in Chapter 12.)

Exhibit 1.10

The Value Chain and Its Support Functions

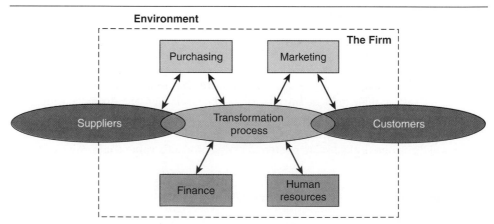

Job Opportunities in Operations Management: Relating OM to Other Business Functions

Exhibit 1.11 lists some of the line and staff jobs that usually fall within the operations function. There are more staff specializations in manufacturing than in services because of the focus on materials management and control.

Operations management is a required course in many business schools, not only because it deals with the basic question of how goods and services are created, but also because many of the concepts developed in OM have direct applications in every other functional area within an organization. As seen in Exhibit 1.12, processes exist within every function. These processes can be continuously improved by applying OM tools and techniques. In addition, as also seen in Exhibit 1.12, each of these functional areas interacts with the OM function. Therefore, to do their jobs correctly, it is important for individuals working in these areas to understand the fundamental concepts of operations management.

Organizational Level	Manufacturing Industries	Service Industries
Upper	Vice president of manufacturing Regional manager of manufacturing	Vice president of operations (airline) Chief administrator (hospital)
Middle	Plant manager Program manager	Store manager (department store) Facilities manager (wholesale distributor)
Lower	Department supervisor Team leader Crew chief	Branch manager (bank) Department supervisor (insurance company) Assistant manager (hotel)
Staff	Production controller Materials manager Quality manager Purchasing agent Work methods analyst Process engineer	Systems and procedures analyst Purchasing agent Inspector Dietician (hospital) Customer service representative

Exhibit 1.11

Line and Staff Jobs in Operations Management

Functional Area	Processes Performed by That Area	Input Provided by OM
Accounting	Asset valuation Financial statements	On-hand inventory Labour and material costs
Finance	Capital investment analysis Cash flow management	Capacity utilization Make-or-buy decisions
Marketing	New product introduction Customer orders	New process requirements Delivery dates
Human resources	Hiring Training	Job descriptions Worker skills requirements
MIS	Software evaluation Hardware requirements analysis	Data requirements Terminal requirements

Exhibit 1.12

Inputs Provided by OM to Other Functional Areas

The Historical Development of Operations Management from an International and Canadian Perspective[11]

Unlike the United States, which evolved from an agricultural base, business in Canada began as a commodity-based colony. Fish, fur, and forests were harvested, then shipped back to France or the U.K. Manufacturing as we know it today did not exist. Items were usually custom-made by skilled artisans who spent many years in apprenticeship learning every facet of how to make a good or provide a service. No two products were ever the same. For many products, trades or guilds were established to provide a common basis of knowledge for these apprenticeship programs.

This cottage industry approach to manufacturing began to change at the beginning of the 19th century. In England, in 1765, Watt invented the steam engine which provided a source of power for manufacturing. In the early 1800s, Eli Whitney introduced the concept of standardized parts, demonstrating by selecting parts at random to assemble and then fire a musket. (Prior to this, every musket was handcrafted with customized parts.) The middle of the 19th century saw the onset of the Industrial Revolution with its large manufacturing facilities powered either by steam or water. However, even with the advent of these large facilities, manufacturing to a large degree remained an art rather than a science.

In the 19th century, industrial development in Canada generally lagged behind that of its neighbour, the U.S., and its colonizer, the U.K., for a variety of reasons. Slow population growth (due to difficult living conditions) in Canada until the beginning of the 20th century resulted in relatively small markets for most products. Secondly, the existence of foreign tariffs meant that export markets were minimal. Thirdly, there was a lack of skilled people in Canada because there were no technical institutions to train them. Finally, it was not until the late nineteenth century that Canada had a cross-continental rail network. This lack of transportation prevented manufacturers from serving distant markets. Thus Canadian manufacturers had neither the skills nor the market economies of scale to invest in new technology and become competitive.

Nevertheless, limited free trade agreements with the U.S. and U.K. (although only for short periods), demand fuelled by the U.S. Civil War, general population growth in the U.S., and the easy availability of natural resources all spurred industrial growth in Canada during this period. By the turn of the twentieth century, the availability of large amounts of cheap hydroelectricity was also proving beneficial to Canada.

scientific management

Systematic approach to increasing worker productivity introduced by Fredrick W. Taylor.

Things changed in manufacturing in general with the introduction of **scientific management** at the beginning of the 20th century. Although one could claim that operations management has existed since the dawn of civilization, scientific management probably was the first historic landmark in the field because it represented for the first time a systematic approach to manufacturing. This concept was developed by Frederick W. Taylor, an imaginative engineer and insightful observer of organizational activities.

The essence of Taylor's philosophy was that scientific laws govern how much a worker can produce per day and that it is the role of management to discover and use

[11]Parts of this section are based on information from the following sources: J. Balakrishnan, J. B. Eliasson, and T. R. C. Sweet, "Factors Affecting the Evolution of Manufacturing in Canada: A Historical Perspective," forthcoming in the *Journal of Operations Management*; and Richard Pomfret, *The Economic Development of Canada* (Toronto: Methuen, 1981).

these laws in its production systems (and that it is the role of the worker to carry out management's wishes without question). Taylor's philosophy was not greeted with approval by all his contemporaries. On the contrary, some unions resented or feared scientific management—and with some justification. Too often, managers of the day were quick to embrace the mechanisms of Taylor's philosophy—time study, incentive plans, and so forth—but ignored their responsibility to organize and standardize the work to be done. In many firms, workers often were viewed as just another interchangeable asset, like plant and equipment. Notable co-workers of Taylor were Frank and Lillian Gilbreth (motion study, industrial psychology) and Henry L. Gantt (scheduling, wage payment plans).

By the early 1900s there were some notable Canadian industries, since mass manufacturing was becoming more feasible due to the increasing population and the general reduction in foreign tariffs leading to exports. The Northern Electric and Manufacturing Company Limited (now Nortel Networks), was incorporated in 1895 and made telephones, wind-up gramophones, and other telecommunications equipment. Massey Harris (later Massey Ferguson) manufactured and won international awards for farm implements. Other current companies that existed at the turn of the 20th century include Frosst (now Merck Frosst), CP Hotels (now Fairmont Hotels), Cara, CP Rail, Bell Canada, Alcan, Imperial Oil, George Weston (bakeries and owner of Loblaws), and McCain Foods. Furthermore, Canadian companies in the early part of the 20th century did not simply implement imported technology, but made their own innovations to these technologies to help growth and development.[12]

In the early 1900s a group of Ontario investors purchased a 49% interest in the Ford Motor Company of Canada and began assembling cars in Chatham, Ontario, from parts imported from Ford's factory in Detroit (the customs duty was lower on imported parts than on fully assembled vehicles). In fact, U.S. companies started establishing branch plants in Canada in the mid-19th century, first in natural products and then in manufacturing, due in part to tariffs that prevented them from exporting to Canada. Although this brought jobs to Canada, R&D usually stayed in the U.S. headquarters. At about the same time, the McLaughlin family, who owned a buggy manufacturing business, formed the McLaughlin Motor Car Company and started assembling motors cars in partnership with Buick. This company later became General Motors of Canada.[13] CCM, known today for sporting equipment, produced automobiles in the early 1900s.[14]

The year 1913 saw the introduction of one of the machine age's greatest technological innovations: the **moving assembly line** for the manufacture of Ford automobiles. (Ford is said to have gotten the idea for an assembly line from observing a Swiss watch manufacturer's use of the technology. Incidentally, all Model-T Fords were painted black. Why? Because black paint dried the fastest.) Before the assembly line was introduced in August of that year, each auto chassis was assembled by one worker in about 12 hours. Eight months later, when the line was in its final form, with each worker performing a small unit of work and the chassis being moved along the line mechanically, the average labour time per chassis was reduced to 93 minutes. This technological breakthrough, coupled with the concepts of scientific management, represents the

moving assembly line

A mass production line in which the product moves along the line while workers at sequential locations add value to the product.

[12]Peter J. Wylie, "Indigenous technological adaptation in Canadian Manufacturing, 1900–1929," *Canadian Journal of Economics*, 23, no. 4 (1990), pp. 856–872.
[13]Heather Robertson, *Driving Force: The McLaughlin Family and the Age of the Car* (Toronto: McClelland and Stewart, 1995).
[14]Ibid.

classic application of labour specialization and still exists today in both manufacturing and service operations.

During both World War I and World War II, Canada's production was geared towards wartime production. After the end of the World War II, Canada and the U.S. prospered because they were among the few industrialized countries whose infrastructure was not destroyed. However, this had some negative consequences for operations. The high demand and lack of international competition meant that companies did not think about operations strategically or as a competitive weapon. The operations function was assigned the responsibility of producing large quantities of standard products at minimum cost regardless of the goals of the firm. Issues such as quality took a back seat. Later, when foreign manufacturers, especially Japanese, entered the market with quality products, North American manufacturers were ill-equipped to respond quickly. This was foreseen by experts in operations, such as Wickham Skinner of the Harvard Business School, who suggested in the late 1960s that companies should place strategic emphasis on operations.[15] Today, of course, companies view operations as a competitive weapon and place great importance on operations management.

In Canada, operations management (OM) evolved under unique circumstances and in response to international influences. The signing of the Canada-U.S. Auto Pact in 1965, (whereby tariffs were reduced if a manufacturer of automobiles or automobile parts did some value-added manufacturing in Canada) gave impetus to growth in the auto industry. Changing processes, whether an adoption of existing technology or improving an existing process, has allowed Canadian companies to produce the same or better product at a lower cost. With the availability of better transportation and communication technology, Canadian firms have become more competitive. Developments in OM such as Materials Requirement Planning (MRP), Just In Time (JIT), Total Quality Management (TQM), and six sigma methods became available to Canadian companies soon after they were introduced. Canada also participates internationally in helping improve operations. The significant role played by the Canadian Standards Association (CSA) in developing international quality management system standards such as the ISO 9000 is a good example. On its 75th anniversary in 2003, the magazine *Canadian Business* profiled what it felt were the best 75 Canadian companies of all time.

The last quarter of the 20th century also saw the rise of Japan and Germany as major economies. Many Japanese companies, through investments in research and development and innovative manufacturing practices, became leaders in industries ranging from automobiles (light and heavy) and electronics to construction and shipbuilding. For example, Sony became a leader in designing and producing innovative electronic goods, while Toyota, with its Just-In-Time (JIT) innovation and high quality manufacturing, became a leader in automobile manufacturing. Chapter 14 is devoted to JIT, sometimes called the biggest revolution in manufacturing since the assembly line. Following their lead, companies from Korea and other Asian countries have also become formidable competitors. Other recent developments that affect international competition include the emergence of Eastern Europe from Communism.

A 1991 report by Professor Michael Porter of Harvard University and a follow-up report in 2004 by Porter and Professor Roger Martin, dean of the Rotman School of Management at the University of Toronto, studied Canadian products and their place in a globally competitive world. The study outlined how Canadian industry and government were doing on global issues. Topics of operational concern included Canadians' apparent

---

[15]C. Wickham Skinner, "Manufacturing—The Missing Link in Corporate Strategy," *Harvard Business Review*, 47, no. 3 (May–June 1969), pp. 136–145.

reliance on raw materials, improving productivity, quality in manufacturing, and government protectionist policy.[16,17]

Exhibit 1.13 gives a summary of the developments in operations management in the 20th century.

Exhibit 1.13

Historical Summary of OM

Year	Concept	Tool	Originator
1910s	Principles of scientific management	Formalized time-study and work-study concepts	Frederick W. Taylor
	Industrial psychology	Motion study	Frank and Lillian Gilbreth
	Moving assembly line	Activity scheduling chart	Henry Ford and Henry L. Gantt
	Economic lot size	Economic Order Quantity (EOQ) applied to inventory control	F. W. Harris
1930s	Quality control	Sampling inspection and statistical tables for quality control	Walter Shewhart, H. F. Dodge, and H. G. Romig
	Hawthorne studies of worker motivation	Activity sampling for work analysis	Elton Mayo and L. H. C. Tippett
1940s–60s	Extensive development of operations research tools	Simulation, waiting-line theory, decision theory, mathematical programming, project scheduling techniques of PERT and CPM	Many researchers globally
1970s	Widespread use of computers in business	Shop scheduling, inventory control, forecasting, project management, MRP	Led by computer manufacturers, in particular, IBM; Joseph Orlicky and Oliver Wight were the major MRP innovators
	Service quality and productivity	Mass production in the service sector	McDonald's restaurants
1980s	Manufacturing strategy paradigm	Manufacturing as a competitive weapon	Harvard Business School faculty
	JIT, TQC, and factory automation	Kanban, poka-yokes, CIM, FMS, CAD/CAM, robots, etc.	Tai-Ichi Ohno of Toyota Motors, W.E. Deming and J. M. Juran and engineering disciplines
1990s	Total quality management	Canada Awards for Excellence, ISO 9000, quality function development, value and concurrent engineering, continuous improvement paradigm	National Quality Institute (NQI), American Society of Quality Control (ASQC), and International Organization for Standardization (ISO)
	Business process reengineering	Radical change paradigm	Michael Hammer and major consulting firms
	Electronic enterprise	Internet, World Wide Web	U.S. government, Netscape Communication Corporation, and Microsoft Corporation
	Supply chain management	SAP/R$_3$, client/server software	SAP, Oracle
2000s	E-commerce	Internet, World Wide Web	Amazon, eBay, Canadian banks

Adapted from: Richard B. Chase, F. Robert Jacobs, and Nicholas J. Aquilano, *Operations Management for Competitive Advantage*, 10th ed. (New York: Irwin McGraw Hill, 2004), p. 16.

---

[16]Michael E. Porter and the Monitor Company, "Canada at the Crossroads: The Reality of a New Competitive Environment," *A Report to the Business Council on National Issues and Minister of Supply and Services* (Ottawa: Business Council on National Issues, 1991), p. 4.

[17]Martin, R. and M. E. Porter, 2001, "Canadian Competitiveness: A Decade after the Crossroads," www.rotman.utoronto.ca/research/competitive1.htm (accessed March 14, 2006).

Conclusion

Operations management is recognized today as a critical functional area within every organization. No longer is operations management considered to be subservient to the finance and marketing areas; instead, it is now treated as an equal. Firms that fail to recognize the significant contribution of the operations management function will lose profits and market share to those firms that do. The once-reactive role of operations management, which concentrated solely on minimizing costs, has been replaced by a more proactive position of maximizing the value added to the goods and services that the organization provides.

Some of the major issues facing operations management executives today in this constantly changing business environment include:

1. Reducing the development and manufacturing time for new goods and services.
2. Achieving and sustaining high quality while controlling costs.
3. Integrating new technologies and control systems into existing processes.
4. Obtaining, training, and keeping qualified workers and managers.
5. Working effectively with other functions of the business (marketing, engineering, finance, and human resources) to accomplish the goals of the firm.
6. Integrating production and service activities at multiple sites in decentralized organizations.
7. Working effectively with suppliers and being user-friendly for customers.
8. Working effectively with new partners formed by strategic alliances (for example, Wal-Mart and Exel Logistics).

All of these issues are interrelated. The key to success is for operations management to do all of these at a level that is competitive in both global and domestic markets.

Key Terms

global economy, global landscape, global village p. 14

moving assembly line p. 21
operations management p. 4
scientific management p. 20

transformation process p. 6
value chain p. 17
virtual enterprise p. 18

Review and Discussion Questions

1. What is operations management and how is it different from operations research?
2. What were the underlying reasons for the lack of emphasis on operations management in the post-World War II years?
3. What are the advantages of bringing customers into the transformation process or technical core?
4. Take a look at the want ads in *The Globe and Mail* and your local newspaper and evaluate the opportunities for an OM major with several years of experience.
5. What are the major factors leading to the resurgence of interest in OM today?
6. Explain the difference, from an operations management perspective, between cost minimization and value maximization.
7. Using Exhibit 1.3 as a model, describe the input–transformation–output relationships found in the following systems.
   a. An airline.
   b. A provincial penitentiary.
   c. A branch bank.
   d. A bakery.
   e. A clothing manufacturer.
   f. A dry cleaner.
   g. An automobile assembly line.
   h. An accounting firm.

8. What do we mean by the expression *value chain,* as it applies to the transformation process of a good or service?

9. Identify a product that is 100 percent goods without any service component.

Identify a product that is 100 percent service without any goods component.

10. Speculate on the future role of the OM function within an organization and the future role of the operations manager.

Internet Exercise

Go to the Online Learning Centre (OLC) Web site at www.mcgrawhill.ca/olc/davis and visit the Web site of one of the companies that provides a virtual plant tour of their operations. Identify the company and describe the various operations presented in the tour. What do you think distinguishes this firm from its competition?

2

Operations Strategy

Chapter Objectives

- Introduce the concept of operations strategy and its various components, and show how it relates to the overall business strategy of the firm.

- Illustrate how operations strategy pertains to adding value for the customer.

- Identify the different ways in which operations strategy can provide an organization with a competitive advantage.

- Introduce the concept of trade-offs between different strategies and the need for a firm to align its operations strategy to meet the needs of the particular markets it is serving.

- Explain the difference between order-qualifiers and order-winners as they pertain to operations strategy.

- Describe how firms are integrating manufacturing and services to provide an overall "bundle of benefits" to their customers.

Steelmaker Dofasco does a Turnaround through Strategic Refocusing

It is no secret that Canadian steelmakers are under pressure. The industry is increasingly facing competition from steelmakers in developing countries such as Brazil, China, and India where labour costs are low. While some other Canadian steelmakers struggle, Hamilton-based Dofasco (a unit of Luxembourg–based Arcelor and Mittal Steel Company), in business since 1912, has turned around its losses from a decade ago through a revised strategy. The company also owns or has partial ownership in facilities in the United States and Mexico.

Until the late 1980s, the company competed on price by producing as much steel as possible at the lowest possible prices. However, by the early 1990s increased competition resulted in Dofasco not being able to compete profitably.

Realizing that the current "competing on cost" strategy (cost leadership) was untenable, Dofasco refocused its strategy to developing new and innovative products, and to providing its customers with solutions for high-quality and specialized applications (product differentiation). The business strategy was called Solutions in Steel and focused on operational excellence, technology and innovation, and intimate customer relationships. By 1999 it was the most profitable steel

producer in North America. In 2000 it was ranked first in North America among thirty steel suppliers in an independent customer satisfaction survey and was rated one of the best Canadian companies to work for by *Report on Business Magazine*.

What did it take to effect a successful transition from the old strategy to the new? Of course, this transformation did not come without effort, resources, or pain. Its workforce was reduced from about 13 000 to 7000. It spends considerable sums on research and development and facility upgrades. Dofasco recognized that employees would be critical to success in such a strategy. Thus employees were provided a variety of training and development opportunities. In addition, the company invested in health, safety, and wellness in the workplace. In 2002, the National Quality Institute awarded Dofasco a Canadian Award for Excellence Healthy Workplace Trophy. Studies have shown that investing in health, safety, and wellness can improve productivity and lower costs. Quality at Dofasco has meant paying attention to environmental concerns also. In 2002, Dofasco's Hamilton facilities achieved ISO 14001 certification. This means that the company's Environmental Management Systems comply with an international set of environmental standards (Chapter 6 discusses quality awards and ISO standards in detail).

The Dofasco story provides an excellent example of the importance of formulating a successful business strategy and implementing supporting operations strategy decisions to ensure long-term survival.

Sources:

Priya Ramu, "Report on Canada's Steel Industry," *World at Six*, CBC Radio, August 6, 2003.

Gordon DiGiacomo, *Case Study: Dofasco's Healthy Lifestyles Program* (Canadian Labour and Business Centre, 2002), www.clbc.ca.

Dofasco Inc., www.dofasco.com.

National Quality Institute, www.nqi.com.

An organization's operations strategy provides an overarching framework for determining how it prioritizes and utilizes its resources to gain a competitive advantage in the marketplace. Today's operations managers face many new challenges with respect to strategy issues, from developing effective strategies to properly implementing them throughout the organization.

As we shall see, there are several external factors that affect operations strategy decisions, including an increase in competition that has resulted from the globalization of business and advances in technology. Consequently, operations managers, in many instances, are now being asked to do more with less: more, in terms of faster delivery times, more variety, and higher quality; less, in terms of lower material costs, lower labour costs, and less available time.

At the same time, managers know all too well that competitors can copy successful strategies and can usually implement them quickly, thereby neutralizing their advantage to some degree. As a result, these same managers from a strategic perspective, must keep a watchful eye to the future, constantly looking for the next strategy that will separate their firms from those of competitors.

Operations Strategy—An Overview

What Is Operations Strategy?

Operations strategy is the development of a long-term plan for using the major resources of the firm in order to achieve a high degree of compatibility between these resources and the firm's long-term corporate strategy. Operations strategy addresses very broad questions about how these major resources should be configured to achieve the desired corporate objectives. Some of the major long-term issues addressed in operations strategy include:

- How large do we make our facilities?
- What type of process(es) do we install to make the products or provide services?
- What will our supply chain look like?
- What will be the nature of our workforce?
- How do we ensure quality?

Each of these issues is addressed in greater detail in subsequent chapters. In this chapter we want to take a macroscopic perspective to better understand how these issues are interrelated. Exhibit 2.1 shows an overall picture of the operations strategy process and its relationship to other strategic processes in the organization.

The Operations Management Strategy Development Process

Today, many corporations, both large, global conglomerates such as General Electric and small ones such as Mississauga, Ontario-based Cara or Toronto-based Onex, consist of several stand-alone businesses that focus on different industries. The conglomerate may have a **vision** and a **mission**. For example the vision of Cara (a company founded in 1883, making it older than some provinces) is "To be Canada's leading integrated restaurant company." Its mission is "Enhancing stakeholder value and building leading businesses, by maximizing our resources and living our values and principles."[1] Within this context, **corporate strategy** defines the specific businesses in which the firm will compete and the way in which resources are acquired and allocated among these various businesses.

The stand-alone businesses within these conglomerates often are referred to as **strategic business units (SBUs)**. SBUs at Cara include, among others, Harvey's and Swiss Chalet in the fast food business, Kelsey's in the restaurant business, Second Cup in

vision

A statement that provides long-term direction and motivation for the organization.

mission

A statement about the organization's business scope and methods of competing.

corporate strategy

Overall strategy adopted by the parent corporation.

strategic business unit (SBU)

Stand-alone business within a conglomerate that operates like an independent company.

---

[1]Cara Operations Limited, www.cara.com.

Exhibit 2.1

**The Operations
Strategy Process**

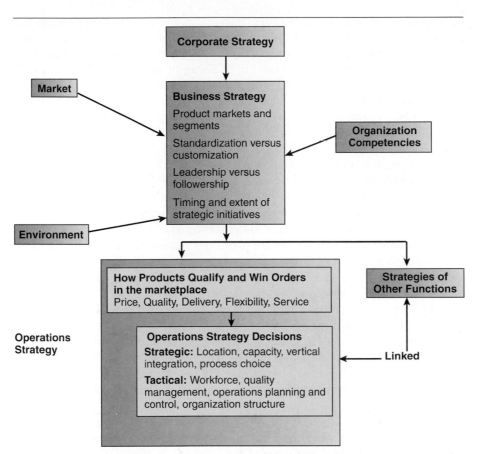

Source: Adapted from Terry Hill, *Manufacturing Strategy* (McGraw Hill Irwin), 2000, p. 32.

specialty coffee, Cara in airline food catering, and Summit in food service distribution. The individual strategy adopted by each SBU, which is referred to as its **business strategy**, defines the scope and boundaries of the SBU, in terms of how it addresses the specific markets that it serves and the products that it provides, the amount of resources to be allocated to innovation, and whether it plans to be a market leader in each of its segments. Decisions regarding when each strategic initiative will be undertaken and its extent are also made at this level.

The business strategy depends on the market requirements (such as customer desires and success criteria in the market), the environment (such as competition, technological advances, and government regulations) and the organizational competencies (such as its core capabilities, its culture, and strengths and weaknesses). Each SBU may also have its own vision and mission.

To not only survive but also to prosper in today's fiercely competitive marketplace, an SBU needs to have a successful strategy. In this type of situation, Michael Porter, a professor at the Harvard Business School, and perhaps today's leading authority on competitive strategy, believes that there are three generic strategies for succeeding in an industry: cost leadership, differentiation, and market segmentation.[2] **Cost leadership** implies that the firm has the ability to successfully underprice its competition. **Differentiation** refers to

cost leadership
Producing the lowest-cost products.

differentiation
Offering products that differ significantly from the competition.

[2]Michael Porter, *Competitive Advantage: Creating and Sustaining Superior Performance* (New York: The Free Press, 1985).

market segmentation

Satisfying the needs of a particular market niche.

ways in which an organization distinguishes its products and services from its competition. For example, a company could offer higher-quality products or services than its competitors. **Market segmentation** refers to the focus of the product or service offering on a segment in the market. An example of focus in the hotel industry would be Toronto-based Four Seasons Hotels, which focuses on the luxury end of the lodging business. Porter believes that to be successful, firms have to trade off among the three. In other words, a company "cannot be all things to all people." Other experts on strategy, such as Henry Mintzberg of McGill University, include cost leadership as a form of differentiation.[3]

functional strategies

Strategy developed by a function within an organization to support the business strategy.

Functional strategies (for example, operations, marketing, human resources) are developed to support or align with the established business strategy. For example, Ethan Allen, a retailer following a business strategy of providing high quality furniture, cannot pursue an operations strategy of achieving low cost by procuring leather that is not of high quality, nor a human resource strategy of not providing training.

operations strategy

How the operations function contributes to competitive advantage.

Operations strategy refers to how the operations management function contributes to a firm's ability to achieve competitive advantage in that marketplace.

Operations strategies are developed from the **competitive priorities** of an organization, which include (*a*) low cost, (*b*) high quality, (*c*) fast delivery, (*d*) flexibility, and (*e*) service. Competitive priorities in turn depend on order qualifiers and winners, which relate to requirements for success in the marketplace.

competitive priorities

How the operations function provides a firm with a specific competitive advantage.

Core competencies are the means by which competitive priorities are achieved. Consequently, core competencies must align directly with competitive priorities. For example, a core competency may relate to research and innovation, such as the ability to design and bring products quickly to market as in the case of Intel, Nortel, or Sony, or effective supply chain management as in the case of Wal-Mart.

Operations strategy decisions can be divided into two major categories: strategic elements, consisting of facility location, capacity, vertical integration, and choice of process; and tactical elements, consisting of the workforce, quality issues, operations planning and control, and organizational structure. The opening story on Dofasco highlighted some of these issues. These decisions have to be consistent with strategic decisions of the other functions, as in the Ethan Allen example.

Operations Strategy Means Adding Value for the Customer

How often have we heard the expression, "Customers want their money's worth"? Unfortunately, from a manager's point of view, it's not that easy. Customers want more than their money's worth, and the more they receive for their money, the more value they see in the goods and services they are purchasing.

In determining the value of a product, be it a good or a service, customers take into consideration all of the benefits derived from the product and compare these to all of the costs of that product. If, in the opinion of the customers, the benefits exceed the costs, then they perceive value in the product. The more the benefits exceed the costs, the more value the product provides.

---

[3]Henry Mintzberg and J. B. Quinn, *The Strategy Process: Concepts and Contexts* (Englewood Cliffs, New Jersey: Prentice Hall, 1992).

In other words,

Perceived customer value = Total benefits − Total costs   (2.1)

When the difference between the benefits and costs is positive, customers perceive value; when it is negative, they believe they have overpaid for the product.

One of the goals in the development of an operations strategy, therefore, should be to maximize the value added to the goods and services that are provided by the firm, as suggested in Exhibit 2.2.

Adding customer value during the transformation process can take many forms and translate into different things to different customers. As seen in Equations 2.1 and 2.2, one way to add value is to reduce the cost of the product, as when you buy books at Indigo.ca. Added value to the customer can also mean that the product is more readily available, such as when you order groceries online or buy a camera over the Internet. Added value can be seen as receiving faster service, as when you use the fast lane on the highway to pay a toll automatically, or it may take the form of information, as when Indigo.ca tells you what other books have been purchased by buyers who have purchased the same book you bought, or when Destina.ca provides you with a list of different airlines going to a particular city and a comparison of their air fares. Added value can also take the form of a more customized product, be it a personal computer from Dell or more personalized service, as when you check into a hotel and they know that you have stayed there before and have certain preferences.

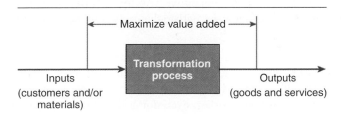

Exhibit 2.2

Maximizing Value Added in Operations

The key element in developing a successful operations strategy is for a firm to provide its customers with additional benefits at an increase in cost that is perceived to be less than those benefits.

Trends Affecting Operations Strategy Decisions

Two major trends that have significantly impacted the role of operations strategy within an organization are increasing globalization of business and advances in technology, especially information technology.

Globalization

As we saw in the first chapter, the world is quickly becoming a global village, caused in large part by technology. As a result of this globalization of business, managers must extend their vision beyond their own national borders when developing operations strategies. This includes the location of manufacturing plants in Southeast Asia because of low labour rates, or the establishment of call centres in Ireland because of a combination of inexpensive labour, an educated workforce, and the necessary technology infrastructure that exists.

Many issues must be evaluated when looking to expand a company's operations globally. For example, the education level of the workforce, the language, and the impact of local laws and customs must be taken into consideration. For example, a major attraction for locating in Ireland is its highly educated workforce. As an another illustration, employees in Germany can work up to 70 hours in some weeks without being paid overtime, and then work as little as 30 hours or less in other weeks, as long as the total hours worked over a given time period (such as 6 or 12 months) meets an agreed-upon amount.

Technology

As discussed in Chapter 1, and as we shall see shortly, technology has also dramatically affected one of the basic concepts in operations strategy: that of making trade-offs between priorities. With advances in technology, managers no longer have to make pure trade-offs between competitive priorities as they once did. Instead, today's technology allows firms to compete on several priorities simultaneously, resulting in shifts to superior performance curves (described later in this chapter).

Competitive Priorities

The key to developing an effective operations strategy lies in understanding how to create or add value for customers. Specifically, value is added through the competitive priority or priorities that are selected to support a given strategy.

Skinner and others initially identified *four basic competitive priorities:* **cost**, **quality**, **delivery**, and **flexibility**. These four priorities translate directly into characteristics that are used to describe various processes by which a company can add value to the products it provides. There now exists a fifth competitive priority—**service**—and it was the primary way in which companies began to differentiate themselves in the 1990s.

Cost

Within most industries, there is a segment of the market that buys strictly on the basis of low cost. To successfully compete in this niche, a firm must necessarily, therefore, be the low-cost producer. But, as noted earlier, even doing this doesn't always guarantee profitability and success.

competitive priorities

cost
Providing low-cost products.

quality
Providing high-quality products.

delivery
Providing products quickly.

flexibility
Providing a wide variety of products.

service
How products are delivered and supported.

Products sold strictly on the basis of cost are typically commodity-like. (Examples of commodities include flour, petroleum, and sugar.) In other words, customers cannot easily distinguish the products made by one firm from those of another. As a result, customers use cost as the primary determinant in making a purchase.

However, this segment of the market often is very large, and many companies are lured by the potential for significant profits, which are associated with large unit volumes of product. As a consequence, the competition in this segment is exceedingly fierce—and so is the failure rate. After all, there can only be one lowest-cost producer, and that firm usually establishes the selling price in the market. For example, Zellers, a unit of Hudson's Bay Company, has found itself under increasing pressure since Wal-Mart entered Canada in 1994. It is estimated that on a sales per square metre basis (a key measure of retail efficiency), Zellers lags well behind Wal-Mart. Thus Zellers will have to improve its efficiency or differentiate itself from Wal-Mart in order to survive.[4]

Quality

Quality can be divided into two categories: product (or design) quality and process (or conformance) quality. The level of quality in a product's design will vary according to the particular market it is aimed to serve. Obviously, a child's first two-wheel bicycle is of significantly different quality than the bicycle of a world-class cyclist. The use of thicker sheetmetal and the application of extra coats of paint are some of the product quality characteristics that differentiate a Mercedes-Benz from a Hyundai. One advantage of offering higher-quality products is that they command higher prices in the marketplace. As mentioned in Chapter 1, Honda sees product safety as a means of achieving competitive advantage.

The goal in establishing the "proper level" of product quality is to focus on the requirements of the customer. Overdesigned products with too much quality will be viewed as being prohibitively expensive. Underdesigned products, on the other hand, will lose customers to products that cost a little more but are perceived as offering much greater benefits.

Process quality is critical in every market segment. Regardless of whether the product is a child's first two-wheeler or a bicycle for an international cyclist, or whether it is a Mercedes-Benz or a Hyundai, customers want products without defects. Thus, the goal of process quality is to produce defect-free products.

Delivery

Another market niche considers speed of delivery to be an important determinant in its purchasing decision. Here, the ability of a firm to provide consistent and fast delivery allows it to charge a premium price for its products. George Stalk Jr., of the Boston Consulting Group, has demonstrated that both profits and market share are directly linked to the speed with which a company can deliver its products relative to its competition.[5] In addition to fast delivery, the reliability of delivery is also important. In other words, products should be delivered to customers with minimum variance in delivery times. This is especially important for those suppliers who supply Just-In-Time (JIT) companies.

Flexibility

From a strategic perspective, in terms of how a company competes, flexibility consists of multiple dimensions, all of which relate directly to how the firm's processes are designed. One element of flexibility is the firm's ability to offer its customers a wide variety of

[4]Zellers Is Stretched in Apparel-Rack War. Analysts Suggest Strategies for Battling Wal-Mart," *Winnipeg Free Press*, August 19, 2002, B6.
[5]George Stalk Jr., "Time and Innovation," *Canadian Business Review* 20, no. 3 (Autumn 1993), pp. 15–18.

ZARA EXCELS ON PRICE, SPEED, AND FLEXIBILITY

Zara, a retail chain of high-fashion boutique clothing stores, has grown rapidly since Amancio Ortega opened his first store in Spain in 1975. Headquartered in northern Spain, Zara, with more than 400 retail stores in 25 countries, now generates sales of more than $3 billion annually, primarily in Europe, but is now beginning to penetrate the Canadian market with nine stores, including stores in Toronto, Vancouver, Montreal, and Calgary. Zara's success is attributed to several factors, including low prices, speed of delivery, and flexibility. Merchandise is delivered to each Zara retail location twice a week. (Merchandise is air-freighted to its stores in Canada.) This fast and almost-continuous replenishment concept reduces the need for significant in-store inventories and the possibility of clothes going out of fashion.

A major factor in Zara's ability to react quickly to changes in the customer buying behaviour is its use of information and technology. Salespeople in each retail location use handheld computers to record buyer preferences and trends. This information, along with actual sales data, is transmitted daily through the Internet to Zara's headquarters in Spain.

In addition, unlike its major competitors which outsource manufacturing, Zara produces most of its merchandise in its state-of-the-art factory in Spain. Products are designed, produced, and delivered to its stores in as little as two weeks after appearing for the first time in a fashion show. By contrast, some competitors such as the GAP require up to nine months' lead time to fill orders from its retail operations. But some of Zara's competitors are not keeping quiet. H&M, a Swedish fashion chain that opened it first Canadian store in Toronto in 2004 and has since expanded, is very good at bringing out the latest fashions at very reasonable prices. In fact, H&M has compressed the time from design to store delivery to three weeks, only a little behind Zara.

Sources:

Kerry Capell and Gerry Khermouch, "Hip H&M the Swedish Retailer Reinvents the World of Affordable Fashion," *Business Week* (Nov 11, 2002), p. 106.

William Echikson, "The Mark of Zara," *Business Week* (May 29, 2000), pp. 98–100.

Jane M. Folpe, "Zara Has a Made-to-Order Plan for Success," *Fortune* (September 4, 2000), p. 80.

Andy Georgiades, "Retailer H&M Is Set to Open Store in Canada," *Wall Street Journal* (March 10, 2004), B.4B.

Richard Heller, "Galician Beauty," *Forbes* (May 28, 2001), p. 98.

Laurent Marchal, "In Their Own Words," *Space* (Winter 2003), p. 4.

Stryker McGuire, "Fast Fashion; How a Secretive Spanish Tycoon Has Defied the Postwar Tide of Globalization, Bringing Factory Jobs from Latin America and Asia back to Europe," *Newsweek*, International Edition (September 17, 2001), p. 36.

---

products. The greatest flexibility along this dimension is achieved when every product is customized to meet the specific requirements of each individual customer. This is often referred to as **mass customization**. (See OM in Practice box on mass customization.)

mass customization
Providing high volume products that are individually customized to meet the specific needs of each customer.

Another dimension of flexibility is how fast a company can change its production facilities to produce a new line of products. This dimension is growing in importance, as product life cycles become shorter and shorter. Sony provides a good example here with its ability to quickly produce new models of its Walkman. Because it has this high degree of changeover flexibility, Sony is able to easily substitute new Walkman models for those models that do not sell well. Yet another dimension of flexibility is the ability to react to changes in volume, such as peak times in restaurants or holiday-season travel.

Service

As product life cycles become shorter and shorter, the actual products themselves tend to quickly resemble those of other companies. As a consequence, these products are often viewed as commodities in which price is the primary determinant in deciding which one to buy. A good example of this is the personal computer (PC) industry. Today, the differences in the products offered between the different PC manufacturers are relatively insignificant, so price is the prime selection criterion.

To obtain an advantage in such a competitive environment, firms are now providing "value-added" service. This is true for firms that provide goods and services. The reason is simple. As Sandra Vandermerwe puts it, "The market power is in the services, because the value is in the results." (Specific examples of how manufacturers are using services as a competitive advantage are presented later in this chapter.)

For example, Fairmont Hotels and Resorts, a Canadian hotel chain that owns luxury hotels and resorts worldwide, has operators answering its toll-free reservation numbers. Although a menu-driven voicemail system is more cost efficient, management knows that its high-income customers prefer a human operator.

Many of Canada's banks are embracing the Internet to provide customers with value-added services. For example, it is quite simple to pay a credit card bill postdated using the bank's Web site. This helps customers avoid forgetting to pay the bill by the due date as well as saving a trip to the mailbox or waiting in line at a branch.

The Next Sources of Competitive Advantage?

Managers are always looking for new ways in which to distinguish their firms from the competition. Currently, four new trends in business appear to be offering firms such an advantage: (1) the use of environmentally friendly processes and environmentally friendly products, (2) corporate responsibility in supply chains, (3) the use of information, and (4) the management of global operations.

Environmentally Friendly Processes and Products

As consumers become more aware of the fragility of the environment, they are increasingly turning towards products that are safe for the environment. The Body Shop, an international retail chain headquartered in England, sells various cosmetics and skin lotions that are made without harming the environment, while Safety-Kleen recycles used motor oil. Calgary-based Suncor has moved from being at the bottom of the oil and gas sector to one of the best in terms of environmental performance.[6] Fishery Products International, a St. John's, Newfoundland and Labrador-based producer of seafood, was recognized in 2000 by the National Fisheries Institute of the United States for its responsible fishing practices. *The Globe and Mail* even gives annual awards to companies that are environmentally friendly. (Chapter 1 discussed other examples of Canadian companies that have become environmentally proactive.)

Companies that can achieve conformance faster to increasingly strict environmental legislation in many countries that mandate reduction of toxic substances such as lead or mercury in products, as well as increased recycling and waste management, will have a competitive advantage. As well, many organizations are realizing that using recycled material (and better environmental practices in general) can reduce costs. As a result, recycled plastic from soft drink bottles is used by Ford Canada for automobile door padding as well as by other companies in products such as T-shirts and sleeping bags. Recycled rubber tires are used across Canada as playing surfaces for sports stadiums[7].

Corporate Responsibility in Supply Chains

Consumers, nongovernmental organizations (NGOs), charities, and other similar organizations have been active in promoting fair trade practices. As a result, companies are also recognizing the importance of corporate responsibility, not only within their own organizations, but also in their supply chains. This helps ensure that companies in the supply chain, especially in developing countries, follow environmentally conscious practices, offer acceptable working conditions, and respect human rights in issues such as child labour. For example, Ten Thousand Villages, a non-profit chain with 43 stores across Canada, sells handicrafts purchased from all over the world that are produced in a fair trade and environmentally friendly manner.

---

[6]A. Nikiforuk, "Saint or Sinner," *Canadian Business* (May 13, 2002).
[7]Diane Peters, "Talking Trash," *Reader's Digest*, December 2005, pp. 105–110.

The Use of Information

Although the term "Information Age" was initially used when the first mass-produced computers were introduced, it wasn't until recently that we actually did enter the information age. This is due in large part to advances in information technology that now allow large quantities of data to be transmitted and stored accurately, and, equally important, inexpensively. As a result, companies are looking to use information in different ways to obtain a competitive advantage in the marketplace. For example, GE Medical Systems sells high-performance products with built-in systems that automatically "call home" when failures occur, or even when potential failures are anticipated. Many times these problems or anticipated problems are repaired remotely, with little or no interruption in product performance. Feedback on existing products can also take the form of the "voice of the customer," as explained in the next chapter. In some instances this information is collected automatically, or through *service guarantees* (explained in detail in Chapter 6.)

Managing Global Operations

As discussed earlier in this chapter, globalization is an important trend affecting operations strategy. With many companies around the world becoming global (whether Magna in Canada or Acer, a computer maker, in Taiwan), managing operations will become more critical. Corporate head offices, marketing facilities, factories, and service centres may become geographically dispersed across different time zones. Each facility may manage the same process differently. Success will depend eventually upon the ability of the company to manage its global capital and human assets ethically and effectively in a multicultural environment, i.e., to provide goods and services efficiently. Other issues that managers will have to address when dealing with global operations are: supply chain strategy (including location), currency fluctuation, the management of risk (including political), compensation, employment standards, vacations, religion, employees' attitudes toward work, local infrastructure, and other cultural diversity issues.

In addition to all this is the issue of ethics. For example, should we locate a facility in a particular country because it has less stringent product labelling laws leading to lower product cost?

Developing an Operations Strategy from Competitive Priorities

Factory Focus and Trade-Offs

The notion of factory focus and trade-offs was central to the concept of operations strategy during the late 1960s and early 1970s. The underlying logic was that a factory could not excel simultaneously on all four competitive priorities. Consequently, management had to decide which priorities were critical to the firm's success, and then concentrate or focus the resources of the firm on those particular characteristics. For firms with very large manufacturing facilities, Skinner suggested the creation of a plant-within-a-plant (PWP) concept, in which different locations within the facility would be allocated to different product lines, each with their own competitive priority. Under the PWP concept, even the workers would be separated to minimize the confusion associated with shifting from one type of priority to another.[8]

---

[8]C. Wickham Skinner, "The Focused Factory," *Harvard Business Review* 52, no. 3 (May–June 1974), pp. 113–122.

The need for focus has been recognized in service operations as well. Hotel chains such as Marriott and Holiday Inn have segmented the hotel industry and now offer a wide variety of products, each focused on a different market segment. For example, within the Marriott group there are Fairfield Inns for economy-minded customers, Marriott Hotels and Resorts for conferences and for customers wanting full-service hotels, Residence Inns for customers wanting more than just a hotel room, and Marriott Courtyards for those wanting certain hotel conveniences such as meals but who are still concerned about price. Similarly, Shouldice Hospital near Toronto (see case at the end of Chapter 7) performs only one type of hernia operation. The benefits of a focused operation can be readily demonstrated at Shouldice hospital. Planning and scheduling is much easier, costs are lower, quality is higher in terms of both medical care and patient service, and patients are treated and discharged much faster than in a less-focused general hospital. However, as a specialist hospital, Shouldice lacks flexibility; that is, it cannot perform other types of medical treatment. Thus there are trade-offs when a company chooses to focus on certain priorities. (See the Lasik Vision case on laser eye surgery at the end of this chapter.)

Questioning the Trade-Offs

With the world becoming a single global village, a group of companies has emerged with an international perspective toward both manufacturing and marketing. Within this global arena, competition is significantly more intense, due both to the greater number of players and the tremendous profit opportunities that exist.

Companies that have excelled on this global level often are referred to as *world class operations*. Events in the world marketplace during the 1970s and 1980s, in terms of the growing intensity in competition, forced these companies to re-examine the concept of operations strategy, especially in terms of the so-called necessary trade-offs. Managers began to realize that they didn't have to make trade-offs to the same extent they had previously thought. What emerged instead was a realization of the need to establish a hierarchy among the different priorities, as dictated by the marketplace. Exhibit 2.3 presents the sequence in which these priorities were introduced over time.

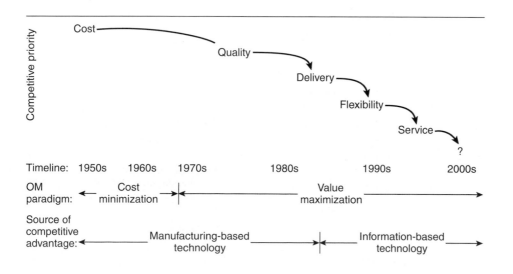

Exhibit 2.3

Timeline for Operations Strategies

Specifically, in the late 1960s and early 1970s, cost was the primary concern, a hold-over from the philosophy of the 1950s that manufacturing's only objective was to minimize production costs. However, as more and more companies began to produce low-cost products, companies needed to develop other ways to differentiate themselves from their competitors. The priority thus shifted to quality. A clear example is the change in the North American automobile industry due to Japanese entrants. Companies at this time obtained a competitive advantage by producing high-quality products, which allowed them to charge more—although price still was a factor in the consumer's buying decision. However, competition again soon caught up, and everyone was offering high-quality products that were reasonably priced.

Companies, looking to obtain another competitive advantage in the marketplace, turned to speed and reliability of delivery as a means of differentiating themselves from the rest of the pack. Now the ante into the game was high-quality products that were reasonably priced *and* that could be delivered quickly and reliably to the customer.

In the 1980s, George Stalk Jr., a leading management guru, identified speed of delivery as a major factor in determining the success of a company.[9] Companies therefore concentrated their resources on reducing product lead times, with dramatic results: Products that once took weeks or months to deliver now were being shipped within hours or days of the receipt of an order.

Eventually, the competition again caught up, and the more aggressive firms looked for still another means to obtain a competitive advantage. This time flexibility was selected, as measured in terms of the firm's ability to produce customized products. Now the marketplace dictated that firms, to be successful, had to produce reasonably priced, customized products of high quality that could be quickly delivered to the customer. (See the OM in Practice box on mass customization.)

As the rules for operations strategy shifted from that of primarily reducing costs to that of including quality, speed of delivery, flexibility, and service, the strategy for the operations management function also shifted. The strategy of minimizing production costs has been replaced with that of maximizing the value added.

This emphasis on being competitive on more than one dimension might lead to the conclusion that there are no longer any trade-offs. This is not the case. As Wickham Skinner said in 1995, "There will always be trade-offs." Today, however, those trade-offs occur on what can be described as a superior performance curve, as shown in Exhibit 2.4.

Exhibit 2.4

Example of Trade-Offs on Superior Performance Curves

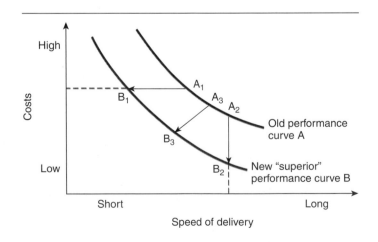

[9]George Stalk Jr., "Time and Innovation," *Canadian Business Review* 20, no. 3 (Autumn 1993), pp. 15–18.

PROCESS FLEXIBILITY + THE INTERNET = MASS CUSTOMIZATION ONLINE

The Internet has made virtually every corner of the world accessible to customers, and in so doing has driven down prices and profits for most products. This hypercompetitive environment has forced businesses to look at new ways to distinguish themselves from their competitors.

To achieve a distinctive market presence, many companies are providing mass-customized products through the Internet. These customized products cannot be stocked in the traditional bricks-and-mortar retail stores. To serve the mass-customization market, firms need flexible manufacturing processes that can accommodate a wide variety of product configurations. For example, Masterfoods, USA, a division of Mars, Inc., can now offer customers a choice of 21 colours of M&Ms in any combination of colours in eight-ounce and five-pound bags (previously, the minimum order size was 40 pounds). These custom-coloured M&Ms, which can also have custom printing on them (It's a Boy!, It's a Girl!, Happy Birthday Harry!), are sold online at a cost almost three times the price of regular M&Ms.

Yankee Candle allows its online customers to custom configure votive candles, choosing among 24 labels, 43 scents, six tulle wrappings, 13 ribbon colours and patterns, and seven silk flower accents—all with customized messages. You can order customized pants from Lands' End, choosing the fabric, the colour, the rise, the front style, the pocket flap style, and a cuff or hem. Lands' End also offers customized shirts, with choices of fabric and colour as well as collar and cuff style, yoke style, and fit according to your measurements and body type descriptions. Reflect.com offers customized cosmetics, including lipsticks and moisturizers. Customers enter information about skin colour and type as well as makeup style preferences, and the interactive site provides guidance about product choices and adds custom ingredients as desired. After you've customized the product, you name the product and it is custom labelled. At Nike ID, Nike's Web site for ordering customized footwear, you choose your favourite colour combinations and personalize your footwear with your name or your favourite slogan. To be able to offer customized footwear, Nike spent six months revamping the manufacturing processes in its Asian factories to increase their flexibility.

Sources:
Lisa Takeuchi Cullen, "Have It Your Way," *Time*, December 23, 2002, pp. 41–42; Faith Keenan, "A Mass Market of One," *Business Week*, December 2, 2002, pp. 68–72; www.yankeecandle.com, accessed April 16, 2004; www.landsend.com, accessed April 16, 2004; www.m-ms.com, accessed April 16, 2004; www.reflect.com, accessed April 16, 2004; www.nikeid.nike.com/nikeid/, accessed April 16, 2004.

In moving to a higher performance curve, managers are no longer only concerned with trade-offs, which take place when one moves along an established curve, such as going from point A_1 to point A_2 on curve A in Exhibit 2.4. Instead, the same speed of delivery can be provided, but at a lower cost, as shown in going from point A_2 to point B_2. Another approach is to improve the speed of delivery while maintaining the same cost, as seen in going from point A_1 to point B_1. A third alternative is to both improve the speed of delivery and reduce cost, as seen in going from point A_3 to point B_3. The important matter here is that in all three examples, the value to the customer is increased significantly, which is the primary purpose for moving to the superior performance curve.

Order-Qualifiers and Order-Winners

Terry Hill of the London Business School has developed the strategic concept of **order-qualifiers** and **order-winners**.[10] Order-qualifiers can be defined as the minimum elements or characteristics that a firm or its products must have even to be considered as a potential supplier or source.

For example, as recently as a few years ago, even an expensive hotel offering an Internet connection in its rooms would have used it as a order-winner. Today, however, almost all types of hotel chains offer in-room Internet connections. Thus in-room Internet has become an order-qualifier, because if a hotel does not offer this facility, many customers will choose another hotel. However, offering a high-definition (HD) television set in the room could be an order-winner.

order-qualifiers
Minimum characteristics of a firm or its products to be considered as a source of purchase.

order-winners
Characteristics of a firm that distinguish it from its competition so that it is selected as the source of purchase.

---

[10]T. Hill, *Manufacturing Strategy: Text and Cases*, 3rd ed. (Burr Ridge, IL: Irwin/McGraw-Hill, 2000).

Basically, when very few firms offer a specific characteristic, such as high quality, customization, or outstanding service, that characteristic can be defined as an order-winner. However, over time, as more and more firms begin to offer that same enhancement, the order-winner becomes an order-qualifier. In other words, it becomes the minimum acceptable level for all competitors. As a result, the customer uses some other new enhancement or characteristic to make the final purchase.

Distinctive (Core) Competencies

critical success factors

The activities, conditions, or other deliverables that are necessary for the firm to achieve its business goals.

distinctive (core) competency

An exceptional capability that creates a preference for a firm and its products or services in the market-place, enabling it to achieve a leadership position over time.

In order to excel at any of the competitive priorities, a firm must determine its **critical success factors:** the activities, conditions, or other deliverables that are necessary for the firm to achieve its business goals—in other words, the things the organization must get right. For example, if the goal of a bank is to achieve a certain percentage of Internet-based transactions, a critical success factor will be a user-friendly Web site that encourages customers to bank online rather than at a branch.

Once the critical success factors have been identified, the firm must develop a set of distinctive (core) competencies. A **distinctive (core) competency** is an exceptional capability that creates a preference for a firm and its products or services in the market-place, enabling it to achieve a leadership position over time. From a strategic perspective, particularly in services, which are relatively easy to copy, it is critical for firms to develop some capabilities in distinctive competencies that are difficult for other firms to replicate. (Note: the terms *distinctive competency*, *core competency*, and *core capability* are often used interchangeably. If there is a difference between them, it is in perspective.) Distinctive competencies are perceived by the customer and hence relate directly to the firm's success in the marketplace. For example, the ability to offer stylish haircuts at a low price may be the distinctive competency perceived by the customer. Core competencies may not be perceived directly by the customer, but they relate to what the customer perceives as distinctive competencies. For example, the distinctive competency of stylish haircuts at a low price may be related to the hair salon chain's core competency to attract and retain well-trained young stylists.

To focus on these core competencies, firms, both in manufacturing and services, have begun to divest themselves of those capabilities that are not considered critical to their success. In manufacturing, more and more components and subassemblies that were previously built in-house are now being subcontracted or outsourced to suppliers. As a result, the material cost in most manufacturing companies, as a percentage of total manufacturing costs, has substantially increased in recent years. On the other hand, the labour cost, as a percentage, has been drastically reduced, often to less than 5 percent of total costs.

This focus on core competencies also has impacted services. More and more service operations are now subcontracting out ancillary support services that were previously provided in-house. Again, this strategy has allowed these services to concentrate on improving their core competencies. For example, some universities subcontract on-campus food services to companies such as Sodexho, Chartwells, or Aramark (this is not without controversy; outsourcing food services at universities has raised concerns from employee and student unions about job losses, working conditions, and food quality). Many Canadian companies have outsourced the maintenance of their employee uniforms to Cintas Corp., which has locations in British Columbia, Alberta, Ontario, and Quebec. High-tech companies such as Cisco Systems, IBM, and NEC have outsourced their manufacturing to contractors such as Toronto-based Celestica, preferring to concentrate on product design and development.

In many instances, the companies that subcontract these support services discover that the subcontractors can perform them better and at a lower cost than when they are done internally. This focus on core capabilities further supports the concept of a *value chain*. Here each company focuses on its core capabilities, thereby allowing it to maximize its value contribution to the end product that is provided to the customer. (A word of caution, however. Casually subcontracting a function that is not viewed as a core competency may result in losing knowledgeable people who know how the broader system operates and who can deal with unexpected emergencies that might shut down a core activity.)

Operations Strategy Decisions

The decisions relating to operations strategy have been classified into two broad categories: strategic decisions, which are more long term; and tactical issues, which are more short term.

Strategic Decisions

Strategic decisions include (*a*) location, (*b*) capacity, (*c*) vertical integration, and (*d*) process choice.

Location

is a major decision that can have a significant impact on the fortunes of a company. Choosing the wrong location can result in operations not being competitive, resulting in loss of market share. It may also mean that the large sum of money spent on locating the facility was wasted. So companies make location decisions only after much thought and strategic analysis. Location is discussed further in Chapter 7.

Capacity

Physical capacity decisions are critically important. Too much capacity is costly, because it represents unnecessary fixed costs, and may reduce profits to the point of bankruptcy. Conversely, too little capacity may create long lead times for manufactured goods and long waiting lines for services that frustrate customers and reduce their loyalty, leading to opportunity costs in the form of lost sales when customers take their business elsewhere. Strategic capacity is discussed in Chapter 7.

Vertical integration

Vertical integration relates to how much of the supply chain is controlled by the organization. Backward integration involves purchasing or controlling the suppliers; forward integration involves purchasing or controlling customers. For example, a coffeehouse chain might purchase coffee bean growers (backward integration) or an airline might purchase a company that provides tours in the cities to which the airline flies (forward integration). Technology has enabled organizations to work together as closely as if they were vertically integrated while still maintaining individual ownerships. This virtual vertical integration makes it possible for organizations to share information and engage in joint planning that produces an advantage for all parties involved. Vertical integration is discussed in Chapter 12.

Process choice

The choice of the process used to produce goods and provide services is very important for most organizations. For example, some restaurants choose to provide table service, while others provide only counter service, and still others have customers serve themselves. Some manufacturing firms choose highly automated, specialized equipment to produce large volumes of a single product, while others may choose more general-purpose equipment that can be used to make a wide range of products. Process choice is discussed in Chapter 3.

Tactical Decisions

Until just recently, tactical decisions were thought to be more quickly changed than strategic decisions, although anyone who has ever had managerial responsibility knows that these decisions cannot be "turned on a dime." The tactical decisions relate to (*a*) workforce, (*b*) quality management, (*c*) operations planning and control, and (*d*) organizational structure.

Workforce

Managers need to establish the skills qualifications for their workers and to determine how the workers will be scheduled, trained, and evaluated. For example, a walk-in medical clinic may choose to staff much of its workforce with nurse practitioners who can assess and treat a wide variety of patients' presenting problems, but whose salaries are likely to be lower than those of physicians. Some restaurants may choose to employ professional waitstaff, and others may choose to employ high school or college students for their major waitstaff pool.

Quality management

Managers also need to decide how quality will be defined, measured, and monitored within their organizations. Bombardier and Imperial Oil are well known for their Six Sigma quality programs, investing in extensive training in statistical analysis and problem solving for their Quality Black Belts. Quality decisions are critically important for every firm, but present particular challenges for service organizations, because of the intangibility of services and the simultaneity of production and consumption. Quality is discussed in Chapter 6.

Operations planning and control

Managers also need to define how the work will be performed and how decisions will be made. These policies and procedures can make a tremendous difference in the quality and efficiency of both manufacturing and service processes. For example, Toyota has been tremendously successful with employing the Toyota Production System to efficiently produce nearly defect-free cars with low levels of inventory. Similarly, one of the reasons for McDonald's success is the consistency of its products and services around the world, which can be attributed in large part to the very clear procedures that have been developed for the way hamburgers and fries should be made and served to customers. Operations planning and control decisions are discussed in Chapters 13 through 16, as well as Chapter 11.

Organizational structure

The hierarchical structure of an organization defines who reports to whom, which in turn determines how the work gets done. For example, manufacturing companies may be organized according to traditional functions, such as operations, marketing, and accounting, or may be organized around product lines with reporting relationships that cross functional boundaries. Similarly, hospitals may be organized according to traditional departments, such as medicine, surgery, nursing, and pharmacy, or they may be organized around service lines, such as women's health care and cardiac care. The way people interact in organizations that are structured differently is likely to be very different.

Clearly, operations strategy decisions are highly interrelated. When these decisions are aligned, the strategy has a good chance of success. When the decisions are not aligned, intraorganizational conflicts arise—and customers can feel the disconnect, too.

The strategy decisions made within the various functions determine how and which processes are established, as well as how performance is measured. Optimally, throughout the strategy development process, information is continuously fed back through the system so that customers' needs are continuously being identified and addressed and performance goals are being achieved. The production or service delivery process, then, is continuously driven by strategy, which is continuously being monitored by the established performance measures.

Integration of Manufacturing and Services

Many firms are now looking to integrated and user-friendly service as a means of obtaining a competitive advantage in the marketplace. In so doing they are recognizing the need to align and integrate the products that are being offered. This is true for both manufacturing and service operations.

Xerox Canada, traditionally a manufacturer of copiers and printers, now calls itself the "document company." To improve their competitiveness, they have moved from providing only hardware to offering solutions that can improve the customer's processing of information, which involves a considerable value-added service aspect. As another illustration, SKF in Sweden no longer produces only ball bearings for its after-market or replacement business. It also provides advice to customers on spare parts management, training, and installation, and suggests good preventative maintenance practices that will extend the life of the bearings.

These services can range from activities in the pre-purchase to purchase and post-purchase phases[11] and even activities downstream from production such as distribution.[12] Hendrix Voeders, traditionally a feed supplier to pig farmers in Holland, now provides a wide range of services including consulting on pig breeding, nutritional management, and logistics. Coca-Cola has taken over some of the bottling and distribution of Coke products, downstream activities that were previously done by independent bottlers.

Some manufacturers provide extensive customer training to accompany the purchase of products. Customers become familiar with the products and learn to use them optimally. In addition this training can act as a competitive barrier. The Foxboro Company uses training to distance itself from the competition. Before its process control products are delivered, customers are invited to Foxboro's manufacturing facility, where their equipment is set up and they learn how to use it under the guidance of Foxboro instructors. This is one of the reasons Foxboro experiences a very high percentage of repeat business from existing customers.

By integrating goods and services into a total package, or a "bundle of benefits," companies are better able to address the overall needs of their customers. The opening vignettes of this chapter and of Chapter 4, in which Dofasco and EllisDon no longer simply make goods, but try to provide complete solutions for their customer needs through various allied services, reemphasize the importance of providing a total package in order to be successful in the twenty-first century.

---

[11]Sandra Vandermerwe, *From Tin Soldiers to Russian Dolls: Creating Added Value Through Services* (Oxford, England: Butterworth-Heinemann, 1993).

[12]Richard Wise and Peter Baumgartner, "Go Downstream: The New Profit Imperative in Manufacturing," *Harvard Business Review* 77, no. 5 (September–October 1999), pp. 133–141.

Conclusion

The concept of operations strategy plays an important role in determining the overall long-term success of an organization. Developing an operations strategy means looking to new ways to add value for the customer in the goods and services that the firm produces and delivers. Value can have many meanings. Managers must therefore align the operations strategy of their firm with the strategies of other functional areas and with the firm's overall business strategy.

The combination of the globalization of business coupled with advances in technology has created a hyper-competitive environment in which managers must constantly be looking for new and innovative strategies to stay ahead of the competition. To properly implement these strategies, managers need to clearly understand the core competencies of their firm and focus their resources on maintaining and improving these capabilities.

Successful firms today are looking to develop strategies that integrate goods and services into a single product offering or "bundle of benefits," which attempts to solve problems for customers rather than just selling them products.

Key Terms

business strategy p. 29

competitive priorities p. 30

   cost p. 32

   delivery p. 32

   flexibility p. 32

   quality p. 32

   service p. 32

corporate strategy p. 28

cost leadership p. 29

critical success factors p. 40

differentiation p. 29

distinctive (core)
   competency p. 40

functional strategies p. 30

market segmentation p. 30

mass customization p. 34

mission p. 28

operations strategy p. 30

order-qualifiers p. 39

order-winners p. 39

strategic business unit (SBU)
   p. 28

vision p. 28

Review and Discussion Questions

1. What is meant by competitiveness?
2. Identify the different types of competitive priorities. How has their relationship to each other changed over the years?
3. For each of the different competitive priorities, describe the unique characteristics of the market niche with which it is most compatible.
4. Describe the difference between order-qualifiers and order-winners. What is the relationship between the two over time?
5. Explain the concept of the core competencies within an organization.
6. In your opinion, do business schools have competitive priorities?
7. Why does the "proper" operations strategy keep changing for companies that are world-class competitors?
8. What is meant by the expression "manufacturing is entering the information age"?

9. What kind of information do you think would add value to the following goods and services?
   a. Used car
   b. Hotel in a foreign city
   c. Cruise ship
   d. College
10. Describe the type of service that would make the following items more attractive to purchase.
    a. Suit of clothes
    b. Used car
    c. Personal computer
    d. Fruits and vegetables
11. For each of the following, what, in your opinion are the order-qualifiers and order-winners?
    a. Selecting an airline to fly on
    b. Deciding in which supermarket to buy groceries
    c. Buying an automobile
    d. Picking a restaurant for Saturday night

Go to the Online Learning Centre (OLC) Web site at www.mcgrawhill.ca/olc/davis and take several company tours for the purpose of describing some of their competitive priorities. For each tour identify the company, the product it makes, and its competitive priorities.

$\boxed{\text{Case 1}}$ Lasik Vision Corp.

At its peak in late 2000, Lasik Vision Corporation had over 30 clinics operating in North America, second only to TLC Laser Eye Centers in Toronto, Ontario, which had 62 clinics. Dr. Hugo Sutton, an eye surgeon and a clinical associate professor at the University of British Columbia, and Michael Henderson founded Lasik Vision in 1997. Since 1978, Sutton had been operating his own eye clinic, initially specializing in cataract surgery. In the intervening years, technological advances such as the excimer laser had transformed refractive surgery (the process of correcting myopia, hyperopia, or astigmatism by altering the contours of the cornea) from a low-tech risky procedure using lathes and sutures into a viable proposition for patients who could spend $5000. After the surgery, they could discard their glasses or contacts. The efficient new procedure eventually allowed surgeons to reduce the fees for this service, making it even more attractive for patients. In 1991, in partnership with two other surgeons, Dr. Sutton set up his own refractive surgery clinic. By 1996, the Lasik technique, sparing patients the months of healing that came with older procedures, became the vogue.

It was at that time that Michael Henderson, a business executive and husband to one of Sutton's patients, approached him. Sutton remembers that "Henderson felt that this was a very powerful technology, a technology that he could take much further. He thought that we were rather pedestrian, slow, and old fashioned." Since Sutton was tiring of doing all the surgeries with little help, the proposal sounded very appealing. In June 1997, Michael Henderson joined Sutton's company,

TMX Laser Vision Canada Inc., as vice president.

Soon it became clear that Henderson was on an efficiency drive. He felt that the way to fortune was to reengineer the traditional model of the refractive surgery process. He let a few employees go, increasing the workload for the remainder. To improve efficiency, he tried not to use expensive equipment. For example, he opposed installing an ultrasound scanner to measure the individual layers of each cornea. This scanner improves the Lasik technique's success ratio. Dr. Sutton overruled him on this idea, but many of Henderson's ideas were implemented.

The traditional model involved acquiring patients through optometrist referrals. These optometrists also provided the postoperative care and received a portion of the $4000 to $5000 fee. In the reengineered model, the optometrists were cut out of the loop. Also, every step in the care delivery system was standardized. Patients were attracted directly with aggressive advertising and a price well below competitors, initially $2995. Henderson's vision of mass volume with low margins was launched in February 1998. Traditionally, other competitors such as TLC ran higher-priced, lower-volume operations (TLC has continued with its model of including the optometrists).

At the same time, Sutton also believed in aggressive treatment. According to one of his colleagues, Dr. Dan Reinstein, "Hugo's nature is pioneering. And so by definition, he is more likely to have less conservative, uh, outcomes." Unfortunately, many patients were not properly informed that they were less-than-ideal candidates for the surgery. In a competitive medical environment, patients emerging from surgery with odd results led to lawsuits. As a result, in August 1998, a rare public statement from the B.C. College of Physicians and Surgeons said that Sutton "has agreed to a modification of his practice and he has voluntarily agreed not to perform these surgical procedures on patients in the higher risk categories."

In light of Sutton's troubles, Henderson became president and CEO in April 1999 and began pushing the company into massive expansion and a public offering. This expansion actually started in Toronto in September 1998, followed by Calgary two months later. Henderson continued expansion until eight more sites had been added by September 1999. Henderson insisted that pricing was the key. In TV advertisements, Henderson personally extolled the Lasik Vision message—Why pay more?—standing next to a large graphic proclaiming "$1475 per eye." By early 1999, the pricing was dropped to $1598 for both eyes, but Henderson preferred to see it even lower. One advertisement he initiated proclaimed a cost of $999 with an asterisk listing another $599 in additional fees in fine print. This prompted Advertising Standards Canada to demand a change.

In December 1999, Henderson announced his intention to step up the pace of expansion. Beginning March 2000, Lasik Vision would start expanding at the pace of one new site per week to open about 20 clinics in the United States. The whole delivery process would be standardized right from the décor of the waiting rooms to the approach in which patients were counselled and corneas were lasered. This was the only way large volumes of patients could be treated with a high level of care. The medical doctors responded to the challenge by devising a hiring and training system that Sutton and the other doctors felt would enable reliable quality across the country.

All this development and expansion was taking place while trouble was brewing between the doctors and Henderson over financial and managerial improprieties. Henderson was aggressively skimming off profits from the company for himself. The last straw came in the spring of 2000 when PriceWaterhouseCoopers grew concerned about Henderson's "unfettered" activities while auditing Lasik's financial statements. In June 2000, Henderson was fired from the company.

Epilogue

Henderson subsequently sued Lasik Vision and Sutton for negligence during an eye surgery performed on his eyes in March 1998, which he claims damaged his vision. Reinstein admits that Henderson had a complication. Henderson's problem, Reinstein insists, is that he does not understand the difference between complication and negligence. "Well, maybe you shouldn't expect him to," he sniffs. "He is not a doctor." Still you have to hand it to him, says Reinstein, "He is an amazing guy. I did learn a lot about doing business from him."

By 2001 the industry was mired in the ugly price war initiated by Lasik Vision, in addition to an advertising war, with many companies spending 10 to 13 percent of revenue on advertising (TLC has even signed professional golfer Tiger Woods to a multi-year contract to endorse his surgery at TLC). Lasik's stock slid from $6 in April 1999 to about a tenth of that by December 2000. As a result of all this, a consolidation spree ensued.

The January 31, 2001, edition of the *Globe and Mail* reported that Lasik Vision had been acquired by another discounter, Icon Laser Eye Centers. At that time Lasik called itself the Dell Computer of laser vision correction—"we offer a high-quality product direct to customers and we cut distribution costs without compromising patient care." However, TLC disagreed: "Clearly it's the utter failure of both their business and clinical models that has forced them into such dire financial circumstances and their marriage of desperation in the first place." At about the same time, Aris Vision of Los Angeles acquired control of Gimbel Vision International of Calgary.

The August 28, 2001, issue of the *Globe and Mail* reported that the two leading laser eye surgery companies, TLC Laser

Centers and St. Louis-based Laser Vision Centers Inc., were merging. It also mentioned that these two companies had refused to participate in the price war initiated by Lasik Vision, which, ironically, had resulted in both Lasik Vision and its acquirer, Icon, going bankrupt.

Questions

1. What was Lasik Vision's competitive priority?

2. Is it an appropriate approach in this industry? What repercussions, actual or perceived, might occur with this priority?

3. What might be some of the external influences on strategy formulation?

4. Given that a company has chosen this priority, what would it have to do to achieve success?

5. What are the order-qualifiers and order-winners in this business?

Source:
This case was adapted by Jaydeep Balakrishnan from an article written by Trevor Cole in *ROB Magazine*, January 2001, and is for discussion purposes only. It is not intended to illustrate the proper or improper management of a situation. Richard B. Chase, F. Robert Jacobs, and Nicholas J. Aquilano, *Operations Management for Competitive Advantage*, 10th ed. (New York: Irwin McGraw-Hill, 2004).

3

New Product and Service Development, and Process Selection

Chapter Objectives

- Illustrate the importance of the development of new products and services to a firm's competitiveness.

- Identify the various types of new products that are developed by companies.

- Introduce the new product design process and the concept of a product's life cycle.

- Demonstrate the necessity of concurrent product and process design as a new product or service is developed.

- Present a framework for understanding how new services are developed and introduced into the marketplace.

Canadian New Product Development Excellence

...in the East

EXFO Electro-Optical Engineering Inc. of Quebec City designs and manufactures fibre-optic test, measurement, monitoring, and automation solutions for the global telecommunications industry. In 2000 it became the first non-U.S. firm to win the Outstanding Corporate Innovator award from the Product Development and Management Association (PDMA). EXFO's strategy is focused on delivering innovative products faster than its competitors. As a result, EXFO has reduced its new product development time from 18–24 months to 9–12 months, an improvement of 50%. Indeed, its new product development process is often benchmarked by other firms. Its success in new product development has resulted in 2000 customer companies in 70 countries around the world. As a result of their market share growth, EXFO received the Growth Strategy Leadership Award in both 2004 and 2005 from a leading market research expert firm in the telecom industry.

...in the West

You may not have heard of Carmanah Technologies of Victoria, B.C., but if you visit Las Vegas, one of those signs inviting you to go in and play blackjack might be made by Carmanah. That is not all it does. Carmanah is a leading integrator of renewable and

energy-efficient technology solutions. The company currently produces solar-powered LED lighting, solar power systems (as backups or in areas where there is no access to power lines), and LED-illuminated signage. Its products are used in transportation, industrial, and domestic applications in many different countries. With manufacturing facilities located in Victoria and Calgary, Carmanah has garnered many awards for innovative lighting products in recent years.

...in an Emerging Industry

One area where Canadian companies have made a good start is in biotechnology. Although challenges exist to maintain competitiveness, Canada currently ranks second in the world behind the United States in terms of the number of biotech companies.

...and is based on Commitment

Successful new product developments such as these come not through good fortune but through long-term investment in new products and processes. For example, CAE of Toronto, a global leader in the design and manufacture of flight simulators for military and civilian aircraft, and control system and training simulators for power plants and marine applications, spends over 20 percent of its annual revenue on research and development.

Sources:

EXFO Electro-Optical Engineering Inc., www.exfo.com.

Visions (January 2001), www.pdma.org/visions/jan01.

James O'Brien, "Survival of the Fittest," Canadian Business (September 2, 2003), pp. 46–49.

Carmanah, www.carmanah.com.

CAE, www.cae.com.

Managerial Issues

A fact of life for most companies and their managers in today's highly competitive environment is that product life cycles are becoming shorter and shorter. To remain competitive and retain overall market share within their respective industries, managers therefore need to focus their resources on developing new products and bringing them to market more quickly and efficiently—and doing it on a continuous basis. From golf shoes to computers, new products often represent the majority of a company's sales. Thus, a failure to introduce new products will ultimately erode a firm's market share and its associated profits.

Why Emphasize New Goods and Services?

Firms today are under more pressure than ever to develop new goods and services more frequently. At the same time, they are also realizing that failure to manage the new product or service development process properly can result in the failure of the product or service in the marketplace because it lacks the features desired by the customer or because competitors introduced the new product or service earlier (See the OMP boxes in this chapter for examples.) Some of the major causes for this increased emphasis on developing new products are (*a*) increased competition, (*b*) advances in technology, (*c*) customer demand, and (*d*) regulation changes.

Increased Competition

As the world becomes a single, global economy, most firms have seen a significant increase in foreign competition in their respective markets. The reasons for this increase in foreign competition are many, including advances in telecommunication technology, a trend to lower trade barriers, and increases in the speed of transportation of goods.

In such a highly competitive environment, the markets for these goods and services tend to reach their maturity much sooner than was previously the case. As a result, these products become commodities much sooner, and their profit margins tend to erode more quickly. Thus firms have to introduce new products to restore profit margins.

Advances in Technology

Rapid advances in technology are causing many products to become obsolete more quickly. The OMP box on Kodak is a good example. The length of time a particular model of any electronic good is stocked has been reduced considerably in recent years. Computers are another good example of products that have been significantly impacted by advances in technology. The speeds and storage capacities of today's computers far exceed anything imaginable 15 years ago, and this trend will most likely continue in the future.

Technology also has impacted the processes by which goods and services are produced and delivered. Computer-aided design (CAD) and computer-aided manufacturing (CAM) systems now provide firms with the ability to significantly reduce the time between product development and production. Another example of how technology has affected the production process is the increased use of robotics on the factory floor. This not only reduces labour costs, but also significantly increases product quality.

Rapid Prototyping (RP) is a computer-aided technique for quickly building physical prototypes from the CAD files used to develop three-dimensional drawings. Using solid-to-the-touch prototypes in developing new products can save time and money because better designs or design flaws can be identified earlier. In one case using RP,

Ford reduced the time required to bring an engine to market by 13 months. In another case the company reduced the cost of a part by 45 percent.[1]

Customer Demand

The combination of increased competition and the greater availability of information has also resulted in more educated consumers who now expect new products to be introduced more frequently. Many publications both in print and online are devoted to comparing existing products and informing customers of new developments. Also, online purchasing has increased product availability from a geographical perspective. Thus, customers are able to better locate and purchase appropriate products. Companies have to respond to ensure that they do not lag behind competitors.

The multi-information display panel on the Toyota Prius, Toyota's fuel-efficient gas/electric car, features a computerized display that includes real-time information on fuel consumption at various speeds.

Regulation Changes

Often changes in government regulations force companies to introduce new products to meet the new regulations. Examples in the auto industry are the regulations that required elimination of lead from gasoline and increased crash safety. Similarly, environmental regulations have forced pesticide manufacturers to change formulations.

The Benefits of Introducing New Products Faster

Greater Market Share

Firms with the ability to bring new products to market quickly have several advantages over their slower competitors. First, as illustrated in Exhibit 3.1A, early market entrants take market share, which is easier to accomplish when there is no competition, compared to trying to take market share away from an entrenched competitor. This is especially true for revolutionary products (which are discussed shortly) for which there are no alternatives. For example, in the semiconductor industry, history has shown that the first two firms to enter a market with a new product tend to capture the majority of the market share for those products. Conversely, in the personal computer industry, one manufacturer estimated a 50 to 75 percent loss in sales due to a six- to eight-month delay in bringing a new product to market. The Apple Ipod is an excellent example of a product that has captured a majority of the market share in its product category.

Price Premiums

Second, when a firm (such as Apple) is the first to bring a new product to market, it has little or no competition, and therefore can charge premium prices, as shown in Exhibit 3.1B,

---

[1]Gary S. Vasilash, "Rapid Prototyping at Ford Saves Time and Money," *Automotive Design & Production*, www.autofieldguide.com/articles, December 8, 2003.

Exhibit 3.1

The Impact of Speed to Market on Market Share, Profit Margins, and Profits over the Product Life Cycle.

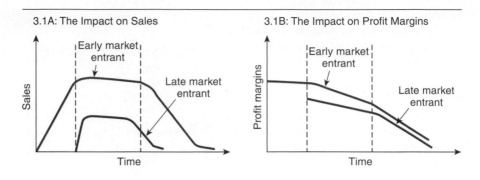

3.1A: The Impact on Sales

3.1B: The Impact on Profit Margins

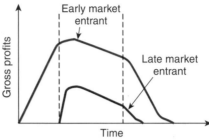

3.1C: The Impact on Gross Profits

while the competition struggles to catch up. This combination of market share and price premiums translates into significant profits, as seen in Exhibit 3.1C (which, in turn, provide the necessary funding to develop and introduce the next round of new products). Thus, the faster a product is introduced into the market ahead of the competition, the more profitable that product is over its entire life cycle. The product life cycle is the time from introduction of the product into the market to its withdrawal (hopefully to be replaced by the next-generation version). In fact, products that are late to market have a much more negative impact on profitability than do cost overruns in either the product development phase or production.[2]

Quick Reaction to Competition

A company that has the resource capability to bring new products to market quickly is also in a much better position to respond quickly to a competitor's surprise announcement of the introduction of a new product. With such resources in hand, the firm can significantly limit the competitive disadvantage usually associated with being a market latecomer.

Set Industry Standards

For revolutionary products, the first firm into the market often has the luxury of setting the standards for that industry. This, in many cases, acts as a barrier to entry, further delaying competitors. Microsoft, first with DOS and then with Windows, provides good examples of this.

---

[2]S. Hamilton, "New-Product Development and Manufacturing Competitiveness: A Hewlett-Packard Perspective" in *Time-Based Competition: The Next Battleground in American Manufacturing*, ed. J. D. Blackburn (Homewood, IL: Business One Irwin, 1991), chap. 8.

Categories of New Products

New products can be grouped according to the degree of innovation associated with them in comparison to existing products. Within this framework, we define three broad categories of new products: (*a*) incremental or derivative products, (*b*) next generation or platform products, and (*c*) breakthrough or radical products. Each of these types of products places specific requirements upon the firm, with those that are the most innovative usually requiring the greatest commitment of resources. Equally important is the fact that each plays an important role in the long-term success of the firm.

Incremental or Derivative Products

On one end of the spectrum are products that have the least amount of innovation. These are often referred to as incremental or *derivative products* and are typically hybrids or enhancements of existing products. These products are often cost-reduced versions of existing products or simply similar products with added features or functions. For example, the minor model-year changes made in the automobile industry can be seen as derivative or incremental products. Such new products require minimal changes in both product design and the manufacturing process. The resource requirements to develop these products are significantly less than those for products that break entirely new ground, because they tend to leverage off of existing products by extending their applicability. Products in this category are crucial to the firm in that they ensure continuing near-term cash flows. They also allow a firm to maintain market share in the short term by continually improving and refining existing product lines.

Next Generation or Platform Products

The middle of these three categories is referred to as *next generation* or *platform products*, which often represent new "system" solutions for the customer. They provide a broad base for a product family that can be leveraged over several years and, therefore, require significantly more resources than do derivative or incremental products. Intel's 286, 386, 486, Pentium, Pentium II, Pentium III, and Pentium 4 microprocessors provide an excellent example of products that fall into this category. Major model changeovers in the automobile industry, like the new Mustang from Ford, are also examples of next generation and platform products. Products in this category are the key to a company's continued growth in revenue in that they provide the necessary foundation for a series of evolutionary products, to which the firm's customers can then migrate over several years.

Breakthrough or Radical Products

At the other end of the new products spectrum are those products that are defined as *breakthrough* or *radical products*. The development of these products typically requires substantial product design and process change. When successfully introduced, this type of product often creates an entirely new product category, which becomes a new core business for the firm. In so doing, it creates an opportunity for it to be the first to enter an entirely new market. The first personal computer, the first laptop, and the first cellular phone are all good examples of breakthrough or radical products. In the development of these breakthrough products, management must recognize that significant process development is required. Products in this category are necessary for the long-term success of the firm. A combination of competitive, environmental, and technological forces often renders existing products obsolete in the long term. Breakthrough products therefore enable the firm to succeed in its current markets as well as in new markets that will be created in the more distant future.

The New Product Development Process

With the trend toward shorter product life cycles, the successful company must be able to (*a*) continuously generate new product ideas, (*b*) convert these ideas into reliable functional designs that are user-friendly, (*c*) ensure that these designs are readily producible, and (*d*) select the proper processes that are most compatible with the needs of the customer. In addition, as seen in the opening vignette, all this must be accomplished within an continuously decreasing time frame. Thus, suggest R. G. Cooper and E. J. Kleinschmidt, formal new products processes (NPDs) are required to ensure the success of new products.[3] The product and price aspects of the 4Ps of marketing (product, price, promotion, place) are critically affected by the NPD process.

Designing new products and delivering them to the market quickly are the challenges facing manufacturers in every industry, from computer chips to potato chips. (See the OM in Practice box on successful product design.) As a result, more successful firms are focusing their resources on reducing the **new product development** (**NPD**) **process** to a fraction of what it once was.

new product development (NPD) process

The method by which new products evolve from conceptualization through engineering to manufacturing and marketing.

The NPD process includes most of the functions within an organization. Marketing (which identifies the target market and forecasts demand for the product), research and development (which develops the technology and subsequently designs the product), and operations (which involves supplier selection and designing the manufacturing process) play the most prominent roles. However, finance, accounting, and information systems also provide important inputs into the process. As seen at the top of Exhibit 3.2, the steps in the NPD process were traditionally conducted in sequence, with the next function usually not beginning its activities until the previous step was completed. This was the major reason the NPD process took so long.

To shorten the NPD process, many of these activities are now done in parallel or concurrently, as seen in the comparison in Exhibit 3.2. This coordinated effort from all of the functional areas is known as **concurrent engineering** (also referred to as concurrent design, simultaneous engineering, or integrated product development).

concurrent engineering

The simultaneous and coordinated efforts of all functional areas, which accelerates the time to market for new products.

Idea Generation

The NPD process begins with an idea for a new product, which can come from one of several sources. Most often it comes from marketing, which developed the idea through its interaction with customers and is often referred to as the **voice of the customer**. When a new product is identified in this manner, it is often called *market pull*, which refers to the primary force driving its development. In other words, the customer's identified need for the product in the market is "pulling" it from the firm. The other major method for generating new products is called *technology push*. In this case, the customers are not even aware of the need for the product; rather, it is developed by the company's R&D function and "pushed" through the company to the marketplace. Polaroid cameras, PCs, and 3M's Post-it notes provide good examples of new products that were the result of technology push.

voice of the customer

Customer feedback used in quality functional deployment process to determine product specifications.

It is important to note that products resulting from technology push also must have a market need in order to be successful. (Polaroid's instant movie system provides a good example of a technology push product for which there was no demand.) At the same time, although technology push products tend to be less common than market pull products, most breakthrough and radical products are the result of technology push.

---

[3]R. G. Cooper and E. J. Kleinschmidt, *Formal Processes for Managing New Products: The Industry Experience* (Hamilton, Ontario: McMaster University, 1991).

Exhibit 3.2

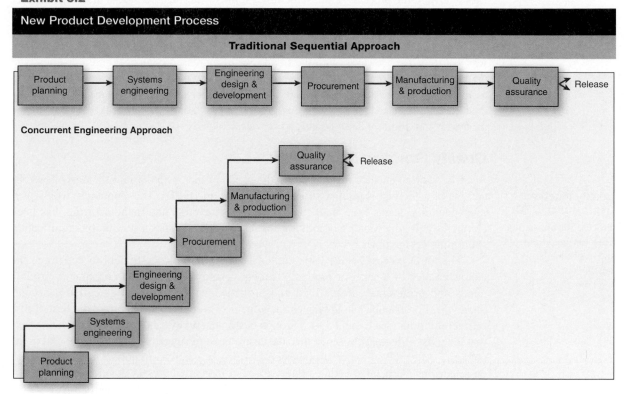

New Product Development Process

Traditional Sequential Approach

Product planning → Systems engineering → Engineering design & development → Procurement → Manufacturing & production → Quality assurance → Release

Concurrent Engineering Approach

Quality assurance → Release

Manufacturing & production

Procurement

Engineering design & development

Systems engineering

Product planning

Source: Clifford F. Gray and Erik W. Larson, *Project Management: The Managerial Process* (New York: McGraw-Hill/Irwin, 2006), p. 175.

Concept Development

Once a new product idea has been generated, it needs to be further developed and tested. This includes an initial design of the product (which is conducted by R&D) along with a detailed analysis of the market and the customers' requirements (which is conducted by marketing). A good example is the new Alberta Children's Hospital in Calgary. Both the exterior (see photo, page 91) and interior were designed based on children's (customer) drawings of what an ideal hospital should look like.[4]

Experimentation is at the heart of new product development. Successful products are created only after many ideas are explored. Harvard Professor Stefan Thomke describes "enlightened experimentation" as using the power of computer and communication technologies to do rapid experimentation early in the stages of product design.[5] Using these high-tech tools allows companies to try out many more new ideas, even those that might seem absurd, without going through the expensive process of building prototypes such as those used for automobiles or aircraft. Drug companies can use computer simulations to eliminate possible ineffective formulations that previously would only have been detected after lengthy clinical trials. Financial institutions can use computer simulations to test whether proposed financial instruments would be successful under predicted market conditions. Thus companies can save considerable amounts of money by detecting design

---

[4]Carey Miller, "Kids at Work," *Apple* (Sept/Oct 2006), pp. 10–11.
[5]Stefan Thomke, "Enlightened Experimentation: The Imperative for Innovation," *Harvard Business Review* (February 2001), pp. 67–75.

flaws early in the process. At the same time, some of the "absurd" ideas that might earlier have never seen the light of day might prove to be viable.

Businesses today recognize the need to involve their customers in all aspects of the design, production, and delivery of the goods and services they offer. In the past, this often was not the case. However, with the trend toward increased competition, companies who do not listen to their customers on a continuous basis will find them taking their business to firms who will. Although there are many approaches for obtaining information from customers, such as surveys and focus groups, we present one that links directly to the processes that produce these goods and services.

Quality Function Deployment

quality function deployment (QFD)

Process for translating customer requirements into a product's design.

A fairly rigorous method for translating the needs of the customer into the design specifications of a product is **quality function deployment (QFD)**. This approach, which uses interfunctional teams from marketing, design engineering, and manufacturing, has been credited by Toyota Motor Corporation for reducing the costs on its cars by significantly shortening design times.

The QFD process begins with studying and listening to customers to determine the characteristics of a superior product. Through market research, the consumers' product needs and preferences are defined and broken down into categories called *customer attributes*. For example, an appliance manufacturer would like to improve the design of a refrigerator door (see Exhibit 3.3). Through customer surveys and interviews, it determines that the most important customer attribute desired in a refrigerator door is that it "seal in the cold air." After the customer attributes are defined, a weighted importance rating for each engineering characteristic that relates to customer attributes is developed. Next, the consumer is asked to compare and rate the company's products with those of its competitors. This process helps the company to determine those product characteristics that are important to the consumer and to evaluate its product in relation to others. The end result is a better understanding and focus on the product characteristics that require improvement.

house of quality

Part of the quality function deployment process that uses customer feedback for product design criteria.

Customer attribute information forms the basis for the matrix in Exhibit 3.3 called the **house of quality**. The matrix depicts (*a*) customer attributes, (*b*) design characteristics required to satisfy customer requirements, (*c*) weighted importance ratings for the design characteristics, (*d*) interrelationships between design characteristics (that could lead to trade-offs), and (*e*) competitor comparisons. By building a house of quality matrix, the cross-functional QFD team can use customer feedback to make engineering, marketing, and design decisions. The matrix helps the team translate customer attribute information into concrete operating or engineering goals. The important product characteristics and goals for improvement are jointly agreed on and detailed in the house. This process encourages the different departments to work closely together and results in a better understanding of one another's goals and issues. However, the most important benefit of the house of quality is that it helps the team to focus on building a product that satisfies customers.

Another important part of this phase of the NPD process includes building models of the new product (both physical models as well as computer-generated models), small-scale testing of the various elements and components of the new product, and conducting detailed investment and financial analyses over the product's anticipated life cycle. In addition, manufacturing and process development personnel should be involved in this phase as early as possible, to ensure optimal compatibility between the new product and the process by which it will be made. The first major hurdle in the NPD process (often referred to as program approval) takes place at the conclusion of this phase, when management has sufficient information to decide whether or not the project should go forward.

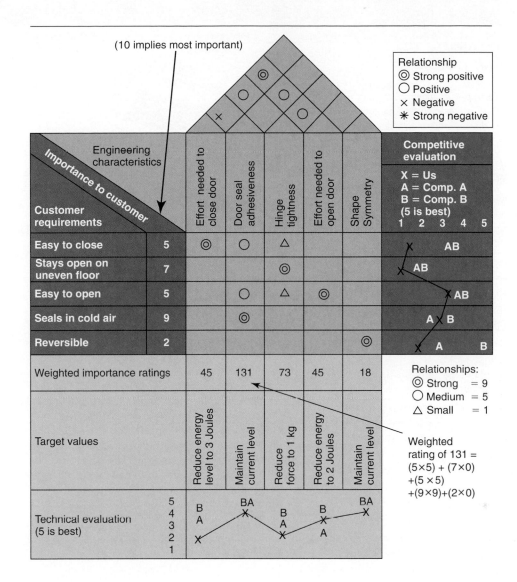

Exhibit 3.3

Completed
House of Quality
Matrix for a
Refrigerator
Door

Design for Manufacturability

In translating the functional product design into a product that can be efficiently manufactured, designers must consider many aspects. They can use a variety of methods and alternative materials to make a product. Furthermore, all of these materials can be formed, cut, and shaped in many ways, along with a very large selection of machining processes.

In designing for manufacturability (DFM), also called design for manufacture or design for manufacture and assembly (DFMA), it is also desirable to keep the number of individual parts to a minimum. For example, Sony plans a massive part standardization by reducing the number of parts it uses from 840 000 to 100 000 within the next few years.[6] In electronics, manufacturers often accomplish this by combining circuits into larger and larger integrated circuits. Not only does this increase the speed, it also reduces the physical

---

[6]Phred Dvorak, "Sony to Slash 20 000 Jobs," *The Globe and Mail*, October 29, 2003, B8.

FACTORS THAT CONTRIBUTE TO SUCCESSFUL PRODUCT DESIGNS

A recent review of successful product designs, ranging from razors and laptop computers to power tools and outdoor grills, identified several factors that these products and their manufacturers shared, including:

- *Design from the outside in.* Make the customer's use of the product the focus of all product development.

- *Partner deeply.* Involve all of the relevant functional areas (e.g., marketing, engineering, purchasing, and manufacturing) early in the design process to assist in defining the new product. (This is often referred to as concurrent engineering.)

- *Partner widely.* With the emergence of the virtual enterprise, organizational boundaries are becoming unclear. Designers, therefore, must partner with all stakeholders—both internal and external.

- *Design the product upfront.* Match the right product to the right market niche. Upfront design analysis will eliminate faulty concepts early.

- *Get physical fast.* Use prototypes to visualize a concept and to obtain quick feedback from both users and managers.

- *Design for manufacturability.* Always design a product that will meet established quality, cost, and delivery parameters. Manufacturing issues are as important to success as ergonomics, aesthetics, and function.

- *Surprise the user.* Always build something extra into the product that will unexpectedly delight the customer. This creates customer loyalty and increases the chances of having a truly "hot" product.

One example of a successful product design is the "smart" bottle cap. Forgetful and/or reluctant patients who don't take their

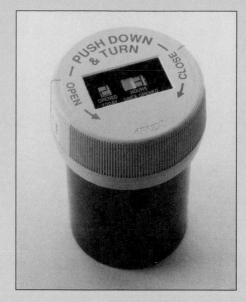

medicine accumulate an estimated $25 billion in avoidable hospital bills annually and billions more in unnecessary nursing home admissions. To reduce these costs, Aprex Corp, located in Fremont, California, now offers a smart bottle cap. Built with a computer chip, alarm clock, and small display panel, the smart cap maintains a record of how frequently the bottle is opened, and is also equipped with a beeper to remind patients who forget to take their medications. The addition of a modem reads the cap's memory and automatically transmits it to Aprex. If the number of times the bottle has been open is incorrect, the patient receives a "reminder call."

Sources:
B. Nussbaum, "Hot Products: Smart Design Is the Common Thread," *Business Week*, June 7, 1993; and Otis Port, "These Bottles Nag You to Take Your Medicine," *Business Week,* February 13, 1995.

---

modular design

Designing a product using standard components and subassemblies to produce customized products.

product's specifications

Output from the design activity that states all criteria for building a product.

size of the product and increases reliability. Exhibit 3.4 shows how to reduce a simple bracket from five parts to one by focusing on the purpose of the part, the fabrication, and the assembly procedure used for its manufacture.

A related concept is called **modular design**. With this approach the end product is designed so that it can be assembled from several individual components that are considered to be standard items. The concept of modularization is used extensively in the computer industry. As an illustration, consider ordering a particular model of computer from the Web site of Dell or HP. If there are four different types of central processors, three different kinds of input/output devices, and two varieties of printers, twenty-four different computer configurations ($4 \times 3 \times 2$) can be sold, while only nine ($4 + 3 + 2$) different products have to be designed and manufactured. Cable companies use the same concept in services in offering packages of TV channels.

The output of the product design activity is the **product's specifications**. These specifications provide the basis for production-related decisions such as the purchase of materials, selection of equipment, assignment of workers, and the size and layout of the

KODAK PRESERVES ITS MOMENTS IN THE PHOTOGRAPHY BUSINESS BY DESIGNING WHAT THE CUSTOMER WANTS

Recently, more-than-a-century-old Eastman Kodak Co. saw its profits tumble when digital cameras began to replace traditional film-based cameras. Why? Traditionally, two-thirds of photographs were taken by women and they ordered most of the prints. Over the years Kodak had successfully courted women with its easy-to-use products.

But digital cameras changed all that. Getting a print was not as easy as dropping off a film, since data first had to be transferred to a computer for printing on a special printer connected to the computer, or saved on a disk for printing at a store—a time-consuming process in either case. Many women, who research shows, want digital photography to be simple but also want high-quality prints, balked at using digital cameras. Research also showed that men were quite happy saving the photographs in digital form and never printing them. Thus men became the primary photographers in the family, not because women have less aptitude for digital photography, but because they are not interested in messing around with cables, interfaces, and storage media. Women had been Kodak's primary customers; it lagged behind its competitors in the male market. And so the company saw its profits drop.

Kodak's response? Total product revamp. Based on its market research regarding female preferences, Kodak redesigned its digital cameras, stressing simple controls and larger display screens. It created a new product category, the stand-alone compact photo printer, which eliminated the need for a computer. Finally, it made digital-image printing simpler through retail kiosks and an online service.

The result has been a slow but steady turnaround for Kodak in digital photography. It has improved its market share in digital cameras from third to first in the U.S. It is also number one in stand-alone photo printers and second in photo paper for printers. And evidence shows that women are returning as its customers.

Source:
William M. Bulkeley, "Softer View: Kodak Sharpens Digital Focus on Its Best Customers: Women; Company Promotes Simplicity and High-Quality Prints; Taking on H-P and Sony; 'A Roach Motel for Pictures,'" *The Wall Street Journal*, July 6, 2005, A1.

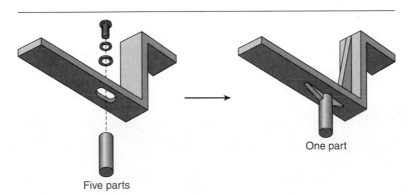

Exhibit 3.4

Design Change to Reduce the Number of Parts in a Bracket

One part

Five parts

Source: Bart Huthwaite. "Managing at the Starting Line: How to Design Competitive Products," Workshop at the University of Southern California–Los Angeles, January 14, 1991, p. 7.

production facility. Product specifications, commonly thought of as blueprints or engineering drawings, often take other forms ranging from precise quantitative and qualitative statements to rather fluid guidelines. Physical products tend to have traditional blueprint specifications; a service firm's design specifications tend to be more general.

While designing for manufacturability, we must remember to design for the consumer. A basic rule in design is to be obvious. Design a product so that a user can look at it, understand it, and figure out how to use it—quickly and without an instruction manual.

Unit Life Cycle Costing-Based Design

Many companies today incorporate **unit life cycle costs** (note that this is different from the product life cycle defined earlier and shown in Exhibit 3.1) in designing a product. This

unit life cycle costs
The cost of each unit of the product over its entire life.

involves designing the product based not only on the initial cost of each unit to the customer, but also on the cost of maintenance, repair, and disposal or reuse of each unit of the product; i.e., the total cost of ownership over the unit's entire life cycle.[7] For example, at least 90% by weight of the Kodak single-use camera is reused or recycled when it is returned to Kodak (www.kodak.com). The ability to reuse such a high percentage is determined at the design stage, based on the type of material and ease of disassembly incorporated into the design. Although some of the incentive for designing products for reuse comes from environmental regulations or concerns, many companies also realize that designing products based on unit life cycle costing can reduce the cost of the product itself over the long term.

Process Selection in Manufacturing

Types of Processes

Manufacturing operations, as shown in Exhibit 3.5, are categorized into three broad types of process structures, each category depending to a large extent on the volume of item(s) to be produced. These three categories are often referred to as **project processes**, **intermittent processes**, and **line-flow processes**. Although we identify three discrete categories, we should emphasize that the different types of manufacturing processes that exist should be viewed as a continuum, and that any one company may incorporate a combination of these processes in the manufacture of its products.

project process

Process that focuses on making one-of-a-kind products.

Project Process

A project-oriented process usually involves the manufacture of a single, one-of-a-kind product. Examples here include the production of a movie and the erection of a skyscraper. Building a customized car to compete in the Molson Indy in Vancouver is another good

Using project-management tools and techniques, Taco Bell was able to construct and open this restaurant in Compton, California, in just two days, compared to the 60 days that is typically required.

[7]Robert S. Kaplan and David P. Norton, *Strategy Maps* (Boston: Harvard Business School Press, 2004), p. 151.

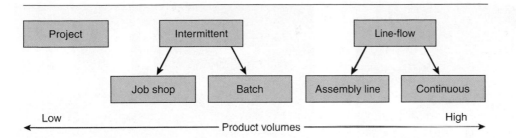

Exhibit 3.5

Types of Processes

example. The major strength of a project-type process is that it is totally flexible to meet the individual needs of the customer. Projects are usually analyzed using network-solving techniques like those presented in Chapter 4.

Variable costs in this category are comparatively very high. On the other hand, fixed costs are negligible or even nonexistent. (In the extreme case, when there is truly only one product to build, all costs are expensed and consequently there are no fixed costs.)

Highly skilled personnel are usually required for this type of process, as they often must work independently, with minimal guidance and supervision. In addition, workers here need to be well trained in a variety of tasks.

Intermittent Process

As shown in Exhibit 3.5, intermittent-type processes can be further subdivided into job shop and batch processes. We define a *job shop* as a process where a specific quantity of a product is produced only once. Numbered prints from a painting, programs for concerts, and T-shirts commemorating specific events are good examples of products made in a job shop process.

A *batch* process produces the same item again and again, usually in specified lot sizes. McDonald's is a good example of a batch process where hamburgers are cooked throughout the day in lot sizes of 12. The manufacture of shoes provides another example of a batch process. Here a batch consists of one size and style of shoe. (Some facilities, such as machine shops, are a combination of job shop and batch processes.)

Variable costs are still relatively high with intermittent processes, although they are usually lower than those of a project-type process. However, higher fixed costs are incurred with these processes. Similarly, worker skills remain high, though somewhat lower than those required for projects.

Line-Flow Process

As with intermittent processes, line-flow processes are frequently subdivided into two processes: assembly line and continuous. Assembly-line processes manufacture individual, discrete products. Examples here include electronic products such as VCRs and CD players, as well as automobiles and kitchen appliances. Continuous processes are exactly what their name implies—continuous, producing products that are not discrete. Petroleum refineries and chemical plants provide good examples of continuous processes.

Line-flows are characterized by high fixed costs and low variable costs, and are often viewed as the most efficient of the three types of processes. Labour skill, especially in assembly-line operations, is typically lower than in other types of processes, since workers are required to learn only a very few simple operations. However, the current trend is to involve the workers in the maintenance of equipment and to give them more responsibility. Line-flows are used for only the highest volumes of products, are very focused, and consequently are the most inflexible of the three processes.

intermittent process
Process that produces products in small lot sizes.

line-flow process
Continuous process that produces high-volume, highly standardized products.

Line-flow processes perform a variety of operations, ranging from processing french fries at McCain Foods to smelting metal at Inco.

The Product-Process Matrix

The relationship between the different types of processes and their respective volume requirements is often depicted on a product-process matrix, shown in Exhibit 3.6, which is adapted from the widely cited Hayes and Wheelwright product-process matrix. In this matrix, as volume increases and the product line narrows (the horizontal dimension), specialized equipment and standardized material flows (the vertical dimension) become economically feasible. This evolution in process structure is frequently related to the different stages of a product's life cycle (introduction, growth, maturity, and decline).

Exhibit 3.6
Matching Major Stages of Product and Process Life Cycles

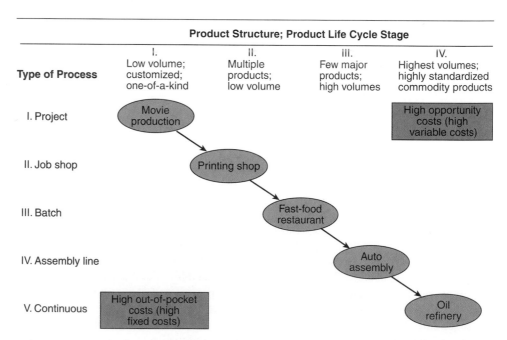

Source: Adapted from Robert Hayes and Steven Wheelwright, *Restoring Our Competitive Edge: Competing through Manufacturing* (New York: John Wiley & Sons, 1984). Copyright © 1984, John Wiley & Sons, Inc. This material is used by permission of John Wiley & Sons, Inc.

The industries listed within the matrix are presented as ideal types that have found their process niche. It certainly is possible for an industry member to choose another position on the matrix, however. For example, Volvo makes cars on movable pallets rather than on an assembly line. Thus, on the matrix it would be at the intersection of process stage II and product stage III. Volvo's production rate is lower than that of its competitors because it is giving up the speed and efficiency of the line. On the other hand, the Volvo system has more flexibility and better quality control than the classic automobile production line. Similar kinds of analysis can be carried out for other types of process-product options through the matrix.

In looking at Exhibit 3.6, it is interesting to note that companies that try to operate in either of the corners opposite the diagonal are doomed to failure. Companies in the upper right-hand corner are too slow to react to changes in the market place. As a result, they try to compete in a market that requires high-volume, low-cost products with a project-type process that not only has very high variable costs, but also has very limited capacity. As a consequence, these firms incur very high opportunity costs from lost sales because high prices encourage customers to take their business elsewhere.

In the lower left-hand corner are companies that anticipated selling greater volumes of product than actually materialized. As a result, these firms have incurred very high out-of-pocket costs in the form of very high fixed costs, which are associated with the capital-intensive processes that were installed.

It may be a little easier to understand the logic of a product-process matrix if we divide it into its component parts. Part A of Exhibit 3.7 shows a traditional product life cycle from product conception through product termination. Part B relates the frequency of changes made in the product design to the stages of the product life cycle. Logically, most of the product changes occur during the initial stages of the life cycle, before major production starts. This suggests that a project-type process is appropriate for this stage. The product then tends to go through many changes: simplification, adding features, newer materials, and so forth. The motivation here is for more performance and perhaps greater appeal to a broader market. The flexibility of an intermittent-type process allows for these changes.

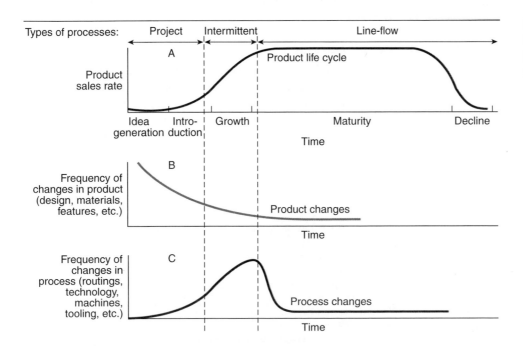

Exhibit 3.7
Product and Process Life Cycles

During the maturity stage of the product, very few additional changes are made and the focus is on low costs, which can be provided by a line-flow process.

Changes in the production process, as shown in Part C of Exhibit 3.7, occur most rapidly during the early stages of production design and start-up. This is where choices are made in the production layout, equipment, tooling, and so on. The goal here is to reduce production costs. Also, both product and process engineers work together to reduce costs and increase product performance. When full production occurs during the maturity phase, few additional changes are made and volumes remain relatively constant. During the decline phase of the product, however, some additional process changes occur; these are due in part to switching the smaller production volumes to different equipment and facilities.

During the early stages in a product's life cycle when production quantities are small (certainly during the product research and development stages), intermittent processes are typically used. Here, all similar machines and processes are grouped together in one location and are used for many different products. As production volumes increase, machines and processes may be grouped in a line-flow process to simplify the product's flow through the factory.

Categories of New Services

As discussed in Chapter 1, services differ from goods in many ways. In comparison to the study and classification of the various types of new products, which began several years ago, the study and classification of the different types of new services is more recent. In addition, services are viewed as being more complex, in that they not only involve the delivery of an end "product," but also include the process by which that product is delivered.

A classification scheme for new services, therefore, should recognize that services involve both. In other words, when attempting to classify the various types of new services, we should categorize them not only by how the end product is changed (that is, what is actually being delivered), but also by how the delivery process of the service has changed. Within this dual framework, illustrated in Exhibit 3.8, we define the following four categories of new services: (*a*) "window dressing," (*b*) breadth of offerings, (*c*) revolutionary, and (*d*) channel development.

"Window Dressing" Services

The lower-left quadrant of Exhibit 3.8 defines those services that have a relatively small increment of change along both dimensions. In other words, the product that is delivered as part of the service does not differ significantly from the company's current offerings, and is delivered in a very similar fashion. Examples of services that we would call "window dressing" include new items on restaurant menus, new routes and destinations for airlines,

Exhibit 3.8

A Framework for Categorizing New Services

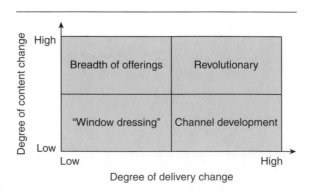

and new courses at colleges and universities. Services that fall into this category usually have a very small impact on the firm's existing service operations and consequently can be brought to market in a relatively short period of time.

Breadth-of-Offering Services

The upper-left quadrant of Exhibit 3.8 represents a significant design change in the content of the service, but it is delivered to the customer in much the same manner as existing services. Air Canada, which had a single airline concept until recently, now has different "products" such as Jetz and Jazz, each focusing on a different market segment. Although the specific content of each segment is different in terms of availability of business class, meals, and other services, the basic method of delivering the service remains the same. For firms developing new products in this category, the challenge is to deliver all of the different types of content to each of the corresponding different market segments in an effective and efficient manner.

Revolutionary Services

The upper-right quadrant of Exhibit 3.8 represents new services that provide both very new content and a very new method of delivery. These services typically take much longer to bring to market and require significantly more of the firm's resources than do any of the other categories. For example, CP Rail introduced a revolutionary service when it developed inter-modal transport, and FedEx introduced overnight delivery service using air freight. Another example, *Epost*, is a joint venture between Canada Post Corporation, the Bank of Montreal, and TELUS Corporation that allows customers to receive and manage their mail online.

Channel Development Services

New services that fall in the lower-right quadrant of Exhibit 3.8 are those in which the service that is provided is the same as that currently offered by the firm, but it is delivered differently through another, often entirely new, channel. The automated teller machine (ATM) provides a good example of services in this category. Traditional bricks-and-mortar retailers that sell their products over the Internet through a Web site provide another example in this category. When developing these new channels, managers need to recognize that process development is critical here, because consumers expect to receive the same level of service quality through the new channel that they have been accustomed to receiving through the older, more traditional channels.

The New Service Development Process

The **new service development (NSD) process** is similar to the NPD process, but with one major difference. When developing a service, you are inherently designing both the product and the process at the same time, because the product is typically inherent in the process. Since services are intangible, rather than something "you can drop on your foot," it is nearly impossible to separate the product from the process. The NSD process typically begins in the same fashion as the NPD process. An idea will come forth, either from marketing/customer (market pull or voice of the customer) or from operations (service operations push). In services, there currently is not the same type and level of R&D as there is for products. The R&D in services occurs primarily in the operations process with respect to how the service is delivered.

The NSD process consists of four stages that are similar to the stages of the NPD process. The first step, *design*, consists of the formulation of the objectives and strategy of

new service development (NSD) process
The method by which new services evolve from conceptualization through to marketing and delivery to the customer.

the new service, followed by concept development and testing of the concept. Concurrently, the *analysis* phase considers the financial implications of the new service and examines the supply chain issues relevant to its delivery. Upon successful completion of these two phases, the new service project is approved for continuation. The third and most resource-intensive phase of NSD is the *development* phase. In this phase, the service design is completed and tested, all the processes that ensure service delivery are fully designed and tested, personnel are trained, and a pilot run of the service is conducted. Once the new service passes the pilot test, *full launch*, the fourth stage in the NSD process, begins when the service is released to the marketplace.

The Customer Contact Approach to Designing Service Processes

Service systems are generally classified along industry lines (financial services, health services, transportation services, and so on). These groupings, though useful in presenting aggregate economic data, are not particularly appropriate for OM purposes because they tell us little about the process. In manufacturing, by contrast, there are, as we have seen, fairly well-defined terms for classifying production activities that transcend industry lines (such as *intermittent* and *continuous production*); when applied to a manufacturing setting, they readily convey the essence of the process. Although it is possible to describe services in these same terms, we need another item of information to reflect the level of customer involvement in the process. That item, which we believe operationally distinguishes one type of service from another in its production function, is the extent of customer contact in the creation of service.

Customer contact refers to the presence of the customer in the system, and *creation of the service* refers to the work process that is involved in providing the service itself. *Extent of contact* here may be roughly defined as the percentage of time the customer must be involved in the system relative to the total time it takes to perform the customer service. Generally speaking, the greater the percentage of contact time between the service system and the customer, the greater the degree of interaction between the two during the production process.

high degree of customer contact

Service operations that require a high percentage of customer contact time.

low degree of customer contact

Service operations that require a low percentage of customer contact time.

From this concept of customer contact, it follows that service systems with a **high degree of customer contact** are usually more difficult to manage and consequently harder to justify than those with a **low degree of customer contact**. In high-contact systems, customers can affect the time of demand, the exact nature of the service, and the quality of the service since they are involved in the process.

Exhibit 3.9 illustrates the differences between high- and low-contact service systems in a bank. Here we see that each design decision is impacted by whether or not the customer is present during the service delivery. We also see that when work is done behind the scenes (in this case, a bank's processing centre), it is performed on substitutes for the customer, that is, customer reports, databases, and invoices. Therefore, we can design these behind-the-scenes operations according to the same principles we would use in designing a factory—that is, to maximize the amount of items processed during the production day.

Obviously, there can be tremendous diversity of customer influence and hence system variability within high-contact service systems. For example, a bank branch offers both simple services such as cash withdrawals that take just a minute or so, as well as complicated services such as loan application preparation that can take in excess of an hour. Moreover, these activities may range from being self-service through an ATM, to co-production where bank personnel and the customer work together as a team to develop the loan application.

Design Decision	High-Contact System (a branch office)	Low-Contact System (a cheque processing centre)
Facility location	Operations must be near the customer.	Operations may be placed near supply, transport, or labour.
Facility layout	Facility should accommodate the customer's physical and psychological needs and expectations.	Facility should focus on production efficiency.
Product design	Environment as well as the physical product define the nature of the service.	Customer is not in the service environment, so the product can be defined by fewer attributes.
Process design	Stages of production process have a direct, immediate effect on the customer.	Customer is not involved in majority of processing steps.
Scheduling	Customer is in the production schedule and must be accommodated.	Customer is concerned mainly with completion dates.
Production planning	Orders cannot be stored, so smoothing production flow will result in loss of business.	Both backlogging and production smoothing are possible.
Worker skills	Direct workforce constitutes a major part of the service product and so must be able to interact well with the public.	Direct workforce need only have technical skills.
Quality control	Quality standards are often in the eye of the beholder and hence variable.	Quality standards are generally measurable and hence fixed.
Time standards	Service time depends on customer needs, and therefore time standards are inherently loose.	Work is performed on customer surrogates (e.g., forms), thus time standards can be tight.
Wage payment	Variable output requires time-based wage systems.	"Fixable" output permits output-based wage systems.
Capacity planning	To avoid lost sales, capacity must be set to match peak demand.	Storable output permits capacity at some average demand level.

Exhibit 3.9

Major Differences between High- and Low-Contact Systems in a Bank

In another attempt to better understand services in general, Roger Schmenner proposes a method for classifying services along two dimensions.[8] The first dimension, degree of customer interaction and customization, closely parallels the degree of customer contact we discuss above. In addition, Schmenner also includes the degree of labour intensity required to deliver the service. On the basis of these two factors he develops a service process matrix, shown in Exhibit 3.10.

Within this matrix, Schmenner defines four broad categories of services:

1. *Service factory* is characterized by a relatively low degree of labour intensity and a relatively low degree of customer interaction and customization.

2. *Service shop* has the same relatively low degree of labour intensity, but has a higher degree of customer interaction and customization.

[8]Roger W. Schmenner, "How Can Service Businesses Survive and Prosper?" *Sloan Management Review* 27, no. 3 (Spring 1986), pp. 21–32, by permission of publisher. Copyright © 1986 by Sloan Management Review Association. All rights reserved.

Exhibit 3.10

The Service Process Matrix

		Relative Degree of Interaction and Customization	
		Low	High
Relative Degree of Labour Intensity	Low	Service factory: 　Airlines 　Trucking 　Hotels 　Resorts and recreation	Service shop: 　Hospitals 　Auto repair 　Other repair services
	High	Mass service: 　Retailing 　Wholesaling 　Schools 　Retail aspects of 　　commercial banking	Professional service: 　Doctors 　Lawyers 　Accountants 　Architects

Source: Roger W. Schmenner, "How Can Service Businesses Survive and Prosper?" *Sloan Management Review* 27, no. 3 (Spring 1986), pp. 21–32, by permission of publisher. Copyright 1986 by Sloan Management Review Association. All rights reserved.

3. *Mass service* is defined by a relatively high degree of labour intensity, but has a relatively low degree of customer interaction.

4. *Professional service* requires both a relatively high degree of labour intensity as well as a relatively high degree of customer interaction and customization.

This type of classification scheme provides service managers with some insights in developing strategies for their respective organizations. For example, services that exhibit a low degree of labour intensity are usually capital intense with high fixed costs. These firms cannot easily adjust capacity to meet changes in demand and therefore must attempt to smooth out the demand during peak periods by shifting it to off-peak times.

The issues confronting service managers with high labour intensity operations require a different focus. Here, workforce management is paramount, with emphasis being placed on hiring, training, and scheduling.

More important, this approach to classifying services cuts across industry lines, providing service managers with a better understanding of the strengths and weaknesses within their own operations. Through this perspective, managers can look to similar operations in other service industries to seek ways for improving their respective operations.

Designing a New Service Organization

Designing a service organization entails the execution of four elements of what James Heskett refers to as the "Service Vision."[9] The first element is identification of the target market (Who is our customer?); the second is the service concept (How do we differentiate our service in the market?); the third is the service strategy (What is our service package and the operating focus of our service?); and the fourth is the service delivery system (What are the actual processes, staff requirements, and facilities by which the service is created?).

Choosing a target market and developing the service package are top management decisions which set the stage for the direct operating decisions of service strategy and delivery system design.

---

[9]James L. Heskett, "Lessons from the Service Sector," *Harvard Business Review* (March–April 1987), pp. 118–126.

Several major factors distinguish service design and development from typical manufactured product development. First, the process and the product must be developed simultaneously; indeed, in services the process is the product. (We make this statement with the general recognition that many manufacturers are using such concepts as concurrent engineering and DFM as approaches to more closely link product design and process design.)

Second, although equipment and software that support a service can be protected by patents and copyrights, a service operation itself lacks the legal protection commonly available to goods production. Third, the service package, rather than a definable good, constitutes the major output of the development process. Fourth, many parts of the service package often are defined by the training individuals receive before they become part of the service organization. In particular, in many professional service organizations, such as law firms and hospitals, prior certification is necessary for hiring. Fifth, many service organizations can change their service offerings virtually overnight. Service organizations such as barbershops, retail stores, and restaurants have this flexibility.

Designing the Customer Service Encounter

Karl Albrecht and Ron Zemke's *Service America!* gets to the heart of the issue of managing service operations when they state: "Every time a customer comes into contact with any aspect of the company it is a "moment of truth," and it can create either a positive or a negative impression about the company."[10] How well these moments of truth or encounters are managed depends on a carefully designed service delivery process. Service encounters can be structured in a number of different ways. They range from the *buffered core* (in which the provider is physically separated from the customer with little contact), through the *permeable system*, (in which the customer can penetrate via phone or face-to-face contact), to the *reactive system* (which is both penetrable and reactive to the customer's requirements).

As one would anticipate, production efficiency decreases as customer contact time increases, thereby giving the customer more influence on the system. To offset this, however, the face-to-face contact provides greater opportunity to sell additional products. Advertising, gourmet restaurants, and personal banking are of this type. Conversely, low contact, such as mail or ATMs, allows the system to work more efficiently because the customer is unable to significantly affect (or disrupt) the system. However, there is relatively little, if any, sales opportunity for additional product sales at this end of the spectrum. Fast food restaurants and Disneyland would fall somewhere in the middle.

By performing this production-efficiency sales-opportunity analysis, trade-offs become more clear-cut, and, more important, at least some of the major design variables are crystallized for analysis purposes. For example, it would make little sense relative to sales for a service firm to invest in high-skilled workers if it plans to operate with low contact and enhance efficiency using standardized procedures.

Process Selection in Services

Types of Service Organizations

The three general approaches to delivering on-site services are the production line approach made famous by McDonald's Corporation, the customer involvement approach

---

[10]Jan Carlzon, president, Scandinavian Airlines System, quoted in Karl Albrecht and Ron Zemke, *Service America! Doing Business in the New Economy* (Homewood, IL: Dow Jones-Irwin, 1985), p. 19.

PRODUCTS SHOULD BE FOR PEOPLE, NOT THE OTHER WAY AROUND

Kim Vicente of University of Toronto in his book, *The Human Factor*, emphasizes the importance of designing products and services that fit the physical and psychological characteristics of humans rather than the other way around. Professor Vicente calls this the "Human-Tech" approach. Often what we think of as "human error" is caused by people trying to adapt to a technology that was not designed with them in mind. For example, in the 1940s many United States military pilots were pulling up the wheels of their planes after landing rather than pulling up the wing flaps (as they should have done in order to slow down the plane). This, of course, was considered "pilot error." An investigation revealed the real reason was that the two related controls were right beside each other on the instrument panel and were almost identical in appearance. The control design was altered to give the wheel switch a rubberized disc (which made it feel like a wheel) and the flap switch a wedge shape (which made it feel like a wing flap). This eliminated the error because there was now a clear, intuitive relationship between the shape of the controls and their functions.

The same concepts apply to processes. Processes have to be designed with physical, psychological, team, organizational, and political considerations in mind. For example, how humans teams work within any setting should be a critical consideration in designing process, especially those in which human life is concerned, such as an operating theatre, an aircraft cockpit, or utilities. Vincente cites the examples of the Chernobyl nuclear disaster in 1986 and the Walkerton, Ontario, e-coli outbreak in 2000—tragedies resulting from processes that did not follow the Human-Tech approach. On the positive side, Vincente cites the creation of the Aviation Safety Reporting System (ASRS) by U.S. government agencies in 1976 as an example of the success of Human-Tech-based systems. Under the ASRS, aviation professionals who are involved in near misses can voluntarily report such incidents without fear of being subject to legal action. These reports can then be used to improve aviation safety. The system works because it avoids the "shoot the messenger of bad news" syndrome would have prevented the pilots from reporting near misses.

Source:
Kim Vicente, *The Human Factor* (Toronto: Knopf Canada, 2003).

---

made famous by ATMs and gas stations, and the personal attention approach made famous by Nordstrom department stores.

The Production Line Approach

 The production or assembly line approach pioneered by McDonald's refers to more than just the steps required to assemble a Big Mac. Rather, as Theodore Levitt notes, it is treating the delivery of fast food as a manufacturing process rather than a service process.[11] Levitt also notes that besides McDonald's marketing and financial skills, the company carefully controls "the execution of each outlet's central function—the rapid delivery of a consistently uniform, high-quality mix of prepared foods in an environment of obvious cleanliness, order, and cheerful courtesy. The systematic substitution of equipment for people, combined with the carefully planned use and positioning of technology, enables McDonald's to attract and hold patronage in proportions no predecessor or imitator has managed to duplicate."

Levitt cites several aspects of McDonald's operations to illustrate the concepts:

- The McDonald's french fryer allows cooking of the optimum number of french fries at one time.
- A wide-mouthed scoop is used to pick up the precise amount of french fries for each order size. (The employee never touches the product.)
- Storage space is expressly designed for a predetermined mix of prepackaged and premeasured products.

---

[11]Theodore Levitt, "Production-Line Approach to Service," *Harvard Business Review* 50, no. 5 (September–October 1972), pp. 41–52.

- Cleanliness is pursued by providing ample trash cans in and outside each facility (larger outlets have motorized sweepers for the parking area).

- Hamburgers are wrapped in colour-coded paper.

- Through painstaking attention to total design and facilities planning, everything is built integrally into the (McDonald's) machine itself—into the technology of the system. The attendant has no choice but to operate it exactly as the designers intended.

The Customer Involvement Approach

In contrast to the production line approach, C. H. Lovelock and R. F. Young propose that the service process can be enhanced by having the customer take a greater participatory role in the production of the service.[12] Automated teller machines (ATMs), self-service gas stations, salad bars, and in-room coffee-making equipment in hotels are examples in which the burden of providing service is shifted to the consumer. Obviously, this philosophy requires some selling on the part of the service organization to convince customers that this is beneficial to them. To this end, Lovelock and Young propose a number of steps, including developing customer trust, promoting the benefits of cost, speed, and convenience, and following up to make sure that the procedures are being effectively used. In essence, this turns customers into "partial employees" who must be trained in what to do and compensated, primarily through lower prices charged for the service.

The Personal Attention Approach

The personal attention approach is basically the concept of mass-customization applied to services. With this approach, each customer is treated as an individual, with the service firm often maintaining a database of each customer's likes and dislikes. These data can be collected manually in "personal books" or more formally by electronic means, as many travel agencies do when they record your meal and seating preferences. In the latter case, this information then becomes available throughout the entire organization.

Tom Peters describes Nordstrom's policies in his book, *Quality!*[13] Nordstrom lives for its customers and salespeople. Salespeople are generously remunerated and are given tremendous leeway in making decisions to help customers. Customers are at the top of the company's only official organization chart, followed by the sales and sales support staff, while the board of directors is at the very bottom. The sales staff's personal books can be bulging, and they have unlimited budgets to send cards, flowers, or thank-you notes to customers. The company also has one of the most liberal returns policies in the business.

Similarly, Harry Rosen, the famous Canadian men's clothier, feels that the key to success, especially in the men's clothing business, is to understand what is going on in the customer's mind even though it is often unexpressed. Although men are often intimidated by shopping for clothes, once you help them overcome their fears and gain their trust, they prefer to do one-stop shopping with your business and let you make decisions for them. Harry Rosen stores keep records of customer purchases and even records of each customer's wardrobe so that their staff can help make good clothing decisions the next time the customer comes in.[14]

---

[12]C. H. Lovelock and R. F. Young, "Look to Customers to Increase Productivity," *Harvard Business Review* 57, no. 2 (May–June 1979), pp. 168–178.

[13]Tom Peters, *Quality!* (Palo Alto, CA: TPG Communication, 1986), pp. 10–12.

[14]Shelagh Rogers, Interview with Harry Rosen, *The Current*, CBC Radio, April 18, 2005.

No matter what approach is taken, seven common characteristics of well-designed service systems have been identified:

1. *Each element of the service system is consistent with the operating focus of the firm.* For example, when the focus is on speed of delivery, each step in the process should help to foster speed.

2. *It is user-friendly.* This means that the customer can interact with it easily—that is, it has good signage, understandable forms, logical steps in the process, courteous service workers that are available to answer questions, and it is easily accessible.

3. *It is robust.* That is, it can cope effectively with variations in demand and resource availability. For example, if the computer goes down, effective backup systems are in place to permit service to continue.

4. *It is structured so that consistent performance by its people and systems is easily maintained.* This means that the tasks required of the workers can be performed repeatedly with a high level of consistency, and the supporting technologies are truly supportive and reliable.

5. *It provides effective links between the back office and the front office so that nothing falls between the cracks.* In other words, barriers between the different functional areas are reduced or eliminated.

6. *It manages the evidence of service quality in such a way that customers see the value of the service provided.* Many services do a great job behind the scenes but fail to make this visible to the customer. This is particularly true when a service improvement is made. Unless customers are made aware of the improvement through explicit communication about it, the improved performance is unlikely to gain maximum impact.

7. *It is cost-effective.* There is minimum waste of time and resources in delivering the service.

Conclusion

Product life cycles are becoming shorter and shorter, as a result of both increased global competition and advances in technology. As a result, businesses need to be able to design, develop, and introduce new goods and services on a continuous and consistent basis. The more quickly a company can introduce a new product ahead of its competition, the more substantial the profits. These profits are attributable both to the premium prices that new products can command while the competition catches up and to the large percentage of the market that is typically captured by the firm that is first to market with its products. To accomplish this, today's companies need to be well-integrated, well-disciplined organizations.

New goods and services fall into one of several categories, the differences between them being dependent on the relative amount of innovation. A company needs to have a portfolio of new offerings from all categories to obtain a balance in both the short term and the long term.

The processes for developing new goods and services are no longer as haphazard as they once were, although new service development still lags new product development in this respect. Firms that have invested the necessary resources in these processes have a significant advantage, in terms of both staying ahead of their competition, and having the ability to react quickly to competitive surprises.

The choice of which process to adopt is also a critical success factor. Goods and services can be produced by any of several different types of processes, each of which has a distinctive set of characteristics. It therefore is important for management to identify these process characteristics when selecting a process to ensure that the goods and services being produced and delivered meet the needs of the firm's customers. In other words, a company's processes should be compatible with the customer requirements of the specific market niche it is trying to serve.

Key Terms

concurrent engineering p. 54

high degree of customer contact p. 66

house of quality p. 56

intermittent process p. 61

line-flow process p. 61

low degree of customer contact p. 66

modular design p. 58

new product development (NPD) process
    p. 54

new service development
    (NSD) process p. 65

product's specifications p. 58

project process p. 60

quality function deployment (QFD) p. 56

unit life cycle costs p. 59

voice of the customer p. 54

Review and Discussion Questions

1. Why it is important for a firm to have an effective new product (or service) development process?

2. What are the benefits to the firm that can develop new products faster than its competition?

3. Describe the three different categories of new products. Discuss how each category differs from the others in terms of resources expended and the impact on the firm's manufacturing processes.

4. Discuss the four different types of new services that are categorized by the amount of change in content and delivery method with respect to a firm's existing services.

5. Describe what is meant by the "voice of the customer."

6. Identify the two methods used by firms to generate new product ideas.

7. Identify and describe the four major phases of the new product development process.

8. What is concurrent engineering and why is it critical for a successful new product development effort? Describe the concept of design for manufacturability and indicate why it is closely connected to concurrent engineering.

9. Identify and describe the four stages of the new service development (NSD) process.

10. What are the three major categories of manufacturing processes and how do they differ in terms of operational characteristics?

11. Why is it important for managers to understand the relationship between the various stages of a product's life cycle and the different types of processes that are available to manufacture that product?

12. Identify the high-contact and low-contact operations that exist in each of the following services:
   a. A dental office
   b. An airline
   c. An accounting office
   d. An automobile dealership

13. Where would you place a drive-in church, a campus food vending machine, and a bar's automatic mixed-drink dispensing machine on the service-system design matrix?

14. a. List specific products that you especially like. What do you like most about them?
   b. Create a list of products that you dislike or are unhappy with. What don't you like about them?
   c. Are there some common reasons for your lists? For example, is it more important for products that you don't see or see very little to be functional rather than attractive (e.g., the furnace or air conditioning in the house, the transmission or engine in the car)? Is good design more important for

things that other people see and relate to you such as your car, your clothes, or your apartment or home furnishings?

Can you formulate some general design guidelines based on your answers?

15. Pick a product and make a list of issues that need to be considered in its design and manufacture. The product can be something such as a stereo, a telephone, a desk, a kitchen appliance, and so on. Consider the functional and aesthetic aspects of design as well as the important concerns for manufacturing.

16. The first step in studying a production process is to develop a description of that process. Once the process is described, we are better able to determine why it works well or poorly and to recommend production-related improvements. Since we are all familiar with fast-food restaurants, try your hand at describing the production process employed at, say, a McDonald's. In doing so, answer the following questions:

   a. What are the important aspects of the service package?
   b. Which skills and attitudes are needed by the service personnel?
   c. How can customer demand be altered?
   d. Can the customer/provider interface be changed to include more technology? More self-serve?
   e. How does it measure up on the seven characteristics of a well-designed service?

Internet Exercise

Go to the Online Learning Centre (OLC) Web site (www.mcgrawhill.ca/olc/davis) and look at the various companies that offer virtual tours of their operations. These firms often highlight their new products on their sites and also have press releases about new products available on their sites. Companies known for their strong ability to introduce new products quickly, such as Gillette, 3M, and Nortel, are also good sources. For at least two of these firms, describe the new products they are currently offering. What type of new product would you categorize them as?

Case 1   The Best Engineered Part Is No Part

Putting together NCR Corp.'s new 2760 electronic cash register is a snap. In fact, William R. Sprague can do it in less than two minutes—blindfolded. To get that kind of easy assembly, Sprague, a senior manufacturing engineer at NCR, insisted that the point-of-sale terminal be designed so that its parts fit together with no screws or bolts.

The entire terminal consists of just 15 vendor-produced components. That's 85 percent fewer parts, from 65 percent fewer suppliers, than in the company's previous low-end model, the 2160. And the terminal takes only 25 percent as much time to assemble. Installation and maintenance are also a breeze, says Sprague. "The simplicity flows through to all of the downstream activities, including field service."

The new NCR product is one of the best examples to date of the payoffs possible from a new engineering approach called "design for manufacturability," mercifully shortened to DFM. Other DFM enthusiasts include Ford, General Motors, IBM, Motorola, Perkin-Elmer, and Whirlpool. Since 1981, General Electric Co. has used DFM in more than 100 development programs, from major appliances to gearboxes for jet engines. GE figures that the concept has netted $200 million in benefits, either from cost savings or from increased market shares.

Nuts to Screws

One U.S. champion of DFM is Geoffrey Boothroyd, a professor of industrial and manufacturing engineering at the University of Rhode Island and the co-founder of Boothroyd Dewhurst Inc. This tiny Wakefield (R.I.) company has developed several computer programs that analyze designs for ease of manufacturing.

The biggest gains, notes Boothroyd, come from eliminating screws and other fasteners. On a supplier's invoice, screws and bolts may run mere pennies apiece, and collectively they account for only about 5 percent of a typical product's bill of materials. But tack on all of the associated costs, such as the time needed to align components while screws are inserted and tightened, and the price of using those mundane parts can pile up to 75 percent of total assembly costs. "Fasteners should be the first thing to design out of a product," he says.

Had screws been included in the design of NCR's 2760, calculates Sprague, the total cost over the lifetime of the model would have been $12 500—per screw. "The huge impact of little things like screws, primarily on overhead costs, just gets lost," he says. That's understandable, he admits, because for new-product development projects "the overriding factor is hitting the market window. It's better to be on time and over budget than on budget but late."

But NCR got its simplified terminal to market in record time without overlooking the little details. The product was formally introduced just 24 months after development began. Design was a paperless, interdepartmental effort from the very start. The product remained a computer model until all members of the team—from design engineering, manufacturing, purchasing, customer service, and key suppliers—were satisfied.

That way, the printed-circuit boards, the molds for its plastic housing, and other elements could all be developed simultaneously. This eliminated the usual lag after designers throw a new product "over the wall" to manufacturing, which then must figure out how to make it. "Breaking down the walls between design and manufacturing to facilitate simultaneous engineering," Sprague declares, "was the real breakthrough."

The design process began with a computer-aided mechanical engineering program that allowed the team to fashion three-dimensional models of each part on a computer screen. The software also analyzed the overall product and its various elements for performance and durability. Then the simulated components were assembled on a computer workstation's screen to assure that they would fit together properly. As the design evolved, it was checked periodically with Boothroyd Dewhurst's DFM software. This prompted several changes that trimmed the parts count from an initial 28 to the final 15.

No Mock-Up

After everyone on the team gave their thumbs-up, the data for the parts were electronically transferred directly into computer-aided manufacturing systems at the various suppliers. The NCR designers were so confident everything would work as intended that they didn't bother making a mock-up.

DFM can be a powerful weapon against foreign competition. Several years ago, IBM used Boothroyd Dewhurst's software to analyze dot-matrix printers it was sourcing from Japan—and found it could do substantially better. Its Proprinter had 65 percent fewer parts and slashed assembly time by 90 percent. "Almost anything made in Japan," insists Professor Boothroyd, "can be improved upon with DFM—often impressively."

Question

1. What development problems has the NCR approach overcome?

Source:
Otis Port, "The Best-Engineered Part Is No Part at All," *Business Week* (May 8, 1989), p. 150.

The Role of Technology in Operations

Supplement Objectives

- Introduce the different ways in which technology can add value to the operations function within an organization.

- Identify the various ways in which technology can be used in a manufacturing company.

- Demonstrate the different ways in which technology can be integrated into service operations.

- Present an introduction to e-tailering.

- Identify organizational challenges when introducing technology.

How Technology Affects Operations

Advances in technology are affecting every aspect of business, and operations management is no exception. From robotics and automation on the factory floor to information technology in the form of enterprise resource planning (ERP) systems and the Internet, technology, and especially information technology, is dramatically changing the way in which both manufacturing and service operations are being designed and managed.

To properly integrate technology into their organizations, operations managers first need to understand what technology can and cannot do. In addition, managers must recognize the need for workers at all levels to be properly trained in the use of the technology, and that this training is not just a one-shot deal, but rather a continuous, ongoing process.

Operations strategy defines the way in which a firm competes in the marketplace. Examples of these strategies include (*a*) low cost, (*b*) quality, (*c*) speed of delivery, and (*d*) customization. As we learned in Chapter 2, managers in the past had to decide which of these strategies was most applicable to the particular market segment they were serving. In so doing, they recognized that there were trade-offs involved, for example, that you couldn't have both low cost and a high degree of customization, or that there was a choice to be made between providing fast product delivery and providing a highly customized product.

These traditional trade-offs are no longer valid for most businesses because technology has "raised the performance bar" by allowing firms to compete on several of these dimensions simultaneously. For example, firms using

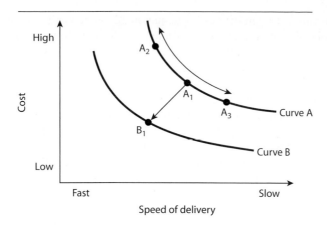

Exhibit S3.1

How Technology Impacts Operational Performance

technology, such as Dell Computer, can now produce and quickly deliver individually customized products, and at very competitive prices. Technology now provides firms with the opportunity to move to a "superior" performance curve, as previously presented in Chapter 2, and shown again in Exhibit S3.1. In moving from A_1 to B_1, for example, a firm can achieve superior performance in terms of both lower cost and also faster service. In comparison, a firm that doesn't use technology must remain on Curve A and consequently must revert to the traditional trade-off where improvement in one dimension is accomplished only at the sacrifice of another dimension (for example, in going from A_2 to A_3 along Curve A, where lower cost is achieved only by providing slower service).

Technology in Manufacturing

Automation

The term *automation* is familiar to all, but a commonly agreed-upon definition still eludes us. Some authorities view automation as a totally new set of concepts that relate to the automatic operation of a production process; others view it simply as an evolutionary development in technology in which machinery performs some or all of the process-control function. Automation is a set of concepts, but it is also evolutionary in the sense that it is a logical and predictable step in the development of equipment and processes.

Some major developments in manufacturing automation include machining centres, numerically controlled machines, industrial robots, computer-aided design and manufacturing systems, flexible manufacturing systems, computer-integrated manufacturing, and islands of automation.

Machining centres not only provide automatic control of a machine but carry out automatic tooling changes as well. For example, a single machine may be equipped with a shuttle system of two worktables that can be rolled into and out of the machine. While work is being done at one table, the next part is mounted on the second table. When machining on the first table is complete, it is moved out of the way and the second part is moved into position.

Numerically controlled (NC) machines are under the control of a digital computer. Feedback control loops determine the position of the machine tooling during the work, constantly compare the actual location with the programmed location, and correct as needed. This eliminates time lost during setups, and applies to both high-volume, standardized types of products as well as low-volume, customized products.

machining centres
Operations where machine tools are changed automatically as part of the process.

numerically controlled (NC) machines
Manufacturing equipment that is directly controlled by a computer.

industrial robots

Programmable machines that can perform multiple functions.

computer-aided (or -assisted) design (CAD)

Designing a product using a specially equipped computer.

computer-aided design and manufacturing system (CAD/CAM)

Integration of design and production of a product through use of a computer.

flexible manufacturing system (FMS)

Manufacturing facility that is automated to some extent and produces a wide variety of products.

computer-integrated manufacturing (CIM)

Integration of all aspects of manufacturing through computer.

Industrial robots are substitutes for human manipulation and other highly repetitive functions. A robot is a reprogrammable machine with multiple functions that can move devices through specialized motions to perform any number of tasks. It is essentially a mechanized arm that can be fitted with a variety of handlike fingers or grippers, vacuum cups, or a tool such as a wrench. Robots are capable of performing many factory operations ranging from machining processes to simple assembly.

One of the major contemporary approaches to the product design process is **computer-aided (or -assisted) design (CAD)**. CAD may be defined as carrying out all structural or mechanical design processes of a product or component at a specially equipped computer. Engineers design through a combination of console controls and a light pen that draws on the computer screen or electronic pad. Different perspectives of the product can be visualized by rotating the product on the screen, and individual components can be enlarged to examine particular characteristics. Depending on the sophistication in software, on-screen testing may replace the early phases of prototype testing and modification.

CAD has been used to design everything from computer chips to potato chips. Frito-Lay, for example, used CAD to design its O'Grady's double-density, ruffled potato chip. CAD is also now being used to custom-design swimsuits. Measurements of the wearer are fed into the CAD program, along with the style of suit desired. Working with the customer, the designer modifies the suit design as it appears on a human form drawing on the computer screen. Once the design is decided upon, the computer prints out a pattern, and the suit is cut and sewn on the spot.

Computer-aided design and manufacturing (CAD/CAM) uses a computer to integrate component design and processing instructions. In current CAD/CAM systems, when the design is finalized, the link to CAM is made by producing the manufacturing instructions. Because of the efficiency of CAD/CAM systems, design and manufacture of small lots can be both fast and low in cost.

Even though CAD/CAM systems are usually limited to larger companies because of the high initial cost, they do increase productivity and quality dramatically. More alternative designs can be produced, and the specifications can be more exact. Updates can be more readily made, and cost estimates more easily drawn. In addition, computer-aided process planning (CAPP) can shorten and, in some cases, even eliminate traditional process planning. A **flexible manufacturing system (FMS)** actually refers to a number of systems that differ in the degree of mechanization, automated transfer, and computer control and are sufficiently flexible to produce a wide variety of products.

A flexible manufacturing module is a numerically controlled (NC) machine supported with a parts inventory, a tool changer, and a pallet changer. A flexible manufacturing cell consists of several flexible manufacturing modules organized according to the particular product's requirements. A flexible manufacturing group is a combination of flexible manufacturing modules and cells located in the same manufacturing area and joined by a materials handling system, such as an automated guided vehicle (AGV).

A flexible production system consists of flexible manufacturing groups that connect different manufacturing areas, such as fabrication, machining, and assembly. A flexible manufacturing line is a series of dedicated machines connected by AGVs, robots, conveyors, or some other type of automated transfer device.

Computer-integrated manufacturing (CIM) integrates all aspects of production into one automated system. Design, testing, fabrication, assembly, inspection, and materials handling may all have automated functions within the area. However, in most companies, communication between departments still flows by means of paperwork. In CIM, these islands of automation are integrated, thus eliminating the need for the paperwork. A computer links all sectors, resulting in more efficiency, less paperwork, and less personnel expense.

Islands of automation refer to the transition from conventional manufacturing to the automated factory. Typical islands of automation include numerically controlled machine tools, robots, automated storage/retrieval systems, and machining centres.

Radio frequency identification (RFID) is another recent technological innovation in manufacturing (and services) for tracking materials within a supply chain. An RFID tag is an inexpensive radio wave responsive device that is attached to a package with a unique identifier (see picture). A radio wave based reader identifies the package by scanning the tag. The identifier then allows the RFID system to access and add data regarding the package, that are then stored on a computer. These could include quantity, supplier details, transit points, destination, etc. Thus they are like bar codes, but better since the RFID scanner does not need to "see" the package for reading, unlike bar code readers. Thus RFID systems can locate packages packed inside containers without the need to have the containers opened, saving time and effort. For example, Canada Post uses RFID to track its mail packages. General Motors and Ford use them in their factories to track and locate inventory and to help production scheduling.[1] Wal-Mart already has many suppliers tagging pallets using RFIDs so that the chain can track shipments.

islands of automation

Automated factories or portions that include NC equipment, automated storage/retrieval systems, robots, and machining centres.

radio frequency identification (RFID)

A system that uses radio waves to identify and track inventory.

Information Technology

The use of information technology in manufacturing operations can be divided into five major groups of software systems: (1) enterprise resource planning (ERP), (2) supply chain management (SCM), (3) new product development (NPD), (4) customer relationship management (CRM), and (5) product life cycle management (PLM). These software packages have significant overlap in terms of their capabilities and what they provide.

Enterprise Resource Planning

Enterprise resource planning (ERP) systems provide a company with a single uniform software platform and database that will facilitate transactions among the different functional areas within the firm, and, in some cases, between firms and their customers and vendors. ERP providers include large organizations such as SAP, and small ones such as Navison. Increasingly ERP providers are producing customized software for different industries. For example, NAVImeat and Wisefish are ERP software packages geared for the meat processing and seafood industry respectively. ERP systems are discussed in detail in Chapter 12.

Supply Chain Management (SCM)

These software systems primarily focus on how firms interact with the suppliers that are part of their overall supply chain. Depending on where the firm is in its supply chain, this also can involve customers. The topic of supply chain management is presented in detail in Chapter 12.

An RFID tag compared to the size of a Canadian loonie. It is paper-thin and lightweight. Thus it can be easily used in tracking any type of package. The tag responds to a RFID scanner which in turn can used to access and enter information about the package. Tag courtesy of Omron Electronics Pte Ltd, Singapore.

New Product Development

New product development (NPD) software focuses on linking the engineering function with the operations function within a firm to facilitate the transfer of new product drawings and models into manufactured products. These software systems include CAD/CAM, which was discussed earlier in this chapter. Some software packages, such as that offered by Parametric Technology, also provide similar

---

[1]Grant Buckler, "Radio Frequency ID Is Key to Auto Industry," *The Globe and Mail*, October 9, 2003, B14.

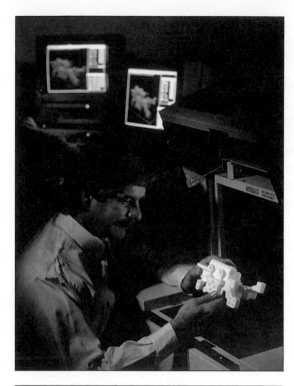

The speed with which a company can design and develop new products is critical to its ability to introduce them quickly into the marketplace. Rapid prototyping machines are a new generation of CAD equipment that can produce three-dimensional prototypes quickly in the initial stages of the product design cycle. These rough draft models result in both higher-quality products and lower development costs.

links with vendors who are directly involved in a firm's new product development process. The topic of new product development is addressed in detail in Chapter 3.

Customer Relationship Management

Customer relationship management (CRM) software, such as that provided by Siebel Systems, focuses on the interface between the firm and its customer. In addition to having order entry capability, these systems collect customer-specific data, which allow the firm to provide customer-specific solutions. These software systems are typically addressed in marketing.

Product Life Cycle

Product life cycle (PLM) management software allows a company to design, analyze, and manage its products from conception to retirement. PLM software can enhance organizational decision making and collaboration and communication between different organizations in design, costing, materials management, quality management, production, market launch, product history tracking, maintenance, and retirement. Thus PLM software can tie into ERP, SCM, NPD, and CRM software.

Technology in Services

Technology Trends in Services

Advances in technology, including improved automated equipment, voice recognition systems, high-speed data transmission lines (like broadband), and faster and more powerful computers, also have had a significant impact on services. Contributing to the growing trend in services is the fact that large amounts of data are readily accessible today and can be transmitted inexpensively over long distances. We identify several major trends in the delivery of services that are a direct result of technology. It is important to note that these trends are not mutually independent; rather, the opposite is true: They are highly dependent on one another.

Increase in Self-Service

Many service industries have seen an increase in self-service operations. Examples include self-service gas stations, ATMs at banks, checkout lanes in grocery stores (see OMP box), and automated toll collections on highways. Self-service also is used extensively in e-businesses, ranging from the purchasing of sweaters from L.L. Bean and airline tickets from WestJet to the purchase of stocks and bonds through BMO Nesbitt Burns and conducting online chequebook transactions with your bank.

The primary reason for the increase in self-service is that it reduces labour costs. With automated self-service equipment, gas station attendants are no longer needed to pump gas, bank tellers are no longer needed to process customer deposits and withdrawals, and customer service representatives are no longer needed to answer telephone calls.

Operations Management in Practice

However, service managers need to recognize that by going entirely to a self-service delivery system, they will exclude certain market segments. For example, some customers do not want to pump their own gas at a gas station; similarly, other individuals prefer to obtain professional advice on investing in the stock market rather than doing their own analysis. Consequently, many service firms offer self-service as only one of several distribution channels for marketing their products.

Inasmuch as it is usually the least costly channel, many service firms will offer customers incentives, often in the form of discounts, to use this channel, or, conversely, charge more when the interaction with an individual is required. Exhibit S3.2 provides some examples of how firms encourage customers to use self-service delivery systems.

Decrease in the Importance of Location

The combination of inexpensive data storage, transmission, and retrieval costs coupled with electronic access to virtually every corner of the world has decreased the importance of location for many services. Online banking services reduce the need for a customer to go to the bank. Home delivery services for groceries, dry cleaning, and so forth eliminate the need for customers to visit these retail locations. Similarly, any purchase made on the Internet, whether it is a book from Amazon.ca or airline tickets from Expedia.ca, eliminates the need for the customer to visit a specific retail location that offers these goods and services. When such services can be conducted remotely, it doesn't matter to the customer where they are located.

The continued development of a worldwide communication network has facilitated the location of back-office service operations to areas where labour costs are relatively inexpensive. As a result, customer call centres can be located anywhere. For example, Moncton, New Brunswick, has an impressive call centre industry in part because of its

Type of Service	Incentive to Use Self-Service
Gas station	Higher price for full-service gas
Investment firm	Higher commission for using a broker
Airline	Reduced fares available only on the Internet
Bank	Additional fee for using a teller

Exhibit S3.2

Methods of Pricing to Encourage Self-Service

bilingual population. Similarly, many North American companies are relocating their call centres to India and other developing countries because of low labour costs. It is important to note, however, that in addition to providing low-cost labour, these locations also must have the necessary communication infrastructure to provide the level of service required by these firms.

Shift from Time-Dependent to Non-Time-Dependent Transactions

There is a growing trend away from time-dependent service transactions toward non-time-dependent transactions. Time-dependent transactions are those transactions that require a service worker to be available at the exact time when the customer requests the service. Examples of time-dependent service transactions include the waitress at a restaurant who is there to serve you when you are hungry, the reservations clerk at an airline call centre who answers the telephone when you call to reserve a flight, the front-desk attendant who is on duty at the hotel when you check in, and your stockbroker who is available when you want to conduct a stock transaction. Non-time-dependent transactions do not require the presence of the service worker at the exact moment when the customer requests service. Examples of non-time-dependent transactions include e-mail, faxes, and voice messages. Time-dependent transactions often are referred to as **synchronous transactions** or communications; non-time-dependent transactions are referred to as **asynchronous transactions** or communications.

There are several reasons for the shift towards non-time-dependent transactions. First, it is more economical from the firm's perspective. As stated above, with time-dependent transactions, service workers must always be available to conduct a customer transaction. To allow for uncertainty in customer demand as well as to minimize customer waiting time, extra workers must be on duty, which adds to the expense. With non-time-dependent activities, a company has greater flexibility in scheduling workers in a more efficient manner, as well as the ability to prioritize the transactions.

Asynchronous transactions are usually more efficient from the customer's perspective too. For example, rather than trying to speak to someone in person, and playing endless rounds of "phone tag," it is much more efficient to send a single e-mail. However, an important point with asynchronous transactions is the need to have a service recovery process in place that assures personal contact when problems do occur.

In addition, with the world quickly becoming a *global village*, single world economy that is linked together electronically, a significant number of transactions do not take place during "regular business hours" (whatever that means these days!). Thus, a customer in Australia who orders something through the Internet from a firm in England can place the order at any time, regardless of what time it is in England, and that order will be processed at the beginning of the next business day. Non-time-dependent transactions permit firms to receive transactions on a 24/7 basis, and then to respond to these transactions efficiently during normal business hours.

Increase in Disintermediation

Stan Davis introduced the term **disintermediation** to mean the elimination of intermediate steps or organizations.[2] Technology allows buyers and sellers to come closer together, often dealing directly with each other without having to go through any intermediate organizations; for example, when travellers purchase airline tickets directly from the airlines through the Internet, eliminating the need for a travel agent. Likewise, trading stocks and bonds on the Internet eliminates the need for a stockbroker. Similarly, many manufacturers

synchronous transactions

Transactions that take place in real time without any time delays, usually between individuals.

asynchronous transactions

Transactions in which there is a delay in time with respect to the communication between the parties involved.

disintermediation

The elimination of intermediate steps or organizations.

---

[2]Stan Davis, *Future Perfect* (Reading, MA: Addison-Wesley, 1987).

now sell their products directly to consumers, eliminating the need for distributors and/or retailers. eBay, the online auction firm, is doing exactly this by providing a network that directly links buyers and sellers.

Integrating Technology into Services

Technology needs to be properly integrated into an organization to provide a competitive advantage, in terms both of increasing the efficiency of the operations as well as better serving its customers. We identify three areas where technology can significantly contribute to the success of an organization.

Strategic Planning

Strategic planning, from an operations perspective, is typically concerned with the long-range view of how an organization conducts business. As we have seen, strategic planning within the operations function of a manufacturing company is concerned with addressing such issues as (*a*) Where do we locate our facilities? (*b*) How big do we make them? (*c*) When do we build them? and (*d*) What processes do we adopt to make our products?

However, a service organization, because it deals directly with its customers, must strategically evaluate how it will interact with them. Service managers also must recognize that technology can significantly alter the way in which a company does business. For example, most of the major airlines now have home pages on the Internet that provide information about special airfare promotions and allow customers to book tickets online. U.S. retailers such as JC Penney have set up Web sites that allow them to test the Canadian market without actually building stores in Canada. If the Canadian market is found not to be viable, the cost of withdrawal will be minimal. Thus, by adopting the proper strategy and associated technology, a firm can substantially increase its revenues and market share. Failure to do so can result in losing customers to competitors.

Improved Performance

Service managers also must recognize that the decision to adopt technology is often driven by the need not only to increase productivity but also to improve the existing performance of their operations. (Improved performance, as defined earlier, includes faster delivery, more product variety, and improved customer responsiveness, to name but a few attributes.) Often, however, with the proper technology, both performance and productivity can be improved, creating a win-win situation for the firm.

Faster service. Technology has allowed service operations to significantly reduce and, in some cases, to totally eliminate the need for customers to wait in line for service. In addition to providing faster service, technology can simultaneously reduce labour costs by entirely eliminating the customer-worker encounter. Automated teller machines (ATMs) and in-room checkout in hotels are examples.

Another example, the use of bar code readers at the checkout counters in supermarkets, has significantly reduced the amount of time a customer can expect to stand in line, while also reducing labour costs and errors in keying in the proper item prices. Barcoding also reduces the need to consistently check inventories, providing managers with better control.

Improved knowledge about customers. In many services, databases now provide managers with detailed information about their customers' purchasing characteristics and their firm's past relationships with these customers. As part of their focus on attention to personal detail, for example, Four Seasons Hotels and Resorts uses a management information system to track individual guest preferences such as preferred bed size, special meals, and desired entertainment equipment. Membership cards of retail chains perform a similar function. Information such as this allows the organization to offer customized promotions. Technology thus can provide a service company with a competitive advantage through its ability to better understand the individual behaviour patterns and past experiences of each of its customers.

Increased product customization. Technology also allows service managers to provide their customers with a wider variety of options than they could previously offer. The terms "microniching" and "mass customization" have evolved, in part, as a direct result of advances in technology that now permit firms to identify and provide customized goods and services to meet the needs of individual customers. An example is the mutual funds division of Toronto-Dominion (TD) Bank Financial Group. In the past, the annual report mailed to individual fund holders contained detailed reports on all the division's mutual funds, making it a thick booklet. This meant extra printing and mailing costs (not to mention the number of trees destroyed). Now, each fund holder receives a much thinner but customized and easier-to-read booklet with summary information about all the mutual funds and detailed information only on his or her order holdings. The entire annual report is available on the bank's Web site.

Increased Efficiency

As stated earlier, the initial motivation for services to adopt technology was the need to reduce operating costs. This is still a major reason for purchasing new technology. Just as capital equipment often is used to reduce costs in a manufacturing company, technology can be similarly applied in a service environment. The two primary ways in which the efficiency or productivity of the operation can be increased are (1) economies of scale and (2) reduced labour costs, recognizing that there is some degree of overlap between the two.

Economies of scale. Advances in communication technology have allowed service companies to reduce the number of locations for many types of activities. For example, reservation operations for hotels, airlines, and car rental agencies have been consolidated in a few central locations. Economies of scale with these larger operations occur, in part, as a result of the ability to schedule a larger number of operators. For example, if the average demand in a given hour (that is, the number of calls received) doubles, the number of operators necessary to provide the same level of service will be less than double. Economies of scale also are reflected in the reduced overhead costs (as measured on a per-unit basis) that are typically associated with larger facilities. As stated earlier, an additional savings that frequently occurs as a result of the firm's ability to locate its operation anywhere is the reduced cost associated with locating in a low-cost-of-living area.

Reduced labour costs. Technology can reduce labour costs in services in two ways. First, it can be used as a total replacement for labour. Alternatively, technology can provide support to existing labour, thereby increasing labour productivity.

For example, ATMs in banks are a total substitute for the traditional bank teller for many routine operations, but cost only a fraction of what a teller costs. Therefore, bank customers should be encouraged to use ATMs when conducting certain types of transactions.

Organizations also can use the Internet to reduce labour costs. Perhaps your university has a system that allows you to register for your courses via the Web. Increased use of the Internet in this manner will reduce long lines at your university's registration office and hopefully reduce its annual operating expenses.

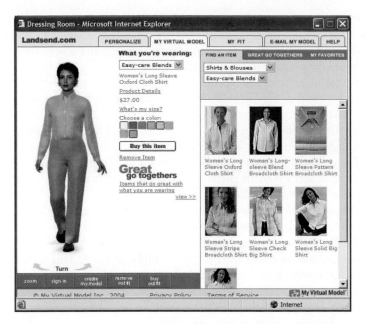

Lands' End Web site allows the customer to create a likeness of him- or herself and "try on" clothing for a custom fit.

Source: www.landsend.com. © 2004 Lands' End,. Inc. and My Virtual Model™.

A note of caution is necessary, however, when contemplating the introduction of totally automated services. First, as noted already, there are some segments of the market that are not comfortable using automation. In addition, although automated equipment usually can do a good job performing routine transactions, there are complex and highly customized transactions that can be resolved only by the customer interacting directly with a knowledgeable employee.

Technology in the form of automation also can be used in service operations to perform repetitive, time-consuming tasks. The use of technology in this manner not only increases worker productivity, but also reduces or eliminates errors. At the same time, it ensures the delivery of a more consistent product to the customer. In some instances, technology also can increase performance in the form of faster service; for example, a timed drink dispenser in a fast food restaurant that with a quick push of a button begins the flow of a specific amount of beverage, permitting the server to assemble the rest of the order while the drink is being poured automatically.

E-Tailering

E-tailering (also called E-tailing) involves providing goods and services through the Internet. Pure e-tailers are those firms that conduct business exclusively through the Internet, such as Amazon.ca, Grocerygateway.com, Etrade.com (stock trading), or ProQuest (document delivery). These services typically have their counterparts in bricks-and-mortar establishments. In many cases, however, e-tail operations are part of a larger organization that also has bricks-and-mortar locations, such as Indigo or Future Shop. Some of these firms (often referred to as *bricks and clicks* or *clicks and mortar)* such as The Gap also provide access to their Web sites at their bricks-and-mortar locations, thereby making the difference between the two even fuzzier.

The major challenge for pure e-tailers is to have the necessary infrastructure in place to efficiently and quickly deliver the goods to its customers. The lack of such infrastructures was clearly evident during the 1999 holiday season when many irate customers who had made purchases through the Internet didn't receive delivery until well into January 2000. Some e-tailers such as Amazon have elected to build their own infrastructures in terms of distribution centres; others have elected to partner with established bricks-and-mortar retail operations.

E-tailers that offer services typically do not need the supply chain infrastructure required by those e-tailers that provide goods. This allows for faster entry into the market, significantly lower investment costs, and, consequently, a quicker return on investment.

Another major challenge for pure e-tailers is the lack of tangibility. With a bricks-and-mortar operation, the customer has a place to go for customer service or to voice a complaint. There is nothing more frustrating than for a customer to wait endlessly on the phone for customer service or for goods to arrive, and to have no other recourse, as is the case when dealing with pure e-tailers.

Equally important for e-tailers is how they can build brand awareness and differentiate themselves in the marketplace. Brand awareness is important for new e-tailers competing with established bricks-and-mortar businesses. Without differentiation, these services offer only commodities, and therefore must compete solely on price. This translates into very small profit margins, which cannot sustain growth.

Revenue-stream issues include pricing, assigning delivery charges, determining whether customers have to take out fee-based memberships, or whether to accept advertising from other companies on their Web site.

Technology-Related Issues

The integration of new technologies into an organization requires a significant amount of training and support in order for both workers and customers to reap the full benefits. The lack of proper training and support, in many instances, not only will fail to yield the expected improvements in performance and/or productivity, but could also prove disastrous financially as frustrated workers quit and unhappy customers take their business elsewhere.

Overcoming Barriers to Entry

As new technologies become available, there are often barriers that prevent customers from using them, and managers need to be aware of these. Such barriers can significantly hinder the growth of the organization. One barrier is the "fear of the unknown" that is often associated with new technologies, a good example being the first time one purchases goods and services over the Internet. Here, because there are no tangibles associated with the firm, customers are concerned about misuse of their credit cards and whether or not they will actually get delivery of the goods or services they have purchased.

Another barrier is the consumer's lack of knowledge in using the service. This is especially true for self-service operations as well as for those services that use new technologies. Self-service gas stations provide a good example here, because there are many individuals who do not know how to operate a gas pump.

ATMs provide a good example of a service involving a new technology in which customers must not only overcome their fear of the unknown, but also must learn how to properly use the technology.

Training and Support

Significant amounts of upfront training must be built into the overall new technology process. This training is often required of both workers and customers. Failure to provide proper training will lead to inefficient operations and frustration. In addition, both workers and customers must have the necessary technical support when questions arise and/or equipment malfunctions occur.

Worker Training

Workers are often required to develop additional skills when a new technology is introduced into the operation. These new skills can be developed through training classes that not only describe the use of the technology but also simulate its use. This allows workers to become familiar with the new equipment and to "debug the process" prior to actually using it online in the presence of a customer. It is important for managers to recognize that worker training is an ongoing process. Many leading-edge firms, such as FedEx, in fact, require their workers to spend a specific number of days each year in training.

Customer Training

Customers also frequently are required to undergo some degree of training when a new technology interacts directly with them. Depending on the type of technology and the level of sophistication required to use it, customer training can vary from a simple pamphlet describing how to use the new technology to attending classes that carefully document the proper use of the technology.

Conclusion

Technology plays a significant role in the successful operation of every organization. With the constant introduction of new state-of-the-art technologies, this trend will most likely continue. However, operations managers must realize that the adoption of technology is not a simple undertaking and therefore must be planned carefully.

In the past, many firms looked to technology primarily to help them increase productivity. However, there are several additional reasons companies elect to incorporate new technologies into their processes, such as building a stronger relationship with their customers and improving their overall performance by providing better customer service.

Finally, the installation of new technology must be accompanied by the proper technical support. In addition, sufficient time must be allocated in the initial start-up phase to provide proper training to both workers and, where necessary, customers. When deciding to purchase new technology, the service manager must ensure that there is compatibility between the desired technology and the overall long-term goals of the firm.

Key Terms

asynchronous transactions p. 82

computer-aided (or -assisted) design (CAD) p. 78

computer-aided design and manufacturing system (CAD/CAM) p. 78

computer-integrated manufacturing (CIM) p. 78

disintermediation p. 82

flexible manufacturing system (FMS) p. 78

industrial robots p. 78

islands of automation p. 79

machining centres p. 77

numerically controlled (NC) machines p. 77

radio frequency identification (RFID) p. 79

synchronous transactions p. 82

www.mcgrawhill.ca/olc/davis

Review and Discussion Questions

1. What are the different ways in which technology can impact an operation? Use examples in both manufacturing and service operations.
2. Identify and compare the perceived benefits and costs for each of the following pairs of services:

Traditional Service	Technology-Driven Service
a. Traditional grocery store	Home delivery grocery service (Grocery Gateway)
b. Neighbourhood travel agent	Internet travel agent (Travelocity)
c. Local bank branch office	Internet bank (ING)
d. Traditional bookstore	Virtual bookstore (Amazon)

3. Describe how technology is adding value for each of the technology-driven services identified in Question 21.
4. What are the benefits of automation in a manufacturing company?
5. Visit any the following services and identify the various ways in which technology is changing how these services are being delivered.
   a. Retail store
   b. Restaurant
   c. Bank office
   d. Supermarket

Internet Exercise

Visit the Web site of a major airline such as Air Canada, British Airways, or Singapore Airlines, and compare the different ways to obtain information on a flight between two major cities of your choosing. Then visit the Web site of an online travel agency such as Expedia.ca, Destina.ca, or Travelocity.ca, and do a similar comparison. What are the advantages and disadvantages of using an airline's Web site? What are the advantages of using an online travel agency's Web site? What are the advantages of ordering airline tickets online versus buying them through your local travel agent, located in a nearby shopping mall?

Case 1 — EMC Uses Technology to Enhance Its Customer Service

The best kind of problem is no problem, or one that is anticipated and fixed before it even occurs. And no one is better at doing this than EMC Corporation, a manufacturer of data storage systems. Using state-of-the-art technology, a wide variety of sensors are installed in its storage systems. These sensors measure almost everything, from the operating environment, such as temperature and vibration, to technical performance, such as faulty sectors on a storage disk or abnormal power surges. In total, there are more than 1000 routine diagnostics. Whenever any of these parameters falls outside of its accepted tolerances, the storage system automatically "calls home" to EMC's call centre in Hopkinton, MA, to report the problem. In fact, more than 80 percent of the 4000 calls received at the call centre each day are not from EMC's customers themselves, but rather from EMC's storage systems. Customer support engineers then either fix the problem remotely from the call centre, or if that is not possible, dispatch a technician to the site. With this ability to anticipate problems before they occur, the first time a customer is even aware of a potential problem is when the technician arrives to replace a potentially faulty component before it actually fails.

One of the key factors in EMC's significant growth over the past decade has been its fanatical devotion to customer service. Providing great customer service, however, requires more than the ability to perform remote diagnostics, it requires commitment from the entire company. For starters, the

customer service call centre is located right in the middle of the engineering department, easily accessible to both hardware and software engineers. If the engineer receiving the call can't resolve the problem in 15 minutes, the responsible design engineer is called in. If it still isn't resolved in another 15 minutes, the vice president for engineering is called in. An unresolved problem will continue to escalate through EMC's organization, to the point where if it isn't solved within eight hours, Mike Ruettgers, EMC's executive chairman and Joe Tucci, EMC's president and CEO, are both notified.

As further evidence of its commitment to service excellence, EMC doesn't treat its customer service organization as a profit centre, as many firms do. By including the service in the cost of the product, customer service is treated as an expense item, without the need to generate profits. This allows customer service to focus entirely on doing whatever is necessary to satisfy the customer.

Does EMC charge more for its products? Absolutely. But its customers believe that EMC products are worth the additional cost. When Forrester Research surveyed 50 big companies about their various technology suppliers, "EMC came out looking like God," says Carl Howe, a director of research at Forrester. "It has the best customer service reviews we have ever seen, in any industry."[1]

In an *Information Week* study conducted on enterprise storage vendors. EMC received a satisfaction score of 8.53 (on a scale of 1 to 10, where 1 is not at all satisfied and 10 is extremely satisfied), compared to scored of 7.21 for Compaq, 7.16 for IBM, and 7.05 for Dell. As further evidence of customer satisfaction, the same study asked customers to rank their enterprise storage vendors in terms of "Service-Level Guarantees" and "After-Sales Service" with the following results.[2]

Customer Rankings of the Enterprise Storage Vendors

Service-Level Guarantees	After-Sales Service
1. EMC	1. EMC
2. Dell	2. Dell
3. IBM	3. IBM
4. Sun Microsystems	4. Sun Microsystems
5. Compaq	5. Compaq

Questions

1. How does technology provide EMC with a competitive advantage in the marketplace?

2. What are some of the concerns that EMC might have when potential problems are fixed remotely without the customer ever knowing about them?

3. What is the role of technology in building customer loyalty at EMC?

[1]Paul C. Judge, "Customer Service: EMC Corp.," *Fast Company* (June 2001), pp. 138–145.

[2]Karyl Scott, "EMC Shores Up Its Offense," Information Week (October 2, 2000), pp. 72–82.

4

Project Management

Chapter Objectives

- Recognize that project management involves both people skills to coordinate and motivate individuals from a range of disciplines and technical skills to properly plan and schedule a project.

- Explain the role of the project manager in organizing and coordinating all activities performed in a project.

- Introduce critical path scheduling as a tool for identifying activities that require immediate attention.

- Identify the time–cost trade-offs involved in expediting the completion of a project.

- Discuss some of the criticisms often associated with project management techniques.

EllisDon Offers Total Project Management

EllisDon is a leading, employee-owned, international construction company completing more than $1 billion in industrial, commercial, institutional, civil, and multi-unit residential construction annually. Founded in London, Ontario in 1951, EllisDon has grown into one of Canada's premier builders, offering services in General Contracting, Construction Management, Project Management, Design-Build, Public/Private Partnerships (P3), and Safety Consulting.

EllisDon has successfully undertaken projects in Europe, the Middle East, Central America, the Caribbean, Malaysia, and the former Soviet Union. The company now has twelve offices across Canada and the United States and worked on projects in Greece for the 2004 Olympics.

In 2006, the *Globe and Mail's Report on Business* named EllisDon one of the 50 Best Companies to Work for in Canada, ranking an impressive third, well ahead of its competition. *The National Post* also named EllisDon as one of the 50 Best Managed Companies in Canada.

Like other types of business, the construction industry has undergone many significant changes over the last few years. Traditionally a construction company, EllisDon had a reputation among both owners and subcontractors for being hard-nosed, which served them well for many years. By the late 1990s, the industry was changing; many clients had downsized and eliminated

in-house experts. They began looking to contractors for more expertise and value-added services. EllisDon embraced this opportunity, changing their role from adversary to team player, and developed the "Client First" program. Under Client First, EllisDon offers guarantees in three aspects of a project that are critical to their clients: performance, price, and schedule.

Furthermore, not having found appropriate software to run all aspects of a successful construction project, it has developed an industry-leading project management software called EdgeBuilder. The EdgeBuilder system allows procurement durations to be reduced while maintaining (and even enhancing) business controls. This is accomplished through the use of online collaborative approval documents. EllisDon created EdgeBuilder in response to industry demand for a single system that addressed the following requirements:

- Flexible, intuitive, and easy to use
- Uses standardized, familiar, and understandable language and terms
- Accessible by all (approved) members of the project team including owners/clients, designers, consultants, contractors, subcontractors, suppliers, and project/construction managers, and even wireless communication with on-site supervisors
- Provides information in "real time"
- Robust and affordable

EdgeBuilder is currently managing over 100 contracts valued at over $1.5 billion.

The company also recognizes the value of their employees. EllisDon encourages employees to build their career within the firm, offering benefits such as a generous profit-sharing plan, training, career development, and tuition reimbursement.

Sources:

M. Gibb-Clark, "EllisDon Rebuilds How It Does Business," *The Globe and Mail*, May 1, 2000, M1.

EllisDon Corporation, www.ellisdon.com.

Photo: Jaydeep Balakrishnan

Managerial Issues

Organizations are increasingly adopting a project approach in many of their activities. Shortened product life cycles, increased competition, technological advancements, and changing customer preferences mean that firms have to create ever-more-sophisticated goods and services ever more quickly, while using fewer resources. Furthermore, more organizations are outsourcing what they used to produce, to focus on their core competencies. Thus collaboration between organizations is increasing, with more emphasis on inter-organizational teams. All this implies that firms no longer have the luxury of inefficient use of time or budget. Project management techniques are useful for ensuring the delivery of quality goods and services on time and within budget.

Many projects are interdisciplinary in nature. Therefore the project team has to deal with the organizational, financial, operational, and informational aspects of managing (planning, scheduling, and controlling) projects. A project also has to deal with its external stakeholders such as the organization, the client, regulatory bodies, etc. In fact, managing a project is like managing a mini-organization. Thus, successfully managing a project requires a talented and capable project leader and team.

From an operations management perspective, identifying the relevant activities, preparing a feasible project plan, determining the project length, identifying crucial activities, and identifying how to reduce project length are important. A variety of software tools are available to schedule and control projects.

Since the word "project" implies that what is being done is unique (different from what has been done previously), uncertainty in time, budget, and outcomes is another crucial issue that the project team must deal with. In addition, with more projects becoming global, cultural issues in project management are becoming more important.

One strategy that many firms, especially those in high-tech industries, adopt to maintain a competitive advantage, is to have the ability to constantly introduce new products that incorporate the latest, state-of-the-art technologies. Intel, which introduces next-generation computer chips while there is still strong demand for current-generation chips, is a good example of these types of firms. The speed with which these firms can introduce new products is often critical to their success.

The ability to react quickly to changing customer demands is also important to services. The design and rollout of an advertising campaign for a new product or service, the purchase and installation of computer hardware or software, the development of a new financial services instrument, and the planning of the Olympics are all examples of services that fall under the heading of projects. Another example of a service that would benefit by using project management concepts is one that designs and develops Web sites for companies.

The design, development, and introduction of a new product or service is viewed as a one-of-kind type activity that is often referred to as a project. The speed with which firms can introduce and provide new goods and services is dependent, in large degree, on management's ability to understand and apply the concepts of project management to all of the required and, very often, dependent activities.

Project management techniques are also appropriate to exactly the opposite type of environment: one in which a product's lead time may be long. The key factor in this case is that when frequency of production is low, each item produced tends to be viewed as a separate project. Examples include construction, shipbuilding, airplane manufacture, and the production of satellites (see the opening vignette).

There are two main components in project management: One heavily emphasizes the organization and the behaviour of *people*; the other focuses on the technology of the *method* (computing start and completion times, critical paths, etc.). In this chapter we address both elements, although we lean more toward describing the technical aspects of project management and leave the people issues to a course on management and organizational behaviour.

Operations Management in Practice

USING PROJECT MANAGEMENT PRINCIPLES TO MANAGE YOUR GROUP TERM PAPER

You might not have thought of it this way, but any group term paper that you do in college is a project. After all, it is expected to be a unique piece of work! In fact, one of the authors has student groups in his class use many of the project management principles you will see in this chapter. Students are expected to break down the project into its constituent parts (called the work breakdown structure or WBS). Furthermore, students are required to use Microsoft Project to come up with a project schedule and to assign responsibility for the various tasks to group members. The milestones (interim deliverables to be submitted to the instructor as well as any others determined by the group) of the project have to be identified in the schedule and the students are expected to meet their deadlines. Conflict in student groups (perhaps one of the project team is not pulling his or her weight), a fact of life in business and industry, are expected to be resolved as much as possible within the group.

Other project management principles are used implicitly. In order to meet a deadline, you might have to take over some of the work initially assigned to your friend because he fell ill. Furthermore, if your group realizes that the paper is behind schedule, you may speed up or "crash" your project by paying an outside party to do some tasks such as proofreading. All this is part of

project control—modifying aspects of the project to get it back on track.

Projects also involve trade-offs between time, cost, and scope. For example, if you hire a proofreader to speed up the project, your costs will go up. Furthermore, though you may have planned to interview someone from industry for this paper, due to lack of time you may have to give up this idea (i.e., reduce the scope of the project in order to avoid delays). Of course this could result in lower customer (instructor) satisfaction and a lower grade!

Once, one of the authors, minutes before the start of the session in which the paper was due, discovered three students from a group standing outside the classroom clutching papers. It turned out they were waiting for the fourth member of their group in order to submit his part, before stapling it and handing it in a few minutes later in class. Suffice to say their project was not one of the better ones the author has seen, a logical outcome for a paper written in four parts by four different people without much collaboration. This is an important lesson in project management that companies have learned the hard way over the years: Projects have to be done in an integrated fashion. For example, if marketing, design, and manufacturing (and other functions in the firm) do not collaborate from the very beginning of a project the result will be rework, delays, and additional costs before the customer gets a satisfactory product. In the worst case, the product will fail in the marketplace, in the same way that a badly planned and executed term paper will receive a poor grade.

Consequently, project managers focus their efforts on three major elements:

- *Time:* How long will the project take from start to finish and will it be completed on schedule?

- *Performance:* Does the project meet or exceed the quality required by the customer?

- *Cost:* What are all of the costs, both direct and indirect, associated with the project, and will it be completed on budget?

Why has studying project management become more important? Companies have realized that poor project management is costing millions or even billions of dollars due to delays or customer dissatisfaction-related rework. Thus more and more professional societies and consultants related to project management are offering training seminars and courses to companies, as are universities and colleges.

Definition of Project Management

A project is basically an organized undertaking to accomplish a specific goal. In a technical sense, a **project** is defined as a series of related jobs or tasks usually directed toward some major output and requiring a significant period of time to perform. *Project*

project
Series of related jobs or tasks focused on the completion of an overall objective.

management can be defined as planning, directing, and controlling resources (i.e., people, equipment, material) to meet the technical, cost, and time constraints of the project.

Although projects are often associated with single, one-of-a-kind type products, the fact is that many projects can be repeated or transferred to other settings or products. The result will be another project output. A contractor building houses or a firm producing customized, low-volume products such as supercomputers, locomotives, or linear accelerators can effectively consider such products as individual projects.

There are some distinct differences between managing ongoing processes and managing projects. One difference relates to organizational structure. Repetitive processes are likely to be managed within the formal organization structure, whereas the group of people working together on a project are often brought together specifically to accomplish the single project and may stop working together when the project is completed. Because project teams are often newly formed groups, it can take time for these groups to become effective, requiring the conscious effort of all those involved as well as a major emphasis on communication.

Another major difference between the management of ongoing processes and project management relates to the tasks themselves. Since projects are by definition not repetitive, flexibility is an important element in successful project management. Unique, first-time tasks cannot always be totally defined or understood until they actually are begun, so project plans must continually evolve over the life of the project. Effective project management requires continuous monitoring, updating, and replanning throughout the life of the project.

A project starts out as a *statement of work (SOW)*. The SOW may be a written description of the objectives to be achieved, with a brief statement of the work to be done and a proposed schedule specifying start and completion dates. It also may contain performance measures in terms of budget and completion steps (milestones) and the written reports to be supplied.

If the proposed work is a very large endeavour, it is frequently referred to as a **program**, although the terms *project* and program are often used interchangeably. A program, which is the highest order of organizational complexity, may take several years to complete, and may consist of interrelated projects completed by many organizations. The development of a new outer-space missile system and the introduction of a new national medical health care system are good examples of programs.

Specific events to be reached at points in time, are called **milestones**. Typical milestones in the introduction of a new product might be the completion of the design phase, the production of a prototype, the completed testing of the prototype, and the approval of a pilot run.

program

Synonym for a project, although it also can consist of several interrelated projects.

milestones

Specific major events to be completed at certain times in the project.

work breakdown structure (WBS)

Method by which a project is divided into tasks and subtasks.

Work Breakdown Structure

The **work breakdown structure (WBS)** is the heart of project management. This subdivision of the objective into smaller and smaller pieces more clearly defines the system in detail and contributes to its understanding and success. Conventional use shows the work breakdown structure decreasing in size from top to bottom and shows this level by indentation to the right in the following format:

Level	
1	Program
2	Project
3	Deliverable
4	Subdeliverable
⋮	⋮
	Work package

HOW DEEP SHOULD THE WORK BREAKDOWN STRUCTURE (WBS) BE?

An important question when developing a WBS is: In how much in detail should one break down the work?

There is no set answer to this question. However, here are some tips given by project managers:

Break down the work until you can do an estimate that is accurate enough for your purposes. If you are doing a ball-park estimate to see if the project is worthy of serious consideration, you probably do not need to break it down beyond major deliverables. On the other hand, if you are pricing a project to submit a competitive bid, then you are likely to go down to the work package level.

The WBS should conform to the way you are going to schedule work. For example, if assignments are made in terms of days, then tasks should be limited as much as possible to one or more days to complete. Conversely, if hours are the smallest unit for scheduling, then work can be broken down into one-hour increments.

If accountability and control are important, then break the work down so that one individual is clearly responsible for the work. For example, instead of stopping at product design, take it to the next level and identify specific components of the design (i.e., electrical schematics, power source, etc.) that different individuals will be responsible for creating.

The bottom line is that the WBS should provide the level of detail needed to manage the specific project successfully.

Source:
Clifford F. Gray and Erik W. Larson, *Project Management: The Managerial Approach* (New York: McGraw-Hill/Irwin, 2006), p. 110.

Exhibit 4.1

Part of a Work Breakdown Structure for Opening a New Restaurant

Level						
1	2	3	4	5		
x					1.0	Open new restaurant
	x				1.1	Human resources
		x			1.1.1	Determine worker requirements
		x			1.1.2	Recruit workers
			x		1.1.2.1	Place advertisements
			x		1.1.2.2	Screen applicants
			x	x	1.1.2.3	Hire workers
				x	1.1.2.2.1	Conduct interviews
		x		x	1.1.2.2.2	Check references
	x				1.1.3	Train workers
		x			1.2	Purchase and install kitchen equipment
			x		1.2.1	Design menu
			x		1.2.1.1	Develop recipes
		x			1.2.1.2	Determine equipment requirements
			x		1.2.2	Purchase equipment
			x		1.2.2.1	Obtain quotes
		x			1.2.2.2	Select vendor
			x		1.2.3	Install equipment
			x		1.2.3.1	Connect electrical
					1.2.3.2	Connect plumbing

Exhibit 4.1 shows part of the work breakdown structure for a project to open a restaurant (not including work packages). Note the ease in identifying deliverables and subdeliverables through the level numbers. For example, determine worker requirements (the third item down) is identified as 1.1.1 (the first item in level 1, the first item in level 2, and the first item in level 3). Similarly, install equipment (the seventeenth item down) is 1.2.3. Exhibit 4.2 shows the same information in tree form.

The lowest level subdeliverable shown in Exhibit 4.2 can be divided into multiple *work packages*. Practice suggests that a work package be limited to about 10 days' worth of work.[1] In the discussion of the network diagram later in this chapter, *tasks* consist of one

---

[1]Clifford F. Gray and Erik W. Larson, *Project Management: The Managerial Process* (New York: McGraw-Hill/Irwin, 2006), pp. 7–11.

Exhibit 4.2

WBS in Tree Form

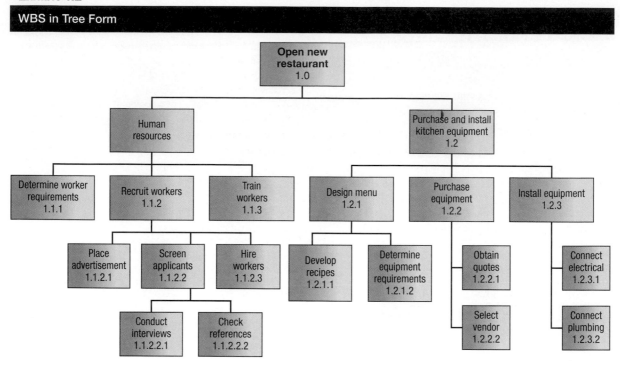

or more work packages. Thus the WBS helps determine what tasks will be needed. Tasks (or activities) have a definite start and finish point, and consume resources and costs. Conversely, the lowest level subdeliverable (above the work package level) in the WBS usually represents a roll-up or aggregation of tasks in the project.

From a cost perspective, similar work packages can be combined into *cost accounts*. Cost accounts are generally under the purview of one department (for example, purchasing) that monitors the cost of the work to ensure it remains within budget.

Another important use for the WBS is to determine the organizational units responsible for performing the work within the time, performance, and cost constraints. This is sometimes called the organization breakdown structure (OBS).

Organizational Considerations in Project Management

As stated previously, the timely completion of successful projects requires an understanding of both the technical and human resource components of project management. The technical component is required to identify the critical activities that affect the overall length of time a project takes to complete. The human resource elements address the issues of leadership and worker motivation within a group or team environment. Web Chapter 17 addresses many of these human resource issues as they pertain to working in teams; our goal here is to present a brief overview of those aspects that appear to exist in most projects.

Sometimes this may involve non-traditional methods of managing the people on the project. (See the OM in Practice box on Group Telecom). Today, with Canadian companies involved around the world, it is important to recognize that there can be significant cultural differences among countries. As well, projects in Canada can involve multi-national teams. For example, a recent major project, the Confederation Bridge linking Prince Edward Island to New Brunswick, was constructed by a consortium that included companies from France, the Netherlands, the United States, and Canada. Project teams may have to be managed with the cultural context in mind.

Role of the Project Manager

Project managers typically have a unique role within the traditional organization structure. Most project management teams are multidisciplinary in nature, involving a wide variety of skills and organizational units. Often these teams include people from engineering, operations, and marketing, and from support services that include risk management, systems operations, auditing, and legal groups. Consequently, today's project managers must often cross traditional functional lines to obtain the support necessary for the completion of a project. In most instances, this support is requested without formal authority. Thus the project manager must create a collaborative culture that relies heavily on social skills as well as technical expertise.

Without the authority of a traditional functional manager and the associated system of rewards and punishments, project managers must earn their authority by building trust, respect, and credibility among project members, as well as by demonstrating sound decision making—all within a stimulating work environment.

High-Performance Project Teams

In today's complex and technologically sophisticated environment, the group has reemerged in importance in the form of project teams. The characteristics of a project team and its ultimate performance depend on many factors that involve both people and structural issues. Although each organization has its own measures of performance, there is general agreement among project managers on which factors are necessary for the creation of a successful project team. These factors are divided into the following four categories:[2]

1. *Task-related variables* are direct measures of task performance, such as the ability to produce quality results on time and within budget, innovative performance, and the ability to change.

2. *People-related variables* affect the inner workings of the team and include good communications, high involvement, the capacity to resolve conflict, and mutual trust and commitment to project objectives.

3. *Leadership variables* are associated with the various leadership positions within the project team. These positions can be created formally, such as the appointment of project managers and task leaders, or emerge dynamically within the work process as a result of individually developed power bases such as expertise, trust, respect, credibility, friendship, and empathy. Typical leadership characteristics include the

---

[2]Hans J. Thamhain, "Managing Technologically Innovative Team Efforts Towards New Product Success," *Journal of Production Innovation Management 7*, no. 1 (March 1990); and Hans J. Thamhain, "Effective Leadership Style for Managing Project Teams," in *Handbook of Program and Project Management*, ed. P. C. Dinsmore (New York: AMACOM, 1992).

ability to organize and direct tasks, facilitate group decision making, motivate, assist in conflict and problem resolution, and foster a work environment that satisfies the professional and personal needs of the individual team members.

4. *Organizational variables* include the overall organizational climate, command-control-authority structure, policies, procedures, regulations, and regional cultures, values, and economic conditions.

It is interesting to note that managers, in describing the characteristics of an effective, high-performing project team, focus not only on task-related skills for producing technical results on time and within budget, but also on team members and leadership qualities.

Barriers to High Team Performance

As a functioning group, the project team is subject to group dynamics. In addition, because it is usually a highly visible and focused work group, the project team often takes on special significance and is accorded high status with commensurate expectations of performance. Although a project team brings significant energy to a task, the possibility of the group malfunctioning is significant. This occurs because there are several barriers to high performance that can exist in a project team. These include (*a*) different points of view, (*b*) role conflicts, and (*c*) power struggles. Each of these barriers must be overcome if the team is to successfully complete its assigned project.

Project Control

The U.S. Department of Defense was one of the earliest large users of project management and has published a variety of useful standard forms. Many are used directly or have been modified by firms engaged in project management. Since those early days, however, graphics software has been written for most computers, so that management, the customer, and the project manager now have a wide choice of how data are presented. Exhibit 4.3 shows a sample of available presentations.

Gantt Chart

Graphical technique that shows the amount of time required for each activity and the sequence in which activities are to be performed.

Exhibit 4.3A is a sample **Gantt chart** showing both the amount of time involved and the sequence in which activities can be performed. For example, "long lead procurement" and "manufacturing schedules" are independent activities and can occur simultaneously. All of the other activities must be done in sequence from top to bottom. Exhibit 4.3B graphically shows the proportion of money spent on labour, material, and overhead. Its value is its clarity in identifying sources and amounts of cost.

Exhibit 4.3C shows the percentage of the project's labour hours that come from the various areas of manufacturing, finance, and so on. These labour hours are related to the proportion of the project's total labour cost. For example, manufacturing is responsible for 50 percent of the project's labour hours, but this 50 percent represents just 40 percent of the total labour dollars charged.

The top half of Exhibit 4.3D shows the degree of completion of these projects. The dotted vertical line signifies today. Project 1, therefore, is already late since it still has work to be done. Project 2, although on schedule, is not being worked on temporarily, which is why there is a space before the projected work. Project 3, also on schedule, continues to be worked on without interruption. The bottom of Exhibit 4.3D shows actual total costs compared to projected costs. The exhibit shows that two cost overruns occurred.

Exhibit 4.3E is a milestone chart. The three milestones mark specific points in the project where checks can be made to see if the project is on time and where it should be. The best place to locate milestones is at the completion of a major activity. In this exhibit,

Exhibit 4.3

A Sample of Graphic Project Reports

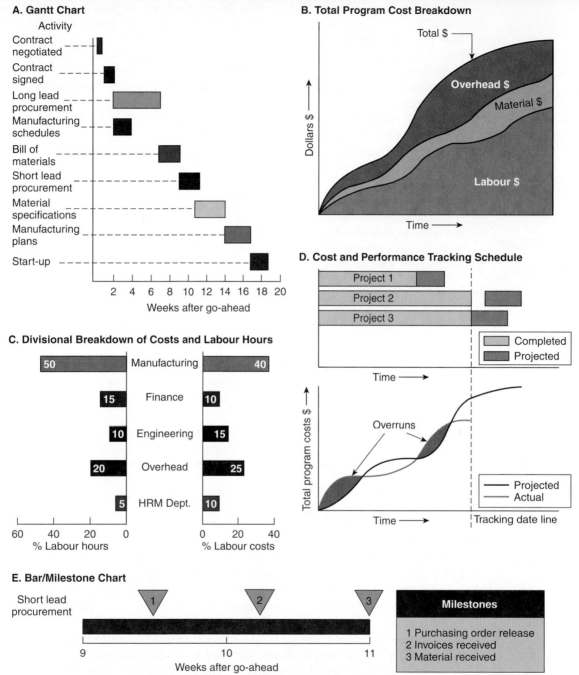

A. Gantt Chart

Activity
- Contract negotiated
- Contract signed
- Long lead procurement
- Manufacturing schedules
- Bill of materials
- Short lead procurement
- Material specifications
- Manufacturing plans
- Start-up

2 4 6 8 10 12 14 16 18 20
Weeks after go-ahead

B. Total Program Cost Breakdown

Total $
Overhead $
Material $
Labour $
Dollars $
Time

C. Divisional Breakdown of Costs and Labour Hours

50	Manufacturing	40
15	Finance	10
10	Engineering	15
20	Overhead	25
5	HRM Dept.	10

60 40 20 0   0 20 40
% Labour hours   % Labour costs

D. Cost and Performance Tracking Schedule

Project 1
Project 2
Project 3

Completed
Projected

Time

Overruns
Total program costs $
Time
Projected
Actual
Tracking date line

E. Bar/Milestone Chart

Short lead procurement

1   2   3

9   10   11
Weeks after go-ahead

Milestones

1 Purchasing order release
2 Invoices received
3 Material received

the major activities completed were "purchasing order release," "invoices received," and "material received."

Other standard reports can be used for a more detailed presentation comparing cost to progress (such as a cost schedule status report—CSSR) or for reports providing the basis for partial payment (such as an "earned value" report).

Critical Path Scheduling

Critical path scheduling refers to a set of graphic techniques used in planning and controlling projects. In any given project, the three factors of concern are time, costs, and resource availability. Here, time refers to the total elapsed time from the beginning of the project until its completion; costs are defined as all of those expenses directly related to the project, including material and labour; resources include the labour available to work on the project, as well as equipment and facilities that can be assigned to the project. Critical path techniques have been developed to deal with each of these, individually and in combination.

PERT (program evaluation and review technique) and **CPM (critical path method)**, the two best-known techniques, were both developed in the late 1950s. PERT was developed under the sponsorship of the U.S. Navy Special Projects Office in 1958 as a management tool for scheduling and controlling the Polaris missile project. CPM was developed in 1957 by J. E. Kelly of Remington-Rand and M. R. Walker of Du Pont to aid in scheduling maintenance shutdowns of chemical processing plants.

Critical path scheduling techniques display a project as a network of nodes and arrows and relate its individual tasks in a way that focuses attention on those tasks that are critical to the project's completion. For critical path scheduling techniques to be most applicable a project must have the following characteristics:

1. It must have well-defined jobs or tasks whose completion marks the end of the project.
2. The jobs or tasks are independent; they may be started, stopped, and conducted separately within a given sequence.
3. The jobs or tasks are ordered; certain ones must follow others in a given sequence.

The construction, aerospace, and shipbuilding industries commonly meet these criteria, and critical path techniques find wide application within them. We previously noted also that the applications of project management and critical path techniques are becoming much more common within firms in rapidly changing industries.

Project management techniques are also becoming more common in health care, with the objective of reducing a patient's overall stay in hospital. Here, each patient is viewed as a project and the various procedures he or she undergoes are considered to be the tasks in that project.

Time-Oriented Techniques

The basic forms of PERT and CPM focus on identifying the longest time-consuming path through a network of tasks as a basis for planning and controlling a project. Both PERT and CPM use nodes and arrows for display. Originally, the basic differences between PERT and CPM were that PERT used the arrow to represent an activity and CPM used the node. The other original difference between these two techniques was that PERT used three estimates—optimistic, pessimistic, and most likely—of an activity's required time, whereas CPM used just a single, best-time estimate. This distinction reflects PERT's origin in scheduling advanced scientific projects (like the lunar missions) that are characterized by uncertainty and CPM's origin in the scheduling of the fairly routine activity of plant maintenance. Thus, PERT was often used when the primary variable of interest was time, whereas CPM was used when the primary variable of interest was cost. As years passed, these two features no longer distinguished PERT from

---

PERT (program evaluation and review technique)

Project scheduling technique using probabilistic activity times.

CPM (critical path method)

Project scheduling technique using deterministic activity times.

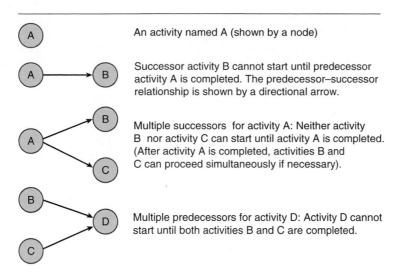

Exhibit 4.4

CPM/PERT Network Conventions

An activity named A (shown by a node)

Successor activity B cannot start until predecessor activity A is completed. The predecessor–successor relationship is shown by a directional arrow.

Multiple successors for activity A: Neither activity B nor activity C can start until activity A is completed. (After activity A is completed, activities B and C can proceed simultaneously if necessary).

Multiple predecessors for activity D: Activity D cannot start until both activities B and C are completed.

CPM. This is because CPM users started to use three time estimates and PERT users often placed activities on the nodes.

We believe the activity on the node is much easier to follow logically than the activity on the arrow. However, the three time estimates are often valuable in obtaining a measure of the probability of completion times. Therefore, in this chapter we use the activity on the node and either a single estimate for activity time or three time estimates, depending on our objective. We use the terms *CPM* and *PERT* interchangeably and mean the same thing, although we tend to use the term *CPM* more frequently.

In a sense, both techniques owe their development to their widely used predecessor, the Gantt chart. Although the Gantt chart is able to relate activities to time in a visually usable fashion for very small projects, the interrelationship of activities, when displayed in this format, becomes extremely difficult to visualize and to work with for projects with more than 25 or 30 activities. Moreover, the Gantt chart provides no direct procedure for determining the critical path, which, despite its theoretical shortcomings, is of great practical value.

CPM with a Single Time Estimate

With the following as an example, we will develop the typical approach taken in project scheduling. The times for each activity have been given as a most likely estimate (rather than three estimates, which will be discussed in a later example). Exhibit 4.4 shows the CPM/PERT conventions that we will use.

Example

Many firms that tried to enter the portable computer market have failed. Suppose your firm believes that there is a big demand in this market because existing products have not been designed correctly. They are either too heavy, too large, or too small to accommodate a standard-size keyboard. Your intended computer will be small enough to carry inside a jacket pocket if need be. The ideal size should be no larger than 8 cm × 20 cm, with a standard typewriter keyboard. It should weigh no more than 400 grams, have a

4- to 8-line $\times$ 80-character back-lit display, and have a micro disk drive and a micro printer. It should be aimed primarily toward word processing use but have plug-in ROMs to accommodate an assortment of computer languages and programs. These characteristics should appeal to travelling businesspeople, but could have a much wider market. If it can be priced to sell retail in the $175–$200 range, the computer should appeal to a wide market.

The project, then, is to design, develop, and produce a prototype of this portable computer. In the rapidly changing computer industry, it is crucial to hit the market with a product of this type in less than a year. Therefore, the project team has been allowed approximately nine months, or 39 weeks, to produce the prototype.

The first assignment of the project team is to develop a project network chart to determine whether or not the prototype computer can be completed within the 39 weeks. Let's follow the steps in the development of this network.

Solution

Step 1: Activity Identification
The project team decides that the following activities constitute the major components of the project: (A) designing the computer, (B) constructing the prototype, (C) evaluating automatic assembly equipment, (D) testing the prototype, (E) preparing an assembly equipment study report, (F) writing methods specifications (to be summarized in a report), and (G) preparing a final report summarizing all aspects of the design, equipment, and methods (see Exhibit 4.5).

Step 2: Activity Sequencing and Network Construction
On the basis of discussion with her staff, the project manager develops the precedence table and sequence network shown in Exhibit 4.5.

Exhibit 4.5

CPM Network for Computer Design Project

CPM Activity/Designations and Time Estimates

Activity	Designation	Immediate Predecessors	Time in Weeks
Design	A	–	21
Build prototype	B	A	4
Evaluate equipment	C	A	7
Test prototype	D	B	2
Write equipment report	E	C, D	5
Write methods report	F	C, D	8
Write final report	G	E, F	2

Using the precedence table, we can construct a network diagram, taking care to ensure that the activities are in the proper order and that the logic of their relationships is maintained. For example, it would be illogical to have a situation in which Activity A precedes Activity B, B precedes C, and then C precedes A.

Step 3: Determine the Critical Path

A path is defined as any sequence of connected activities through the network.

The **critical path** is defined as the longest sequence of connected activities through the network. In other words, the shortest time in which the project can be completed is determined by the length of the critical path. To find the critical path, we simply identify all of the paths through the network, from beginning to end, and calculate their respective completion times. The path with the longest completion time is, by definition, the critical path. For our example, the different paths and their respective completion times are as follows:

Path	Completion Time (in weeks)
A–C–F–G	$21 + 7 + 8 + 2 = 38$
A–C–E–G	$21 + 7 + 5 + 2 = 35$
A–B–D–F–G	$21 + 4 + 2 + 8 + 2 = 37$
A–B–D–E–G	$21 + 4 + 2 + 5 + 2 = 34$

Path A–C–F–G takes the longest to complete—38 weeks—and is therefore the critical path for this project. Consequently, this project as it now exists cannot be completed in fewer than 38 weeks. Inasmuch as the project has been allowed 39 weeks to be completed, there appears to be no problem. If the project were required to be completed in fewer than 38 weeks, then one or more of the activities on the critical path would have to be "crashed" or accelerated to meet the required project completion date.

Step 4: Determine Slack Times

The total **slack time** for an activity is defined as that amount of time that an activity can be delayed without affecting the overall completion time of the project (see the OMP on slack before you continue). To calculate the slack time for each activity, the following terms are defined:

t_i: *Time required to complete activity i*

ES_i: *Early start time of an activity i*, the earliest possible time that the activity can begin

$EF_i = ES_i + t_i$: *Early finish time of an activity i*, the early start time plus the time needed to complete the activity

LF_i: *Late finish time*, the latest possible time that an activity can end without delaying the project

$LS_i = LF_i - t_i$: *Late start time*, the late finish time minus the time needed to complete the activity

$S_i = LF_i - EF_i$ or $LS_i - ES_i$: *The slack for an activity i*

critical path
Longest sequence of activities that determines the overall length of the project.

slack time
Amount of time an activity can be delayed without affecting the completion date of the overall project.

Step 4.1: Find the ES and EF for Each Activity

The ES time for each activity is determined with a "forward pass" through the network, beginning with the first activity A,

We set the $ES_A = 0$ (representing the start of the project). Then

$$ES_A = 0$$

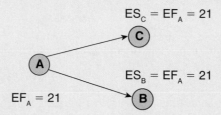

$$EF_A = ES_A + t_A \quad \text{or} \quad EF_A = 0 + 21 = 21$$

Proceeding to the two immediate successors of A (i.e., B and C) to get their ES times.

$$ES_C = EF_A = 21$$

$$ES_B = EF_A = 21$$

$$EF_A = 21$$

Now we can calculate the EF times for activities B and C as shown.

$$ES_C = 21$$

$$EF_C = 21 + 7 = 28$$

$$ES_B = 21$$

$$EF_B = 21 + 4 = 25$$

This procedure is repeated for each activity in the network. How do we select the EF when more than one activity precedes the activity being evaluated? The procedure is shown for activity F.

$$ES_F = MAX(EF_C, EF_D) \quad \text{or}$$
$$ES_F = MAX(28, 27) = 28 \text{ weeks}$$

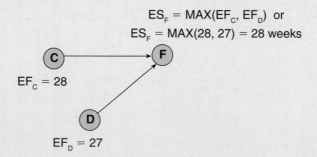

$$EF_C = 28$$

$$EF_D = 27$$

So, although activity D is completed by week 27, since we have to wait for both C and D to be completed before F can begin, the earliest we could start activity F is 28 weeks after we begin the project. Given that F takes 8 weeks to do, the earliest it can finish is week 36. The early start and finish times for all the activities in the computer design project are shown in both the table and network diagram in Exhibit 4.6.

Step 4.2: Find the LS and LF for Each Activity

To obtain the LS for each activity we simply reverse the procedure for calculating the ES, beginning at the end of the project. Since we start at the end of the network and work our way back to the beginning, this is called a "backwards pass" through the network.

We begin with the last activity, G. As we determined earlier, the critical path for the project is 38 weeks.

Therefore, set the $LF_G = 38$ (representing the end of the project). Now we can calculate the latest time that activity G can start without delaying the project as

$$LS_G = LF_G - t_G \quad \text{or} \quad LS_G = 38 - 2 = 36$$

$$\boxed{G}$$

$$LF_G = 38$$

As seen, the latest that we could start activity G (and still complete the project in 38 weeks) is 36 weeks, since it takes two weeks to do activity G.

Proceeding to the two immediate predecessors of G (i.e., F and E) we get the LF times for activities E and F.

Therefore both activities E and F must be completed at the latest by week 36 if the project is not to be delayed.

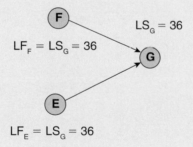

$$LF_F = LS_G = 36$$

$$LS_G = 36$$

$$LF_E = LS_G = 36$$

Now we can calculate the LS times for activities E and F as

$$LS_F = 36 - 8 = 28$$

$$\boxed{F}$$

$$LF_F = 36$$

$$LS_E = 36 - 5 = 31$$

$$\boxed{E}$$

$$LF_E = 36$$

The LS times for the remaining activities are likewise calculated. The procedure for determining the LF when more than one activity follows the activity being evaluated is shown for activity C.

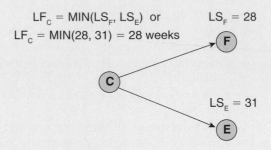

$$LF_C = MIN(LS_F, LS_E) \text{ or}$$
$$LF_C = MIN(28, 31) = 28 \text{ weeks}$$

Thus, though activity E can start as late as week 31, activity F has to begin by week 28 so as not to delay the project. This means that C has to be completed by week 28 and has to start by week 21 at the latest.

The latest start and the latest finish times for all of the activities in the computer design project are shown in both the table and network diagram in Exhibit 4.6.

Step 4.3: Determine the Total Slack Time for Each Activity

As stated previously, the total slack time for each activity is defined as either LS – ES or LF – EF (see Exhibit 4.6). In the computer design project, the slack time for activity E

Exhibit 4.6

CPM Network for Computer Design Project

					Slack Calculations and Critical Path Determinations		
Activity	**ES**	**EF**	**LS**	**LF**	**LS – ES**	**Slack**	**On Critical Path**
A	0	21	0	21	0 − 0	0	Yes
B	21	25	22	26	22 − 21	1	No
C	21	28	21	28	21 − 21	0	Yes
D	25	27	26	28	26 − 25	1	No
E	28	33	31	36	31 − 28	3	No
F	28	36	28	36	28 − 28	0	Yes
G	36	38	36	38	36 − 36	0	Yes

[CPM network diagram]

Activity C (7): 21, 21 / 28, 28
Activity F (8): 28, 28 / 36, 36
Activity A (21): 0, 0 / 21, 21
Activity G (2): 36, 36 / 38, 38
Activity B (4): 21, 22 / 25, 26
Activity D (2): 25, 26 / 27, 28
Activity E (5): 28, 31 / 33, 36

Key: A
ES, LS
EF, LF

Operations Management in Practice

EVERYBODY USES SLACK TIME; THE KEY IS TO USE IT WISELY[3]

Let us continue with our example, using project management principles in your term paper. Assume that your project is due in the assignment dropoff box at noon today and it is currently 8 a.m. All paths in your project have been completed, except one. There are two tasks left on this path—proofreading the document and printing. This is a major paper worth a significant proportion of your grade. Thus careful proofreading is essential. You calculate this task will take you two hours. Printing in colour on a laser jet printer will take another hour. So if you start now (the earliest time possible), you get the early start schedule, shown on the accompanying Gantt chart.

The proofreading task starts at 8 a.m. and ends at 10 a.m. The printing task starts at 10 a.m. and ends at 11 a.m.

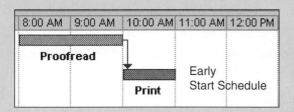

Now, let's say you had something else urgent to do now (at 8 a.m.). You figure you could work on that urgent task for an hour now and delay starting the proofreading until 9 a.m. at the latest and still complete both tasks by noon. This is called a late-start schedule. Here is what a Gantt chart of the schedule would look like:

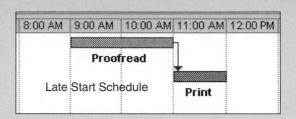

The proofreading task starts at 9 a.m. and ends at 11 a.m. The printing task starts at 11 a.m. and ends at noon. The project is still on time.

The maximum time you can delay an activity without affecting the required project completion time is the slack time. In other words, slack time is the difference in start times between the late and early start schedules. In this case the tasks together have a slack time of one hour.

Note that the slack time allows you to reschedule activities to make more effective use of your time. This is useful when project team members may be working on multiple projects at the same time. Note, however, that with the late start schedule you cannot have any delays. For example, with the early start schedule, if your printer ran out of ink you would have time to fix it and still be on time. This will not be possible with the late start schedule. So good project managers use slack wisely, as a buffer against uncertainty. Perhaps it might be better to work on your other project for only 30 minutes. Then you could start the proofreading task at 8:30 a.m. and be done with the project at 11:30 a.m., leaving some time for delays.

is three weeks, and for activities B and D, one week each. Notice that the activities on the critical path (i.e., A, C, F, and G) do not have any slack times, because, in fact, they are all on the critical path and any delay in these activities will therefore affect the overall project's completion time. Typically, the project completion time is calculated using network analysis and then compared with the desired deadline. Thus, although there is no slack in any of the activities on the critical path with respect to the calculated project completion time, there can be slack in the critical path when the desired deadline is longer. In this example if the desired deadline is 39 weeks and the calculated project completion time remains at 38 weeks, there is a one-week slack time in the critical path. As seen in the OMP on slack time, these slack times represent flexibility and should be used wisely. Note that activity slack times on a particular path in the network are correlated. So an increase or decrease in the slack time of one activity will affect the slack time of the other activities in that path.

[3]The authors are thankful to Brent Snider of the Haskayne School of Business, University of Calgary, for suggesting that we use the paper submission deadline example to explain the concept of slack time.

> **Early Start and Late Start Schedules**
> An early start schedule is one that lists all of the activities by their early start times. A late start schedule lists the activities to start as late as possible without delaying the completion date of the project.

PERT (CPM with Three Activity Time Estimates)

If a single estimate of the time required to complete an activity is not reliable, the alternative is to use three time estimates. By incorporating three estimates for each activity, we have the opportunity to obtain a probability for the completion time for the entire project. Briefly, the procedure using this approach is as follows: The estimated activity time is a weighted average, with more weight given to the best estimate and less to the maximum and minimum times. The estimated completion time of the network is then computed using basic statistics.

We continue with the computer design project (see Exhibit 4.5), only now each of the activities has three time estimates associated with it, and the seven-step procedure for solving this problem is as follows:

Step 1: Identify Each Activity to Be Done in the Project (which is identical to the CPM method with a single time estimate).

Step 2: Determine the Sequence of Activities and Construct a Network Reflecting the Precedence Relationships (again, this is identical to the CPM method with a single time estimate).

Step 3: Define the Three Time Estimates for Each Activity.
The three time estimates for each activity are defined as:

a = *Optimistic time:* the minimum reasonable period of time in which the activity can be completed. (There is only a small probability, typically assumed to be about 1 percent, that the activity can be completed in a shorter period of time.)

m = *Most likely time:* the best guess of the time required. Since m would be the time thought most likely to appear, it is also the mode of the beta distribution (which is discussed in the next step).

b = *Pessimistic time:* the maximum reasonable period of time the activity would take to be completed. (There is only a small probability, typically assumed to be about 1 percent, that it would take longer.)

Typically, the information about the three estimates is obtained from those people who are to perform the activity or others with expertise about the activity.

Step 4: Calculate the Expected Time (ET) for Each Activity.
The formula to calculate the expected activity completion time is:

$$\text{ET} = \frac{a + 4m + b}{6}$$

This formula is developed from the beta probability distribution and weights the most likely time (m) four times more than either the optimistic time (a) or the pessimistic time (b). The beta distribution is an extremely flexible distribution. It can take on a variety of forms that typically arise in project management activities, and it has finite end points,

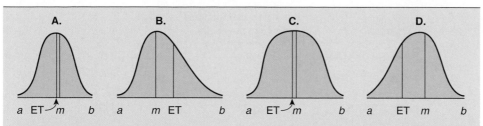

Exhibit 4.7

Typical Beta Curves

Curve A indicates very little uncertainty about the activity time, and since it is symmetrical, the expected time (ET) and the most likely or modal time (*m*) fall along the same point.

Curve B indicates a high probability of finishing the activity early, but if something goes wrong, the activity time could be greatly extended.

Curve C is almost a rectangular distribution, which suggests that the estimator sees the probability of finishing the activity early or late as equally likely, and $m \cong$ ET.

Curve D indicates that there is a small chance of finishing the activity early, but it is more probable that it will take an extended period of time.

Exhibit 4.8

Activity Expected Times and Variances

Activity	Activity Designation	Time Estimates			Expected Times (ET) $\dfrac{a + 4m + b}{6}$	Activity Variances (σ^2) $\left(\dfrac{b - a}{6}\right)^2$
		a	*m*	*b*		
Design	A	10	22	28	21	9.00
Build prototype	B	1	4	7	4	1.00
Evaluate equipment	C	4	6	14	7	2.78
Test prototype	D	1	2	3	2	0.11
Write report	E	1	5	9	5	1.78
Write methods report	F	7	8	9	8	0.11
Write final report	G	2	2	2	2	0.00

which limit the possible activity times to the area between *a* and *b*. In the simplified version, this formula permits a straightforward computation of the activity mean and standard deviation. Four typical beta curves are illustrated in Exhibit 4.7.

Step 5: Calculate the Variance (σ^2) for Each Activity.

The variance, σ^2, associated with each ET is computed using the following formula:

$$\sigma^2 = \left(\frac{b - a}{6}\right)^2$$

As you can see, the variance is the square of one-sixth the difference between the two extreme time estimates, and, of course, the greater this difference, the larger the variance. A summary of the expected time and variance for each activity involved in making the portable computer discussed previously is presented in Exhibit 4.8.

Step 6: Identify All of the Paths in the Network and Their Estimated Completion Times and Variances.

The expected path completion time and path variance are calculated as follows:

$$\text{ET}_p = \text{ET}_A + \text{ET}_B + \ldots + \text{ET}_N$$
$$\sigma_p^2 = \sigma_A^2 + \sigma_B^2 + \ldots + \sigma_N^2$$

Exhibit 4.9

Path Estimated
Completion
Times and
Variances

Path	Expected Completion Time (ET$_p$ in weeks)	Variance (σ_p^2)
A–C–E–G	35	13.56
A–B–D–F–G	37	10.22
A–B–D–E–G	34	11.89
A–C–F–G	38	11.89

where

$\quad$ ET$_p$ = Expected completion time for path

$\quad$ σ_p^2 = Variance for the path

$\quad$ ET$_A$, ET$_B$, … , ET$_N$ are the expected times for each activity on the path

$\quad$ σ_A^2, σ_B^2, … , σ_N^2 are the variances for each activity on the path

Using the data in Exhibit 4.8, the path variances are calculated and summarized in Exhibit 4.9, along with the path expected completion times.

Step 7: Determine the Probability of Completing the Project by a Given Date.

The probability of completing the project by a given date is dependent on the probability of each path in the network being completed by that date. In our example, the desired completion time for the project is 39 weeks. In other words, we want to calculate the probability of completing the project in 39 weeks or less. To do this we need to calculate the probability of each of the paths in the network being completed in 39 weeks or less. All of the paths need to be completed in 39 weeks or less for the project to be completed within that same time period. Thus, the probability of the project being completed within a given time is equal to the minimum of the probabilities of the different paths.

Using the data in Exhibit 4.9, we can now construct the probability distribution for each path and calculate the probability of each path being completed in 39 weeks or less. This is shown graphically in Exhibit 4.10. Note that to calculate the probability of completing each path in 39 days or less, we use σ_p, which is the square root of the variance, σ_p^2.

In Exhibit 4.10, the shaded area to the left of the line representing 39 weeks is the probability of that path being completed within the 39-week period. To obtain the value of that probability, we use the normal table in Appendix B or C. To be able to use this table we need to calculate a Z-value associated with each path, indicating how many standard deviations the 39 weeks is from the expected completion time for that path. The formula for this is:

$$Z = \frac{D - ET_p}{\sigma_p}$$

where

$\quad$ D = Desired completion date for the project

$\quad$ ET$_p$ = Expected completion time for the path

$\quad$ σ_p = Standard deviation for the path

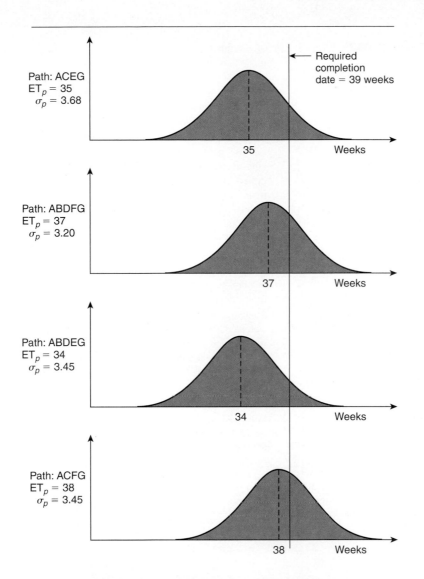

Exhibit 4.10

Probability of Each Path Being Completed in 39 Weeks or Less

Path	Z-Value	Completion Probability
A–C–E–G	1.09	0.8621
A–B–D–F–G	0.63	0.7357
A–B–D–E–G	1.45	0.9265
A–C–F–G	0.29	0.6141

Exhibit 4.11

Path Z-Values and Probabilities of Completing Each Path in 39 Weeks or Less

In this manner, the Z-value for each path is calculated and presented in Exhibit 4.11, along with the corresponding probability that we obtain from the normal table in Appendix B or C. As an approximation, one can determine the probability of completing the project within 39 weeks or less as the minimum of the individual path probabilities, or

THE ATHENS 2004 OLYMPICS PROJECT

In the realm of event project management, the Olympic Games rank as one of the premier achievements.

Project Definition

Objective: To stage the Year 2004 Summer Olympic Games at specified locations in Greece beginning August 13 at a cost of $5.2 billion.

Client: Activities are underwritten by the Greek government. Many stakeholders and customers, e.g., citizens of Athens, local and national governments, the Greek people, the International Olympic Organization, the international community as a whole, the athletes, and Greek and international business communities.

Scope: Organizing all games and ceremonies. Putting in place all technology and resources required to stage the Games. Handling public relations and fundraising.

Criteria for success: Trouble-free performance of Games. Level of public enthusiasm and enjoyment. Economic activity generated within Athens and Greece. Continued interest in future Olympic Games.

Project team: Athens Organizing Committee Olympic Games (AOCOG) was appointed as the project managers by legislation. Other organizations directly contributing to the success of the Games, such as the International Olympic Committee, Greek Olympic Committee, Athens City Council, and Olympic Coordination Authority (Greek government) have been made party to the Host City Contract. Olympic Coordination Authority is responsible for all the infrastructure projects, most of which are either already under way or are being reprogrammed to accommodate the Games. Completion of these projects on time is vital to the success of the Olympic Games.

WBS: The work breakdown structure for the project includes the following major areas: events; venues and facilities including accommodation; transport; media facilities and coordination; telecommunications; security arrangements; medical care; human resources including volunteers; cultural olympiad; pre-games training; information technology projects; opening and closing ceremonies; public relations; financing; test games and trial events; and sponsorship management and control of ambush marketing. Each of these items could be treated as a project in its own right. Precision coordination will be necessary to ensure that these, and therefore the entire Games project, are delivered on time.

Time, obviously, is the most critical dimension of the Athens 2004 Olympic Games project. Early on, initial delays and confusion caused the IOC to consider moving the Olympics to a different city. This threat galvanized the Greek efforts. At the end of a three-year, around-the-clock construction blitz, Olympic organizers finally silenced critics with all the venues ready for the August 13 opening ceremony. As in the past, cost was the dimension sacrificed, with the projected cost doubling to the $8 to 12 billion range. The Greeks were also forced to scale back the scope of construction and compromise on quality. Although the glass roof centerpiece for the Olympic Stadium was preserved, delays caused cancellation of a similar roof for the aquatic centre. Secondary projects designed to spruce up the city had to be scaled back or cut. Unfinished work was hidden behind huge banners. Ribbons and flags were used to divert attention from sidewalks that were never smoothed out or the dreary concrete buildings that didn't get fresh paint.

Source:
Clifford F. Gray and Erik W. Larson, *Project Management: The Managerial Process* (New York: McGraw-Hill/Irwin, 2006), pp. 106–107.

$$\text{Prob (Proj} < 39) = \text{MIN}[(0.8621), (0.7357), (0.9265), (0.6141)] = 0.6141$$

Thus, the probability of completing this project within 39 weeks is 61.41 percent, even though its expected completion time, as determined by the average activity times on the critical path, is 38 weeks.

Maintaining Ongoing Project Schedules

It is important to keep a project schedule accurate and current. The schedule tracks the progress of the project and identifies problems as they occur while time to correct the situation may still be available. In some situations, for example, it may be necessary to shift limited resources, be they labour, equipment, or facilities, from noncritical activities that are not on the critical path, and therefore have some slack time, to critical activities without slack time that are on the critical path. The schedule also monitors the progress of the costs and is often the basis for partial payments. In practice, however, schedules are often sloppily kept, or even totally abandoned.

Perhaps the most important reason for this happening is that managers are not committed enough to the technique to insist that the schedules be kept up to date. The resulting poor schedules consequently give project scheduling a bad name. Experience in project scheduling techniques is important and this job should not be carelessly relegated to the closest warm body. The project manager must support the schedule and see to it that it is maintained.

Time–Cost Trade-Off Models

In practice, project managers are as much concerned with the cost to complete a project as they are with the time to complete the project. For this reason, **time–cost trade-off models** have been devised. These models, which are extensions of PERT and CPM, attempt to develop a minimum-cost schedule for the entire project and to control budgetary expenditures during the project.

Minimum-Cost Scheduling (Time–Cost Trade-Off)

The basic assumption in minimum-cost scheduling is that there is a relationship between activity completion time and the cost of a project. On the one hand, it costs money to expedite an activity; on the other hand, it costs money to sustain (or lengthen) the project. The costs associated with expediting activities to shorten their completion times, termed *activity direct costs*, add to the project's direct costs. These additional costs that are included when an activity is accelerated or fast-tracked also are referred to as **crash costs**. Worker-related crash costs include overtime pay to reduce the overall completion time. Another example of crash costs would be the additional expenses incurred in shipping items by air freight to expedite their delivery, instead of through slower, more normal distribution channels such as the mail or on trucks.

The costs associated with sustaining the project are termed *project indirect costs*: overhead, facilities, and resource opportunity costs, and, under certain contractual situations, penalty costs or lost incentive payments. Since *activity direct costs* and *project indirect costs* are opposing costs dependent on time, the scheduling problem is essentially one of finding that project duration that minimizes their sum or, in other words, finding the optimum point in a time–cost trade-off.

The procedure for finding this point consists of the following five steps and is illustrated using the simple four-activity network that is shown in Exhibit 4.12. Assume in this example that the indirect costs remain constant for eight days and then increase at the rate of $5 per day.

time–cost trade-off models

Models that develop the relationship between direct project costs, indirect costs, and time to complete the project.

crash costs

Additional costs of an activity when time to complete it is shortened.

Step 1: Prepare a CPM-Type Network Diagram

For each activity this diagram should list

a. Normal cost (NC): The lowest expected activity cost (these are the lesser of the cost figures shown under each node in Exhibit 4.12).

b. Normal time (NT): The time associated with each normal cost.

c. Crash time (CT): The shortest possible activity time.

d. Crash cost (CC): The cost associated with each crash time.

Step 2: Determine the Cost per Unit of Time (Assume Days) to Expedite (or Crash) Each Activity

The relationship between activity time and cost may be shown graphically by plotting CC and CT coordinates and connecting them to the NC and NT coordinates by a concave,

Exhibit 4.12

Example of
Time–Cost
Trade-Off
Procedure

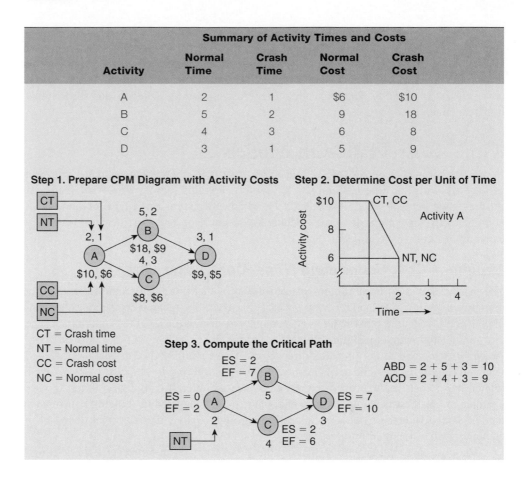

Summary of Activity Times and Costs				
Activity	**Normal Time**	**Crash Time**	**Normal Cost**	**Crash Cost**
A	2	1	$6	$10
B	5	2	9	18
C	4	3	6	8
D	3	1	5	9

Step 1. Prepare CPM Diagram with Activity Costs

CT = Crash time
NT = Normal time
CC = Crash cost
NC = Normal cost

Step 2. Determine Cost per Unit of Time

Step 3. Compute the Critical Path

ABD = 2 + 5 + 3 = 10
ACD = 2 + 4 + 3 = 9

convex, or straight line—or some other form, depending on the actual cost structure of the activity's performance, as shown in Exhibit 4.12. For Activity A, we assume a linear relationship between time and cost. This assumption is common in practice and facilitates the derivation of the cost per day to expedite since this value may be found directly by taking the slope of the line using the formula: Slope $= (CC - NC) \div (NT - CT)$. (When the assumption of linearity cannot be made, the cost of expediting must be determined graphically for each of the days the activity may be shortened.)

The calculations needed to obtain the cost of expediting the remaining activities are shown in Exhibit 4.13.

Step 3: Compute the Critical Path

For the simple network we have been using, this schedule would take 10 days. The critical path is A–B–D.

Step 4: Shorten the Critical Path at the Least Cost

The easiest way to proceed is to start with the normal schedule, find the critical path, and reduce the path time by one day using the lowest-cost activity. Then recompute and find the new critical path and reduce it by one day also. Repeat this procedure until the time of

Exhibit 4.13

Calculation of
Cost per Day to
Expedite Each
Activity

Activity	CC − NC	NT − CT	$\dfrac{CC - NC}{NT - CT}$	Cost per Day to Expedite	Number of Days Activity May Be Shortened
A	$10 − $6	2 − 1	$\dfrac{\$10 - 6}{2 - 1}$	$4	1
B	$18 − $9	5 − 2	$\dfrac{\$18 - \$9}{5 - 2}$	$3	3
C	$8 − $6	4 − 3	$\dfrac{\$8 - \$6}{4 - 3}$	$2	1
D	$9 − $5	3 − 1	$\dfrac{\$9 - \$5}{3 - 1}$	$2	2

Exhibit 4.14

Reducing the Project Completion Time One Day at a Time					
Current Critical Path(s)	Remaining Number of Days Activity May Be Shortened	Cost per Day to Expedite Each Activity	Least-Cost Activity to Expedite	Total Cost of All Activities in Network	Project Completion Time
A–B–D	All activity times and costs are normal			$26	10
A–B–D	A–1, B–3, D–2	A–4, B–3, D–2	D	28	9
A–B–D	A–1, B–3, D–1	A–4, B–3, D–2	D	30	8
A–B–D	A–1, B–3	A–4, B–3	B	33	7
A–B–D, A–C–D	A–1, B–2, C–1	A–4, B–3, C–2	A*	37	6
A–B–D, A–C–D	B–2, C–1	B–3, C–2	B & C†	42	5‡

*To reduce both critical paths by one day, reduce either A alone, or B and C together at the same time (since either B or C by itself modifies the critical path without shortening it).

†B & C must be crashed together to reduce both critical paths by one day.

‡Since path A–C–D cannot be crashed anymore, five days is the minimum length of the project.

completion is satisfactory, or until there can be no further reduction in the project completion time. Exhibit 4.14 shows the reduction of the network one day at a time.

Step 5: Plot Project Direct, Indirect, and Total-Cost Curves and Find Minimum-Cost Schedule

Exhibit 4.15 shows the indirect cost plotted as a constant $10 for the first eight days and increasing $5 per day thereafter. The direct costs are plotted from Exhibit 4.14 and the total project cost is shown as the total of the two costs.

Summing the values for direct and indirect costs for each day yields the project total cost curve. As you can see, this curve is at its minimum for an eight-day schedule, which costs $40 ($30 direct + $10 indirect).

Exhibit 4.15

Plot of Costs and Minimum Cost Schedule

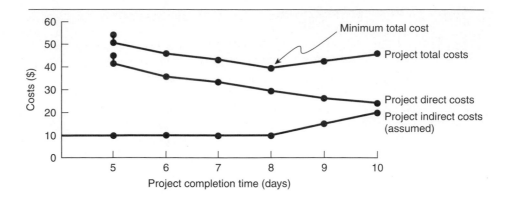

CPM and PERT in Practice

As with many other methods, basic CPM or PERT analysis may have to be modified to fit situations encountered in practice. Thus, management must be sure that the people charged with planning, monitoring, and controlling activities have a general understanding of how these methods should be used in practice.

Both methods assume that project activities can be identified as entities (that is, there is a clear beginning and ending point for each activity). In practice, projects, especially complex ones, change in content over time, and therefore a network made at the beginning may be inaccurate later on. Also, activities can be conditional, i.e., be contingent upon the occurrence or non-occurrence of a previous activity. Therefore, monitoring the network during project progress and updating when appropriate are important aspects of project management and control (some project management software can actually incorporate conditional activities). Controlling the project is important not only for the schedule but also for cost and scope.

Though CPM and PERT focus on the critical path, it is important to remember that delays and uncertainties in activities can cause the critical path to change during the project. For this reason it has been suggested that a *critical activity* concept replace the critical path concept as a focus of managerial control. With this approach, attention would centre on those activities that have a high potential variation and lie on a *near-critical path*. A near-critical path is one that though it has slack, could become critical if one or a few activities along it were to be delayed. Obviously, the more parallelism in a network, the more likely that one or more near-critical paths exist. Conversely, the more a network approximates a single series of activities, the less likely it is to have near-critical paths.

Furthermore, the assumption that all activity times in PERT follow the beta distribution, with the variance of the project assumed to be equal to the sum of the variances along the critical path is not always true. Fortunately, these days some of the project management software packages can actually do a Monte Carlo computer simulation of the project without having to use these two assumptions. In Monte Carlo simulation the computer 'does' the project virtually, thousands if not tens of thousands of times. Each time it generates a different activity completion time for uncertain activities based on any distribution that the user specifies. Thus it is more flexible and provides more realistic and more detailed results than those that can be obtained by using PERT. For example, Monte Carlo simulation can give the probability that a near-critical path will become critical. Obviously, if this probability is very high, it means that this activity has to be monitored carefully.

Finally, the cost of applying critical path methods to a project sometimes is used as a basis for concern. However, the cost of applying PERT or CPM rarely exceeds 2 percent of the total project cost. When used with added features of a WBS and various reports, it is more expensive but rarely exceeds 5 percent of the total project costs. This added cost is generally justified by the additional savings resulting from improved scheduling and the resulting reduction in project time.

Gray and Larson[4] suggest that smaller projects (with less than 100 activities) can be effectively developed using Post-It type stickers, erasable markers, and a whiteboard. This is a flexible and visual way for the project team to create network diagrams.

The critical path techniques of PERT and CPM have proven themselves for more than four decades and promise to be of continued value in the future. With the rapidly changing business environment and the high costs associated with these changes, management needs to be able to both quickly and efficiently plan and control the activities of the firm. The inherent value of a tool that allows management to structure complex projects in an under-standable way, to pick out possible sources of delay before they occur, to isolate areas of responsibility, and, of course, to save time in costly projects virtually ensures that the use of project management will expand.

Project Management Software

Project management software is a necessity for today's project managers. No longer do project managers have to be dependent on manually drawn networks that are arduously updated at great time and expense to reflect the latest project changes and status. Instead there are now a large number of project management software packages available in different price ranges which can readily incorporate changes in the project, thereby providing the manager with fast updates on a frequent basis. Even products that fall in the lower end of this range can simulate the project and have the ability to reschedule activities to optimize results, based on the latest developments. With many projects, budgets are an important consideration, and project management therefore needs to include estimates of the labour required to complete them. Software in this category has the ability to schedule and track labour hours and costs. The cost of software in this category can range from $300 to $500, with Microsoft Project and Primavera products being the market leaders.

The high end of the software market ranges from $400 to $20 000 and, as one might expect, differs considerably in terms of what it provides. These software packages are typically for project managers who are managing more than one project simultaneously. Products that are available in this category include Microsoft Project 2002 (with Project Central), Primavera Project Planner, Open Plan, Cobra, and Enterprise PM.

Exhibit 4.16 shows two views of the same project created using Microsoft Project. Exhibit 4.16A shows a Gantt chart (with arrows showing precedence, thus combining a traditional Gantt chart with the CPM diagram; Exhibit 4.15B is the CPM (Network) diagram. Note that activities and precedence arrows on the critical path are shown in red in both diagrams and that weekends have been specified as nonworking.

---

[4]Clifford F. Gray and Erik W. Larson, *Project Management: The Managerial Process* (New York: McGraw-Hill/Irwin, 2006), pp. 7–11.

Exhibit 4.16

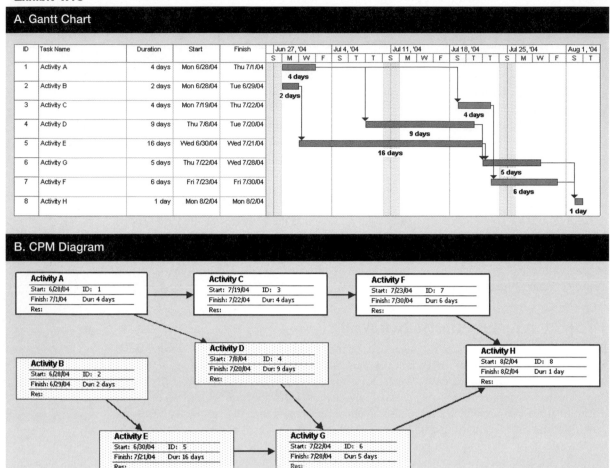

Conclusion

Product life cycles are becoming shorter as more new products are continuously being introduced into the marketplace. A key factor in the ability of a company to introduce these products quickly, add new facilities, or make major operational changes of any kind is an understanding of project management concepts and techniques.

Successful projects require both technical skills and people skills. Technical skills identify the critical activities on which the project team should focus its efforts. People skills provide the motivation and team efforts that are necessary for the project to be completed in a timely manner.

Although much of this chapter has dealt with network solving techniques used in project management, effective project management involves much more than simply setting up a CPM or PERT schedule. It requires, in addition, clearly identified project responsibilities, a simple and timely progress reporting system, and good people-management practices.

Projects fail for a number of reasons. The most significant reason is that those involved do not take project scheduling seriously. Often, personnel who have been newly exposed and those who have had unsatisfactory experiences do not comply with the procedure. They may neither spend the time to properly develop their parts of the network, nor even submit good time and cost estimates. This attitude usually continues throughout the project with a reluctance to revise schedules.

A good resource for furthering your project management skills is the Project Management Institute (www.pmi.org), a global association (with chapters in Canada) of industry and academic project management professionals.

Key Terms

CPM (critical path method) p. 100

crash costs p. 113

critical path p. 103

Gantt chart p. 98

milestones p. 94

PERT (program evaluation and review technique) p. 100

program p. 94

project p. 93

slack time p. 103

time–cost trade-off models p. 113

work breakdown structure (WBS) p. 94

Review and Discussion Questions

1. Define project management.
2. Describe or define work breakdown structure, program, project, task, subtask, and work package.
3. How does the role of a project manager differ from that of a traditional functional manager?
4. What are some of the key characteristics of high performance work teams?
5. What are some of the reasons project scheduling is not done well?
6. Discuss the graphic presentations in Exhibit 4.3. Are there any other graphic outputs you would like to see if you were the project manager?
7. Which characteristics must a project have for critical path scheduling to be applicable? What types of projects have been subjected to critical path analysis?
8. What are the underlying assumptions of minimum-cost scheduling? Are they equally realistic?
9. "Project control should always focus on the critical path." Comment.
10. Why would subcontractors for a government project want their activities on the critical path? Under which conditions would they try to avoid being on the critical path?
11. What is meant by "crashing a project," and when do you do this?

Internet Exercise

The increasing application of project management techniques has resulted in the development of a large number of project management software packages. Your boss has asked you to conduct a search on the Internet to identify six different project management software packages that are currently available. She has requested that you prepare a one-page memo (plus any additional pages for exhibits, if necessary) that evaluates these different packages. You should include in your software evaluation the following information:

- Name of software
- Name and location of company offering the software
- Price
- Computer requirements
- Description
- Unique features
- Unique applications

Suggested key words to help you in your search are PROJECT, MANAGEMENT, and SOFTWARE.

Solved Problems

Problem 1

A project has been defined to contain the following list of activities, along with their required times for completion:

Activity	Immediate Predecessors	Time (days)	Activity	Immediate Predecessors	Time (days)
A	–	1	F	C, D	2
B	A	4	G	E, F	7
C	A	3	H	D	9
D	A	7	I	G, H	4
E	B	6			

a. Draw the critical path diagram.

b. Show the early start and early finish times.

c. Show the critical path.

d. What would happen if Activity F were revised to take four days instead of two?

Solution

The answers to *a*, *b*, and *c* are shown in the following diagram.

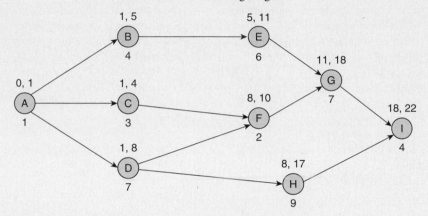

d. New critical path: A–D–F–G–I. Time of completion = 23 days.

Problem 2

The following are the precedence requirements, normal and crash activity times, and normal and crash costs for a construction project:

Activity	Preceding Activities	Required Time (weeks)		Cost	
		Normal	Crash	Normal	Crash
A	–	4	2	$10 000	$11 000
B	A	3	2	6 000	9 000
C	A	2	1	4 000	6 000
D	B	5	3	14 000	18 000
E	B, C	1	1	9 000	9 000
F	C	3	2	7 000	8 000
G	E, F	4	2	13 000	25 000
H	D, E	4	1	11 000	18 000
I	H, G	6	5	20 000	29 000

a. What are the critical path and the estimated completion time?

b. To shorten the project by three weeks, which tasks would be shortened and what would the final total project cost be?

Solution

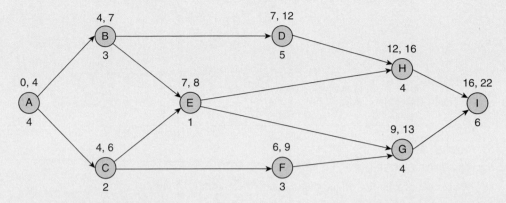

a. Critical path A–B–D–H–I.

Normal completion time = 22 weeks.

b.

Activity	Crash Cost	Normal Cost	Normal Time	Crash Time	Cost per Week	Possible Number of Weeks to Decrease
A	$11 000	$10 000	4	2	$ 500	2
B	9 000	6 000	3	2	3 000	1
C	6 000	4 000	2	1	2 000	1
D	18 000	14 000	5	3	2 000	2
E	9 000	9 000	1	1		0
F	8 000	7 000	3	2	1 000	1
G	25 000	13 000	4	2	6 000	2
H	18 000	11 000	4	1	2 333	3
I	29 000	20 000	6	5	9 000	1

1. 1st week: CP = A–B–D–H–I. Cheapest activity is A at $500. Critical path stays the same.

2. 2nd week: A is still the cheapest at $500. Critical path stays the same.

3. 3rd week: Since A is no longer available, the choices are B (at $3000), D (at $2000), H (at $2333), or I (at $9000).

Therefore, choose D at $2000.

Total cost for the project shortened three weeks is:

A	$11 000
B	6 000
C	4 000
D	16 000
E	9 000
F	7 000
G	13 000
H	11 000
I	20 000
	$97 000

Problem 3

The following represents a project that should be scheduled using CPM:

		Time (Days)		
Activity	Predecessors	a	m	b
A	–	2	4	5
B	–	1	2	6
C	A	1	3	4
D	A	2	3	5
E	B	3	4	10
F	C, D	3	4	5
G	D, E	1	3	6
H	F, G	2	3	5

a. Draw the network.

b. What is the critical path?

c. What is the probability of completing the project within 16 days?

Solution

a.

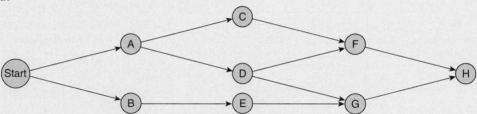

b. Critical path is A–D–F–H with an expected duration of 14.17 days as shown below.

c.

		Activity	
		ET	Variance
	Activity Times	$\dfrac{(a + 4m + b)}{6}$	$\left[\dfrac{b - a}{6}\right]^2$
	a	m	b
A	2	4	5	3.83	0.25
B	1	2	6	2.50	0.69
C	1	3	4	2.83	0.25
D	2	3	5	3.17	0.25
E	3	4	10	4.83	1.36
F	3	4	5	4.00	0.11
G	1	3	6	3.17	0.69
H	2	3	5	3.17	0.25

Paths	ET_p	σ^2_p	σ_p	$z = \left[\dfrac{16 - ET_p}{\sigma_p}\right]$	Probability of path completion in 16 days
ACFH	13.83	0.86	0.93	2.33	0.9901
ADFH	14.17	0.86	0.93	1.98	0.9761
ADGH	13.33	1.44	1.20	2.22	0.9868
BEGH	13.67	3.00	1.73	1.35	0.9115

Probability of completion of project within 16 days = MIN (0.9901, 0.9761, 0.9868, 0.9115) =   0.9115 or 91.5%

Note that though ADFH is the critical path, BEGH has a lower completion probability because of higher variance due to more uncertainty in activity durations. Thus, when activity durations are uncertain, paths other than the critical path have to be monitored carefully also.

1. The following activities are part of a project to be scheduled using CPM:

Activity	Immediate Predecessors	Time (weeks)
A	–	6
B	A	3
C	A	7
D	C	2
E	B, D	4
F	D	3
G	E, F	7

a. Draw the network.

b. What is the critical path?

c. How many weeks will it take to complete the project?

d. How much slack time does Activity B have?

2. Halifax Steam Turbine and Generator Company manufactures electric power–generating systems for the major electric power companies. Turbine/generator sets are made to specific order and generally require a three- to five-year lead time. Costs range from $8 to $15 million per set.

Management has been planning their production using traditional planning techniques such as planning charts, Gantt charts, and other shop floor control methods. However, management would now like to introduce CPM project planning and control methods where each turbine/generator set is considered a separate project.

The following is a segment of the total activities involved in the turbine/generator production:

Activity	Immediate Predecessors	Time (weeks)
a	–	8
b	a	16
c	a	12
d	a	7
e	b, c	22
f	c, d	40
g	e, f	15
h	–	14
i	h	9
j	i	13
k	i	7
l	j	36
m	k	40
n	l, m	9
o	g, n	10

a. Draw the network.

b. Find the critical path.

c. Which activities would you decrease to cut the project time by two weeks?

d. Which activities would you decrease to cut the project time by 10 weeks?

3. The R&D department of Crowchild Avionics is planning to bid on a large project for the development of a new communication system for commercial planes. The table below shows the activities, times, and sequences required.

Activity	Immediate Predecessors	Time (weeks)
A	–	3
B	A	2
C	A	4
D	A	4
E	B	6
F	C, D	6
G	D, F	2
H	D	3
I	E, G, H	3

   a. Draw the network diagram.

   b. What is the critical path?

   c. Supposing you wanted to shorten the completion time as much as possible, and had the option of shortening any or all of B, C, D, and G each two weeks (in effect, activity G takes zero time to complete). Which would you shorten?

   d. What are the new path and earliest completion time?

4. A construction project is broken down into the 10 activities listed below.

Activity	Preceding Activity	Time (weeks)
1	–	4
2	1	2
3	1	4
4	1	3
5	2, 3	5
6	3	6
7	4	2
8	5	3
9	6, 7	5
10	8, 9	7

   a. Draw the precedence diagram.

   b. Find the critical path.

   c. If activities 1 and 10 cannot be shortened, but activities 2 through 9 can be shortened to a minimum of 1 week each at a cost of $10 000 per week per activity, which activities would you shorten to shorten the project by four weeks?

5. The TPJ company has received a special order for a number of units of a special product that consists of two component parts, X and Y. The product is a nonstandard item that the firm has never produced before, and scheduling personnel have decided that the

application of CPM is warranted. A team of manufacturing engineers has prepared the following table:

Activity	Description	Immediate Predecessors	Expected Time (days)
A	Plan production	–	5
B	Procure materials for Part X	A	14
C	Manufacture Part X	B	9
D	Procure materials for Part Y	A	15
E	Manufacture Part Y	D	10
F	Assemble Parts X and Y	C, E	4
G	Inspect assemblies	F	2
H	Completed	G	0

    a. Construct a graphic representation of the CPM network.

    b. Identify the critical path.

    c. What is the length of time to complete the project?

    d. Which activities have slack time and how much?

6. The following is a CPM network with activity times in weeks:

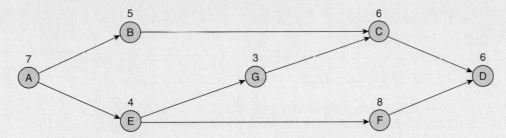

    a. Determine the critical path.

    b. How many weeks will the project take to complete?

    c. Supposing F could be shortened by one week and B by two weeks. What effect would this have on the completion date?

7. The following represents a plan for a project:

Job No.	Predecessor Job(s)	a	m	b
1	–	2	3	4
2	1	1	2	3
3	1	4	5	12
4	1	3	4	11
5	2	1	3	5
6	3	1	2	3
7	4	1	8	9
8	5, 6	2	4	6
9	8	2	4	12
10	7	3	4	5
11	9, 10	5	7	8

a. Construct the appropriate network diagram.

b. Identify the critical path.

c. What is the expected completion time for the project?

d. What is the probability that the project will be completed in 30 days or less?

8. A project manager has compiled a list of major activities that will be required to install a computer information system in her firm. The list includes estimated completion times for activities and precedence relationships.[5]

Activity	Successors	Time (weeks)		
		a	m	b
A	D, F	2	4	6
D	E	6	8	10
E	H	7	9	12
H	End	2	3	5
F	G	3	4	8
G	End	5	7	9
B	I	2	2	3
I	J	2	3	6
J	K	3	4	5
K	End	4	5	8
C	M	5	8	12
M	N	1	1	1
N	O	6	7	11
O	End	8	9	12

If the project is finished within 27 weeks of its start, the project manager will receive a bonus of $1000; if the project is finished within 28 weeks of its start, the bonus will be $500. Find the probability of each bonus.

9. The following is a network with the activity times shown above the nodes in days:

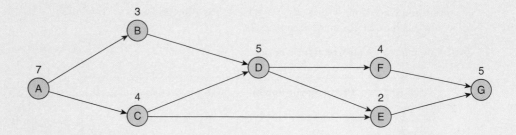

a. Find the critical path.

b. The following table shows the normal times and the crash times, along with the associated costs for each of the activities.

---

[5]Adapted from William J. Stevenson and Mehran Hojati, *Operations Management* 2nd ed. (Toronto: McGraw-Hill Ryerson, 2004).

Activity	Normal Time	Crash Time	Normal Cost	Crash Cost
A	7	6	$7 000	$ 8 000
B	3	2	5 000	7 000
C	4	3	9 000	10 200
D	5	4	3 000	4 500
E	2	1	2 000	3 000
F	4	2	4 000	7 000
G	5	4	5 000	8 000

If the project is to be shortened by four days, show which activities, in order of reduction, would be shortened and the resulting total project costs.

10. The home office billing department of a chain of department stores prepares monthly inventory reports for use by the stores' purchasing agents. Given the following information, use the critical path method to determine

   a. How long the total process will take.

   b. Which jobs can be delayed without delaying the early start of any subsequent activity.

	Job and Description	Immediate Predecessors	Time (hours)
A	Start	–	0
B	Get computer printouts of customer purchases	A	10
C	Get stock records for the month	A	20
D	Reconcile purchase printouts and stock records	B, C	30
E	Total stock records by department	B, C	20
F	Determine reorder quantities for coming period	E	40
G	Prepare stock reports for purchasing agents	D, F	20
H	Finish	G	0

11. For the network and the data shown:

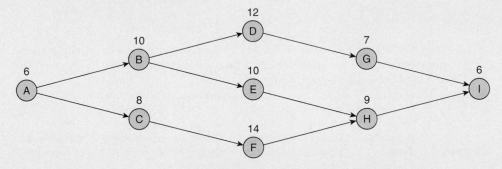

   a. Determine the critical path and the early completion time for the project.

Activity*	Normal Time (weeks)	Normal Cost	Crash Time (weeks)	Crash Cost
A	6	$ 6 000	4	$12 000
B	10	10 000	9	11 000
C	8	8 000	7	10 000
D	12	12 000	10	14 000
E	10	10 000	7	12 000
F	14	14 000	12	19 000
G	7	7 000	5	10 000
H	9	9 000	6	15 000
I	6	6 000	5	8 000

*An activity cannot be shortened to less than its crash time.

   b. Reduce the project completion time by four weeks. Assume a linear cost per day shortened and show, step by step, how you arrived at your schedule. Also indicate the critical path.

12. The following CPM network has estimates of the *normal time* listed for the activities:

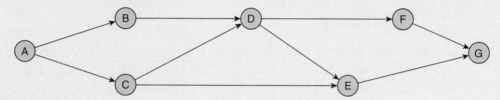

   a. Identify the critical path.

   b. What is the length of time to complete the project?

   c. Which activities have slack, and how much?

Activity	Time (weeks)
A	7
B	2
C	4
D	5
E	2
F	4
G	5

   d. The following is a table of normal and crash times and costs. Which activities would you shorten to cut two weeks from the schedule in a rational fashion? What would be the incremental cost? Is the critical path changed?

Activity	Normal Time	Crash Time	Normal Cost	Crash Cost	Possible Number of Weeks Decrease	Cost/Week to Expedite
A	7	6	$7 000	$ 8 000		
B	2	1	5 000	7 000		
C	4	3	9 000	10 200		
D	5	4	3 000	4 500		
E	2	1	2 000	3 000		
F	4	2	4 000	7 000		
G	5	4	5 000	8 000		

Case 1 — Whistler Ski Resort Project

Given the coming 2010 Winter Olympics in Vancouver and Whistler, BC, and the fact that the number of skiing visitors to Whistler has been increasing at an exciting rate, the Whistler Ski Association has been considering construction of another ski lodge and ski complex. The results of an economic feasibility study just completed by members of the staff show that a winter resort complex near the base of Whistler Mountain could be a very profitable venture. The area is accessible by car, bus, train, and air. The board of directors has voted to build the ten-million dollar complex recommended in the study. Unfortunately, due to the short summer season, the complex will have to be build in stages. The first stage (year 1) will contain a day lodge, chair lift, rope tow, generator house (for electricity), and a parking lot designed to accommodate 400 cars and 30 buses. The second and third stages will include a hotel, ice rink, pool, shops, two additional chair lifts, and other attractions. The board has decided that stage one should begin no later than April 1 and be completed by October 1, in time for the next skiing season. You have been assigned the task of project manager, and it is your job to coordinate the ordering of materials and construction activities to ensure the project's completion by the required date.

After looking into the possible sources of materials, you are confronted with the following time estimates: Materials for the chair lift and rope tow will take 30 days and 12 days, respectively, to arrive once the order is submitted. Lumber for the day lodge, generator house, and foundations will take 9 days to arrive. The electrical and plumbing materials for the day lodge will take 12 days to arrive. The generator will take 12 days to arrive. Before actual construction can begin on the various facilities, a road to the site must be build; this will take 6 days. As soon as the road is in, clearing can begin concurrently on the sites of the day lodge, generator house, chair lift, and rope tow. It is estimated that the clearing task at each site will take 6 days, 3 days, 36 days, and 6 days, respectively. The clearing of the main ski slopes can begin after the area for the chair lift has been cleared; this will take 84 days.

The foundation for the day lodge will take 12 days to complete. Construction of the main framework will take an additional 18 days. After the framework is completed, electrical wiring and plumbing can be installed concurrently. These should take 24 and 30 days, respectively. Finally, the finishing construction on the day lodge can begin; this will take 36 days.

Installation of the chair lift towers can begin once the site is cleared, lumber delivered, and the foundation completed; all this takes 6 days, and the towers take 67 days. Also, when the chair lift site has been cleared, construction of a permanent road to the upper towers can be started; this will take 24 days. While the towers are being installed, the electric motor to drive the chair lift can be installed; the motor can be installed in 24 days. Once the towers are completed and the motor installed, it will take 3 days to install the cable and an additional 12 days to install the chairs.

Installation of the towers for the rope tow can begin once the site is cleared and the foundation is built and poured; it takes 4 days to build the foundation, pour the concrete and let it cure, and 20 days to install the towers for the rope tow. While the towers are being erected, installation of the electric motor to drive the rope tow can begin; this activity will take 24 days. After the towers and motor are installed, the rope tow can be strung in 1 day. The parking lot can be cleared once the rope tow is finished; this task will take 18 days.

The foundation for the generator house can begin at the same time as the foundation for the lodge; this will take 6 days. The main framework for the generator house can begin once the foundation is completed; framing will take 12 days. After the house is framed, the diesel generator can be installed in 18 days.

Finishing construction on the generator house can then begin and will take 12 more days.

A list of the activities, with associated normal times, crashing (the maximum number of days the activity can be shortened by; for example, ordering material for chair lift can be shortened from 30 days to 26 days at most) and the per day cost of crashing each activity are given below. Note that activities with an '-' cannot be crashed at all.

Assignment:

1. In how many days will the project be completed?

2. The Association would like to reduce the length of the project by eight days. Which activities would you crash and in what sequence? What is the additional cost?

3. If each day the project were reduced there were a benefit of $5000 due to additional revenue from starting early, how many days should they crash the project?

Adapted from Clifford F. Gray and Erik W. Larson, *Project Management: The Managerial Process* (New York: McGraw-Hill/Irwin, 2006), pp. 186–187.

Activity	Normal Time Time (days)	Crashing (days)	Per Day Crash cost ($)
Start	0	–	–
Order material for chair lift (CL)	30	4	4600
Order material for rope tow (RT)	12	2	5000
Order lumber	9	1	4200
Order electrical and plumbing material	12	2	2500
Order generator	12	1	7500
Build road	6	1	7000
Clear day lodge (DL) site	6	1	3400
Clear generator house (GH) site	3	–	–
Clear CL site	36	1	8000
Clear RT site	6	5	5000
Clear main slope	84	7	3000
Foundation – DL	12	3	4500
Construction – DL	18	3	1000
Electrical – DL	24	6	1500
Plumbing – DL	30	1	2500
Finishing – DL	36	5	8000
Foundation – CL	6	1	3500
Install towers – CL	67	5	1500
Build permanent road	24	–	2000
Install electric motor – CL	24	2	2500
Install cable	3	–	–
Install chairs	12	2	5500
Foundation – RT	4	–	–
Install towers – RT	20	–	–
Install electric motor – RT	24	3	6000
Install RT cable	1	–	–
Clear parking lot	18	2	3500
Foundation – GH	6	1	2300
Frame – GH	12	1	1900
Install generator	18	2	3600
Finish GH	12	1	2600
End	0	–	–

Case 2 Brunswick United Soccer Club

Nicolette Larson was loading the dishwasher with her husband, Kevin, and telling him about the first meeting of the Tournament Organizing Committee. Larson, a self-confessed "soccer mom," had been elected tournament director and was responsible for organizing the club's first summer tournament.

Brunswick United Soccer Club (BUSC) was formed in 1992 as a way of bringing recreational players to a higher level of competition and preparing them for the Provincial Olympic Development Program and/or high school teams. The club currently has 24 boys and girls (ranging in age from under 9 to 16) on teams affiliated with the New Brunswick Soccer Association. The club's board of directors decided in the fall to sponsor a summer invitational soccer tournament to generate revenue. Given the boom in youth soccer, hosting summer tournaments has become a popular method for raising funds. BUSC teams regularly compete in three to four tournaments each summer at different locales in Eastern Canada. These tournaments have been reported to generate between $50 000 and $70 000 for the host club.

BUSC needs additional revenue to refurbish and expand the number of soccer fields at the Rock Rimmon soccer complex. Funds would also be used to augment the club's scholarship program, which provides financial aid to players who cannot afford the $450 annual club dues.

Nicolette gave her husband a blow-by-blow account of what transpired during the first tournament committee meeting that night. She started the meeting by having everyone introduce him- or herself and by proclaiming how excited she was that the club was going to sponsor its own tournament. She then suggested that the committee brainstorm what needed to be done to pull off the event; she would record their ideas on a flipchart.

What emerged was a free-for-all of ideas and suggestions. One member immediately stressed the importance of having qualified referees and spent several minutes describing in detail how his son's team had been robbed in a poorly officiated championship game. This was followed by other stories of injustice on the soccer field. Another member suggested that they needed to quickly contact the local colleges to see if they could use their fields. The committee spent more than 30 minutes talking about how they should screen teams and how much they should charge as an entry fee. An argument broke out over whether they should reward the winning teams in each age bracket with medals or trophies. Many members felt that medals were too cheap; others thought trophies would be too expensive. Someone suggested that they seek local corporate sponsors to help fund the tournament. The proposed sale of tournament T-shirts and sweatshirts was followed by a general critique of the different shirts parents had acquired at different tournaments. One member advocated that they recruit a native artist he knew to develop a unique silk-screen design depicting First Peoples' art for the tournament. The meeting adjourned 30 minutes late with only half of the members remaining until the end. Nicolette drove home with seven sheets of ideas and a headache. As Kevin poured a glass of water for the two aspirin Nicolette was about to take, he tried to comfort her by saying that organizing this tournament would be a big project not unlike the projects he works on at his engineering and design firm. He offered to sit down with her the next night and help her plan the project. He suggested that the first thing they needed to do was to develop a WBS for the project.

Questions

1. Develop a draft of the work breakdown structure (WBS) for the tournament that contains at least three levels of detail.

2. What are the major deliverables associated with hosting an event such as a soccer tournament?

3. How would developing a WBS alleviate some of the problems that occurred during the first meeting and help Nicolette organize and plan the project?

4. Where can Nicolette find additional information to help her develop a WBS for the tournament?

5. How could Nicolette and her task force use the WBS to generate cost estimates for the tournament? Why would this be useful information?

Adapted from C. F. Gray, and E. W. Larson, *Project Management: The Managerial Process* (New York: McGraw-Hill, 2002).

Process Measurement and Analysis

Chapter Objectives

- Illustrate how all activities within an organization are actually processes that need to be managed.

- Present the various measures of performance that can be used to evaluate a process.

- Show how process analysis can provide managers with an in-depth understanding of how a process is performing, while at the same time identifying areas for improvement.

- Present the concept of service blueprinting and illustrate how it is used to evaluate processes within a service environment.

- Introduce the concept of business processes and show how they are providing managers with a broader perspective for managing their organizations.

- Present the concepts of benchmarking and reengineering, and show their roles in creating world-class operations.

Faster Service Has Benefits and Costs

Saying "Himayltakeyourorderplease?" takes only one second for the drive through greeter at Wendy's Old-Fashioned Hamburgers. This is two seconds faster than Wendy's guidelines and illustrates the effort fast food chains are putting into speeding up their drive-through pick-up windows. Cars spent on average 150.3 seconds at the leader in this category, Wendy's, which made it 16.7 seconds and 21 seconds faster than McDonald's and Burger King respectively. Yet, far from resting on its laurels, Wendy's is working hard to reduce this time even further.

Why this emphasis on reducing process and waiting times? The drive-through business has been growing at a faster rate than on-premise sales. Since the growth in the number of new restaurants is slowing, the big chains are focusing on this newer battleground, drive-through sales. Using product development, employee retraining, and new technology, McDonald's, Burger King, Arby's, Taco Bell, and others are battling to be the fastest in the business. It is estimated that increasing drive-through efficiency by 10 percent bolsters sales for the average fast-food restaurant by about 10 percent per year.

Wendy's and Burger King are building special drive-through kitchens, while McDonald's is experimenting with windshield

transponders that can automatically bill the purchaser's account, making the cash transaction redundant. McDonald's estimates that it can shave off 15 seconds from its drive-through time and boost sales by 2 percent. Timers, kitchen choreography designed to eliminate unnecessary movement, and wireless headsets that let all workers hear customer orders are other initiatives. Sounding alarms such as beeps, sirens, and even voices congratulating or admonishing crews are also being used.

Is there a trade-off in speeding up the service? The same survey that placed Wendy's on top in speed also ranked it eleventh in accuracy. University student Clint Toland and his girlfriend recently drove through a Taco Bell to get a late-night meal of nachos with meat but no beans only to discover back at home that the order contained beans and no meat. Says he, "I am never coming back."

Speed can also be stressful for employees. After nine months at a drive-through, night manager Tiffany Swan Holloway vows never to work again in fast food. Her small night crew had a hard time keeping up with the 60-second service goal, and the beepers irritated her too.

This is a good illustration of some of the trade-offs in process design. Although faster processes are desirable, ultimately they are not desirable at the cost of lower quality or higher server stress.

Source:
Jennifer Ordonez, "Next! An Efficiency Drive: Fast-Food Lanes Are Getting Even Faster—Big Chains, Vying for Traffic, Use High-Tech Timers, 'Kitchen Choreography'—Mesclun in a Milkshake Cup?" *Wall Street Journal*, May 18, 2000, A1.

Managerial Issues

The primary role of managers, in essence, is to manage processes, including the individuals involved in those processes. And what managers are now recognizing is that every set of activities represents a process. Examples include *processing* a payroll, *processing* an application for employment, *processing* a purchase order, *processing* a customer complaint, and *processing* a product design change. In addition, managers also are acknowledging that these individual processes do not operate in a vacuum, but rather are linked to other processes in other functional areas, thereby creating larger, more complex business processes, which by definition span these functional areas within an organization.

As we learned earlier in the book, the choice of what type of process to adopt is part of operations strategy. Once this decision has been made and the process has been installed, it must then be managed. Management means identifying the critical performance measures of the process and monitoring them on a regular basis to ensure established standards or goals are being achieved. Management here also includes taking the necessary corrective actions when these measures indicate there is a problem. Process performance measures are divided into two major categories: those that pertain to all processes and those that are specific to individual processes. Both are necessary.

Standards of performance are constantly being raised. New products are being designed and introduced faster. They also are being delivered faster to customers and are of higher quality than was the previous norm. As a result, processes must constantly be improved. To assist managers in doing this, benchmarking (defined in detail later in this chapter) often is used to identify how a firm's process performance compares to that of other firms. Such comparisons provide managers with the information necessary to create world-class operations. When significant differences are identified, the process often is reengineered with the goal of improving its overall performance.

Process Analysis

process

Actual conversion of inputs to output.

As seen in Exhibit 1.2 in Chapter 1, a **process** involves taking inputs and converting them to outputs. Of course, one of the objectives of a process is to be as efficient as possible, by minimizing the amount of non-valued parts in the conversion or transformation. Process analysis allows us to identify the value-added and non-value-added parts of the process so that we can eliminate the latter. Furthermore, a manager may have different types of processes to choose from in providing the particular product or service. Process analysis also provides us with some insight into the trade-offs (see opening vignette) we face as managers when selecting one particular process over another, allowing us to select the best possible process given the operations strategy.

process flow chart

Schematic diagram describing a process.

A **process flow chart** is a schematic diagram which describes a process. It provides management with an opportunity to view the entire process step by step. The traditional symbols used in drawing a process flow chart are presented in Exhibit 5.1. The flow chart for Burger King's process of preparing hamburgers is shown in Exhibit 5.2. In the case of Burger King, the beef patties are cooked and kept in work-in-process (WIP) inventory. From these some popular (high-volume) types of burgers are completely assembled and kept in a

Exhibit 5.1

Elements in a process Flow Chart

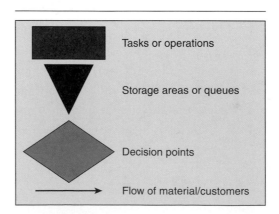

Tasks or operations

Storage areas or queues

Decision points

Flow of material/customers

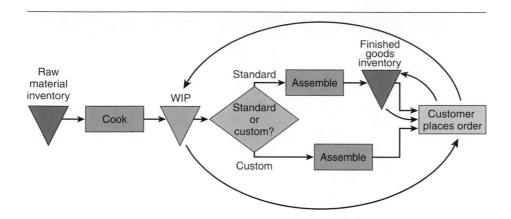

Exhibit 5.2

**Process Flow
Charts for
Making
Hamburgers**

finished goods inventory so that a customer can receive them immediately on placing an order. Yet the process also allows for customized burgers, assembled only when the customer specifies the exact type of burger needed. Of course, the customer won't get it immediately. But, since the patties have already been cooked and are in the WIP inventory (where they are kept heated and fresh) the customer will not need to wait long. Competitors of Burger King such as Harvey's or McDonald's may follow a different process, depending on their strategy.

Process Measurement

A key factor in the success of every organization is its ability to measure performance. Such feedback on a continuous basis provides management with the data necessary to determine if established goals or standards are being met. As Peter Drucker, a well-known management guru, has said, "If you can't measure it, you can't manage it." Without proper measures of performance, managers cannot assess how well their organizations are doing or compare their performance with that of their competitors. Without these performance measures, managers would be like ships' captains, adrift on the ocean with no land in sight and no compass or other navigational instruments to guide them.

However, with a growing number of performance measures available, managers today must be selective in choosing only those measures that are critical to their firm's success. Depending on the specific industry and market niche within that industry, some measures of performance are more important to management than others. For example, in a fast-food outlet, a key performance indicator is the speed with which food is delivered to the customer. In an upscale restaurant, however, key performance measures might be the variety of items offered on the menu and the quality of food served.

In today's information-intense environment, managers, like everyone else, are deluged with reams of reports containing data on all aspects of a company's performance. It is essential, therefore, for management to identify those key indicators that measure the parameters that are critical to the success of their firms.

Types of Performance Measures

Productivity

The efficiency with which inputs are transformed into outputs is a measure of the process's **productivity**. In other words, productivity measures how well we convert inputs into outputs. In its broadest sense, productivity is defined as

$$\text{Productivity} = \frac{\text{Outputs}}{\text{Inputs}}$$

productivity
Efficiency of a process.

Exhibit 5.3

**Partial Measures
of Productivity**

Type of Business	Productivity Measure (Output/Input)
Restaurant	Customers (meals)/labour hour
Retail store	Sales/square metre
Chicken farm	Kilograms of meat/kilogram of feed
Utility plant	Kilowatts/tonne of coal
Paper mill	Tonnes of paper/cord of wood

Exhibit 5.3

**Partial Measures
of Productivity**

Ideally, we would like to measure the total productivity of a process, which would be the total outputs divided by the total inputs. Unfortunately, the inputs come in various forms. For example, labour is measured in hours, a building is measured in square meters, raw material is measured in kilograms, units, and so forth. It therefore would be impossible to obtain a measure for the total inputs into a process unless we converted all of the inputs to a common denominator such as money. However, in doing so, the operations manager loses an understanding of how the process is performing. Consequently, management will adopt one or more partial measures of productivity, which is the output of the process (in either revenues or units) divided by a single input. Some commonly used partial measures of productivity are presented in Exhibit 5.3. Such measures give managers the necessary information in familiar units, thereby allowing them to more easily relate to the actual performance of the operation. As noted in the exhibit, productivity can be measured for many factors, including labour, facilities, and equipment.

Productivity is what we call a *relative measure*. In other words, to be meaningful it needs to be compared to something else. For example, what can we learn from the fact that we operate a restaurant, and that its productivity last week was 8.4 customers/labour hour? (Nothing!)

Productivity comparisons can be made in two ways. First, a company can compare itself to similar operations within its industry, or can use industry data when they are available (e.g., comparing productivity among the different stores in a franchise).

Another approach is to measure productivity over time within the same operation. Here we compare productivity in one time period with that of the next.

Capacity

capacity

Output of a process in a given time period.

The output capability of a process is referred to as the **capacity** of the process. This performance measure is typically presented in units of output per unit of time, although, as we shall see later in the section, this is not always practical. Examples of measures of capacity are shown in Exhibit 5.4.

As noted by these examples, measures of capacity exist for both manufacturing and services. The major difference between manufacturing and services, in terms of measuring capacity, is that with service operations the measures of capacity usually include the

Exhibit 5.4

**Measures of
Capacity**

Type of Operation	Measure of Capacity
Fast-food restaurant	Customers per hour
Brewery	Barrels of beer per year
Hotel reservation call centre	Telephone calls per hour
Automobile assembly plant	Cars per hour
Paper mill	Tonnes of paper per year
College	Students per class period

Exhibit 5.4

**Measures of
Capacity**

customer, because the customer is typically an integral part of the process. (Because customers often participate in the service delivery process, they can be viewed as both an input and an output.)

Design capacity is defined as the ideal output rate at which a firm would like to produce under normal circumstances and for which the system was designed. Depending on the product or process and goals of the company, design capacity could even be established using a five-day-a-week, single-shift operation. *Maximum capacity* is used to define the maximum potential output rate that could be achieved when productive resources are used to their maximum. Typically, most firms can operate effectively at maximum capacity for only short periods of time. Operating at maximum capacity, for example, results in higher energy costs, the need for overtime wage premiums, and increased machine breakdowns due to the lack of time to conduct scheduled preventive maintenance. In addition, worker fatigue resulting from extended hours on the job can cause an increase in defective products as well as a decrease in labour productivity.

The degree to which a firm utilizes its productive capacity is referred to as **capacity utilization**, which is defined as follows:

capacity utilization
Percentage of available capacity that is actually used.

$$\text{Capacity utilization} = \frac{\text{Actual output}}{\text{Design capacity}}$$

For example, if an automobile assembly plant had a design capacity of 3600 cars per week, and actually produced only 2700 cars in one week, then its capacity utilization for that week would be

$$\text{Capacity utilization} = \frac{2700}{3600} = 75\%$$

With this definition of capacity utilization, it is possible to have utilization rates that are in excess of 100 percent, which should be a warning to management that excessive production costs are being incurred.

So far, we have measured capacity in terms of units of output per unit of time, which is appropriate as long as the output is relatively homogeneous (e.g., cars, stereos, etc.). However, when the output units are highly variable, especially in terms of process requirements, a more meaningful measure of capacity is often expressed in terms of one of the inputs. Consider, for example, a flexible machining centre that can make parts that take anywhere from five minutes to two hours to produce. The capacity of the centre, in terms of units produced per week, could vary significantly depending on which particular units were being produced. In this case, a better measure of capacity utilization would be:

$$\text{Capacity utilization} = \frac{\text{Actual machine hours used}}{\text{Total machine hours available}}$$

Such measures of capacity utilization will become more popular as the flexibility of processes increases to permit wider varieties of products to be made. This approach to measuring capacity utilization is also more applicable to many service operations that have a very high labour content and also require that labour to perform a wide variety of tasks. Examples here include medical doctors, whose tasks can vary from performing surgical operations to having office visits and attending required meetings. College professors provide another good example. In addition to teaching students, they also are required to conduct research and be of service to the college and the community. In both these instances, capacity as measured in terms of available hours per week is clearly the appropriate measure.

Quality

The quality of a process usually is measured by the defect rate of the products produced. Defects include those products that are identified as nonconforming, both internally (prior to shipping the product to the customer) as well as externally (i.e., products whose defects are found by the customer). The topic of process quality measurement and control is presented in greater detail in Chapter 6 and its supplement.

There are additional measures of a process's overall quality. With increasing awareness and concern for the environment, for example, the amount of toxic waste generated is also a measure of a process's quality. Similarly, the amount of scrap and waste material produced is another process quality indicator.

Speed of Delivery

Companies are experiencing increased pressure with respect to speed of delivery. Firms that once took weeks and months to deliver a product are now delivering products in hours and days. Purolator provides a good example of a firm that adds value by providing fast overnight delivery of packages.

Speed of delivery has two dimensions to measure. The first is the amount of time from when the product is ordered to when it is shipped to the customer, known as a product's *lead time*. Companies that produce standard products significantly reduce lead times by producing products for finished goods inventory. For such situations, orders are immediately filled from existing inventories. Companies that produce customized products, however, do not have the luxury of a finished goods inventory. Firms producing such products typically require a significant lead time before the finished product can be shipped.

Variability of Delivery

Another dimension in measuring delivery is the variability in delivery time. In many cases this dimension is more critical than the estimated delivery time itself. In other words, customers, whether they are other companies or end users, do not like uncertainty. Uncertainty negatively affects work scheduling, capacity utilization, inventory management, and so forth, which reduces the overall efficiency of the process. For example, imagine a store that is not sure when it will receive the goods it orders. It is likely to hold more safety inventory to compensate for the additional uncertainty in delivery times, increasing costs. Thus the less variability in delivery times, the better.

Flexibility

agile manufacturing

Ability of a manufacturing process to respond quickly to the demands of the customer.

Currently, the competitive advantage for many companies lies in their ability to produce customized products to meet individual customer needs. The capability of a company to provide such customized products in a timely manner is often referred to as **agile manufacturing**. Flexibility is the measure of how readily the company's transformation process can adjust to meet the ever-changing demands of its customers.

There are multiple dimensions to flexibility. One type of flexibility indicates how quickly a process can convert from producing one product or family of product(s) to another. For example, many Canadian automobile assembly plants still require a minimum of several weeks' shutdown annually to convert from one model year to the next, indicating a degree of inflexibility in this area.

Another measure of a process's flexibility is its ability to react to changes in volume. Processes that can accommodate large fluctuations in volume are said to be more flexible than those that cannot. Most service operations need to be very flexible in this dimension because of their inability to inventory demand. (For example, customers wanting to eat at a restaurant on Saturday night will not wait until Monday morning.) Thus, service operations such as retail stores, restaurants, and health clinics must have the ability to adjust to meet the demand from a few customers per hour to several hundred customers per hour. The typical assembly-line operation in a manufacturing facility cannot similarly adjust. The volume of output from an assembly line is fixed, and consequently companies with this type of process must resort to other means of balancing supply and demand. For example, appliance makers and automobile companies offer discounts and low-cost financing to encourage consumer buying during slow periods of demand, in part because of their inability to adjust the outputs of their manufacturing facilities without shutting them down entirely.

Yet another dimension of flexibility is the ability of the process to produce more than one product simultaneously. Thus, the more products a process can produce at a time, the more flexible it is said to be. This dimension of flexibility is especially important in producing customized products. For example, the flexibility of Dell's computer assembly processes allows it to custom-build computers to meet the individual requirements of each customer.

Process Velocity

A relatively new measure of performance is **process velocity**. Also referred to as *manufacturing velocity*, process velocity is the ratio of the actual throughput time from it takes for a product to go through the process divided by the value-added time required to complete the product or service. (Value-added time is defined as that time when work is actually being done to complete the product or deliver the service.)

process velocity
Ratio of total throughput time for a product to the value-added time.

For example, if the throughput time for a product is six weeks, and the actual value-added time to complete the product is four hours, then the process velocity of this product is

$$\text{Process velocity} = \frac{\text{Total throughput time}}{\text{Value-added time}}$$

$$\text{Process velocity} = \frac{6 \text{ weeks} \times 5 \text{ days per week} \times 8 \text{ hours per day}}{4 \text{ hours}} = 60$$

A process velocity of 60, in this case, means that it takes 60 times as long to complete the product as it does to do the actual work on the product itself. In other words, process velocity is like a golf score—the lower, the better.

Process velocities in excess of 100 are not uncommon. For example, University Microfilms, Inc. (UMI), which provides microfilming services for libraries and dissertations, took 150 days to process a manuscript, although only two hours were actually spent adding value to the manuscript. For UMI, the process velocity for a manuscript was therefore:

$$\text{Process velocity} = \frac{150 \text{ days per manuscript} \times 8 \text{ hours per day}}{2 \text{ hours}} = 600$$

UMI was able to reduce the throughput time to 60 days, thereby lowering its process velocity to 240.[1]

James Womack and Daniel Jones provide another good example of measuring process velocity. In their book *Lean Thinking*, they analyze the value stream of a carton of cola.[2] In their analysis, they identify only three hours in which value is actually being added to the product, although the overall process takes 319 days. In this case, the process velocity for a carton of cola is

$$\text{Process velocity} = \frac{319 \text{ days} \times 8 \text{ hours per day}}{3 \text{ hours}} = 851$$

---

[1]A. Bernstein, "Quality Is Becoming Job One in the Office, Too," *Business Week* (April 29, 1991).
[2]James P. Womack and Daniel T. Jones, *Lean Thinking: Banish Waste and Create Wealth in Your Corporation* (New York: Simon and Shuster, 1996), p. 43.

As noted by the above examples, the concept of process velocity is equally applicable to manufacturing and services. Process velocity also can be applied to any particular segment of the process or to the overall process. For example, a firm may want to focus only on its manufacturing velocity, in which case it would look at the throughput time from when the product is first begun to when it is completed and ready to ship. A broader perspective might measure process velocity from the time when the customer first places the order for product to when payment is finally received and the cheque has cleared.

In the past, many companies focused primarily on increasing the efficiency of the value-added time, which often constitutes only a very small portion of a product's overall time in the process.

Process Analysis Definitions

As a first step in understanding the important characteristics of processes, we define here some of the more commonly used terms.

Make-to-Stock versus Make-to-Order

make-to-stock system
Process for making highly standardized products for finished goods inventory.

make-to-order system
Process for making customized products to meet individual customer requirements.

The type of process chosen for each stage dependent on the firm's operations strategy and the type of product being manufactured. A **make-to-stock system** (see Exhibit 5.5A) is compatible with producing a highly standardized product that can be stored in a finished goods inventory for quick delivery to the customer. As a result, these products are usually forecasted in anticipation of future customer orders. In contrast, a **make-to-order system** (see Exhibit 5.5B) focuses on producing customized items that have already been ordered by the customer. It is important to note here that a make-to-order system requires more flexibility than a make-to-stock system, and as a result tends to be slower and more inefficient and, therefore, more expensive.

However, a make-to-stock system tends to limit the number of product variations to a few highly standardized items. To achieve maximum process efficiency while at the same time increasing product variety, firms will delay the customization step until the last possible moment. A good example of this application is the mixing of custom-coloured paints at home improvement centres while customers wait.

Modularization

modularization
Use of standard components and subassemblies to produce customized products.

Another approach that attempts to combine process efficiency with some degree of customization is called **modularization**. In Chapter 3, we introduced the concept of a modularly designed product. Such products can be produced using a modularized process (see Exhibit 5.5C). Modularization also has application in services. For example, an Italian restaurant can offer its customers a choice of 60 different dishes by combining four types of pasta, three types of sauces, and five varieties of meat ($4 \times 3 \times 5$). (For another example see the OM in Practice box on surveillance cameras). Key trade-offs in modularization are speed of design, quality, and reliability versus uniqueness. For example, although Daimler-Chrysler realized that having every Mercedes Benz model as different as possible (differentiating between the various models) was important to a luxury car brand, having too many unique parts in each model can bring its own problems. Designing unique parts requires time, increasing the time needed to design a new model. This could be a disadvantage if a competitor such as Lexus or BMW were to introduce a state-of-the art model more quickly. Also, new and untested parts have a higher risk of unanticipated failure in the field, resulting in product recalls, whereas using common parts that have already been field tested would be more reliable. At the same time however, Daimler-Chrysler wants to keep its reputation for innovation in each model. Thus it does not want too many common components either. So it is using limited modularization.[3]

Exhibit 5.6 compares make-to-stock, make-to-order, and modularized production processes.

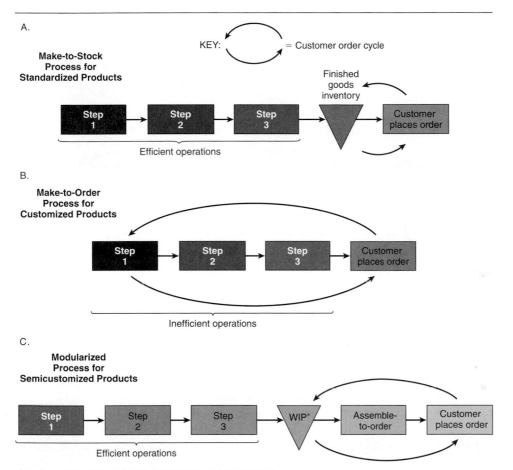

Exhibit 5.5

A Comparison of Make-to-Stock, Make-to-Order, and Modularized Processes

* WIP consists of standardized components and subassemblies.

Process Type	Unit Cost	Flexibility	Speed	Quality (Product/Process)
Make-to-order	High	Very high	Very slow	High/variable
Make-to-stock	Low	Low	Fast	Low/consistent
Modularized	Medium	Medium	Medium	Medium/consistent

Exhibit 5.6

Comparison of Processes

[3]Stephen Power, "Betting on the S, Mercedes Looks to New Model of Flagship S-Class to Reverse an Image of Sagging Quality," *Wall Street Journal*, July 11, 2005, B.1.

DESIGN YOUR OWN SURVEILLANCE CAMERA ON THE WEB

Silent Witness Ltd. (a unit of Honeywell), a Surrey, B.C.-based company with locations in Canada, the United States, and the United Kingdom, designs and manufactures a full range of video monitoring technology for the global marketplace, including high-performance closed circuit television (CCTV) cameras, digital and analog storage solutions, digital processing technologies, and network-based remote video surveillance. You can design your preferred surveillance camera by going to their Web site. With about 19 types of housings, 12 types of cameras, and 6 types of lenses (each for two different types of television systems), and some other options, you can have more than 1000 camera configurations, yet the company needs to produce and carry only a little more than 40 stock keeping units (SKUs). So they don't have to forecast demand and manage the supply chain for 1000 items, only for 40 items. This is a good example of how modular design gives the customer more choices while making operations management easier for the provider.

Source:
www.honeywellvideo.com/support/configurators/modular/index.html

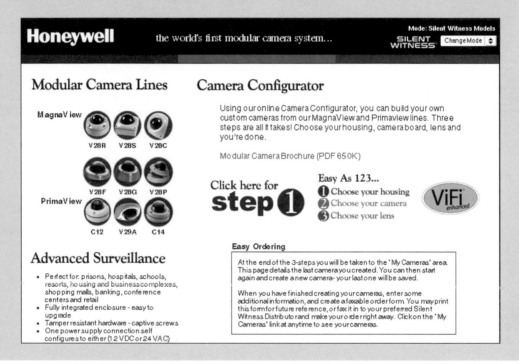

Hybrid Process

Most of the processes we encounter consist of more than one stage or step to produce the required goods or services. These are often referred to as **multistage processes**. Within a multistage process, a different type of process can exist at each stage. When this occurs, these multistage processes are frequently referred to as **hybrid processes**. For example, Cavendish Farms (a Moncton, New Brunswick-based producer of frozen potato products for both retail and restaurant/institutional markets around the world) produces frozen french fries at its processing plant in Annan, Prince Edward Island. There the potatoes are washed, peeled, and cut in a continuous process, cooked in a batch process, and then packaged in an assembly-line type of operation.

Within a given industry, different firms may adopt different types of processes to produce the same or similar products. For example, some potato chip manufacturers cook their potatoes with a continuous process instead of a batch process.

multistage process
Process that consists of more than one step.

hybrid process
Multistage process that consists of more than one type of process.

Tightness and Dependence

The relationship between the various stages in a process is frequently referred to as the degree of *tightness* in the process. Processes that are considered very tight, such as assembly lines, have a great deal of *dependence* between stages. In other words, if production stops due to a machine breakdown at an early stage in the process, work ceases almost immediately at all of the subsequent operations. This high degree of dependence among the stages is caused by a lack of buffer inventories between adjacent stages. The greater the buffer inventories, the greater the independence between stages and the "looser" the process. Batch processes typically exhibit a high degree of independence between stages, as shown by the large amounts of buffer inventories in the form of work-in-process (WIP). With these types of processes, a failure at one stage in the process does not impact any other stages until the WIP between them is depleted.

Bottlenecks

The capacity of each stage in a multistage process often varies for several reasons, including dissimilar output rates of the different pieces of equipment that comprise the overall process. In these situations, the stage of the process with the lowest capacity is referred to as the **bottleneck** in the process. Adding additional capacity to alleviate the bottleneck at one stage in the process often will shift the bottleneck to another stage. When this occurs, the full capacity potential of the additional equipment may not be realized. Bottlenecks are discussed further in Chapter 11, "Scheduling." The example on the next page illustrates the relationship between the bottleneck and process capacity.

bottleneck
Stage or stages that limit the total output of a process.

Capacity versus Demand

In the above example, we focused entirely on the available capacity of the process without considering the demand for the bread. It is important when analyzing the capacity requirements for a process that we not confuse the capacity of the process with the demand for the firm's products. For example, if the demand for a product is less than the capacity of the smallest stage, then no bottleneck exists (in the bakery example, if demand were less than 150 kilograms per hour, there would not be a bottleneck). As a result, no additional equipment is needed. Only when demand exceeds the capacity at one or more stages do we have to address the problem of a bottleneck and consider installing additional equipment.

The use of process flow charts in conjunction with a capacity analysis of each stage in the process provides management with a thorough understanding of the major process issues that need to be addressed. In addition, as part of the process analysis, it is often necessary to draw three different flow charts. These three flow charts define (*a*) what the official or documented method is, (*b*) how the work is actually being performed, and (*c*) what the proper procedures should be.

Value Stream Mapping

A concept closely related to process analysis is **value stream mapping (VSM)**.[4] VSM, a concept developed by Toyota, involves developing a flow chart that helps users see and understand the flow of material and information as products make their way from raw material to the customer (the value stream). Both value-adding and non-value-adding activities are included in the chart. Once the chart has been drawn, the next step is to identify the activities that do not add value and eliminate them.

Exhibit 5.7 shows the value stream map for a product assembled from components. Note that some of the steps in the process are clearly non-value added. Moving the components

value stream mapping (VSM)
Developing a flow chart to eliminate wasteful activities and improve the process.

---

[4]Jared Lovelle, "Mapping the Value Stream," *IIE Solutions*, 33, 2 (February 2001), pp. 26–32.

Example

A commercial bread bakery wants to evaluate its capacity, in terms of how many kilograms of bread it can produce per hour. A simplified version of the process is shown below:

In the mixing stage, all of the ingredients are combined to form the dough. The dough must then rise in a controlled environment called a proofing box or proofing oven, which monitors humidity and temperature. Following the proofing, the bread is then formed into loaves and baked. In the final stage, the bread is packaged prior to distribution to retail outlets. The bakery currently has the following equipment:

Stage	Capacity (kg/hr/machine)	Number of Machines
Mixing	60	3
Proofing	25	6
Baking	40	4
Packaging	75	3

a. What is the current capacity of the bakery in kilograms of bread per hour?

b. Where is the bottleneck in the process?

c. If an additional piece of equipment were purchased to increase the capacity of the bottleneck, what would be the new capacity of the bakery?

Solution

a. The total capacity of the bakery is determined by calculating the total capacity at each stage of the process as follows:

Stage	Equipment Capacity (kg/hr/machine)	Number of Machines	Total Capacity (kg/hr)
Mixing	60	3	180
Proofing	25	6	150
Baking	40	4	160
Packaging	75	3	225

The overall capacity of the bakery is 150 kilograms per hour, as determined by the proofing operation, which is the stage with the smallest capacity.

b. Currently, the bottleneck is at the proofing stage because that stage has the smallest hourly capacity.

c. If another proofing oven were purchased, the capacity of the proofing stage would now be 175 kilograms per hour. However, with the addition of the new proofing oven, the bottleneck in the process now would shift to the baking stage because that has the lowest capacity of 160 kilograms per hour. Thus the new overall capacity of the bakery with the addition of another proofing oven would be only 160 kilograms per hour.

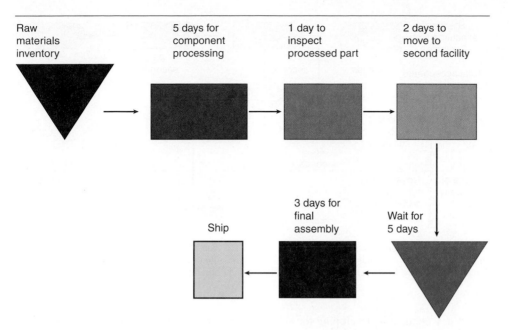

Exhibit 5.7

Process Improvement Using Value Stream Mapping

from one facility to another and having them wait before being assembled are steps that are clearly adding time and cost without any value to the customer (waste) and should be removed through process redesign. Even non-value-added activities that may appear to be needed such as inspection should be candidates for elimination. If the process before inspection was failsafe (discussed later), so that no errors were produced, then the inspection step could be a waste and therefore could be eliminated. In addition, a company may be able to reduce the raw material inventory by going to a just-in-time system (discussed in Chapter 13). Thus carrying excess inventory can also be a waste since holding inventory costs money. If the company manages to eliminate the inspection, as well as the move and the wait at the second facility, the customer will get the product eight days earlier, a fifty percent reduction in lead time! Note that Exhibit 5.7 shows only the part of the product's value stream within our own facility. If we could collaborate with our suppliers, customers, and logistics providers to map the entire value stream, more waste could be identified.

Service Blueprinting

As with manufacturing process analysis, the standard tool for service process analysis is the flow chart. In 1978, Lynn Shostack added to the standard process flow chart the concept of the *line of visibility* and emphasized the identification of potential fail points in her version of the flow chart, calling it a **service blueprint**.[5] She also has made a compelling argument for having blueprints on every aspect of a service, and for having the "keeper of the blueprint" as a specific job function in any large service organization. Current practice in some companies is to have blueprints available on computers so that when problems arise, senior managers can zero in on any portion of a service process, thereby making more informed decisions about how to resolve them. One example is the service blueprint for providing a shoeshine, as shown in Exhibit 5.8. Note that the service blueprints don't use the standard flow chart notation shown in Exhibit 5.1.

service blueprint
Process flow chart for services that includes the customer.

[5]G. Lynn Shostack, "Designing Services That Deliver," *Harvard Business Review* 62, no. 1 (January–February 1984), p. 135.

Exhibit 5.8

Blueprint for a Corner Shoeshine

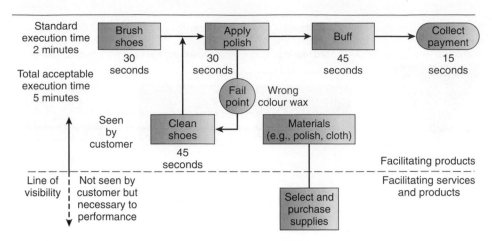

A key element in developing the service blueprint is the *line of visibility*. All activities above the line take place in direct contact with the customer. Those activities below the line are considered to be backroom operations, taking place without the customer's presence. Activities above the line of visibility, therefore, need to focus on providing good service; backroom operations, however, should focus on process efficiency.

For example, the steps involved in developing a blueprint for a simple shoeshine process, including a profitability analysis, are as follows:

1. *Identify processes.* The first step in creating such a blueprint is mapping the processes that constitute the service. Exhibit 5.8 maps out the various steps in providing a shoeshine. Because the service is simple and clear-cut, the map is straightforward. It might be useful to specify how the proprietor will perform the step called *buff*.

2. *Isolate fail points.* Having diagrammed the processes involved, the designer now can see where the system might go awry. For example, the shoeshiner might pick up and apply the wrong colour wax, so the process designer must build in a subprocess to correct this possible error. The identification of fail points and the design of fail-safe processes are critical. The consequences of service failures can be greatly reduced by analyzing fail points at the design stage.

3. *Establish a time frame.* Since all services depend on time, which is usually the major cost determinant, the process designer should establish a standard execution time.

4. *Analyze profitability.* Any delay in getting a customer's shoes shined affects profits negatively, regardless whether the delay is due to other customers already waiting for service, rework due to errors, slower than usual shoe shining, or a combination of the three. Exhibit 5.9 quantifies the cost of delay; at four minutes the proprietor loses money. A service designer must establish a time-of-service-execution standard to ensure a profitable business.

Exhibit 5.10 provides a more complicated blueprint, that of a cash account at a discount brokerage.

	Execution Time		
	2 Minutes	**3 Minutes**	**4 Minutes**
Price	$.50	$.50	$.50
Costs			
Time @ $.10 per minute	.20	.30	.40
Wax	.03	.03	.03
Other operating expenses	.09	.09	.09
Total costs	$.32	$.42	4.52
Pretax profit	$.18	$.08	($.02)

Exhibit 5.9

Shoeshine Profitability Analysis

Source: Reprinted by permission of *Harvard Business Review*. From G. Lynn Shostack, "Designing Services That Deliver" (January–February 1984), p. 134. Copyright © 1984 by the Harvard Business School Publishing Corporation; all rights reserved.

Fail-Safing

Services processes typically involve the customer. Consequently, any errors that occur during the process take place in front of the customer, thereby providing management with little or no opportunity to correct the situation before the customer is affected by it. In many of these situations, especially where self-service is involved, a concept of **fail-safing** or foolproofing has been developed, often referred to by its Japanese name, *poka-yoke.*

One example of fail-safing is the bathroom in an airplane. To avoid possible embarrassment resulting from an unlocked door, the light will not go on until the bathroom door is actually locked. Another example of fail-safing is provided in some hotels that require that the room card be placed in a specific slot for the electricity in the room to be turned on. In this way, the guest always knows where the room card is while in the room, and at the same time, the electricity is shut off when the guest is not in the room, thereby saving the hotel money in terms of reduced energy costs.

fail-safing

Designing a service process so as to make it error free or foolproof.

Business Processes

We define a **business process** as "a logical set of tasks or activities that *crosses functional boundaries* and recognizes its *interdependence* with other processes or business processes." In other words, business processes cut across "the white spaces" in an organizational chart, linking the various functional areas to accomplish a common task or goal. Exhibit 5.11 identifies some of the more common business processes and the respective functional areas they link.

business process

A set of sequential tasks or activities that cross functional boundaries and recognize their interdependence with other processes or business processes.

Business Process Analysis

The analysis of business processes uses basically the same methodology described earlier in this chapter with respect to process analysis. In addition, however, as noted above, business process analysis recognizes that the business process being analyzed is dependent on the outputs of other business processes (or processes) and similarly, other business processes (or processes) are dependent on the output of the business process under evaluation. The analysis of a business process involves benchmarking and reengineering, both of which are explained in detail in the following sections.

Likewise, the performance measures for business processes are similar to those used to evaluate processes. In addition to the operational-oriented measures described earlier in this chapter, there often are additional measures of performance specific to each business process. Examples of these business process–specific measures are presented in Exhibit 5.12.

Exhibit 5.10

Service Blueprint for a Cash Account at a Discount Brokerage

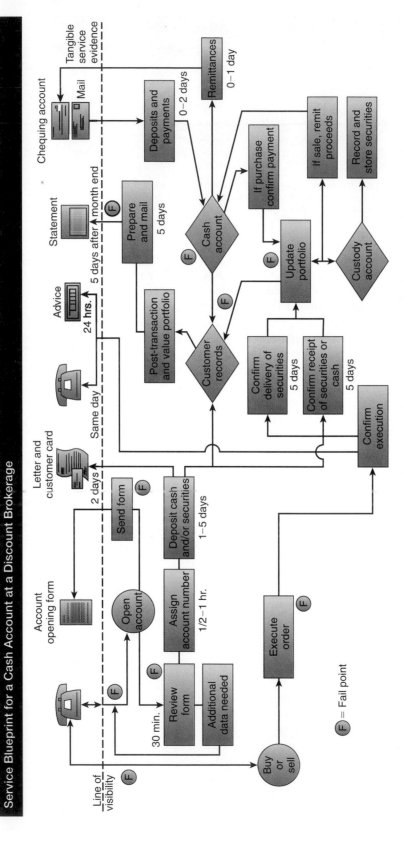

Source: Reprinted by permission of *Harvard Business Review.* From G. Lynn Shostack, "Designing Services That Deliver," *Harvard Business Review* 62, no. 1 (January–February 1984), p. 138. Copyright © 1984 by the Harvard Business School Publishing Corporation; all rights reserved.

Business Process	Functional Areas That Are Linked
New product development	Operations, marketing, finance, engineering
Order fulfillment	Marketing, operations, accounting
Supply chain management	Purchasing, operations, accounting
Asset management	Operations, accounting, finance
Recruitment	Human resources, operations, accounting

Exhibit 5.11

Examples of Business Processes

Business Process	Specific Measures of Performance
Order fulfillment	Service level (percentage of orders filled from stock) Lead time (time between receipt of customer order and delivery)
Supply chain management	Percentage of on-time deliveries Lead time (time between placement of vendor order and delivery)
New product development	Time to market (time from product conception to availability) Market share (percentage of market captured by new product)
Human resource management	Employee turnover rate Employee satisfaction

Exhibit 5.12

Measures of Performance for Specific Business Processes

The first step in analyzing a business process is to define the process boundaries. It is extremely important to clearly establish (*a*) where the process begins and ends, (*b*) the inputs and outputs of the process, and (*c*) the other processes in the organization that either impact on or are impacted by the process under evaluation. In determining the process boundaries, the scope of the process is defined, which is critical. Process analyses that have too wide a scope are often too complex to analyze properly, and therefore become unmanageable. The resulting analysis, in these cases, is very often difficult to understand, measure, and ultimately change. On the other hand, processes that are too narrow in scope have only limited potential for improvement.

Business process analysis can take place at various levels within an organization. The degree of detail used in the analysis is often referred to as **granularity**. Business process analysis that is conducted at a high level but does not get into a great amount of detail is said to be of large granularity, whereas an analysis that is done in greater detail is referred to as being of small granularity.

granularity
A term used to describe the level of detail that is used in analyzing a process.

Once the boundaries of the business process being analyzed are established, the firm must then link its overall corporate strategies to the process. In other words, the firm must clearly understand how the process under evaluation contributes to its competitive advantage. For example, if a company competes by being low cost and providing fast delivery, the process must be analyzed with respect to how it contributes to low cost and fast delivery. By linking strategy to the business process, the firm can more easily identify the key measures it will use to evaluate the process.

The third step is mapping the process. Here a process flow chart is developed, providing a visual context for analyzing the process. This chart provides both the analyst and the process owner with a clear understanding of the boundaries of the process and the various steps involved. When mapping the process, it is important to understand the specific order in which the steps are performed, how long each step takes, and the resources that are required. As part of the mapping process, the various steps that are required are often

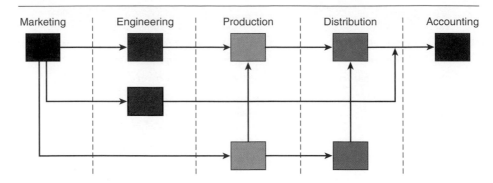

grouped by functional area to more clearly illustrate the cross-functionality of the process, as shown in Exhibit 5.13.

As stated above, the firm's strategies provide a basis for determining which key measures are to be used to evaluate the process. After the process is evaluated, it is *benchmarked* to determine how it compares to similar processes both internally (within the firm) and externally (those of other firms). The combination of performance measures and benchmarking provides management with some clear insight into identifying the major problems with the process that need to be corrected.

In the last step, the process is improved through *reengineering*, which identifies and addresses the root causes of the problem. However, determining how the process is to be reengineered is not sufficient. The successful implementation of the necessary process changes is just as important as the changes themselves. As a final note, these process evaluations should be conducted on a periodic basis to ensure that the process continues to perform in the desired manner.

Benchmarking

benchmarking

Comparison of a
company's measures
of performances with
those of firms
considered to be
world class.

Benchmarking is simply a comparison of a company's performance in certain areas with that of other firms in its industry and/or with those firms that are identified as world-class competitors in specific functions and operations.[6] Benchmarking can cut across traditional industry lines, providing opportunities for new and innovative ways to increase performance. For example, Xerox, in its desire to deliver products quickly, studied how L. L. Bean of Freeport, Maine, a mail-order company well-known for fast and accurate service, accomplished this.

Firms that want to compete as world-class organizations in the highly competitive global arena must attain *best of breed* status in those performance parameters that are critical for success in their respective industries and market segments. This can be accomplished only through measuring and comparing their performance with that of others, and then instituting the necessary actions for improvement. Many Canadian companies, large, small, and in different industries, use benchmarking to improve quality and productivity. Some examples are Ford Canada (automobiles), Nortel (telecommunications), Suncor (petroleum), MedcomSoft (computer software), Aeronautical and Technical Services (see opening vignette of Chapter 6), and Delta Hotels (travel). Many Canadian business schools benchmark by being accredited by the Association to Advance Collegiate Schools

---

[6]This section draws heavily on: Robert C. Camp, *Benchmarking: The Search for Industry Best Practices That Lead to Superior Performance* (Milwaukee, WI: ASQC Quality Press, 1989), and Robert C. Camp, *Business Process Benchmarking: Finding and Implementing Best Practices* (Milwaukee, WI: ASQC Quality Press, 1995).

PROCESS MANAGEMENT AT FEDEX

Process management at FedEx is viewed as a systematic examination of how the actual work of operating a business gets done. This approach, which cuts across divisional, functional, and departmental lines, entails collaborative investigation, analysis, and then refinement of the basic processes, activities, and tasks by which a business operates.

The five core business processes defined at FedEx are (1) providing direction; (2) acquiring and retaining customers; (3) servicing customers; (4) moving, tracking, and delivering the product; and (5) invoicing and collecting payment. Process management at FedEx is customer-driven. It focuses first on customer requirements to assure that the process is designed to meet the expectations of the customer. It utilizes analytical techniques to identify high-leverage opportunities for standardizing work processes, as well as for creating opportunities for continuous improvement.

Measurement is also important at FedEx. The old business maxim, "You cannot manage what you cannot measure," has been an inspiration for measuring both customer satisfaction and service quality. Measurement is accomplished through the use of process quality indicators (PQIs), which measure the outputs of processes, as well as other process indicators, which measure such factors as the quality of the process results, the cycle time of each operation within a process, and the cost of the process. An example of a PQI within the moving, tracking, and delivering the product core process is "the total number of conveyances (trucks and aircraft) arriving late at hubs, destination ramps, and destination stations, which is measured on a daily basis at the corporate level."

FedEx recognizes that its future success depends on many factors, including its ability to improve its business processes. It believes that only if it can adopt and fully utilize analytical business

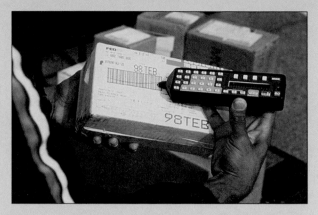

tools, such as process management, to improve operations will it be able to compete against other companies in the marketplace. However, the full utilization of the techniques of process management depends on the motivation and competencies of its front-line management. Its managers must have analytical, communication, and decision-making skills, and Fed-Ex provides training to ensure that these managers obtain these required skills.

FedEx has also been in the forefront, using technologies such as the Internet and wireless for managing its processes which have become even more complex with the addition of value-added services. For example, FedEx acquired Kinko's, a chain of copying stores, in 2004 and also provides supply chain management services to its customers.

Sources:
Adapted from a letter from Fred Smith, CEO, FedEx, to FedEx management, October 7, 1996.
www.fedex.com, Rick Brooks, "FedEx to Buy Kinko's for $2.2 Billion," *Wall Street Journal*, Dec. 31, 2003, A3.

of Business (AACSB), an international accreditation association representing the highest standards of achievement for business schools worldwide.

David T. Kearns, CEO of Xerox Corporation, defines benchmarking as follows:

Benchmarking is the continuous process of measuring products, services, and practices against the toughest competitors or those companies recognized as industry leaders.[7]

Several key elements in this definition should be emphasized. "Continuous measuring" implies that benchmarking is an interactive process with no end. With competition constantly raising the bar, levels of performance accepted today will not be tolerated by the customer tomorrow. Only through constant monitoring of our performance and that of our competitors will we be able to know where we stand at any point in time. One of the implied requirements of the Canadian Awards for Excellence (CAE), a national quality award issued by the National Quality Institute, is that companies benchmark against other companies.

---

[7]Camp, *Business Process Benchmarking*, p. 10.

John Deere, the farm equipment manufacturer, uses technology to be more responsive to its customers. This technology allows dealers and farmers to communicate directly with John Deere warehouses, providing them with ready access to parts and equipment.

Benchmarking means measurement. This can be accomplished internally (within the organization) as well as externally (with competitors and world-class firms). It is important for management to be aware that benchmarking is not limited only to manufacturing, but can also be applied to other functional areas in an organization.

Benchmarking should not be limited only to direct competitors. Rather it should focus on those firms or business functions or operations within firms that have achieved recognition as world-class operations. In other words, as Robert Camp states in the title of his book, "benchmarking is the search for best practices that leads to superior performance."[8]

Regardless which business a company is in, it may want to look at EXFO (see the opening vignette of Chapter 3) for benchmarking the new product development process, at GE for information systems, and at Toyota for consistent process quality.

What Should We Benchmark?

Benchmarking can be applied to many areas within an organization. Robert Camp identifies three of these: (1) goods and services, (2) business processes, and (3) performance measures.

Goods and Services

Benchmarking identifies the features and functions of the goods and services that are desired by the firm's customers. This information is incorporated into product planning, design, and development in the form of product goals and technology design practices.

Business Processes

Benchmarking in this area provides the basis for business process improvement and reengineering. These changes should be an integral part of the continuous quality improvement initiative.

---

[8]Ibid.

Performance Measures

The end result of benchmarking goods, services, and processes is to establish and validate objectives for the key performance measures that have been identified as critical to the success of the organization.

Business Process Reengineering

For many years, dating well back into the nineteenth century, companies were organized and structured both to maximize efficiency and to control growth.[9] However, with the emergence of a single world economy and increased competition from all corners of the globe, today's competitive priorities for success have shifted from efficiency to innovation, speed, service, and quality.

To increase efficiency in the factory, job design was dominated by the division-of-labour concept in which the work to be done was subdivided into a series of tasks that could be performed by less-skilled individuals. However, this approach, although increasing productivity among lower-skilled workers, had its disadvantages. With each individual focusing primarily on his or her assigned task, no one assumed overall responsibility for the process itself. The result was that these conventional process structures were fragmented and piecemeal, and consequently lacked the integration necessary to support the current competitive priorities, for example, quality and service. This shift in priorities has forced managers to rethink how their firms operate, and to focus on redesigning their core business processes. This is the goal of reengineering. To accomplish this, we need to "get back to the basics," by applying some of the concepts presented in this chapter that allow us to better understand these processes.

Reengineering Defined

This process of rethinking and restructuring an organization is often referred to as **reengineering**. Reengineering literally means starting from the beginning with a clean sheet of paper in terms of how we design our organizations to better serve our customers. It focuses on processes, not individuals performing individual tasks. A key element of reengineering is the notion of "discontinuous thinking"—identifying and discarding antiquated rules and assumptions that are often the foundation for current business operations, and that continue to exist when only small, incremental changes are made.

reengineering
Process of rethinking
and restructuring an
organization.

A cornerstone of reengineering is the use of computer technology. With advances in database management, speed of processing, and networking capabilities, today's computers should be used to formulate new approaches that are based on the computer's strengths. Instead, many companies simply transfer existing manual systems onto computers and wonder why their problems still exist even though they have "automated" their systems.

An example of reengineering is Ford's desire to reduce its accounts payable department in the early 1980s. Initially, through traditional methods, management determined that the 500-person department should be reduced by 100 people (a 20 percent reduction in that workforce). However, investigation revealed that Mazda's accounts payable department consisted of only five people. Even though Mazda was smaller than Ford, this didn't explain the tremendous difference in department sizes. Subsequently, Ford decided to completely rethink its accounts payable department.

---

[9]Adapted from Michael Hammer and James Champy, *Reengineering the Corporation: A Manifesto for Business Revolution* (New York: HarperCollins, 1993).

Under the old system, the 500 workers in accounts payable were constantly shuffling paper—matching vendor invoices to purchase orders and receiving documents, for example. Most of their time was spent trying to reconcile the paperwork when it didn't match up. This was the biggest cause of delayed payments. Under the new system, all of the paperwork has been virtually eliminated, thanks to the computer. When goods are received, a clerk on the dock uses the computer to instantly reconcile each delivery with its purchase order. The clerk now has the authority to accept the goods and to issue an order to the computer to pay the vendor. As a result, the bill is paid when the goods are received, not when the invoice is received. With the significant reduction in paperwork, the accounts payable department has been reduced to 125 people (a 75 percent reduction), who can now accomplish the same work previously done by 500 people, and do it faster.

Characteristics of a Reengineered Process

Based on their many years of experience with companies that have successfully reengineered their processes to better meet the needs of the marketplace, Michael Hammer and James Champy have identified several characteristics of reengineered processes, described below, that they have observed on a recurring basis.

Several Jobs Are Combined into One

Assembly lines are no longer used because of their inherent fragmentation of work. Specialists are replaced by "case workers," who have responsibility for overseeing the entire process. This is referred to as horizontal work compression. By combining tasks and jobs under one person, errors that occur in transferring information from one individual to another are eliminated. In addition, the cycle time is significantly reduced because only one person has responsibility.

Workers Make Decisions

Decision making becomes a part of every person's job, eliminating the need for the traditional, costly hierarchical organizational structure with its many layers of management. This is referred to as vertical work compression. The benefits include faster customer response, lower overhead costs, and increased worker empowerment.

The Steps in the Process Are Performed in a Natural Order

With reengineering, processes no longer have to be forced into a sequential order. Instead, a natural sequence of events is permitted, based on what needs to be done next. This allows many jobs to be performed simultaneously, thereby reducing the throughput time.

Processes Have Multiple Versions

Unlike assembly lines, which are totally inflexible and therefore can produce only standardized products, reengineered processes have several versions to meet the unique requirements of different market niches as well as individual customers. An advantage of the multiple-version approach is that these processes tend to be relatively simple in comparison to the traditional assembly processes, which are usually quite complex. For example, IBM Credit, which finances products and services that IBM sells, has multiple versions for the credit issuance process. Straightforward application cases are dealt with entirely using a computer. Medium-difficulty cases need intervention by a generalist employee; hard cases involve the intervention of specialist advisors.

Work Is Performed Where It Makes the Most Sense

This involves shifting work across traditional functional boundaries. No longer, for example, are all purchases made by the purchasing department. For small purchases, such as office supplies, it may be more efficient to have each department do its own purchasing.

	Tactical	Strategic
Scope	Function	Strategic business unit (SBU)
Focus	Single process	All critical core processes
Targets	Process workflow	Holistic: workflow, systems, structure, incentives, culture
Role	Isolated improvement initiative	Focused vision for all improvement initiatives
Results	Decrease in expense, headcount, space	Increase in profit, return, market share

Source: Gateway Management Consulting.

Exhibit 5.14

Comparison between Strategic and Tactical Deployment Techniques for Reengineering

Issues with Reengineering

In recent years, both manufacturing and service companies have adopted business process reengineering in an attempt to be more responsive to the marketplace as well as to increase the overall efficiency of their operations. However, very few of these reengineering efforts have been successful. One reason for this is the inability of management to link the reengineering effort to the overall corporate strategy. The result is often a piecemeal approach in which the reengineering program has to compete for scarce resources with other management initiatives such as total quality management, self-directed work teams, and outsourcing.

A successful reengineering program must be linked to the corporate strategy of the firm. In other words, reengineering is a strategic issue that must be addressed by the entire organization, at least at the strategic business unit (SBU) level, rather than being viewed as a tactical program. The differences in these two approaches to implementing reengineering are shown in Exhibit 5.14.[10]

As with all major projects that require significant organizational change, the successful implementation of a reengineering effort is highly dependent upon the commitment and participation of top management.

---

[10]Raymond L. Manganelli and Steven R. Raspa, "Why Reengineering Has Failed," *Management Review* (July 1995), pp. 39–43.

Processes exist in every type of business environment, be it manufacturing or service, and the type of processes used and how well they perform are directly related to the success of every organization. Managers, therefore, need to understand how these processes work and measure their performance on a continuous basis. An integral part of managing processes is process analysis, which is used to identify weaknesses in the process or areas for improvement.

For every process there are a multitude of performance measures. It is essential therefore for managers to identify those key performance measures that best provide them with the proper information that will allow intelligent and effective decision making.

To be most meaningful, performance measures should be compared with something. Traditionally these comparisons have been made within an organization, looking at trends over a period of time. Other comparisons were made with industry data that were readily available.

Conclusion

More recently, however, companies have begun looking outside their industries to find those firms that have the best practices in a particular functional area or in a specific type of process. This policy of seeking out the best of the best is referred to as benchmarking.

Proper performance measurement and benchmarking are critical elements for firms that want to compete successfully in the global marketplace. In such a fiercely competitive environment, where rules are constantly changing and standards are constantly being raised, only those firms that are cognizant of both their capabilities and those of their competitors will survive.

Managers now recognize that there are many processes that cross functional lines. Process flow charts and analysis, which were once used solely within the manufacturing function, also can be applied to these business processes.

The lessons learned in manufacturing also can be applied in a service environment. Here, however, the customer's direct interaction with the service process must be taken into consideration. This type of analysis of service operations is often referred to as service blueprinting.

In an effort to improve processes, in terms of both effectiveness and efficiency, business process reengineering often starts from ground zero in redesigning a process. This approach provides an opportunity for new and innovative ideas to be introduced while at the same time taking advantage of the latest technology available.

Key Terms

agile manufacturing p. 140

benchmarking p. 152

bottleneck p. 145

business process p. 149

capacity p. 138

capacity utilization p. 139

fail-safing p. 149

granularity p. 151

hybrid process p. 144

make-to-order system p. 142

make-to-stock system p. 142

modularization p. 142

multistage process p. 144

process p. 136

process flow chart p. 136

process velocity p. 141

productivity p. 137

reengineering p. 155

service blueprint p. 147

value stream mapping
   (VSM) p. 145

Review and Discussion Questions

1. Why are performance measures important?
2. What do we mean when we say productivity is a "relative" measure?
3. What are the typical performance measures for quality, speed of delivery, and flexibility?
4. What should the criteria be for management to adopt a particular performance measure?
5. What is benchmarking? Why is it important for firms that want to compete globally to adopt benchmarking?
6. What is the difference between a make-to-stock and a make-to-order process?
7. How does modularization allow a company to increase efficiency while at the same time providing its customers with a wide variety of products?

8. What is the definition of *bottleneck*? How does a bottleneck impact the output of a process?
9. Identify the major elements in a process flow chart.
10. How does service blueprinting differ from process flow analysis?
11. How does a business process differ from a process?
12. Describe the order fulfillment business process for purchasing a book from Amazon.ca, and map the process in a flow chart.
13. What is meant by *business process reengineering*? Why have so many of these types of projects failed in recent years?

Go to the Online Learning Centre (OLC) at www.mcgrawhill.ca/olc/davis and take a plant tour. Describe the firm's process in detail and draw a process flow chart for the operation.

Problem

A potato chip manufacturer in Saskatoon produces "Prairie-style, kettle-cooked" potato chips for distribution throughout Canada to retail outlets as well as to hotels and resort areas. The process of making potato chips is relatively simple. Raw potatoes, which are delivered once a week to the factory, are first washed and peeled. After a visual inspection to ensure all of the peel and eyes are removed, the potatoes are then sliced and immediately fried in a large kettle. (The peeling and frying operations are done in batches; the slicing is a continuous operation.) After frying, the cooked chips are inspected and any burnt ones are removed. The chips are then salted and stored in large cartons. This first phase of the process is done on two shifts of eight hours each. By contrast, the packaging operation is run only eight hours a day because of the large capacity of the equipment. The cooked chips are packaged in either 50 g or 250 g packages. The last step in the process places the packages in cartons for delivery. (There are twenty-four 50 g packages to a carton and twelve 250 g packages to a carton.)

The following information is given about the capacities of the different stages in the operation:

Stage	Capacity per Machine	Number of Machines
Peeling	275 kg/hr	2
Slicing	680 kg/hr	1
Cooking	115 kg/hr	2
Packaging (50 g)	160 pkgs/min	2
Packaging (250 g)	30 pkgs/min	1
Cartoning (50 g)	5 cartons/min	1
Cartoning (250 g)	4 cartons/min	1

The weekly demand is 17 500 cartons of 50 g chips and 5000 cartons of 250 g chips.

a. Draw the flow chart for this operation.
b. Using Excel, set up a worksheet that shows all of the stages involved in producing potato chips and determine the capacity of each stage in kilograms per week.
c. Identify the bottleneck(s) in the process.
d. Make recommendations for eliminating the bottleneck(s).

Solution

a.

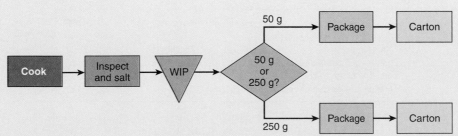

b. See spreadsheet.

Prairie Potato Chip Production Process

	Demand		Cartons	kg					
	50g		17 500	21 000			=E8+E9		
	250g		5 000	15 000					

Stage	Capacity per machine		No. of Mach.	kg/hr. per machine	Cap. (kg/hr.)	Cap. (kg/wk.)	Demand (kg/wk.)	Over/Under Capacity	
Peeling	275	kg/hr.	2	275	550	44 000	36 000	8 000	kg
Slicing	680	kg/hr.	1	680	680	54 400	36 000	18 400	kg
Cooking	115	kg/hr.	2	115	230	18 400	36 000	(17 600)	kg
Pack (50g)	160	pkgs/min.	2	480	960	38 400	21 000	17 400	kg
Pack (250g)	30	pkgs/min.	1	450	450	18 000	15 000	3 000	kg
Carton (50g)	5	ctns/min.	1	360	360	14 400	21 000	(6 600)	kg
Carton (250g)	4	ctns/min.	1	720	720	28 800	15 000	13 800	kg

=(C20*12*250*60)/1000

=E20*F20

=40*G20

=H20-I20

c. The bottlenecks are the cooking stage and the cartoning of the 50 g packages, because the demand in each case exceeds the available capacity.

d. Add two additional fryers for cooking the potatoes, and one additional operation for putting the 50 g package into cartons.

Problems

1. Your parents are visiting you, and you decide to take them out to dinner at a fancy restaurant. As you drive up to the restaurant, a parking attendant greets you and takes your car to the parking lot. Upon entering the restaurant, you give your name to the hostess, who tells you there will be a short wait. You go into the lounge where you order drinks. Your name is called shortly thereafter, and you are seated in the main dining room where all of you enjoy your meal.

   a. Draw a service blueprint for your visit to this restaurant. Be sure to include the line of visibility and identify all of the processes associated with your visit.

   b. Identify what you think are the strengths and weaknesses of this process.

2. You have just dropped your car off at the local gas station for an oil change and tune-up. When you pick up your car, you drive up to a gas pump and fill up. You then pay for the gas and the work that you had done. Draw a service blueprint for your visit to this gas station, including the line of visibility.

3. As the regional manager of a small chain of pizza stores, you have just received the following data from two of your locations:

	Store A	Store B
Sales (week)	$8 500	$12 500
Number of customers (week)	2 150	4 175
Total labour hours worked (week)	440	535
Total square metres of operation	128	165

   a. Define at least three measures of productivity for these two operations and calculate the productivity for each of these measures for the two stores.

    b. Based on these productivity measures, briefly analyze and compare these two operations.

    c. What might be some of the reasons for the differences in productivity?

4. The Churchill Popcorn Company produces high-quality gourmet popcorn that is delivered to independently owned specialty food shops. Currently, the weekly demand is 6000 cartons of 100 g bags and 5000 cartons of 400 g packages. (There are twenty-four 100 g packages and twelve 400 g packages per carton.) The facility where the popcorn is made operates on a five-day-a-week, eight-hour-a-day schedule. Currently, this facility has the following equipment and respective capacities:

Equipment	Capacity	Batch Time	Number
Corn popper	40 kg/batch	6 min	3
Packaging (100 g)	40 pkgs/min		2
Packaging (400 g)	20 pkgs/min		1
Carton operation (100 g)	1 min/carton		2
Carton operation (400 g)	1 min/carton		2

    a. Draw a process flow chart for producing and packaging the popcorn.

    b. Determine the capacity utilization of each stage in the process when the daily demand is produced, and identify any bottlenecks that exist.

    c. If bottleneck(s) do exist, what are your recommendations for meeting the daily demand?

5. Speedy Tax Service offers low-cost tax preparation services in many locations throughout Prince Edward Island. To efficiently expedite a client's tax return, Speedy's operations manager has established the following process: Upon entering a tax preparation location, each client is greeted by a receptionist who, through a series of short questions, can determine which type of tax service the client needs. This takes about five minutes. Clients are then referred to either a professional tax specialist, if their tax return is complicated, or a tax preparation associate, if the return is relatively simple. The average time for a tax specialist to complete a return is one hour; the average time for an associate to complete a return is 30 minutes. During the peak of tax season, an office is typically staffed by six specialists and three associates, and is open 10 hours a day. After the tax returns have been completed, the clients are then directed to see a cashier (there are two at each location) to pay for having their tax return prepared. This takes about six minutes per client to complete. During the peak of tax season, an average of 100 clients per day come into a location, of which 70 percent require the services of a tax specialist.

    a. Draw a flow chart for the above process.

    b. Identify any bottleneck(s) that exist during tax season.

    c. Calculate the average client throughput times (assuming there is no waiting) for a client seeing a specialist and for a client seeing an associate.

6. The Dainty Donuts Store has both a take-out section and an eat-in area. The take-out section consists of four stations, and there are 10 seats in the eating area. The average take-out order takes about three minutes to fill. The average eat-in customer consumes his or her coffee and donut(s) in an average time of 12 minutes, although the server is only required to spend two minutes to complete these orders. The peak hour of the day is from 7:00 a.m.–8:00 a.m., during which approximately 100 customers will typically arrive. Of these, 60 percent are take-out orders.

    a. To prevent worker burn-out, management believes that worker utilization should not exceed 80 percent. Using this criterion, how many workers should be scheduled during the peak hour of 7:00 a.m.–8:00 a.m.?

   b. Determine the capacity utilization for both the take-out counters and the seats during this peak period.

7. The walk-in clinic at a hospital in a U.S. city has received a grant from the state government to analyze how well it is treating its patients. To conduct this analysis, a business student has been hired to identify and define the various steps required to process a patient through the clinic. Her report contains the following information:

> Upon entering the clinic, each patient is given a form to complete, which takes about five minutes, and then has to wait an additional three minutes before being seen by a triage nurse, who assesses the severity of the patient's illness. This step in the process takes about two minutes per patient. Based on the nurse's evaluation, the patient is assigned to see either a doctor or a nurse practitioner or is sent immediately to the hospital's emergency room.
>
> Patients assigned to see a doctor wait an average of about 12 minutes before actually seeing the doctor. The average treatment time with a doctor is 15 minutes. Patients directed to nurse practitioners wait an average of 18 minutes. With nurse practitioners, the average treatment time is 17 minutes.
>
> Following treatment by either the doctor or nurse practitioner, each patient then must check out with a cashier to settle how they are going to pay for their visit. The wait to see a cashier is five minutes, and the time spent with the cashier is approximately six minutes.

   a. What is the average throughput time in the walk-in clinic for a patient seeing a doctor? For a patient seeing a nurse practitioner? For a patient who is transferred to the emergency room?

   b. Determine the process velocity for a patient seeing a doctor and for a patient seeing a nurse practitioner.

Case 1   Kristen's Cookie Company (A)

You and your roommate are preparing to start Kristen's Cookie Company in your on-campus apartment. The company will provide fresh cookies to starving students late at night. You need to evaluate the preliminary design for the company's production process to figure out many variables, including what prices to charge, whether you will be able to make a profit, and how many orders to accept.

Business Concept

Your idea is to bake fresh cookies to order, using any combination of ingredients that the buyer wants. The cookies will be ready for pickup at your apartment within an hour.

Several factors will set you apart from competing products such as store-bought cookies. First, your cookies will be completely fresh. You will not bake any cookies before receiving the order; therefore, the buyer will be getting cookies that are literally hot out of the oven.

Second, like Steve's Ice Cream,[1] you will have a variety of ingredients available to add to the basic dough, including chocolate chips, M&M's, Crispy Crunch bars, coconut, walnuts, and raisins. Buyers will telephone in their orders and specify which of these ingredients they want in their cookies. You guarantee completely fresh cookies. In short, you will have the freshest, most exotic cookies anywhere, available right on campus.

The Production Process

Baking cookies is simple: mix all the ingredients in a food processor; spoon out the

---

[1] Steve's Ice Cream was started in the Boston area by a young entrepreneur to provide make-to-order ice cream, using mix-ins.

cookie dough onto a tray; put the cookies into the oven; bake them; take the tray of cookies out of the oven; let the cookies cool; and, finally, take the cookies off the tray and carefully pack them in a box. You and your roommate already own all the necessary capital equipment: one food processor, cookie trays, and spoons. Your apartment has a small oven that will hold one tray at a time. Your landlord pays for all the electricity. The variable costs, therefore, are merely the cost of the ingredients (estimated to be $.60/dozen), the cost of the box in which the cookies are packed ($.10 per box; each box holds a dozen cookies), and your time (what value do you place on your time?).

A detailed examination of the production process, which specifies how long each of the steps will take, follows. The first step is to take an order, which your roommate has figured out how to do quickly and with 100 percent accuracy. (Actually, you and your roommate devised a method using the Internet to accept orders and to inform customers when their orders will be ready for pickup. Because this runs automatically on your personal computer, it does not take any of your time.) Therefore, this step will be ignored in further analysis.

You and your roommate have timed the necessary physical operations. The first physical production step is to wash out the mixing bowl from the previous batch, add all of the ingredients, and mix them in your food processor. The mixing bowls hold ingredients for up to three dozen cookies. You then dish up the cookies, one dozen at a time, onto a cookie tray. These activities take six minutes for the washing and mixing steps, regardless of how many cookies are being made in the batch. That is, to mix enough dough and ingredients for two dozen cookies takes the same six minutes as one dozen cookies. However, dishing up the cookies onto the tray takes two minutes per tray.

The next step, performed by your roommate, is to put the cookies in the oven and set the thermostat and timer, which takes about one minute. The cookies bake for the next nine minutes. So total baking time is 10 minutes, during the first minute of which your roommate is busy setting the oven. Because

the oven only holds one tray, a second dozen takes an additional 10 minutes to bake.

Your roommate also performs the last steps of the process by first removing the cookies from the oven and putting them aside to cool for five minutes, then carefully packing them in a box and accepting payment. Removing the cookies from the oven takes only a negligible amount of time, but it must be done promptly. It takes two minutes to pack each dozen and about one minute to accept payment for the order.

That is the process for producing cookies by the dozen in Kristen's Cookie Company. As experienced bakers know, a few simplifications were made in the actual cookie production process. For example, the first batch of cookies for the night requires preheating the oven. However, such complexities will be put aside for now. Begin your analysis by developing a process flow diagram of the cookie-making process.

Key Questions to Answer Before You Launch the Business To launch the business, you need to set prices and rules for accepting orders. Some issues will be resolved only after you get started and try out different ways of producing the cookies. Before you start, however, you at least want a preliminary plan, with as much as possible specified, so that you can do a careful calculation of how much time you will have to devote to this business each night, and how much money you can expect to make. For example, when you conduct a market survey to determine the likely demand, you will want to specify exactly what your order policies will be.

Therefore, answering the following operational questions should help you:

1. How long will it take you to fill a rush order?

2. How many orders can you fill in a night, assuming you are open four hours each night?

3. How much of your own and your roommate's valuable time will it take to fill each order?

4. Because your baking trays can hold exactly one dozen cookies, you will

produce and sell cookies by the dozen. Should you give any discount for people who order two dozen cookies, three dozen cookies, or more? If so, how much? Will it take you any longer to fill a two-dozen cookie order than a one-dozen cookie order?

5. How many food processors and baking trays will you need?

6. Are there any changes you can make in your production plans that will allow you to make better cookies or more cookies in less time or at lower cost? For example, is there a bottleneck operation in your production process that you can expand cheaply? What is the effect of adding another oven? How much would you be willing to pay to rent an additional oven?

Problems for Further Thought

1. What happens if you are trying to do this by yourself without a roommate?

2. Should you offer special rates for rush orders? Suppose you have just put a tray of cookies into the oven and someone calls up with a "crash priority" order for a dozen cookies of a different flavour.

Can you fill the priority order while still fulfilling the order for the cookies that are already in the oven? If not, how much of a premium should you charge for filling the rush order?

3. When should you promise delivery? How can you look quickly at your order board (list of pending orders) and tell a caller when his or her order will be ready? How much of a safety margin for timing should you allow?

4. What other factors should you consider at this stage of planning your business?

5. Your product must be made to order because each order is potentially unique. If you decide to sell standard cookies instead, how should you change the production system? The order-taking process?

Source:

Copyright 1986 by the President and Fellows of Harvard College, Harvard Business School.

Case 9-686-093. This case was prepared by Roger Bohn with the assistance of K. Somers and G. Greenberg as the basis for class discussion rather than to illustrate either effective or ineffective handling of an administrative situation. Reprinted by permission of the Harvard Business School.

S5

Work Performance Measurement

Supplement Objectives

- Introduce the more common types of work methods practised in the workplace.

- Understand the fundamental issues involved in developing work measurements.

- Identify the basic elements associated with conducting a time study.

- Determine how to design a work sampling study and apply it to an actual operation.

Work needs to be properly designed and measured, regardless of the type of organization in which it is done, be it manufacturing or services. The proper design of work ensures that tasks are completed with a minimum of wasted effort. Proper work design, as discussed in the previous chapter, also ensures that the work is accomplished without causing injury to the employee.

Work measurement is equally important for several reasons. First, it is used to determine the labour cost, which is usually a major component of the overall cost of producing a good or a service. Second, knowing how long it takes to complete a specific task or assignment provides management with the ability to determine the number of workers needed to meet a given level of demand. For example, the number of customer service representatives that Aliant, a major telecommunications provider in Atlantic Canada, needs at its call centres is dependent on the demand as expressed by the number of calls it receives daily and the length of time to process each call, which is referred to as the average handling time (AHT). A third reason for work measurement is to identify those workers who are meeting or exceeding standards and who should be appropriately recognized and rewarded. It also identifies those who fall below the standards and require additional training.

In the early part of this century, beginning with Frederick W. Taylor and continuing with Frank and Lillian Gilbreth, work measurements were done almost exclusively in manufacturing companies. Although the specific methodology associated with work measurement has basically not changed since its inception with Taylor, the manner in which work measurements are conducted and used has changed significantly (see OM in Practice: Work Measurement Then and Now).

Work Methods

An integral part in the development and design of processes is the definition of the tasks that must be accomplished. But how should these tasks be done? Years ago, production workers were craftspeople who had their own (sometimes secret) methods for doing things. However, over time products became more complicated, as mechanization of a higher order was introduced, and output rates increased. As a result, the responsibility for work methods has been transferred to management. It is no longer logical or economically feasible to allow individual workers to produce the same product by different methods. Work specialization brought much of the concept of craftwork to an end, as less-skilled workers were employed to do the simpler tasks.

In some large companies, the responsibility for developing work methods is typically assigned to either a staff department designated *methods analysis* or an industrial engineering department; in small firms this activity is often performed by consulting firms that specialize in work methods design. However, as illustrated in the OM in Practice example, more firms are allowing their workers to design their own jobs and also to determine how long they should take.

The principal approach to the study of work methods is the construction of charts, such as operations charts, worker-machine charts, simo (simultaneous motion) charts, and activity charts, in conjunction with time-study or standard-time data. The choice of which charting method to use depends on the activity level of the task; that is, whether the focus is on (*a*) the overall operation, (*b*) the worker at a fixed workplace, (*c*) a worker interacting with equipment, or (*d*) a worker interacting with other workers (see Exhibit S5.1).

Overall Operation

The objective in studying the overall production system is to identify non-value-added time delays, transport distances, processes, and processing time requirements, with the goal of simplifying the entire operation. The primary objective here is to eliminate any step in the process that does not add value to the product. The approach is to develop a process flow chart and then ask the following questions:

What is done? Must it be done? What would happen if it were not done?

Where is the task done? Must it be done at that location or could it be done somewhere else?

When is the task done? Is it critical that it be done then or is there flexibility in time and sequence? Could it be done in combination with some other step in the process?

Exhibit S5.1

Work Methods and Design Aids

Activity	Objective of Study	Study Techniques
Overall production system	Eliminate or combine steps; shorten transport distance; identify delays	Flow diagram, service blueprint, process chart
Worker at fixed workplace	Simplify method; minimize motions	Operations charts, simo charts; apply principles of motion economy
Worker interacts with equipment	Minimize idle time; find number or combination of machines to balance cost of worker and machine idle time	Activity chart, worker-machine charts
Worker interacts with other workers	Maximize productivity, minimize interference	Activity charts, gang process charts

Operations Management in Practice

WORK MEASUREMENT THEN AND NOW

Job Design Then . . .

Frederick W. Taylor recounts his "motivation" of his trusty worker, Schmidt (in *Principles of Scientific Management,* 1910):

> "Schmidt, are you a high-priced man?"
>
> "Vell, I don't know vat you mean."
>
> "Oh yes you do. What I want to know is whether you are a high-priced man or not. . . . What I want to find out is whether you want to earn $1.85 a day or whether you are satisfied with $1.15, just the same as all those cheap fellows are getting?"
>
> "Vell, yes I vas a high-priced man."
>
> "Now come over here. You see that pile of pig iron?"
>
> "Yes."
>
> "You see that car?"
>
> "Yes."
>
> "Well, if you are a high-priced man, you will load that pig iron on that car tomorrow for $1.85."
>
> "You see that man over there? . . . Well, if you are a high-priced man, you will do exactly as this man tells you tomorrow, from morning till night. When he tells you to pick up a pig and walk, you pick it up and you walk, and when he tells you to sit down and rest, you sit down. You do that straight through the day. And what's more, no back talk."

And Now . . .

Researcher Jacques Bélanger studied job control at a unionized Canadian transportation equipment plant. General control by management involved fragmenting the manufacturing process into relatively short operations. Based on work measurements, technicians grouped the various operations into eight-hour jobs. The workers, however, had much discretion over execution. They could re-group the tasks and re-sequence them in the most economical way to reduce the non-value added time as much as possible. This sometimes also involved sharing or redistributing some tasks among two or more working group members. The uniqueness of the system was that once the workers had finished the eight-hour job, though they could not leave the factory, they could use any remaining shift time for leisure activities. This method of balanced control, which gives labour autonomy and social reward, has contributed to a high level of productivity at the factory.

Source:

J. Bélanger, "Job Control and Productivity: New Evidence from Canada," *British Journal of Industrial Relations*, 27, no. 3 (1989), pp. 347–364; "Return of the Stopwatch," The Economist (January 23, 1993), p. 69.

How is the task done? Why is it done this way? Is there another way?

Who does the task? Can someone else do it? Should the worker be of a higher or lower skill level?

These types of questions usually help to eliminate much unnecessary work, as well as to simplify the remaining work, by combining a number of processing steps and changing the order of performance.

Use of the process chart is valuable in studying an overall operation, though care must be taken to follow the same item throughout the process. The subject may be a product being manufactured, a service being provided, or a person performing a sequence of activities. An example of a process chart (and flow diagram) for a clerical operation is shown in Exhibit S5.2. Common notation in process charting is given in Exhibit S5.3.

Worker at a Fixed Workplace

There are many jobs that require workers to remain at a specified workstation to complete their assigned tasks. This applies to both manufacturing and services. When the nature of the work is primarily manual (such as sorting, inspecting, making entries, or assembly operations), the focus of work design is on simplifying the work method and making the required operator motions as few and as simple as possible.

The same concepts also apply to services. For example, a customer service representative at a call centre is trained to ask specific questions in a given order so that a customer's inquiry is processed as efficiently as possible. With services, however, the issue is further complicated by the presence of the customer in the process. Here efficiency cannot be achieved at the expense of angering the customer, who may perceive an efficient operator as being curt or rude.

There are two basic ways to determine the best method for performing an essentially manual task. The first is to search among the various workers performing that task and find

Exhibit S5.2

Flow Diagram and Process Chart of an Office Procedure— Present Method*

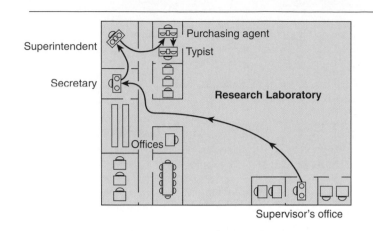

Superintendent

Purchasing agent

Typist

Secretary

Research Laboratory

Offices

Supervisor's office

Present Method ☒ Proposed Method ☐	**PROCESS CHART**
SUBJECT CHARTED Requisition for small tools	DATE _____
Chart begins at supervisor's desk and ends at	CHART BY J.C.H.
typist's desk in purchasing department	CHART NO. R136
DEPARTMENT Research laboratory	SHEET NO. 1 OF 1

DIST. IN FEET	TIME IN MINS.	CHART SYMBOLS	PROCESS DESCRIPTION
		●⇨□D▽	Requisitions written by supervisor (one copy)
		O⇨□▶▽	On supervisor's desk (awaiting messenger)
65		O◀□D▽	By messenger to superintendent's secretary
		O⇨□▶▽	On secretary's desk (awaiting typing)
		●⇨□D▽	Requisition typed (original requisition copied)
15		O◀□D▽	By secretary to superintendent
		O⇨□▶▽	On superintendent's desk (awaiting approval)
		O⇨■D▽	Examined and approved
		O⇨□▶▽	On superintendent's desk (awaiting messenger)
20		O◀□D▽	To purchasing department
		O⇨□▶▽	On purchasing agent's desk (awaiting approval)
		O⇨■D▽	Examined and approved
		O⇨□▶▽	On purchasing agent's desk (awaiting messenger)
5		O◀□D▽	To typist's desk
		O⇨□▶▽	On typist's desk (awaiting typing of purchase order)
		●⇨□D▽	Purchase order typed
		O⇨□▶▽	On typist's desk (awaiting transfer to main office)
		O⇨□D▽	
105		3 4 2 8	Total

*Requisition is written by supervisor, typed by secretary, approved by superintendent, and approved by purchasing agent; then a purchase order is prepared by a stenographer.

Source: Ralph M. Barnes, *Motion and Time Study*, 8th ed. (New York: John Wiley & Sons, 1980), pp. 76–79. Copyright © John Wiley & Sons. This material is used by permission of John Wiley & Sons, Inc.

Exhibit S5.3

Common Notation in Process Charting

the one who performs the job best. That person's method is then accepted as the standard, and the other workers are trained to perform it in the same way. This was basically F. W. Taylor's approach. The second method is to observe the performance of a number of workers, analyze in detail each step of their work, and pick out the superior features of each worker's performance. This results in a composite method that combines the best elements of the group studied. This was the procedure used by Frank Gilbreth, the father of motion study, to determine the "one best way" to perform a work task.

Taylor observed actual performance to find the best method; Frank Gilbreth and his wife Lillian relied on movie film. Through micromotion analysis—observing the filmed work performance frame by frame—the Gilbreths studied work very closely and defined its basic elements, which was termed **therbligs** ("Gilbreth" spelled backward, with the *t* and *h* transposed). They also used the motion model—a wire representation of the path of a motion. Their study led to the rules or principles of motion economy listed in Exhibit S5.4.

Once the various motions for performing a task have been identified, an *operations chart* is then developed, listing the individual operations and their sequence of performance. For greater detail, a *simo* (simultaneous motion) *chart* may be constructed, listing not only the operations but also the times for both left and right hands. This chart may be assembled from the data collected with a stopwatch, from analysis of a film of the operation, or from predetermined motion-time data (such as developed by the Gilbreths, discussed later in this chapter). Many aspects of poor design become immediately obvious with this technique—a hand being used as a holding device (rather than a jig or fixture), an idle hand, or an exceptionally long time for positioning.

therbligs
Basic units of measurement used in micromotion analysis.

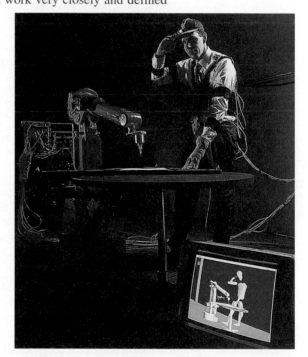

Worker Interacting with Equipment

When a person and equipment operate together to perform a given set of tasks, interest focuses on the efficient use of both the person's time and the equipment's time. When the working time of the operator is less than the equipment run time, a worker-machine chart is a useful device in analysis. If the operator can operate several pieces of equipment, the problem is to find the most economical combination of

Software from Deneb Robotics is designed to help companies strategically plan to meet production goals. Wearing a harness with 11 sensors, Brian Christensen of Deneb demonstrates software that helps engineers maximize efficiency on a production line by coordinating movements of humans and robots that work side by side (see the monitor).

Using the human body the way it works best:
1. The work should be arranged to provide a natural rhythm that can become automatic.
2. The symmetrical nature of the body should be considered:
   a. The motions of the arms should be simultaneous, beginning and completing their motions at the same time.
   b. Motions of the arms should be opposite and symmetrical.
3. The human body is an ultimate machine and its full capabilities should be employed:
   a. Neither hand should ever be idle.
   b. Work should be distributed to other parts of the body in line with their ability.
   c. The safe design limits of the body should be observed.
   d. The human should be employed at its highest use.
4. The arms and hands as weights are subject to the physical laws, and energy should be conserved:
   a. Momentum should work for the person and not against him or her.
   b. The smooth, continuous arc of the ballistic is more efficient.
   c. The distance of movements should be minimized.
   d. Tasks should be turned over to machines.
5. The tasks should be simplified:
   a. Eye contacts should be few and grouped together.
   b. Unnecessary actions, delays, and idle time should be eliminated.
   c. The degree of required precision and control should be reduced.
   d. The number of individual motions should be minimized along with the number of muscle groups involved.

Arranging the workplace to assist performance:
1. There should be a definite place for all tools and materials.
2. Tools, materials, and controls should be located close to the point of use.
3. Tools, materials, and controls should be located to permit the best sequence and path of motions.

Using mechanical devices to reduce human effort:
1. Vises and clamps can hold the work precisely where needed.
2. Guides can assist in positioning the work without close operator attention.
3. Controls and foot-operated devices can relieve the hands of work.
4. Mechanical devices can multiply human abilities.
5. Mechanical systems should be fitted to human use.

Source: Frank C. Barnes, "Principles of Motion Economy: Revisited, Reviewed, and Restored,"
Proceedings of the Southern Management Association Annual Meeting, Atlanta, GA, 1983,
p. 298. Reprinted by permission.

operator and equipment, such that the combined cost of the idle time of the equipment and the idle time for the worker are at a minimum.

Worker-machine charts are always drawn to scale, the scale being time as measured by length. Exhibit S5.5 gives an example of a worker-machine chart in a service setting.

With many services, however, the "machine" that the worker interacts with often is a computer, which is simultaneously providing and collecting information (as in the case of making an airline or hotel reservation). In designing these types of processes, the goal is to provide the necessary information as quickly as possible to both the worker and the customer, and also to provide a format for collecting customer data that is both accurate and fast. This is accomplished by having significantly large computer capacity, which is relatively inexpensive in comparison to the cost of the worker.

Workers Interacting with Other Workers

Increasingly, work in both manufacturing and services is being performed by teams. The degree of interaction may be as simple as one operator handing a part to another, or as complex as a cardiovascular surgical team consisting of doctors, nurses, an anesthesiologist,

	PERSON				MACHINE	
	Customer	Time in sec.	Clerk	Time in sec.	Coffee Grinder	Time in sec.
0	1. Ask grocer for 500 g of coffee (brand and grind)	5	Listen to order	5	Idle	5
10	2. Wait	15	Get coffee and put in machine, set grind, and start grinder	15	Idle	15
20 / 30	3. Wait	21	Idle while machine grinds	21	Grind coffee	21
40 / 50	4. Wait	12	Stop grinder, place coffee in package, and close it	12	Idle	12
60 / 70	5. Receive coffee from grocer, pay grocer, and receive change	17	Give coffee to customer, wait for customer to pay for coffee, receive money, and make change	17	Idle	17

Summary

	Customer	Clerk	Coffee grinder
Idle time	48 sec.	21 sec.	49 sec.
Working time	22	49	21
Total cycle time	70	70	70
Utilization as a percentage	Customer utilization = $\frac{22}{70} \approx 31\%$	Clerk utilization = $\frac{49}{70} = 70\%$	Machine utilization = $\frac{21}{70} = 30\%$

The customer, the clerk, and the coffee grinder (machine) are involved in this operation. It required 1 minute and 10 seconds for the customer to purchase 500 g of coffee in this particular store. During this time the customer spent 22 seconds, or 31 percent of the time, giving the clerk his order, receiving the ground coffee, and paying the clerk for it. He was idle during the remaining 69 percent of the time. The clerk worked 49 seconds, or 70 percent of the time, and was idle 21 seconds, or 30 percent of the time. The coffee grinder was in operation 21 seconds, or 30 percent of the time, and was idle 70 percent of the time.

the operator of the artificial heart machine, an X-ray technician, standby blood donors, and the pathologist (and perhaps a minister to pray a little).

To facilitate analysis of team efforts, an activity or a gang process chart is used to plot the activities of each individual on a time scale similar to that of the worker-machine chart. A gang process chart is usually employed to trace the interaction of a number of workers with machines of a specified operating cycle, to find the best combination of workers and machines. An activity chart is less restrictive and may be used to follow the interaction of any group of operators, with or without equipment being involved. Such charts are often

Exhibit S5.6

Activity Chart of Emergency Tracheotomy

Time in minutes	Nurse	First Doctor	Orderly	Second doctor	Nurse supervisor	Scrub nurse	
0	Detects problem; notifies doctor						0
1							1
2	Gets mobile cart						2
3		Makes diagnosis					3
4							4
5	Notifies nurse supervisor						5
6	Notifies second doctor	Assists patient to breathe			Opens OR; calls scrub nurse		6
7	Notifies orderly			Assures availability of laryngoscope and endotracheal tube			7
8	Moves patient to OR	Moves to OR	Moves patient to OR			Moves to OR; sets up equipment	8
9		Scrubs					9
10		Dons gown and gloves		Operates laryngoscope and inserts endotracheal tube			10
11							11
12		Performs tracheotomy		Calls for IPPB machine			12
13							13
14							14
15							15
16							16

Source: Data taken from Harold E. Smalley and John Freeman, *Hospital Industrial Engineering* (New York: Reinhold, 1966), p. 409.

used to study and define each operator in an ongoing repetitive process, and they are extremely valuable in developing a standardized procedure for a specific task. Exhibit S5.6, for example, shows an activity chart for a hospital's emergency routine in performing a tracheotomy (an operation for opening a patient's throat surgically to allow him or her to breathe), where detailed activity analysis is of major importance because any unnecessary delay could be fatal.

Work Measurement

work measurement

Methodology used for establishing time standards.

The subject of **work measurement** for establishing time standards has been controversial since the days of Taylor. With the widespread adoption of Deming's ideas (see Chapter 6), it has become the subject of renewed criticism. (Deming argued that work standards and quotas inhibit process improvement, focusing all of the worker's efforts on speed rather than quality.) Nevertheless, all organizations need some form of standard time estimates for planning and budgeting, and many companies use them with success in work design.

Type of Work	Major Methods of Determining Task Time
Very short interval, highly repetitive	Videotape analysis
Short interval, repetitive	Stopwatch time study: predetermined motion-time data
Task in conjunction with machinery or other fixed-processing-time equipment	Elemental data
Infrequent work or work of a long cycle time	Work sampling

It is therefore important to understand the basic industrial engineering methods used to set standards:

1. Time study (stopwatch and micromotion analysis).
2. Elemental standard time data.
3. Predetermined motion-time data.
4. Work sampling.

Each method has its advantages over the others and has particular areas of application. Exhibit S5.7 lists these methods and relates them to a general class of jobs.

Time Study

A **time study** is generally conducted with a stopwatch, either on the job site or by analyzing a videotape of the job. Procedurally, the job or task to be studied is separated into measurable parts or elements, and each element is timed individually. After a number of repetitions, the collected times are averaged. (The standard deviation may be computed to give a measure of variance in the performance times.) The averaged times for each element are then added together, and the result is the observed performance time for the operator. However, to make this operator's time applicable to all workers, a measure of speed, which is expressed as a *performance rating* and which reflects how hard the observed operator is working, also must be included to "normalize" the job. The application of a rating factor provides what is called *normal time.*

time study
Determination, with use of a stopwatch, of how long it takes to complete a task or set of tasks.

Example

An industrial engineer conducts a time study on an operator and determines that a specific task takes about two minutes to complete. The engineer estimates that the particular operator that she is observing is working about 20 percent faster than normal. The company has an allowance factor of 15 percent of job time for personal needs, delays, and fatigue. Calculate the standard time for this task.

Solution

Normal time = Observed performance time per unit ($\overline{T}$) × Performance rating

In this example, denoting normal time by NT,

$NT = 2(1.2) = 2.4$ minutes

When an operator is observed over a long period of time, the number of units produced during this time, along with the performance rating, gives the normal time as

$$NT = \frac{\text{Total time observed}}{\text{Number of units produced}} \times \text{Performance rating}$$

Standard time is derived by adding allowances to normal time. These allowances include personal needs (washroom and coffee breaks, and so forth), unavoidable work delays (equipment breakdown, lack of materials, and so forth), and worker fatigue (physical or mental). There are two equations for calculating standard time:

Standard time = Normal Time + (Allowance × Normal time)

or

$$ST = NT(1 + \text{Allowances}) \tag{S5.1}$$

and

$$ST = \frac{NT}{1 - \text{Allowances}} \tag{S5.2}$$

Equation S5.1 is used most often in practice. Here the allowances are stated as a percentage of the "job time." In other words, the allowance factor is added to the job time to obtain the standard time. However, if the allowances are stated as a percentage of the total "work time," then Equation S5.2 is the correct one to use.

In this example, the normal time to perform a task is 2.4 minutes and the allowances for personal needs, delays, and fatigue total 15 percent of the job time; then by Equation S5.1,

$$ST = 2.4(1 + 0.15) = 2.76 \text{ minutes}$$

In an eight-hour day, a worker would produce 8 × 60/2.76 = 174 units. This implies 174 × 2.4 minutes per unit (normal time) = 417.6 minutes working and 480 − 417.6 = 62.4 minutes for allowances.

However, if the allowance factor is stated as a percentage of the total work time, then we would use Equation S5.2:

$$ST = \frac{2.4}{1 - 0.15} = 2.82 \text{ minutes}$$

In the same eight-hour day, using Equation S5.2, 8 × 60/2.82 (or 170) units are produced with 408 working minutes and 72 minutes for allowances. Depending on how the allowance factor is specified, there is a difference of four units produced and also approximately 10 minutes in the daily allowance time.

Work measurement is particularly important when workers are paid by the amount of work they actually complete, referred to as *piece-rate*. Using the above example, if the hourly rate for an employee is $12.00 per hour, then that employee, if on piece-rate, would be paid as follows:

60/2.82 = 21.277 pieces per hour is the standard.

$12.00 per hour/21.277 per hour = $0.564/piece.

Thus, a person working at 100 percent of standard would earn $12.00 per hour; a person working at 110 percent of standard would earn $13.20 per hour.

A major problem with the piece-rate system is that it tends to reward quantity at the expense of quality. As a result, firms that have adopted the piece-rate system usually will pay only for good parts that are produced.

Before a time study is conducted, each task is broken down into elements or parts. Some general rules for the breakdown of a task are:

1. Define each work element to be short in duration but sufficiently long enough so that each can be timed with a stopwatch and the time written down.

2. If the operator works with equipment that runs separately—the operator performs a task and the equipment runs independently—separate the actions of the operator and that of the equipment into different elements.

3. Define any delays by the operator or equipment into separate elements.

How many observations are enough? Time study is really a sampling process; that is, we take a relatively small number of observations as being representative of many subsequent cycles to be performed by the worker. A great deal of analysis and experience indicates that the number of observations is a function of cycle length and the number of repetitions of the job over a one-year planning period.

Elemental Standard-Time Data

Elemental standard-time data are obtained from previous time studies and codified in tables in a handbook or computer data bank. Such data are used to develop time standards for new jobs or to make time adjustments to reflect changes in existing jobs. They are more correctly viewed as normal-time data, because tabled values have been modified by an average performance rating, and allowances must be added to obtain a standard time.

Calculating a **time standard** for a new job using elemental standard-time data tables entails the following steps:

1. Break down the new job into its basic elements.

2. Match these elements to the time for similar elements in the table.

3. Adjust element times for special characteristics of the new job. (In metal cutting, for example, this is often done by a formula that modifies the time required as a function of type of metal, size of the cutting tool, depth of the cut, and so forth.)

4. Add element times together and add delay and fatigue allowances as specified by company policy for the given class of work.

The obvious benefit of elemental standard data is cost savings because it eliminates the need for a new time study every time there is a new job. This saves staff time and avoids disruption of the workforce. The main practical requirement of the approach is that the elemental data must be kept up to date and easily accessible.

time standard
Established time for completing a job, used in determining labour costs associated with making a product.

Predetermined Motion-Time Data

As with elemental standard-time data, predetermined motion-time data tables create a time standard for a job or task. There are, however, significant differences between the two approaches. Whereas the elemental standard-time data tables provide times for job-specific work elements, the predetermined motion-time data tables provide times for basic motions such as a "reach of a given length" or "the grasp of an object of a given weight." These motions, in their most basic elements, can be defined in terms of therbligs, which were described earlier in this chapter. Because they are generic in nature, predetermined motion-time data can be applied to a wide range of manual tasks. By comparison, the elemental standard-time data tables typically are specific to a given company or industry.

Work Sampling

Whereas work measurement is concerned with how long it takes to perform a specific task or activity, **work sampling** is primarily concerned with how workers spend their time among

work sampling
Technique for estimating how workers allocate their time among various activities throughout a workday.

several tasks or activities. For example, we may want to know how much time workers spend on indirect activities such as material handling to determine whether or not more cost-efficient material handling equipment should be purchased. In a hotel reservation call centre, we would want to know what percentage of time is actually spent on the telephone. Work sampling provides us with a method for determining the time spent on these activities, and involves observing a portion or sample of the work activity. Then, based on the findings in this sample, statements can be made about how the employee or employees spend their time.

For example, if we were to observe a fire department rescue squad 100 random times during the day and found that it was involved in a rescue mission for 30 of the 100 times (en route, on site, or returning from a call), we would estimate that the rescue squad spends approximately 30 percent of its time directly on rescue mission calls. (The time it takes to make an observation depends on what is being observed. Often only a glance is needed to determine the activity; the majority of studies require only several seconds' observation.)

Observing an activity even 100 times, however, may not provide the accuracy desired in the estimate. To refine this estimate, three main issues must be decided (these points are discussed later in this section, along with an example):

1.   What level of statistical confidence is desired in the results?
2.   How many observations are necessary?
3.   Precisely when should the observations be made?

The number of observations required in a work sampling study can be fairly large, ranging from several hundred to several thousand, depending on the activity and the desired degree of accuracy. The formula for computing the required number of observations is

$$N = \frac{Z^2 p(1-p)}{E^2} \tag{S5.3}$$

where

N = Number of observations to be made

Z = Number of standard deviations associated with a given confidence level

p = Estimated proportion of time that the activity being measured occurs

E = Absolute error that is desired

Example

For example, we want to determine what percentage of the time the front desk clerks at a hotel are idle. We want our results to be 95 percent confident within an error of 3 percent. Our initial estimate of the clerks' idle time is 20 percent.

In this example:

Z = 1.96 (corresponding to 95% confidence)

p = 0.20 (estimated percentage idle time)

E = 0.03 (absolute error)

Solution

Substituting these values into the above formula, we obtain the following:

$$N = \frac{(1.96)^2 (0.2)(1 - 0.2)}{(0.03)^2}$$

$$N = \frac{(3.84)(0.16)}{(0.0009)}$$

N = 682.95 or 683 observations. (*Note:* We always round up here to ensure that we meet the minimum requirements of the study.)

Thus, with the above work sampling study, we can state that we are 95 percent confident that the true percentage of time that the clerks are idle falls within 3 percent of the study results.

However, we don't always have an initial estimate of the proportion of time spent on a given activity (in fact, that is often why we are doing the work sampling study in the first place!). In these situations, we use $p = 0.5$ which will give us a worst case scenario. (If p is equal to anything other than 0.5 we have, in effect, overestimated the sample size.)

As an illustration, suppose in the above example we don't have an initial estimate for the proportion of time the front desk clerks are idle. In this case we would use $p = 0.5$, and the calculation of the sample size would be as follows:

$$N = \frac{(1.96)^2(0.5)(1-0.5)}{(0.03)^2}$$

$$N = \frac{(3.84)(0.25)}{(0.0009)}$$

$N = 1067.11$, or 1068 observations.

The specific steps involved in conducting a work sampling study are:

1. Identify the specific activity or activities that are the main purpose for the study. For example, determine the percentage of time equipment is working, idle, or under repair.

2. If possible, estimate the proportion of time of the activity of interest to the total time (e.g., the equipment is working 80 percent of the time). These estimates can be made from the analyst's knowledge, past data, reliable guesses from others, or a pilot work-sampling study. If no estimate can be made, assume, as stated above, that the proportion is 0.50.

3. State the desired accuracy in the study results.

4. Determine the specific times when each observation is to be made.

5. If you are using an estimated time, recompute the required sample size at two or three intervals during the study period by using the data collected thus far. Adjust the number of observations if appropriate.

The number of observations to be taken in a work sampling study is usually divided equally over the study period. Thus, if 500 observations are to be made over a 10-day period, the observations are usually scheduled at 500/10, or 50 per day. Each day's observations are then assigned a specific time by using a random number generator. The need to divide the observations equally over the data collection period is even more important in service operations, where workers can be extremely busy during certain periods and less busy at other times.

Example

There has been a long-standing argument that a large percentage of nurses' time in a hospital is spent on non-nursing activities. This, the argument goes, creates an apparent shortage of well-trained nursing personnel, a significant waste of talent, a corresponding loss of efficiency, and increased hospital costs because nurses' wages are the highest single cost in the operation of a hospital. Furthermore, pressure is growing for hospitals and hospital administrators to contain costs. With that in mind, let us use work sampling to test the hypothesis that a large portion of nurses' time is spent on non-nursing duties.

Assume at the outset that we have made a list of all the activities that are part of nursing and will make our observations in only two categories: nursing and non-nursing activities. (An expanded study could list all nursing activities to determine the portion of time spent in each.) Therefore, when we observe nurses during the study and find them performing one of the duties on the nursing list, we simply place a tally mark in the nursing column. If we observe a nurse doing anything besides nursing, we place a tally mark in the non-nursing column.

Solution

We now can proceed to design the work sampling study. Assume that we (or the nursing supervisor) estimate that nurses spend 60 percent of their time on nursing activities. Also assume that we would like to be 95 percent confident that the findings of our study are within the absolute error range of plus or minus 3 percent. In other words, if our study shows nurses spend 60 percent of their time on nursing duties, we are 95 percent confident that the true percentage lies between 57 and 63 percent. Using the above formula, we calculate that 1025 observations are required for 60 percent activity time and ±3 percent error. If our study is to take place over 10 days, we start with 103 observations per day.

To determine when each day's observations are to be made, we assign specific numbers to each minute and a random number table is used to set up a schedule. If the study extends over an eight-hour shift, we can assign numbers to correspond to each consecutive minute. The list in Exhibit S5.8 shows the assignment of numbers to corresponding minutes. For simplicity, because each number corresponds to one minute, a three-number scheme is used, with the second and third numbers corresponding to the minute of the hour. A number of other schemes also would be appropriate. (If a number of studies are planned, a computer program may be used to generate a randomized schedule for the observation times.)

If we refer to a random number table and list three-digit numbers, we can assign each number to a time. The random numbers shown in Exhibit S5.9 demonstrate the procedure for seven observations.

This procedure is followed to generate 103 observation times, and the times are rearranged chronologically for ease in planning. Rearranging the times determined in Exhibit S5.9 gives the total observations per day shown in Exhibit S5.10 (for our sample of seven).

To be perfectly random in this study, we also should "randomize" the nurse we observe each time (the use of various nurses minimizes the effect of bias). In this study, our first observation is made at 7:13 a.m. for Nurse X. We walk into the nurse's area and

Exhibit S5.8

Assignment of Numbers to Corresponding Minutes

Time	Assigned Numbers
7:00–7:59 a.m.	100–159
8:00–8:59 a.m.	200–259
9:00–9:59 a.m.	300–359
10:00–10:59 a.m.	400–459
11:00–11:59 a.m.	500–559
12:00–12:59 p.m.	600–659
1:00–1:59 p.m.	700–759
2:00–2:59 p.m.	800–859

Random Number	Corresponding Time from the Preceding List
669	Nonexistent
831	2:31 p.m.
555	11:55 a.m.
470	Nonexistent
113	7:13 a.m.
080	Nonexistent
520	11:20 a.m.
204	8:04 a.m.
732	1:32 p.m.
420	10:20 a.m.

Exhibit S5.9

Determination of Observation Times

Observation	Scheduled Time	Nursing Activity (✓)	Non-Nursing Activity (✓)
1	7:13 a.m.		
2	8:04 a.m.		
3	10:20 a.m.		
4	11:20 a.m.		
5	11:55 a.m.		
6	1:32 p.m.		
7	2:31 p.m.		

Exhibit S5.10

Observation Schedule

check either a nursing or a non-nursing activity, depending on what we observe. Each observation need be only long enough to determine the class of activity—in most cases only a glance. At 8:04 a.m. we observe Nurse Y. We continue in this way to the end of the day and the 103 observations. At the end of the second day (and 206 observations), we decide to check for the adequacy of our sample size.

Let's say that we made 150 observations of nurses working and 64 of them not working, which gives 70.1 percent working. Again, using the formula given above, we calculate that the required number of observations is now 895. Inasmuch as we have already taken 206 observations, we need to take only another 689 over the next eight days, or 86 per day. This recalculation of the sample size should be done several times during the data collection period.

If at the end of the study we find that 66 percent of nurses' time is involved with what has been defined as nursing activities, there should be an analysis to identify the remaining 34 percent. Approximately 12 to 15 percent is justifiable for coffee breaks and personal needs, which leaves 20 to 22 percent of the time that must be justified and compared to what the industry considers ideal levels of nursing activity. To identify the non-nursing activities, a more detailed breakdown could have been built into the sampling plan. Otherwise, a follow-up study might be in order.

ANATOMY OF SURGERY

"... I was transferred to the Military Hospital whose Surgical Division was headed by Colonel R. H. Rose-Innes and for some years came under the influence of this truly remarkable surgeon. It was he who taught me that every surgical instrument was designed for a purpose, and that if we used an instrument we should at least know what it was that prompted the designer to shape the instrument in the way he did. It was he who taught me that to waste movements during an operation was to waste time and to jeopardize the well being of the patient. It was this obsession not to waste movements and to use correct instruments and to discard what was unnecessary that has driven me since, constantly to try to improve upon the techniques of long ago handed down to us by our teachers. It was this same obsession that led to the use of instruments from all fields of surgery that were appropriate to the task to be done by that instrument; and finally it prompted the introduction of Time and Motion Studies into the operating theatre which led to a breakaway from the usually acceptable routines, and to the exploring of new ideas or ideas that were new to me and apparently new to a large number of colleagues from all over the world who have seen them done."

In his book, *Abdominal and Vaginal Hysterectomy: New Techniques Based on Time and Motion Studies*, Dr. Joel-Cohen also describes the suggested layout of the theatre, including where doctors, nurses, and equipment and instruments should be stationed. He also analyzes required pharmaceutical and other materials, and the steps in each type of surgery and in postoperative care.

Source:
S. Joel-Cohen, *Abdominal and Vaginal Hysterectomy: New Techniques Based on Time and Motion Studies* (London: William Heinemann Medical Books, 1977).

Conclusion

Most readers of this book will encounter questions of work methods and measurement in the service sector. It appears that in services, as well as in manufacturing, the new performance metric will be speed, achieved through improved work methods and teamwork. Interestingly enough, modern examples of work performance measurement epitomize some of the fundamental ideas that Fredrick W. Taylor introduced almost a century ago.

Key Terms

therbligs p. 169

time study p. 173

work sampling p. 175

time standard p. 175

work measurement p. 172

Review and Discussion Questions

1. Why are work measurement and time study activities still necessary today?
2. How do the latest approaches for determining time standards (as shown in the OM in Practice box on Taylor on page 167, fit with the concepts of worker empowerment and team work?
3. What are the major differences between work measurement and work sampling? What are the objectives in each case?
4. Is there an inconsistency when a company requires precise time standards and, at the same time, encourages job enrichment?
5. Automated systems such as voice recognition units (VCUs) increase the efficiency of a call centre, but what are the disadvantages of these systems?

Problem 1

Felix Unger is a very organized person and wants to plan his day perfectly. To do this, he has his friend Oscar time his daily activities. The following are the results of Oscar timing Felix on polishing two pairs of black shoes. What is the standard time for polishing one pair? (Assume a 5 percent allowance factor for Felix to get Oscar an ashtray for his cigar. Account for noncyclically recurring elements by dividing their observed times by the total number of cycles observed.) All times shown are in minutes.

Element	Observed Times Shoe 1	Shoe 2	Shoe 3	Shoe 4	Observed Time	$\bar{T}$	Performance Rating	NT
Get shoeshine kit	0.50						125%	
Polish each shoe	0.94	0.85	0.80	0.81			110	
Put away kit				0.75			80	

Solution

	Observed Time	$\bar{T}$	Performance Rating	NT
Get shoeshine kit	0.50	0.50/2 = 0.25	125%	0.31
Polish shoes (2 pair)	3.40	3.40/2 = 1.70	110	1.87
Put away kit	0.75	0.75/2 = 0.375	80	0.30
Normal time for one pair of shoes				2.48

Standard time for the pair $= 2.48 \times 1.05 = 2.61$ minutes

Problem 2

A total of 15 observations have been taken of a head baker for a school district. The numerical breakdown of her activities is as follows:

Make Ready	Do	Clean Up	Idle
2	6	3	4

Based on this information, how many work sampling observations are required to determine how much of the baker's time is spent in "doing"? Assume a 5 percent desired absolute error and 95 percent confidence level.

Solution

Since 95 percent confidence is required, use $Z = 1.96$. Also,

$p =$ "Doing" $= 6/15 = 40\%$

$E = .05$ (given)

To calculate the number of observations required, we use the following formula:

$$N = \frac{Z^2 p(1-p)}{E^2} = \frac{(1.96)^2(0.4)(1-0.4)}{(0.05)^2} = 369 \text{ observations}$$

Problems

1. As a time-study analyst, you have observed that a worker has produced 40 parts in a one-hour period. From your experience, you rate the worker as performing slightly faster than 100 percent—so you estimate performance at 110 percent. The company allows 15 percent of job time for fatigue and delay.
   a. What is the normal time?
   b. What is the standard time?
   c. If a worker produces 300 units per day and has a base rate of $10.00 per hour, what would the day's wages be for this worker if the company operates on a piece-rate payment plan?

2. A time study was made of an existing job to develop new time standards. A worker was observed for a period of 45 minutes. During that period, 30 units were produced. The analyst rated the worker as performing at a 90 percent performance rate. Allowances in the firm for rest and personal time are 12 percent of job time.
   a. What is the normal time for the task?
   b. What is the standard time for the task?
   c. If the worker produced 300 units in an eight-hour day, what would the day's pay be if the basic rate was $12.00 per hour and the firm used a piece-rate payment system?

3. A time-study analysis has obtained the following performance times by observing a worker over 15 operating cycles:

Performance Number	Time (seconds)	Performance Number	Time (seconds)
1	15	9	14
2	12	10	18
3	16	11	13
4	11	12	15
5	13	13	16
6	14	14	15
7	16	15	11
8	12		

The worker was rated as performing at 115 percent. Allowances for personal time and fatigue in the company are 10 percent of job time. The base rate for the worker is $9.00 per hour and the company operates on a piece-rate payment plan.
   a. What is the normal time?
   b. What is the standard time?
   c. If the worker produced 2500 units in a day, what would the gross pay for the day be?

4. A work sampling study is to be conducted over the next 30 consecutive days of an activity in the city fire department. Washing trucks, the subject of the study, is to be observed, and it is estimated that this occurs 10 percent of the time. A 3.5 percent accuracy with 95 percent confidence is acceptable. State specifically when observations should be made on one day. Use a 10-hour day from 8:00 a.m. to 6:00 p.m.

5. In an attempt to increase productivity and reduce costs, Rho Sigma Corporation is planning to install an incentive pay plan in its manufacturing plant.
   In developing standards for one operation, time-study analysts observed a worker for a 30-minute period. During that time the worker completed 42 parts. The analysts rated the worker as producing at 130 percent. The base wage rate of the worker is $5 per hour. The firm has established 15 percent as a fatigue and personal time allowance (as a percentage of job time).
   a. What is the normal time for the task?
   b. What is the standard time for the task?

    c. If the worker produced 500 units during an eight-hour day, what wages would the worker have earned?

6. Since new regulations will greatly change the products and services offered by a certain bank, time studies must be performed on tellers and other personnel to determine the number and types of personnel needed and incentive wage payment plans that might be installed.

    As an example of the studies that the various tasks will undergo, consider the following problem and come up with the appropriate answers:

    A hypothetical case was set up in which the teller (to be retitled later as an *account adviser*) was required to examine a customer's portfolio and determine whether it was more beneficial for the customer to consolidate various investments into a single mutual fund or to leave the portfolio unaltered. A time study was made of the teller, with the following findings:

Time of study	90 minutes
Number of portfolios examined	10 portfolios
Performance rating	130 percent
Rest for personal time	15 percent of job time
Teller's proposed new pay rate	$12 per hour

    a. What is the normal time for the teller to do a portfolio analysis for the mutual fund?

    b. What is the standard time for a portfolio analysis?

    c. If the bank decides to pay the new tellers on a piece-rate basis, how much would a teller earn for a day in which he or she analyzed 50 customer portfolios?

7. It is estimated that a bank teller spends about 10 percent of his time in a particular type of transaction. The bank manager would like a work-sampling study that shows, within plus or minus 3 percent, whether the clerk's time is really 10 percent (i.e., from 7 to 13 percent). The manager is well satisfied with a 95 percent confidence level.

    You estimate that, for the first "cut" at the problem, a sample size of 400 is indicated for the 10 percent activity time and ± 3 percent absolute error.

    State how you would perform the work-sampling study. If the study were to be made over a five-week period with five days per week from the hours of 9:00 to 5:00, specify the exact time (in minute increments) that you would make Monday's observations.

8. The call centres of a major express delivery service receive an average of 500 000 calls a day. The average time an operator spends on the phone with a customer is 3.77 minutes, which is referred to as the average handling time (AHT). In addition, a work-sampling study revealed that the operators spend an additional 1.25 minutes per call performing other tasks related to the call, such as researching the location of a lost package.

    a. If the firm allows the operators a personal allowance factor of 15 percent of their job time, how many operators does the firm need to answer the calls for an average day?

    b. The firm has decided to institute a menu-driven call answering system, which will reduce the operator's time on the phone to 3.25 minutes, although the amount of "non-telephone time" is expected to remain the same. If the operators are paid $16.00 per hour, including fringe benefits, how much money will the new answering system save the firm on a daily basis?

9. A mail-order catalogue company that specializes in high-quality outdoor clothing and accessories processes 125 000 orders a day during its peak season just before Christmas. The average time for a customer to place an order on the phone is 5.88 minutes. In addition, the customer service representative who takes the order requires an additional 2.00 minutes after completing the call to complete the necessary paperwork for the order.

a. If the representatives are paid an average of $12.00 per hour and the firm provides them a personal allowance factor of 14 percent of total time worked, how many representatives are needed on a daily basis to take phone orders during the peak season (based upon an eight-hour work day)?

b. Considering only the representatives' time, what is the cost to place an order?

c. The company is currently planning to install a Web site that will allow customers to place orders online. If the firm receives 20 percent of its orders online, how much money will it save in labour during its three-month peak season? (Assume that the labour cost to place an order online is zero and that the peak season is 90 days long.)

6

Quality Management

Chapter Objectives

- Define quality and identify the different dimensions of quality as they relate to both goods and services.

- Introduce those individuals, often referred to as quality gurus, who have played a significant role in the evolution of quality management, and describe their specific contributions.

- Define the various elements that comprise the cost of quality.

- Describe the more successful management quality initiatives such as total quality management (TQM) and Six Sigma.

- Present the various quality awards and recognition that promote and encourage firms to provide high-quality goods and services.

Total Quality Initiatives in Aeronautical Charting

Most people may not have heard of Aeronautical and Technical Services (ATS), a division of Natural Resources Canada, though it is vital to aviation in Canada. ATS publishes Canada's official aeronautical charts, providing specialized cartographic imaging and printing services to the Government of Canada's map agencies. In addition to its importance to pilots and air traffic controllers, in the past ATS has played a role in crises. For example, during the 1997 Manitoba floods and the 1998 ice storm in Central Canada, employees at ATS worked round the clock to prepare precise maps for emergency workers (this role has since been transferred to another government department).

Like other public service organizations, ATS had to downsize during the mid 1990s, having to maintain quality with fewer resources, although it has since grown to keep up with increasing demand. ATS undertook two key quality initiatives to meet client requirements for increased quality. The first was to become ISO 9000 certified, which helps ensure that a quality process is used throughout the map-making process. The second was to enter into a partnership with the National Quality Institute (NQI). This involved among other tasks, going through

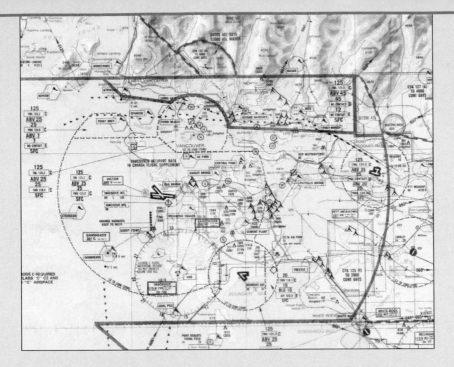

NQI assessments, benchmarking NQI's Canada Award for Excellence winners, and participating in the NQI's Tour de Force visits to gain valuable knowledge about quality.

ATS's basic approach to quality involved decentralizing the ownership of documentation and key processes. This resulted in the ISO elements, production procedures, and NQI criteria being sponsored by individuals. Although this took longer to do, the buy in was better and the long-term payback much greater.

ATS also realized that getting a quality process implemented as quickly as possible and then improving it is better than attempting to make it perfect first. Thus they followed a plan–do–check–act cycle (see Exhibit 6.2). This greatly reduced the implementation times.

The greatest effect of these quality initiatives was the increase in the confidence stakeholders and clients had in ATS and the confidence and pride the employees had in knowing that they were doing things right.

Quality improvement is not limited to for-profit business organizations. Not-for-profit institutions in education, government, health care, and other fields are taking steps to improve quality. Additional examples can be found in Exhibit 6.9 and in the OM in Practice box on school attendance in the chapter supplement.

Sources:

N. G. Grant and L. J. Taylor, "Case Study: Canada Awards for Excellence Trophy Recipient," *Excellence Magazine* (Winter 2001), www.nqi.com.

Joseph Peter and Katie Davidman, "Aeronautical and Technical Services—Natural Resources Canada," Discussion Paper No. W/08, Canadian Policy Research Networks, 1999, www.cprn.org/cprn.html.

Managerial Issues

Quality will always matter to customers—so it should be a high priority for every manager. This is true for both manufacturing operations and services. Defining quality from the customer's perspective, however, is very difficult because it can mean different things to different people. This represents one of the major challenges facing managers today. At the same time, the level of quality of the goods and services being sold today continues to increase, due in part to a combination of increased global competition and an increased knowledge of customers. Service quality is especially difficult to manage, for a variety of reasons. Unlike product quality, service quality is often highly subjective, varying from customer to customer even under identical circumstances. As a result, good service quality to one customer may be viewed as poor service quality by another.

The reason that quality is difficult to define is that it is a very broad concept that encompasses many dimensions, which vary for both goods and services. Good managers will identify those quality dimensions that are most important to their customers.

Another reason managers should be concerned with quality is that quality and cost are closely related. There are significant costs associated with producing bad products. Similarly, there are costs related to providing poor service to customers. Bad quality results in dissatisfied customers who eventually take their business elsewhere. Thus, high quality in goods and services is essential to maintaining customer loyalty and long-term customer relationships, which has been shown to significantly increase profits.

With the growth in global competition, the market for goods and services has shifted from being a producers' market, where customers are at the mercy of the firms that are providing the goods and services, to being a consumers' market, where customers have a wide variety of sources from which to buy the goods and services they desire. This trend is expected to increase as more and more consumers purchase goods and services on the Internet from every corner of the world. In such a highly competitive environment, managers are acknowledging the importance of customer loyalty, and recognize that a key element in maintaining customer loyalty is the ability to provide the highest quality goods and services. It is no longer acceptable merely to satisfy customers; now customer loyalty depends on the ability of a firm to delight its customers. However, as we shall see, quality can have many meanings, and each firm therefore needs to identify the specific elements of quality that are most important to the particular market on which it is focusing.

From a historical perspective, the quality movement can trace its roots back to the 1920s when Walter Shewhart developed the concept of statistical process control for measuring and monitoring the quality of a process. However, Shewhart's concepts were not widely accepted by industry until World War II, when, by necessity, firms began to apply his ideas because of both the vast quantities of material being produced to support the war effort and the critical shortage of labour.

Following World War II, consumer demand, which had been building during the war years, was unleashed, creating an unprecedented demand for products in North America. In such an environment, companies focused their efforts on turning out high volumes of goods to meet this demand, often sacrificing quality. During this same time period, W. Edwards Deming and Joseph Juran, two of the quality gurus presented in this chapter, were teaching managers in Japan to lower costs and improve quality by "doing it right the first time." As a result of their efforts, the quality of Japanese goods increased significantly, to the point that by the 1970s they were considered to be among the best in the world. Canadian, U.S., and European organizations spent the next two decades catching up. At the same time companies from newly industrialized countries such as South Korea, Brazil, and Taiwan started producing quality goods.

Today, providing high-quality goods and services is a mandatory for the long-term success of every organization, both to retain customers, and, as seen in the Dofasco vignette in Chapter 2, as a competitive weapon.

Defining Quality

For many years following World War II, quality was viewed primarily as a defensive function rather than as a competitive weapon for use in developing new markets and increasing market share. In this role, the quality emphasis was on quality control (QC): reducing the number of customer complaints received. As a result, there was a heavy reliance on inspection (sorting the good from the bad) rather than on prevention. Identifying defective output and either fixing it (rework) or disposing of it (scrap) incurred costs. It was therefore believed that higher quality must be more costly. Quality control managers often reported to manufacturing managers, who were measured primarily on output; consequently they had little or no power to either halt production or delay the shipment of faulty products.

Today, however, more and more companies are recognizing that quality can be defined in many ways. With the realization that quality has many dimensions, firms are now able not only to identify new market niches, but also to increase their market share in existing ones.

Quality in Goods

David Garvin has identified eight different **quality dimensions** with respect to goods on which a company can compete: (1) performance, (2) features, (3) reliability, (4) durability, (5) conformance, (6) serviceability, (7) aesthetics, and (8) perceived quality.[1]

Performance

Performance is a measure of a product's primary operating characteristics. Since performance usually can be measured in specific quantitative terms, a product's performance characteristics are often compared and ranked with those of the competition. With an automobile, for example, performance characteristics include how fast it can accelerate from 0 to 100 kph and its fuel efficiency in terms of litres per 100 km. For a personal computer, performance characteristics include operating speed and random access memory (RAM) capacity.

Features

Features are the "bells and whistles" that are offered with a product. Although features are not the primary operating characteristics of a product, they may, nonetheless, be very important to the customer. For example, a moon roof and stereo system may be the deciding factors for a new car buyer, while a specific type of refrigerator may appeal to a customer because it offers an icemaker and water dispenser.

Reliability

The reliability of a product relates to the probability that the product will fail within a specified time. Reliability is often measured as the mean time between failures (MTBF) or the failure rate per unit of time or other measure of usage. High product reliability is important in such products as airplanes, computers, and copying machines. Toyota vehicles are known for their reliability. The bored Maytag repairman with no service calls and Sears' Die Hard battery offer additional examples of product reliability.

Durability

The durability dimension of quality relates to the expected operational life of a product. In some instances, as with a light bulb, the filament eventually burns out and the entire product must be replaced. In other cases, such as with an automobile, the consumer must evaluate the trade-off between replacing the product entirely versus spending money on repairs to the existing one.

Conformance

A product's conformance to design specifications is primarily process oriented, in that it reflects how well the product and its individual components meet the established standards.

Serviceability

Serviceability is concerned with how readily a product can be repaired and the speed, competence, and courtesy associated with that repair. This dimension of quality is sometimes overlooked in the design stage. For example, in the 1970s Chevrolet designed a car in which one of the spark plugs could not be removed without pulling out the entire engine. The speed of the repair is also important, in that it affects the overall number of products needed for those businesses that require constant coverage. Using a city's paramedic service as an example, the frequency and the amount of time a paramedic vehicle requires repair and maintenance impact directly on the total number of vehicles the city needs to provide the proper level of coverage.

quality dimensions
Recognition that quality can be defined in many ways and that companies can use quality as a competitive advantage.

---

[1]David Garvin, "Competing on the Eight Dimensions of Quality," *Harvard Business Review* (November–December 1987), pp. 101–110.

Aesthetics

Aesthetics is a dimension of quality for which there is a high degree of individual judgment that is highly subjective. In fact, in terms of aesthetics, good quality to one group of customers might even be perceived as poor quality to another group. Companies, therefore, have an opportunity with this quality dimension to seek out a very specific market niche.

Perceived Quality

According to David Garvin, perceived quality is directly related to the reputation of the firm that manufactures the product. Often, total information about the various quality aspects of a product is not available, especially when it is a new product being introduced for the first time. Consequently, customers rely heavily on the past performance and reputation of the firm making the product, attaching a perceived value based on the previous performance of the company's other products.

Quality in Services

Parasuraman, Zeithaml, and Berry (1990, 1994)[2] identified the following five factors or dimensions that contribute to the level of service quality a firm provides to its customers:

Reliability

This refers to the ability to perform the promised service dependably and accurately. This is the most important of the five factors, because little else will matter to a customer if a service is unreliable. For example, no amount of friendliness or sincere apologies from the staff will compensate for a delayed flight that makes a client miss an important meeting. Generally, companies are more deficient on reliability than on any other dimension. FedEx provides a good example of a firm that provides highly reliable service.

Responsiveness

This refers to the willingness and/or readiness of employees to provide service. How easily you can get the attention of the clerk at The Bay department store is a measure of responsiveness. The time it takes to receive a return call on a complaint or a solution to a problem is also a measure of a firm's responsiveness.

Assurance

The knowledge and courtesy of employees play a major role in the success of the business. Their ability to convey trust and confidence helps ensure that the customer will return. For example, when a customer buys a mutual fund from a bank, it is important that the employee have good knowledge of the mutual fund industry and be able to help the client choose the appropriate fund. Such attributes are also critical in the case of lawyers and doctors.

Empathy

In many businesses, caring, individualized attention is very important to customers. Imagine a doctor who cannot empathize with a patient or an insurance adjuster interested only in the company's bottom line, with no concern for the injuries suffered by a client in an automobile accident. The Nordstrom and Harry Rosen examples from Chapter 3 in which the focus is on individual attention, are good examples of this factor. The personalized entertainment systems and comfortable seating that Singapore Airlines provides even in its economy class to make its long flights more comfortable is another example.

---

[2]L. L. Berry, A. Parasuraman, and V. A. Zeithaml, "Improving Service Quality in America: Lessons Learned," *The Academy of Management Executive*, 8, no. 2 (May 1994), pp. 32–52; and L. L. Berry, V. A. Zeithaml, and A. Parasuraman, "Five Imperatives for Improving Service Quality," *Sloan Management Review* 29 (Summer 1990), pp. 29–38.

Tangibles

This refers to the appearance of the physical facilities, equipment, personnel, and communication materials. The boxy, brown UPS truck or the red and blue Canada Post truck is any easily recognizable tangible. The cleanliness of the uniforms of the restaurant's wait-staff or an instruction manual for a product that is easy to read and understand are other examples.

Additional Views of Quality

Technical Quality versus Functional Quality

In service operations, as in manufacturing operations, it is important to note the distinction between *technical quality*, which relates to the core element of the good or service, and *functional quality*, which relates to the customers' perception of how the good functions or the service is delivered. For example, the appropriateness of the medical treatment ordered by a physician for a patient's ailment is a measure of the technical quality of the care. The physician's "bedside manner"—how empathetic he or she is, how well he or she listens and explains, how much care he or she takes to make the patient comfortable both physically and psychologically—is a measure of the functional quality of the care.

Customers can readily assess functional quality because it relates primarily to the interaction between the firm providing the good or service and its customers. Technical quality, however, may not be something that customers are able to assess because they do not have the technical knowledge required to do so. For example, unless they know a great deal about automobiles, customers may be uncertain about what the technical specifications of a new car mean or whether a mechanic has appropriately identified and solved their car problems. Similarly, most of us who are not trained in dentistry are unable to tell whether our dentists know a cavity in a tooth from a hole in the wall! To compensate for not having the knowledge required to assess technical quality, customers often will use some measures they hope are objective to help them make those assessments. For example, when we evaluate the quality of physicians, we may consider where they trained, how much experience they have, and whether they are certified by a specialty board. When we evaluate an MBA program, we may look to see if the school is accredited and at the percentage of faculty with doctoral degrees as measures of technical quality. The inability of most customers to properly assess technical quality makes functional quality all the more important. Good managers care about both aspects of quality.

Expectations and Perceptions

Another approach used to define quality in services is to measure how satisfied the customer is with the service received. Customers' satisfaction with service is related to both their prior expectations about the service and their perception of how well the service was provided. Customers develop a certain set of expectations based on a variety of inputs. They

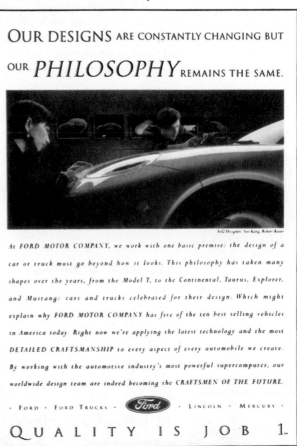

OUR DESIGNS ARE CONSTANTLY CHANGING BUT OUR *PHILOSOPHY* REMAINS THE SAME.

At FORD MOTOR COMPANY, we work with one basic premise: the design of a car or truck must go beyond how it looks. This philosophy has taken many shapes over the years, from the Model T, to the Continental, Taurus, Explorer, and Mustang: cars and trucks celebrated for their design. Which might explain why FORD MOTOR COMPANY has five of the ten best selling vehicles in America today. Right now we're applying the latest technology and the most DETAILED CRAFTSMANSHIP to every aspect of every automobile we create. By working with the automotive industry's most powerful supercomputer, our worldwide design team are indeed becoming the CRAFTSMEN OF THE FUTURE.

· FORD · FORD TRUCKS · *Ford* · LINCOLN · MERCURY ·

QUALITY IS JOB 1.

A Ford quality ad with a focus on the application of the most current technology when building cars.

consider their previous experience with services in general and with each specific kind of service they have encountered. For example, customers might have specific expectations about service in a retail clothing store that provides a basis for what they should expect when they speak with an employee on the phone—as well as when they are served in another retail clothing store. Customers also develop expectations when they hear about services from others. If you hear that your friend was delighted with her stay at a particular hotel, you're more likely to expect a similar level of service if you stay there. Customers also form expectations based on a service provider's advertisements and promotions. Promises of positive service bring in customers—but a promise isn't enough. Customers will be satisfied only if the service meets or exceeds their expectations. And the service performance is coloured by the customer's perceptions of the quality of service, so that the relationship between expectations, service performance, and the perception of that performance can be described in the following equation:

$$\text{Satisfaction} = (\text{Perception of performance}) - (\text{Expectation})$$

The equation shows that there are two ways to increase satisfaction: improve the customers' perception of performance or decrease their expectations. But what happens to expectations for the next service encounter when satisfaction is high? It is likely that the customer will expect that high level of service again, thereby raising the stakes for the service provider.

The service satisfaction equation is therefore a dynamic one: Each encounter affects customer expectations for the next encounter, so managing both performance and expectations is important for achieving high levels of customer satisfaction. Before managers can think about managing service performance, however, they must understand what service quality is. What is it customers want? How can their needs be met consistently?

The Quality Gurus

Over the years there have been many individuals involved in the quality revolution. Several have been recognized as **quality gurus** for their valuable contributions and forward thinking. Walter A. Shewhart, W. Edwards Deming, Joseph M. Juran, Shigeo Shingo, Kaoru Ishikawa, Armand Feigenbaum, Philip Crosby, and Genichi Taguchi are a few notable examples. Although they have much in common in terms of how they view quality, each has left his unique stamp on the quality movement. Consequently, their philosophical approaches to quality are significantly different.

Walter A. Shewhart

Walter A. Shewhart was a statistician at Bell Laboratories who studied randomness in industrial processes. He developed the foundations of modern **statistical process control (SPC)**, discussed in supplement 6. Shewhart also developed the "plan–do–check–act" (PDCA) cycle shown in Exhibit 6.1. Prior to the PDCA cycle, organizations typically managed activities as though they had identifiable beginning and end points. The PDCA cycle uses a circular model to emphasize the need for continuous improvement. Shewhart's pioneering work in statistical process control had a strong influence on both Deming and Juran.

W. Edwards Deming

A thorough understanding of statistical process control is the basic cornerstone of Deming's approach to quality. Deming emphasized the importance of having an overall organizational approach for quality management. He therefore insisted that top managers attend his

quality gurus

Individuals who have been identified as making a significant contribution to improving the quality of goods and services.

statistical process control (SPC)

Methods, such as control charts, that signal shifts in a process that will likely lead to products and/or services not meeting customer requirements.

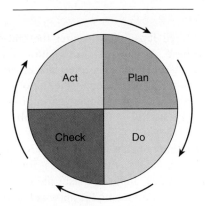

Exhibit 6.1

Shewhart's Plan–Do–Check–Act (PDCA) Cycle

Source: "The PDCA Cycle" from *Deming Management at Work* by Mary Walton, copyright © 1990 by Mary Walton. Used by permission of G. P. Putnam's Sons, a division of Penguin Putnam, Inc.

lectures, knowing that the QC staff by itself could not support and sustain an ongoing organizationwide quality effort. The Japanese recognized Deming's tremendous contribution to the success of their companies, naming their highest award for industrial excellence after him—the Deming Prize in 1951, decades before such awards were created in North America.

One of Deming's major contributions focused on disproving the fallacy that it costs more to make better-quality products. He demonstrated that just the opposite is true: A high-quality process is, in fact, less costly than a low-quality one. When products are made properly the first time, substantial savings accrue from the elimination of unnecessary labour for rework and repairs and the cost to scrap nonconforming material.

According to Deming, 85 percent of the quality problems generated by a company can be attributed to management, because they have the power to make the decisions that impact on the current systems and practices. Over the years, Deming identified 14 points he believed critical to improving quality. These 14 points are presented in Exhibit 6.2.

1. Create constancy of purpose for improvement of product and service.
2. Adopt the new philosophy.
3. Cease dependence on mass inspection.
4. End the practice of awarding business on the price tag alone.
5. Improve constantly and forever the system of production and training.
6. Institute training.
7. Institute leadership.
8. Drive out fear.
9. Break down barriers between staff areas.
10. Eliminate slogans, exhortations, and targets for the workforce.
11. Eliminate numerical quotas.
12. Remove barriers to pride in workmanship.
13. Institute a vigorous program of education and retraining.
14. Take action to accomplish the program.

Exhibit 6.2

Deming's 14-Point Program for Improving Quality

Source: "14 Point System" from *Deming Management at Work* by Mary Walton, copyright © 1990 by Mary Walton. Used by permission of G. P. Putnam's Sons, a division of Penguin Putnam, Inc.

Joseph M. Juran

Like Deming, Juran also visited Japan shortly after the end of World War II to assist in rebuilding its industrial base. Also like Deming, Juran emphasized the importance of producing quality products, and thus directed his efforts while in Japan toward teaching quality concepts and their application to the factory floor. Based on his experience with Japanese companies, Juran developed an approach to quality that focuses primarily on three areas: (1) quality planning, (2) quality control, and (3) quality improvement.

According to Juran, the quality of a product is defined as its fitness for use, as viewed by the customer. In evaluating a product's fitness for use, Juran takes into account the total life cycle of each unit of the product. Juran also uses the cost of quality, discussed in the next section, as his framework for introducing his approach to quality.

Shigeo Shingo

Shigeo Shingo is credited (along with Taiichi Ohno, former vice-president of Toyota Motors) with helping revolutionize the way goods are manufactured.[3] In terms of quality his most important contribution was the development of *poka-yoke* and source inspection systems. Source inspection is used to identify errors before they become defects so that the process can be adjusted to prevent errors. This occurs at every stage of the process by monitoring potential error sources. *Poka-yoke* systems involve mistake proofing, and are discussed later in this chapter. Shingo's philosophy was focused on defect prevention or "zero defects."

Kaoru Ishikawa

Kaoru Ishikawa is best known as a pioneer of the quality circle movement in Japan in the early 1960s.[4] Although quality circles originated in the West, it was only after Ishikawa's work that they became popular in the West. He managed to convince management of the potential for a significant contribution from the workforce to quality, productivity, and other work-related issues. He also emphasized statistical control tools, (discussed in supplement 6). The cause and effect (or fishbone) diagram is named after him. He was one of the earliest quality experts to focus on the next stage in a process, the internal customer. Many of these quality control tools are discussed in detail in the supplement to this chapter.

He also believed strongly in organizationwide methods of quality improvement. Ishikawa saw organizationwide quality as applying not only to design and production of goods but also to after-sales service, wasteful processes, the quality of management, and interpersonal relations.

Armand Feigenbaum

In 1956, Armand Feigenbaum proposed the concept of "total quality control," which begins with the recognition that quality is the responsibility of everyone in the organization. He stressed interdepartmental communication, particularly with respect to product design control, incoming material control, and production control. Like Juran, he believed in the power of the cost-of-quality framework, and emphasized careful measurement and reporting of these costs.

---

[3]Department of Trade and Industry, U.K. Government, www.dti.gov.uk/mbp/bpgt/m9ja00001/m9ja0000112.html.
[4]Department of Trade and Industry, U.K. Government, www.dti.gov.uk/mbp/bpgt/m9ja00001/m9ja000019.html.

Philip Crosby

Crosby's philosophy, which is similar in some respects to Deming's, states that any organization can reduce its total overall costs by improving the quality of its processes. In one of his first books, Crosby preached that "quality is free." According to Crosby, the cost of providing poor-quality goods and services is significant. He estimated that the cost of producing poor quality can run as high as 25 percent of revenues for manufacturing companies and 40 percent of operating expenses in service operations. Crosby also claims that companies that have successfully implemented quality programs can expect to reduce their costs of quality to less than 2.5 percent of sales.[5]

Genichi Taguchi

Taguchi takes an engineering approach to design quality, focusing on the design of experiments to improve both the yield and performance quality of products. He emphasizes the minimization of variation (discussed in supplement 6), which is also the cornerstone of his philosophical approach. While Juran emphasizes the cost of quality to the firm, Taguchi is concerned also with the cost of quality to society as a whole. He takes Juran's concept of external failure much further, including not only the cost to the firm that ships the defective product, but also the cost to the firm that accepts it, the customer that buys and uses it, and so on.

The Cost of Quality

Following Juran's model, we divide the **cost of quality** into three major categories: (1) cost of prevention, (2) cost of detection/appraisal, and (3) cost of failure. The third category, the cost of failure, is further subdivided into internal failure costs and external failure costs.

The total cost of quality is the sum of the costs in all three categories. The typical percentages of total quality costs that are estimated for each of the three categories are shown in Exhibit 6.3.

The cost of poor quality includes detection/appraisal costs and both internal and external failure costs, and can range from 15 to 25 percent of the total cost of a product. These costs of poor quality include the more traditional, visible items such as waste, rework, inspections, and recalls, as well as the often-overlooked "invisible" categories such as customer allowances, complaint handling, lost or wasted capacity, and excessive overtime.[6]

cost of quality

Framework for identifying quality components that are related to producing both high-quality products and low-quality products, with the goal of minimizing the total cost of quality.

Category	Feigenbaum	Juran and Gryna
Prevention costs	5%–10%	0.5%–5%
Detection/appraisal costs	20%–25%	10%–50%
Failure costs	65%–70%	Internal: 25%–40%
		External: 20%–40%
Total cost of quality	100%	100%

Exhibit 6.3

Typical Quality Cost Ratios

Source: A. V. Feigenbaum, Total Quality Control, 3rd ed. (New York: McGraw-Hill, 1983), p. 112; and Joseph M. Juran and F. M. Gryna, Quality Planning and Analysis (New York: McGraw-Hill, 1970), p. 60.

---

[5]Philip B. Crosby, *Quality Is Free* (New York: New America Library, 1979), p. 15.
[6]Joseph A. DeFeo, "The Tip of the Iceberg," *Quality Progress* (May 2001), pp. 29–37.

Cost of Prevention

cost of prevention
Costs associated with the development of programs to prevent defectives from occurring in the first place.

Costs of prevention, by definition, are those costs incurred by an organization in its effort to prevent defective goods and services from being produced. Included in this category are investments in machinery, technology, as well as education and training programs, which are designed to reduce the number of defects that the process produces. Also included in this category are the costs to administer the firm's quality program, data collection and analysis, and vendor certification. All of the quality gurus strongly support investments in this category because the returns are so high, including the benefits gained from increasing customer satisfaction and reducing scrap losses and rework expenses.

Cost of Detection/Appraisal

cost of detection/ appraisal
Costs associated with the test and inspection of subassemblies and products after they have been made.

Costs of detection or **appraisal** are those costs associated with evaluating the quality of the product. Costs included in this category are incoming material inspection, tests and inspection throughout the transformation process, test equipment maintenance, and products destroyed during destructive testing.

Cost of Failure

cost of failure
Costs associated with the failure of a defective product.

internal failure costs
Costs associated with producing defective products that are identified prior to shipment.

external failure costs
Costs associated with producing defective products that are delivered to the customer.

Costs of failure pertain to nonconforming and nonperforming products. Also included in this category are the costs associated with the evaluation and disposition of customer complaints. As stated earlier, we further subdivide failure costs into internal and external failure costs.

Internal failure costs are identified as those costs that are incurred when defects are produced within the system. They include only those costs attributed to defects that are found before the products are delivered to the customer. Examples of internal failure costs include scrap, rework/repair, retesting of reworked/repaired products, downtime, yield losses due to process variability, and the disposition of the defective items.

External failure costs are those costs that are incurred after the product has been delivered to the customer. Included in this category are the cost of returned material, warranty charges, field survey costs, legal expenses from lawsuits, customer dissatisfaction, loss of revenues due to downgrading products as seconds, and costs of allowances/concessions made to customers. (See the OM in Practice Box on the cost of poor quality.)

It is now generally recognized that increased spending on prevention provides significant returns in the form of reductions in detection/appraisal and failure costs—and in the overall cost of quality. Thus the old adage, "An ounce of prevention is worth a pound of cure" is also most appropriate for quality.

At the same time, Deming suggested that total quality costs can be decreased by improving the process itself. An improved process reduces both the number of defects produced and the costs of prevention and appraisal. A comparison of Deming's model with the previously traditional view toward quality is presented in Exhibit 6.4.

When defective products or services are eliminated, there are two direct effects. First, there are more good units produced (and capacity is therefore increased) and second, each unit produced costs less because the cost of the failures is both reduced and also spread over a larger number of nondefective goods or services. For example, if a plastic injection moulding process scraps 15 defective pen barrels out of every 100 that are produced, the cost to produce the 15 scrapped units must be spread over the remaining 85 units—and there are only 85 units available to sell. If the quality of the process is improved and only five units are scrapped per 100 produced, then there are 95 units that are available for sale, and the cost of only the five scrapped units is now spread over the 95 good units rather than 85 as was previously the case.

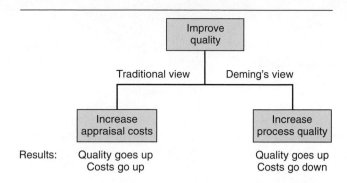

Exhibit 6.4

Two Views of the Cost of Improved Quality

For example, a bank that set out to improve quality and reduce its costs found that it also had boosted productivity. The bank developed this productivity measure for the loan processing area: the number of loans processed divided by the resources required (labour cost, computer time, loan forms). Before the quality improvement program, the productivity index was 0.2660 [2080/($11.23 × 640 hours + $0.05 × 2600 forms + $500 for systems costs)]. After the quality improvement project was completed, labour time fell to 546 hours and the number of forms processed increased to 2100 for a change in the index to 0.3088, or an increase in productivity of 16 percent.

Service Guarantees

Warrantees are common for products such as automobiles, washing machines, and televisions. Such warrantees guarantee that these products will work throughout a stated period of time or else they will be either repaired or replaced free of charge. Less common are guarantees for services. Nevertheless, Christopher Hart has suggested that the service guarantee can be a powerful tool for obtaining feedback from customers on how service operations are performing.

For a service guarantee to be effective, it must contain the following elements: It must be (a) unconditional, (b) easy to understand and communicate, (c) meaningful, (d) easy and painless to invoke, and (e) easy and quick to collect on. For example, Canada Post will refund the mailing charge for guaranteed delivery services if your package is not delivered on time. Many stores will refund your money within a certain period after purchase if you are not satisfied with the product no matter what the reason. One federal government-appointed commission on health care has proposed guaranteeing medical procedure wait times for Canadians (see OM in Practice Box in Chapter 10).

From a quality standpoint, the unconditional service guarantee provides management with continuous customer feedback. If it is easy to invoke and collect on, then customers will use the service guarantee to voice their complaints rather than simply taking their business elsewhere.

Organizationwide Quality Initiatives

As the quality movement gained momentum, managers looked to develop initiatives that would allow them to integrate quality throughout their entire organizations. The purpose of these initiatives is to provide a common framework for identifying quality issues with the goal of improving the overall quality of the firm's goods and services. Two of the more successful quality initiatives that been adopted by many firms are total quality management and six sigma.

COST OF POOR QUALITY

The following examples highlight the need for defect prevention (fail-safing or poka-yoke) in different organizations

A misaligned row of information in an electronic spreadsheet used to bid for electricity transmission contracts in New York state will cost Calgary-based TransAlta Corp U.S.$24 million. This is expected to wipe out 10 percent of the company's annual profit. The error meant that TransAlta overpaid for certain transmission contracts as well as buying more capacity than it intended in certain cases. Since New York state rules do not allow bids to be changed even in the event of human blunder, TransAlta will have to honour the contracts that it does not need.

A misrouted order at high-tech brokerage house ITG Canada Corp to buy and sell $30 million worth of stocks at the Toronto Stock Exchange (TSX) meant thousands of dollars in losses to the company. Trades are done through an electronic network. Said a Bay Street veteran, "what is interesting is that ITG did not have a fail-safe system that worked."

The cost of quality can be described in human terms, too. In Canadian health care, it is estimated that annually there are about 70 000 injuries caused to health care workers (mostly nurses) by needles and other sharp objects. As many as 300 of these result in the transmission of serious diseases such as HIV-AIDS and hepatitis C. At the same time, research in the United States shows that the use of safety-engineered devices such as retractable needles and self-sheathing scalpels can reduce injuries by more than 50 percent. In 2004, Saskatchewan became the first province to introduce regulations making it mandatory for health-care facilities to use retractable needles and other safety-engineered medical devices. It is expected this will result in savings of $1.4-million annually in treating the aftermath of needle injuries.

Sources:

Patrick Brethour, "Human Error Costs TransAlta $24-Million on Contract Bids," *The Globe and Mail*, June 4, 2003, B11.

Andrew Willis, "High-Tech Broker Hurt by Misrouted Order," *The Globe and Mail*, June 5, 2003, B1.

André Picard, "A Tiny Pinprick, a Deadly Outcome," *The Globe and Mail,* December 1, 2003, A1.

André Picard, "Saskatchewan to be first province to insist on safer needles," *The Globe and Mail*, November 2, 2004, A15.

Total Quality Management

total quality management (TQM)
Approach to integrating quality at all levels of an organization.

Total quality management (TQM) can be viewed as an organizationwide approach that focuses on producing high-quality goods and services. TQM, when properly used, is an integral part of an organization, not a separate, stand-alone program, and it encompasses all of the functional areas and levels within the organization, including suppliers.

Elements of TQM

There are four primary elements that are integral to every successful TQM program: (1) leadership, (2) employee involvement, (3) product/process excellence, and (4) customer focus.

Leadership. The leadership provided by an organization's management is a major cornerstone in the development and implementation of a successful TQM program. When properly executed, a TQM program is companywide, transcends the traditional functional areas, and involves all of the firm's employees. It therefore requires vision, planning, and communication, all of which are the responsibility of top management. Studies have indicated that total commitment from management is a critical element in successfully implementing such programs.

Top management can demonstrate its commitment to a TQM program in several ways. These include incorporating TQM into the firm's overall strategy and demonstrating by actions as well as words that quality is the number one operating priority of the organization (see the OM in Practice Box on High Liner Food).

Employee involvement. Employee involvement is another critical element in successfully implementing a TQM program. By involving all employees in the decision-making process, management is able to receive inputs from those nearest the problems and in the

TQM AND LEADERSHIP AT HIGH LINER FOODS

High Liner Foods (formerly National Sea Products) is a 100-year-old food processing company based in Lunenburg, Nova Scotia. It is a company that has weathered the decline in fish stocks on the East Coast by launching new products, eliminating unprofitable lines, acquiring non-seafood based businesses, and focusing on total quality management (TQM). Today its profits are increasing and the company is successfully penetrating U.S. markets, where it lists major grocery chains, club stores, and Wal-Mart among its customers. In fact Fisher Boy, the company's U.S. and Mexican seafood brand, was the best selling fish stick in the United States in 2002. In 1995 the Canadian grocery trade gave a "Best New Product Award" to the company's Gourmet Fillets. Since then it has won the Grand Prix Awards (grocery industry Junos or Grammys) from the Canadian Council of Grocery Distributors for different products.

A few years earlier the company had launched a TQM campaign. Top management recognized that leadership would be a key in the success of the campaign. Said President and CEO Henry Demone "When you launch something like this (TQM) in a company, you have to assume that the people in middle management and front lines are going to be skeptical. Okay (they say), the guys went to a seminar or they read a book and this is the flavour of the month. They test your commitment and you have to prove your commitment by your actions day to day."

Demone also introduced a broad and regular consultation process for planning to improve communication and decision making in an era where tough decisions had to be made, such as getting out of some seafood businesses, laying off employees, and reorganizing.

For example, at the company's Arnold's Cove plant in Newfoundland, employees organized themselves into work teams along with management "coaches" to learn new processing skills and interact with technology.

Today, Demone considers quality and innovation to be key parts of the company's competitive strengths.

Sources:

Quality Imperative, VHS (Ottawa, Ontario: Stonehaven Productions, 1991).

Casey Mahood, "National Sea Stock Hits 52-Week High, CEO Suggest Investors Eyeing Its New Product and Strategic Success," *The Globe and Mail*, April 29, 1997, B17.

Kevin Cox, "High Liner Charts a Sea Change," *The Globe and Mail*, February 5, 1999, B25.

Henry Demone, Address to Shareholders, May 1, 2003, www.highlinerfoods.com.

best position to recommend viable solutions. Employee involvement, which appears to be prevalent in most world-class operations, also takes advantage of the skills and knowledge of all employees.

A key element in employee involvement is that each worker assumes the responsibility for inspecting the quality of his or her own work. This is referred to as quality at the source and extends beyond the worker to include the work group, all departments, and the suppliers of parts and services to the organization. This view changes the often-adversarial practice of having a QC inspector, typically from the QC department, making decisions about good or bad quality.

Product/process excellence. Product/process excellence involves the quality of the product's design and analysis of field failures. It also includes statistical process control (SPC) and other analytical tools (discussed later in this chapter and in Supplement 6).

Process control is concerned with monitoring quality *while the product is being produced or the service is being performed.* Typical objectives of process control plans are to provide timely information on whether currently produced items are meeting design specifications and to detect shifts in the process that signal that future products may not meet the customer's requirements. The actual control phase of process control occurs when corrective action is taken, such as when a worn part is replaced, a machine is overhauled, or a new supplier is found. Process control concepts, especially statistically based control charts, are used in services as well as in manufacturing.

An underlying philosophy in achieving product/process excellence is the concept of **continuous improvement**. This has a general meaning as well as a specific TQM meaning. Its general meaning is an ongoing effort to improve in every part of the organization

continuous improvement

Concept that recognizes that quality improvement is a journey with no end and that there is a need to look continuously for new approaches for improving quality.

and all of its outputs. Its more specific meaning focuses on continual improvement in the processes by which work is accomplished.

In Japanese companies, the concept of continuous improvement is referred to as *kaizen*. It can be interpreted as a systematic approach to eliminating errors and improving the quality of the product that is delivered to the customer. One of the ways kaizen is achieved is through the use of **poka-yoke** (foolproofing or fail-safing the methods that are used to make the products). In manufacturing, poka-yoke often requires that a part be redesigned so that it can fit only one way. As stated earlier, a good example of poka-yoke in services is the bathroom onboard an airplane. Here the light will not go on until the door is locked, ensuring privacy. Also, height bars at amusement parks ensure proper height for the rides (see the OM in Practice Box on the cost of poor quality).

Customer focus. The customer's perception of quality must be taken into account in setting acceptable quality levels. In other words, a product isn't reliable unless the customer says it's reliable and a service isn't fast unless the customer says it's fast. Translating customer quality demands into specifications requires marketing research (or product development) to accurately determine what the customer wants and product designers to develop a product (or service) that can be produced to consistently achieve that desired level of quality. This, in turn, requires that we have an operational definition of quality, an understanding of its various dimensions, and a process for including the voice of the customer in those specifications. The quality of a product or service may be defined by the quality of its design (product quality) and the quality of its conformance to that design (process quality). **Design quality** refers to the inherent value of the product in the marketplace and is thus a strategic decision for the firm, as discussed earlier.

Conformance quality refers to the degree to which the product or service meets design specifications. It, too, has strategic implications, but the execution of the activities involved in achieving conformance are of a tactical day-to-day nature. It should be evident that a product or service can have high design quality but low conformance quality, and vice versa.

The operations function and the quality organization within the firm are primarily concerned with quality of conformance. Achieving all the quality specifications is typically the responsibility of manufacturing management (for products) and branch operations management (for services).

Both design quality and conformance quality should provide products that meet the customer's objectives for those products. This is often termed the product's *fitness for use*, and it entails identifying those dimensions of the product (or service) that the customer wants and developing a quality control program to ensure that these dimensions are met.

Implementing TQM

As seen in Exhibit 6.5, companies have adopted several approaches to implementing TQM. However, only when quality is totally integrated into the day-to-day operations of the firm can a TQM program be truly successful.

The implementation of a successful quality program throughout an organization is not a simple undertaking. As a result, there have been many failed attempts. Edward Fuchs identifies two major causes for the inability of firms to successfully adopt an organization-wide quality program: "lack of focus on strategic planning and core competencies, and obsolete, outdated cultures."[7]

---

[7]Edward Fuchs, "Total Quality Management from the Future," *Quality Management Journal* (October 1993), pp. 26–34.

poka-yoke

Simple devices, such as automatic shutoff valves or fixtures to orient parts, that prevent defects from being produced.

design quality

Specific characteristics of the product that determine its value in the marketplace.

conformance quality

Defines how well the product is made with respect to its design specifications.

Exhibit 6.5

Three Schools of Total Quality Management Programs

	Total Quality Harangue	Total Quality Tools	Total Quality Integration
Noticeable characteristics	Exhortation, lots of talk about quality; generally a marketing campaign intended to create buying signals without incurring the expense of fundamental changes	Introduction of specific tools; viz., statistical process control, employee involvement programs, and/or quality circles	Serious review of all elements of the organization; efforts to involve suppliers and customers
Rationale	Management may believe that quality is better than generally known or may be creating a smoke screen; viz., "everybody's doing it," "it's the thing to do these days"	Valued customers insist on implementation of a team program; or competitors have introduced successful programs creating a "bandwagon" effect	Systematic effort to improve earnings through differentiation based on quality
Responsibility for quality	Unchanged; specific function within organization assigned responsibility for quality	Lower-level members of organization regardless of function	Shared responsibility; senior management accepts responsibility to create an environment encouraging quality
Structural changes	None; the organization remains unchanged	Incremental changes within functional areas or processes	Dramatic changes integrating functions within the organization and involving customers and suppliers in the total production process
Representative employee attitudes and behaviours	Total quality is just a fad, "this too shall pass"; smart employees learn to keep their heads down—they talk about quality when expected to but know that business continues as usual	"It's a nice idea, too bad management isn't really serious about quality"; clever employees participate in seminars and use appropriate tools to fix obvious flaws in their areas of responsibility, but are careful not to rock the boat	"At last, we've got a chance to do it right"; committed employees study the total quality vision, actively search for opportunities to improve performance across the organization, challenge conventional assumptions, and seek to involve customers and suppliers
Role of the quality professional	Police officer, watchdog	Resident expert, advisor	Strategic leaders, change agent

Source: Eric W. Skopec, Strategic Visions Inc. (used by permission).

In addition to these two underlying causes, companies have identified the following obstacles that need to be addressed if a quality program is to be truly successful within an organization:[8]

- Lack of a companywide definition of quality
- Lack of a formalized strategic plan for change
- Lack of a customer focus
- Poor interorganizational communication
- Lack of real employee empowerment

[8]Gary Salegna and Farzaneh Fazel, "Obstacles to Implementing Quality," *Quality Progress* (July 2000), pp. 53–57.

- Lack of employee trust in senior management
- View of quality program as a quick fix
- Drive for short-term financial results
- Politics and turf issues

Six Sigma

Six Sigma

A statistically based, structured methodology for identifying and eliminating causes of errors in a process.

Motorola, in large part in response to the very-high-quality products that were being manufactured in Japan, introduced a quality improvement program during the 1980s known as **Six Sigma**. The goal of a Six Sigma program is to reduce process variation to the point where there are only 3.4 defects per million opportunities. (The quantitative analysis associated with Six Sigma is presented in the supplement to this chapter.) Six Sigma is especially important for those businesses such as services and high-volume manufacturing firms that involve a very large number of operations or transactions on a continuous basis. For example, if the following processes were only 99 percent reliable (which corresponds to 4σ quality), they would have the following numbers of defects:

- 20 000 pieces of mail lost every hour
- Unsafe drinking water almost 15 minutes every day
- 5000 incorrect surgical operations every week
- Two short or long landings at most major airports each day
- 200 000 incorrect drug prescriptions filled every year
- No electricity for almost seven hours every month[9]

For comparison purposes, Exhibit 6.6 provides some benchmarks for the quality of various processes in terms of their relative levels of performance.

Over the years, Six Sigma has evolved into a management tool to reduce all forms of waste within an organization. The methodologies of a Six Sigma program provide a common language and set of goals that can be used throughout an organization.

To ensure that customers' requirements are being met on a consistent basis, organizations need to develop processes that are capable of meeting these requirements. The managerial thrust of a Six Sigma program is to effectively provide a framework and

Exhibit 6.6

Quality Performance Levels for Various Processes (Based on U.S. Data)

Process Description	Quality Performance Level
IRS phone-in tax advice	2.2σ
Restaurant bills, doctors' prescription writing, payroll processing	2.9σ
Average company	3.0σ
Airline baggage handling	3.2σ
Best-in-class companies	5.7σ
U.S. Navy aircraft accidents	5.7σ
Watch off by 2 seconds in 31 years	6.0σ
Airline industry fatality rate	6.2σ

Source: Dave Harrold, "Designing for Six Sigma Capability," *Control Engineering*, January 1999.

---

[9]*Source:* Motorola.

SIX SIGMA IS CATCHING ON IN CANADA

The highest profile company in the world to employ Six Sigma is GE. GE's goal is to train all employees (including those in Canada) to at least the basic, or "green belt" level of the methodology, and to apply the program across all its operations, from plastics to financial services.

A high-profile Canadian company that uses Six Sigma is Bombardier Inc. Mining company Noranda, Maple Leaf Foods, Air Canada, Imperial Oil, Celestica, and Ford Canada are other Canadian companies that have adopted Six Sigma. Bombardier adopted a stepwise approach in implementing the program, rolling it out division by division.

A good example of how Six Sigma was applied at Bombardier related to the problems of paint peeling off brand new jet planes. The defective paint would then have to be sanded down and the jets repainted, a huge waste of resources. A Six-Sigma team identified the root cause of the five-year-old problem in five months (it was related to the thickness of the undercoat) and the company fixed it, resulting in savings of millions of dollars a year. Bombardier is also encouraging suppliers to become knowl-

edgeable about Six Sigma. By 2000, more than 12 000 Canadian employees had been trained at different levels. (Six Sigma uses martial arts terms such as "green belt" and "master black belt" to indicate progression in training, though Bombardier uses different labels that work both in English and French and that avoid warlike connotations). The company had also spent $50 million in licence fees and training. In the year ended January 31, 2000, Bombardier realized $83 million in savings from the Six-Sigma program.

Sources:
"Six Sigma, Bombardier Style," *The Globe and Mail*, September 26, 1997, P64.

Wayne Lilly, "Where Do CEOs Come from, Who Hired Them—and How Do They Stay at the Top? The Elusive Grail: Six Sigma Is But the Latest Twist in the Search for Management Excellence," *National Post*, November 1, 2001.

Michael Legault, "Achieving Perfection," *Canadian Plastics* (November 1998): 35–37.

Allan Swift, "Blackbelts in Problem Solving: Bombardier and Noranda Profit from the Six Sigma Management Technique," *The Ottawa Citizen*, March 2, 2000, B3.

Bombardier Inc., www.bombardier.com.

---

associated methodologies to analyze and evaluate business processes with the overall goal of reducing waste. The Six Sigma improvement process typically begins with identifying a problem to be solved and then defining a project to solve that problem. The process used by the project team is often referred to as DMAIC, which stands for **d**efine, **m**easure, **a**nalyze, **i**mprove, and **c**ontrol.

Six Sigma, as with any organizational quality initiative, requires the commitment of top management and the alignment of incentives for it to succeed. At organizations such as General Electric, many top executives have their incentive bonuses tied to Six Sigma performance.

A key element in the successful implementation of a Six Sigma program involves the selection and training of the workforce throughout the organization so that the philosophy of reducing variation and waste and improving output is a part of everyone's everyday work. To accomplish this, key employees, referred to as "Black Belts" are chosen to lead the major improvement projects. These Six Sigma project leaders receive intensive training in quantitative improvement tools using statistical software and are also trained in teamwork and communication.

Another key ingredient in the success of Six Sigma programs is the impressive cost savings that have been achieved as a direct result of their implementation. At Honeywell, the cost savings are more than US$2 billion since it first implemented Six Sigma in 1994. At GE, six sigma generated more than US$2 billion in savings in 1999 alone, and Black and Decker's Six Sigma productivity savings increased to US$75 million in 2000.[10] Some organizations have used Six Sigma methods in combination with other techniques to achieve good results (see the OM in Practice Box on IMC Global).

---

[10]Joseph A. DeFeo, "The Tip of the Iceberg," *Quality Progress* (May 2001), pp. 29–37.

SASKATCHEWAN MINES USE A COMBINATION OF TECHNIQUES TO CONTINUOUSLY IMPROVE

IMC Global Inc. is a mining company that produces and supplies concentrated phosphates and potash fertilizers. The company is also one of the world's largest manufacturers of salt for road de-icing, food processing, water conditioning, and other applications. It has Canadian facilities in Esterhazy, Colonsay, and Belle Plain, all in Saskatchewan. IMC Global is a good example of a company combining different types of continuous improvement processes. After it invested in the Six Sigma continuous improvement model, John Biedry, vice president for continuous improvement, felt the need for a method to target improvements that do not need the rigour of Six Sigma.

With the help of the Action Workout method from Leap Technologies, the company's potash mining facility in Saskatchewan was able to achieve impressive results. In the Action Workout method, workout teams made up of five to seven employees operate for 60 days or less, relying on structured improvement processes to guide their work. In Saskatchewan, one team evaluated miners' shift utilization to find inconsistencies and best practices—a process that resulted in reducing labour and materials costs by U.S.$59 000. An energy conservation team focused on reducing the use of natural gas and electricity in the mining facility and produced U.S.$68 000 in gains based on frontline employee ideas. A load-out productivity team investigated how loads of potash were being transported. That team made improvements in scheduling, routing, and loading procedures, saving the company U.S.$33 000.

Sources:
"Mining Company Accelerates Return on Six Sigma with Action Workout," *Quality Digest* (March 2002), www.qualitydigest.com/mar02/html/apps1.html.

IMC Global Inc., www.imcglobal.com.

Recognizing and Rewarding Quality

To encourage and promote high-quality goods and services, government and quasi-government organizations have begun recognizing those firms that provide outstanding levels of quality in the goods and services that they provide. Many countries, in fact, have some sort of quality award to recognize outstanding companies. In Japan for example, it is the Deming Prize; in the European Union it is the European Quality Award. Some of these national awards, such as the Canadian Awards for Excellence (CAE) and the Malcolm Baldrige National Quality Award (MBNQA) in the United States, recognize outstanding firms in several categories. Other forms of recognition, such as ISO 9000 and ISO 14000, which are international, take the form of certification.

Canada Awards for Excellence

The Canada Awards for Excellence (CAE) are quality awards given annually to Canadian organizations by the National Quality Institute (NQI) on behalf of the Canadian government.[11] The CAE are Canada's awards for recognizing outstanding achievement across major functions of the organization. Although some awards are unidimensional, the **CAE criteria** are broad based and look at many factors to ensure that excellence is evident throughout an organization. The seven main criteria are shown in Exhibit 6.7. The criteria are leadership, planning, customer focus, people focus, process management, supplier/partner focus, and overall business performance. Each of the seven main criteria have sub-criteria. Since its inception in 1984, hundreds of organizations have been honoured for their impressive accomplishments (see the OM in Practice Box on the NQI).

CAE criteria

Criteria for assessing overall quality of an organization and determining the winner(s) of the CAE awards.

---

[11]*Canadian Framework for Business Excellence* (Toronto: National Quality Institute, 2000).

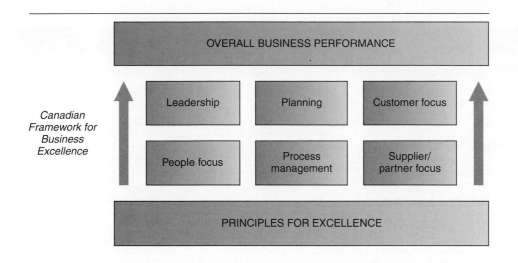

Exhibit 6.7

The Integrated Framework for the Canadian Awards for Excellence

Categories

There are three categories of Canada Awards for Excellence, adjudicated according to various NQI criteria:

Quality Award

● For public sector organizations; this award is adjudicated according to the Canadian Quality Criteria for Public Sector Excellence.

● For private sector businesses; this award is adjudicated according to the Canadian Framework for Business Excellence—Strategic Quality Approach.

Healthy Workplace Award

● This award is adjudicated according to the Canadian Healthy Workplace Criteria. This award evaluates employee well-being. See the opening vignette of Chapter 2 for the Dofasco example.

Education Award

● Starting in 2004, institutions involved in Kindergarten to K12 education can apply for a new education quality award.

● This award is adjudicated according to the Canadian Excellence in Education Criteria.

Forms of Recognition for the Awards

The Canada Awards for Excellence Gold trophy is awarded to organizations that have fully met the intent of the NQI criteria, with documented overall achievements and results.

The Canada Awards for Excellence Silver and Bronze are awarded to organizations that have completed some good work toward meeting the intent of the NQI criteria, but need some more time to get desired documented results, and are usually one or two years away from Gold Trophy recognition.

A list of recent winners in different categories is given in Exhibit 6.8a (the categories were revised in 2004; see Exhibit 6.8b). They include manufacturing and service organizations, both for-profit and not-for-profit, from different parts of the country.

Exhibit 6.8a

Recent Winners of the Canadian Awards for Excellence		
Year **Quality Trophy**	**Healthy Workplace Trophy**	**Certificate of Merit**
2003 College of Physicians and Surgeons of Nova Scotia, Halifax, Nova Scotia	Statistics Canada	Envision Financial, British Columbia
2002 Dana Canada Inc., Spicer Driveshaft Group, Magog, Quebec Canada Post, Saskatoon Operations Homewood Health Centre, Guelph, Ontario Mullen Trucking, Aldersyde, Alberta	Dofasco Inc., Hamilton, Ontario NCR, Mississauga, Ontario	CAE, Saint Laurent, Quebec
2001 Cardiac Care Network of Ontario, Toronto, Ontario Dana Corporation, Spicer Driveshaft Division, Thorold, Ontario Diversicare Canada Management Services Co., Inc., Ontario Division—Mississauga, Ontario IBM Solution Delivery Services, Markham Ontario Dana Canada Inc., Structural Solutions Division— Automotive Systems Group, Virgil, Ontario	Amex Canada Inc.	Gleneagles Elementary School, West Vancouver, BC Honeywell (FRAM) Consumer Products Group, Stratford, Ontario
2000 Aeronautical and Technical Services— Government of Canada British Columbia Transplant Society Delta Hotels Honeywell Water Controls Business Unit, Toronto		Lawrence Heights Middle School, Toronto District School Board SKF Canada
1999 Telus Operator Services, BC	MDS Nordion, TELUS—Corporate Health Services, BC	Neill & Gunter Limited, Fredericton, NB Celestica International Inc.
1998 Amex Canada Inc. Flemington Public School, Toronto, Ontario John Deere Limited TELUS Mobility Inc.		Honeywell Ltd., Hydronics Business Unit Trade Electric Supply Ltd.

Source: National Quality Institute Web site (www.nqi.com)

Exhibit 6.8b

Year Quality Award	Healthy Workplace Award	Customer Service Award for Small Business	Education Award
2005 **Gold Trophy** 3M Canada Company, NuComm International, St. Catharines, ON Xerox North American TeleWeb, Saint John, NB and Dartmouth, NS Telus, Vancouver, BC **Silver Award** Real Estate Board of Greater Vancouver, Vancouver, BC **Bronze Award** Purolator Courier Ltd., Mississauga, ON	**Gold Trophy** Homewood Health Centre, Guelph, ON **Gold Trophy** **Small Organization** Buffett Taylor & Associates Ltd., Whitby, ON	**Gold Trophy** Print Audit, Calgary, AB Venngo Inc., Toronto, ON Vubiz Ltd, Mississauga, ON	**Gold Trophy** R. H. King Academy, Scarborough, ON **Silver Award** Vincent Massey Public School, Ottawa, ON St. Luke Catholic Elementary School, Mississauga, ON
2004 **Gold Trophy** Polywheels Manufacturing Ltd., Oakville, ON **Silver Award** Formation Construction Engineering Maritime Forces Atlantic (Department of National Defence), Halifax, NS Region of Peel, ON Calian Technology, Kanata, ON	**Gold Trophy** DaimlerChrysler Canada and the Canadian Auto Workers, Delta Hotels **Bronze Award** **Small Organization** M&M Meat Shops Ltd. (Head Office), Kitchener, ON	**Silver Award** Strus & Associates Inc, Mississauga, ON **Bronze Award** Print Audit, Calgary, AB	**Silver Award** Henry Hudson Sr. Public School, Toronto, ON R. H. King Academy, Scarborough, ON

NQI PROGRESSIVE EXCELLENCE PROGRAM

Created in 1992, the National Quality Institute (NQI) is a not-for-profit organization that provides strategic focus and direction for Canadian organizations to achieve excellence in quality and healthy workplace practices. Funds are generated through memberships and the sales of products and services. The services are all focused on assisting Canadian organizations, both public and private, to increase productivity, heighten the level of organizational excellence, and develop healthy workplaces.

The NQI also offers four levels of Progressive Excellence Program (PEP) certification, giving companies a roadmap to implement NQI criteria into their organization in stages. Unlike the Canadian Awards for Excellence (CAE), which are one-time awards, these are certifications that have to be maintained through periodic assessments. At each level, the organizations are assessed every two years at which time they can also move up a level. In that respect they are similar to the ISO standards. Currently, organizations can be certified at different levels in the following categories: quality, healthy workplace, tourism, education, and Progressive Aboriginal Relations (PAR). The PAR certifications indicate a commitment by the organization to Canada's aboriginal peoples.

In addition to for-profit organizations, governmental organizations such as the municipalities of St. John, New Brunswick (Canada's oldest incorporated city), and Markham, Parry Sound, Sault. Ste. Marie, and Peel, all in Ontario, have achieved various levels of PEP certification. St. Luke Elementary School in Mississauga, Ontario recently became the first school in Canada to be certified. Details on these and other certified organizations can be found on the Web site of the NQI (www.nqi.com).

Sources:

David Helwig, "City of Sault Ste. Marie on PEP Journey," *SooToday.com*, April 9, 2003.

John Stewart, "Quality Marks Life at St. Luke," Mississauga News, March 3, 2003.

Dan Corbett, "PEP in the City," *Excellence Magazine*, National Quality Institute, November 29, 2002.

National Quality Institute, www.nqi.com.

Malcolm Baldrige National Quality Award (MBNQA)

Background

The Malcolm Baldrige National Quality Improvement Act was passed in 1987 to recognize total quality management in American industry. The Malcolm Baldrige National Quality Award (MBNQA), named after Malcolm Baldrige, who served as secretary of commerce from 1981 until his death in 1987, represents the United States government's endorsement of quality as an essential part of successful business strategy.

Without question, the MBNQA and its comprehensive criteria for evaluating total quality in an organization have had considerable impact. Initially the MBNQA was awarded in three categories: manufacturing, services, and small

business. Beginning in 1999, two additional categories were added: health care and education. For the most part, the MBNQA criteria are similar to the CAE criteria shown in Exhibit 6.7. The weights for the different criteria in the MBNQA are shown in Exhibit 6.9.

Benefits of the CAE and MBNQA Quality Criteria

For companies using them, the criteria serve many purposes. Indeed, part of the Baldrige criteria's power lies in the fact that they can be applied in many different ways to organizations whose quality improvement programs are of different maturities.

Exhibit 6.9

2001 MBNQA
Award Criteria—
Item Listing

Categories/Items	Points Values
1.0 Leadership	120
2.0 Strategic planning	85
3.0 Customer and market focus	85
4.0 Information and analysis	90
5.0 Human resource focus	85
6.0 Process management	85
7.0 Business results	450
Total Points	1000

Source: *2002 Criteria for Performance Excellence*, U.S. Dept. of Commerce,
Baldrige National Quality Program, National Institute of Standards and Technology,
Gaithersburg, MD 20899. (www.quality.nist.gov)

As a practical tool for assessing operations, the CAE and MBNQA guidelines can be used to:

1. Help define and design a total quality system
2. Evaluate ongoing internal relationships among departments, divisions, and functional units within an organization
3. Assess and assist outside suppliers of goods and services to a company
4. Assess customer satisfaction

Early-stage companies can use the guidelines as a checklist or blueprint to help them design their overall quality programs. Middle-stage companies can use them as a road map to guide them down the road to continued quality improvement. Finally, advanced-stage companies can use them as an evaluative tool to help fine-tune their quality programs and benchmark them against other industry and world leaders.

The guidelines also provide a common language for discussing quality across companies, functional areas, industries, and disciplines. By providing a broad, flexible approach to assessing total quality, the CAE and MBNQA systems foster improved information sharing and overall communications. These activities, in turn, lead employees and management to develop a shared meaning of total quality that can be built into the organization's goals and policies. From such shared meaning develops an organizational value system that is customer-focused, quality-driven, and central to the culture of the company.

ISO Standards

During the 1980s and into the 1990s, organizations around the world became more concerned about efficiently and effectively meeting the needs of their customers. Although national quality awards such as the Canadian Awards for Excellence and the Malcolm Baldrige National Quality Award in the United States had been bestowed on companies that had achieved high quality in their goods and services, increasing international trade made universal standards for quality more important. However, until 1987, there was no standardized way for supplier organizations around the world to demonstrate their quality practices or to improve the quality of their manufacturing or service processes. In that year, the International Organization for Standardization (ISO) published its first standards for quality management.

The International Organization for Standardization

ISO, headquartered in Geneva, Switzerland, is made up of representatives from each of the national standards bodies from over 90 countries. The Standards Council of Canada (SCC), a federal Crown corporation, is the Canadian member body of the ISO. As such, the SCC co-ordinates Canada's participation in the development of the ISO standards. ISO and the International Electrotechnical Commission (IEC), both nongovernmental organizations, work together to develop and publish voluntary standards, introducing as many as 800 new and revised standards each year. In 1986, after several years of development, ISO Technical Committee 176 completed the **ISO 9000 series quality standards**. It immediately became apparent that the ISO 9000 standards were different from the usual engineering standards, which often related to units of measure, standardization of terminology, and methods of testing. Instead, these new standards incorporated the belief that management practice can be standardized to the benefit of both the producers of goods and services and their customers.

ISO 9000 series quality standards
International set of standards for managing the processes that an organization uses to produce its goods and services.

The ISO 9000 Series of Standards

The purpose of the ISO 9000 standards is to satisfy the customer organizations' quality assurance requirements and to increase the level of confidence of the customer organizations in their suppliers. The series does not provide specific quality indicators or describe ways of achieving them, since these depend on the specific industry. Instead, the documents provide generic frameworks and general principles that can be applied to any organization of any size in any industry. The first major revisions to the ISO 9000 standards were completed in December 2000 with the issuance of the following three new standards that replaced the previously existing standards:[12]

- *ISO 9001:2000—Quality Management Systems—Requirements.* This standard is used to demonstrate the conformity of a quality management system to the requirements of customers and third parties. This standard is used for the certification of a firm's quality management systems.

- *ISO 9004:2000—Quality Management Systems—Guidelines for Performance Improvement.* This standard provides organizations with guidelines that can be used to establish a quality management system that is focused not only on meeting customer requirements but also on improving performance.

- *ISO 9000:2000—Quality Management Systems—Fundamentals and Standards.* This standard provides the terminology and definitions used in the first two standards.

ISO 9000 standards played a particularly important role in the formation of the European Union because they promoted a single, worldwide quality standard that would foster international trade and co-operation. Before long, organizations recognized that service management also could be improved through the application of the fundamentals of management practice that were set forth in the ISO 9000 standards.

ISO 9000 Certification

Registration procedures to become certified differ depending on the country.[13] In Canada, although it is possible for organizations to self-declare conformity, most companies are assessed by third-party quality system registrars for ISO 9000 certification, since most

---

[12]John E. West, "Implementing ISO 9001:2000," *Quality Progress* (May 2001), pp. 65–70.
[13]This section is based on the Standards Council of Canada (SCC) Web site (www.scc.ca) and conversations with Canadian Standards Association (CSA) personnel.

customers prefer their supplier to be independently assessed. The Standards Council of Canada (SCC) is the accreditation body for registrars.

The role of the registrars. The registrar is an external organization. Registrars apply to the SCC before auditing a firm. The SCC reviews their application information to determine if there is a conflict of interest (for example, a consultant organization that has been advising a company on ISO certification cannot be a registrar for that company). The individuals from the registrar who conduct the assessment are called auditors.

The ISO 9000 certification process. Companies follow a fairly straightforward process to obtain ISO 9000 certification. First, the firm submits an application to a registrar. Generally this involves providing information about the size and locations of the company, its products, what products will be included in the scope of the certification, who the firm's ISO contact people will be, and how the 20 elements of the standard are documented and supported by procedures. The registrar reviews the Quality Manual prior to the on-site audit.

The next step in the audit is a preliminary assessment, which is an on-site, mock audit lasting several days. The preliminary assessment determines the current state of operations at the firm. The registrar provides feedback to the firm and suggestions for corrective action. Once the issues of concern have been addressed, a full audit is performed.

The full audit typically takes two or three auditors two to four days to complete. Auditors review the company's facility and determine how processes have been documented. The auditor's final report is submitted to the registrar's Review Board, which makes a final determination about certification. If the company is not approved for certification, it has the right to appeal, first to the registrar, then to the SCC.

Once a firm has been certified, it has the right to use its registrar's mark on stationery and advertising, along with the mark of the SCC. However, it may not use these marks on its products because ISO 9000 certifies processes rather than products. There are companies that publish the list of certified companies to help organizations search for certified suppliers. For example, WedTech Inc., a plastics manufacturer with plants in Calgary, Alberta, and Brantford, Ontario, caught the attention of new customers after it achieved ISO 9002 certification.[14]

Although SCC's accreditation of a company does not mean that the certification is recognized worldwide, mutual agreements signed between the SCC and its counterparts in other countries mean participating accreditation bodies (which include those of most of Canada's major trading partners) will recognize the SCC's accreditation program as equivalent to their own.

Certification audits cost between $15 000 and $45 000. Companies will typically take 12 to 18 months to prepare for and undergo the registration process to become certified. Some companies undertake the registration process on their own; others engage outside consultants. The usual certification period is three years, after which the company has to seek recertification, although this can vary by registrar. During the certification period, surveillance audits are conducted once every year.

ISO 14000 Series

ISO 14000
International set of standards for managing processes that an organization uses for environmental management.

The **ISO 14000** series is a set of international standards and guidance documents for environmental management. Environmental management refers to the practice of managing the impact of an organization's activities on the environment. The ISO 14000 series provides a

[14]"Compounders Define Goals," *Canadian Plastics* (October 1994), pp. 6–11.

set of tools for determining the environmental aspects of an organization's activities, establishing goals and targets for those aspects, evaluating how well those goals and targets are being achieved, and for auditing, labelling, and continuously improving performance. Since the standards apply to all industries, the ISO 14000 series does not provide specific environmental targets or describe ways of achieving them. Instead, the documents provide generic frameworks and general principles. The series covers aspects such as consumption of natural resources and energy, and measuring and managing emissions, effluents, and other waste streams.

Having ISO 14000 does not necessarily indicate that a company's environmental performance is better than that of its competitors. However, since establishing and maintaining an environmental management system (EMS) requires a significant investment of time and resources, the registration indicates a company's commitment to monitoring, managing, and improving its environmental performance on an ongoing basis. To maintain its registration, the company must show not only consistency, but also improvement in its performance over time. As mentioned in Chapter 1, EPCOR in the electricity generating industry, and Canfor and Domtar in the forestry industry, have already become partially or fully certified. In 1999, Suncor's Sarnia Refinery became the first refinery in Canada to receive ISO 14001 certification, and every one of the company's operating businesses is expected to implement the ISO 14001 requirements.[15] In 2002, Dofasco's Hamilton steel plant became ISO 14001 certified.[16] In both cases these steps form a part of the company's goal to become more environmentally friendly.

Toward a Global Market

At the end of 1999, more than 340 000 ISO 9000-series and more than 14 000 ISO 14000-series registration certificates had been issued around the world. Slightly less than 10 000 ISO 9000 and about 200 ISO 14000 registrations were Canadian. Europe and the Far East led in the number of the registrations compared to North America, where the growth was slower.[17]

When customer organizations have an objective way to evaluate the quality of a supplier's processes, the risk of doing business with that supplier is significantly reduced. When quality standards are truly standardized around the world, customer firms can be more confident that supplier firms will produce the goods and services that will satisfy their needs.

Other standards While the ISO 9000 standards are generic to any industry, other quality system standards are specific to different industries. For example, the ISO/TS 16949 is a quality standard for the automotive industry, developed jointly by the ISO and International Automotive Task Force which is composed of international manufacturers and associations from across the automobile industry.[18] The ISO/TS 16949 standard specifies the quality system requirements for the design, development, production, and installation/servicing of automotive-related products.

[15]Suncor Energy Inc., www.suncor.com.

[16]Dofasco Inc., www.dofasco.com.

[17]*Management Systems Standards*: *The Story So Far. Canada's Experience with ISO 9000, ISO 14000 and QS-9000* (Ottawa, Ontario: Standards Council of Canada, 2000), p. 1.

[18] www.thewindow.to/iso9000/ts-16949.htm Accessed, December 10, 2005.

Conclusion

The production and delivery of high-quality goods and services are critical elements in determining the long-term success of an organization. No longer is quality looked upon only from the narrow perspective of defects. Rather, managers are now recognizing that quality has many dimensions and that they need to identify the dimensions that are most important to the specific market segments they serve.

The quality of the goods and services now being provided has increased significantly over the last several decades, due in large part to increased global competition. With competition expected to continue in the near future, we can expect the quality of goods and services to increase.

Thus, quality management as a strategic issue should not be approached with an off-the-shelf program devised by others. Quality must be integrated internally and externally. Managers are paid to use new quality concepts, but more important, to lead customization and integration of these concepts into their organizations.

Key Terms

CAE criteria p. 204

conformance quality p. 200

continuous improvement
   p. 199

cost of detection/appraisal
   p. 196

cost of failure p. 196

cost of prevention p. 196

cost of quality p. 195

design quality p. 200

external failure costs p. 196

internal failure costs p. 196

ISO 9000 series quality
   standards p. 209

ISO 14000 p. 210

poka-yoke p. 200

quality dimensions p. 189

quality gurus p. 192

Six Sigma p. 202

statistical process control
   (SPC) p. 192

total quality management
   (TQM) p. 198

Review and Discussion Questions

1. Is quality free? Debate!
2. Identify the quality dimensions for each of the following:
   a. IBM personal computer
   b. School registration process
   c. Steakhouse
   d. University
   e. Travel agency
   f. Television
3. An agreement is made between a supplier and a customer such that the supplier must ensure that all parts are within tolerance before shipment to the customer. What is the effect on the cost of quality to the customer?
4. In the situation described in Question 3, what would be the effect on the cost of quality to the supplier?
5. If line employees are required to assume the quality control function, their productivity will decrease. Discuss this.

6. "You don't inspect quality into a product; you have to build it in." Discuss the implications of this statement.
7. How could you apply the CAE criteria to your college or university?
8. How is the CAE award process beneficial to companies who do not win?
9. What is the major contribution of the ISO 9000 standards?
10. Compare the ISO certification process with the CAE award criteria. What are the main differences?
11. What are some of the reasons that quality initiatives fail in organizations? How can these be overcome?
12. What are some of the major reasons for the success of Six Sigma?
13. Find out if your province or territory has a quality award, and if it does, describe it.

Internet Exercise

Compare the European Quality Award and the Deming Prize with the CAE and MBNQA.

Case 1

Death on the Highway: Quality Problems at Ford and Firestone

On August 9, 2000, Bridgestone/Firestone, Inc., officially announced that it was voluntarily recalling 6.5 million of its Wilderness AT tires, a large portion of which had been installed on Ford's very popular sports utility vehicle (SUV), the Explorer. In the ensuing months, it was revealed that Ford Explorers that were equipped with Firestone's Wilderness AT tires had been involved in a significant number of rollover accidents resulting in more than 170 deaths and over 700 injuries on U.S. highways, and more than 40 deaths elsewhere in the world.[1]

Both Ford and Firestone began firing off verbal salvos to the media and public, each blaming the other for the accidents. Congressional investigations were also initiated to determine the causes of these accidents, with the heads of both firms called to testify. In the period following Bridgestone/Firestone's initial recall it was revealed that multiple product-liability lawsuits had been filed against both companies.

In May 2001, 10 months after the initial recall announcement, Bridgestone/Firestone announced that it would no longer supply tires to Ford, citing "significant concerns" relating to the safety of the Explorer. A day later, Ford's then CEO Jacques Nasser announced the recall of 13 million Firestone Wilderness AT tires that had been installed on Ford Explorers and pickup trucks, noting a lack of confidence in "the future performance of these (Firestone) tires in keeping our customers safe."[2]

Without warning, when an Explorer is travelling at relatively high speeds, the tread on the Wilderness AT tires can separate from the tire, resulting in a noisy blowout. The Explorer, a heavy vehicle like many SUVs, has a high centre of gravity and much of its weight is over its axles. Consequently, when a blowout occurs, the Explorer has a tendency to roll over, often causing death or serious injury to one or more of the vehicle's occupants.

In designing the Explorer to combine ruggedness, room, comfort, and a smooth ride, Ford mounted the cabin, which has all of the luxury of a relatively expensive car, on a narrow truck frame. To accomplish this, Ford needed to set both higher load limits and also lower tire pressure requirements for the Explorer. Unfortunately, while this combination may have met consumer preferences pertaining to size and aesthetics, it ignored the reality of American driving habits: Americans tend to drive fast, with little attention to tire maintenance, and to rely heavily on built-in safety features such as seatbelts, airbags, and rollbar construction to keep them from harm in the event of an accident. While there is little or no margin of safety from vehicle rollover with underinflated tires on a vehicle such as the Explorer, Ford recommended tire pressure of 26 psi (pounds per square inch), which was lower than Firestone's recommendation of 30 psi.[3] In addition, little effort was made by either Ford or Firestone to emphasize to Explorer owners (or owners of any vehicle for that matter) the importance of maintaining adequate tire pressure. In cool weather, tires can lose 1 to 2 pounds of air pressure per month, and more in warmer weather. To compound this problem, car owners seldom check tire pressure. In fact, it was reported that 8 percent of the tires replaced during Firestone's 2000 recall had tire pressure below 23 psi.[4]

Financial Impact

Since voluntarily recalling 6.5 million tires in August 2000, Bridgestone/Firestone, Inc., Bridgestone's U.S. subsidiary and builder of the recalled tires, has posted a $510 million loss for fiscal year (FY) 2000, resulting from special charges of $750 million associated with the recall and anticipated liability damage claims. Bridgestone officials also anticipated a $200 million loss for its U.S. subsidiary in FY 2001. Shares of Japan's Bridgestone stock have lost more than half their value since the August 2000 tire recall, and Bridgestone's consolidated net profit for FY 2000 was 80 percent lower than for the previous fiscal year and its lowest profit in the past 10 years. In January 2001, the sales of Firestone replacement tires were down 40 percent from January 2000.[5]

The tire recall in August 2000 cost Ford $550 million and the company currently faces hundreds of lawsuits seeking cumulative damages of more than $590 million. Subsequent to the August 2000 recall, Ford announced a recall of more than one million Firestone tires that had been installed on Ford Explorers after August 2000, and in May 2001 it recalled an additional 13 million Wilderness AT tires that were original equipment on its SUVs and pickup trucks. It is estimated that Ford will spend $3 billion replacing these tires, and Ford has indicated that it will take a charge of $2.1 billion in the second quarter of 2001. Ford officials have indicated that they expect a second quarter loss of 35 cents a share and have suspended their share repurchase program. Furthermore, the shortage of tires due to the May 2001 recall caused Ford to shut down its operations at the Ford Ranger truck plant for two weeks, and two Ford Explorer plants were idled for one week each.[6]

Automobile Design and Manufacture

The creation of a new automobile model involves many trade-offs. In attempting to respond to both consumer desires and competitive pressures, auto manufacturers often face many conflicting choices between their marketing, engineering, and manufacturing functions, and, unfortunately, safety. In designing the rugged, roomy, comfortable Explorer, Ford SUV engineers, due to previous management decisions, mounted the plush cabin on a narrow truck frame and front-end suspension system that was designed in the 1960s.

During prototype design and testing of the Explorer in the late 1980s, Ford was in the midst of responding to more than 800 lawsuits resulting from accidents involving rollovers of its Bronco II, which were eventually settled for approximately $2.4 billion. The Bronco II had a higher centre of gravity and was a less aerodynamically stable vehicle with its unique "Twin I-Beam" suspension system.

In spite of these problems, Ford decided to use this same suspension system on the Explorer because it allowed Ford to manufacture its new SUV on existing assembly lines. The end result was a heavy vehicle with a high centre of gravity, much of its weight above the axles, a rigid ladder frame, and extremely flexible leaf springs that when unsprung could release weight with great force—all precursors to rollover when a vehicle is driven too fast through tight turns and sudden changes of direction.[7]

Internal Ford memos and e-mails pertaining to the Explorer and Firestone Wilderness AT tire, which were made public during congressional investigations, revealed that Ford was aware, as early as 1987, that "light truck rollovers are 2 to 4 times the car rate" and that the developers of the SUV were urged to contemplate "any design actions that improve vehicle stability or help maintain the passenger safety in the vehicle." Ford engineers struggled with decisions relating to the Explorer's stability and handling, including its suspension system, weight and height, steering characteristics, and tire pressure. A 1989 internal Ford engineering report indicated that the Explorer prototype "demonstrated a rollover response ... with a number of tire, tire pressure (and) suspension configurations," and a test report revealed that during handling maneuvers, this prototype had a greater tendency than even the Bronco II to lift its wheels off the ground while turning. In addition, although the safety record of the Bronco II was suspect, the test report noted that the Explorer had to be "at least equivalent to the Bronco II in these maneuvers to be considered acceptable for production." Still another internal Ford report included an observation that the Explorer's "relatively high engine position ... prevents further significant improvement in the Stability Index (a measure of resistance to tipping) without extensive suspension, frame, and sheet metal revisions." Ford engineers offered the following four alternatives for improving the stability of the Explorer as the 1990 production date approached: (1) widen the chassis by two inches, (2) lower the engine, (3) lower the recommended tire pressure, and (4) stiffen the springs. Ford's management chose to recommend a lower tire pressure of 26 pounds per square inch (psi) (although Bridgestone/Firestone's recommendation was 30 psi) and stiffen the springs.

By 1995, Ford had replaced the twin I-beam suspension, although they did not lower the engine or make the chassis wider. The new, lighter suspension system, however, raised, rather than lowered, the Explorer's centre of gravity.

Ford chose to equip the Explorer with Firestone's Wilderness AT P235 tire, although internal Ford documents revealed that the Consumer Union (CU) tests that the Explorer underwent indicated "a high confidence of passing CU with Firestone's P225 tires and less confidence on the Firestone's P235" and that Ford's "management is aware of the potential risk with the P235 and has accepted that risk; the CU test is generally unrepresentative of the real world and I see no real risk in failing the CU test except what may result in the way of spurious litigation."[8]

Tire Design and Manufacture

The Wilderness AT tires that were mounted on the Explorer were produced by Firestone to Ford's specifications. Among the many decisions made when specifying tire characteristics is heat resistance. The heat resistance standards used at the time of the design of the Explorer to rate tires were established in 1968, nearly 20 years earlier, and were based on the ways in which motorists drove at that time. While nearly all SUV manufacturers equip these vehicles with "B" rated tires, Ford's specifications called for a lower-heat-resistant "C" rated tire. "C" rated tires must meet the standard of being able to endure two hours at 50 m.p.h. and an additional 90 minutes at speeds of up to 85 m.p.h. when the tire is inflated to the manufacturer's recommended pressure and the vehicle load is within the recommended load limit. The tire pressure recommended by Ford for the Wilderness AT was 26 psi, in spite of the fact that Firestone recommended a higher inflation pressure of 30 psi.[9]

Many manufacturers of steel-belted radial tires install a nylon layer between the steel belts and tread to decrease the steel belt's chafing on the tread rubber. This safety feature reduces the chance of tread separation in an otherwise properly constructed tire. During the investigation of the cause of the Explorer rollover accidents, tire experts testified that cost is the only reason not to install the nylon caps and it has been estimated by consumer advocates that the cost to include the nylon cap can range from pennies to as much as $1.00 per tire. The Firestone Wilderness AT tires that were on Explorers did not include this nylon safety layer.[10]

Introduced in the United States in the 1960s, steel-belted tires, which are stronger, last longer, and contribute to improved gas mileage, were considered to be a technology breakthrough in the tire industry. One of the problems, however, that tire makers have continuously attempted to overcome through changes in the way the belts are constructed and bonded is having the steel and rubber properly adhere to each other, which is somewhat akin to mixing oil and water. The fresher the rubber, the more adhesive it is, and the more adhesive the rubber, the better it adheres to the steel belts and other tire components.

Tires are highly engineered products with more than a dozen parts, such as treads and sidewalls, requiring very sophisticated equipment to manufacture. To achieve the low costs demanded by automakers, tire manufacturers utilize highly automated, sprawling plants to obtain significant economies of scale. As a consequence, separate tire parts are often made in multiple locations throughout the plant, requiring large quantities of work-in-process inventory throughout the facility. The various parts are typically brought together and added, one by one, in the final assembly and fabrication operation, which takes place on massive tire machines. Scattered throughout the plant, inventories of sticky rubber often can pick up debris that can decrease the strength of the rubber.

Although the Firestone P235/75R-15 Wilderness AT tire is made at several Firestone plants in the United States, the highest level of tread separation complaints were for those tires made at Firestone's Decatur, Illinois, facility. During 1996, Firestone received

10 times more complaints related to tires made in Decatur than for the same size and model tire made at its other plants. Such complaints did fall by approximately 50 percent during 1997 and were much lower for tires built in Decatur during 1998 and 1999.[11]

With the exception of the Decatur plant, Firestone utilizes a slab system in which long sheets of the rubber used to coat the steel belts are extruded. The Decatur plant utilizes a process known as pelletizing, where rubber pellets are churned out and blended with a lubricant to create the rubber components. It has been reported that Firestone has discovered that rubber made by the pelletizing process was chemically different and weaker than that created by the slab system, with the lubricant apparently contributing to rubber breakdown and tread separation.

Former Firestone employees, including both production workers and tire inspectors at the Decatur plant during the period in which the allegedly flawed tires were produced, have made statements or have given testimony during litigation or government investigations that raise serious doubts about both the production and quality processes there. Among these assertions are that

- Workers punctured air bubbles that developed in the skim coat and sidewalls in some tires during production, after which, if the tire passed an air-leak test, it was returned to the production process.

- A chemical solvent, benzene, was added to old, dry rubber after it sat too long to restore its tackiness (excessive use of benzene can reduce the quality of the tire material).

- Relations between labour and management have been strained during and since a bitter $2\frac{1}{2}$ year strike by the United Steelworkers of America, the union representing the tire workers.

- The ability and skills of replacement workers employed by Firestone during the strike were suspect.

- The 12-hour shifts required of workers coupled with high production quotas and the payment of an hourly rate based on meeting tire-production quotas caused lack of attention to quality.

- Tire inspectors often were required to examine 100 tires per hour and, consequently, tires often received little or no inspection.[12]

In addition to these issues, the president of Bridgestone has acknowledged that the same quality control criteria were not applied equally to both its Bridgestone and Firestone tires. "If there was a problem with a Bridgestone tire, our technology staff in Tokyo would rush to the site" overseas to help out, he said. "But if a problem arose with a Firestone tire, they wouldn't do anything."[13]

Questions

1. In addition to the financial costs mentioned, what are some of the other costs, both internal and external to the firms, that can be associated with the poor quality of the Firestone tires and Ford Explorers?

2. Identify some of the management decisions at both Ford and Firestone that may have contributed to poor quality. What was the rationale for these decisions?

3. For both Ford and Firestone, identify the potential causes for the accidents that occurred.

Source:

Copyright © by James Salsbury and Mark Davis.

This case describes an actual business situation and was prepared using information obtained from public sources. Neither Ford nor Firestone was contacted directly and asked to present their views on this matter.

Endnotes

1 John Greenwald, "Tired of Each Other," *Time* (June 4, 2001): 51–52.
2 Ibid.
3 Milo Geyelin, "Theories Mount Regarding Root of Tire Defects," *The Wall Street Journal*, Aug. 23, 2000, p. B9.
4 Stephen Powers, and Timothy Aeppel, "Firestone Ties Accidents to Weight of Explorer—Ford Denies that Load Increased Significantly," *Asian Wall Street Journal*, December 23, 2000, p. 1.

5 Todd Zaun, "Bridgestone's Net Fell 80% Last Year—Results Reflect Huge Loss at U.S. Unit After Firestone Recall—Outlook for Subsidiary's Sales and Bottom Line Remains Grim," *Asian Wall Street Journal*, February 23, 2001, p. 4.

6 David Kiley, "Ford Bites $3B Bullet to Replace Tires Firestone Viewed as Risk," *USA Today*, May 23, 2001, p. B1.

7 Royal Ford, "Ford Lightens Up on Explorer for Safety's Sake," *Boston Globe*, December 16, 2000, p. D1.

8 Greenwald, John, "Tired of Each Other," *Time*, June 4, 2001, p. 52.

9 Holman W. Jenkins Jr., "Tires and Torts: Parsing Out the Firestone Blame," *Asian Wall Street Journal*, May 31, 2001, p. 6.

10 James R. Healey and Sara Nathan, "Could $1 Worth of Nylon Have Saved People's Lives? Experts: Caps on Steel Belts May Help Stop Shredded Tires," *USA Today*, August 9, 2000, p. B1.

11 Earle Eldridge and Sara Nathan, "Data Point to Firestone Tires Made at Illinois Factory—Ford Analysis Shows High Rate of Warranty Claims from Decatur Plant," *USA Today*, August 14, 2000, p. B1.

12 Thomas A. Fogarty, "Retirees Cite Production Practices—Depositions in '92 Case May Shed Light on Recent Problems, but Company, Unions Dispute Claims," *USA Today*, August 24, 2000, p. B3; Timothy Aeppel, "Ex-Firestone Workers to Testify in Suit—Retired Decatur Employees Are Expected to Call Tire Inspection Rushed," *The Wall Street Journal*, August 23, 2000, p. A3; Hames R. Healey and Sara Nathan, "Could $1 Worth of Nylon Have Saved People's Lives? Experts: Caps on Steel Belts May Help Stop Shredded Tires," *USA Today*, August. 9, 2000, p. B1.

13 Miki Tanikawa, "Bridgestone President Admits Tire Quality-Control Problems," *The New York Times*, September 10, 2000, p. C12.

S6

Quality Control Tools for Improving Processes

Supplement Objectives

- Introduce the different quality control tools that are used for analyzing and improving the quality of processes.

- Describe in detail the two major approaches —acceptance sampling and statistical process control—in which statistical analysis can be used to improve process quality.

- Define the two different types of errors that can occur when statistical sampling is used.

- Distinguish between attributes and variables with respect to the statistical analysis of processes.

- Discuss Taguchi methods and how they are different from traditional statistical quality control methods.

- Describe the quantitative methodology behind six sigma.

The Basic Quality Control Tools

There are a number of tools that can be used to collect, present, and analyze data about any kind of process, including service processes. Some of the tools described in this section are simple and straightforward to use; others require some understanding of statistics. Whatever tool is used, the goal in using it is to provide management with the proper information to make better decisions about how to design and improve process performance.

Within the quality literature, seven basic tools have been identified that can assist managers in improving the quality of their processes. These seven basic quality control (QC) tools are: (1) process flow charts (or diagrams), (2) bar charts and histograms, (3) Pareto charts, (4) scatterplots (or diagrams), (5) run (or trend) charts, (6) cause-and-effect (or fishbone) charts, and (7) statistical process control. The first six tools are presented in this section, along with checksheets, another tool used to collect data. Statistical process control is presented in detail later in this supplement.

Process Flow Charts (or Diagrams)

Process flow diagrams or *flow charts* show each of the steps required to produce either a good or a service. As described in Chapter 5, tasks are typically depicted as rectangles, waits or inventories as inverted triangles, and decision points as diamonds. Arrows connecting these activities show the direction of flow in the process. In service operations, flow charts often are referred to as "service blueprints."

The primary purpose for using flow chart analysis in Chapter 5 is to properly sequence the

various tasks required to produce a given product or service and to identify any bottlenecks in the process that limit its overall capacity. The purpose of flowcharting, from a quality improvement perspective, is to identify those steps in the process that could be potential sources of error.

Checksheets

Most of us have collected data about some process by noting how frequently an event occurs and making a tick mark for a particular category in a *checksheet*. For example, if a company wanted to collect information about the various customer complaints it received on a product such as a vacuum cleaner, it would identify the different types of complaints and then note the frequency with which each complaint was made, as shown in Exhibit S6.1.

As another example of a checksheet, restaurant managers might want to collect information about the type of demand coming into the restaurant, in terms of group size, so they can determine how to arrange tables more effectively. To collect these data, the host or hostess would use a checksheet to record the size of each group as it arrives, as shown in Exhibit S6.2.

What is most important about checksheets is that the categories not overlap and that all categories be listed; in other words, categories should be mutually exclusive and collectively exhaustive. An example of a confusing checksheet at the same restaurant would be one that, instead of listing group size, listed "couples, families, groups of friends." These categories don't capture all possibilities (business groups, for example, might not fit into any of those categories) and it is possible that the categories could overlap (families with friends). In addition, the different people collecting the data may not all make the same determination of which categories to put the same group into—and the data, when finally collected, most likely would not be very useful.

Type of Complaint	Frequency
Cord too short	ⅢⅢ ⅢⅢ
Dirt bags hard to change	ⅢⅢ
Too heavy	ⅢⅢ ⅢⅢ
Breaks down a lot	ⅢⅢ ‖
Accessories don't always work	‖‖
Other	‖‖‖

Exhibit S6.1

Checksheet for Recording Complaints

Customers in Party	Count
1	‖‖‖
2	ⅢⅢ ⅢⅢ ⅢⅢ ⅢⅢ ‖‖
3	ⅢⅢ ⅢⅢ ‖‖
4	ⅢⅢ ⅢⅢ ⅢⅢ ⅢⅢ ⅢⅢ ⅢⅢ‖
5	ⅢⅢ ⅢⅢ ⅢⅢ
6	ⅢⅢ ‖‖
>6	‖‖

Exhibit S6.2

Checksheet for Group Sizes in a Restaurant

Bar Charts and Histograms

Bar charts and *histograms* visually display data variation. A bar chart is used to graph nominal data (also called "categorical" or "attribute" data), which are data that can be categorized and counted, rather than measured. For example, a manager might count the number of units produced each day on an assembly line, as shown in Exhibit S6.3.

Histograms are used to display continuous data that can be measured. For example, a quality control inspector might measure the diameter of a hole on a part. Because the scale is continuous, we need to first determine how to divide it into intervals. In this case, we could use intervals of .010, .025, .050, or .100 cm, depending on how much variation there is in the diameters of the hole. If the intervals are too small, we will only have one data point in each cell; at the other extreme, if the interval is too large, we will have all the data in one cell. Histogram intervals (which also are referred to as "buckets" or "bins") must all be the same size and must not overlap (see Exhibit S6.4).

Pareto Charts

Pareto charts (sometimes referred to as *Pareto analysis*) are specialized bar charts. As illustrated in Exhibit S6.5, the frequency of occurrence of errors is sorted in descending order and a cumulative percentage line is typically added to make it easier to determine how the errors add up. Pareto charts can help to establish priorities for action, focusing attention on those errors that occur most frequently.

Exhibit S6.3

Bar Chart of Daily Units Produced

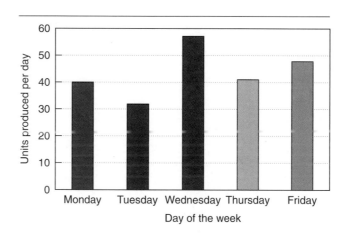

Exhibit S6.4

Histogram of Hole Diameters

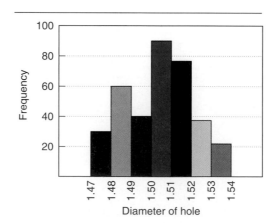

Operations Management in Practice

PRIORITIZING ERRORS AT FEDEX

To ensure the highest possible quality of delivery of its packages, FedEx measures its delivery performance every day in every facility, using a service quality index (SQI). The SQI for each location is calculated by multiplying the frequency of each of the errors that occurred in a given day by their respective weights. Using weights is a modification of the traditional Pareto chart, which is unweighted. Weights may be estimated by gauging the importance of that error type to a customer through surveys. To illustrate how the SQI is calculated, the various errors that could occur are shown below along with their actual respective weights and a theoretical number of times each error occurred in a hypothetical region.

If the errors were unweighted, then the manager, using Pareto analysis, would assign priority to the traces, because they occurred the most often. By weighting each of the errors as shown above, the manager's first priority is to eliminate lost packages.

Source:
Special thanks to Bob Wall, FedEx.

Type of Error	Weight	Frequency	Weighted Value
Lost package	50	1	50
Damaged package	30	1	30
Overnight wrong day	10	2	20
Other wrong day late	10	2	20
Traces	3	5	15
International priority inbound wrong day late	10	1	10
Complaint reopened	10	1	10
Late pickup stops	3	3	9
Package not cleared for international destination	3	2	6
Abandoned calls	1	4	4
Domestic right day late	1	2	2
Missing proof of delivery	1	2	2
International right day late	1	1	1
Invoice adjustment	1	1	1

SQI for region: 180

Exhibit S6.5 is a Pareto chart that shows the responses to an internal hospital survey about what factors need to be changed in emergency room processes.

However, there are times when the frequency of occurrence by itself does not determine how important an error problem might be. For example, when making a bar chart of student complaints about a university food service, it might be known that complaints about waiting in line are twice as common as complaints about food availability, but that students consider food availability to be five times more important than waiting. The Pareto diagram can weight the factors being considered to enable managers to take action on those items that most need attention, as illustrated in the following OM in Practice box.

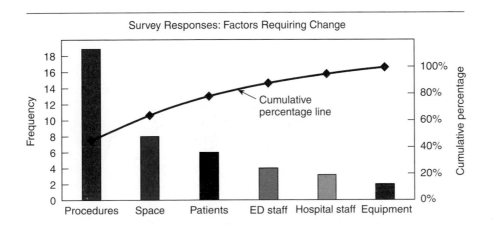

Exhibit S6.5

Pareto Chart of Factors in an Emergency Room

221

Scatterplots (or Diagrams)

Scatterplots show the relationship between two measured (not counted) variables. For example, in an upscale restaurant, you may want to understand the relationship between how long customers wait to have their orders taken and how satisfied they are with their service. You could measure the wait time to order in minutes and you could assess customer satisfaction with a survey, using a scale of 1 to 10. It is likely that for this restaurant, you would see a relationship resembling the one shown in Exhibit S6.6; that is, customers are less satisfied when waits are either too short or too long. If the wait is too short, customers may feel that they are being rushed because they do not have enough time to study the menu and make a decision about what they want to order; if it is too long, they may be frustrated by the slow responsiveness of the service staff.

Run (or Trend) Charts

Run charts show the behaviour of some variable over time. For example, suppose a plant manager would like to keep track of the number of errors that occur each day with respect to manufacturing a given product. The manager would record the number of errors that occurred each day and plot them on a run chart, as shown in Exhibit S6.7. The run chart shows that after the week ending July 20, there was a significant reduction in the number of errors that occurred. (Additional investigation might reveal that the workers had completed a training course that week on how to use the new equipment that had been installed.)

Exhibit S6.6

Scatterplot of Customer Satisfaction and Waiting Time in an Upscale Restaurant

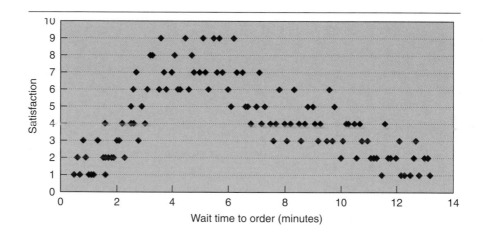

Exhibit S6.7

Run Chart of the Number of Daily Errors

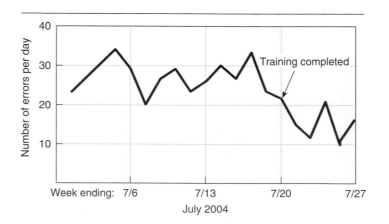

Cause-and-Effect (or Fishbone) Diagrams

Cause-and-effect diagrams (also known as *fishbone diagrams* or *Ishikawa diagrams*) are used to identify the causes that lead to a particular outcome or effect. Major categories of the causes are first identified; then, for each cause, "Why?" is asked until the root cause for that category can be identified. Exhibit S6.8 shows a cause-and-effect diagram for customer complaints in a restaurant. If customers complain about server rudeness, the cause of the rudeness must be discovered before the proper action can be taken. In this example, the servers might be rude because they are rushed, and they are rushed because they are assigned too many tables. The table assignment process should be the target of managerial action, then, rather than admonishing servers to be more polite.

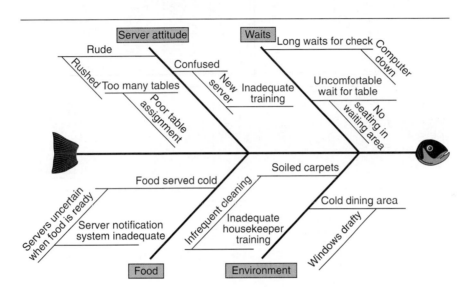

Exhibit S6.8

Cause-and-Effect Diagram for Customer Complaints in a Restaurant

Advanced Quality Tools

Shigeru Mizuno described several advanced quality tools, among them the affinity diagram, the interrelationship digraph (or relations diagram), the tree diagram, and the matrix diagram.[1] Like the seven basic quality tools, the advanced quality tools focus users on the issues, rather than their feelings about the issues, and present information in such a way that patterns are easy to identify.

Affinity Diagram

Affinity diagrams are used to structure the ideas generated from a discussion or brainstorming session. They clarify ideas by organizing them according to their affinity, or similarity, to each other. To build an affinity diagram, participants write their ideas on pieces of paper or sticky notes, one idea to a note. They collect the notes and spread them out on a table or wall, then arrange them into related groups. After all the ideas are grouped, participants name each category and look for the relationships between them.

For example, a group of faculty held a working session on team learning and used an affinity diagram to organize their ideas about what students should learn from teamwork. They generated a list of items, grouped them into categories, and finally arranged the categories to show the relationships between them, as shown in Exhibit S6.9.

---

[1]Shigeru Mizuno, *Management for Quality Improvement: The Seven New QC Tools* (Cambridge, MA: Productivity Press, 1988).

Exhibit S6.9

Affinity Diagram of Team Learning Objectives

Team Learning: Skills and Dimensions

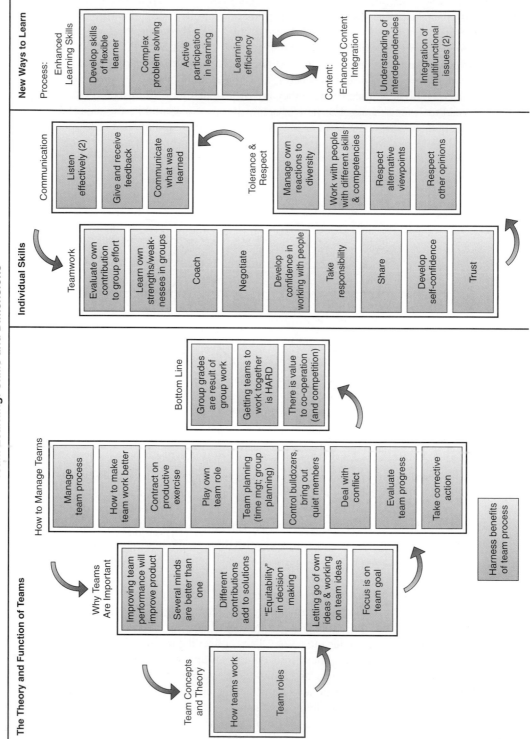

Interrelationship Digraph

Like an affinity diagram, an *interrelationship digraph* helps to sort out cause-and-effect relationships. Interrelationship digraphs are used when there are a large number of interrelated issues that need to be better understood. They help to focus discussion and build a deeper understanding of how factors affect each other. Interrelationship digraphs are built by agreeing on the issues, identifying the elements that are important and showing them on the diagram, and connecting related elements with arrows that point from the factor that influences to the factor that is influenced. If two elements influence each other, the arrow is depicted in a way that shows which element has greater influence. When the exercise is completed, the elements with the most outgoing arrows are shown to be the drivers or causes that lead to the outcomes or results, which are the elements with the most incoming arrows. Exhibit S6.10 shows an interrelationship digraph for late discharge from a hospital surgical unit. "No preplanning for discharge" is clearly a driver for several other issues that contribute to late discharges.

Tree Diagram

A *tree diagram* helps users to systematically determine ways to efficiently and effectively meet objectives. The tree diagram breaks down the main goal into subgoals and actions and promotes agreement among group members by clearly identifying and displaying the strategy to be taken. Exhibit S6.11 shows the basic structure of a tree diagram.

Matrix Diagram

A *matrix diagram* is used to organize information that can be compared on a variety of characteristics in order to make a comparison, selection, or choice. The diagram arranges elements of a problem or event in rows and columns on a chart that shows relationships among each pair of elements. The information is easy to visualize and comprehend. Exhibit S6.12 shows a matrix diagram for different plans that can be implemented to achieve a goal. Each plan is evaluated according to established performance criteria.

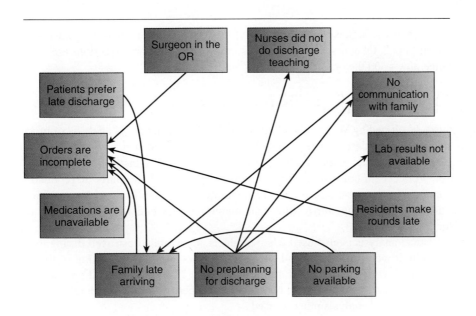

Exhibit S6.10

Relations Diagram for Late Hospital Discharge

Exhibit S6.11

Basic Structure of a Tree Diagram

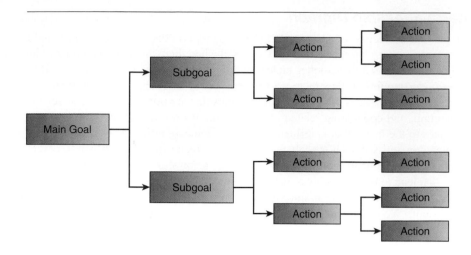

Exhibit S6.12

Matrix Diagram

Plan \ Criteria	Strategic fit	Feasibility	Time	Cost	Total
Plan 1	◉	◯	△	◉	22
Plan 2	◉	◉	◉	△	28
Plan 3	◯	◯	◯	△	10
Plan 4	◯	△	◯	◉	16
Plan 5	△	◯	△	◉	14

◉ Excellent = 9
◯ Fair = 3
△ Poor = 1

Plan 2 achieves the highest score on the performance criteria, so it would make sense to implement Plan 2. Of course, the criteria according to which plans or actions are evaluated determine how good the outcome of matrix analysis will be.

Statistical Analysis of Processes

Although developed by Walter Shewhart in the 1920s, the statistical analysis of processes was not put into widespread use until World War II, and then it was used only out of necessity. At that time, it was realized that the testing and/or inspection of a sample of parts or products (in comparison to testing/inspecting all of the parts or products) was both faster and more economical because it required significantly less labour. With a significant labour shortage during the war, manufacturers had little choice but to use statistical analysis.

Statistical analysis is also used when products are actually destroyed during the tests. For example, it would not have made sense to conduct 100 percent testing of the bombs and bullets that were manufactured during World War II. Similarly, food products cannot be 100 percent taste-tested, nor can batteries be 100 percent tested for durability. In such situations, statistical analysis must be used.

There are two broad categories of statistical tools: (1) acceptance sampling, which assesses the quality of the parts or products after they have been produced, and (2) statistical process control, which assesses whether or not an ongoing process is performing within established limits. The mathematical calculations are the same for each category, although the interpretation of results is different, as we shall see shortly.

Attributes and Variables

Within each of these broad categories, statistical quality control methods can be further divided into two additional categories: The first approach uses **attribute data** (that is, data that are counted, such as the number of defective parts produced or the number of dissatisfied customers); the second approach uses **variable data** (that is, data that are measured, such as the length of a wire or the weight of a package of cereal). Each approach can be used in either acceptance sampling or statistical process control, as shown in Exhibit S6.13.

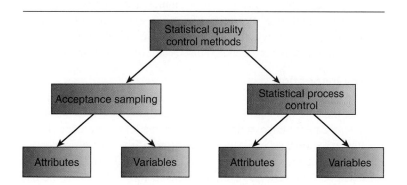

Exhibit S6.13

Statistical Quality Control Methods

Sampling Errors

When we use a sample from a larger population or from the output generated by a process instead of monitoring the entire population or output, there is the possibility that the sample results are not representative of the actual population or process. When this occurs, we have a sampling error. There are two types of sampling errors that can occur, as shown in Exhibit S6.14. The first occurs when the population is considered bad or the process is considered out of control, when neither is the case. This type of error is referred to as an

Exhibit S6.14

Types of Sampling Errors

		The population or process is actually:	
		Good or in control	Bad or out of control
The sample says that the population or process is:	Good or in control	In agreement	β or Type II error
	Bad or out of control	α or Type I error	In agreement

types of sampling errors:

α error, Type I error, or producer's risk
Occurs when a sample says parts are bad or the process is out of control when the opposite is true.

β error, Type II error, or consumer's risk
Occurs when a sample says parts are good or the process is in control when just the reverse is true.

α error, Type I error, or producer's risk. The second type of sampling error occurs when the population is considered good or the process is considered in control, when they really are not. This type of error is referred to as a **β error**, **Type II error**, or **consumer's risk**. Balancing the risk of occurrence between the Type I and Type II errors is a major consideration in determining the sample size and the control limits.

Acceptance Sampling

Designing a Sampling Plan for Attributes

Acceptance sampling, as previously stated, is performed on goods that already exist to determine if they conform to specifications. These products may be items received from another company and evaluated by the receiving department or they may be components that have passed through a processing step and are evaluated by company personnel either in production or later in the warehousing function.

Acceptance sampling is executed through a sampling plan. In this section, we illustrate the planning procedures, with respect to attributes, for a single sampling plan—that is, a plan in which the quality is determined from the evaluation of one sample. (Other plans may be developed using two or more samples. See J. M. Juran and F. M. Gryna's *Quality Planning and Analysis* for a detailed discussion of these plans.)

Costs to Justify Inspection

Total or 100 percent inspection is justified when the cost of a loss incurred by not inspecting is greater than the cost of inspection. For example, suppose a faulty item results in a $10 loss. If the average percentage of defective items in a lot is 3 percent, the expected cost of faulty items is $0.03 \times \$10$, or $0.30 each. Therefore, if the cost of inspecting each item is less than $0.30, the economic decision is to perform 100 percent inspection. Not all defective items will be removed, however, since inspectors will pass some bad items and reject some good ones.

The purposes of a sampling plan are to test the lot to either (*a*) find its quality or (*b*) ensure that the quality is what it is supposed to be. Thus, if a quality control supervisor already knows the quality (such as the 0.03 given in the example), he or she does not sample for defects. Either all of the items must be inspected to remove the defects or none of them should be inspected, and the rejects pass into the process. The choice simply depends on economics in terms of the cost to inspect versus the cost incurred by passing a reject.

A single sampling plan when we are looking at attributes is defined by n and c, where n is the number of units in the sample and c is the acceptance number. The size of n may vary from one to all the items in the lot (usually denoted as N) from which it is drawn. The acceptance number c denotes the maximum number of defective items that can be found in the sample before the lot is rejected. Values for n and c are determined by the interaction of four factors (AQL, α, LTPD, and β) that quantify the objectives of the product's producer and its consumer. The objective of the producer is to ensure that the sampling plan has a low probability of rejecting good lots. Lots are defined as good if they contain no more than a specified level of defectives, termed the **acceptable quality level (AQL)**.[2] The objective of the consumer is to ensure that the sampling plan has a low probability of

acceptable quality level (AQL)
Maximum percentage of defects that a company is willing to accept.

---

[2]There is some controversy surrounding AQLs, based on the argument that specifying some acceptable percentage of defectives is inconsistent with the philosophical goal of zero defects. In practice, even in the best companies, there is an acceptable quality level. The difference is that it may be stated in parts per million rather than in parts per hundred. This is the case in Motorola's Six Sigma quality standard, which holds that no more than 3.4 defects per million parts are acceptable.

At the Volkswagon factory in Brazil, inspectors do a final check of the finished vehicles.

accepting bad lots. Lots are defined as bad if the percentage of defectives is greater than a specified amount, termed *lot tolerance percent defective* (LTPD). As presented earlier, the probability associated with rejecting a good lot is denoted by the Greek letter alpha (α) and is termed the *producer's risk*. The probability associated with accepting a bad lot is denoted by the Greek letter beta (β) and is termed the *consumer's risk*. The selection of particular values for AQL, α, LTPD, and β is an economic decision based on a cost trade-off or, more typically, on company policy or contractual requirements.

There is a humorous story supposedly about Hewlett-Packard during its first dealings with Japanese vendors, who place great emphasis on high-quality production. HP had insisted on 2 percent AQL in a purchase of 100 cables. During the purchase agreement some heated discussion took place wherein the Japanese vendor did not want this AQL specification; HP insisted that they would not budge from the 2 percent AQL. The Japanese vendor finally agreed. Later, when the box arrived, there were two packages inside. One contained 100 good cables. The other package had 2 cables with a note stating: "We have sent you 100 good cables. Since you insisted on 2 percent AQL, we have enclosed two defective cables in this package, though we do not understand why you want them."

The following example, using an excerpt from a standard acceptance sampling table, illustrates how the four parameters—AQL, α, LTPD, and β—are used in developing a sampling plan.

Example

Values of n and c

Brandon Industries manufactures Z-Band radar scanners used to detect speed traps. The printed circuit boards in the scanners are purchased from an outside vendor. The vendor produces the boards to an AQL of 2 percent defectives and is willing to run a 5 percent risk (α) of having lots of this level or fewer defectives rejected. Brandon considers lots of 8 percent or more defectives (LTPD) unacceptable and wants to ensure that it will accept such poor-quality lots no more than 10 percent of the time (β). A large shipment has just been delivered. What values of n and c should be selected to determine the quality of this lot?

c	LTPD ÷ AQL	n · AQL	c	LTPD ÷ AQL	n · AQL
0	44.890	0.052	5	3.549	2.613
1	10.946	0.355	6	3.206	3.286
2	6.509	0.818	7	2.957	3.981
3	4.890	1.366	8	2.768	4.695
4	4.057	1.970	9	2.618	5.426

Solution

The parameters of the problem are AQL = 0.02, $\alpha = 0.05$, LTPD = 0.08, and $\beta = 0.10$. We can use Exhibit S6.15 to find c and n.

First divide LTPD by AQL ($0.08 \div 0.02 = 4$). Then find the ratio in column 2 that is equal to or just greater than that amount (i.e., 4). This value is 4.057, which is associated with $c = 4$.

Finally, find the value in column 3 that is in the same row as $c = 4$ and divide that quantity by AQL to obtain n ($1.970 \div 0.02 = 98.5$).

The appropriate sampling plan is $c = 4$, $n = 99$.

Operating Characteristic Curves

Although a sampling plan such as the one just described meets our requirements for the extreme values of good and bad quality, we cannot readily determine how well the plan discriminates between good and bad lots at intermediate values. For this reason, sampling plans are generally displayed graphically through the use of **operating characteristic (OC) curves**. These curves, which are unique for each combination of n and c, simply illustrate the probability of accepting lots with varying percentages of defectives. The procedure we have followed in developing the plan, in fact, specifies two points on an OC curve: one point defined by AQL and $1 - \alpha$, and the other point defined by LTPD and β. Curves for common values of n and c can be computed or obtained from available tables[3] (see Exhibit S6.16).

A sampling plan discriminating perfectly between good and bad lots has an infinite slope (vertical) at the selected value of AQL. In Exhibit S6.16, a percentage of defectives to the left of 2 percent would always be accepted and to the right, always rejected. However, such a curve is possible only with complete inspection of all units and thus is not a possibility with a true sampling plan.

An OC curve should be steep in the region of most interest (between the AQL and the LTPD), which is accomplished by varying n and c. If c remains constant, increasing the sample size n causes the OC curve to be more vertical. While holding n constant, decreasing c (the maximum number of defective units) also makes the slope more vertical, moving closer to the origin.

The size of the lot from which the sample is taken has relatively little effect on the quality of protection. Consider, for example, that samples—all of the same size of 20 units—are taken from different lots ranging from a lot size of 200 units to a lot size of infinity. If each lot is known to have 5 percent defectives, the probability of accepting the lot based on the sample of 20 units ranges from about 0.34 to about 0.36. This means

operating characteristic (OC) curves

Curves that show the probability of accepting lots that contain different percentages of defectives.

---

[3]See, for example, H. F. Dodge and H. G. Romig, *Sampling Inspection Tables—Single and Double Sampling* (New York: John Wiley & Sons, 1959), and *Military Standard Sampling Procedures and Tables for Inspection by Attributes* (MIL-STD-105D) (Washington, DC: U.S. Government Printing Office, 1983).

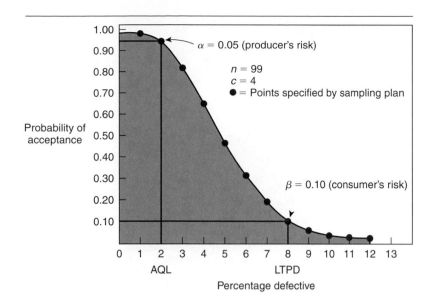

Exhibit S6.16

Operating Characteristic Curve for AQL = 0.02, α = 0.05, LTPD = 0.08, β = 0.10

that as long as the lot size is several times the sample size, it makes little difference how large the lot is. It seems a bit difficult to accept, but statistically (on the average in the long run) whether we have a carload or box full, we'll get about the same answer. It just seems that a carload should have a larger sample size.

Designing a Sampling Plan for Variables

When we use variables to determine if we should accept an entire lot, we again take a sample of the items. However, instead of counting the number of defectives in the sample, we measure the variable of interest for each item in the sample and compute the mean for the sample. We then compare the mean of the sample with **control limits** that have been previously established to determine whether or not we accept the entire lot.

There are three factors that must be taken into consideration in designing a sampling plan for an item where variables are used as the criterion for acceptance. These are: (1) the probability of rejecting a lot that is actually good (that is, committing an α error), (2) the probability of accepting a lot that is actually bad (that is, committing a β error), and (3) the sample size, n.

control limits
Points on an acceptance sampling chart that distinguish between the accept and reject region(s). Also, points on a process control chart that distinguish between a process being in and out of control.

Example

Ramos Electronics Company buys a 50-ohm resistor from an outside vendor. (A resistor is a component used in electrical circuits to retard current. An ohm is the measure of how much a resistor retards the current.) From historical data, the standard deviation for this resistor is 3 ohms. Determine the appropriate control limits if we use a sample size of $n = 100$ and we want to be 95 percent confident that the sample results are truly representative of the total population. (In other words, the probability of committing an α error is $1 - 0.95$ or 5 percent.)

Solution

The equation for determining the control limits (CL) is

$$CL = \mu \pm z_{\alpha/2}\frac{\sigma}{\sqrt{n}} \tag{S6.1}$$

Exhibit S6.17

Establishing Control Limits for Acceptance Sampling Using Variables

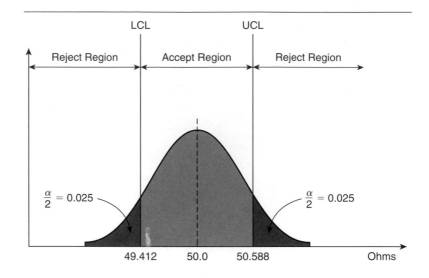

where

μ = The desired mean of the population.

$z_{\alpha/2}$ = The number of standard deviations from the mean that corresponds to the given level of α. ($\alpha/2$ indicates that this is a two-tailed test and that the α error is equally divided between the two tails of the distribution.) The value of z is obtained from the normal distribution table in Appendix B or C at the end of this book. (As noted in the table, the z-value for a two-tailed test with 95 percent confidence is 1.96.)

σ = The value of the population's standard deviation.

Substituting, we have

$$CL = 50 \pm 1.96 \frac{(3)}{\sqrt{100}}$$

$$= 50 \pm 0.588$$

The lower control limit (LCL) is therefore 49.412 and the upper control limit (UCL) is 50.588, as shown in Exhibit S6.17.

The inspection procedure for this resistor therefore is to (*a*) take a random sample of 100 resistors, (*b*) measure the number of ohms in each resistor in the sample, (*c*) compute the mean of the sample, and finally (*d*) compare the sample mean with the established control limits; in other words, if the sample mean falls within the range of 49.412–50.588, the lot is accepted; otherwise the lot is rejected.

Example

Continuing with the resistor problem, we can tolerate some variation in the number of ohms in each resistor. However, if the number of ohms falls below 49, then we would have a serious problem in our electrical circuit. What is the probability of our accepting a lot when the average resistance is 49 ohms or less?

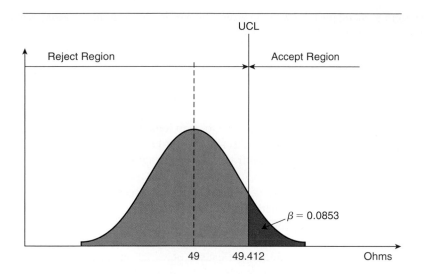

Exhibit S6.18

Determining the Probability of Committing a β Error

Solution

This situation is depicted in Exhibit S6.18. It is important to note that the control limits that were previously established do not change. The probability of accepting a bad lot or committing a β error is defined by that percentage of the area under the curve with a mean of 49 that falls within the acceptance range. (Note that this is a one-tailed test because the β error occurs only in the right tail under the curve.)

The probability of committing this error is determined as follows:

$$\text{LCL} = \mu + z_\beta \frac{\sigma}{\sqrt{n}}$$

where

z_β = The number of standard deviations from the mean that corresponds to the given level of β

Substituting, we have

$$49.412 = 49 + z_\beta \frac{(3)}{\sqrt{100}}$$

$$0.412 = (z_\beta)0.3$$

$$z_\beta = 1.373$$

Again, using the normal distribution table at the end of this book, we look up the value of $z = 1.373$ and find the corresponding area under the curve of 0.0853. Thus the probability of committing a β error under these conditions is 8.53 percent.

Statistical Process Control

Statistical process control (SPC) is a quantitative method for monitoring a repetitive process to determine whether that process is operating properly. SPC uses process data collected in real time and compares current measures to baseline process performance measures. It then applies simple statistical techniques similar to those used in acceptance sampling to determine whether or not the process has changed. SPC allows management

statistical process control (SPC)

Statistical method for determining whether a particular process is in or out of control.

and workers to distinguish between random fluctuations inherent in the process and variation that might indicate that the process has changed.

At its core, SPC is about understanding the variation that occurs in a process. Every process varies in some unique way. Some processes vary a great deal; some vary only slightly. A careful analysis of the inherent variation in a given process makes it possible to compare its current performance with its expected performance, as determined by how the process has performed in the past.

As an illustration, a person uses an axe to chop logs into 30 cm lengths for firewood. Over many days of chopping, he has discovered that he consistently chops the logs into lengths that can vary as much as 8 cm from his target length of 30 cm (in other words, the lengths he chops are 30 cm plus or minus 8 cm). It could be said that the expected variation—due to the random variation in his chopping process—is 8 cm from the target. He would expect that unless something in his chopping process changes, he would continue to chop pieces of length 30 ± 8 cm. If suddenly he were producing pieces shorter than 22 cm and/or longer than 38 cm, he might question why his usual process has changed. He might look for nonrandom causes of variation: Is he tired or distracted? Has he changed his chopping style? Has his axe become dull? Is the wood he is currently chopping somehow different from the wood he has consistently cut within 8 cm of the target?

This simple example demonstrates the difference between the inherent, random variation that can be associated with a particular process and the nonrandom, or assignable, causes of variation. Assignable causes usually can be categorized as relating to either the worker, the equipment, or the materials being used.

SPC uses statistics—in particular, the power of sampling—to refine this basic understanding of variation in processes. The *central limit theorem* tells us that no matter what the actual shape of a distribution is, when samples of a given size are repeatedly drawn from that distribution and the means of the samples are calculated and plotted on a graph, these sample means will be normally distributed. If you are not convinced of this, think about a deck of cards. If each of the cards takes its face value (an ace = 1, numbered cards take their number value, a jack = 11, a queen = 12, and a king = 13), the deck represents a uniform distribution of cards: There are four of each value. The overall average value of a card in a deck would be seven. If you draw several samples of four cards each from the deck, how many of these samples will have an mean value of one? It will be a very rare sample that contains four aces. How many samples will have an mean value of 13? Again, only four kings will produce that sample mean, so that outcome will also be very rare. On the other hand, think of how many ways a sample mean of seven could be produced: four sevens, three sixes and one nine, and so on in many different combinations. If you shuffle the deck, draw a sample, calculate its mean, plot the sample mean on a graph, reshuffle the deck and begin again, you will find that your sample mean distribution will quickly take on the shape of a bell (or normal) curve, rather than the uniform flat shape of the underlying distribution of cards in the deck.

What about distributions other than the uniform? Does the central limit theorem hold true? You can do the same experiment with cards, assigning the value of four to all red cards and 10 to all black cards. The overall or grand mean of the deck is still seven, but the shape of the distribution of cards is now bimodal. Draw samples as before, calculate the mean value of each sample, plot the means on a graph, and the graph will shortly begin to look bell-shaped. Of course, the larger the sample size, the smoother the curve.

If the distribution of sample means is assumed to be normal, then we can use the well-understood properties of the normal distribution to understand variation in processes. For example, as shown in Exhibit S6.19, we know that if we have a normal distribution:

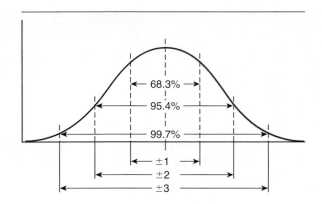

Exhibit S6.19

Areas under the Normal Distribution Curve Corresponding to Different Numbers of Standard Deviations from the Mean

- The distribution is bilaterally symmetrical
- 68.3 percent of the distribution lies between plus and minus one standard deviation from the mean
- 95.4 percent of the distribution lies between plus and minus two standard deviations from the mean
- 99.7 percent of the distribution lies between plus and minus three standard deviations from the mean

If we plot the means of successive samples drawn from a process whose long-run pattern of variation is known, we can look at the pattern of the sample means and decide whether the process is behaving the way we expect it to behave, or whether it has changed.

Statistical control means that a process is exhibiting only its inherent random variation and that it is not showing any signs of "assignable" variation. Statistical control does *not* mean that a process is producing goods or services that are good or bad.

SPC Charts

SPC charts are actually a specialized category of run charts that are based on the central limit theorem. The mean value for the process is calculated (usually from past performance) and, for the sample size being used, control limits are calculated. These control limits usually are established at three standard deviations above and below the mean because plus and minus three standard deviations from the mean value encompasses 99.7 percent of the area under a normal distribution. The *x*-axis of the SPC chart is time; the y-axis is the variation from the mean value for the process. The centre line of an attribute chart is the long-run average for that attribute, such as percentage defective, and the centre line of a variables chart is the mean value for the process.

For each sample, we calculate the sample mean (either the percentage of an attribute that occurs in the sample or the average measured value) and plot that point on the graph. As each sample mean is plotted, we look to see if the process is exhibiting variation that does not look random. For example, we would expect to see the points distributed around the centre line in the proportion described above because of what we know about normal distributions. If we see too little or too much variation, it may indicate that there is a nonrandom factor affecting the process. If we see evidence that the points are not distributed symmetrically around the centre line, it also may indicate that there is a nonrandom factor affecting the process. If we see patterns such as several points in a row going up or several points in a row going down, it again may indicate that there is a nonrandom factor affecting

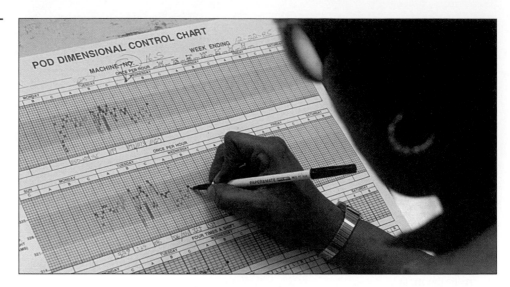

the process. When we look at an SPC chart, we are looking for evidence of nonrandom behaviour—the process behaving in a way we would not expect it to behave, given what we know about it.

Because points on an SPC chart are plotted as the samples are drawn, the ambiguity of "too little or too much variation" or "evidence of a nonrandom pattern" has prompted the development of rules of thumb for interpreting control charts, as shown in Exhibit S6.20. These rules of thumb, or heuristics, are simply methods of standardizing the way variation in a control chart is interpreted.

A process that exhibits nonrandom variation is said to be "out of control." (Remember that "out of control" does not mean that the process is producing bad output. A process can be out of control and producing fewer defects than usual. The key is that the process is not behaving in the way it is expected to behave given what is known about the process.) When we see evidence of nonrandom variation in a process, we try to identify the factors that may have caused that variation. In other words, we look for assignable cause: changes in workers, equipment, or materials.

SPC Using Attribute Measurements

Attribute data are data that are counted, such as good or bad units produced by a machine. If we draw samples during our production run on that machine, we can count, for each sample, the number of units that are good and the number of units that are bad, based on our quality criteria. We can then compare the number of bad units in each sample to the long-run percentage of bad units for that particular machine and determine whether the process is behaving the way we expect it to behave. A process can be in control and producing bad output. For example, if the long-run percentage of defectives for a particular process is 20 percent, that means that 20 percent of the output is bad! The process may continue to produce the same level of defectives—in other words, be in control—but the defectives are still being produced. On the other hand, if a process usually produces 20 percent defectives and something changes so that the process now produces only 5 percent defectives, the process is out of control—but has improved! The goal is to find the cause of

Exhibit S6.20

**Control Chart
Evidence for
Investigation**

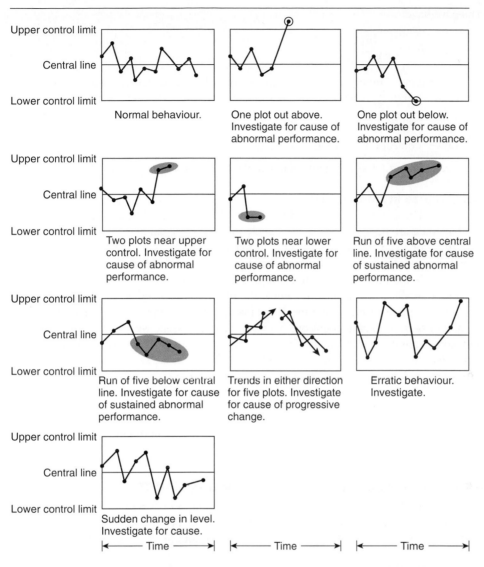

Source: Bertrand L. Hansen, *Quality Control: Theory and Applications*, © 1963, p. 65. Reprinted by permission of Pearson Education, Inc., Upper Saddle River, NJ.

any nonrandom variation and either eliminate it (if it is producing more defects) or sustain it (if it has resulted in process improvement).

Calculating Control Limits

The centre line for an attribute chart is the long-run average for the attribute in question. For example, for a p-chart, or percentage defective chart, the centre line is $\bar{p}$ (pronounced "p-bar"), the long-run average percentage defective.

Centre line = $\bar{p}$ = Long-run average

Standard deviation of sample = $s_p = \sqrt{\dfrac{\bar{p}(1-\bar{p})}{n}}$

Thus, we have

$$CL = \overline{p} \pm z_{\alpha/2} \sqrt{\frac{\overline{p}(1-\overline{p})}{n}} \tag{S6.2}$$

The upper control limit (UCL) and the lower control limit (LCL) are usually established at plus and minus three standard deviations from $\overline{p}(z_{\alpha/2} = 3)$. Thus:

Upper control limit $= \text{UCL} = \overline{p} + 3s_p$

Lower control limit $= \text{LCL} = \overline{p} - 3s_p$

If the calculated LCL is a negative number, the LCL is set equal to zero.

Sample Size in Attribute SPC

The size of a sample is extremely important for successful SPC implementation. If attribute data are being collected, the sample must be large enough to be able to count the attribute. For example, if we know that a machine produces, in the long-run, 5 percent defects and we have a sample size of five, we are very unlikely to be able to answer the question: "Is the process producing defects at the rate it usually does." The usual rule of thumb for attribute SPC is that the sample should be large enough to be able to include the attribute twice, on average. So if the defect rate is 5 percent, the sample size would need to be at least 40 to expect to count two defects. Of course, since we are not looking at every unit, some samples, just by chance, will have more than two defects, while some will have fewer than two. We are looking for a pattern of defects in the samples over time that will tell us whether the process is exhibiting nonrandom variation.

Determining the Long-Run Attribute Level

Because the long-run attribute percentage is critical in determining the centre line and for calculating the control limits for the SPC chart, it is important to have adequate historical information about the process.

Variable Measurements Using $\overline{X}$ and R Charts

Variable data are data that are measured, such as length or weight. There are four main issues in creating a control chart that uses variable data: (1) the size of the sample, (2) the number of samples, (3) the frequency of the samples, and (4) the control limits.

Size of Samples

For industrial applications in process control, it is preferable to keep the sample size small. There are two main reasons: First, the sample needs to be taken within a reasonable length of time, otherwise the process might change while the sample is being taken. Second, the larger the sample, the more it costs to take.

Sample sizes of four or five units seem to be the preferred numbers. The *means* of samples of this size have an approximately normal distribution, no matter what the distribution of the parent population looks like. Sample sizes greater than five give narrower control limits and thus are more sensitive. For detecting finer variations of a process, it may be necessary, in fact, to use larger sample sizes. However, when sample sizes exceed 15 or so, it would be more appropriate to use the standard deviation (σ) and $\overline{X}$ charts rather than R and $\overline{X}$ charts. One advantage of using the R charts is that the range is easier to calculate than the standard deviation.

Number of Samples

Once the chart has been set up, each sample taken can be compared to the chart and a decision can be made about whether the process is acceptable. To set up the charts, however, prudence (and statistics) suggest that 25 or more samples be taken.

Frequency of Samples

How often to take a sample is a trade-off between the cost of sampling (along with the cost of the unit if it is destroyed as part of the test) and the benefits of adjusting the system. Usually, it is best to start off with frequent sampling of a process and then decrease the sampling frequency as confidence in the process increases. For example, one might start with a sample of five units every half hour and end up feeling that one sample per day is adequate.

Control Limits

Standard practice in statistical process control for variables is to set control limits at three standard deviations above the mean and three standard deviations below. This means that 99.7 percent of the sample means are expected to fall within these control limits (i.e., within a 99.7 percent confidence interval). Thus, if one sample mean falls outside this wide band, we have strong evidence that the process is out of control.

How to Construct $\overline{X}$ and R Charts

An $\overline{X}$ chart tracks the changes in the means of the samples by plotting the means that were taken from a process. $\overline{X}$ is the average of the means.

An R chart tracks the changes in variability by plotting the range within each sample. The range is the difference between the highest and the lowest values in that sample. As stated earlier, R values provide an easily calculated measure of variation used like a standard deviation. $\overline{R}$ is the average of the ranges of each sample. More specifically, these terms are defined:

$$\overline{X} = \frac{\sum_{i=1}^{n} X_i}{n} \tag{S6.3}$$

where

$\overline{X}$ = Mean of the sample
i = Item number
n = Total number of items in the sample

$$\overline{\overline{X}} = \frac{\sum_{j=1}^{m} \overline{X}_j}{m} \tag{S6.4}$$

where

$\overline{\overline{X}}$ = The average of the means of the samples
j = Sample number
m = Total number of samples

Exhibit S6.21

Factors for Determining from $\bar{R}$ the 3-Sigma Control Limits for $\bar{X}$ and R Charts

Number of Observations in Subgroup n	Factor for $\bar{X}$ Chart A_2	Factors for R Chart	
		Lower Control Limit D_3	Upper Control Limit D_4
2	1.88	0	3.27
3	1.02	0	2.57
4	0.73	0	2.28
5	0.58	0	2.11
6	0.48	0	2.00
7	0.42	0.08	1.92
8	0.37	0.14	1.86
9	0.34	0.18	1.82
10	0.31	0.22	1.78
11	0.29	0.26	1.74
12	0.27	0.28	1.72
13	0.25	0.31	1.69
14	0.24	0.33	1.67
15	0.22	0.35	1.65
16	0.21	0.36	1.64
17	0.20	0.38	1.62
18	0.19	0.39	1.61
19	0.19	0.40	1.60
20	0.18	0.41	1.59

Upper control limit for $\bar{X} = UCL_{\bar{x}} = \bar{\bar{X}} + A_2\bar{R}$　　Upper control limit for $\bar{R} = UCL_R = D_4\bar{R}$

Lower control limit for $\bar{X} = LCL_{\bar{x}} = \bar{\bar{X}} - A_2\bar{R}$　　Lower control limit for $\bar{R} = LCL_R = D_3\bar{R}$

Note: All factors are based on the normal distribution.

Source: E. L. Grant, *Statistical Quality Control*, 6th ed. (New York: McGraw-Hill, 1988). Reprinted by permission of McGraw-Hill, Inc.

$$\bar{R} = \frac{\sum\limits_{j=1}^{m} R_j}{m} \tag{S6.5}$$

where

$\bar{R}$ = Average of the measurement differences R for all samples

R_j = Difference between the highest and lowest values in sample j

E. L. Grant and R. Leavenworth computed a table that allows us to easily compute the upper and lower control limits for both the $\bar{X}$ chart and the R chart.[4] These are defined as

Upper control limit for $\bar{X} = \bar{\bar{X}} + A_2\bar{R}$

Lower control limit for $\bar{X} = \bar{\bar{X}} - A_2\bar{R}$

Upper control limit for $R = D_4\bar{R}$

Lower control limit for $R = D_3\bar{R}$

where the values for A_2, D_3, and D_4 are obtained from Exhibit S6.21.

---

[4]E. L. Grant and R. Leavenworth, *Statistical Quality Control* (New York: McGraw-Hill, 1964), p. 562. Reprinted by permission.

We would like to create an $\overline{X}$ and an R chart for a process. Exhibit S6.22 shows the measurements that were taken of all 25 samples. The last two columns show the average of the sample $\overline{X}$ and the range R.

Upper control limit for $\overline{X} = \overline{\overline{X}} + A_2\overline{R}$
$$= 10.21 + 0.58(0.60) = 10.56$$

Lower control limit for $\overline{X} = \overline{\overline{X}} - A_2\overline{R}$
$$= 10.21 - 0.58(0.60) = 9.86$$

Upper control limit for $R = D_4\overline{R}$
$$= 2.11(0.60) = 1.26$$

Lower control limit for $R = D_3\overline{R}$
$$= 0(0.60) = 0$$

Sample Number	Each Unit in Sample					Average $\overline{X}$	Range R
1	10.60	10.40	10.30	9.90	10.20	10.28	.70
2	9.98	10.25	10.05	10.23	10.33	10.17	.35
3	9.85	9.90	10.20	10.25	10.15	10.07	40
4	10.20	10.10	10.30	9.90	9.95	10.09	.40
5	10.30	10.20	10.24	10.50	10.30	10.31	.30
6	10.10	10.30	10.20	10.30	9.90	10.16	.40
7	9.98	9.90	10.20	10.40	10.10	10.12	.50
8	10.10	10.30	10.40	10.24	10.30	10.27	.30
9	10.30	10.20	10.60	10.50	10.10	10.34	.50
10	10.30	10.40	10.50	10.10	10.20	10.30	.40
11	9.90	9.50	10.20	10.30	10.35	10.05	.85
12	10.10	10.36	10.50	9.80	9.95	10.14	.70
13	10.20	10.50	10.70	10.10	9.90	10.28	.80
14	10.20	10.60	10.50	10.30	10.40	10.40	.40
15	10.54	10.30	10.40	10.55	10.00	10.36	.55
16	10.20	10.60	10.15	10.00	10.50	10.29	.60
17	10.20	10.40	10.60	10.80	10.10	10.42	.70
18	9.90	9.50	9.90	10.50	10.00	9.96	1.00
19	10.60	10.30	10.50	9.90	9.80	10.22	.80
20	10.60	10.40	10.30	10.40	10.20	10.38	.40
21	9.90	9.60	10.50	10.10	10.60	10.14	1.00
22	9.95	10.20	10.50	10.30	10.20	10.23	.55
23	10.20	9.50	9.60	9.80	10.30	9.88	.80
24	10.30	10.60	10.30	9.90	9.80	10.18	.80
25	9.90	10.30	10.60	9.90	10.10	10.16	.70
				$\overline{\overline{X}} =$		10.21	
				$\overline{R} =$			.60

Exhibit S6.22

Measurements in Samples of Five from a Process

Exhibit S6.23 shows the $\overline{X}$ chart and R chart with a plot of all the sample means and ranges of the samples. All the points are well within the control limits, although sample 23 is close to the $\overline{X}$ lower control limit. The $\overline{X}$ chart shows how well the process is centred about the target mean. The R chart demonstrates the degree of variability in the process.

Exhibit S6.23

X̄ Chart and R Chart

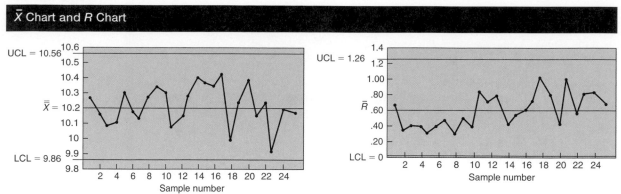

A Framework for Applying the Tools

Each of the different tools presented in this supplement provides a manager with specific information about a process. However, it is not just a matter of selecting the right tool. Equally important, the manager needs to understand how these various tools work together to improve the quality of a process.

Exhibit S6.24 provides a framework for the logical integration of these various tools. (Also see the OM in Practice Box on using these tools in a school setting.) As suggested in Exhibit S6.20, these tools are used on a continuous basis to identify sources of error in a process.

Exhibit S6.24

A Framework for Applying the Different Quality Control Tools

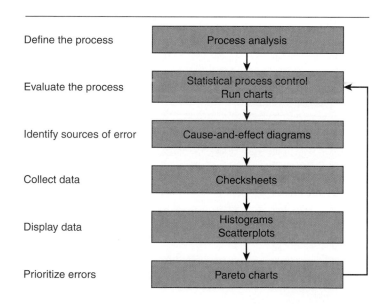

Process Capability

Process control chart limits can be compared to design specification limits to determine if the process itself is capable of making products within design specification (or tolerance) limits. In Exhibit S6.25 concentric circles represent sample means which are compared to

Operations Management in Practice

AN ARIZONA SCHOOL USES QUALITY IMPROVEMENT TOOLS TO ADDRESS ATTENDANCE ISSUES

Sharron Walker, the principal of a small high school in Sells, Arizona, was facing a school attendance problem. Rewards for regular attendance and punishment for continual absence only addressed the symptoms. Because schools are not process-oriented, they have few methods and tools to help them measure how their processes function over time. Ms. Walker decided to use quality improvement tools to investigate the root causes of the problem.

Through a brainstorming process with stakeholders, a cause-and-effect diagram was drawn up. The diagram revealed diverse factors that affected school attendance, such as having to wait all day at the hospital in case of illness.

Surveys were conducted among students to identify causes for absenteeism. Pareto diagrams based on the survey output indicated that babysitting, illnesses, disciplinary infractions, and a few other reasons were major causes of absenteeism.

The team used statistical process control to measure the attribute: "Whether the student was present or absent." Results from the *p*-charts revealed that 60 percent of the points were outside the control limits, as well as a declining roller coaster pattern in the points. This pattern of nonrandomness indicated that there might be common elements among the students missing school. Similar patterns were seen at other local schools when analyzed.

Checksheets were then used to determine the profile of a "truant" student. By collecting data on aspects such as grade level, age, and gender, among others, a profile of the typical truant student was built. Checksheets also revealed that most disciplinary infractions were committed during lunch and class changes.

The team probed deeper by developing Pareto diagrams, which indicated that students were most likely to be absent on Mondays, and that February and March had the highest monthly absentee rates. The team was able to identify different causes for these phenomena.

Through the use of these control charts, cause-and-effect diagrams, Pareto analyses, checksheets, graphs, and surveys, a number of recommendations were made to address the root cause of the low attendance problem.

Source:
Sharron Walker, "Special Report: Quality in Education on the Move. Using Statistical Process Control to Improve Attendance," *Quality Digest* (1995), www.qualitydigest.com/sep/control.html.

the LCL/UCL, and dots represent individual values which are compared to the LSL/USL. In Exhibit S6.25A, we see a process that on average is producing items within the control limits, but its variation is such that it can't meet specifications for all items. Exhibit S6.25B shows reduction in this variability, but the process is still deficient. Finally, in Exhibit S6.25C, we see that the process variability has been brought under control. Thus Exhibits S6.25A to S6.25C indicate increasing process capability. How is this accomplished?

A. Process Not Capable, but in Statistical Control	B. Process Variance Reduced, but Still Not Capable of Defect-Free Production	C. Process Capable of Defect-Free Production
	One individual measure out	Upper specification limit (USL)
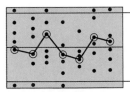	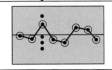	Upper control limit (UCL)
		Lower control limit (LCL)
		Lower specifications limit (LSL)
Normal variance pattern, but variance is too great for all individual unit measurements to be within tolerance limits. (Seven of 35 are outside.)	Variance is reduced so that control limits for sample means are inside the tolerance limits, but individual units will still be produced outside the tolerance limits through normal variation.	Variance now is so greatly reduced that no individual measurements should fall outside tolerance even if the central tendency of the process is not centred in the tolerance range.

Exhibit S6.25

Reducing Process Variance So That All Parts Are within Specification (Tolerance)*

*Tolerance: The range within which all individual measurements of units produced is desired to fall.
Source: Robert W. Hall, *Attaining Manufacturing Excellence: Just-in-Time Manufacturing, Total Quality, Total People Involvement* (Homewood, IL: Dow Jones–Irwin, 1987), p. 66. By permission of The McGraw-Hill Companies.

By working to improve the performance of each source of variance: workers, machine, tooling, setup, material, and the environment.

Process Capability Ratio

For a process to be both in control and within tolerance, the part tolerance limits must be equal to or wider than the upper and lower limits of the process control chart. Since these control limits are at plus or minus three standard deviations, the tolerance limits must exceed six standard deviations. A quick way of making this determination is through the use of a process capability ratio. This ratio is calculated by dividing the tolerance width by six standard deviations (the process capability), as shown in the following formula in which s, the sample standard deviation, is substituted for σ, the population standard deviation.

$$\text{Process capability ratio} = C_p = \frac{\text{Upper tolerance limit} - \text{Lower tolerance limit}}{6s} \quad \text{(S6.6)}$$

The larger the ratio, the greater the potential for producing parts within tolerance from the specified process. A ratio that is greater than 1 indicates that the tolerance limit range is wider than the actual range of measurements. If the ratio is less than 1, then some parts will be out of tolerance. The minimum capability ratio is frequently established at 1.33. Below this value, design engineers have to seek approval from manufacturing before the product can be released for production.

Capability Index

The process capability ratio does not indicate specifically how well the process is performing relative to the target dimension. Thus, a second performance index, called C_{pk}, must be employed to determine whether the process mean is closer to the upper specification limit, USL, or the lower specification limit, LSL.

$$C_{pk} = \min\left[\frac{\bar{X} - \text{LSL}}{3s}, \frac{\text{USL} - \bar{X}}{3s}\right] \quad \text{(S6.7)}$$

When C_{pk} equals the capability ratio (C_p), then the process mean is centred between the two specification limits. Otherwise, the process mean is closest to the specification limit corresponding to the minimum of the two C_{pk} ratios. Consider the following example:

Example

A manufacturing process produces a certain part with a mean diameter of 2 cm and a standard deviation of 0.03 cm. The upper specification limit equals 2.05 cm, and the lower specification limit equals 1.9 cm.

Solution

From this information, a process capability ratio (C_p) and a capability index (C_{pk}) were calculated.

$$\text{Process capability ratio} = C_p = \frac{2.05 - 1.90}{6(0.03)} = 0.833$$

Exhibit S6.26

The Goal of Six Sigma

A. Process Variation Equals Design Tolerance

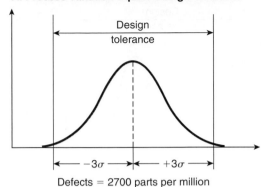

Defects = 2700 parts per million

B. Process Variation is 50 Percent of Design

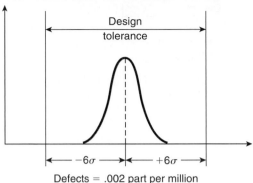

Defects = .002 part per million

$$C_{pk} \text{ for LSL} = \frac{2 - 1.90}{3(0.03)} = 1.11$$

$$C_{pk} \text{ for USL} = \frac{2.05 - 2}{3(0.03)} = 0.56$$

From the process capability ratio, we can conclude that the process is not capable of producing parts within the design's specification. The C_{pk} analysis points out that the process mean is closer to the upper tolerance limit. Given this information, work can be done on the manufacturing process to increase the process capability ratio and also to centre the mean between the two specification limits. This may involve, for example, a simple adjustment of a machine tool setting.

Six Sigma: Application

As seen in Exhibit S6.26A, the design tolerance is equal to the process variation, as defined by $\pm 3\sigma$, and the design mean equals the process mean. The process capability ratio (C_p) therefore is equal to 1. Under these conditions, we would expect the process to yield 99.74 percent good parts or, conversely, 2700 defects per million.

With Six Sigma, the goal is to reduce the process variation to 50 percent of the design tolerance, as shown in Exhibit S6.26B. (Again, the design mean equals the process mean.) This results in a $C_p = 2.0$. Under these conditions, the defect rate is 2 parts per billion (ppb). However, to determine the number of defects associated with Six Sigma, we also must take into consideration the movements (shifts) in actual mean of the process relative to the design mean, which is reflected in the capability index (C_{pk}). From historical data on a wide variety of processes, we know that actual process means can vary as much as 1.5σ from the design mean, as shown in Exhibits S6.27A and S6.27B. This amount of variation (1.5σ) between the two means is a major assumption in the calculation of the defect rates that are presented in a Six Sigma program, and

Exhibit S6.27A

Impact of 1.5σ Shift on 3σ Process

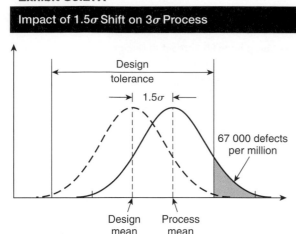

Design tolerance

1.5σ

67 000 defects per million

Design mean   Process mean

Exhibit S6.27B

Impact of 1.5σ Shift on 6σ Process

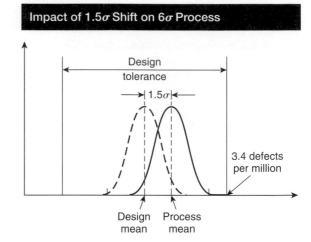

Design tolerance

1.5σ

3.4 defects per million

Design mean   Process mean

Exhibit S6.28

Defect Rates for Different Levels of Sigma (σ) Assuming a 1.5 Shift in Actual Mean from Design Mean

Sigma Level of Quality	Defects per Million
1.5σ	500 000
2.0σ	308 300
2.5σ	158 650
3.0σ	67 000
3.5σ	22 700
4.0σ	6 220
4.5σ	1 350
5.0σ	233
5.5σ	32
6.0σ	3.4

which are also presented in Exhibit S6.28. Thus "Six Sigma" is not the same as plus or minus six standard deviations ($\pm 6\sigma$).

Taguchi Methods

Throughout this chapter we have discussed statistical quality control methods from the point of view of acceptance sampling and process adjustments. In what many have termed a revolution in quality thinking, Genichi Taguchi of Japan has suggested the following: Instead of constantly fiddling with production equipment to ensure consistent quality, design the product to be robust enough to achieve high quality despite fluctuations on the production line. This simple idea has been employed by such companies as Ford Motor Company, ITT, and IBM; as a result, they have saved millions of dollars in manufacturing costs.

Taguchi methods

Statistical technique for identifying the cause(s) of process variation that reduces the number of tests that are necessary.

Taguchi methods are basically statistical techniques for conducting experiments to determine the best combinations of product and process variables to make a product. *Best* means lowest cost with highest uniformity. This can be a complicated, time-consuming procedure. For example, in designing the process for a new product, one might find that a single processing step with only eight process variables (machine speed, cutting angle, and so on) could be combined in up to 5000 different ways (which is referred to as a full factorial design). Thus, finding the combination that makes the product with the highest uniformity at the lowest cost can't be done efficiently by trial and error. Taguchi has found a way around this problem by focusing on only a fraction of the combinations that represent the overall spectrum of product/process outcomes. He developed a visual way to choose the best subset of the full number of experiments. This approach makes use of fractional factorial design, which is significantly easier for people who do not have extensive training in statistics.

Taguchi also is known for the development of the concept of a *quality loss function* (QLF) that relates the cost of quality directly to the variation in a process. Essentially, with this function Taguchi is saying that any deviation from the target quality level results in a loss to society. For example, if a defective tire goes flat, society loses the productive time of the owner who needs to either change it and/or have it repaired. If the owner doesn't change the tire, society loses the time the repairperson spends on fixing the tire because he or she could have been doing work that was not repair, but instead contributed value to society (either by producing value or enjoying leisure). The following discussion from an article by Joseph Turner develops this concept in detail.

Is an Out-of-Spec Product Really out of Spec?

Variation around Us

It is generally accepted that, as variation is reduced, quality is improved. Sometimes that knowledge is intuitive. If a train is always on time, schedules can be planned more precisely. If clothing sizes are consistent, time can be saved by ordering from a catalogue. But rarely are such things thought about in terms of the value of low variability. With engineers, the knowledge is better defined. Pistons must fit cylinders, doors must fit openings, electrical components must be compatible, and boxes of cereal must have the right amount of raisins—otherwise quality will be unacceptable and customers will be dissatisfied.

However, engineers also know that it is impossible to have zero variability. For this reason, designers establish specifications that define not only the target value of something, but also acceptable limits about the target. For example, if the target value of a dimension is 10 cm, the design specifications might then be 10.00 cm $\pm$ 0.02. This would tell the manufacturing department that, although it should aim for exactly 10 cm, anything between 9.98 cm and 10.02 cm is OK.

The traditional way of interpreting such a specification is that any part that falls within the allowed range is equally good, while any part falling outside the range is totally bad. This is illustrated in Exhibit S6.29. (Note that the cost in this model is zero over the entire specification range, and then there is a quantum leap in cost once the limit is violated.)

Taguchi has pointed out that such a view is nonsense for two reasons:

1. From the customer's view, there is often practically no difference between a product just inside specifications and a product just outside. Conversely, there is a far greater

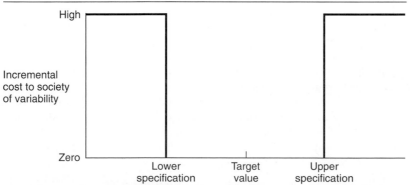

Exhibit S6.29

A Traditional View of the Cost of Variability

Source: Adapted from Joseph Turner, "Is an Out-of-Spec Product Really out of Spec?" *Quality Progress,* December 1990, pp. 57–59.

Exhibit S6.30

Taguchi's View of the Cost of Variability

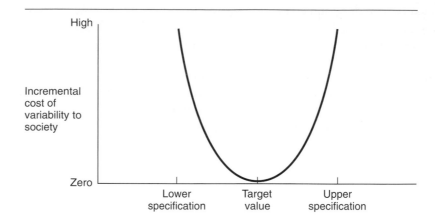

difference in the quality of a product that is at the target and the quality of one that is near a limit.

2. As customers become more demanding, there is pressure to reduce variability. The underlying philosophy in Exhibit S6.25 does not recognize this pressure.

Taguchi suggests that a more accurate picture of the loss is shown in Exhibit S6.30. Notice that in this graph the cost is represented by a smooth curve. There are dozens of illustrations of this notion: the meshing of gears in a transmission, the speed of photographic film, the temperature in a workplace or department store. In nearly anything that can be measured, the customer sees not a sharp line, but a gradation of acceptability. Customers see the loss function as Exhibit S6.26 rather than Exhibit S6.25.

What are the elements of loss to society? Internally, the more variable the manufacturing process, the more scrap generated and the more a company will have to spend on testing and inspecting for conformance. Externally, customers will find that the product does not last as long or work as well if it is not close to target. Perhaps, when used in adverse situations, the product will not perform at all, even though it meets specifications that were developed based on normal usage.[5]

---

[5]Joseph Turner, "Is an Out-of-Spec Product Really out of Spec?" *Quality Progress* (December 1990), pp. 57–59. Copyright © 1990, American Society for Quality. Reprinted with permission.

Conclusion

The different quality control tools presented in this supplement provide the necessary foundation for producing high-quality goods and services. Within this group, statistical quality methods play a very significant role. Acceptance sampling provides us with a method for evaluating products after they have been made. The purpose of statistical process control is to focus on the process while the product is made.

If the inherent variation of a process is understood, managers and workers can watch the process to make sure that it is performing as expected. When the process exhibits nonrandom variation, the cause of the variation (assignable cause) needs to be sought and eliminated (if the process has deteriorated) or continued (if the process has improved). Because variation can easily be seen on an SPC chart, managers and workers can readily identify nonrandom variation and look for its assignable causes.

The introduction of quality improvement concepts such as Six Sigma and Taguchi methods provide us with additional ways to continuously "raise the bar" by improving the quality of processes still further.

acceptable quality level (AQL) p. 228

control limits p. 231

operating characteristic (OC) curves p. 230

statistical process control (SPC) p. 233

Taguchi methods p. 246

types of data:

attribute data p. 227

variable data p. 227

types of sampling errors:

α error, Type I error, or producer's risk p. 228

β error, Type II error, or consumer's risk p. 228

Control limits for a variable

$$CL = \mu \pm z_{\alpha/2} \frac{\sigma}{\sqrt{n}} \tag{S6.1}$$

Control limits for an attribute

$$CL = \bar{p} \pm z_{\alpha/2} \sqrt{\frac{\bar{p}(1-\bar{p})}{n}} \tag{S6.2}$$

Mean of a sample

$$\bar{X} = \frac{\sum\limits_{i=1}^{n} X_i}{n} \tag{S6.3}$$

Average of means of all samples

$$\bar{\bar{X}} = \frac{\sum\limits_{j=1}^{n} \bar{X}_j}{m} \tag{S6.4}$$

Average range of all samples

$$\bar{R} = \frac{\sum\limits_{j=1}^{m} R_j}{m} \tag{S6.5}$$

Process capability ratio

$$C_p = \frac{\text{Upper tolerance limit} - \text{Lower tolerance limit}}{6s} \tag{S6.6}$$

Capability index

$$C_{pk} = \min\left[\frac{\bar{X} - \text{LSL}}{3s}, \frac{\text{USL} - \bar{X}}{3s} \right] \tag{S6.7}$$

1. Discuss the trade-off between achieving a zero AQL (acceptable quality level) and a positive AQL (e.g., an AQL of 2 percent).
2. The capability index allows for some drifting of the process mean. Discuss what this means in terms of product quality output.
3. Discuss the purposes and differences between p-charts and $\bar{X}$ and R charts.
4. In an agreement between a supplier and a customer, the supplier must ensure that

all parts are within tolerance before shipment to the customer. What is the effect on the cost of quality to the customer?

5. In the situation described in Question 4, what would be the effect on the cost of quality to the supplier?

6. Discuss the logic of Taguchi methods.

7. Can you think of a way to use a deck of cards to simulate other distributions and test the central limit theorem?

8. What is the difference between a Type I error and a Type II error?

9. What is the difference between a Pareto chart and a histogram?

10. Using a checksheet, record the different colours of 40 automobiles that are in the parking lot at your school or at a shopping mall. Plot the results in a bar chart.

11. Take the results in Question 10 and plot a Pareto chart.

12. Using a checksheet, record the storage space for each of 20 document files that you and/or your classmates have for Word, Excel, and PowerPoint (or their equivalents), for a total of 60 data points. Choosing the appropriate interval, plot each of the three sets of data on a histogram. What conclusions can you draw from this histogram?

Internet Exercise

Go to the Bombardier Web site (or that of any other company that has successfully implemented six sigma) and describe the role of six sigma within that organization and how it has contributed to the overall improvement of the firm. You can also use other sources that discuss six sigma in this organization using an Internet search.

Solved Problem

Problem

Completed forms from a particular department of the Yellowknife Insurance Company were sampled on a daily basis as a check against the quality of performance of that department. To establish a tentative norm for the department, one sample of 100 units was collected each day for 15 days, with these results:

Sample	Sample Size	Number of Forms with Errors	Sample	Sample Size	Number of Forms with Errors
1	100	4	9	100	4
2	100	3	10	100	2
3	100	5	11	100	7
4	100	0	12	100	2
5	100	2	13	100	1
6	100	8	14	100	3
7	100	1	15	100	1
8	100	3			

a. Develop a p-chart using a 95 percent confidence interval.

b. Plot the 15 samples collected.

c. What comments can you make about the process?

Solution

Insurance company forms.

a. $\bar{p} = \dfrac{46}{15(100)} = 0.031$

$$s_p = \sqrt{\frac{\overline{p}(1-\overline{p})}{n}} = \sqrt{\frac{0.031(1-0.031)}{100}} = \sqrt{0.0003} = .017$$

$$\text{UCL} = \overline{p} + 1.96 s_p = 0.031 + 1.96(0.017) = 0.064$$

$$\text{LCL} = \overline{p} - 1.96 s_p = 0.031 - 1.96(0.017) = -0.002 \text{ or zero}$$

b. The defectives are plotted here.

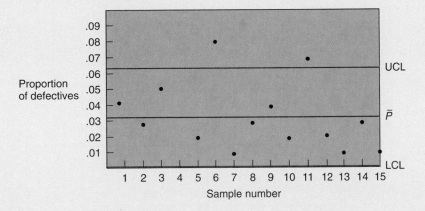

c. Of the 15 samples, 2 were out of the control limits. Since the control limits were established as 95 percent, or 1 out of 20, we would say that the process is out of control. It needs to be examined to find the cause of such widespread variation.

Problems

1. A metal fabricator produces connecting rods with an outer diameter that has a 1 ± .01 cm specification. A machine operator takes several sample measurements over time and determines the sample mean outer diameter to be 1.002 cm with a standard deviation of 0.003 cm.

    a. Calculate the process capability ratio and the capability index for this example.

    b. What do these figures tell you about the process?

2. Ten samples of 15 parts each were taken from an ongoing process at the Noelle Pradeep Company to establish a p-chart for control. The samples and the number of defects in each are shown here.

Sample	n	Number of Defects in Sample
1	15	3
2	15	1
3	15	0
4	15	0
5	15	0
6	15	2
7	15	0
8	15	3
9	15	1
10	15	0

a. Develop a p-chart for 95 percent confidence.

b. Based on the plotted data points, what comments can you make?

3. Resistors for electronic circuits are being manufactured at the Falenda Company on a high-speed automated machine. The machine is being set up to produce a large run of resistors of 1000 ohms each.

    To set up the machine and to create a control chart to be used throughout the run, 15 samples were taken with 4 resistors in each sample. The complete list of samples and their measured values are as follows:

Sample Number	Readings (in ohms)			
1	1010	991	985	986
2	995	996	1009	994
3	990	1003	1015	1008
4	1015	1020	1009	998
5	1013	1019	1005	993
6	994	1001	994	1005
7	989	992	982	1020
8	1001	986	996	996
9	1006	989	1005	1007
10	992	1007	1006	979
11	996	1006	997	989
12	1019	996	991	1011
13	981	991	989	1003
14	999	993	988	984
15	1013	1002	1005	992

Develop an $\bar{X}$ chart and an R chart and plot the values. From the charts, what comments can you make about the process? (Use the table in Exhibit S6.21.)

4. You are the newly appointed assistant administrator at a local hospital, and your first project is to investigate the quality of the patient meals put out by the food-service department. You conducted a 10-day survey by submitting a simple questionnaire to the 400 patients with each meal, asking that they simply check off either that the meal was satisfactory or unsatisfactory. For simplicity in this problem, assume that the response was 1000 returned questionnaires from the 1200 meals each day. The results ran as follows:

	Number of Unsatisfactory Meals	Sample Size
December 1	74	1 000
December 2	42	1 000
December 3	64	1 000
December 4	80	1 000
December 5	40	1 000
December 6	50	1 000
December 7	65	1 000
December 8	70	1 000
December 9	40	1 000
December 10	75	1 000
	600	10 000

a. Construct a *p*-chart based on the questionnaire results, using a confidence interval of 95.4 percent, which is two standard deviations.

b. What comments can you make about the results of the survey?

5. The provincial and local police departments are trying to analyze crime rate areas so that they can shift their patrols from decreasing crime rate areas to areas where rates are

increasing. The city has been geographically segmented into areas containing 5000 residences. The police recognize that all crimes and offenses are not reported; people either do not want to become involved, consider the offenses too small to report, are too embarrassed to make a police report, or do not take the time, among other reasons. Every month, because of this, the police are contacting by phone a random sample of 1000 of the 5000 residences in one area for data on crime (the respondents are guaranteed anonymity). The data collected for the past 12 months for one area are as follows:

Month	Crime Incidence	Sample Size	Crime Rate
January	7	1000	0.007
February	9	1000	0.009
March	7	1000	0.007
April	7	1000	0.007
May	7	1000	0.007
June	9	1000	0.009
July	7	1000	0.007
August	10	1000	0.010
September	8	1000	0.008
October	11	1000	0.011
November	10	1000	0.010
December	8	1000	0.008

Construct a *p*-chart for 95 percent confidence and plot each of the months. If the next three months show the number of crime incidences (out of 1000 residences sampled) in this area as

January = 10   February = 12   March = 11

What comments can you make regarding the crime rate?

6. Some of the citizens complained to city council members that there should be equal protection under the law against the occurrence of crimes. The citizens argued that this equal protection should be interpreted as indicating that high-crime areas should have more police protection than low-crime areas. Therefore, police patrols and other methods for preventing crime (such as street lighting or cleaning up abandoned areas and buildings) should be used in proportion to crime occurrence.

In a fashion similar to Problem 5, the city has been broken down into 20 geographical areas, each containing 5000 residences. The 1000 sampled from each area showed the following incidence of crime during the past month:

Area	Number of Crimes	Sample Size	Crime Rate
1	14	1000	0.014
2	3	1000	0.003
3	19	1000	0.019
4	18	1000	0.018
5	14	1000	0.014
6	28	1000	0.028
7	10	1000	0.010
8	18	1000	0.018
9	12	1000	0.012
10	3	1000	0.003
11	20	1000	0.020
12	15	1000	0.015
13	12	1000	0.012
14	14	1000	0.014
15	10	1000	0.010

Area	Number of Crimes	Sample Size	Crime Rate
16	30	1000	0.030
17	4	1000	0.004
18	20	1000	0.020
19	6	1000	0.006
20	30	1000	0.030
	300		

Suggest a reallocation of crime protection effort, if indicated, based on a *p*-chart analysis. To be reasonably certain of your recommendation, select a 95 percent confidence level.

7. The St. Catharines Beverage Company has developed a line of sophisticated beverages targeted for couples who both work and have no children. This segment of the consumer market is often referred to as "DINKs" (i.e., Double Income, No Kids). This new line of beverages is thus being produced under the label "Drinks for Dinks." The bottles for this product are filled on automatic equipment that has been adjusted so that the average fill per bottle is 300 ml. Historically, it has been determined that the standard deviation of the filling equipment is 4.36 ml. Every hour, a sample of 36 bottles is taken at random from the process, and the average volume is calculated and plotted on an $\bar{X}$ chart.

   a. Draw an $\bar{X}$ process control chart with limits of ±3 standard deviations, correctly labelling the UCL and LCL.

   b. The average sample volumes for Monday morning were as follows:

Hour	7:00 AM	8:00 AM	9:00 AM	10:00 AM	11:00 AM
Average volume	302.45	298.64	295.09	301.64	306.27

   Plot the average volume for each hour on the process control chart. Do you think that the process is in control?

8. Allison Danielewicz, the manager of the 800-number reservation service for a nationwide chain of luxury hotels, is concerned about the productivity of her operation. Analysis of past data shows that it should take an average of five minutes to properly process a reservation and that the standard deviation is 30 seconds. Every day, Allison randomly samples how long it takes to make each of 25 reservations.

   a. Set up a process control chart with 95 percent confidence limits.

   b. If the sample results show that the average reservation time is significantly above the upper control limit, what might be some of the causes for the longer reservation times? How would you correct these problems?

   c. Should Allison have any concern if the average reservation time was significantly below the lower control limit? Why?

9. You have just returned from a trip to Victoria where you stayed at a first-class hotel. After spending $250 per night for the room plus an additional $35 per night to park your car, you are very unhappy with the level of service you received during your stay at this hotel.

   a. Draw a fishbone diagram identifying the major causes of your dissatisfaction and possible secondary causes within each of these categories (do not include price).

   b. You call the hotel to voice your complaint, and the manager asks you if you would be willing to collect some data for her so she can get at the root cause of the problem. You collect the following data on 100 complaints:

Cause (Select from part *a*)	Frequency
1. _____	16
2. _____	11
3. _____	27
4. _____	42
5. _____	4

c. Draw a Pareto diagram for the above data, labelling the axes appropriately. How does this information assist the manager in improving the service quality of her operation?

10. You have just returned from an airline trip to Spain and are very unhappy with your onboard experience.

a. Draw a fishbone diagram identifying the different possible primary causes (within each of these categories) for your dissatisfaction with your trip. Also identify several possible secondary causes.

b. You call the airline to voice your complaint and the manager asks if you will collect some data for him so that he can get at the root cause of the problem. You collect the following data on 100 complaints:

Cause (Select from part *a*)	Frequency
1. _____	6
2. _____	22
3. _____	14
4. _____	43
5. _____	10
6. _____	5

c. Draw a Pareto diagram for the above data, labelling the axes appropriately. How does this information assist the manager in improving the service quality of his operation?

Case 1 Shortening Customers' Telephone Waiting Time

This case illustrates how a bank applied some of the basic seven quality tools discussed in this supplement and storyboard concepts to improve customer service. It is the story of a Quality Circle (QC) program implemented in the main office of a large bank. An average of 500 customers call this office every day. Surveys indicated that the callers tended to become irritated if it took too long for the call to be answered and for the caller to be transferred to the appropriate person. By contrast, prompt service reassured the customers and made them feel more comfortable doing business by phone. The bank feared that dissatisfied customers might move their business to another bank.

Selection of a Theme

A QC team was formed to address the telephone reception issue. Telephone reception was chosen as a QC theme for the following reasons: (*a*) Telephone reception is the first impression a customer receives from the company; (*b*) this theme coincided with the company's telephone reception slogan, "Don't make customers wait, and avoid needless switching from extension to extension"; and (*c*) it also coincided with a companywide campaign being promoted at that time that advocated being friendly to everyone one met.

First, the team discussed why the present method of answering calls made callers wait.

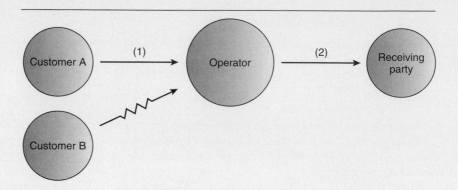

Case Exhibit CS6.1 illustrates a frequent situation, where a call from customer B comes in while the operator is talking with customer A. Let's see why the customer has to wait.

At (1), the operator receives a call from the customer but, due to lack of experience, does not know where to connect the call. At (2), the receiving party cannot answer the phone quickly, perhaps because he or she is unavailable, and no one else can take the call. The result is that the operator must transfer the call to another extension while apologizing for the delay.

Situation Analysis

To fully understand the situation, the QC members decided to brainstorm regarding the reasons for poor service. Some of the reasons identified for customers having to wait too long before they were connected to the appropriate person were:

1. The receiving party is out of the office for the day on other business, or is absent that day, or is not at the desk at present (these are considered three reasons). In these cases the operator would have to try somebody else who could help the caller.

2. Sometimes the customer engages the operator in lengthy conversation or spends a long time complaining to the operator.

3. Often customers are not aware whom they should contact within the bank.

4. Sometimes the delay is system related. As is common in queues, sometimes there is a high call volume, at other times it is light. If they call at lunchtime there is usually only one operator since the only other operator would be at lunch.

5. Sometimes the operator cannot find an alternative person to receive calls since everybody in the section is unavailable.

6. One or the other of the operators is sometimes absent due to illness or vacation.

7. In some cases operators may lack knowledge about the job responsibilities within the company and thus may not transfer the caller to the appropriate person at the first try. The caller would then have to be transferred again. In other cases operators have difficulty understanding customer requests.

Operators were then asked to keep checksheets on several points to tally the reasons for poor service spanning 12 days from June 4 to 16. (See Figure CS6.2A.) The data recorded on the checksheets unexpectedly revealed that "only one operator (partner out of the office)" topped the list by a big margin, occurring a total of 172 times. In this case, the operator on duty had to deal with large numbers of calls when the phones were busy. A total of 351 customers had to wait a long time (experienced poor service), which accounted for about 6 percent of the calls received. (See Figure CS6.2B).

A. Checksheet—Designed to Identify the Problems

Reason Date	No one present in the section receiving the call	Receiving party not present	Only one operator (partner out of the office)	Total
June 4	\\\\	⊬⊬⊤ \	⊬⊬⊤ ⊬⊬⊤ \	24
June 5	⊬⊬⊤	⊬⊬⊤ \\\	⊬⊬⊤ ⊬⊬⊤ \\\\	32
June 6	⊬⊬⊤ \	\\\\	⊬⊬⊤ ⊬⊬⊤ \\	28
June 15	⊬⊬⊤	⊬⊬⊤	⊬⊬⊤ \\\	25

B. Reasons Why Callers Had to Wait

Cause type	Description	Number of occurrences
A	Customer does not know whom to contact regarding concern	19
B	Receiving party not present in office	73
C	No one present in section	61
D	One operator (partner out of office)	172
E	Lengthy conversation	16
F	Other reasons	10
	Total	351

System Improvement

The bank implemented a number of suggestions made by the QC. As a result the customer waiting time improved considerably. Exhibit CS6.3 shows data from a recent 12-day period comparable to the June 4 to 16 analysis, where the details on all calls considered to be poorly served (defective calls) are shown. As seen, although the poorly serviced calls could not be reduced to zero, all items presented showed a marked improvement. The total number of calls dropped from 351 to 59. The major cause of delays—"one operator"—plummeted from 172 incidents to 15 in the follow-up survey.

Questions

1. Create a fishbone diagram using the reasons given in the situation analysis. Use four main categories: Receiving party, Customer, System, and Operator.

2. Using the data in Exhibit S6.2B prepare a Pareto diagram for the six reasons.

Explain how it can help you improve the system.

3. How would you have solved these problems?

4. With the improved system and the data in Exhibit CS6.3, prepare the following:

   a. checksheet for poorly serviced calls, similar to CS6.2A, in the format shown below.

Day	Reasons						Total
	A	B	C	D	E	F	
1							
2							
.							
.							
12							

   b. bar chart for the daily total number of poorly serviced calls during the 12 days.

Exhibit CS6.3

Defective Call #	Day	Reason	Defective Call #	Day	Reason
1	1	One operator	31	7	Receiving party not present
2	1	One operator	32	7	One operator
3	1	Receiving party not present	33	7	No one in section
4	1	No one in section	34	7	No one in section
5	1	Lengthy conversation	35	8	Receiving party not present
6	1	Customer does not know whom to contact	36	8	One operator
7	1	No one in section	37	8	Customer does not know whom to contact
8	2	Other reasons	38	8	Receiving party not present
9	2	Lengthy conversation	39	8	No one in section
10	2	One operator	40	8	One operator
11	3	Receiving party not present	41	8	Receiving party not present
12	3	No one in section	42	9	One operator
13	3	Receiving party not present	43	9	No one in section
14	3	No one in section	44	10	Receiving party not present
15	3	Receiving party not present	45	10	One operator
16	3	One operator	46	10	No one in section
17	4	No one in section	47	10	One operator
18	4	Receiving party not present	48	10	No one in section
19	4	No one in section	49	10	Receiving party not present
20	4	Receiving party not present	50	10	No one in section
21	4	No one in section	51	10	No one in section
22	4	One operator	52	11	One operator
23	5	Receiving party not present	53	11	Receiving party not present
24	5	No one in section	54	11	No one in section
25	5	Receiving party not present	55	11	Customer does not know whom to contact
26	5	No one in section	56	12	No one in section
27	6	One operator	57	12	No one in section
28	6	One operator	58	12	Receiving party not present
29	6	Receiving party not present	59	12	Customer does not know whom to contact
30	6	One operator			

    c. Pareto diagram of the improved system using the six reasons.

5. Using the data given, comment on the overall and specific improvements in the system.

6. What would be the next step in improving the system even further?

Hint: It is related to Exhibit 6.2 in Chapter 6.

Source:

From "The Quest for Higher Quality—the Deming Prize and Quality Control," Ricoh Company, Ltd., in Masaaki Imai, *Kaizen: The Key to Japan's Competitive Success* (New York: The McGraw-Hill Companies, 1986), pp. 54–58.

7

Strategic Facility Decisions: Location and Capacity

Chapter Objectives

- Present a framework for evaluating alternative site locations.

- Identify the various factors, both quantitative and qualitative, to take into consideration when selecting a location for a manufacturing or service organization.

- Distinguish between factors that are important for locating a manufacturing facility and those that are important for locating a service operation.

- Discuss strategic capacity issues.

Toyota Chooses Woodstock, Ontario, for its New Assembly Plant

October 11, 2005: Toyota President, Katsuaki Watanabe and Canadian Prime Minister Paul Martin attend the sod-turning ceremony for Toyota's latest planned North American plant in Woodstock, a small town located between Toronto and London. When completed the plant will employ 2000 workers and churn out 200 000 automobiles per year.

What made Woodstock attractive to Toyota? Location and aggregate capacity are major decisions and thus are made on the basis of multiple factors, not cost alone. In the case of Toyota, one factor would have been that Ontario is now the number one jurisdiction for assembling automobiles in North America (a distinction it wrested from Michigan in 2004), with a very strong auto parts industry as well. Besides, southwestern Ontario, along with the geographically proximal U.S. Midwest, traditionally forms the heart of the North American auto industry. Thus developing suppliers close by that can deliver parts frequently and in small batches, something crucial to its Just-In-Time (JIT) system (discussed in Chapter 13) is feasible at Woodstock.

Another important factor is the existence of another Toyota plant nearby in Cambridge,

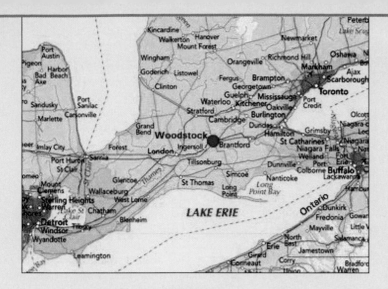

Ontario. As Toyota gears up to attempt to overtake General Motors and become the world's biggest automaker, it will have to rely on its existing plants to train new employees in the new plants in its JIT system which focuses on waste elimination. So having Cambridge nearby was a plus.

Also rural locations close to big cities are ideal since the cost of land is lower than in the city, yet highways make it easy to get parts in and vehicles out to cities such as Toronto, a road, rail, air, and sea transportation hub. In addition, the major North American markets of central Canada and the midwestern, eastern, and south-eastern U.S. are nearby.

It helped that the Ontario government contributed $70 million in incentives to help land the deal and that the federal government chipped in another $55 million. Lobbying by top ministers in Ontario and the federal government (including the Prime Minister) probably helped also.

Another advantage of Woodstock is the many universities and technical institutions nearby from which Toyota can recruit skilled employees. Canada's socialized health system is also a plus since Toyota won't be burdened as much by employee health care costs as it would be in the United States. Furthermore, general liberalization of trade rules means that Toyota can take advantage of a good location in Canada and yet not be limited by Canada's small market. It can export Woodstock-built vehicles to the United States and beyond.

Source:
Greg Keenan, "Toyota may double output, boost hiring at new plant," *Globe and Mail*, October 12, 2005, B1.
Norihiko Shirouzu, "Mean but Lean, Toyota Seeks Outside Help; With In-House Quality Gurus in Short Supply, Auto Maker Turns to Its Assembler Affiliates," *Wall Street Journal*, July 14, 2005, B4.

Senior management makes a long-term commitment whenever it decides to build a manufacturing facility. Such facilities typically require a substantial investment in capital, the recovery of which takes many years. As discussed earlier in Chapter 2, the construction of a facility involves several strategic decisions, which include (*a*) how big to make it, (*b*) when to build it, (*c*) where to build it, and (*d*) what type(s) of process(es) to install. For example, when Enbridge decided to invest in wind power generation in Saskatchewan, when Toyota decided to build a plant in Cambridge, Ontario, and when Texas-based EDS decided to move a call centre from North Carolina to Cape Breton, Nova Scotia, these are some of the factors they would have considered. Each of these decisions significantly impacts operational decisions for many years, and consequently it also can have a significant impact on the overall success of the firm.

Back-of-the-house services similarly require large capital investments. An example of such a facility is Shopper's Drug Mart's distribution hub in Calgary. On the other hand, the capital investment is usually much smaller for front-of-the-house operations that interact directly with the customer. However, the risks associated with selecting sites for front-of-the-house operations tend to be much higher, as the success of an operation at a given location is significantly affected not only by the customer demographics within its immediate area but also by the unique characteristics of the site. To illustrate the importance of selecting the right site for these types of services, there is a saying in the restaurant business that "The three most important factors for success are Location, Location, and Location."

For manufacturing companies and back-of-the-house service operations, management must address many issues when adding capacity. These include: Should we close the existing facility? Can we expand the existing facility? Should the new facility have a different process from existing operations? The primary consideration in making these decisions is to minimize costs. In contrast, the decision to locate a front-of-the-house service facility is primarily driven by its revenue potential.

The globalization of business further complicates the location decision. Local customs, tax rates, tax incentives, and laws must be taken into consideration, along with infrastructure in terms of roads, telecommunications, and supporting businesses. Ireland, for example, is attracting both manufacturing and service organizations because of its relatively low cost and educated workforce, infrastructure, and tax incentives. Another example is the creation of *maquiladora* businesses in Mexico along the U.S. border. With the establishment of the North American Free Trade Agreement (NAFTA), these firms are now able to ship products duty-free into the United States and Canada. As a result, U.S. and Canadian companies have relocated operations there due to the significantly lower labour costs in Mexico.

An incorrect site location decision is very expensive for both manufacturing and service firms. Because it is a long-term decision, management must live with the consequences of that decision for many years. Thus, a decision to build in the wrong location, at the wrong time, with the wrong capacity or the wrong process(es) can have significant negative implications for the profits of the firm. If management elects subsequently to sell off the facility as a result of recognizing a bad decision, a substantial portion of the initial investment frequently will not be recoverable because the facility is usually built for a unique purpose. Consequently, management must take a very hard look at these types of decisions.

Locating Manufacturing Operations

The location decision, whether in manufacturing or services, involves determining the location of a facility or facilities as well as the capacity of each facility. The facility location decision answers the strategic question: "Where should we build our firm's facilities and how large should each one be?"

The facility location decision for a manufacturing firm usually involves the location of both the manufacturing plant and the warehouse or distribution facilities. As a general rule, products that decrease in weight and volume during the manufacturing process tend to be located near the sources of raw material. An example of this would be a lumber mill that is located in a forest where the trees are being harvested. In this case, the reduction is so significant that the mill is often moved every few years, to be closer to the trees being cut down. On the other hand, products that increase in weight and volume during the manufacturing process tend to be located near the consumers. An example of this is a soft drink bottler that is located near a major city. In both of these cases, the goal is to reduce distribution costs.

At the same time, as the world continues toward a single, global economy, businesses need to take a more international perspective with respect to locating their manufacturing facilities, as seen in the OM in Practice on Palliser Furniture's global location decisions. The low labour costs provided by faraway countries often more than offset the additional transportation costs. However, there are many other factors besides costs that are involved in selecting a site. As a result, the complexity of the decision-making process increases severalfold when a firm decides to shift from a national to an international site location strategy. In weighing the advantages and disadvantages of alternative sites, the analysis therefore should include an evaluation of both qualitative and quantitative factors.[1] (One method for comparing the qualitative factors for different locations is known as factor-rating systems, which is presented in detail later in this chapter.) Location decisions can be broken down into country-specific, region-specific, and site-specific decisions. Each of these would consider the different qualitative and quantitative factors discussed below, but would place different emphasis on the different factors.

Qualitative Factors

The qualitative factors include (*a*) local infrastructure, (*b*) worker education, culture, and skills, (*c*) product content requirements, and (*d*) political/economic stability.

Local Infrastructure

The local infrastructure that is necessary to support a manufacturing operation can be divided into two broad categories: institutional and transportational. With manufacturing operations becoming more flexible and responsive to customer requirements, there is a growing dependence on local institutions or suppliers to be more flexible and responsive. In addition, the local transportation network that links the suppliers to the manufacturer must be efficient and reliable. For example, the lack of an adequate and reliable transportation infrastructure in the Former Soviet Union (FSU) or the People's Republic of China would impede a firm that uses just-in-time (JIT) concepts from locating in these areas.

Worker Education, Culture, and Skills

The increased sophistication of today's manufacturing processes requires that the workforce be highly educated and equipped with a wide variety of skills. Increased emphasis on automation requires specific worker skills to operate and maintain equipment. Modern manufacturing processes such as just-in-time (JIT) also require a well-educated workforce. As an illustration, the significant growth of business in Singapore in recent years can be attributed, in large part, to the investment of its government in educating and training its population. Compatibility of the location's business culture with the organization's corporate culture may also be important.

Product Content Requirements

Content requirements state that a minimum percentage of a product must be produced within the borders of a country for that product to be sold in that country. This assures jobs in the local economy while reducing the difference between imports and exports. For example, for a car to be sold in the Philippines, it must be assembled there. Consequently, each of the major car manufacturers that wants to sell cars in the Philippines has an assembly plant there, even though demand for cars in that country is sufficiently small to suggest that importing them would be more economical.

content requirements

Requirement that a percentage of a product must be made within a country for it to be sold there.

---

[1]Alan D. MacCormack, Laurence J. Newman III, and Donald B. Rosenfeld, "The New Dynamics of Global Manufacturing Site Location," *Sloan Management Review* (Summer 1994), pp. 69–80.

EVOLUTION OF A GLOBAL LOCATION STRATEGY AT A WINNIPEG FURNITURE MAKER

Palliser Furniture, which originated as a woodworking shop in 1944 in a Winnipeg basement, is Canada's largest furniture manufacturer, employing about 5000 people worldwide. With suppliers on four continents, and factories in Canada, the United States, Mexico, and Indonesia, it stands among the industry leaders in global presence. As this example describes, the company chose these global locations after careful consideration and for various strategic reasons.

It was only in 1981 that Palliser opened its first international plant in Fargo, North Dakota, allowing it to secure a beachhead in the United States, the world's largest furniture market. The U.S. expansion also allowed it to hedge against currency fluctuations. In 1991 another plant in North Carolina was established and the Fargo plant closed in 1994. The arrival of the Free Trade Agreement (FTA) in 1984 and the North American Free Trade Agreement (NAFTA) in 1994 and the resulting lowering of tariffs had a profound effect on Palliser. These agreements brought tremendous opportunities since the U.S. and Mexican markets were now more accessible. At the same time the Canadian market was no longer protected. Thus Palliser had to become more competitive. As a result the company redefined its markets, rationalized its distribution locations, and shifted its manufacturing locations. Mexico was seen as an attractive location because of its cheap labour. By the late 1990s Palliser had established a factory in Saltillo, a city close to Monterey, as its Mexican location. Saltillo has a stable economic base, including manufacturing operations of Chrysler, GM, Lear Seating, Fruit of the Loom, etc. Thus the city also had experience in tanning, cutting, and sewing operations, skills valuable to Palliser.

In 2000, it opened it first Asian factory in Indonesia because of the country's highly skilled labour force and its wood processing tradition, among other reasons. The plant produces wood components for furniture to be assembled in Winnipeg. With the ability to design, produce, and source in different parts of the

globe (it also has a partnership with a Lithuanian company), Palliser can come to market with both inexpensive offerings and pricier goods. Also as important, with three plants in North America it has the ability to juggle production between plants for the important North American market. It can provide two- to four-week deliveries on even custom orders, which its Asian competition cannot match. Palliser has not abandoned its Canadian base, however. Currently four (three in Winnipeg and one in Alberta) of its seven locations are in Canada.

Sources:

Michael Chazin, "The New Global Reality," *Upholstery Design and Management* (December 2002), pp. 12–16.

Anthony Goerzen, *Palliser Furniture* (London, Ontario: University of Western Ontario, Ivey Management Services, 1998).

Geoff Kirbyson, "Winnipeg Furniture Maker Sets Up Shops in Asia, Europe," *Winnipeg Free Press*, August 11, 2000, B5.

"Palliser Looks for 400-M in Canadian Sales," *Winnipeg Free Press*, March 5, 1999, B12.

Palliser Furniture, www.palliser.com.

Political/Economic Stability

The stability of a region refers to the number and intensity of economic and political fluctuations that might occur there. The dissolution of the former Soviet Union provides ample evidence of the problems associated with locating a business in unstable economies. Toronto-based Bata, the world's largest shoe company, relocated to Canada from Europe more than 60 years ago under pressure from war and communism.

Quantitative Factors

The quantitative factors include (*a*) labour costs, (*b*) distribution costs, (*c*) incentives, (*d*) exchange rates, and (*e*) tax rates.

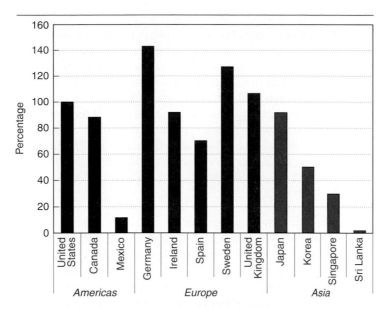

Exhibit 7.1

Comparison of 2004 Hourly Wages for Production Workers

Source: U.S. Department of Labor, Bureau of Labor Statistics, November 2005.

Labour Costs

Labour costs can vary dramatically, depending on location. In Western Europe, the United States, Canada, and Japan, labour costs are quite high compared to Mexico and parts of Asia (see Exhibit 7.1). An important factor that must be considered is the skill requirements of the worker. Although the cost of labour in many areas is very low, the workers in these very same regions often lack adequate education and skills.

Distribution Costs

As we become more global, distribution and transportation costs take on added importance. In addition to the cost of transportation, the time required to deliver the products also must be taken into consideration. Consequently, in many cases the low costs associated with manufacturing products in Asia are offset by the long lead times and the high cost of delivery to markets in North America and Europe.

Incentives

Countries often offer incentives in the form of low-cost manufacturing facilities to attract companies. For example, within the People's Republic of China (PRC) many **special economic zones (SEZ)** have been established that are exempt from tariffs and duties—provided that the products made there are sold outside the PRC. In some countries, the local government will enter into a partnership with a firm, with the government providing the land, the building, and perhaps the training of the workforce.

special economic zones (SEZ)

Duty-free areas in a country established to attract foreign investment in the form of manufacturing facilities.

Forgivable loans and grants from the federal and Nova Scotia governments induced Electronic Data Systems to move a call centre from the United States to Cape Breton.[2] The Ontario and Federal governments are considering incentives including research and development funds to compete with the incentives being offered by many U.S. states to maintain auto industry investment in Ontario.[3]

[2]Mark Mackinnon, "Prayers Answered for Cape Bretoners: 900 to 1500 new Jobs," *The Globe and Mail,* March 31, 2000, A7.
[3]Simon Tuck, "Ottawa, Ontario Rev Up Interest in Auto Industry," *The Globe and Mail,* April 21, 2003, B1.

Exchange Rates

The volatility of the exchange rates between countries can have a significant impact on sales and profits. In fact, Exhibit 7.1 would have looked quite different in 2002. Between 2002 and 2004, the U.S. dollar depreciated relative to the Canadian dollar. Thus, compared to that of the U.S., the wage rate in Canada (and many other countries) was relatively lower in 2002. For example, the wage level in Canada was at 78% of the U.S. level. By 2004, as seen in the exhibit, the Canadian wage level had risen to 94% of the U.S. level, partly due to the depreciation of the U.S. dollar. This will decrease the price competitiveness of Canadian products in the United States while increasing the ability of U.S. products to compete in Canada. On the other hand, the depreciation of the Canadian dollar from almost US$0.90 to about US$0.65 during the 1990s had the opposite effect.

Tax Rates

Tax rates can differ significantly between countries, and even within a country. For example, in Canada, the provincial sales tax and income tax can vary significantly between provinces. Other taxes that need to be considered include property taxes and payroll taxes. In many western European countries, such as France and Germany, payroll taxes can be as high as 50 percent. To attract businesses, many countries and states will offer significant tax incentives. For example, a country may exempt a firm from paying income taxes during its first 5 or 10 years of operation, after which normal tax rates will apply.

Locating Service Operations

Many of the issues manufacturing companies have to address when expanding their operations internationally also must be addressed by service operations. (See the OM in Practice on Toys "Я" Us in Japan.) For example, when McDonald's opened its first restaurant in Moscow, the lack of an existing institutional infrastructure to support its operation required that it build a central commissary. This commissary prepared everything for the retail outlet, from hamburger patties to rolls and french fries. In addition, the Russian farmers had to be shown how to grow vegetables such as potatoes and lettuce that would meet McDonald's high-quality product specifications. In contrast, the opening of a McDonald's in the United States or Western Europe would only require a call to established, local suppliers.

Interestingly, George A. Cohon, founder and senior chairman of McDonald's Restaurants of Canada Limited, spearheaded the opening of McDonald's in the former Soviet Union in 1990. In doing so he had to deal with unique supply chain, quality management, and human resources and currency challenges. He is currently founder and senior chairman of McDonald's in Russia, which is controlled by McDonald's of Canada.[4]

Location Strategies

In an effort to better serve customers, service operations have adopted a variety of location strategies, depending on the particular customer requirements they are trying to address. Exhibit 7.2 presents several approaches to satisfying these customer needs.

Computer Programs for Site Selection

With the growth in **geographic information systems (GIS)**, service operations are able to conduct location analysis more quickly and with greater accuracy than was previously

geographic information systems (GIS)

Computer tool that assesses alternative locations for service operations.

---

[4]McDonald's Corporation, www.mcdonalds.ca; Geoffrey York, "Golden Arches Stretching over Russia," *The Globe and Mail*, December 3, 1998, B10; Youngeme Moon and Kerry Herman, *McDonald's in Russia: Managing a Crisis* (Cambridge, MA: Harvard Business School Publishing, 2003).

Operations Management in Practice

TOYS "Я" US IN JAPAN

Toys "Я" Us has successfully entered the Japanese toy market through private-sector help—in this case, with the help of Nintendo.

On December 20, 1991, Toys "Я" Us—the world's largest toy retailer—opened its first retail store in Japan. What may now sound like an American success story in Japan travelled a difficult road for two years. The retailer had established locations in Canada, the United Kingdom, Germany, France, Singapore, Hong Kong, Malaysia, and Taiwan well before it attempted to enter the Japanese market.

In January 1990, Toys "Я" Us formally applied to open its first (large) toy store in Niigata, Japan. This caused local toy retailers to proclaim their opposition by invoking provisions contained in the Large-Scale Retail Store Act. Then they organized a lobbying group to mobilize support against the American firm. Toys "Я" Us appealed for help directly through the U.S. trade representative and other channels. Sustained American political pressure and widespread publicity finally forced MITI to confront the local lobby and limit to 18 months the application process under the restrictive retail law. It was April 1990, and Toys "Я" Us had overcome its first major hurdle.

But there was another hurdle to cross. Toys "Я" Us succeeds in large part by selling below suggested retail price. It accomplishes this mainly through exploiting economies it obtains through volume purchases. Anticipating the threat posed by that strategy to their own profit margins, Japanese toy manufacturers banded together and vowed not to sell their wares to Toys "Я" Us. But Nintendo depends heavily on Toys "Я" Us for the distribution of its products in the United States and other major markets. Nintendo's defection triggered an ultimate end to this boycott.

Private-sector countermeasures consciously adopted by numerous major Japanese corporations are replacing the falling barriers to entry of public-sector regulation.

Source:

Mark Mason, "United States Direct Investment in Japan: Trends and Prospects," Copyright © 1992, by the Regents of the University of California. Reprinted from the California Management Review, Vol. 35, No. 1. By permission of the Regents.

Customer Requirements	Strategy
Customers are hungry because airlines no longer serve food on short flights.	Locate "real" restaurants in airports (e.g., the restaurants of the Delta Calgary Airport Hotel or the Fairmont Vancouver Airport, which are attached to the airports).
Customers want more convenient locations to save time.	Combine previously separate service operations into one location (e.g., ATMs and convenience stores with gas stations).
Customers are reluctant to shop frequently in large megastores because they are time consuming.	Add other services to increase convenience such as fast food and banking (e.g., McDonald's in Wal-Mart, Starbucks in Chapters, and Tim Horton's in Rona).

Exhibit 7.2
Customer Requirements and Location Strategies for Service Operations

Source: Adapted from Hal Reid, "Retailers Seek the Unique," *Business Geographics* 5, no. 2 (February 1997), pp. 32 35.

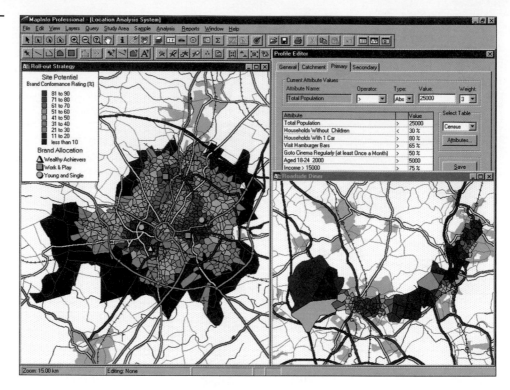

possible. GIS allows large databases to be displayed graphically, thereby providing the service manager with a "bird's-eye view" of a particular region of interest. These regional maps can display a wide variety of demographic data, depending on the needs of the service manager. Exhibit 7.3A, for example, shows the location of housing loans for a bank, including a breakdown by income of the different areas served by the bank. Exhibit 7.3B analyzes the percentage of total sales that would be generated from different areas if a regional mall were to be built. Exhibit 7.3C identifies the gap between the demand for noncritical emergency room visits and the availability of clinics and physicians to meet that demand.

In addition to GIS, there are many nongraphic computer programs available to assist the service manager in evaluating alternative site locations. Many of these models incorporate forecasting techniques such as regression analysis, which will be introduced in Chapter 9.

Types of Service Facilities

The decision where to locate a service facility is highly dependent on the specific type of service that is being provided and how it is delivered to the customer. We identify the following three types of service facilities, based upon the degree and type of contact each has with the customer:

- Facilities with direct interface with the customer
- Facilities with indirect customer contact
- Facilities with no customer contact

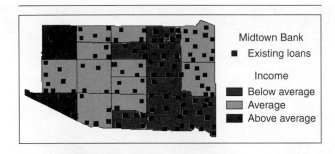

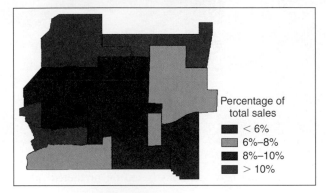

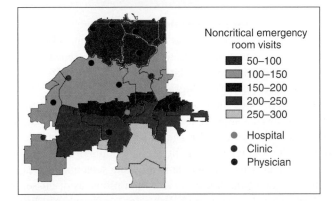

Source: Getting to Know Arc View GIS (Redlands, CA: Environmental Systems Research Institute, Inc., 1997). Reprinted with permission.

Exhibit 7.3

A. Distribution of a Bank's Housing Loans in an Area

B. Distribution of Sales for a Regional Mall by Area

C. Demand for Health Care in a Region and the Services that Are Available

Facilities with Direct Interface with the Customer

Businesses that require the actual presence of the customer as part of the service process are often referred to as **bricks-and-mortar operations** because of their physical structures. Examples of these types of services include restaurants, hotels, branch offices of banks, hospitals, and traditional retail operations such as supermarkets, large department stores, and small clothing boutiques. For firms with these types of decentralized facilities, the critical success factor is the amount of sales that a given location can generate. Consequently, many multilocation services have developed sophisticated forecasting models for predicting the sales that potential new locations can generate. (Forecasting models that

bricks-and-mortar operation

A front-of-the-house service that requires a physical structure to interact directly with the customer.

At a Dell call centre, employees provide assistance to customers.

are used to evaluate potential new locations based on predicted sales are presented in Chapter 9.)

Facilities with Indirect Customer Contact

Services such as telephone call centres and virtual firms that only link to the customer through a Web site do not require the customer's physical presence to deliver the service. Examples of the wide variety of services that have call centres include hotels, airlines, and car rental agencies (for reservations); brokerage and financial services (for trading transactions); and mail order businesses such as Sears Canada (for customer orders). Call centres also provide customer service support for both services and manufacturing companies. These same services often provide a Web site as an alternative channel of communication with the customer. With these types of facilities, the choice of location, in terms of being near the customer, is not an issue. Consequently, the site selection process in these cases is very similar to that of back-of-the-house service operations, as discussed in the following section. In fact, both the call centres and Web sites are frequently located in the same facility to take advantage of economies of scale.

Facilities with No Customer Contact

back-of-the-house

A service facility, or that part of the service process, that does not come in contact with the customer.

Services that have no direct interaction with the customer are often referred to as **back-of-the-house** operations. Because the customer is absent from the process, these services, in many respects, tend to resemble a manufacturing operation. Services with these characteristics can be further divided into two broad categories: (1) the processing (sometimes) and distribution of physical goods (as illustrated by a central commissary for a restaurant chain) and (2) the processing and distribution of information (as illustrated by a credit card billing operation). As in selecting a manufacturing site, the location of a physical distribution centre needs to consider not only the facility's operating costs but also the distribution or delivery costs, with the goal of minimizing the combined costs of both. Canadian Tire's regional distribution centres provide a good example of this type of facility.

In addition to distributing products, some of these back-of-the-house facilities also include, to some extent, manufacturing processes and are therefore often referred to as

quasi-manufacturing operations. Some pizza chains have central commissaries where the pizza dough is mixed and rolled into appropriate size balls (but not rolled into the flat circular pizza shape). This is a good example of a quasi-manufacturing operation.

However, for those back-of-the-house services that are exclusively involved in processing information, there are only the facility operating costs to minimize, because the differences in delivery costs between alternative locations are usually nonexistent or negligible. For example, the cost of long-distance telephone calls is the same throughout Canada, as is the cost of mail delivery. Thus, the site selection criteria for a cheque processing operation of a bank, or a customer billing operation for a retail chain or credit card company, will focus primarily on minimizing facility operating expenses.

As with manufacturing operations, managers need to consider both qualitative and quantitative factors in evaluating potential sites. These factors will vary in both type and relative importance, depending on the type of service facility for which the location is being evaluated. From an operational perspective, these factors are the same as those used in evaluating a manufacturing site. This is especially true for back-of-the-house operations. In addition, front-of-the-house operations need to consider customer-related factors that can impact sales at a location. Depending on the service, some of these factors include (*a*) average family income, (*b*) average family size, (*c*) population density, and (*d*) pedestrian and/or automobile traffic.

Methods for Evaluating Potential Locations

Both qualitative and quantitative methods are available for evaluating and comparing potential site locations. These include the factor-rating system and the centre-of-gravity methods, both of which are described here in detail. In, addition, there are forecasting models that use regression analysis to predict sales for **front-of-the-house** operations. (See Chapter 9 on forecasting.) Often, a combination of these methods is used so that management can evaluate sites from several perspectives.

Factor-Rating Systems

Factor-rating systems are probably one of the most widely used location selection techniques because they can combine very diverse issues (multiple criteria) into an easy-to-understand format. At the same time, it is important to recognize that although the end result from this type of analysis is a quantitative number, factor-rating systems are used to evaluate both qualitative and quantitative factors.

Another reason that the factor-rating system approach is so popular is that it is relatively simple to use, requiring only six steps:

1. Identify the specific criteria or factors, often called critical success factors (CSFs), to be considered in selecting a site (see OM in Practice box on Criteria for Selecting a Location for a Back-of-the-House Service Operation).

2. Assign a weight to each factor indicating its importance relative to all of the other factors being considered.

3. Select a common scale for rating each factor (for example, 1–100).

4. Rate each potential location on each of the factors.

5. Multiply each factor's score by the weight assigned to that factor.

6. Sum up the weighted scores for all of the factors and select the location with the highest total score.

quasi-manufacturing operation

A service firm's dedicated production and distribution facility that supplies its retail operations.

front-of-the-house

A service facility, or that part of the service process, that interacts directly with the customer.

factor-rating systems

A qualitative approach for evaluating alternative site locations.

Example

To illustrate the factor-rating system, consider The Regina Low-Credit Card Interest Bank, which is looking to locate its credit card operations. Two potential sites have been identified. Management has decided to use the following criteria, as suggested in the OM in Practice box, and has assigned the following weights to each based upon their relative importance. The two locations are then rated on each of these factors and a total score for each location is calculated.

Solution

We construct a spreadsheet as follows, and calculate the score for each of the two locations under consideration:

Factor	Weight	Rating Site A	Rating Site B	Score Site A	Score Site B
Size and education of workforce within 25 km	20	60	75	1200	1500
Availability of part-time workers (students)	10	45	20	450	200
Distance to telecommunications infrastructure	25	80	90	2000	2250
Distance to higher-education facilities	5	50	35	250	175
Cost-of-living index	15	85	80	1275	1200
Cultural amenities	10	65	40	650	400
Crime statistics	15	95	90	1425	1350
Totals	100			7250	7075

Using this evaluation as a criterion, Site A, with the higher score, should be selected. Because the factor-rating system is a highly qualitative technique, the use of an electronic spreadsheet, such as Excel, will allow management to easily vary the factor weights to see their overall impact on the decision.

It should be noted that although the weights for the factors in this example totalled 100, this is not a requirement. What is important is that the weights assigned to each factor reflect their relative importance in selecting a site. Equally important, the scale for rating each factor, as stated earlier, should be the same. Also, in determining a rating for each factor for a specific location, the actual value assigned is not as critical as its relative value in comparison to the other sites under consideration.

Other, more sophisticated multi-factor or multi-criteria decision models for handling more complex decisions are available commercially. For example Expert Choice software uses the Analytic Hierarchy Process (AHP), a multi-criteria decision process.

Cost-Based Analysis

Location decisions can also be made by building mathematical or computer models that minimize costs. In order to build such a model for a potential facility or a network of potential facilities, the analyst has to obtain the quantitative information discussed earlier such as labour and distribution costs, incentives, exchange rates, and tax rates for potential locations. For bigger organizations this process is complex, and sophisticated mathematical and computer models are built to identify appropriate locations. In many cases the cost of doing this sophisticated analysis is well worth it because choosing the wrong location can result in the company experiencing excessive costs for many years.

CRITERIA FOR SELECTING A LOCATION FOR A BACK-OF-THE-HOUSE SERVICE OPERATION

Fluor Global Location Strategies has identified the following general criteria for selecting a location for an office, be it for a company headquarters, an R&D facility, or a back-of-the-house operation:

- Population characteristics (size, education, diversity, etc.)
- Workforce characteristics (size, type/distribution, education, number employed, etc.)
- Availability of alternative workforces (military spouses, students, underemployed, etc.)

- Distance to commercial airports (including "direct-service" international airports)
- Distance to population centres
- Distance to telecommunications infrastructure (COs, PoPs, fibre networks, etc.)
- Distance to higher-education facilities
- Quality-of-life characteristics:
    - Quality-of-living index
    - Cost-of-living index
    - Cultural amenities
    - Crime statistics

Source:
Special thanks to Fluor Global Location Strategies.

The computer models used will generally try to minimize the sum of fixed costs and variable costs. For example, the fixed costs of building five different warehouses of 50 000 square metres is higher than building one warehouse of 250 000 square metres, though the total area is the same. However, having five different warehouses means we can have a warehouse close to the different demand centres, reducing transportation costs. Thus, there is often a trade-off between different types of costs. There are many software packages, such as CAST, SLIM, and MANUGISTICS, that do this type of computer modelling.

Centre-of-Gravity Method

The evaluation of alternative regions, subregions, and communities is commonly termed *macro-analysis*, while the evaluation of specific sites in a selected community is often termed *micro-analysis*. One technique used in micro-analysis is the **centre-of-gravity method**. The centre-of-gravity method is a quantitative technique that can be used to determine the optimal location of a facility based upon minimizing the transportation costs between where the goods are produced and where they are sold or redistributed. A manufacturing firm might use this method to determine where to locate its factory relative to its distribution facilities. Services also would use this method. For example, Domino's Pizza, Burger King, and Taco Bell all have commissaries that prepare food that is then distributed to their respective retail operations. Zellers' distribution centres provide an example of a service operation that delivers only manufactured goods.

The centre-of-gravity method also can be used to select locations for traditional bricks-and-mortar retail operations such as supermarkets, department stores, and wholesale discount operations such as Costco. For these services, the location is usually dependent on the population density and the average sales per customer for the different areas to be served.

The first step in the centre-of-gravity method is to locate each of the existing retail operations on an X and Y coordinate grid map. The purpose of the grid map is to establish relative distances between the locations. Exhibit 7.4 illustrates such a grid map as part of the example presented below.

The centre of gravity or the location for the supporting or distribution facility is then found by calculating the X and Y coordinates that result in minimizing the distribution

centre-of-gravity method

A quantitative approach for determining the optimal location for a facility based upon minimizing total distribution costs.

costs among all facilities. To determine this location on the grid map, the following formulas are used:

$$C_x = \frac{\sum x_i V_i}{\sum V_i} \tag{7.1}$$

$$C_y = \frac{\sum y_i V_i}{\sum V_i} \tag{7.2}$$

where

C_x = X coordinate of the centre of gravity

C_y = Y coordinate of the centre of gravity

x_i = X coordinate of the ith location

y_i = Y coordinate of the ith location

V_i = Volume of good transported to the ith location

Example

Ye Olde Bake Shoppe Company currently has four retail locations within the metropolitan area of a major city. Currently, each retail outlet makes all of its own breads and pastries from scratch (that is, prepared from basic ingredients such as flour, sugar, shortening, etc.). These locations are shown on the grid map in Exhibit 7.4. Management, to reduce costs and ensure consistency of the firm's products among all of the locations, has decided to build a central commissary where the products will be prepared and subsequently distributed to the four retail stores. The question now is where to locate this commissary.

The estimated amounts of product sold weekly (in kilograms) in each store along with its respective grid coordinates are provided in the table below.

Store Location	X Coordinate	Y Coordinate	kg of Product Sold
A	125	100	1250
B	250	75	3000
C	450	300	2750
D	200	350	1500

Exhibit 7.4

Grid Map of Ye Olde Bake Shoppe's Retail Locations

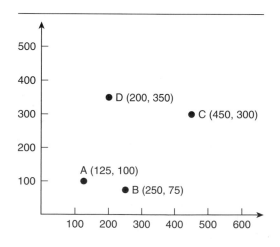

To determine the centre of gravity, which will be the ideal location for the commissary, we set up the spreadsheet for applying Equations 7.1 and 7.2:

	A	B	C	D	E	F	G	H	I	J	K
1		Ye Olde Bake Shoppe									
2											
3											
4			Location	x_i	y_i	V_i	$x_i{}^*V_i$	$y_i{}^*V_i$			
5											
6			A	125	100	1,250	156,250	125,000			
7			B	250	75	3,000	750,000	225,000			
8			C	450	300	2,750	1,237,500	825,000 ←			
9			D	200	350	1,500	300,000	525,000			
10										=E8*F8	
11				Totals:		8,500	2,443,750	1,700,000			
12										=SUM(G6.G9)	
13				C(x) =		287.50					
14											
15				C(y) =		200.00 ←				=H11/F11	
16											
17											

This provides management with the *X* and *Y* grid coordinates for the centre of gravity, which serve as a starting point for locating the new commissary.

A Spreadsheet Approach to Locating Facilities

Although the centre-of-gravity method provides an optimal solution for minimizing distribution costs, the resulting solution is often unrealistic. The location chosen by this method might be in a residential neighbourhood, or might not have access to major highways, or might already be occupied by another business. (It does, however, provide a good starting point for searching for a location.) A more realistic approach to selecting a site, therefore, is to identify several sites that are both available and also meet the requirements of the firm. Each site is then evaluated using the same criterion as in the centre-of-gravity approach; that is, to minimize the total costs of distribution. However, unlike the centre-of-gravity approach which has an infinite number of solutions, this approach will be limited to a choice among the sites selected for evaluation.

We use the Ye Olde Bake Shoppe chain of retail stores again to illustrate this approach and to provide a basis of comparison between the two methods. Management has identified two potential sites on which to locate the commissary. With production costs estimated to be the same at both sites, management's goal in selecting a site is to minimize distribution costs. The following information is provided on each site:

Store Location	kg of Product Sold	Distance to Site 1 (km)	Distance to Site 2 (km)
A	1250	19.5	23.0
B	3000	17.5	12.5
C	2750	20.6	18.0
D	1500	11.2	25.0

Solution

Using the same logic as in the centre-of-gravity method, we set up the following spreadsheet to calculate the total distribution costs associated with each site. (For consistency with the centre-of-gravity method, we define distribution costs here as total kg-km.)

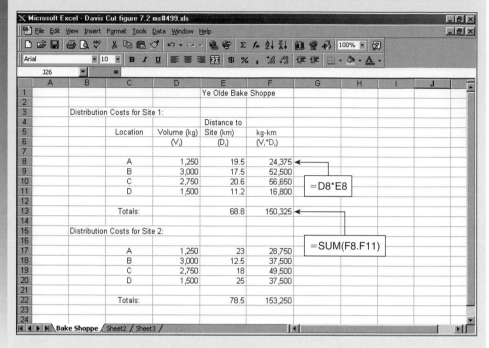

Based on the above analysis, site 1 appears to have the lower distribution cost, and therefore should be selected as the site for the new commissary.

Strategic Capacity Decisions

The capacity of the production system defines the firm's competitive boundaries. Specifically, it sets the firm's response rate to the market, its cost structure, its workforce composition, its level of technology, its management and staff support requirements, and its general inventory strategy. If capacity is inadequate, a company may lose customers through slow service or by allowing competitors to enter the market. If capacity is excessive, a company may have to reduce its prices to stimulate demand, underutilize its workforce, carry excess inventory, or seek additional, less-profitable products to stay in business.

Capacity-related issues are also discussed in other chapters such as process analysis (Chapter 5), facility layout (Chapter 8), waiting line management (Chapter 10), scheduling (Chapter 11), aggregate planning (Chapter 14) and dependent demand inventory management (Chapter 16). In this chapter we focus on strategic or long-range capacity decisions, which often involve major investments.

Factors Affecting Capacity

Capacity is affected by both external and internal factors. The external factors include (*a*) government regulations (working hours, safety, pollution), (*b*) union agreements, and (*c*) supplier capabilities. The internal factors include (*a*) product and service design, (*b*) personnel and jobs (worker training, motivation, learning, job content, and methods),

Exhibit 7.5

Comparing
Capacity and
Demand in a
Service
Operation

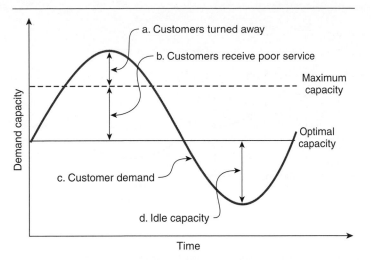

Source: Managing Services, 2/e by Lovelock, Christopher © 1992. Adapted by permission of Pearson Education, Inc., Upper Saddle River, NJ.

(*c*) plant layout and process flow, (*d*) equipment capabilities and maintenance, (*e*) materials management, (*f*) quality control systems, (*g*) product-mix decisions, and (*h*) management capabilities.

Important Capacity Concepts

In service operations we often distinguish between *maximum capacity* and *optimum capacity* because of the customer's direct interaction with the service facility. Christopher Lovelock has identified four different situations that the service manager may encounter in trying to match customer demand with the existing capacity of the operation. These situations, illustrated in Exhibit 7.5, are (*a*) demand exceeds maximum capacity causing customers to be turned away; (*b*) demand, although less than maximum capacity, exceeds optimum capacity resulting in customers who receive poor service; (*c*) demand equals optimum capacity; and (*d*) demand is less than optimum capacity, resulting in idle capacity.

Best Operating Level
The *best operating level* is that capacity for which the average unit cost is at a minimum. This is depicted in Exhibit 7.6. Note that as we move down the unit cost curve for each plant size, we achieve economies of scale until we reach the best operating level, and then we encounter diseconomies of scale as we exceed this point.

Economies and Diseconomies of Scale
The concept of economies of scale is well known: As product volumes increase, the average cost per unit decreases. This concept can be related to a best operating level for a given plant size. As shown in Exhibit 7.6, economies of scale (as well as diseconomies of scale) are found not only between the cost curves for each plant, but within each one as well.

Exhibit 7.6 also shows the best operating levels, V_A, V_B, V_C, and V_D, for plant sizes A, B, C, and D, respectively. Economies of scale occur for several reasons. As volumes increase, fixed costs are spread out over a greater number of units, thereby reducing the amount of overhead that is allocated to each product. With large volumes, a firm also can take advantage of quantity discounts, thereby reducing material costs. Scale factors, which

Exhibit 7.6

Economies of Scale

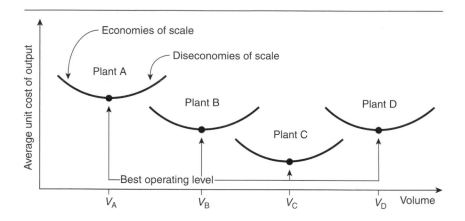

are associated with larger facilities, are a third source of economies of scale. For example, with processing operations such as breweries and refineries, doubling the capacity of a facility increases its costs by about 40 percent, which reflects the ratio of change in the volume in a cylinder or pipe to its outside area (in other words, to double the volume through a pipe requires about 141 percent more material for the larger pipe).

Diseconomies of scale also can occur for several reasons. When the best operating level in a plant is exceeded, additional costs are incurred. These added costs can take the form of overtime, inefficient scheduling, and machine breakdowns resulting from a lack of time to perform preventive maintenance. Diseconomies of scale also can occur with larger plants, as indicated by Plant D in Exhibit 7.6. This could be due to an inability to efficiently coordinate material flows and schedule workers. Organizational factors also can contribute to diseconomies of scale. With larger facilities, the contribution of each individual is diminished. Management and workers become more segregated and communicate less with each other. In operations that have a labour union, for example, grievances per 100 employees tend to increase in relation to the size of the plant.

Although finding the best size and operating level is illusive, managers often set policies regarding the maximum size for any one facility. As a result, the real challenge is predicting how costs will change for different output rates and facility sizes. This assessment requires careful attention to the different causes of economies of scale for each situation.

In the past several years, we have begun to see that diseconomies of scale come much sooner than we previously anticipated. This recognition, along with technological capability to do more in a plant, has resulted in a shift toward small facilities. The steel industry, with its declining number of large, integrated plants and its corresponding shift toward minimills, is a well-known case in point.

capacity flexibility

Ability to provide a wide range of products and volumes with short lead times.

agile manufacturing

Ability of a manufacturing process to respond quickly to changes in the marketplace.

Capacity Flexibility

Having the capability to deliver what the customer wants within a relatively short lead time is how we define **capacity flexibility**. Such flexibility is achieved through flexible plants, processes, workers, and strategies that use the capacity of other organizations. **Agile manufacturing** is another term that reflects the ability of a facility to react quickly to changes in the marketplace.

Flexible plants. Perhaps the ultimate in plant flexibility is the *zero-changeover-time* plant. Using movable equipment, knockdown walls, and easily accessible and reroutable utilities, such a plant can adapt to change in real time. An analogy to a familiar service business captures the flavour quite well—a plant with equipment "that is easy to install and easy to tear down and move—like the Ringling Bros., Barnum and Bailey Circus in the old tent-circus days" (or like today's Quebec-based entertainment company, Cirque du Soleil).[5]

Flexible processes. Flexible processes are epitomized by flexible manufacturing systems on the one hand and simple, easy-to-set-up equipment on the other. Both of these technological approaches permit rapid low-cost switching from one product line to another, enabling what is sometimes referred to as *economies of scope.* (By definition, economies of scope exist when multiple products can be produced at a lower cost in combination than they can separately.)

Flexible workers. Flexible workers have multiple skills and the ability to switch easily from one kind of task to another. They require broader training than specialized workers and need managers and staff support to facilitate quick changes in their work assignments.

Use of external capacity. Two common strategies for creating flexibility by using the capacity of other organizations are subcontracting and sharing capacity. An example of subcontracting is Air Canada's subcontracting its ticketing, check-in, and ground services in a foreign destination to that country's national carrier. Another example of sharing capacity is airlines sharing codes. For example, the same flight between Vancouver and Auckland, for instance, may have an Air New Zealand flight number and an Air Canada fight number and each airline will be assigned seats on the flight that they can sell. Another interesting example of sharing capacity (and flexible processes) is the "night market" in the Kowloon area of Hong Kong. After business hours every day, the roads that are used by vehicles during business hours become an outdoor shopping centre with shops that can be erected and dismantled quickly (using scaffolding). Naturally, only products that can be moved and stored easily, such as clothing and jewellery, are sold in these shops.

Capacity Balance

In a perfectly balanced plant, the output of Stage 1 provides the exact input requirement for Stage 2, the output of Stage 2 provides the exact input requirement for Stage 3, and so on. In practice, however, achieving such a perfect design is usually both impossible and undesirable. One reason is that the best operating levels for each stage generally differ. For instance, Department 1 may operate most efficiently over a range of 90 to 110 units per month while Department 2, the next stage in the process, is most efficient at 75 to 85 units per month, and Department 3, the third stage, works best over a range of 150 to 200 units per month. Another reason is that variability in product demand and the processes themselves generally leads to imbalance except in automated production lines, which, in essence, are just one big machine. There are various ways of dealing with imbalance. One is to add capacity to those stages that are bottlenecks. This can be done by temporary measures such as scheduling overtime, leasing equipment, or going outside the system and purchasing additional capacity through subcontracting. A second way is through the use of buffer inventories in front of the bottleneck stage to assure that it always has something to work on. A third approach involves duplicating the facilities of that department that is the cause of the bottleneck (which, in essence, eliminates the bottleneck).

Capacity Strategies

For organizations, there are two polar strategies for adding capacity: proactive and reactive. Each has its strengths and weaknesses. The company may also choose a strategy that

---

[5]See R. J. Schonberger, "The Rationalization of Production," *Proceedings of the 50th Anniversary of the Academy of Management* (Chicago: Academy of Management, 1986), pp. 64–70.

falls between these poles. Which strategy to adopt is dependent, to a large extent, on the operating characteristics of the facility, and the overall strategy of the firm.

Proactive

With a proactive strategy, management anticipates future growth and builds the facility so that it is up and running (with significant excess capacity) when the demand is there, as seen in Exhibit 7.7A. With this strategy, opportunity costs resulting from lost sales due to an inability to meet demand are minimized, although the firm does have to allocate fixed costs over a relatively small volume of units during the plant's initial period of operation. Retail chains and airlines that have aggressively expanded would be examples of this strategy. Naturally, if the expected future growth occurs, the company would be in an excellent position to capture market share. On the other hand, if the expected future growth does not occur, the company would be saddled with non-performing assets. Also, managing a large expansion can be a challenge in itself. A recent example is the Montreal-based airline, Jetsgo. Jetsgo stopped flying without prior notice on March 11, 2005, after having expanded too aggressively. This left many passengers and ticket holders (including children going to Disney World and honeymoon couples to Las Vegas) stranded, as well as employees who were informed only after midnight not to come to work in the morning.[6]

Reactive

When a reactive strategy is adopted, capacity lags behind demand. The plant may use overtime, temporary increased labour, and other measures to satisfy as much demand as possible, as shown in Exhibit 7.7B. Capacity is increased in small chunks, perhaps by expanding current facilities. Automaker Honda is an example. Honda's plants tend to start off on a small scale and grow as necessary.[7] This strategy avoids the disadvantages of the proactive strategy. However, one problem with this strategy is how best to meet the unfilled demand before the expansion is in operation. Another problem is that due to lack of capacity the firm may surrender market share to a firm following the proactive strategy if significant market growth occurs.

Combination

A firm can also follow a capacity strategy between the two extremes. As seen in Exhibit 7.7C, capacity is added when existing capacity is strained somewhat (but not as strained as in the reactive case). When the capacity expansion is complete, there is more than adequate capacity but not as much excess as in the proactive case. Some airports fall into this category. When the new airport is built, capacity of the airport is planned with future growth in mind. Thus, when the new airport opens, there may be existing unused capacity to cater to future growth or the ability to expand later if needed. The issue here, as with reactive strategy (though to a lesser extent), is how best to satisfy demand before the new or expanded facility is up and operating. But, like the proactive strategy, though to a smaller extent, the firm also has to be careful to avoid expanding too much.

Capacity Planning

capacity planning
Determination of which level of capacity to operate at to meet customer demand in a cost-efficient manner.

The objective of **capacity planning** is to specify which level of capacity will meet market demands in a cost-efficient way. Capacity planning can be viewed in three time durations: long range (greater than one year), intermediate range (the next 6 to 12 months), and short range (less than six months).

---

[6]CBC Radio, Calgary Eye-Opener, March 11, 2005.
[7]L. J. Krajewski and L. P. Ritzman, *Operations Management* (Upper Saddle River, NJ: Prentice Hall, 2002), p. 336.

Exhibit 7.7

**Strategies for
Adding Capacity**

A. Proactive

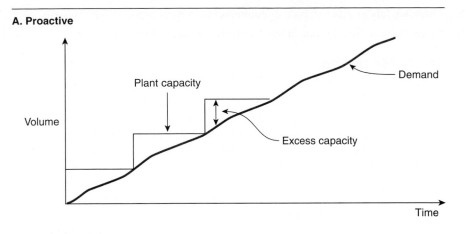

B. Reactive

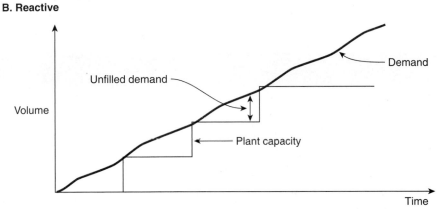

C. Combination

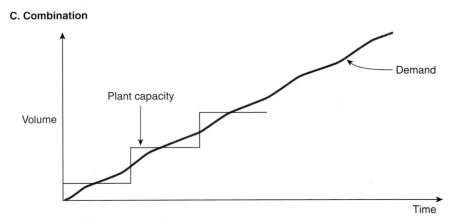

As mentioned earlier, our focus in this chapter is on long-range capacity planning, in which the firm makes its major investment decisions. In addition to planning large chunks of capacity (such as a new factory), typical long-range capacity planning efforts also must address the demands for individual product lines, individual plant capabilities, and allocation of production throughout the plant network. Typically, these are carried out according to the following steps:

1. Forecast sales for each product line.
2. Forecast sales for individual products within each product line.

3. Calculate labour and equipment requirements to meet product line forecasts.

4. Project labour and equipment availabilities over the planning horizon.

Capacity Measures

As described in detail in Chapter 5, capacity is the output of a process or facility over a given time period. For a manufacturing plant, examples of capacity include: televisions per week, barrels of oil per year, and gallons of laundry detergent per month. For a service operation, capacity is usually measured over shorter time periods, because time is more critical due to the customer's interaction with the process. Examples here include customers per hour in a restaurant, calls per hour in a call centre, and guests per hour at the front desk of a hotel.

Capacity utilization, also described in Chapter 5, defines what percentage of the available capacity is actually being used. For example, a call centre might have 1200 workstations, but, on a given day, only have 600 of them staffed with operators. In this case, the call centre would be working at 600/1200 or 50 percent capacity utilization that day.

Conclusion

The decisions regarding where and when to locate a facility and how big to make it are critical to the success of every business, be it a manufacturing or service operation. As a result, significant analysis and planning are required to ensure that a potential location will properly support the long-term strategy and objectives of the firm. In addition, deciding where to locate a new facility is complex, involving both qualitative and quantitative factors.

Like so many topics in operations management today, location decisions and capacity planning are being significantly influenced, not only by advances in information technology, but also by the trend toward globalization. As more firms continue to focus on their core competencies, management has changed its perspective on available capacity, while at the same time becoming more dependent on its suppliers. The growth in international markets, as well as cheaper labour and other incentives offered by foreign countries, also has significantly affected decisions about where to locate new operations.

Key Terms

agile manufacturing p. 278

back-of-the-house p. 270

bricks-and-mortar operation p. 269

capacity flexibility p. 278

capacity planning p. 280

centre-of-gravity method p. 273

content requirements p. 263

factor-rating systems p. 271

front-of-the-house p. 271

geographic information systems (GIS) p. 266

quasi-manufacturing operation p. 271

special economic zones (SEZ) p. 265

Key Formulas

Centre of gravity

$$C_x = \frac{\sum x_i V_i}{\sum V_i} \qquad (7.1)$$

$$C_y = \frac{\sum y_i V_i}{\sum V_i} \qquad (7.2)$$

1. List some practical limits to economies of scale; that is, when should a plant stop growing in size?

2. What are some capacity balance problems faced by the following organizations or facilities?
   a. An airline terminal
   b. A university computing centre
   c. A clothing manufacturer

3. What are the primary capacity planning considerations for foreign companies locating their facilities in Canada?

4. What are some major capacity considerations of a hospital? How do they differ from those of a factory?

5. What are some of the location factors that a manufacturer needs to take into consideration in locating a factory in a foreign country?

6. In what respects is facility layout a marketing problem in services? Give an example of a service system layout designed to maximize the amount of time the customer is in the system.

7. Identify some of the site selection criteria that should be considered by a high-end, full-service hotel chain such as the Delta, Fairmont, or Four Seasons. (By full-service we mean that the hotel has a restaurant, cocktail lounge, meeting rooms, and catering facilities to accommodate large functions such as conferences and weddings.)

8. Identify some of the site selection factors that should be considered for a budget motel that primarily provides only rooms, such as Motel 6, Days Inn, and EconoLodge.

9. What are some of the factors that should be taken into consideration when evaluating potential sites for a distribution centre of quasi-manufacturing operation that directly supports retail operations?

Internet Exercise

Visit the Web site of an ASP (application service provider) that will give you detailed maps that include the distance and time between any two locations. What is the estimated time it takes to go from your home to your school and how many miles is it? Use the same ASP to determine how far it is from your school to the nearest McDonald's.

Solved Problems

Problem 1

Maple Leaf Hotels, Inc., is looking to relocate its reservations call centre and has identified the following factors and respective weights for evaluating each potential site:

Factor	Weight
Available workforce	30
Level of skills	15
Telecommunications infrastructure	45
Cost of labour	50
Access to major highways	25
Total	165

A consultant has identified the following three sites and has rated each of these locations on the above factors as follows:

Factor	Ratings Site A	Ratings Site B	Ratings Site C
Available workforce	65	80	90
Level of skills	50	45	75
Telecommunication infrastructure	90	70	40
Cost of labour	75	90	85
Access to major highways	80	85	55

a. Which site would you recommend for locating the call centre?
b. How much does the rating for the labour cost factor have to increase for site A so that the scores for sites A and B are the same?
c. How much does the weight for the infrastructure factor have to increase before site A becomes the preferred location for the call centre?

Solution

a. We set up the following spreadsheet to calculate the scores for each location:

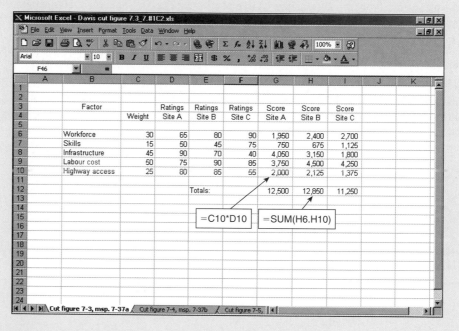

Based upon this analysis, we recommend that the new call centre be located at site B, which has the highest score of 12 850.

b. To determine the rating for the labour cost factor at site A that makes the scores for sites A and B identical, we again use a spreadsheet and increase the labour cost rating for site A until the scores for the two sites are the same. The desired labour cost rating for site A is 82, as illustrated in the following spreadsheet:

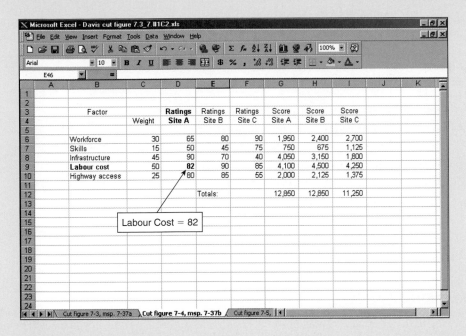

c. As shown in the spreadsheet below, the weight for the infrastructure has to be increased to 63 before site A becomes the preferred location.

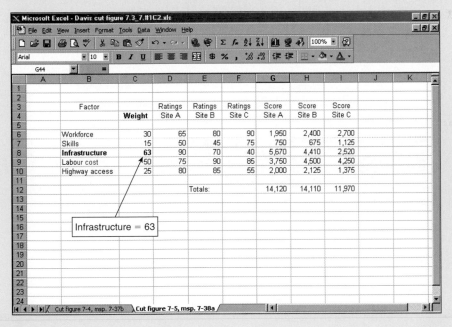

Problem 2

Personal Nursing Services (PNS) provides individualized nursing care to patients in three hospitals in the metropolitan area of a major city. For a variety of reasons, assignments often change at the last minute in terms of the number of patients to be cared for at each hospital.

As a result, the nurses working for PNS report each morning to PNS's headquarters for their daily assignments. PNS then provides vans to take the nurses to their respective hospitals. The vans also pick them up at the end of the day and return the nurses to the headquarters so that they can file their reports before going home. Consequently, the vans make two round trips a day to each hospital. The location of each hospital is indicated on the grid map at right.

PNS has experienced rapid growth in the demand for its services and is therefore looking to move into larger facilities.

a. Using the centre-of-gravity method, determine the ideal location for its new headquarters.

b. PNS has submitted a proposal to a fourth hospital that is located at coordinates $X = 20$, $Y = 5$. If it is awarded the contract for this hospital, where should its headquarters building now be located?

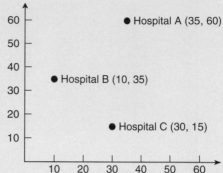

Solution

Looking at the grid map, we calculate the coordinates of each of three hospitals now being served as follows:

Hospital	X Coordinate	Y Coordinate
A	35	60
B	10	35
C	30	15

a. Using a spreadsheet and based upon the three hospitals that are currently under contract, we calculate the coordinates for the new headquarters as follows:

Hospital	x_i	y_i	V_i	$x_i * V_i$	$y_i * V_i$	
A	35	60	2	70	120	=E8*F8
B	10	35	2	20	70	
C	30	15	2	60	30	
		Totals:	6	150	220	
		C(x) =	25.00			=SUM(G6.G8)
		C(y) =	36.67			=H10/F10

Thus, the new headquarters' location should be at coordinates $X = 25.0$, $Y = 36.7$.

b. To add the fourth hospital, we simply update the spreadsheet with the fourth hospital's coordinates and recalculate the X and Y coordinates for the new headquarters' location.

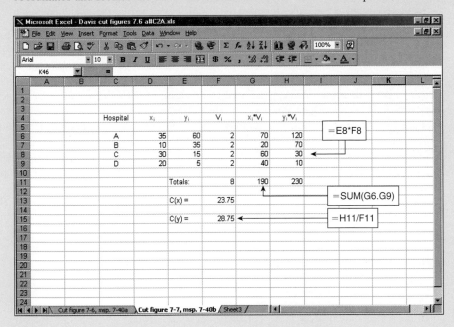

Thus, if PNS is awarded the contract for the fourth hospital, then the ideal location for its new headquarters would be at coordinates $X = 23.8$ and $Y = 28.8$.

1. The Speedy Ambulance Service is searching for a location that will serve both as its headquarters and as a garage for its ambulances. You have been asked to chair the site selection search team. The team has identified the following factors that need to be considered in choosing a location, and also has assigned the following weights to these factors:

Factor	Weight
Proximity to hospitals	25
Population over age 65	30
Access to major highways	15
Number of nursing homes	20
Local tax incentives	10
Total	100

The search team has found three sites and has assigned the following factor ratings to each:

Factor	Ratings Site A	Ratings Site B	Ratings Site C
Proximity to hospitals	30	45	75
Population over age 65	60	55	35
Access to major highways	80	90	65
Number of nursing homes	45	60	55
Local tax incentives	85	70	80

Problems

a. Which site would you recommend to the search committee?

b. What is the impact on the site selection if the weight of the "access to major highways" factor is reduced to 5 and the weight of the "local tax incentives" factor is increased to 20?

2. Edtoys.com is a virtual company that offers a wide variety of educational children's toys through its Web site. When an order is received, it is immediately sent electronically to the manufacturer for direct shipment to the customer. With this type of structure, Edtoys.com does not have to maintain inventories of toys or become involved in their delivery. Management is therefore focusing primarily on making its Web site as customer friendly as possible and expanding its number of product offerings.

Edtoys.com has seen tremendous growth in the past several years and needs to find a new and larger location for its offices. Based on conversations with several members of Edtoys.com's top management team, a consulting firm has identified the following factors that should be taken into consideration in choosing a new site for its offices, and also has assigned the following weights to each of these factors:

Factor	Weight
Proximity to business schools	20
Access to highways	20
Telecommunications infrastructure	40
Quality of Life	30
Proximity to major airport	25
Total	135

The consulting firm has identified two possible locations and has assigned each the following factor ratings:

Factor	Rating Site A	Rating Site B
Proximity to business schools	70	55
Access to highways	40	75
Telecommunications infrastructure	75	90
Quality of life	60	85
Proximity to major airport	80	50

Which site should the consulting firm recommend to Edtoys.com?

3. Patorano's Pizza, a chain of Italian pizza restaurants, wants to expand its operations into Asia, specifically in the Peoples' Republic of China (PRC). Unfortunately, due to a lack of food purveyors and suppliers, management must build its own distribution centre and commissary, where many of the foods used in the restaurant will be either partially or fully prepared. (For example, the dough for the pizza will be mixed and portioned at the commissary.) The first stage of its business plan has identified specific locations for the first three restaurants to be opened. The X and Y coordinates and estimated annual sales for each of these three locations are presented below:

Location	X Coordinate	Y Coordinate	Forecasted Sales (in yuan)
A	20	45	2 500 000
B	35	15	4 000 000
C	5	50	1 800 000

a. Draw a grid map and locate each of the planned restaurants on it.

b. Assuming that the volume of products to be shipped is directly proportional to sales, calculate the coordinates for the central commissary that will minimize distribution costs. Plot these coordinates on the grid map.

c. The second phase of the business plan calls for two more locations at the following grid locations and with estimated sales shown below:

Location	X Coordinate	Y Coordinate	Forecasted Sales (in yuan)
D	45	10	3 200 000
E	30	30	1 400 000

What is the impact of these additional restaurants on the location of the central commissary?

4. Sharif's Office Supplies is a small retail chain that sells high-priced designer office supplies to senior executives. It has recently opened three locations in the metropolitan Edmonton area that are currently being supplied from the corporate warehouse in Vancouver. The *X* and *Y* coordinates for these locations are provided in the table below along with the annual sales that each location generates. To reduce shipping costs, management has decided to open a distribution centre in the Edmonton area.

Store Location	X Coordinate	Y Coordinate	Annual Sales
Downtown Edmonton	60	53	$745 000
St. Albert	13	78	$483 000
Millwood	21	42	$612 000

a. Draw a grid map and locate each of the three stores on it.

b. Assuming that the volume of products to be shipped is directly proportional to sales in each store, calculate the coordinates for the distribution centre that will minimize distribution costs. Plot these coordinates on the grid map.

5. Having determined the optimal location for its distribution facility, Zahira Sharif, the president of Sharif's Office Supplies, found two sites that were available. The distance each site is from each of the three retail locations is as follows:

Retail Location	Distance from Site A (km)	Distance from Site B (km)
Downtown Edmonton	17	14
St. Albert	10	12
Millwood	25	18

Which location should Zahira choose to minimize her distribution costs?

6. Gourmet Specialty Foods, an upscale grocery chain that caters to high-income families, wants to build a new supermarket that will service three affluent communities. A market research study revealed that the average weekly food purchases per family are the same for each of these three communities.

Community	Number of Families	X Coordinate	Y Coordinate
Smithtown	12 800	93	81
Jonesville	17 300	27	116
Moore City	9 500	75	34

Determine the optimal grid location for the supermarket.

7. A real estate consulting firm has found two locations that will meet Gourmet Specialties's requirements. The distance each of the locations is from the three communities is as follows:

Community	Site A (km)	Site B (km)
Smithtown	7.5	9.7
Jonesville	4.6	3.1
Moore City	8.0	6.2

On which site should Gourmet Specialties build its new supermarket?

8. Cool Air, a manufacturer of automotive air conditioners, currently produces its XB-300 line at three different locations, Plant A, Plant B, and Plant C. Recently, management decided to build all compressors, a major product component, in a separate dedicated facility, Plant D.
    a. Using the centre-of-gravity method and the information displayed in Exhibits 7.8 and 7.9, determine the best location for Plant D. Assume a linear relationship between volumes shipped and shipping costs (no premium charges).
    b. Refer to the information given in Part (a). Suppose management decides to shift 2000 units of production from Plant B to Plant A. Does this change the proposed location of Plant D, the compressor production facility? If so, where should Plant D be located?

Exhibit 7.8

Plant Location Matrix

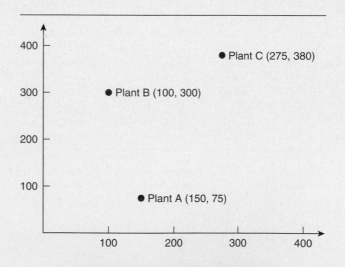

Exhibit 7.9

Quantity of Compressors Required by Each Plant

Plant	Compressors Required per Year
A	6000
B	8200
C	7000

Case 1   Oh's Bagel Bakeries

Founded in 1983 in Windsor, Ontario, Oh's Bagel Bakeries is a retail bagel concept that has grown to more than 100 neighbourhood bagel bakeries in southwestern Ontario. These stores are located in major downtown areas, suburban strip shopping centres, and easy-to-drive-to, quick-service locations. In addition to bagels, the bakeries also offer a wide variety of cream cheeses, soups, coffees, and deli-style sandwiches that customers either can enjoy on the premises or take out.

Every Oh's bakery bakes its own bagels throughout the day, providing customers with fresh hot bagels. However, to ensure that only the highest quality bagels are served and that there is consistency in both the quality and size of the bagels among its many retail locations, Oh's initially prepares the raw bagels at central commissaries. These commissaries are responsible for mixing the dough, forming the bagels and proofing them (that is, allowing them to rise properly under a controlled temperature and humidity environment). The raw bagels are then distributed to individual locations where they are first boiled in water and then baked.

Currently, Oh's has more than 20 retail locations in the greater Windsor area, most of them located in downtown Windsor and in the suburbs south and east of Windsor. There are also four stores that are located in west Windsor. The addresses for each of these bakeries and the average number of dozens of bagels that each receives daily are shown below:

Address	Average Number of Dozens of Bagels Delivered per Day
45 Kenora Boulevard	180
356 Sudbury Avenue	135
2100 Thunder Bay St.	165
211 North Bay St.	120

Currently these four locations are provided with bagels from a central commissary that is located in east Windsor. Because this commissary is reaching its maximum capacity, management has decided to locate a new commissary in south Windsor to provide bagels for these four locations. (It also is expected that there will be additional future locations in south Windsor that also will be served by this commissary.)

Sheri Oh, founder and current CEO at Oh's, working with a real estate consultant, has identified two potential locations for this commissary:

The distances and times from these locations to the four stores are shown below.

Commissary Location—67 Timmins St.

Location of Bakery	Distance (km)	Time (min)
Kenora Blvd.	14.95	19
Sudbury Ave.	9.9	14
Thunder Bay St.	5.66	11
North Bay St.	6.26	25

Commissary Location—9156 Nipigon Ave.

Location of Bakery	Distance (km)	Time (min)
Kenora Blvd.	8.99	16
Sudbury Ave.	3.95	11
Thunder Bay St.	12.73	20
North Bay St.	5.79	21

Questions

1. One alternative is for Sheri to subcontract out the delivery of the bagels to a local food delivery service that has quoted a delivery charge of five cents per dozen bagels per kilometer. Using this cost as a criterion, which site should Sheri select for the commissary?

2. Another option is to use a company truck, which is available, for the deliveries. With this alternative, Sheri estimates that the driver will have to make one delivery per day to each of the four locations, and that the driver and truck will cost $30.00 per hour, including the driver's benefits. Under this scenario, which commissary site should Sheri select?

3. Which of these two alternative methods of delivery (that is, outsourcing or keeping it in-house) do you recommend and why?

4. What additional factors should Sheri take into consideration in selecting a new commissary site in south Windsor?

Source:
© 2001 James Salsbury and Mark M. Davis. This case describes an actual company and its business environment, although some of the data presented here may be disguised and/or modified for proprietary reasons or to emphasize a specific teaching objective.

Case 2 | Shouldice Hospital—A Cut Above

"Shouldice Hospital, the house that hernias built, is a converted country estate which gives the hospital 'a country club' appeal."

A quote from *American Medical News*

Shouldice Hospital in Canada is widely known for one thing—hernia repair! In fact, that is the only operation it performs, and it performs a great many of them. Over the past two decades this small 90-bed hospital has averaged 7000 operations annually. Last year, they had a record year and performed nearly 7500 operations. Patients' ties to Shouldice do not end when they leave the hospital. Every year the gala Hernia Reunion dinner (with complimentary hernia inspection) draws in excess of 1000 former patients, some of whom have been attending the event for over 30 years.

A number of notable features in Shouldice's service delivery system contribute to its success. (1) Shouldice only accepts patients with the uncomplicated external hernias, and it uses a superior technique developed for this type of hernia by Dr. Shouldice during World War II. (2) Patients are subject to early ambulation, which promotes healing. (Patients literally walk off the operating table and engage in light exercise throughout their stay, which lasts only three days.) (3) Its country club atmosphere, gregarious nursing staff, and built-in socializing make a surprisingly pleasant experience out of an inherently unpleasant medical problem. Regular times are set aside for tea, cookies, and socializing. All patients are paired up with a roommate with similar background and interests.

The Production System

The medical facilities at Shouldice consist of five operating rooms, a patient recovery room, a laboratory, and six examination rooms. Shouldice performs, on average, 150 operations per week, with patients generally staying at the hospital for three days. Although operations are performed only five days a week, the remainder of the hospital is in operation continuously to attend to recovering patients.

An operation at Shouldice Hospital is performed by one of the 12 full-time surgeons assisted by one of 7 part-time assistant surgeons. Surgeons generally take about one hour to prepare for and perform each hernia operation, and they operate on four patients per day. The surgeons' day ends at 4 p.m., although they can expect to be on call every fourteenth night and every tenth weekend.

The Shouldice Experience

All patients undergo a screening exam prior to setting a date for their operation. Patients in the Toronto area are encouraged to walk in to have the diagnosis done. Examinations are done between 9 a.m. and 3:30 p.m. Monday through Friday, and between 10 a.m. and 2 p.m. on Saturday. Out-of-town patients are mailed a medical information questionnaire (also available over the Internet), which is used for the diagnosis. A small percentage of the patients who are overweight or otherwise represent an undue medical risk are refused treatment. The remaining patients receive a confirmation card with the scheduled date for their operation. A patient's folder is transferred to the reception desk once an arrival date is confirmed.

Patients arrive at the clinic between 1 p.m. and 3 p.m. the day before their surgery. After a short wait, they receive a brief preoperative examination. They are then sent to see an admissions clerk to complete any necessary paperwork. Patients are next directed to one of the two nurses' stations for blood and urine tests and then are shown to their rooms. They spend the remaining time before orientation getting settled and acquainting themselves with their roommate.

Orientation begins at 5 p.m., followed by dinner in the common dining room. Later in the evening, at 9 p.m., patients gather in the lounge area for tea and cookies. Here, new patients can talk with patients who have already had their surgery. Bedtime is between 9:30 and 10 p.m.

On the day of the operation, patients with early operations are awakened at 5:30 a.m. for preoperative sedation. The first operations begin at 7:30 a.m. Shortly before an operation starts, the patient is administered a local anesthetic, leaving him alert and fully aware of the proceedings. At the conclusion of the operation, the patient is invited to walk from the operating table to a nearby wheelchair, which is waiting to return him to his room. After a brief period of rest, he is encouraged to get up and start exercising. By 9 p.m. that day, he is in the lounge having cookies and tea, and talking with new, incoming patients.

The skin clips holding the incision together are loosened, and some are removed the next day. The remainder are removed the following morning just before the patient is discharged.

When Shouldice Hospital started, the average hospital stay for hernia surgery was three weeks. Today, many institutions push "same day surgery" for a variety of reasons. Shouldice Hospital firmly believes that this is not in the best interests of patients, and is committed to their three-day process. Shouldice's post-op rehabilitation program is designed to enable the patient to resume normal activities with minimal interruption

and discomfort. Shouldice patients frequently return to work in a few days. The average total time off is eight days.

"It is interesting to note that approximately 1 out of every 100 Shouldice patients is a medical doctor."

Future Plans

The management of Shouldice is thinking of expanding the hospital's capacity to serve considerable unsatisfied demand. To this effect, the vice president is seriously considering two options. The first involves adding one more day of operations (Saturday) to the existing five-day schedule, which would increase capacity by 20 percent. The second option is to add another floor of rooms to the hospital, increasing the number of beds by 50 percent. This would require more aggressive scheduling of the operating rooms.

The administrator of the hospital, however, is concerned about maintaining control over the quality of the service delivered. He thinks the facility is already getting very good utilization. The doctors and the staff are happy with their jobs and the patients are satisfied with the service. According to him, further expansion of capacity might make it hard to maintain the same kind of working relationships and attitudes.

Questions

Exhibit C7.1 is a room-occupancy table for the existing system. Each row in the table follows the patients that checked in on a given day. The columns indicate the number of patients in the hospital on a given day. For example, the first two of the table shows that 30 people checked in on Monday and were in the hospital for Monday, Tuesday, and Wednesday. By summing the columns of the table for Wednesday, we see that there are 90 patients staying in the hospital that day.

1. How well is the hospital currently utilizing its beds?

2. Develop a similar table to show the effects of adding operations on Saturday. (Assume that 30 operations would still

Exhibit C7.1

Operations
with 90 Beds
(30 patients
per day)

Check-in day	Beds Required						
	Monday	Tuesday	Wednesday	Thursday	Friday	Saturday	Sunday
Monday	30	30	30				
Tuesday		30	30	30			
Wednesday			30	30	30		
Thursday				30	30	30	
Friday							
Saturday							
Sunday	30	30					30
Total	60	90	90	90	60	30	30

be performed each day.) How would this affect the utilization of the bed capacity? Is this capacity sufficient for the additional patients?

3. Now look at the effect of increasing the number of beds by 50 percent. How many operations could the hospital perform per day before running out of bed capacity? (Assume operations are performed five days per week, with the same number performed on each day.) How well would the new resources be utilized relative to the current operation? Could the hospital really perform this many operations? Why? (Hint: Look at the capacity of the 12 surgeons and the 5 operating rooms.)

4. Although financial data are sketchy, an estimate from a construction company indicates that adding bed capacity would cost about $100 000 per bed. In addition, the rate charged for the hernia surgery varies between $900 to $2000 (U.S. dollars), with an average rate of $1300 per operation. The surgeons are paid a flat $600 per operation. Due to all the uncertainties in government health care legislation, Shouldice would like to justify any expansion within a five-year time period.

Source:
Adapted from R. Chase et al, Operations Management for Competitive Advantage (New York: McGraw-Hill/Irwin, 2005) pp. 446–448.

8

Facility Decisions: Layouts

Chapter Objectives

- Introduce the different types of facility layouts that can be used in designing manufacturing and service operations.

- Present a methodology for designing a process-oriented layout.

- Introduce the concept of take time and its relationship to the output capacity of a product-oriented layout.

- Identify the various steps and elements that are involved in balancing an assembly line.

- Discuss the current trends in facility layouts given today's shorter product life cycles and customers' increasing desire for customized products.

Layout Redesign is Key to Improved Customer Service at Standard Aero

Winnipeg's Standard Aero is one of the world's largest independent small gas turbine engine and accessory repair and overhaul facilities. With operations around the globe, the company provides a unique mix of management and MRO (maintenance, repair, and overhaul) services to regional airline, business aviation, helicopter, government/military, marine, and industrial customers. Customers include Rolls Royce, United Express, Bombardier, and the U.S. Air Force.

In their quest for excellence, Standard Aero worked to reduce turnaround times to customers. When they first broke down this time into its components such as workmanship, inspection, and so on, what they least expected to find was that a majority of the time was spent in queues in front of machines! This clearly showed the amount of non-value-added time in the process.

To provide faster customer service, they implemented a continuous improvement program. This included changing the factory layout. Traditionally in Standard Aero (as in many other companies), the different machines were grouped by type into departments. Since each order tends to be different, and thus each customer order had different

processing requirements, the flow of any particular order was unpredictable, and orders were often assigned to machines in each department arbitrarily. This is shown in the figure on the top, and resulted in workplace disorganization leading to queues and long turnaround times. Standard Aero reorganized the machines into cells that process similar groups of customer orders. This led to more organized flow, fewer queues, and ultimately faster turnaround. This is shown in the figure on the bottom and in the accompanying photo, where the flow is much more organized.

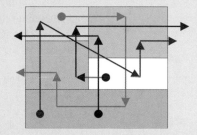

The cells were designed by teams of employees from the shop floor. Tabletop simulations were done to assess the performance of the proposed cells, and computer simulations were done to test variations. Cell leaders and members were given substantial training for their new roles as co-managers of an entire cell instead of just being in charge of their own machines. When the cells were implemented, each station was labelled, and cleanliness and openness were given priority (as seen in the accompanying picture). Each cell also had a board set up for productivity measures to be posted regularly (as can be seen in the photo). As a result of layout and other continuous improvement measures, the turnaround time for engines decreased considerably. (Manufacturing cells are discussed in more detail under Group Technology Layout in this chapter as well as in Chapter 13.)

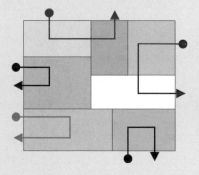

Sources:
Leon Dodd, Jr., "The Team Approach to ISO 9000:2000 at Standard Aero Alliance," *The Journal for Quality and Participation* (Spring 2002), pp. 41–44.

Paul Soubry, Presentation by the President of Standard Aero to the APICS Winnipeg Chapter, April 18, 2002.

Standard Aero Limited, www.standardaero.com.

Managerial Issues

Managers need to take many factors into consideration when determining which type of facility layout is most appropriate for their operations. This applies to manufacturing and service operations alike. Product-oriented layouts such as assembly lines, as we shall see, are highly efficient but tend to be very inflexible. Process-oriented layouts, on the other hand, are very flexible in terms of the wide variety of products that can be made but, as we saw at Standard Aero in the opening vignette, they typically have significant work-in-process inventories and are relatively inefficient and slow.

The choice of which type of layout to adopt cannot be made lightly because it can significantly impact a company's long-term success, both in terms of product costs and its ability to compete successfully in the marketplace. In addition, the investment costs associated with installing a particular layout, in terms of time and money, are substantial.

The manager's goal in selecting a layout is to provide a smooth flow of material through the factory, or an uncomplicated traffic pattern for both customers and workers in a service operation. Today, there are many software packages available to assist managers in designing a layout that is both efficient and effective, as illustrated in the next OM in Practice box.

Types of Manufacturing Layouts

It is estimated that over $250 billion is spent annually in the United States alone on facilities planning and replanning.[1] Furthermore, between 20 and 50 percent of the total costs in manufacturing are related to material handling. Effective planning can reduce these costs by 10 to 30 percent.[2] Thus, effective layouts can generate significant bottom line savings.

There are three basic types of layouts that have been identified in manufacturing plants: (1) process layout, (2) product layout, and (3) fixed-position layout. In addition, there is one hybrid, referred to as a group technology or cellular layout, which is a combination of process and product layouts. We discuss these in detail except for the fixed-position layout. As a starting point for this discussion, Exhibit 8.1 presents the general characteristics of a good layout for both manufacturing and service operations.

Exhibit 8.1

Characteristics of a Good Layout

Manufacturing and Back-Office Service Operations	Face-to-Face Services
1. Straight-line flow pattern (or adaptation).	1. Easily understood service-flow pattern.
2. Backtracking kept to a minimum.	2. Proper waiting facilities.
3. Production time predictable.	3. Easy communication with customers.
4. Little interstage storage of materials.	4. Customer surveillance easily maintained.
5. Open plant floors so everyone can see what's going on.	5. Clear exit and entry points with sufficient checkout capabilities.
6. Bottleneck operations under control.	6. Departments and processes arranged so that customers see only what you want them to see.
7. Workstations close together.	7. Balance between waiting areas and service areas.
8. Minimum material movement.	8. Minimum walking.
9. No unnecessary rehandling of materials.	9. Lack of clutter.
10. Easily adjustable to changing conditions.	10. High sales volume per square foot of facility.

[1]J. A. Tompkins, J. A. White, Y. A. Bozer, and J. M. A. Tanchoco, *Facilities Planning* (New York: Wiley, 2003), p. 10.
[2]Ibid.

298

SOFTWARE HELPS FIRMS DESIGN FACTORY LAYOUTS AND MANAGE MATERIALS FLOWS

Factory CAD is a new technology developed by UGS PLM Solutions for factory layout and design. Factory CAD allows designers to drag-and-drop common factory elements to create virtual 3D layouts—much like working with 3D plastic models that represent the actual facility. Only Factory CAD ensures that the pieces don't just physically fit together, but also function appropriately together. Its technique enables engineers and managers to bring product, tooling, and plant geometry all into a single 3D visual depiction that is much easier to understand than the usual 2D drawing.

Factory CAD allows engineers to spend more of their time designing instead of drawing. Because Factory CAD makes layout creation, modification, and visualization easy, potential problem areas with process and material flows can be eliminated earlier—prior to building the physical factory. The layout models can also be used for simulating production events and material flows, saving time and eliminating redundant work. With this approach to designing layouts, firms can save millions of dollars because they make fewer design changes after the facility has been constructed and are able to begin production sooner.

After designing the factory layout, manufacturing firms need to plan the flow of materials. This includes: (*a*) how many loading docks to have, (*b*) where to locate them, (*c*) where within the plant inventories should be held, and (*d*) how materials will be moved. In addition, managers need to track the costs associated with inventory, including: (*a*) purchasing, (*b*) receiving, (*c*) storage, and (*d*) movement within the plant.

Factory Flow, another UGS PLM Solutions product, is an integrated material handling software product that permits engineers to visualize material flows and to optimize layouts based on material flow distances, frequency, and costs. Engineers input information about material flows for different layout alternatives and Factory Flow compares them and identifies the best configuration.

Material flow information is stored in the Factory Flow database, allowing the program to generate diagrams that show material movement, both in straight lines and according to the actual paths that exist in the plant. The information can be used to identify where to best store materials and how workers should move through the layout to access them.

Factory Flow customers can often recover their investment in software and training in just a few months. By using it, they usually also achieve significant reductions in factory floor space requirements, manufacturing cycle time, and work-in-process inventories.

Source:

Adapted from two papers provided by Shreekanth Moorthy, Product Manager, UGS PLM. "Material Handling & Optimization Using Factory Flow," and "3-D Plant Modeling Using Factory CAD."

Three Dimensional Factory Layout Generated by Factory CAD.

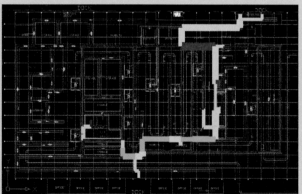

Material Flows through a Factory Generated by Factory Flow.

In a **process layout** (also called a *job-shop layout* or *layout by function*), shown in Exhibit 8.2A by a path followed by a particular job, similar equipment or functions are grouped together, such as in a machine shop where all the saws are in one area and all the grinding machines are in another. A part being worked on travels from one area to the next, according to the specific sequence of operations required. This type of layout is often

process layout
Similar operations are performed in a common or functional area, regardless of the product in which the parts are used.

Exhibit 8.2

Group Technology versus Departmental Specialty

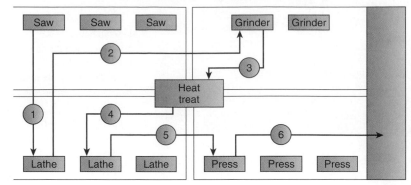

A. Process-oriented layout by department speciality

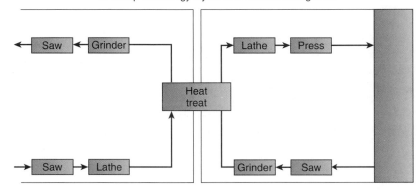

B. Group technology layout with manufacturing cells

product layout

Equipment/operations are located according to the progressive steps required to make the product.

group technology (G/T) or cellular layout

Groups of dissimilar machines brought together in a work cell to perform tasks on a family of products that share common attributes.

found in high-mix, low-volume manufacturing plants that have an intermittent process (see the opening vignette in this chapter). Thus it has the advantages and disadvantages of an intermittent process, as discussed in Chapter 3 (see Exhibits 3.5 and 3.6).

A **product layout** (also called a *flow-shop layout*), shown in the accompanying picture and in Exhibit 8.10, is one in which equipment or work processes are arranged according to the progressive steps by which the product is made. If equipment is dedicated to the continual production of a narrow product line, this is usually called a *production line* or *assembly line*. Examples are the manufacture of small appliances (toasters, irons, beaters), large appliances (dishwashers, refrigerators, washing machines), electronics (computers, CD players), and automobiles. Thus it has the advantages and disadvantages of a line flow process as discussed in Chapter 3 (see Exhibits 3.5 and 3.6).

A **group technology (GT) or cellular layout**, shown in Exhibit 8.2B, brings together dissimilar machines into work centres (or cells) to work on products that have similar shapes and processing requirements. A GT layout is similar to process layout, in that the cells together can handle a variety of products, and it is similar to product layout in that each cell is dedicated to a limited range of products. Thus it combines some of the advantages of both product and process layouts. Often the cell is arranged in a U-shape, as shown in the exhibit and opening vignette, to allow workers to move more easily from one station to another. Cells can also share equipment that is expensive to duplicate such as heat treatment equipment.

In a **fixed-position layout**, by virtue of its bulk or weight, the product remains stationary at one location. The manufacturing equipment is moved to the product rather than vice versa. Shipyards and construction sites are good examples of this format.

Manufacturing facilities often may have a combination of layout types. For example, a given floor may be laid out by process, another floor by product. It is also common to find an entire plant arranged according to general product flow (fabrication, subassembly, and final assembly), coupled with process layout within fabrication and product layout within the assembly department. Likewise, group technology frequently is found within a department that itself is located according to a plantwide process-oriented layout.

An operation's layout continually changes over time because the internal and external environments are dynamic. As demands change, so can layout. As technology changes, so can layout. In Chapter 3, we discussed a product/process matrix indicating that as products and volumes change, the most efficient layout is also likely to change. Therefore, the decision on a specific layout type may be a temporary one.

fixed-position layout
The product, because of its size and/or weight, remains in one location and processes are brought to it.

Process Layout

The most common approach for developing a process layout is to arrange departments consisting of similar or identical processes in a way that optimizes their relative placement. In many installations, optimal placement often translates into placing departments with large amounts of interdepartmental traffic adjacent to one another. The primary goal in designing a layout for a manufacturing or distribution facility is to minimize material handling costs. In a service organization, the main objective is to minimize customer and worker travel time through the process.

Minimizing Interdepartmental Movement Costs

Consider the following simple example:

> Suppose that we want to arrange the six departments of a toy factory to minimize the interdepartmental material handling cost. [We use a method similar to one called Computerized Relative Allocation of Facilities Technique (**CRAFT**),[3] which performs intelligent pairwise exchanges of departments and locations. Many other types of algorithms are also available to solve the process layout problem.] Initially, let us make the assumption that all departments have the same amount of space, say 40 m by 40 m, and that the building is 80 m wide and 120 m long (and thus compatible with the department dimensions). The first thing we would want to know is the nature of the flow between departments and the way the material is transported. If the company has another factory that makes similar products, information about flow patterns might be obtained from these records. On the other hand, if this is a new product, such information would have to come from routing sheets or from estimates by knowledgeable personnel such as process or industrial engineers. Of course these data, regardless of their source, have to be adjusted to reflect the nature of future orders over the projected life of the proposed layout.
>
> Let's assume that this information is available. We find that all available material is transported in a standard-size crate by forklift truck, one crate to a truck (which constitutes one "load"). Now suppose that the transportation cost to move one load one

Example

CRAFT
Computerized relative allocation of facilities technique (CRAFT) performs intelligent pairwise exchanges of departments and locations.

[3]E. S. Buffa, G. C. Armour, and T. E. Vollmann, "Allocating Facilities with CRAFT," *Harvard Business Review*, 42, no. 2 (1964), pp. 136–158.

Exhibit 8.3

Interdepartmental Flow

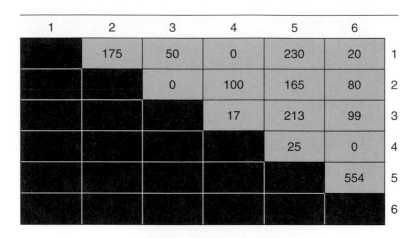

Exhibit 8.4

Building Dimensions and Departments

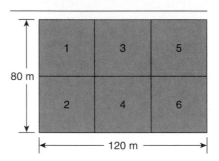

metre is $0.10. This is also called the cost to move a unit load a unit distance. The expected loads between departments for the first year of operation are tabulated in Exhibit 8.3; the available factory space is depicted in Exhibit 8.4. The bidirectional arrows in Exhibit 8.4 represent aisles in the middle of the departments, indicating that the movement between departments is along the aisles only in either direction. Thus, to move from department 2 to department 5, the forklift has to go along the aisle in one direction. This is called rectilinear movement. Another method of movement (not used in this example) is diagonal, in which the shortest distance between the centres of departments is used. We also assume that there is two-way traffic between departments. For example, the 554 loads shown between departments 5 and 6 in Exhibit 8.3 reflect flow from department 5 to department 6 as well as in the reverse direction.

Solution

Steps in Improving a Process Layout

The information in Exhibits 8.3 and 8.4 is always required in order to improve a process layout. Once we have this information, the following steps are needed to design a better layout:

Step 1   Illustrate the interdepartmental flow by a model.

Exhibit 8.5, for example, is a combination of Exhibit 8.3 and Exhibit 8.4. This provides the basic layout pattern which we are trying to improve.

Step 2   Determine the annual cost of this layout.

Step 2a

Annual Cost of Flow between Each Pair of Departments = Material Handling Cost per Unit Load per Unit Distance × Distance between Department Pair × Number of Loads Moved between Department Pair

The data required for this can be found in Exhibits 8.3 to 8.5. For example, the annual cost of moving material between departments 1 and 2 is given by

$0.10 × 40 m × 175 loads = $700

Similarly, the annual cost of moving material between departments 2 and 5 (using the aisle via departments 4 and 6 or 1 and 3) is given by:

$0.10 × 120 m × 165 loads = $1980

With six departments, we have fifteen possible department pairs. The annual cost of flow for every department pair is shown in Exhibit 8.6.

Step 2b
Annual Cost of Flow in the Layout = Sum of the Annual Costs of Flow between Each Pair of Departments

Here the flow cost of each pair of departments calculated in Step 2a is added to obtain the total cost of the layout. As seen in Exhibit 8.6, the annual cost of flow in the layout is $10 128.

Step 3 Find the layout with the lowest annual cost of flow.

There are many methods to do this. But for layouts with many departments (more than 15) it is difficult to determine mathematically the layout with the lowest flow cost. For example, in a six-department problem there are 6!

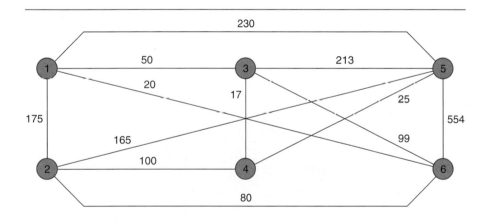

Exhibit 8.5

Interdepartmental Flow Graph with Number of Annual Movements

	1	2	3	4	5	6	
		700	200	0	1840	240	1
			0	400	1980	640	2
				68	852	792	3
					200	0	4
						2216	5
							6

Total cost: $10 128

Exhibit 8.6

Cost Matrix— First Solution

(or 720) possible layout arrangements. A fifteen-department problem would have 15! possible arrangements—a very large number (you can determine this using your calculator). So it is not possible to evaluate the flow cost of every possible layout arrangement.

Therefore, in practice, methods mentioned earlier, such as CRAFT, attempt to find a good solution but not necessarily the lowest cost solution. CRAFT involves switching pairs of departments intelligently to examine whether the cost can be reduced. How does this work? Consider the costs in Exhibit 8.6. Note in Step 2a that the flow cost between each department pair depends on the flow between them as well as the distance. In Exhibit 8.5 we see that interdepartmental flows between department 5 and departments 1, 2, and 3 are 230, 165, and 213—quite high. Yet we see that department 5 is tucked away in the top right corner of the layout. Thus each of the 165 loads between departments 2 and 5 has to travel 120m, resulting in a cost of $1980 in Exhibit 8.6. At the same time the flow between department 4 and other departments is relatively low. Thus, from a flow cost perspective it might make more sense to switch departments 5 and 4 to locate 5 more centrally.

Exhibit 8.7 shows the building layout for this revised solution. Exhibit 8.8 shows the revised cost matrix. The total flow costs have been reduced to $9608. Notice that because department 5 is more centrally located, the flow between departments 2 and 5 costs only $660 instead of $1980, a saving of $1320. However, since department 4 is now farther away from 2, the flow cost between these two departments has increased from $400 to $1200, an increase of $800. The rest of the flow costs in the layout have not changed. So the net benefit is $1320 − $800 = $520, which is equal to the cost decrease from $10 128 to 9608.

Of course there are many other possible department switches, and for most practical size layouts, we would need a computer to do all the calculations. Methods

Exhibit 8.7

Revised Building Layout

| 1 | 3 | 4 |
| 2 | 5 | 6 |

Exhibit 8.8

Cost Matrix— Revised Solution

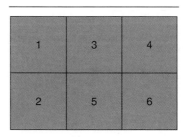

	1	2	3	4	5	6	
		700	200	0	1840	240	1
			0	1200	660	640	2
				68	852	792	3
					200	0	4
						2216	5
							6

Total cost: $9608

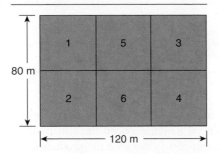

Exhibit 8.9

**Lowest Cost
Building Layout**

such as CRAFT do pairwise switches as long as the switch decreases costs. As mentioned earlier, for larger problems, there is no guarantee that the solution generated by CRAFT or other methods will be the lowest cost one. In the example shown here however, since there are only 720 possibilities, each was evaluated using a computer. Exhibit 8.9 shows the lowest cost layout, with a flow cost of $8748.[4]

Product Layout

When product demand is sufficiently high and sustainable over a long period of time, it is usually cost effective to rearrange resources from a process layout to a product layout as defined by the sequence of steps required to make the product. We often call these *assembly* lines, although the ratio of direct manual labour to machine work can vary widely. Assembly lines can vary from virtually 100 percent parts assembly by workers, to the other extreme, an *automated transfer* line, where all direct work is done by machine. In between are all types: Automobile lines have tools ranging from simple hammers and wrenches to robotic welding and painting; assembly lines in electronics can range from manual parts assembly to equipment for automatic parts insertion, automatic soldering, and automatic testing.

Assembly Lines

Assembly lines are a special case of product layout. In a general sense, the term assembly line refers to a progressive assembly linked by some type of material handling device. The usual assumption is that some form of pacing is present, and the allowable processing time is equivalent for all workstations. Within this broad definition, there are important differences among line types. A few of these are material handling devices (belt or roller conveyor, overhead crane), line configuration (U-shape, straight, branching), pacing (machine, human), product mix (one product or multiple products), workstation characteristics (workers may sit, stand, walk with the line, or ride the line), and length of the line (few or many stations).

The range of products partially or completely assembled on lines includes toys, appliances, autos, food and drink, garden equipment, perfumes and cosmetics, and a wide variety of electronic components. In fact, it is probably safe to say that virtually any product with multiple parts and produced in large volume uses assembly lines to some degree. Clearly, assembly lines are an important technology; to really understand their managerial requirements one must have some familiarity with how a line is balanced.

An important consideration that should not be overlooked in designing assembly lines is the human factor. Early assembly lines were machine paced; that is, they moved at a predetermined pace, regardless of whether or not the work was completed at a station. Under this structure, workers who fell behind had to rush to complete their assigned tasks, with the result often being faulty workmanship.

---

[4]The authors are thankful to Sherry Oh of the Haskayne School of Business for her Excel software that did the computations.

Exhibit 8.10

Illustrating Takt Time and Throughput Time on an Assembly Line

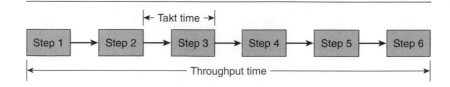

In recent years, worker-paced assembly lines, advocated initially by Japanese manufacturers, have replaced machine-paced lines in many facilities. With the worker-paced line, the operator continues to work on the product until the work assigned is satisfactorily completed. Only then is the product allowed to move on to the next station. The quality of the products made on a worker-paced line is significantly higher than that of products made on a comparable machine-paced line. When a Japanese manufacturer took over the production of televisions from a U.S. company, the number of defects dropped from 160 defects per 100 TVs to 4 defects per 100 TVs, even though the output per day and the workforce remained virtually unchanged. This dramatic increase in quality was attributed, in large part, to the installation of a worker-paced assembly line to replace the existing machine-paced line.[5]

Definitions. Before we begin our analysis of assembly lines, there are two terms that need to be defined, as illustrated in Exhibit 8.10.

- *Product interval time.* The product interval time is the actual time between products being completed at a station. This is often referred to as *cycle time,* or more recently, **takt time** (from the German word meaning "the baton that an orchestra conductor uses to regulate the beat of the music").[6] As we shall see shortly, the takt time for an assembly line determines the capacity of that line. We will use takt time to describe the product interval time in our analyses.

takt time

The time interval between stations on an assembly line.

- *Product duration time.* The overall time it takes to complete an individual product, from start to finish, is known as the product's **throughput time**, and is important, especially when looked at from the customer's perspective for the delivery of customized products. We will use throughput time to describe the product duration time.

throughput time

The overall elapsed time from when the manufacture of a product is first begun to when that specific product is completed.

Assembly Line Balancing

An assembly line consists of a series of workstations, each with a uniform time interval referred to as a takt time (which is also the time between successive units coming off the end of the line). At each workstation, work is performed on a product by adding parts and/or by completing an assembly operation. The work performed at each station is made up of many *tasks* (also referred to as *elements*, or *work units*). Such tasks are described by motion-time analysis. Generally, they are groupings that cannot be subdivided on the assembly line without paying a high penalty in extra motions.

assembly line balancing

Assignment of tasks to workstations within a given cycle time and with minimum idle worker time.

The total work to be performed at a workstation is equal to the sum of the tasks assigned to that workstation. The **assembly line balancing** problem is one of assigning all of the tasks required to a series of workstations so that the time required to do the work at each station does not exceed the takt time, and at the same time, the unassigned (i.e., idle) time across all workstations is minimized. An additional consideration in designing the line is to assign the tasks as equitably as possible to the stations. The problem is further complicated by the relationships among tasks imposed by product design and process

---

[5]Lloyd Dobyns and Frank Reuven, *If Japan Can, Why Can't We?* (New York: NBC-TV News Presentation, June 24, 1980).

[6]Robert W. Hall, "Time Prints and Takt Times," *Target: Innovation at Work* 14, no. 3 (1998), pp. 6–13.

technologies. This is called the precedence relationship, which specifies the order in which the tasks must be performed in the assembly process.

Steps in assembly line balancing. The sequence of steps required to balance an assembly line is straightforward:

1. Specify the sequential relationship among tasks using a precedence diagram. The diagram consists of circles and arrows. Circles represent individual tasks; arrows indicate the order of task performance.

2. Determine the required takt time (T), using the following formula:

    $$T = \frac{\text{Production time per day}}{\text{Output per day (in units)}}$$

3. Determine the lower bound on the number of workstations (i.e., the theoretical minimum number of workstations, N_t) required to satisfy the takt time constraint, using the following formula:

    $$N_t = \frac{\text{Sum of task times}\,(S)}{\text{Takt time}\,(T)}$$

4. Select a primary rule by which tasks are to be assigned to workstations and a secondary rule to break ties. (Both primary and secondary rules usually are selected from a list of logical heuristic rules or rules-of-thumb. Common rules include the shortest operation time rule, the longest operation time rule, and the largest number of following tasks rule. Research has shown that some rules are better than others for certain problem structures. If the problem is not large we could also try different rules to determine which provides the best solution.)

5. Assign tasks, one at a time, to the first workstation until the sum of the task times is equal to the takt time, or no other tasks are feasible because of time or sequence restrictions. Repeat the process for Workstation 2, Workstation 3, and so on, until all tasks are assigned.

6. Evaluate the efficiency of the resulting assembly line using the following formula:

    $$\text{Efficiency} = \frac{\text{Sum of task times}\,(S)}{\text{Actual number of workstations}\,(N_a) \times \text{Takt time}\,(T)}$$

7. If efficiency is unsatisfactory, rebalance the line using a different decision rule.

Example

A toy company produces a Model J Wagon that is to be assembled on a conveyor belt. Five hundred wagons are required per day. The company is currently operating on a one-shift, eight-hour-a-day schedule, with one hour off for lunch (i.e., net production time per day is seven hours). The assembly steps and times for the wagon are given in Exhibit 8.11. Assignment: Find the balance that minimizes the number of workstations, subject to takt time and precedence constraints.

Solution

1. Draw a precedence diagram. Exhibit 8.12 illustrates the sequential relationships identified in Exhibit 8.11. (The length of the arrows has no meaning.)

2. Takt time determination. Here we have to convert to seconds since our task times are in seconds.

    $$T = \frac{\text{Production time per day}}{\text{Output per day}} = \frac{7 \text{ hrs/day} \times 60 \text{ min/hr} \times 60 \text{ sec/min}}{500 \text{ wagons}}$$

    $$= \frac{25\,200}{500} = 50.4 \text{ seconds}$$

Exhibit 8.11

Assembly Steps and Times for Model J Wagon

Task	Performance Time (in seconds)	Description	Tasks that Must Precede
A	45	Position rear axle support and hand fasten four screws to nuts	—
B	11	Insert rear axle	A
C	9	Tighten rear axle support screws to nuts	B
D	50	Position front axle assembly and hand fasten with four screws to nuts	—
E	15	Tighten front axle assembly screws	D
F	12	Position rear wheel #1 and fasten hub cap	C
G	12	Position front wheel #2 and fasten hub cap	C
H	12	Position front wheel #1 and fasten hub cap	E
I	12	Position rear wheel #2 and fasten hub cap	E
J	8	Position wagon handle shaft on front axle assembly and hand fasten bolt and nut assembly and hand fasten bolt and nut	F, G, H, I
K	9	Tighten bolt and nut	J
	195		

Exhibit 8.12

Precedence Graph for Model J Wagon

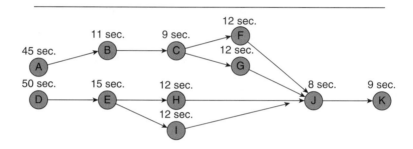

3. The theoretical minimum number of workstations required (the actual number may be greater):

$$N_t = \frac{S}{T} = \frac{195 \text{ seconds}}{50.4 \text{ seconds}} = 3.86 \text{ stations} \rightarrow 4 \text{ stations}$$

(Since we cannot have a fraction of a station, we always round up to the next whole integer. For this example, the minimum number of stations is four.)

4. Select assignment rules. In this case, we use as our primary rule

   a. Assign tasks in order of the largest number of following tasks. Our secondary rule, to be invoked when ties exist from our primary rule, is

   b. Assign tasks in order of longest operating time.

Task	Total Number of Following Tasks	Following Tasks
A	6	B, C, F, G, J, K
B or D	5	C, F, G, J, K (for B)
C or E	4	H, I, J, K (for E)
F, G, H, or I	2	J, K
J	1	K
K	0	—

Exhibit 8.13A

Balance Made According to Largest Number of Following Tasks Rule

	Task	Task Time (in seconds)	Remaining Unassigned Time (in seconds)	Feasible Remaining Tasks	Task with Most Followers	Task with Longest Operation Time
Station 1	A	45	5.4 idle	None		
Station 2	D	50	0.4 idle	None		
Station 3	B	11	39.4	C, E	C, E	E
	E	15	24.4	C, H, I	C	
	C	9	15.4	F, G, H, I	F, G, H, I	F, G, H, I
	F*	12	3.4 idle	None		
Station 4	G	12	38.4	H, I	H, I	H, I
	H*	12	26.4	I		
	I	12	14.4	J		
	J	8	6.4 idle	None		
Station 5	K	9	41.4 idle	None		

*Denotes task arbitrarily selected when there is a tie between longest operation times.

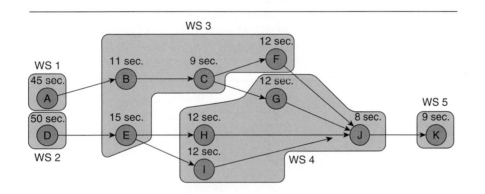

Exhibit 8.13B

Precedence Graph for Model J. Wagon

Exhibit 8.13C

Efficiency Calculation

$$\text{Efficiency} = \frac{S}{NT}$$

$$= \frac{195}{(5)(50.4)} = 0.77, \text{ or } 77\%$$

5. Make task assignments to form Workstation 1, Workstation 2, and so forth, until all tasks are assigned. The actual assignment is given in Exhibit 8.13A and is shown graphically in Exhibit 8.13B.

6. Calculate the efficiency. This is shown in Exhibit 8.13C.

7. Evaluate the solution. An efficiency of 77 percent indicates an imbalance or idle time of 23 percent ($1.0 - 0.77$) across the entire line. From Exhibit 8.13A we can see that there are 57 total seconds of idle time, and the "choice" job is at Workstation 5.

Is a better balance possible? In this case, yes. Try balancing the line with rule *b* and breaking ties with rule *a*. (This will give you a feasible four-station balance.)

Often the longest required task time dictates the shortest possible takt time for the production line. This task time becomes the lower time bound, unless it is possible to split the task into two or more workstations.

Example

Consider the following illustration: Suppose that an assembly line contains the following task times in seconds: 40, 30, 15, 25, 20, 18, 15. The line runs for 7½ hours per day and the required output is 750 wagons per day.

Solution

The takt time required to produce 750 wagons per day is 36 seconds ([7½ × 60 minutes × 60 seconds]/750). How do we deal with the task that is 40 seconds long?

There are several ways that we may be able to accommodate the 40-second task in a line with a 36-second takt time. The possibilities include:

1. *Split the task.* Can we split the task so that complete units are processed in two workstations?

2. *Duplicate the station.* By duplicating the task at two stations, the effective task time is reduced by 50 percent. If necessary, additional stations can be assigned to the same task to further lower the effective task time. With this approach, several tasks may be combined into one station to increase efficiency. In the example given, the first two tasks with 40 and 30 seconds each would be combined into one station, which would then be duplicated. The effective takt time for this station is then 35 seconds ([40 + 30]/2), which is below the required cycle time of 36 seconds.

3. *Share the task.* Can the task somehow be shared so an adjacent workstation does part of the work? This differs from the split task in the first option because the adjacent station acts to assist, not to do some units containing the entire task.

4. *Use a more skilled worker.* Since this task exceeds the cycle time by just 11 percent, a faster worker may be able to meet the 36-second time.

5. *Work overtime.* Producing at a rate of one unit every 40 seconds would produce 675 wagons per day, 75 short of the needed 750. The amount of overtime required to do the additional 75 wagons is 50 minutes (75 × 40 seconds/60 seconds).

6. *Redesign.* It may be possible to redesign the product to reduce the task time slightly.

Other possibilities to reduce the task time include equipment upgrading, a roaming helper to support the line, a change of materials, and multiskilled workers to operate the line as a team rather than as independent workers.

Flexible line layouts. As we saw in the preceding example, assembly line balancing frequently results in unequal workstation times. In fact, the shorter the takt time, the greater the probability of a higher percentage of imbalance in the line. Flexible line layouts such as those shown in Exhibit 8.14 are a common way of dealing with this problem. In our toy company example, the U-shaped line with work sharing at the bottom of the figure could help resolve the imbalance.

Mixed-model line balancing. To meet the demand for a variety of products and to avoid building high inventories of one product model, many manufacturers often schedule several different models to be produced over a given day or week on the same line. To illustrate how this is done, suppose our toy company has a fabrication line to bore holes in

Exhibit 8.14

Flexible Line Layouts

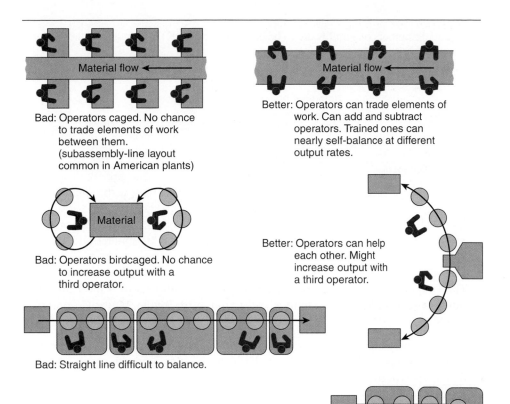

Bad: Operators caged. No chance to trade elements of work between them. (subassembly-line layout common in American plants)

Better: Operators can trade elements of work. Can add and subtract operators. Trained ones can nearly self-balance at different output rates.

Bad: Operators birdcaged. No chance to increase output with a third operator.

Better: Operators can help each other. Might increase output with a third operator.

Bad: Straight line difficult to balance.

Better: One of several advantages of U-line is better operator access. Here, five operators were reduced to four.

Source: Robert W. Hall, *Attaining Manufacturing Excellence* (Homewood, IL: Dow Jones-Irwin, 1987), p. 125.

its Model J Wagon frame and its Model K Wagon frame. The time required to bore the holes is different for each wagon type.

Example

Assume that the final assembly line downstream requires equal numbers of Model J and Model K wagon frames. Also assume that we want to develop a takt time for the fabrication line which is balanced for the production of equal numbers of J and K frames. Of course, we could produce Model J frames for several days and then produce Model K frames until an equal number of frames has been produced. However, this would build up unnecessary work-in-process inventory.

If we want to reduce the amount of work-in-process inventory, we could develop a cycle mix that greatly reduces inventory buildup while keeping within the restrictions of equal numbers of J and K wagon frames.

Solution

Process times: 6 minutes per J and 4 minutes per K.
The day consists of 480 minutes (8 hours × 60 minutes).

$$6J + 4K = 480$$

Since equal numbers of J and K are to be produced (or J = K), produce 48J and 48K per day, or 6J and 6K per hour.

The following shows one balance of J and K frames.

Balanced Mixed-Model Sequence

Model sequence	J J	K K K	J J	J J	K K K	Repeats
Operation time	6 6	4 4 4	6 6	6 6	4 4 4	8 times
Minitakt time	12	12	12	12	12	per day
Total takt time			60			

This line is balanced at six wagon frames of each type per hour with a minitakt time of 12 minutes.

Another balance is J K K J K J, with times of 6, 4, 4, 6, 4, 6. This balance produces three J and three K every 30 minutes with a minitakt time of 10 minutes (JK, KJ, KJ).

The simplicity of mixed-model balancing (under conditions of a level production schedule) is seen in Yasuhiro Mondon's description of Toyota Motor Corporation's operations:

1. Final assembly lines of Toyota are mixed product lines. The production per day is averaged by taking the number of vehicles in the monthly production schedule classified by specifications and dividing by the number of working days.

2. In regard to the production sequence during each day, the cycle time of each different specification vehicle is calculated and, in order to have all specification vehicles appear at their own cycle time, different specification vehicles are ordered to follow each other.[7]

The mixed-model line appears to be a relatively straightforward sequencing problem. This is because in our example the two models fit nicely into a common time period that also matched demand. From a mathematical standpoint, designing a mixed-model line is very difficult, and no technique exists to provide the optimum assignment of tasks to workstations. This is because the mixed-model line involves multiple lot sizes, lot sequencing, setup times for each lot, differing workstation sizes along the line, and task variations. The problem is to design the assembly line and workstations and to specify exactly which tasks are to be done in each.

The objectives of a mixed-model line design are to minimize idle time as well as the inefficiencies caused by changing from model to model. Researchers have used integer programming, branch and bound techniques, and simulation. They still have not been able to find the optimal solution for a realistic-size, real-world problem.

Current Thoughts on Assembly Lines

The widespread use of assembly-line methods in manufacturing has dramatically increased output rates. Historically, the focus almost always has been on full utilization of human labour; that is, to design assembly lines minimizing human idle times. Equipment and facility utilization stood in the background as much less important. Past research tried to find optimal solutions, as if the problem existed in a never-changing world.

---

[7]S. Manivannan and Dipak Chudhuri, "Computer-Aided Facility Layout Algorithm Generates Alternatives to Increase Firm's Productivity," *Industrial Engineering* (May 1984), pp. 81–84.

IMPROVED LAYOUTS HELP ANY FACILITY— MANUFACTURING, DISTRIBUTION, OR SERVICE

In the mid-1980s Western Glove Works of Winnipeg, a private label jean manufacturer (whose U.S. customers include Macy's and Nordstrom) was located in two 70-year-old buildings located about five blocks apart. Work in process (WIP) moved slowly within each facility and had to be trucked between buildings. Production was inefficient and costs were excessive because of the additional moves for products and employees and because of poor communication. The company decided that it needed a new facility to improve its competitiveness.

The initial plan for the layout for the integrated facility, showing every machine and work area, was created in consultation with management and production staff. Then the plan was displayed in a high traffic area and employees were invited to comment on the plan. One change based on these comments was inclusion of a daycare facility. The plan was also evaluated for possible future changes. Since the layout plan implemented was based on so much thought and analysis, the basic design of the facility remained unchanged for more than a decade and was able to handle the tripling of volume (and quadrupling of sales) the company experienced. Says Michael Silver, president of Western Glove Works Silver Jeans division, "Planning that involved all staff was instrumental in creating a great design that has stood the test of time."

Spartan Plastics is a London, Ontario-based, medium-sized company that extrudes plastic parts primarily for the auto industry. The company realized that its inefficient warehouse layout resulted in employees walking in excess of 500 kilometres every year to fill orders. Furthermore, an ABC analysis (described in Chapter 16) revealed that the top twenty items alone generated 40 percent of sales. Previously, the warehouse shelves had been organized by item serial number, so that items could be located easily The company rearranged the warehouse by placing the most popular items closest to the packing and shipping area, at eye level and within arm's reach. Less popular items were placed farther away from the packing area. Finally, the shelf location was computerized. As a result of all these layout changes walking time was reduced.

When investment dealer CIBC Wood Gundy moved to its new facility in BCE Place in Toronto, the new layout design had to incorporate many considerations. In addition to the data and communication cabling, the new trading floor had to accommodate the needs of traders, support staff, offices, and meeting rooms. For example, to help communicate verbally, dealers were located near those whose work was most closed related to theirs. Says Don Gibson, vice-president of office services at Wood Gundy, "I have done about a dozen trading floors here in Canada, and this is the first time there has been no negative feedback from *anybody.*"

Sources:
Gene Barbee, "The Best Laid Plans: Part II," *Bobbin*, 37, no. 12 (1996), pp. 107–110.
Narendar Sumukadas and Chris Piper, *Spartan Plastics* (London, Ontario: University of Western Ontario, Ivey Management Services, 1997).
Patricia Fernberg, "Focus on Facilities: Wood Gundy BCE Place," *Modern Office Technology* (March 1991), pp. 53–54.

Newer views of assembly lines take a broader perspective. Intentions are to incorporate greater flexibility in the number of products manufactured on the line, more variability in workstations (such as size, number of workers), improved reliability (through routine preventive maintenance), and high-quality output (through improved tooling and training). (See the opening vignette of Chapter 1.)

Group Technology (Cellular) Layout

A group technology (or cellular) layout, shown in Exhibit 8.2B, allocates dissimilar machines into cells to work on products that have similar weights, shapes, and processing requirements. Group technology (GT) layouts are now widely used in metal fabricating, computer chip manufacture, and assembly work. The overall objective is to gain the benefits of product layout in job-shop kinds of production. These benefits include:

1. *Better human relations.* Cells consist of a few workers who form a small work team; a team turns out complete units of work.

2. *Improved operator expertise.* Workers see only a limited number of different parts in a finite production cycle, so repetition means quick learning.

3. *Less work-in-process inventory and material handling.* A cell combines several production stages, so fewer parts travel through the shop.

4. *Faster production setup.* Fewer jobs mean reduced tooling and hence faster tooling changes.

Developing a GT Layout

Shifting from process layout to a GT cellular layout entails three steps:

1. Grouping parts into families that follow a common sequence of operations, which requires developing and maintaining a computerized parts classification and coding system. This is often a major expense with such systems, although many companies have developed short-cut procedures for identifying parts-families.

2. Identifying dominant flow patterns of parts-families as a basis for location or relocation of processes.

3. Physically grouping machines and processes into cells. Often some parts cannot be associated with a family and specialized machinery cannot be placed in any one cell because of its general use. These unattached parts and machinery are placed in a "remainder cell."

Facility Layouts for Services

The overall goal in designing a layout for a service facility, from an operations perspective, is to minimize travel time for workers, and, often, also for customers when they are directly involved in the process. From a marketing perspective, however, the goal is usually to maximize revenues. Frequently these two goals are in conflict with each other. It is therefore management's task to identify the trade-offs that exist in designing the layout, taking both perspectives into consideration. For example, the prescription centre in a pharmacy is usually located at the rear, requiring customers to walk through the store. This encourages impulse purchases of nonprescription items, which usually have higher profit margins.

Types of Service Layouts

We use the three basic types of manufacturing facility layouts described earlier in this chapter as a framework for identifying the different types of layouts that exist in service operations.

Process Layout

The support services for an emergency room in a hospital offer a good example of a *process layout*, with radiology, blood analysis, and the pharmacy each being located in a specific area of the hospital. Patients requiring any of these specific services therefore must go to the locations where these services are provided. The kitchen of a large restaurant also can be viewed as a process layout. Here all of the desserts and breads are prepared in the bake shop; fruits and vegetables are peeled, sliced, and diced in the prep area; and raw meats and seafood are prepared for cooking in the butcher shop. Even the cooking line often is subdivided by type of process, with all of the frying taking place in one area, broiling and roasting in another, and sauteed dishes in a third.

Product Layout

A good service example of a *product layout* is a cafeteria line where all of the various stations (for example, salads, hot and cold entrees, desserts, and beverages) are arranged in a specific order, and customers visit each station as they move through the line.

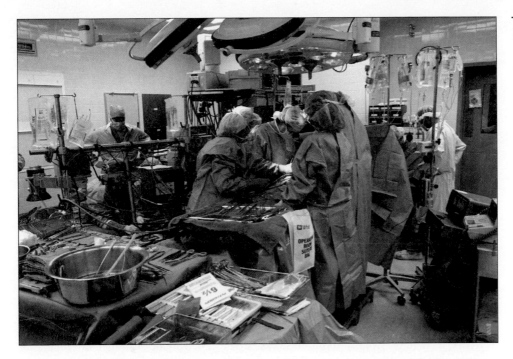

An operating room provides a good example of a fixed-position layout in a service environment. Here the patient remains "fixed" on the operating table, and doctors, nurses, and equipment are brought in to the operating room as they are needed.

Fixed-Position Layout

Examples of *fixed-position layouts* in services include (*a*) an automobile repair shop (where all of the processes such as brake repair, oil change, etc., typically take place in the same location), (*b*) an operating room in a hospital (where the patient remains in a given location on the operating table), and (*c*) a table at a restaurant where all of the different courses in a meal are brought to the customer (and in some cases even prepared at the table in front of the customer).

Layout Considerations in Services

In designing facility layouts for service operations, additional, service-unique issues need to be taken into consideration. First, the cost per square foot for retail locations is usually very expensive (in comparison to that for a manufacturing facility). Service retail operations, therefore, must design their facilities to maximize the sales generated per square foot (or square meter). To accomplish this, operations such as restaurants have reduced the percentage of area devoted to back-of-the-house operations, such as the kitchen, to allow for additional seating. One way this is accomplished, as discussed in an earlier chapter, is through the use of a quasi-manufacturing facility or central commissary where food can be economically prepared in a relatively low-cost area. Another approach is taken by Benihana's of Tokyo, a chain of Japanese steak houses. There the strategy is to move the kitchen to the front of the house so customers can actually participate in the food preparation process.

Another service-unique factor that needs to be taken into consideration is the customer's presence in the transformation process. As a result, the decor package of the service operation plays an important role in determining the customer's overall satisfaction with the service encounter.

servicescape

Describes the physical surroundings in a service operation that can affect a customer's perception of the service received.

Mary Jo Bitner has introduced the expression **servicescape** to describe the physical surroundings in which the service takes place.[8] The servicescape of an operation comprises three major elements: (1) the ambient conditions, (2) the spatial layout and functionality, and (3) the signs, symbols, and artifacts.

Ambient Conditions

These refer to the background characteristics of the operation, including noise level, lighting, and temperature. (It often is said that the prices in restaurants are inversely related to the amount of lighting—the darker the restaurant, the more expensive the food.) Hanging lights over tables, seen in some better restaurants, suggests privacy; recessed lighting in ceilings, on the other hand, seen in many fast-food operations, sends different signals to the customer.

Spatial Layout and Functionality

Unlike manufacturing firms where the goal in designing a layout is to minimize the cost of moving material between areas, one of the goals of a service operation is to minimize the travel time of employees (see the OM in Practice on layout redesign), and, in some instances, of customers. At the same time, the service firm is trying to maximize revenues per customer by exposing them to as many opportunities as possible to spend their money. For example, most grocery stores have magazines and candy located at checkout counters so that customers waiting to pay will be tempted to make an impulse purchase. Layouts in IKEA, a chain of Swedish furniture stores, are designed so the customer, after entering the store, must go through the entire facility to exit, not unlike a maze with a single path through it.

Signs, Symbols, and Artifacts

These refer to aspects of the service operation that have social significance. For example, bank buildings often include columns and stone to give the feeling of security. The offices of large law firms and consulting practices are frequently decorated in dark woods and thick carpets to connote success and traditional values. Waiters in tuxedos or waiters in white shirts, hats, and aprons—each gives certain signals, in terms of establishing the customers' expectations of the operation.

Computer Software for Facility Layout

The OM in Practice Box on using FactoryFLOW illustrated the use of computer software in facility layout. Since layout problems in practice can be quite complex, software is required for designing effective layouts. FactoryFLOW, FactoryPLAN, FactoryOPT, and LAYOPT are examples of commercial software that can help design manufacturing and service facility layouts. These packages generally have the ability to incorporate many of the practical considerations that need to be included in designing a layout. These could include fixed locations such as elevators and washrooms, uneven department shapes, and aisles. Some incorporate qualitative factors other than material handling cost (the only factor we considered in process layouts in this chapter) such as noise factors, dust, and so on. Many use embedded mathematical algorithms to evaluate different layout configurations to determine the more effective ones. *Industrial Engineer* is a publication that periodically surveys facility layout software available in the market.

---

[8]Mary Jo Bitner, "Servicescapes: The Impact of Physical Surroundings on Customers and Employees," *The Journal of Marketing* (April 1992), pp. 57–71.

Conclusion

As we saw in the opening vignette, the choice of which type of facility layout to adopt can have a significant impact on the long-term success of a firm. This decision, therefore, should not be made lightly, but only after an in-depth analysis of the operational requirements has been completed.

A major issue to be addressed in facility layout decisions in manufacturing is: How flexible should the layout be to adjust to future changes in product demand and product mix? Some argue that the best strategy is to have movable equipment that can be shifted easily from place to place to reduce material flow time for near-term contracts. However, although this is appealing in general, the limitations of existing buildings and permanently anchored equipment, as well as the general plant disruption that is created, make this a very costly strategy.

In service systems, particularly with multi-location chains, the study of layout has become extremely important because the selected layout can be replicated at hundreds or even thousands of facilities. Indeed, a layout error in a fast-food chain has a more immediate, and generally a more far-reaching, impact on profits than a layout error in a factory.

Key Terms

assembly line balancing p. 306

CRAFT p. 301

fixed-position layout p. 301

group technology (G/T) or cellular layout p. 300

process layout p. 299

product layout p. 300

servicescape p. 316

takt time p. 306

throughput time p. 306

Review and Discussion Questions

1. What kind of layout is used in a health club?
2. What is the objective of assembly line balancing? How would you deal with a situation in which one worker, although trying hard, is 20 percent slower than the other 10 people on a line?
3. How do you determine the idle-time percentage from a given assembly line balance?
4. What is the essential requirement for mixed-model lines to be practical?
5. Why might it be difficult to develop a group technology layout?
6. In what respects is facility layout a marketing problem in services? Give an example of a service system layout designed to maximize the amount of time the customer is in the system.
7. Visit a major hotel in your area and describe the layout of its operations.
8. Describe the layout of a branch office of a bank.
9. How might you design the layout for a walk-in clinic?
10. Visit two different supermarkets. What similarities do their layouts share in common? What differences did you notice?

Internet Exercise

Using PLANT and LAYOUT as suggested key words, search the Web to identify and describe in detail the plant layout for an individual company. As an alternative, go to the McGraw-Hill Operations Management homepage at www.mcgrawhill.ca/olc/davis and take a plant tour of a company, then describe the physical layout of the operation.

Solved Problems

Problem 1

A university advising office has four rooms, each dedicated to specific problems: petitions (Room A), schedule advising (Room B), grade complaints (Room C), and student counselling (Room D). The office is 40 m long and 10 m wide. Each room is 10 m by 10 m. The present location of rooms is A, B, C, D; that is, a straight line. The contact summary shows the number of contacts that each advisor in a room has with other advisors in the other rooms. Assume that all advisors are equal in this value.

Contact summary: AB = 10, AC = 20, AD = 30,
BC = 15, BD = 10, CD = 20.

a. Evaluate this layout according to one of the methods presented in this chapter.

b. Improve the layout by exchanging functions within rooms. Show your amount of improvement using the same method as in *a.*

Solution

a. Evaluate this layout according to one of the methods in the chapter.

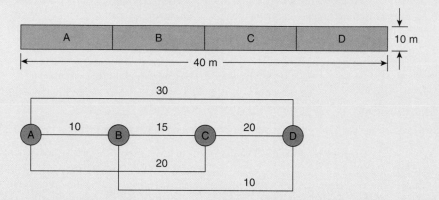

Using the material handling cost method shown in the toy company example (pages 301–305), we obtain the following costs, assuming $1 per contact between adjacent rooms and an additional $1 per contact for each room in between.

AB = 10 × 1 = 10
AC = 20 × 2 = 40
AD = 30 × 3 = 90
BC = 15 × 1 = 15
BD = 10 × 2 = 20
CD = 20 × 1 = 20
        Current cost = 195

b. Improve the layout by exchanging functions within rooms. Show your amount of improvement using the same method as in *a.* A better layout would be either BCDA or ADCB.

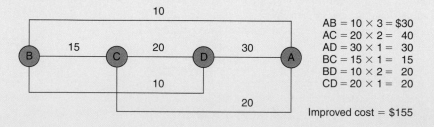

AB = 10 × 3 = $30
AC = 20 × 2 =   40
AD = 30 × 1 =   30
BC = 15 × 1 =   15
BD = 10 × 2 =   20
CD = 20 × 1 =   20

Improved cost = $155

Problem 2

The following tasks must be performed on an assembly line in the sequence and times specified.

Task	Task Time (seconds)	Tasks that Must Precede	Task	Task Time (seconds)	Tasks that Must Precede
A	50	—	E	20	C
B	40	—	F	25	D
C	20	A	G	10	E
D	45	C	H	35	B, F, G

a. Draw the schematic diagram.

b. What is the theoretical minimum number of stations required to meet a forecasted demand of 400 units per eight-hour day?

c. Use the longest-operating-time rule and balance the line in the minimum number of stations to produce 400 units per day.

d. Compute the efficiency of the line.

e. Does your solution generate any managerial concerns?

Solution

a. Draw the schematic diagram.

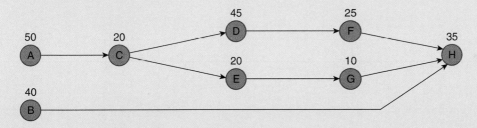

b. Theoretical minimum number of stations to meet D = 400 is

$$N_t = \frac{S}{T} = \frac{245 \text{ seconds}}{\left(\dfrac{60 \text{ seconds} \times 480 \text{ minutes}}{400 \text{ units}}\right)} = \frac{245}{72} = 3.4 \rightarrow \quad 4 \text{ stations}$$

c. Use the longest-operating-time rule and balance the line in the minimum number of stations to produce 400 units per day.

	Task	Task Time (seconds)	Remaining Unassigned Time	Feasible Remaining Tasks
Station 1	A	50	22	C
	C	20	2	None
Station 2	D	45	27	E, F
	F	25	2	None
Station 3	B	40	32	E
	E	20	12	G
	G	10	2	None
Station 4	H	35	37	None

d. $Efficiency = \dfrac{S}{N_a \times T} = \dfrac{245}{4(72)} = 85\%$

e. Yes. Station 4 is only half as busy as the other three stations.

Problems

1. An assembly line makes two models of trucks: a Buster and a Duster. Busters take 12 minutes each and Dusters take 8 minutes each. The daily output requirement is 24 of each per day. Develop a balanced mixed-model sequence to satisfy demand.

2. The tasks and the order in which they must be performed according to their assembly requirements are shown in the following table. These are to be combined into workstations to create an assembly line.

   The assembly line operates 7½ hours per day. The output requirement is 1000 units per day.

Task	Preceding Tasks	Time (seconds)
A	—	15
B	A	24
C	A	6
D	B	12
E	B	18
F	C	7
G	C	11
H	D	9
I	E	14
J	F, G	7
K	H, I	15
L	J, K	10

   a. What is the takt time?

   b. Balance the line based on the 1000-unit forecast, stating which tasks would be done in each workstation. [Use the shortest operating time (SOT) rule].

   c. For *b* above, what is the efficiency of your assembly line?

   d. After production was started, Marketing realized they underestimated demand and needed to increase output to 1100 units. What action would you take? Be specific in quantitative terms, if appropriate.

3. An assembly line operates seven hours per day and produces 420 units per day. The following tasks are required with their respective performance times and preceding tasks:

Task	Time (seconds)	Preceding Tasks
A	15	None
B	15	None
C	45	A, B
D	45	C

   Compute the takt time and the theoretical minimum number of workstations, and prepare an initial line configuration. Determine the efficiency of your assembly line.

4. An initial solution has been given to the following process layout problem. Given the flows described and a transportation cost of $2.00 per unit per meter, compute the total cost for

the layout. Each location is 100 m long and 50 m wide, as shown on the figure below. Use the centres of departments for distances and compute using rectilinear distances.

Department

		A	B	C	D
	A	0	10	25	55
Department	B		0	10	5
	C			0	15
	D				0

```
        100 m  100 m  100 m
50 m  ┌──────┬──────┬──────┐
      │  A   │  B   │  C   │ 50 m
      └──────┴──────┼──────┤
                    │  D   │ 50 m
                    └──────┘
```

5. An assembly line will operate eight hours per day and produce 480 units per day. The task times and precedence relationships are summarized below. Prepare an initial assembly-line configuration using the longest-operating-time rule, and determine the efficiency of your layout.

Task	Time (seconds)	Preceding Tasks
A	20	None
B	40	A
C	35	B
D	35	B
E	35	C, D

6. An assembly line at CeeCee Industries is to be designed that will operate 7½ hours per day and supply a steady demand of 300 units per day. The following are the tasks and their task performance times:

Task	Preceding Tasks	Performance Time (seconds)
a	—	70
b	—	40
c	—	45
d	a	10
e	b	30
f	c	20
g	d	60
h	e	50
i	f	15
j	g	25
k	h, i	20
l	j, k	25

   a. Draw the precedence diagram.
   b. What is the takt time?
   c. What is the theoretical minimum number of workstations?
   d. Assign tasks to workstations, stating what your logic rule is.
   e. What is the efficiency of your line balance?
   f. Suppose demand increases by 10 percent. How would you react to this?

7. Given the following data on the task precedence relationships for an assembled product and assuming that the tasks cannot be split, what is the theoretical minimum takt time?

Task	Performance Time (minutes)	Tasks that Must Precede
A	3	—
B	6	A
C	7	A
D	5	A
E	2	A
F	4	B, C
G	5	C
H	5	D, E, F, G

    a. Determine the minimum number of stations needed to meet a takt time of 10 minutes according to the "largest number of following tasks" rule.

    b. Compute the efficiency of the balances achieved.

8. Simon's Mattress Factory is planning to introduce a new line of pillow-top mattresses. Current plans are to produce the mattresses on an assembly line. Mattresses will be built on individual platforms pulled by a chain in a track in the floor. This will allow workers to completely walk around the mattress. Tools will be suspended from the ceiling, so that there will be no problem with tangling cords or wrapping them around the platform.

    The assembly-line process starts with the basic spring foundation and builds the mattress as it progresses down the line. There are 12 operations required, and their times and process sequence are as follows:

Operation	Time (minutes)	Tasks that Must Precede
A	1	—
B	3	A
C	4	B
D	1	B
E	5	C
F	4	D
G	1	E, F
H	2	G
I	5	G
J	3	H
K	2	I
L	3	J, K

    Tentative plans are to operate the line 7½ hours per day. Demand for the mattresses is expected to be 70 per day.

    a. Draw the schematic diagram.

    b. What is the takt time?

    c. What is the theoretical minimum number of workstations?

    d. Create a reasonably balanced assembly line.

    e. Supposing the plan was to produce these in a job shop layout. Discuss and compare the characteristics, pros, cons, and so forth of a job shop versus assembly line for this mattress production.

9. Bodnarchuk Manufacturing Company received a contract for 20 000 units of a product to be delivered in equal weekly quantities over a six-month period. Bodnarchuk works 250 days per year on a single-shift, 40-hour work week.

    The table below states the tasks required and their precedence sequence and task times in seconds.

Task	Task that Must Precede	Time (seconds)
A	—	150
B	A	120
C	B	150
D	A	30
E	D	100
F	C, E	40
G	E	30
H	F, G	100

   a. Develop an assembly line that meets the requirements.

   b. State the takt time.

   c. What is the efficiency of the line?

   d. Supposing the vendor asked you to increase output by 10 percent. State specifically how you would respond to this.

10. The following tasks are to be performed on an assembly linc:

Task	Time (seconds)	Tasks that Must Precede
A	20	—
B	7	A
C	20	B
D	22	B
E	15	C
F	10	D
G	16	E, F
H	8	G

The workday is 7 hours long and the demand for completed product is 750 units per day.

   a. Find the takt time.

   b. What is the theoretical number of workstations?

   c. Draw the precedence diagram.

   d. Balance the line using the longest-operating-time rule.

   e. What is the efficiency of the line balanced as in *d*?

   f. Suppose that demand rose from 750 per day to 800 units per day. What would you do?

   g. Suppose that demand rose from 750 per day to 1000 units per day. What would you do?

11. A Whitehorse Credit Union branch has six departments with a from-to (trip or flow) matrix as follows:

From/To	1	2	3	4	5	6
1 Bank Tellers	—					70
2 Bank Reps	20	—			45	
3 Commercial Tellers		10	—	15		20
4 Information Desk	20			—	40	
5 Bank Manager		30		30	—	
6 Cash Department	10		70			

Current Block Plan:

2	4	3
6	5	1

The distance between the centres of each department is five metres horizontally and four metres vertically. Design a better layout that reduces the interdepartmental movement cost. Assume that the cost per trip between departments is $1.

Case 1   First Detect: Linking Product Design and Process Layout

FirstDetect designs and manufactures fire safety monitoring equipment for corporate customers in the North American market. Their equipment can detect a fire less than a half second after ignition through a technology that identifies specific light waves known to be emitted by the ignition of a fire, based on the accelerant involved (natural gas, propane, ammonia, sulphur, hydrogen, etc.). Furthermore, their fire detection equipment can be integrated into a facility's fire suppression system, enabling a fire to be detected and actively suppressed within seconds of ignition. This equipment provides a company with a safer work environment, reduces the probability of fire damage and corresponding production downtime, while also reducing insurance premiums.

With growing demand for such fire detection equipment, new competitors have entered the market in recent years. A market for "standardized" models of this fire detection equipment developed in which suppliers such as FirstDetect manufacture and stock finished models that are most frequently desired by customers. More recently, a competitor from China has aggressively targeted the North American market by offering its version of the standardized models for prices below FirstDetect's production costs for their equivalent model. As a result, FirstDetect's sales have declined steadily, and management is discussing alternative strategies for the new market conditions in which they find themselves.

Currently, FirstDetect manufactures standardized fire detection models in an assembly line process. Employees work exclusively at one of the component machining or final assembly stages (each of which is similar in nature to Exhibit 8.10). Production commences when a shop employee withdraws the required materials from the central stockroom. The fixtures used at the machining stages are old, and dedicated to one product model each. When they want to manufacture a different model, all fixtures must be disassembled and removed, and then the fixtures required for the next model are installed and assembled. Because of the significant setup, or switchover times, production scheduling staff consolidate common customer orders as much as possible before providing a bulk production order to the shop. Furthermore, production scheduling often bumps up the quantity on the production order if customer demand quantity is deemed too low. Although this helps to spread out the setup costs over a higher volume, FirstDetect then has finished goods inventory, and must trust that another customer eventually will order that model. FirstDetect also has a work-in-process inventory to store batches that are machined but not scheduled immediately for final assembly. All customer orders are currently entered into the computer system by selecting information such as the finished standard model item number, quantity, and delivery date.

At a recent management meeting, sales manager Farima Hashemi commented that more customers are requesting fire detection equipment other than FirstDetect's standard offering. In the past, FirstDetect occasionally accepted custom orders, since some customers are willing to pay a significant premium to get a product that fits their specific requirements. To avoid confusion with regular production, custom orders were machined and assembled in a separate area (similar in nature to Exhibit 8.2A) by a single shop employee who had completed a general engineering diploma at a local technical college. After the meeting, accounting manager Aidan Richards performed a cost analysis on some recent custom orders and found that although the sales price per unit was significantly higher than for standard models, excessive engineering administration costs related to preparing a complete drawing and production (machining and assembly) instructions for each custom order exceeded the increase in sales price. The result was a financial loss in the majority of the custom orders analyzed. Based on these findings, accounting recommended a significant price increase for future custom orders. However, the sales manager is concerned that the price increase proposed by accounting might deter customers from choosing First-Detect for their custom order requirements.

With foreign competitors significantly undercutting their prices for their standard models, FirstDetect's management team began investigating the strategic option of focusing on the growing custom order market and essentially vacating the standard market. Farima and the engineering manager, Shari Vandelee, determined that their custom order requests were actually various configurations of the three purchased subcomponents (housing, signal range, and accelerant type) that were machined and assembled into a finished fire detector. Further investigation revealed that over 95% of custom order requests could be configured by selecting one of 20 possible housings, one of 5 possible detection ranges, and one of 15 possible accelerant types (although some restrictions would apply depending on which housing was selected). Upon presenting these findings to the management team, the operations manager, Fal Levin, commented that the scenario sounds ideal for the concept of modular design. Intrigued by a quick summary of the concept, the management team asked the operations manager to provide a brief report on what would be involved in implementing modular design at FirstDetect. The management team requested the following information:

a. Given the rectangular facility in Case Exhibit 1, where do you think the different areas should be located in relation to each other given the current situation? Assume that in addition to the manufacturing areas (machining, assembly and custom manufacturing) described, there are raw material/purchased components, work in process, and finished goods inventory areas.

b. Briefly explain where the current manufacturing processes would appear on the Product-Process matrix in Chapter 3.

c. What are some of the pros and cons of modular design for both the customer and for FirstDetect (as compared to FirstDetect's current process for handling custom orders)?

d. Briefly explain where a manufacturing process that supports the modular design concept would appear on the Product-Process matrix.

e. Assume that as they move to a modular designed product, they would like to implement a group technology (GT) layout. Would you first implement it in the component machining or final assembly stages? Why?

f. Considering FirstDetect's current production capabilities, what operational changes would be required so that operations could effectively support a modular design approach for the growing custom order market? Consider equipment, employees, layout, information systems procedures, and inventory management.

Source:
This case was written for classroom discussion by Brent Snider of the Haskayne School of Business at the University of Calgary. It is based on a real situation.

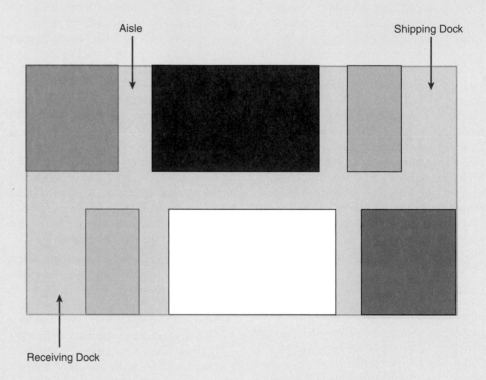

9

Forecasting

Chapter Objectives

- Introduce the basic concepts of forecasting and its importance within an organization.

- Identify several of the more common forecasting methods and how they can improve the performance of both manufacturing and service operations.

- Provide a framework for understanding how forecasts are developed.

- Demonstrate that errors exist in all forecasts and show how to measure and assess these errors.

- Discuss some of the software programs that are available for developing forecasting models.

Krispy Kreme Uses Forecasting Models throughout All Levels of Its Organization

Since 1999, Krispy Kreme, which began making doughnuts in 1937, has grown from 140 to more than 320 locations in 37 states within the United States as well as in Canada and Australia. Additional Krispy Kreme locations are planned for the United Kingdom, New Zealand, Spain, Japan, and South Korea.

To maintain control over its fast-growing network of retail locations, Krispy Kreme has installed a Web-based system that links all of its stores with corporate headquarters. In addition to keeping track of doughnut mixes and ensuring the colours of sprinkles, the new system has also been able to reduce ordering errors by 90 percent while increasing productivity significantly.

Integral elements of this new Web-based system are the forecasting techniques Krispy Kreme has incorporated throughout its organization with the objective of improving the overall efficiency and performance of its retail stores. At the corporate level, Krispy Kreme has developed a sophisticated causal forecasting model to predict sales for potential new store locations. Inasmuch as Krispy Kreme customers come from all income levels, the average family income in an area is not a major

factor in projecting sales for a proposed site. Some of the factors that are included in the Krispy Kreme site location model are population density within a given number of miles of the site and automobile and/or pedestrian counts (depending on the type of location).

Once the store is up and operating, the corporate office develops a monthly financial forecast of demand for individual stores. Factors included in this time-series forecast are seasonality of sales and the percentage breakdown of the two major categories of sales: on-premises sales and off-premises sales. (Off-premises sales include both packaged and unpackaged doughnuts and doughnuts in branded forms that are delivered to convenience stores, supermarkets, and mass merchants.

At the individual store level, daily sales forecasts determine the number of batches, the size of batches, and the scheduling times for production. To ensure that each store has the proper inventories of fresh doughnuts available when customers want them, additional sales forecasts are developed on an hourly basis, again using time-series analysis. Hourly forecasts are also used to determine worker requirements and weekly shift schedules. Forecasting doughnut sales at this level is critical because the doughnut mix and other ingredients are delivered on a just-in-time basis to the stores from Krispy Kreme's distribution centres. (The doughnut mix ingredients are blended together at these central facilities to ensure consistent product quality at every location.)

Sources:

Deborah Silver, "Dollars to Doughnuts," *Restaurants and Institutions*, May 15, 2000, pp. 165–169; Brad Wall, "Evolution in the Forecasting Process at Krispy Kreme," *Journal of Business Forecasting*, Spring 2002, pp. 15–16; Tricia Bisoux, "The Sweet Taste of Success," *BizEd*, May/June 2003, pp. 16–20; Andy Serwer, "The Hole Story," *Fortune*, July 7, 2003, pp. 53–62; Charles Haddad, "Customer Service: Krispy Kreme," *Business Week*, November 24, 2003, p. 88; and interviews with Brad Wall, director of forecasting and planning at Krispy Kreme.

The importance of forecasting as a business tool has grown significantly in recent years, both in manufacturing and services. According to a 1998 survey conducted by the Institute of Business Forecasting, 77 percent of the firms replying said that they only began hiring full-time forecasting professionals during the previous 10 years. In fact, 62 percent indicated that they only began hiring full-time forecasting persons during the previous five years. For example, Levi Strauss has a full-time forecasting department of 30 people. Duracell, the battery manufacturer, has a staff of eight full-time forecasters.

Managers now use forecasting models at all levels in their organizations, as illustrated at FedEx in the OM in Practice box. From a strategic, long-range perspective, forecasting the demand for products provides management with the ability decide when to add capacity in the form of new manufacturing facilities; similarly, forecasting customer demand helps service managers decide where to locate retail service outlets for maximum sales.

For manufacturing firms, forecasting demand at the tactical or intermediate level is a major input into the managerial decision-making process. For example, intermediate forecasting plays an important role in determining what portion of the workforce should be permanent and what portion should be temporary workers. Accurate forecasting is also a critical element in supply-chain management and the determination of proper inventory levels, as illustrated in the opening vignette about Krispy Kreme.

Short-term forecasting is especially important in services, where customer demand is often unknown and capacity in the form of front-line workers must be available when and where customers require it.

However, although forecasting can provide managers with future information that will allow them to run their operations more effectively and efficiently, managers also must recognize that forecasts are not perfect. Inaccuracies in forecasting occur because there are too many factors in the business environment that cannot be predicted or controlled with certainty. Rather than search for the perfect forecast, it is far more important for managers to establish the practice of continually reviewing these forecasts and to learn to live with their inaccuracies. This is not to say that we should not try to improve the forecasting model or methodology, but that we should try to find and use the best forecasting method available, *within reason*. In this respect, it is important to note that the cost of obtaining small improvements in forecasting accuracy is very high after *reasonable* forecasts have been developed, as illustrated in Exhibit 9.1.

The goal of this chapter is to present an introduction to several different forecasting techniques and models (both qualitative and quantitative) that are commonly used in business, recognizing that additional and more sophisticated forecasting techniques and models are available to people seeking more in-depth knowledge in this area. We address primarily time series techniques and causal relationships, including a discussion of the sources of errors and their measurement.

Chaman L. Jain, "Explosion in the Forecasting Function in Corporate America," *The Journal of Business Forecasting* (Summer 1999), pp. 2, 28.

The Importance of Forecasting

The opening vignette illustrates why forecasting is an important aspect of operations. It often is on the basis of forecasts that planners order material and schedule employees. Poor forecasts can result in excess inventories or shortages of material. In the case of staffing, poor forecasting can result in an excess or shortage of available employees. In the case of perishable materials or items that become obsolete quickly, excess inventories can result in significant losses. Similarly, if the company has excess staff on duty it will be paying out unnecessary wages. On the other hand, shortages will result in poor customer service, with

Exhibit 9.1

Comparing the Costs and Benefits of Forecasting

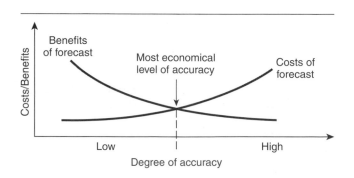

the possible loss of customers. Furthermore, the large amount of data being gathered electronically makes it possible to use more sophisticated techniques than in the past to arrive at accurate forecasts in a timely manner. Thus, companies are starting to pay a lot more attention to forecasting.

Types of Forecasting

Forecasting techniques can be classified into three broad categories: *qualitative, time-series analysis,* and *causal relationship forecasting.*

Qualitative techniques are subjective or judgmental in nature, and are based on estimates and opinions. Such techniques are used primarily when there are no data available. **Time-series analysis**, the main focus of this chapter, is based on the idea that data describing past demand can be used to predict future demand. In other words, the time-related trends that generated demand in the past will continue to generate demand in the future. **Causal relationship forecasting**, on the other hand, assumes that demand is related to some underlying factor or factors in the environment, and that cause-and-effect relationships are at work.

Time-series analysis typically is used in short-range situations, such as forecasting worker requirements for the next week. Causal relationship forecasting is usually used for longer-term issues, such as selecting a site for a retail operation. Exhibit 9.2 briefly describes some of the different varieties of the three basic types of forecasting models. In this chapter we present three of the time-series analysis methods listed in the exhibit and the first of the causal relationship forecasting techniques.

qualitative techniques

Nonquantitative forecasting techniques based upon expert opinions and intuition. Typically used when there are no data available.

time-series analysis

Analyzing data by time periods (for example, hours, days, weeks) to determine if trends or patterns occur.

causal relationship forecasting

Relating demand to an underlying factor other than time.

Exhibit 9.2

Forecasting Techniques and Common Models

I. Qualitative	*Subjective, judgmental. Based on intuition, estimates, and opinions.*
Delphi method	An interactive learning process involving a group of experts who respond to a questionnaire. A moderator compiles results and formulates a new questionnaire that is again submitted to the same group of experts.
Market research	Collects customer data in a variety of ways (surveys, interviews, etc.) to test hypotheses about the market. This information is typically used to forecast long-range and new-product sales.
Historical analogy	Ties what is being forecast to a similar product. Important in planning new products when a forecast may be derived by using the history of a similar existing product.
Panel consensus	A panel of experts arrives at a consensus value for the forecast.
Executive judgment	Relies on the intuition, experience, and knowledge of the manager to arrive at the forecast.
II. Time-Series Analysis	*Based upon the idea that the history of occurrences over time can be used to predict the future.*
Simple moving average and weighted moving average	The data points from several time periods are averaged by dividing the sum of the point values by the number of data points. These points may be weighted equally or unequally, as seen fit by experience.
Exponential smoothing	Recent data points are weighted more, with weighting declining exponentially as data become older.
Linear regression	Fits a straight line to past data generally relating the data values to time. Most common fitting technique is least squares.
Trend projections	Fits a mathematical trend line to the data points and projects it into the future.

III. Causal Relationships	*Tries to understand the system underlying and surrounding the item being forecast. For example, sales may be affected by advertising, quality, and competitors.*
Regression analysis	Similar to least squares method in time series but may contain multiple variables. Basis is that forecast is caused by the occurrence of other events or factors.
Input/output models	Focuses on sales of each industry to other firms and governments. Indicates the changes in sales that a producer industry might expect because of purchasing changes by another industry.
Leading indicators	Statistics that move in the same direction as the series being forecast but move before the series, such as an increase in the price of gasoline indicating a future drop in the sale of large cars.

Exhibit 9.3

Comparison of Forecasting Techniques

Technique	Time Horizon	Model Complexity	Data Requirements
I. Qualitative			
Delphi method	Long	High	High
II. Time Series			
Moving average	Short	Very low	Low
Exponential smoothing	Short	Low	Very low
Linear regression	Long	Medium high	High
III. Causal Relationships			
Regression analysis	Long	Fairly high	High

Exhibit 9.3 shows a comparison of the strengths and weaknesses of these different forecasting methods. The moving-average and exponential-smoothing methods tend to be the best and easiest techniques to use for short-term forecasting with little data required. The long-term models are more complex and require much more data. In general, the short-term models compensate for random variation and adjust for short-term changes (such as consumers' responses to a new product). Medium-term forecasts are useful for seasonal effects, and long-term models identify general trends and are especially useful in identifying major turning points. Which forecasting model or models a firm should adopt depends on several factors, including: (*a*) forecasting time horizon, (*b*) data availability, (*c*) accuracy required, (*d*) size of the forecasting budget, and (*e*) availability of qualified personnel.

Components of Demand

In most cases, the demand for products or services can be broken down into five components: (1) average demand for the period, (2) trends, (3) seasonal influence, (4) cyclical elements, and (5) random variation. Exhibit 9.4 illustrates a plot of demand over a four-year period, showing the trend, cyclical, and seasonal components, and randomness (or error) around the smoothed demand curve.

Cyclical factors are more difficult to determine since either the time span or the cause of the cycle may not be known. For example, cyclical influence on demand may come from such occurrences as political elections, war, economic conditions, or sociological pressures.

Random variations are caused by chance events. Statistically, when all the known causes for demand (average, trend, seasonal, and cyclical) are subtracted from the total

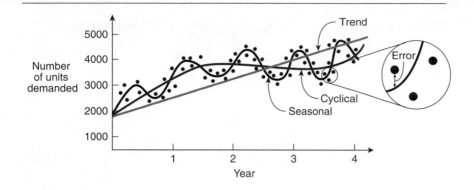

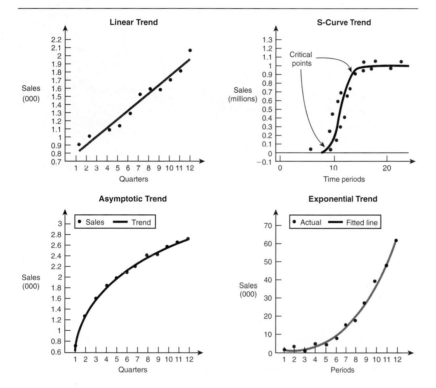

Exhibit 9.5

Common Types of Trends

demand, what remains is the unexplained portion of demand. If one is unable to identify the cause of this remainder, it is assumed to be purely random chance. This unexplained portion is often referred to as the error or *noise* in the forecast.

In addition to these five components there is often autocorrelation, which denotes the persistence of occurrence. More specifically, the demand expected at any point is highly correlated with its own past values. For example, if demand has been high during December for the past 10 years, then one would expect high demand during December in the coming year. When demand is random, the demand from one time period to another may vary widely. When high autocorrelation exists, the demand is not expected to change very much from one time period to the next.

Trend lines are the usual starting point in developing a forecast. These trend lines are then adjusted for seasonal effects, cyclical, and any other expected events that may influence the final forecast. Exhibit 9.5 shows four of the most common types of trends. A linear trend reflects a straight continuous relationship. An S-curve is typical of a product's

Operations Management in Practice

OUTSTANDING CUSTOMER SERVICE AT FEDEX STARTS WITH FORECASTING

FedEx is the world's largest express transportation company. To support its global transportation network, FedEx has established 51 customer service call centres throughout the world. The 16 call centres located in the United States handle about 500 000 calls a day. The service-level goal for all of its call centres is to answer 90 percent of all calls within 20 seconds or less. There are three major networks that are supported by these call centres: domestic, international, and freight.

For each network, FedEx has developed four types of forecasts, based on forecasting horizons. The strategic or long-range plan, which is revised and updated once a year, forecasts the number of incoming calls, the average handling time per call, staffing requirements, and the number of technology-handled calls (i.e., calls not requiring a customer service representative). The business plan addresses the same items as in the strategic plan but is revised on an as-needed basis, as decided by upper management. The tactical forecast provides a daily forecast of incoming calls and is done once a month. The lowest level of forecasting, the operational forecast, forecasts the number of incoming calls and average handling time in half-hour increments for each day of the week using historical data as shown. This forecast is done weekly.

How might forecasting help FedEx? The long-term forecasts ensure that FedEx has enough employees on its payroll to handle aggregate call volumes. For example, if call volumes

increase significantly due to business growth, unless employees are hired months in advance it would difficult for existing staff to meet the new volume. This could lead to a drop in

growth and maturity cycle. The critical points on the S-curve are where the trend makes a transition from slow growth to fast growth and from fast to slow. An asymptotic trend starts with the highest demand growth at the beginning, which then tapers off. Such a curve could happen when a firm enters an existing market with the objective of saturating and capturing a large share of the market. An exponential curve is common in products with explosive growth, as is often experienced with new high-technology products (See the OM in Practice Box on HP.). The exponential trend suggests that sales will continue to increase rapidly for some period of time—an assumption that is questionable for longer time periods.

Time-Series Analysis

Time-series forecasting models attempt to predict the future based on past data. For example, sales figures collected for each of the past six weeks can be used to forecast sales for the seventh week. Quarterly sales figures collected for the past several years can be used to forecast sales in future quarters.

We present here three types of time-series forecasting models: (1) simple moving average, (2) weighted moving average, and (3) exponential smoothing. To determine which model is most appropriate to use, the data should first be plotted on a graph. For example, if the data points appear to be relatively level, a moving average or exponential smoothing model would be appropriate; if the data points show an underlying trend, then

Historical Data for FedEx Call Centre

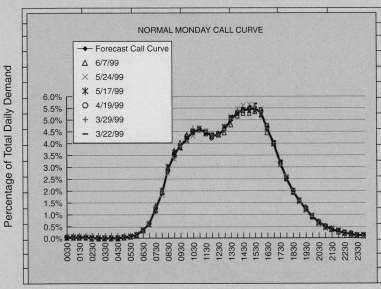

NORMAL MONDAY CALL CURVE

Percentage of Total Daily Demand

Legend:
- ◆ Forecast Call Curve
- △ 6/7/99
- ✕ 5/24/99
- ✳ 5/17/99
- ○ 4/19/99
- + 3/29/99
- − 3/22/99

Hour of the Day

service levels or to employee stress if they are overworked. The tactical and operational forecasts allow FedEx to prepare detailed schedules and plan for emergencies, allowing schedulers to decide how many part-time employees to schedule during each hour within a shift or to decide how to handle short sudden spikes in demand or employee illness effectively without affecting service levels. Thus forecasting helps FedEx maintain service levels while containing costs.

Source:

Weidong Xu, "Long Range Planning for Call Centers at FedEx," *The Journal of Business Forecasting* (Winter 1999–2000), pp. 6–11.

exponential smoothing with trend adjustment would be appropriate. In addition, the errors associated with each model should be calculated and the resulting errors compared.

Simple Moving Average

If the demand for a product is neither growing nor declining rapidly, and also does not have any seasonal characteristics, a **simple moving average** can be very useful in identifying a trend within the data fluctuations. For example, if we want to forecast sales in June with a five-month moving average, we can take the average of the sales in January, February, March, April, and May. When June passes, the forecast for July would be the average of February, March, April, May, and June. The formula for a simple moving average forecast is

simple moving average

Average over a given number of time periods that is updated by replacing the date in the oldest period with those in the most recent period.

$$F_t = \frac{A_{t-1} + A_{t-2} + \cdots + A_{t-n}}{n} \qquad (9.1)$$

where

F_t = Forecasted sales in period t
A_{t-1} = Actual sales in period $t - 1$
n = Number of periods in the average

Example

Solution

Suppose we want to forecast weekly demand for a product using both a three-week and a nine-week moving average, as shown in Exhibits 9.6 and 9.7. These forecasts are computed as follows:

To illustrate, the three-week forecast for week 4 is

$$\frac{1000 + 1400 + 800}{3} = 1067$$

and the nine-week forecast for week 10 is

$$\frac{1300 + 1500 + 1500 + \cdots + 800}{3} = 1367$$

Exhibit 9.6

Forecast Demand Based on a Three- and a Nine-Week Simple Moving Average

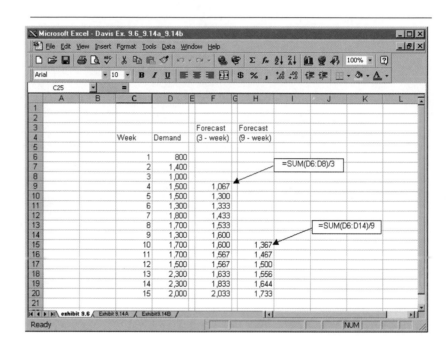

Exhibit 9.7

Moving Average Forecast of Three- and Nine-Week Periods versus Actual Demand

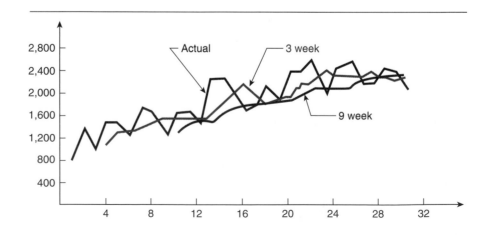

FORECASTING SALES AT TACO BELL REDUCES LABOUR COSTS

Labour is a major cost component at Taco Bell, a large fast-food chain specializing in Mexican food, averaging 30 percent of sales. Scheduling the proper number of workers for a given time period therefore is critical in the highly competitive fast-food industry. Too many workers results in excessive costs and reduced profits. Too few workers, on the other hand, results in lost sales and/or poor service. With the demand being highly variable throughout the day (52 percent of daily sales occur between 11:00 a.m. and 2:00 p.m.), Taco Bell needs to accurately forecast sales to schedule the proper number of workers.

After evaluating several forecasting techniques, Taco Bell adopted a six-week moving average. The number of customer transactions are recorded in 15-minute time intervals for each day of the week. For example, the forecasted number of customers to be served next Friday between 10:30 a.m. and 10:45 a.m. is the six-week average of the number of customers served in that same time period for the previous six Fridays.

This forecasting model is a major element in Taco Bell's labour-management system, which is estimated to have saved Taco Bell US$16.4 million in labour costs in 1996 (in comparison to the previously existing management system).

Source:
Jackie Hueter and William Swart, "An Integrated Labor-Management System for Taco Bell," *Interfaces* 28, no. 1 (January–February 1998), pp. 75–91.

As noted in the OM in Practice box above, it is important to select the proper number of periods to include in the moving average. In determining the right number of periods to use, management must take into consideration several conflicting effects. As noted in Exhibit 9.6, the larger the number of periods included in the average, the greater the random elements are "smoothed," which may be desirable in some cases. However, if a trend exists in the data—either increasing or decreasing—the resulting moving average has the adverse affect of constantly lagging this trend. Therefore, although a smaller number of periods in the moving average produces more oscillation, the resulting forecast will more closely follow the existing trend. Conversely, the inclusion of more periods in the moving average will give a smoother forecast but it will lag the trend by a greater amount.

Exhibit 9.7 graphs the data shown in Exhibit 9.6, illustrating how the number of periods used in the moving average can impact the forecast. Note that the growth trend appears to level off at about the 23rd week. The three-week moving average responds better in following this change than the nine-week, although overall, the nine-week average is smoother.

The main disadvantage in calculating a moving average is that all the individual elements used in the average must be carried as data since a new forecast period involves adding the newest data and dropping the oldest data. For a three- or six-period moving average, this is not too severe; but plotting a 60-day moving average of the daily demand for each of 20 000 items in inventory would involve a significant amount of data. At the same time, today's PCs are fast and efficient at doing multiproduct moving averages for a long time period. For example, using a 60-day moving average for 20 000 products would require 61 calculations per product ×20 000 products, or 1 220 000 calculations. With today's PCs these calculations would probably take one or two seconds, at most, to complete.

Weighted Moving Average

Whereas the simple moving average gives equal weight to each component of the moving-average database, a **weighted moving average** allows each element to be weighted by a factor, where the sum of all the weighting factors equals one. The formula for a weighted moving average forecast is

$$F_t = w_{t-1} - A_{t-1} + w_{t-2}A_{t-2} + \cdots + w_{t-n}A_{t-n} \tag{9.2}$$

weighted moving average

Simple moving average in which weights are assigned to each time period in the average. The sum of all of the weights must equal one.

where

F_t = Forecasted sales in period t

A_{t-1} = Actual sales in period $t - 1$

w_{t-1} = Weight assigned to period $t - 1$

n = Number of periods in the moving average

An additional constraint when using this equation for the weighted moving average forecast is

$$\sum_{i=1}^{n} w_{t-i} = 1$$

Example

A department store may find that in a four-month period the best forecast is derived by using 40 percent of the actual sales (in units) for the most recent month, 30 percent of two months ago, 20 percent of three months ago, and 10 percent of four months ago. The actual unit sales were as follows:

Month 1	Month 2	Month 3	Month 4	Month 5
100	90	105	95	?

Solution

The forecast for month 5 therefore would be

$F_5 = 0.40(95) + 0.30(105) + 0.20(90) + 0.10(100)$

$= 38.0 + 31.5 + 18.0 + 10.0$

$= 97.5$ units

Suppose sales for month 5 actually turned out to be 110; then the forecast for month 6 would be

$F_6 = 0.40(110) + 0.30(95) + 0.20(105) + 0.10(90)$

$= 44.0 + 28.5 + 21.0 + 9.0$

$= 102.5$ units

The weighted moving average has a definite advantage over the simple moving average because it can vary the effects between older data and more recent data. With the forecasting software now available, there is little computational difference between using a weighted moving average and a simple moving average. Both can be obtained in "real time." If there is a disadvantage to the weighted moving average, it is that someone must determine the weights to be used.

Exponential Smoothing

exponential smoothing

Time-series forecasting technique that does not require large amounts of historical data.

In the two forecasting methods just presented, a major issue is the need to continually carry a large amount of historical data. Nevertheless, in many applications (perhaps even in most), the most recent data points tend to be more indicative of the future compared to those in the distant past. If this premise is valid—that the importance of data diminishes as the past becomes more distant—then **exponential smoothing** may be the most logical and easiest method to use.

The reason it is called "exponential smoothing" is that each increment in the past is decreased by $(1 - \alpha)$, as shown below:

	Weighting at $\alpha = 0.20$
Most recent weighting $= \alpha(1 - \alpha)^0$	0.2000
Data 1 time period older $= \alpha(1 - \alpha)^1$	0.1600
Data 2 time periods older $= \alpha(1 - \alpha)^2$	0.1280
Data 3 time periods older $= \alpha(1 - \alpha)^3$	0.1024

Therefore, the exponents 0, 1, 2, 3 ... , and so on give this method its name.

Exponential smoothing is the most commonly used of all forecasting techniques. It is an integral part of virtually all computerized forecasting programs, and is widely used for ordering inventory in retail firms, wholesale companies, and other service operations.

Exponential smoothing accomplishes virtually everything that can be done with moving average forecasts, but requires significantly less data. The **exponential smoothing constant alpha (α)** is a value between 0 and 1. If the actual demand tends to be relatively stable over time, we would choose a relatively small value for α to decrease the effects of short-term or random fluctuations, which is similar to having a moving average that involves a large number of periods. If the actual demand tends to fluctuate rapidly, we would choose a relatively large value for α to keep up with these changes. This is similar to using a moving average with a small number of periods.

The major reasons that exponential smoothing techniques have become so well accepted are:

1. Exponential smoothing models are surprisingly accurate.
2. Formulating an exponential smoothing model is relatively easy.
3. The user can readily understand how the model works.
4. There is very little computation required to use the model.
5. Computer storage requirements are small because of the limited use of historical data.

In the exponential smoothing method, only three pieces of data are needed to forecast the future: the most recent forecast, the actual demand that occurred for that forecast period, and a smoothing constant alpha (α). As described above, this smoothing constant determines the level of smoothing and the speed of reaction to differences between forecasts and actual occurrences. The value for the constant is arbitrary and is determined by both the nature of the item being forecasted and the manager's sense of what constitutes a good response rate. However, error measuring techniques such as MAD (discussed later in this chapter) can be used to evaluate different values for α until that value is found that minimizes the historical error. For example, if a firm produced a standard item with relatively stable demand, the reaction rate to differences between actual and forecast demand would tend to be small, perhaps just a few percentage points. However, if the firm were experiencing growth, it would be desirable to have a higher reaction rate, to give greater importance to recent growth experience. The more rapid the growth, the higher the reaction rate should be. Sometimes users of the simple moving average switch to exponential smoothing but like to keep the forecasts about the same as the simple moving average. In this case, α is approximated by $2 \div (n + 1)$ where n was the number of time periods that were used in the moving average.

The equation for an exponential smoothing forecast is

$$F_t = F(1 - \alpha) F_{t-1} + \alpha A_{t-1}$$

or rewritten as

$$F_t - F_{t-1} + \alpha(A_{t-1} - F_{t-1}) \tag{9.3}$$

exponential smoothing constant alpha (α)

Value between 0 and 1 used in exponential smoothing to minimize the error between historical demand and respective forecasts.

where

F_t = Exponentially smoothed forecast for period t
F_{t-1} = Exponentially smoothed forecast made for the prior period
A_{t-1} = Actual demand in the prior period
α = Desired response rate, or smoothing constant

This equation states that the new forecast is equal to the old forecast plus a portion of the error (the difference between the previous forecast and what actually occurred).[1]

When exponential smoothing is first introduced, the initial forecast or starting point may be obtained by using a simple estimate or an average of preceding periods. If no historical forecast data are available, then the forecast for the previous period (that is, last month) is set equal to the demand for that period.

Example

To demonstrate how the exponential smoothing method works, assume that the long-run demand for a given product is relatively stable and a smoothing constant (α) of 0.05 is considered appropriate. If the exponential smoothing method were used as a continuing policy, a forecast would have been made for last month. Assume that last month's forecast (F_{t-1}) was 1050 units, and 1000 units were actually demanded (A_{t-1}).

Solution

The forecast for this month then would be calculated as follows:

$$F_t = F_{t-1} + \alpha(A_{t-1} - F_{t-1})$$
$$= 1050 + 0.05(1000 - 1050)$$
$$= 1050 + 0.05(-50)$$
$$= 1047.5 \text{ units}$$

Because the smoothing coefficient is relatively small, the reaction of the new forecast to an error of 50 units is to decrease the next month's forecast by only 2.5 units.

Example

Vinny da Silveira owns a small restaurant that is open seven days a week. Until just recently he forecasted the daily number of customers using his "gut feel." However, he wants to open another restaurant and recognizes the need to adopt a more formal method of forecasting that can be used in both locations. He decides to compare a three-week moving average and exponential smoothing with $\alpha = 0.7$ and $\alpha = 0.3$. The actual sales for the past three weeks are shown below, along with his forecast for last week.

Customers per Day							
Week	**Sun**	**Mon**	**Tue**	**Wed**	**Thu**	**Fri**	**Sat**
Actual:							
3 weeks ago	138	183	182	188	207	277	388
2 weeks ago	143	194	191	200	213	292	401
Last week	157	196	204	193	226	313	408
Forecast:							
Last week	155	191	192	198	204	286	396

---

[1]Some writers prefer to call F_t a smoothed average.

a. Forecast sales for each day of the next week using:
- A three-week moving average
- Exponential smoothing with $\alpha = 0.7$
- Exponential smoothing with $\alpha = 0.3$

b. The actual sales for the next week are as follows:

			Customers per Day				
Week	Sun	Mon	Tue	Wed	Thu	Fri	Sat
Actual:	160	204	197	210	215	300	421

Evaluate each of the three forecasting techniques based on the one week's data. Which technique would you recommend to Vinny?

Solution

a. The forecasts for each of the three methods are presented below.

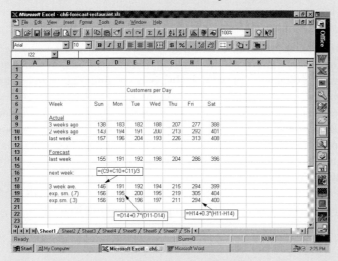

b. Using the average mean absolute deviation (MAD) as a criterion for measuring error, a comparison of the three forecasting methods is presented below:

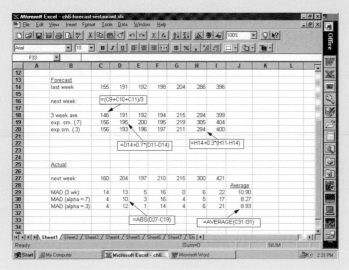

> Based upon this analysis, Vinny should use the exponential smoothing method with $\alpha = 0.7$, because that method has the lowest average MAD of 8.27. (MAD, which is a measure of how much the forecasted demand differs from the actual demand, is discussed in detail later in this chapter.)

As discussed above, exponential smoothing has the shortcoming of lagging changes in demand. Exhibit 9.8 shows actual data plotted as a smooth curve to show the lagging effects of the exponential forecasts. The forecast lags the actual demand during an increase or decrease, but overshoots actual demand when a change in the direction occurs. Note that the higher the value of alpha, the more closely the forecast follows the actual. To more closely track actual demand, a trend factor may be added. In addition, the value of alpha can be adjusted to improve the accuracy of the forecast. This is termed *adaptive forecasting*. Both trend effects and adaptive forecasting are briefly explained in the following sections.

Trend Effects in Exponential Smoothing

As stated earlier, an upward or downward trend in data collected over a sequence of time periods causes the exponential forecast to always lag behind (that is, to be above or below) the actual amount. Exponentially smoothed forecasts can be corrected somewhat by including a trend adjustment. To correct for the trend, we now need two smoothing constants. In addition to the smoothing constant α, the trend equation also requires a **trend smoothing constant (δ)**. Like alpha, delta is limited to values between 0 and 1. The delta reduces the impact of the error that occurs between the actual and the forecast. If both alpha and delta are not included, the trend would overreact to errors.

To initiate the trend equation, the trend value must be entered manually. This first trend value can be an educated guess or computed from past data.

trend smoothing constant delta (δ)

Value between 0 and 1 that is used in exponential smoothing when there is a trend.

Exhibit 9.8

Exponential Forecasts versus Actual Demands for Units of a Product over Time Showing the Forecast Lag

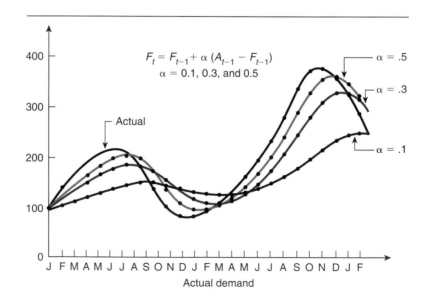

$$F_t = F_{t-1} + \alpha (A_{t-1} - F_{t-1})$$
$$\alpha = 0.1, 0.3, \text{ and } 0.5$$

Actual demand

The equation to compute the forecast including trend (FIT) is

$$\text{FIT}_t = F_t + T_t \tag{9.4}$$

where

$$F_t = \text{FIT}_{t-1} + \alpha(A_{t-1} - \text{FIT}_{t-1}) \tag{9.5}$$

$$T_t = T_{t-1} + \alpha\delta(A_{t-1} - \text{FIT}_{t-1}) \tag{9.6}$$

Example

Assume an initial starting point for F_t of 100 units, a trend of 10 units, an alpha of 0.20, and a delta of 0.30. If the actual demand turned out to be 115 rather than the forecast 100, calculate the forecast for the next period.

Solution

Adding the starting forecast and the trend, we have

$$\text{FIT}_{t-1} = F_{t-1} + T_{t-1} = 100 + 10 = 110$$

The actual A_{t-1} is given as 115. Therefore,

$$F_t = \text{FIT}_{t-1} + \alpha(A_{t-1} - \text{FIT}_{t-1})$$

$$= 110 + 0.2(115 - 110) = 111.0$$

$$T_t = T_{t-1} + \alpha\delta(A_{t-1} - \text{FIT}_{t-1})$$

$$= 10 + (0.2)(0.3)(115 - 110) = 10.3$$

$$\text{FIT}_t = F_t + T_t = 111.0 + 10.3 = 121.3$$

If, instead of 121.3, the actual turned out to be 120, the sequence would be repeated and the forecast for the next period would be

$$F_{t+1} = 121.3 + 0.2(120 - 121.3) = 121.04$$

$$T_{t+1} = 10.3 + (0.2)(0.3)(120 - 121.3) = 10.22$$

$$\text{FIT}_{t+1} = 121.04 + 10.22 = 131.26$$

Determining Alpha (α) with Adaptive Forecasting

A key factor in accurate forecasting with exponential smoothing is the selection of the proper value of alpha (α). As stated previously, the value of alpha can vary between 0 and 1. If the actual demand appears to be relatively stable over time, then we would select a relatively small value for alpha, that is, a value closer to zero. On the other hand, if the actual demand tends to fluctuate rapidly, as in the case of a new product that is experiencing tremendous growth, then we would select a relatively large value of alpha that is nearer one.

Regardless of the initial value selected, α will have to be adjusted periodically to ensure that it is providing accurate forecasts. This is often referred to as *adaptive forecasting*. There are two approaches to adjusting the value of alpha. One uses various values of alpha; the other uses a tracking signal (discussed later in the chapter).

1. *Two or more predetermined values of alpha.* The amount of error between the forecast and the actual demand is measured. Depending on the degree of error, different values of alpha are used. For example, if the error is large, alpha is 0.8; if the error is small, alpha is 0.2.

2. *Computed values of alpha.* A tracking signal computes whether the forecast is keeping pace with genuine upward or downward changes in demand (as opposed to random changes). The tracking signal is defined here as the exponentially smoothed actual error divided by the exponentially smoothed absolute error. Alpha is set equal to this tracking signal and therefore changes from period to period within the possible range of 0 to 1.

In logic, computing alpha seems simple. In practice, however, it is quite prone to error. There are three exponential equations: one for the single exponentially smoothed forecast as done in the previous section of this chapter, one to compute an exponentially smoothed actual error, and the third to compute the exponentially smoothed absolute error. Thus, the user must keep three equations running in sequence for each period. Furthermore, assumptions must be made during the initial time periods until the technique has had a chance to start computing values. For example, alpha must be given a value for the first two periods until actual data are available. Also, the user must select a second smoothing constant, in addition to alpha, that is used in the actual and absolute error equations. Clearly, those who use adaptive forecasting on a regular basis rely on technology for the calculations.

Forecasting Errors in Time-Series Analysis

When we use the word *error*, we are referring to the difference between the forecast value and what actually occurred. So long as the forecast value is within the confidence limits, as we discuss below in "Measurement of Error," this is not really an error. However, common usage refers to the difference as an error.

Demand is generated through the interaction of a number of factors that are either too complex to describe accurately in a model or are not readily identifiable. Therefore, all forecasts contain some degree of error. In discussing forecast errors, it is important to distinguish between *sources of error* and the *measurement of error.*

Sources of Error

Errors can come from a variety of sources. One common error many forecasters are unaware of is caused by the projection of past trends into the future. For example, when we talk about statistical errors in regression analysis, we are referring to the deviations of observations from our regression line. It is common practice to attach a confidence band to the regression line to reduce the unexplained error. However, when we subsequently use this regression line as a forecasting device by projecting it into the future, the error may not be correctly defined by the projected confidence band. This is because the confidence interval is based on past data; consequently it may or may not be valid for projected data points and therefore cannot be used with the same confidence. In fact, experience has shown that the actual errors tend to be greater than those predicted by forecasting models.

Errors can be classified as either bias or random. *Bias errors* occur when a consistent mistake is made; that is, the forecast is always too high or always too low. Sources of bias include (*a*) failing to include the right variables, (*b*) using the wrong relationships among variables, (*c*) employing the wrong trend line, (*d*) mistakenly shifting the seasonal demand from where it normally occurs, and (*e*) the existence of some undetected trend. *Random errors* can be defined simply as those that cannot be explained by the forecast model being used. These random errors are often referred to as "noise" in the model.

Operations Management in Practice

FORECASTING FOR SHORT-LIVED PRODUCTS AT HEWLETT PACKARD

Traditional forecasting methods assume that product life cycles are long, at least a few years. For Hewlett Packard (HP) in North America, this long-life assumption is no longer valid. Many HP products have life cycles of between 9 to 18 months, a short life cycle. To complicate matters further, these products have high uncertainty in demand and a steep obsolescence curve. HP found that traditional forecasting methods were ill-suited to these products. So the company's Strategic Planning and Modelling Group (SPaM) developed a Product Life Cycle (PLC) forecasting method specifically for these types of products.

SPaM recognized that the usual short life cycle product demonstrated the following characteristics: well-defined life cycle phases from introduction to maturity and then to end of life, a high demand spike during the introduction phase followed by a gradual downward levelling off during maturity, and finally, a steep end-of-life drop-off often caused by planned product rollovers. These characteristics formed the basis of the forecasting method (historical data from similar products served as a good starting point). To these were added templates for seasonality, price drops, and special promotions. The method was developed with the involvement of forecasters and included development of a good user interface, ensuring that it was actually used. It is estimated that the increased forecast accuracy saves HP U.S.$15 million or so annually.

Source:
Jim Burruss and Dorothea Kuettner, "Forecasting for Short Lived Products: Hewlett Packard's Journey," *Journal of Business Forecasting* (Winter 2002–2003), pp. 9–14.

Measurement of Error

Several of the common terms used to describe the degree of error associated with forecasting are *standard error, mean squared error* (or *variance*), and *mean absolute deviation.* In addition, *tracking signals* may be used to indicate the existence of any positive or negative bias in the forecast.

Standard error is discussed in the section on linear regression later in the chapter. Since the standard error is the square root of a function, it is often more convenient to use the function itself. This is called the *mean square error*, or variance.

The **mean absolute deviation (MAD)** was at one time very popular, but subsequently was ignored in favour of the standard deviation and standard error measures. In recent years, however, MAD has made a comeback because of its simplicity and usefulness in obtaining tracking signals. MAD is the average error in the forecasts, using absolute values. It is valuable because MAD, like the standard deviation, measures the dispersion (or variation) of observed values around some expected value.

mean absolute deviation (MAD)

Average forecasting error based upon the absolute difference between the actual and forecast demands.

MAD is computed using the differences between the actual demand and the forecast demand without regard to whether it is negative or positive. It therefore is equal to the sum of the absolute deviations divided by the number of data points, or, stated in equation form:

$$\text{MAD} = \frac{\sum_{t=1}^{N} |A_t - F_t|}{n} \qquad (9.7)$$

where

t = Period number

A_t = Actual demand for period t

F_t = Forecast demand for period t

n = Total number of periods

$||$ = A symbol used to indicate the absolute value of a number, thus disregarding positive and negative signs

Exhibit 9.9

A Normal Distribution with a Mean = 0 and a MAD = 1

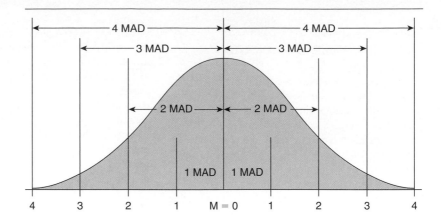

When the errors that occur in the forecast are normally distributed (which is usually assumed to be the case), the mean absolute deviation relates to the standard deviation as

$$1 \text{ standard deviation} = \sqrt{\frac{\pi}{2}} \times \text{MAD, or approximately 1.25 MAD}$$

Conversely,

$$1 \text{ MAD} \approx 0.8 \text{ standard deviation}$$

The standard deviation is the larger measure. If the MAD for a set of points was found to be 60 units, then the standard deviation would be 75 units. And, in the usual statistical manner, if control limits were set at ±3 standard deviations (or ±3.75 MADs), then 99.7 percent of the points would fall within these limits. (See Exhibit 9.9.)

tracking signal

Measure of error to determine if the forecast is staying within specified limits of the actual demand.

A **tracking signal** is a measurement that indicates whether the forecast average is keeping pace with any genuine upward or downward changes in demand. As used in forecasting, the tracking signal is the *number* of mean absolute deviations that the forecast value is above or below the actual occurrence. Exhibit 9.9 shows a normal distribution with a mean of zero and a MAD equal to one. Thus, if we compute a tracking signal and find it equal to −2, we can conclude that the forecast model is providing forecasts that are quite a bit above the mean of the actual occurrences.

A tracking signal can be calculated using the arithmetic sum of forecast deviations divided by the mean absolute deviation, or

$$TS = \frac{RSFE}{MAD} \tag{9.8}$$

where

RSFE = Running sum of forecast errors

MAD = Mean absolute deviation

It is important to note that although the MAD, being an absolute value, is always positive, the tracking signal can take on positive and negative values.

Exhibit 9.10 illustrates the procedure for computing MAD and the tracking signal for a six-month period where the forecast had been set at a constant 1000 and the actual demands that occurred are as shown. In this example, the forecast, on the average, was off by 66.7 units and the tracking signal was equal to 3.3 mean absolute deviations.

Exhibit 9.10

| | Demand | | | | | Sum of | | $TS = \dfrac{RSFE}{MAD}$ |
Month	Forecast	Actual	Deviation	RSFE	Abs Dev	Abs Dev	MAD*	
1	1000	950	−50	−50	50	50	50	−1.00
2	1000	1070	+70	+20	70	120	60	0.33
3	1000	1100	+100	+120	100	220	73.3	1.64
4	1000	960	−40	+80	40	260	65	1.23
5	1000	1090	+90	+170	90	350	70	2.43
6	1000	1050	+50	+220	50	400	66.7	3.31

Computing MAD, RSFE, and the Tracking Signal from Forecast and Actual Data

*Mean absolute deviation (MAD). For Month 6, MAD = 400 ÷ 6 = 66.7.

†Tracking signal $= \dfrac{RSFE}{MAD}$. For Month 6, $TS = \dfrac{RSFE}{MAD} = \dfrac{220}{66.7} = 3.3 \, MADs$.

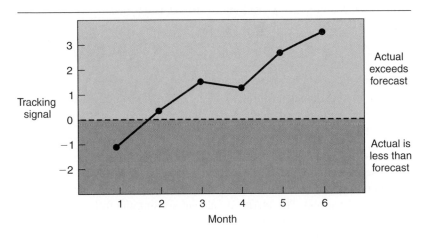

Exhibit 9.11

A Plot of the Tracking Signals Calculated in Exhibit 9.10.

We can obtain a better interpretation of the MAD and tracking signal by plotting the points on a graph. Although not completely legitimate from a sample size standpoint, we plotted each month in Exhibit 9.11 to show the drifting of the tracking signal. Note that it drifted from −1 MAD to +3.3 MADs. This occurred because the actual demand was greater than the forecast in four of the six periods. If the actual demand doesn't fall below the forecast to offset the continual positive RSFE, the tracking signal will continue to rise and we would conclude that the assumption that demand is 1000 is a bad forecast. When the tracking signal exceeds a pre-established limit (for example, ±2.0 or ±3.0), the manager should consider changing the forecast model or the value of α.

Acceptable limits for the tracking signal depend on the size of the demand being forecast (high-volume or high-revenue items should be monitored frequently) and the amount of personnel time available (narrower acceptable limits cause more forecasts to be out of limits and therefore require more time to investigate). Exhibit 9.12 shows the area within the control limits for a range of zero to four MADs.

In a perfect forecasting model, the sum of the actual forecast errors would be zero; that is, the errors that result in overestimates would offset the errors that are underestimates. The tracking signal then also would be zero, indicating an unbiased model that neither leads nor lags the actual demands.

Exhibit 9.12

The Percentages of Points Included within the Control Limits for a Range of 0 to 4 MADs

	Control Limits		Percentage of Points Lying within Control Limits
Number of MADS		Related Number of Standard Deviations	
= 1		0.798	57.048
= 2		1.596	88.946
= 3		2.394	98.334
= 4		3.192	99.856

Often, MAD is used to forecast errors. It might then be desirable to make the MAD more sensitive to recent data. A useful technique to do this is to compute an exponentially smoothed MAD (often identified as MAD_t) to forecast the next period's error range. The procedure is similar to single exponential smoothing, presented earlier in this chapter. The value of the MAD_t forecast is to provide a range of errors; in the case of inventory control, this is useful in establishing safety stock levels. MAD_t is defined as

$$MAD_t = (1 - \alpha)\,MAD_{t-1} + \alpha\,|A_{t-1} - F_{t-1}| \tag{9.9}$$

where

MAD_t = Forecast MAD for the tth period
α = Smoothing constant (normally in the range of 0.05 to 0.20)
A_{t-1} = Actual demand in the period $t - 1$
F_{t-1} = Forecast demand for period $t - 1$

There are occasions when it is more desirable to assess the accuracy of the forecast model in relative terms rather than in absolute terms, as presented above. When this occurs, we use the **mean absolute percentage error (MAPE)** to determine the forecasting errors as a percentage of the actual. The MAPE is calculated using the following formula:

mean absolute percentage error (MAPE)

The average absolute difference between the actual and forecast demands expressed as a percentage of the actual demand.

$$MAPE = \frac{\sum_{t=1}^{n} \dfrac{|A_t - F_t|}{F_t}}{n} \times 100 \tag{9.10}$$

where

A_t = Actual demand
F_t = Forecasted demand
n = Number of periods in the forecast

Example

Using the data presented in Exhibit 9.10, we calculate the MAPE as follows:

Period	Forecast Demand (F_t)	Actual Demand (A_t)	Deviation ($A_t - F_t$)	Absolute Deviation $|A_t - F_t|$
1	1000	950	−50	50
2	1000	1070	+70	70
3	1000	1100	+100	100
4	1000	960	−40	40
5	1000	1090	+90	90
6	1000	1050	+50	50

$$\text{MAPE} = \frac{\sum_{t=1}^{n} \frac{|A_t - F_t|}{F_t}}{n} \times 100$$

$$\text{MAPE} = \frac{\frac{50}{950} + \frac{70}{1070} + \frac{100}{1100} + \frac{40}{960} + \frac{90}{1090} + \frac{50}{1050}}{6} \times 100$$

$$\text{MAPE} = \frac{0.053 + 0.065 + 0.091 + 0.042 + 0.082 + 0.048}{6} \times 100$$

$$\text{MAPE} = \frac{0.381}{6} \times 100 = 6.4\%$$

Linear Regression Analysis

As with previous techniques, regression analysis for forecasting uses historical demand data to predict future demand. It is different from the other techniques in that the functional relationship used to predict future demand (called the dependent variable) is based on minimizing the sum of squared distances between the functional relationship line and the historical demand values. Thus the historical demand values (called the independent variables) are used to determine the functional relationship line. When the functional relationship line is linear, the method is called linear regression. (This technique is discussed further in the OLC.)

linear regression analysis

Type of forecasting technique that assumes that the relationship between the dependent and independent variables is a straight line.

Causal Relationship Forecasting

The techniques discussed so far use historical demand data to forecast future demand. For example, we may use historical demand for new homes to predict future demand for new homes. In causal relationship forecasting, we use historical data from one or more influential factors (independent variables) to predict the future values for demand (dependent variable). For example, since demand for new homes may depend on interest rates, we say that interest rates have a causal or influential effect on the building of new homes. Using the historical relationship between interest rates and new home building, we can try to predict demand for new homes given current interest rates. (These techniques are discussed in the OLC.)

Neural Networks

Neural networks represent a relatively new and growing area of forecasting. Unlike the more common statistical forecasting techniques such as time-series analysis and regression analysis, neural networks simulate human learning. Thus, over time and with repeated use, neural networks can develop an understanding of the complex relationships that exist between inputs into a forecasting model and the outputs. For example, in a service operation these inputs might include such factors as historic sales, weather, time of day, day of week, and month. The output would be the number of customers that are expected to arrive on a given day and in a given time period. In addition, neural networks perform computations much faster than traditional forecasting techniques. For example, the Southern Company, a utility company that provides electricity throughout the south, currently uses neural networks to forecast short-term power requirements a week to

neural networks

A forecasting technique simulating human learning that develops complex relationships between model inputs and outputs.

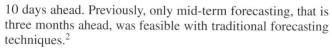

10 days ahead. Previously, only mid-term forecasting, that is three months ahead, was feasible with traditional forecasting techniques.[2]

The Application of Forecasting in Service Operations

Service managers are recognizing the important contribution forecasting can make in improving both the efficiency and the level of service in a service operation. Point-of-sale (POS) equipment can now provide the service manager with historical sales data in time increments as small as 15 minutes. The availability of these data permits accurate forecasting of future sales in similar time increments, thereby permitting the service manager to schedule workers more efficiently. Davis and Berger[3] point out that, in addition to forecasting sales, such models also can forecast product usage, which reduces the spoilage of perishable items that have a short shelf life.

A meteorologist analyzes computer weather patterns to improve the accuracy of forecasting the weather.

Forecasting is also an integral part of *yield management* (also known as revenue management), discussed in more detail in a later chapter. In brief, yield management attempts to maximize the revenues of those service operations that have high fixed costs and small variable costs. Examples of such service businesses include airlines, car rental agencies, and hotels. The goal of yield management is to maximize capacity utilization, even if it means offering large price discounts, when necessary, to fill available capacity. At the same time, the manager does not want to turn away a full-paying customer because the capacity had been previously sold to a discount customer. To accomplish this successfully, the manager must be able to forecast demand patterns for different market segments.

Forecasting Software Programs

There are many forecasting software programs now available. Some of these programs exist as library routines within a mainframe computer system; some may be incorporated or "bundled" as part of a larger program package. Still other programs can be purchased separately from software companies specializing in this area. Many of these programs are also available for PCs.

No longer does one have to be an expert in statistical forecasting techniques to use these programs; most are easy to understand and user friendly. In fact, anyone with working knowledge of an electronic spreadsheet such as Lotus 1-2-3®, Quattro Pro®, or Excel® can create a forecast on a PC.

A wealth of information concerning forecasting is available on the Internet. This includes reviews of different forecasting programs. Because this is a fast-changing area, you should conduct your own search on the Internet to obtain the latest information on forecasting programs. A recent survey on forecasting can be found in *ORMS Today*.[4]

[2]Karl Moore, Robert Burbach, and Roger Heeler, "Using Neural Networks to Analyze Qualitative Data," *Marketing Research* 7 (January 1, 1995), p. 34.
[3]Mark M. Davis and Paul D. Berger, "Sales Forecasting in a Retail Service Environment," *The Journal of Business Forecasting* (Winter 1989), pp. 8–17.
[4] Jack Yurkiewicz, "Forecasting Software Survey," *ORMS Today* (February 2003), pp. 44–51, www.orms-today.com.

Conclusion

Forecasting is fundamental to any operational planning effort. In the short run, a forecast is needed to predict the requirements for materials, products, services, or other resources to respond to changes in demand. Forecasts permit adjusting worker schedules and varying labour and materials. In the long run, forecasting is required as a basis for strategic changes, such as developing new markets, developing new products or services, and expanding or creating new facilities.

For long-term forecasts that lead to heavy financial commitments, great care should be taken to derive an accurate forecast. Several approaches should be used. Causal methods such as regression analysis or multiple regression analysis are beneficial because they provide a basis for discussion. Economic factors, product trends, growth factors, and competition, as well as a myriad of other possible variables, need to be considered and the forecast adjusted to reflect the influence of each.

Short- and intermediate-term forecasting, such as is required for inventory control and labour and material scheduling, may be satisfied with simpler models, such as exponential smoothing, perhaps with an adaptive feature or a seasonal index. In these applications, thousands of items are usually being forecast. The forecasting routine therefore should be simple and run quickly on a computer. The routines should also detect and rapidly respond to identifiable short-term changes in demand while at the same time ignoring occasional spurious demands. Exponential smoothing, when monitored by management to adjust the value of alpha, is also an effective technique.

A Chinese fortune cookie once stated that "Forecasting is difficult, especially about the future." A perfect forecast is like a hole-in-one in golf: great to get, but we should be satisfied just to get close to the cup—or, to push the metaphor, just to land on the green. The ideal philosophy for managers is to create the best forecast possible and then have sufficient flexibility in the system to adjust for the inevitable forecasting errors. Managers must recognize the trade-offs that exist in developing forecasting models: The greater the accuracy required, the more expensive the model. At some point, the cost of improved accuracy cannot be justified economically.

Key Terms

causal relationship forecasting p. 331

exponential smoothing p. 338

exponential smoothing constant alpha (α) p. 339

linear regression analysis p. 349

mean absolute deviation (MAD) p. 345

mean absolute percentage error (MAPE) p. 348

neural networks p. 349

qualitative techniques p. 331

simple moving average p. 335

time-series analysis p. 331

tracking signal p. 346

trend smoothing constant delta (δ) p. 342

weighted moving average p. 337

Key Formulas

Simple Moving Average Forecast

$$F_t = \frac{A_{t-1} + A_{t-2} + \cdots + A_{t-n}}{n} \tag{9.1}$$

Weighted Moving Average Forecast

$$F_t = w_{t-1}A_{t-1} + w_{t-2}A_{t-2} + \cdots + w_{t-n}A_{t-n} \tag{9.2}$$

and

$$\sum_{t=1}^{n} w_{t-i} = 1$$

Exponential Smoothing

$$F_t = F_{t-1} + \alpha(A_{t-1} - F_{t-1}) \tag{9.3}$$

Exponential Smoothing with Trend Effects

$$\text{FIT}_t = F_t + T_t \tag{9.4}$$

$$F_t = \text{FIT}_{t-1} + \alpha(A_{t-1} - \text{FIT}_{t-1}) \tag{9.5}$$

$$T_t = T_{t-1} + \alpha\delta(A_{t-1} - \text{FIT}_{t-1}) \tag{9.6}$$

Mean Absolute Deviation (MAD)

$$\text{MAD} = \frac{\sum_{t=1}^{n}|A_t - F_t|}{n} \tag{9.7}$$

Tracking Signal

$$\text{TS} = \frac{\text{RSFE}}{\text{MAD}} \tag{9.8}$$

Exponentially Smoothed MAD

$$\text{MAD}_t = (1 - \alpha)\text{MAD}_{t-1} + \alpha|A_{t-1} - F_{t-1}| \tag{9.9}$$

Mean Absolute Percentage Error (MAPE)

$$\text{MAPE} = \frac{\sum_{t=1}^{n}\frac{|A_t - F_t|}{F_t}}{n} \times 100 \tag{9.10}$$

Review and Discussion Questions

1. Examine Exhibit 9.3 and suggest which forecasting technique you might use for (*a*) bathing suits, (*b*) demand for new houses, (*c*) electrical power usage, (*d*) new plant expansion plans.

2. In terms of the errors, why would the operations manager wish to use the least squares method when doing simple linear regression?

3. All forecasting methods using exponential smoothing, adaptive smoothing, and exponential smoothing including trend require starting values to initialize the equations. How would you select the starting value for, say, F_{t-1}?

4. From the choice of simple moving average, weighted moving average, exponential smoothing, and simple regression analysis, which forecasting technique would you consider the most accurate? Why?

5. What is the main disadvantage of daily forecasting using regression analysis?

6. What are the main problems with using adaptive exponential smoothing in forecasting?

7. What is the purpose of a tracking signal?

8. What are the main differences between traditional forecasting techniques and neural networks?

9. Discuss the basic differences between the mean absolute deviation (MAD) and the standard error of the estimate.

10. What implications does the existence of forecast errors have for the search for ultrasophisticated statistical forecasting models such as neural networks?

Internet Exercise

The Wharton School at the University of Pennsylvania has a Web site devoted to forecasting at www-marketing.wharton.upenn.edu/forecast/welcome.html. Visit this Web site and select a firm that provides business forecasting software. Visit that firm's Web site and perform the following:

● Describe the company.

● Select one of its forecasting software products and describe it in detail, including costs.

● Identify specific applications for which this program would be most suitable.

Problem 1

Sunrise Baking Company markets doughnuts through a chain of food stores and has been experiencing over- and underproduction because of forecasting errors. The following data are their daily demands in dozens of doughnuts for the past four weeks. The bakery is closed Saturday, so Friday's production must satisfy demand for both Saturday and Sunday.

	4 Weeks Ago	3 Weeks Ago	2 Weeks Ago	Last Week
Monday	2200	2400	2300	2400
Tuesday	2000	2100	2200	2200
Wednesday	2300	2400	2300	2500
Thursday	1800	1900	1800	2000
Friday	1900	1800	2100	2000
Saturday } Sunday	2800	2700	3000	2900

Make a forecast for this week on the following basis:

a. Daily, using a simple four-week moving average.

b. Daily, using a weighted average of 0.40 for last week, 0.30 for two weeks ago, 0.20 for three weeks ago, and 0.10 for four weeks ago.

c. Sunrise is also planning its purchases of ingredients for bread production. If bread demand had been forecast for last week at 22 000 loaves and only 21 000 loaves were actually demanded, what would Sunrise's forecast be for this week using exponential smoothing with $\alpha = 0.10$?

d. Supposing, with the forecast made in (*c*), this week's demand actually turns out to be 22 500. What would the new forecast be for the next week?

Solution

a. Simple moving average, 4 weeks.

Monday $\qquad \dfrac{2400 + 2300 + 2400 + 2200}{4} = \dfrac{9300}{4} = 2325$ doz.

Tuesday $\qquad = \dfrac{8500}{4} = 2125$ doz.

Wednesday $\qquad = \dfrac{9500}{4} = 2375$ doz.

Thursday $\qquad = \dfrac{7500}{4} = 1875$ doz.

Friday $\qquad = \dfrac{7800}{4} = 1950$ doz.

Saturday and Sunday $\qquad = \dfrac{11\,400}{4} = 2850$ doz.

b. Weighted average with weights of 0.40, 0.30, 0.20, and 0.10.

	(0.40)		(0.30)		(0.20)		(0.10)		
Monday	960	+	690	+	480	+	220	=	2 350
Tuesday	880	+	660	+	420	+	200	=	2 160
Wednesday	1 000	+	690	+	480	+	230	=	2 400
Thursday	800	+	540	+	380	+	180	=	1 900
Friday	800	+	630	+	360	+	190	=	1 980
Saturday and Sunday	1 160	+	900	+	540	+	280	=	2 880
	5 600		4 110		2 660		1 300		13 670

c. $F_t = F_{t-1} + \alpha(A_{t-1} - F_{t-1})$

$\qquad = 22\,000 + 0.10(21\,000 - 22\,000)$

$\qquad = 22\,000 - 100$

$\qquad = 21\,900$ loaves

d. $F_{t+1} = 21\,900 + \alpha(22\,500 - 21\,900)$

$\qquad = 21\,900 + 0.10(600)$

$\qquad = 21\,960$ loaves

Problem 2

A specific forecasting model was used to forecast demands for a product. The forecasts and the corresponding demands that subsequently occurred are shown below.

Month	Actual	Forecast
October	700	660
November	760	840
December	780	750
January	790	835
February	850	910
March	950	890

Use the MAD and tracking signal technique to evaluate the forecasting model.

Solution

Evaluate the forecasting model using MAD, MAPE, and tracking signal.

Month	Actual Demand	Forecast Demand	Actual Deviation	Cumulative Deviation (RSFE)	Absolute Deviation
October	700	660	40	40	40
November	760	840	−80	−40	80
December	780	750	30	−10	30
January	790	835	−45	−55	45
February	850	910	−60	−115	60
March	950	890	60	−55	60
				Total dev. =	315

$$MAD = \frac{315}{6} = 52.5$$

$$MAPE = \frac{\dfrac{40}{700} + \dfrac{80}{760} + \dfrac{30}{780} + \dfrac{45}{790} + \dfrac{60}{850} + \dfrac{60}{950}}{6} \times 100$$

$$MAPE = \frac{0.058 + 0.105 + 0.038 + 0.057 + 0.070 + 0.063}{6} \times 100$$

$$MAPE = \frac{0.39}{6} \times 100 = 6.5\%$$

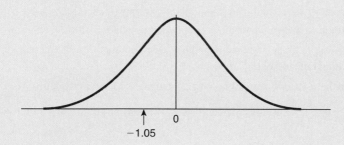

$$\text{Tracking signal} = \frac{-55}{52.5} = -1.05$$

Forecast model is well within the distribution.

Problems

1. Demand for stereo headphones and CD players for joggers has caused Nina Industries to experience a growth of almost 50 percent over the past year. The number of joggers is continuing to expand, so Nina expects demand for headsets to also expand.

   Demands for the stereo units for last year were as follows:

Month	Demand (units)	Month	Demand (units)
January	4200	July	5300
February	4300	August	4900
March	4000	September	5400
April	4400	October	5700
May	5000	November	6300
June	4700	December	6000

   a. Using least squares regression analysis, what would you estimate demand to be for each month next year? Follow the general format in the OLC.

   b. To be reasonably confident of meeting demand, Nina decides to use three standard errors of estimate for safety. How many additional units should be held to meet this level of confidence?

2. The historical demand for the number of employees required in a facility is:

Month	Demand
January	12
February	11
March	15
April	12
May	16
June	15

    a. Using a weighted moving average with weights of 0.60 for June, 0.30 for May, and 0.10 for April, find the July forecast for number of employees.

    b. Using a simple three-month moving average, find the July forecast.

    c. Using single exponential smoothing with $\alpha = 0.2$ and a June forecast = 13, find the July forecast. Make whatever assumptions you wish. List these assumptions.

    d. Using simple linear regression analysis, calculate the regression equation for the preceding demand data.

    e. Using the regression equation in (*d*), calculate the forecast for July.

3. The following tabulations are actual sales of units for six months and a starting forecast in January.

	Actual	Forecast
January	100	80
February	94	
March	106	
April	80	
May	68	
June	94	

    a. Calculate the forecast for the remaining five months using simple exponential smoothing with alpha = 0.2.

    b. Calculate the MAD for the forecasts.

    c. Calculate the MAPE for the forecasts.

4. Sales data for two years are given below. The data are aggregated with two months of sales in each period.

Period	Sales	Period	Sales
January–February	109	January–February	115
March–April	104	March–April	112
May–June	150	May–June	159
July–August	170	July–August	182
September–October	120	September–October	126
November–December	100	November–December	106

    a. Plot the data on a graph.

    b. Fit a simple linear regression model to the sales data.

    c. Using the results from part (*b*), prepare bimonthly forecasts for the next year.

5. The tracking signals that were computed using the past demand history for three different products are shown below. Each product used the same forecasting technique.

	TS 1	TS 2	TS 3
1	−2.70	1.54	0.10
2	−2.32	−0.64	0.43
3	−1.70	2.05	1.08
4	−1.1	2.58	1.74
5	−0.87	−0.95	1.94
6	−0.05	−1.23	2.24
7	0.10	0.75	2.96
8	0.40	−1.59	3.02
9	1.50	0.47	3.54
10	2.20	2.74	3.75

Discuss the tracking signals for each product and what the implications are.

6. Prepare a forecast, using simple linear regression, for each quarter of the next year from the following past two years' quarterly sales information.

Quarter	Sales
1	160
2	195
3	150
4	140
5	215
6	240
7	205
8	190

7. Kitchener fast food manager Kiri Yuthevong would like to determine the number of employees to schedule on May 30. The number of customers who were served every hour in the previous four weeks (on the same day of the week) is shown below. Each employee can serve 10 customers each hour. Assume the employees can work as little as an hour on May 30. The restaurant is open from 8 a.m. to 8 p.m.

Hour	May 1	May 8	May 15	May 23	Hour	May 1	May 8	May 15	May 23
8:00–9:00 a.m.	70	90	60	110	2:00–3:00 p.m.	110	100	90	80
9:00–10:00 a.m.	50	60	50	40	3:00–4:00 p.m.	60	60	40	50
10:00–11:00 a.m.	40	30	20	20	4:00–5:00 p.m.	40	30	40	30
11:00–Noon	60	80	70	100	5:00–6:00 p.m.	60	70	90	80
Noon–1:00 p.m.	120	150	130	130	6:00–7:00 p.m.	130	150	150	140
1:00–2:00 p.m.	140	160	180	170	7:00–8:00 p.m.	80	90	70	60

a. Using a simple moving average, forecast the employee requirements for each hour on May 30.

b. Using a weighted moving average, forecast the employee requirements for each hour on May 30. Assume a weight of 0.1 for May 1, 0.2 for May 8, 0.3 for May 15 and 0.4 for May 23.

8. The following are the actual tabulated demands for an item for a nine-month period, from January through September. Your supervisor wants to test two forecasting methods to see which method was better over this period.

Month	Actual
January	110
February	130
March	150
April	170
May	160
June	180
July	140
August	130
September	140

   a. Forecast April through September using a three-month simple moving average.

   b. Use simple exponential smoothing to estimate April through September. (Use $\alpha = 0.3$ and assume that the forecast for March was 130.)

   c. Use MAD to decide which method produced the better forecast over the six-month period.

9. A particular forecasting model was used to forecast maintenance hours in a six-month period. The forecasts and the actual hours that resulted are as follows:

Month	Hours (Forecasted)	Hours (Actual)
April	250	200
May	325	250
June	400	325
July	350	300
August	375	325
September	450	400

   Calculate the tracking signal and state whether you think the model being used is giving acceptable answers. Justify your conclusion.

10. Lethbridge Industries has a very simple forecasting model: Take the actual demand for the same month last year and divide that by the number of fractional weeks in that month, producing the average weekly demand for that month. This weekly average is used as the weekly forecast this year.

   The following eight weeks show the forecast (based on last year) and the demand that actually occurred:

Week	Forecast Demand	Actual Demand
1	140	137
2	140	133
3	140	150
4	140	160
5	140	180
6	150	170
7	150	185
8	150	205

a. Compute the MAD and the MAPE.

b. Using the RSFE, compute the tracking signal.

c. Based on your answers to (*a*) and (*b*), what comments can you make about Lethbridge's method of forecasting?

11. The historical demand for a product is January, 80; February, 100; March, 60; April, 80; and May, 90.

   a. Using a simple four-month moving average, what is the forecast for June? if June experienced a demand of 100, what would your forecast be for July?

   b. Using exponential smoothing with $\alpha = 0.20$, if the forecast for January had been 70, compute what the exponentially smoothed forecast would have been for the remaining months through June.

   c. Using the least squares method, compute a forecast for June, July, and August.

   d. Using a weighted moving average with weights of 0.30 (May), 0.25 (April), 0.20 (March), 0.15 (February), and 0.10 (January), what is June's forecast?

12. In this problem, you are to test the validity of your forecasting model. The following are the forecasts for a model you have been using along with the actual demands that occurred:

Week	Forecast	Actual
1	800	900
2	850	1000
3	950	1050
4	950	900
5	1000	900
6	975	1100

Compute the MAD, the MAPE, and the tracking signal and draw a conclusion as to whether the forecasting model you have been using is giving reasonable results. Justify your conclusion.

13. Assume that your stock of sales merchandise is maintained based on the forecast demand. If the distributor's sales personnel call on the first day of each month, compute your forecast sales for each of the three methods requested here.

Month	Actual
June	140
July	180
August	170

   a. Using a simple three-month moving average, what is the forecast for September?

   b. Using a weighted moving average, what is the forecast for September with weights of 0.20, 0.30, and 0.50 for June, July, and August, respectively?

   c. Using simple exponential smoothing and assume that the forecast for June had been 130, calculate the forecasts for September with a smoothing constant alpha of 0.30.

14. The historical demand for a product is:

Month	Demand
April	60
May	55
June	75
July	60
August	80
September	75

    a. Using a simple four-month moving average, calculate a forecast for October.

    b. Using simple exponential smoothing with $\alpha = 0.2$ and a September forecast = 65, calculate a forecast for October.

15. A forecasting method you have been using to predict product demand is shown in the following table along with the actual demand that occurred.

Forecast	Actual
1500	1550
1400	1500
1700	1600
1750	1650
1800	1700

    a. Compute the tracking signal using the MAD and running sum of forecast errors (RSFE).

    b. Calculate the MAPE.

    c. Comment on whether you feel the forecasting method is giving good predictions.

16. Sales during the past six months have been as follows:

January	115
February	123
March	132
April	134
May	140
June	147

    a. Using a simple three-month moving average, make forecasts for April through July. What is the main weakness of using a simple moving average with data that are patterned like this?

    b. Using simple exponential smoothing with $\alpha = 0.70$, if the forecast for January had been 110, compute the exponentially smoothed forecasts for each month through July. Compare the forecasts for April through July with those obtained in part (*a*). Is this method more accurate for these data? Why or why not?

17. Actual demand for a product for the past three months was:

Three months ago	400 units
Two months ago	350 units
Last month	325 units

    a. Using a simple three-month moving average, what would the forecast be for this month?

    b. If 300 units actually occurred this month, what would your forecast be for the next month?

    c. Using simple exponential smoothing, what would your forecast be for this month if the exponentially smoothed forecast for three months ago was 450 units and the smoothing constant was 0.20?

18. After using your forecasting model for a period of six months, you decide to test it using MAD and a tracking signal. The following are the forecasted and actual demands for the six-month period:

    a. Calculate the tracking signal.

Period	Forecast	Actual
May	450	500
June	500	550
July	550	400
August	600	500
September	650	675
October	700	600

    b. Decide whether your forecasting routine is acceptable.

19. Consolidated Edison Company of New York, Inc., sells electricity, gas, and steam to New York City and Westchester County. Sales revenue for the years 1989 to 1999 are shown below. Forecast the revenues for 2000 through 2003. Use your own judgment, intuition, or common sense concerning which model or method to use, as well as the period of data to include. Obtain the actual revenues for three years and evaluate your forecasting model.

Year	Revenue ($ millions)
1989	5550
1990	5739
1991	5873
1992	5933
1993	6020
1994	6260
1995	6537
1996	6960
1997	7121
1998	7093
1999	7491

20. Erika Eckstein recently graduated from a business school and has taken a position as the assistant manager at a small hotel with 35 rooms. One of her first assignments is to develop a model to forecast the number of room-nights that are expected to be sold in each month in 2004. (A room-night is the sale of one room for one night.) She has collected the following historical data on how many room-nights have been sold for each month in each of the past three years:

	Room-Nights Sold		
Month	2001	2002	2003
January	307	275	316
February	257	209	251
March	290	304	338
April	323	312	370
May	425	469	472
June	589	548	593
July	791	734	777
August	643	658	702
September	454	420	513
October	725	690	766
November	547	493	639
December	605	584	668

a. Using exponential smoothing with an electronic spreadsheet, develop a forecast for the number of room-nights to be sold in each month of 2004. Since this is the first time Erika is doing this forecast, use $\alpha = 0.3$ and $\alpha = 0.7$ and develop two forecasts. (Assume that the forecast for each month in 2001 is equal to the actual demand.)

b. Which α would you recommend using and why?

21. A customer service call centre for a major appliance manufacturer has collected the following data for the last four Mondays on incoming calls:

Time	Four Mondays Ago	Three Mondays Ago	Two Mondays Ago	Last Monday
6:00–8:00 a.m.	35	42	39	33
8:00–10:00 a.m.	66	71	78	80
10:00–Noon	90	105	112	98
Noon–2:00 p.m.	99	123	114	107
2:00–4:00 p.m.	87	101	96	94
4:00–6:00 p.m.	55	43	51	38
6:00–8:00 p.m.	25	31	34	30

a. Use exponential smoothing with $\alpha = 0.6$ and $\alpha = 0.1$ to forecast the number of calls for next Monday.

b. Using MAD as a criterion, which of the two values of α do you recommend?

c. Construct a table to calculate the average MAD for values of $\alpha = 0.1, 0.2, 0.3, \ldots, 0.9$. Which value of α do you recommend be used?

Note: This problem should be done using Excel or a comparable electronic spreadsheet. The data for this problem are in an Excel spreadsheet on the disc included with the book.

22. Chez Lopez is a haute cuisine restaurant that is only open for dinner. To determine the proper number of waitstaff to schedule for each meal, Aspen Wang, the dining room manager, needs to forecast the number of meals that will be served. To do this, she has collected the following data:

Day of the Week	Four Weeks Ago	Three Weeks Ago	Two Weeks Ago	Last Week
Sunday	56	44	63	65
Monday	87	72	79	81
Tuesday	90	93	88	95
Wednesday	101	92	107	102
Thursday	120	114	106	118
Friday	125	131	143	157
Saturday	166	152	178	179

a. Use exponential smoothing with $\alpha = 0.4$ and $\alpha = 0.8$ to forecast the number of calls for next Monday.

b. Using MAD as a criterion, which of the two values of α do you recommend?

c. Construct a table to calculate the average MAD for values of $\alpha = 0.1, 0.2, 0.3, \ldots, 0.9$. Which value of α do you recommend be used?

Note: This problem should be done using Excel or a comparable electronic spreadsheet. The data for this problem are in an Excel spreadsheet on the disc included with the book.

10

Waiting Line Theory

Chapter Objectives

- Introduce the major characteristics that exist in waiting lines and describe how they can impact a customer's waiting time.

- Identify the various constraints and/or conditions that waiting line theory and its associated equations require for the results to be valid.

- Present waiting line theory in the form of a set of equations that represent various types of waiting line configurations that can be encountered.

Vancouver International Airport Authority Uses Queuing Simulation to Determine Staffing Levels at Security Points

After September 11, 2001, security measures at most major international airports increased significantly. This increase in passenger screening often resulted in longer lines to get through the security checkpoints, to the point where it was not unheard of for a passenger to spend more time in the security lines than actually flying.

These long lines of passengers waiting to get through the security checkpoints provided a team of students, faculty, and staff from the Centre for Operational Excellence (COE) at the University of British Columbia with an opportunity to conduct a queuing simulation study for the Vancouver International Airport Authority. The objective of the study was to determine the most efficient way to schedule workers at the various security checkpoints throughout the airport so that 90 percent of the passengers could expect to wait no longer than ten minutes prior to going through security (90-10 service criterion).

To collect data for the simulation study, COE team members spent several days, sometimes starting at 5:00 a.m., observing the airport's four preboarding security locations. They observed the flow of passengers through

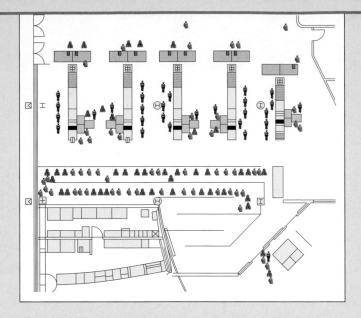

the entire security screening process, collecting data on how much time passengers spent at each of the steps in the process. (These observations alone identified some areas for immediate improvement, such as improved signage for paying special airport fees and asking passengers to boot up their laptops and place their metal possessions in special containers before entering the security screening area.)

Passenger arrivals at the security checkpoints were generated by the daily flight departure schedule, which included each flight's departure time, gate number, and passenger capacity. These data, combined with the anticipated load factor for each flight, were converted by a simulation model using a simple triangular distribution into an estimate of the number of passengers expected to arrive at each of the four security checkpoints during each ten-minute time interval throughout the day.

After the passenger arrival patterns were generated, the next step in the simulation was to develop a look-up table for each of the four security locations that listed the expected passenger demand for each ten-minute time interval and the corresponding number of security staff required to achieve the 90-10 service criterion. Simulation was used extensively in this part of the study. If the 90-10 service criterion was exceeded over the length of the simulation, then the staffing level was reduced; if it wasn't, the staffing was increased. For each time period, the simulation was run until the minimum staffing level to meet the 90-10 service criterion was determined.

The final step in this project was to convert the staffing requirements for each ten-minute time period into minimum-cost worker shift schedules for the security checkpoints.

Source:
Based on the article, "Right on Queue," by Derek Atkins, Mehmet A. Begen, Bailey Kluczny, Anita Parkinson, and Martin L. Puterman, which appeared in the April 2003 issue of *OR/MS Today*. Reprinted with permission.

aiting lines form whenever an item or a person seeks a process that is fully occupied with other items or persons. In manufacturing, waiting lines occur when parts arrive at a machine and that machine is busy working on other parts. In services, waiting lines occur when customers arrive at a service facility and that facility is already engaged serving other customers. Specific examples of waiting lines in services include (*a*) waiting to check in at an airline reservations counter,

(*b*) waiting on a telephone to make a hotel reservation, and (*c*) waiting to be seated in a restaurant.

Customer waiting lines are a fact of life that every manager must address. Even with manufacturing companies, as technology in the form of the Internet brings customers closer to the factory, customer waiting issues take on increasing importance with respect to product delivery and subsequent customer service support. Dell Computer provides a good example of this.

The analysis of waiting lines is a key element of process analysis and improvement discussed in Chapter 5. Once we have mapped the process we can determine the effectiveness of the process based in part on waiting line measures such as how long a customer waits for service or how often an employee is idle. Then we can make decisions about how to improve the process if necessary. Perhaps we may need to hire another employee or introduce technology to reduce wait times. We may also decide to train the employee to alternate between two processes in order to avoid employee idle time.

The Web supplement to this chapter primarily addresses the management of the customer's satisfaction with waiting in line. Here we focus on the management of the actual length of the wait, as measured in time, be it seconds, minutes, or hours.

In this chapter we introduce the basic elements of waiting line problems and provide standard steady-state formulas for solving them. These formulas, developed through queuing theory, enable facility designers, managers, and planners to analyze service requirements and establish service facilities appropriate to stated conditions. Queuing theory is broad enough to cover such dissimilar delays as those encountered by customers in a shopping mall or by aircraft awaiting landing slots.

Queuing theory is used extensively in both manufacturing and service environments, and is a standard tool of operations management in areas such as service delivery system design, scheduling, and machine loading.

Waiting Line Characteristics

The waiting line (or queuing) phenomenon consists essentially of six major components: (1) the source population, (2) the way customers arrive at the service facility, (3) the physical line itself, (4) the way customers are selected from the line, (5) the characteristics of the service facility itself (such as how the customers flow through the system and how much time it takes to serve each customer), and (6) the condition of the customers when they exit the system (back to the source population or not?). These six elements, shown in Exhibit 10.1, are discussed separately in the following sections.

Population Source

Arrivals at a service system may be drawn from either a *finite* or an *infinite* population. The distinction is important because the analyses are based on different premises and require different equations for their solution.

Finite Population

A *finite population* refers to the limited size of the customer pool, which is the source that will use the service, and at times form a line. The reason this finite classification is important is because when a customer leaves his/her position as a member of the population

Exhibit 10.1

Framework for Viewing Waiting Line Situations

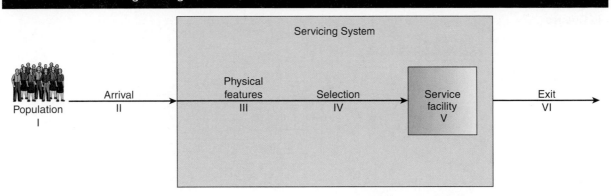

of users, the size of the user group is reduced by one, which reduces the probability of a customer requiring service. Conversely, when a customer is serviced and returns to the user group, the population increases and the probability of a user requiring service also increases. This finite class of problems requires a separate set of formulas from that of the infinite population case.

Infinite Population

An infinite population is one that is sufficiently large in relation to the service system that any changes in the population size caused by subtractions or additions to the population (e.g., a customer needing service or a serviced customer returning to the population) do not significantly affect the system probabilities. If, for example, there were 100 machines that were maintained by one repairperson, and one or two machines broke down and required service, the probabilities for the next breakdowns would not be very different and the assumption could be made without a great deal of error that the population, for all practical purposes, was infinite. Nor would the formulas for "infinite" queuing problems cause much error if applied to a physician who has 1000 patients, or a department store that has 10 000 customers.

Arrival Characteristics

Another determinant in the analysis of waiting line problems is the *arrival characteristics* of the queue members. As shown in Exhibit 10.2, there are four main descriptors of arrivals: the *pattern of arrivals* (whether arrivals are controllable or uncontrollable); the *size of arrival units* (whether they arrive one at a time or in batches); the *distribution pattern* (whether the number of arrivals within a given time interval or the time between arrivals is constant or follows a statistical distribution such as a Poisson, exponential, or even Erlang; and the *degree of patience* (whether the arrival stays in line or leaves). We describe each of these in more detail.

Poisson Distribution

A type of discrete distribution describing the number of occurrences of an event within a given interval where the mean and variance are always equal.

Exponential Distribution

When the number of occurrences of an event within a given interval follows a Poisson distribution, the time between successive occurrences of the event follows an exponential

Exhibit 10.2

Arrival Characteristics in Queues

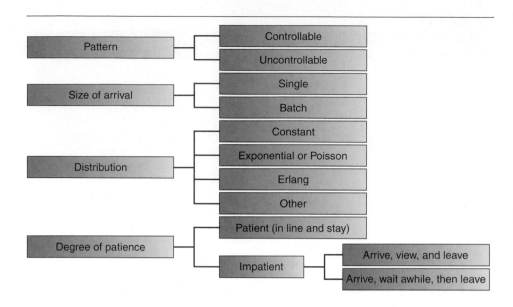

distribution. The exponential distribution is a continuous distribution and the variance is always the square of the mean. For example, if the number of arrivals in an hour follows a Poisson distribution, then the time between two successive arrivals follows an exponential distribution.

Erlang Distribution

A continuous distribution that can be used to describe the distribution of the sum of random variables generated from the exponential distribution. For example, if time between arrivals is exponentially distributed, the Erlang distribution can be used to describe the time between the first arrival and the nth arrival, where n could be any number.

Arrival Patterns

The arrivals at a system are far more *controllable* than is generally recognized. Hair salons, as an illustration, may decrease their Saturday arrival rate (and hopefully shift it to other days of the week) by charging an extra $1 for adult haircuts or charging adult prices for children's haircuts. Department stores run sales during the off season or one-day-only sales in part for purposes of control. Airlines offer excursion and off-season rates for similar reasons. The simplest of all arrival-control devices is the posting of business hours.

Some service demands are clearly *uncontrollable*, such as emergency medical demands on a city's hospital facilities. However, even in these situations, the arrivals at emergency rooms in specific hospitals are controllable to some extent by, say, keeping ambulance drivers in the service region informed of the status of their respective host hospitals.

Size of Arrival Units

A *single arrival* may be thought of as one unit (a unit is the smallest number handled). A single arrival at the Toronto Stock Exchange (TSX) is one transaction (usually greater than 100 shares of stock), while at an automobile workshop it may be one vehicle.

A *batch arrival* is some multiple of a unit, such as a whole family coming into a hair salon for service (instead of just one member of the family coming in for service). In a manufacturing plant it may be a container of parts arriving at the same time instead of a single part.

Distribution of Arrivals

Waiting line formulas generally require an **arrival rate**, or the average number of customers or units per time period (e.g., 10 per hour). The time between arrivals is referred to as the interarrival time (such as an average of one every six minutes). A *constant* arrival distribution is periodic, with exactly the same time period between successive arrivals. In production processes, probably the only arrivals that truly approach a constant interarrival period are those that are subject to machine control. Much more common are *variable* random arrival distributions. The variable or random distribution patterns that occur most frequently in system models are described by the *negative exponential*, *Poisson*, or *Erlang* distributions.

arrival rate

Rate at which customers arrive into a service delivery system, usually expressed in terms of customers per hour.

Degree of Patience

A *patient* arrival is one who waits as long as necessary until the service facility is ready to serve him or her. (Even if arrivals grumble and behave impatiently, the fact that they wait is sufficient to label them as patient arrivals for purposes of waiting line theory.)

There are two classes of *impatient* arrivals. Members of the first class arrive, survey both the service facility and the length of the line, and then decide to leave. Those in the second class arrive, view the situation, and join the waiting line, and then, after some period of time, depart. The behaviour of the first type is termed *balking*, and the second is termed *reneging.*

Physical Features of Lines

Length

In a practical sense, an infinite line is very long in terms of the capacity of the service system. Examples of *infinite potential length* are a line of vehicles backed up for miles at the tollbooths on a highway and customers who must form a line around the block as they wait to purchase tickets for a concert to see a popular singer.

Gas stations, loading docks, and parking lots have *limited line capacity*, which is often defined by legal restrictions or physical space characteristics. This complicates the waiting line problem not only in service system utilization and waiting line computations, but also in the shape of the actual arrival distribution as well. The arrival who is denied entry into the line because of lack of space may rejoin the population at a later time or may seek service elsewhere. Either action makes an obvious difference in the finite population case.

Number of Lines

A *single line* or single file, of course, means that there is only one line. The term *multiple lines* refers either to the single lines that form in front of two or more servers or to single lines that converge at some central redistribution point.

Customer Selection

Queuing Discipline

A queuing discipline is a priority rule, or set of rules (some of which are listed in Exhibit 10.3), for determining the order of service to customers who are waiting in line. The rules selected can have a dramatic effect on the system's overall performance. The number of customers in line, the average waiting time, the range of variability in waiting time, and the efficiency of the service facility are just a few of the factors affected by the choice of priority rules.

Exhibit 10.3

Factors in a
Queuing
Discipline

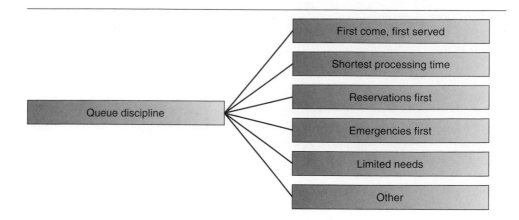

Probably the most common priority rule, especially in service operations, is *first come, first served* (FCFS), also known as first in, first out (FIFO). This rule states that the customers in line are served on the basis of their chronological arrival; no other characteristics have any bearing on the selection process. This is popularly accepted as the fairest rule, even though in practice it discriminates against the customer requiring a short service time.

Reservations first, emergencies first, highest-profit customer first, largest orders first, best customers first, longest waiting time in line, and soonest promised date are other examples of priority rules. Each has its advantages as well as its shortcomings.

Directives such as "single transactions only" (as in a bank) or "cash only" express lanes (as in a supermarket) seem similar to priority rules, but in reality they are methodologies for structuring the line itself. Such lines are formed to serve a specific class of customers with similar characteristics. Within each line, however, priority rules still apply (as before) to the method of selecting the next customer to be served. A classic case of line structuring is the supermarket with the fast checkout line for customers with 12 items or less.

Processing Facility Structure

Several types of processing facility structures are presented in Exhibit 10.4, four of which are discussed in detail in the following sections. The physical flow of items or customers to be processed (serviced) may go through a single line, multiple lines, single or multiple steps (phases), or some combination of these. The choice of format depends partly on the volume of customers (or items requested by them, as in a factory) served, partly on physical constraints, and partly on the restrictions imposed by sequential requirements governing the order in which the process must be performed.

Single Channel, Single Phase
This is the simplest form of waiting line structure, and straightforward formulas are available to solve the problem for standard distribution patterns of arrival and service. When the distributions are nonstandard, the problem is easily solved by computer simulation. A typical example of a single-channel, single-phase situation is the one-person barbershop.

Single Channel, Multiphase
A car wash provides a good illustration for a series of services—vacuuming, wetting, washing, rinsing, drying, window cleaning, and parking—performed in a fairly uniform

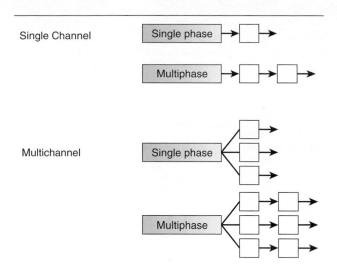

Exhibit 10.4

**Service Facility
Structure Types**

sequence. A critical factor in the single-channel case with service in series is the amount of buildup of items allowed in front of each service, which in turn constitutes separate waiting lines.

Multichannel, Single Phase

Tellers' windows in banks and checkout counters in supermarkets and high-volume department stores exemplify this type of structure. The difficulty with this format is that the uneven service time given each customer results in unequal speed or flow among the lines. This results in some customers being served before others who arrived earlier, as well as in some degree of line shifting. Varying this structure to assure the servicing of arrivals in chronological order would require forming a single line, from which, as a server becomes available, the next customer in the queue is assigned. This type of line structure is now commonly used at airport ticket counters and banks.

Multichannel, Multiphase

This situation is similar to the preceding one except that two or more services are performed in sequence. The admission of patients in a hospital follows this pattern because a specific sequence of steps is usually required: initial contact at the admissions desk, filling out forms, making identification tags, obtaining a room assignment, escorting the patient to the room, and so forth. Since several servers are usually available for this procedure, more than one patient at a time may be processed.

Service Rate

Waiting line formulas generally define **service rate** as the capacity of the server in terms of the number of units served per time period (such as 12 customers per hour) and *not* as service time, which might average five minutes each. A *constant* service time rule states that each service takes exactly the same time. As in constant arrivals, this characteristic is generally limited to machine-controlled operations. As with arrival rates, Erlang and exponential distributions represent variable service times.

The *exponential* distribution is frequently used to approximate the actual service distribution at each phase. Some services also have some practical minimum time. A clerk in a checkout line may have a three-minute average service time but a one-minute

service rate

Capacity of a service station, usually expressed in terms of customers per hour. The reciprocal of the service rate is the average time to serve a customer.

TO BE GUARANTEED OR NOT TO BE ... THAT IS JUST ONE OF THE QUESTIONS FACING CANADIAN HEALTH CARE

"I waited for six months for my first hip, and it was awful because I was in constant pain," Linda Wilhelm told the *Globe and Mail* in Saint John, New Brunswick. She has undergone a dozen joint-replacement operations and knows what it's like to be on a waiting list. For a spinal-fusion operation, she had to scrounge air miles for a trip to Toronto.

That this is not an isolated case is confirmed by a recent study of the MRI system in Alberta that revealed that the waiting lines for MRIs continue to grow despite additional capacity. As more capacity is added, there is also a corresponding increase in demand. This demand comes not just from population growth, but also an ever-growing list of patient conditions for which MRIs are an indicated procedure.

A recent Senate standing committee report written by Senator Michael Kirby recommends that patients such as Ms. Wilhelm should be offered a Care Guarantee. Under such a plan the government would provide Canadians with guaranteed access to specific medical procedures within prescribed time frames. If the procedures are not carried out within those time frames, patients should be transferred to another province, or even to the United States, with all costs paid. The committee also identified the trade-offs facing health care waiting list management: Make people wait longer for care, make them pay on their own, or spend more tax money on health. However, another national commission, headed by former Saskatchewan Premier Roy Romanow, supports better waiting list management but without a guarantee, concluding that such a guarantee would not be feasible.

Sources:

Sherry Oh, Erhan Erkut, Dan Haight, and Armann Ingolfsson, "Managing Line-ups for Alberta's MRIs: An Overview of the Issues Facing Edmonton and Calgary's Health Regions," *45th Annual Meeting of the Canadian Operation Research Society*, Vancouver, B.C., June 2003.

André Picard, "Patients Hail Proposals on Drug Costs, Waiting Lists," *The Globe and Mail*, October 26, 2002, A4.

Michael Decter, "Now the Hard Part Begins: From Romanow to a Deal," *Winnipeg Free Press*, December 8, 2002, B4.

"The Kirby Solution," *Winnipeg Free Press*, October 26, 2002, A16.

minimum time because of having to wait for the receipt to print. Likewise in a hair salon, although the average service time may be 30 minutes, a person is rarely finished in less than 20 minutes or more than an hour. Hence, these and similar types of services are poorly characterized by the exponential curve.

Capacity Utilization

capacity utilization

Percentage of time a service station is busy serving a customer.

The percentage of time that a service station is busy attending to the needs of a customer is referred to as the **capacity utilization** of that station. This is the percentage of time that the station is busy. The remainder of the time there are no customers to be waited on and the station is, therefore, considered to be idle. In single-channel service systems, the capacity utilization is simply the ratio of the arrival rate to the service rate. For example, if customers arrive into a system at the rate of eight per hour and the service rate is 12 customers per hour, then the capacity utilization of this service station is 8/12 or 66.7 percent. It is important to note that in determining the capacity utilization for a station, both the arrival rate and the service rate must be expressed in the same units.

Exit

Once a customer is served, two exit scenarios are possible: (1) the customer may return to the source population and immediately become a competing candidate for service again or (2) there may be a low probability of reservice. The first case can be illustrated by a machine that has been routinely repaired and returned to duty but may break down again; the second by a machine that has been overhauled or modified and has a low probability of reservice over the near future. We might refer to the first as the "recurring-common-cold case" and to the second as the "appendectomy-only-once case."

It should be apparent that when the population source is finite, any change in the service performed on customers who return to the population modifies the arrival rate at

Exhibit 10.5

Properties of Some Specific Waiting Line Models								
Model	Layout	Service Phase	Source Population	Arrival Pattern	Queue Discipline	Service Pattern	Permissible Queue Length	Typical Example
1	Single channel	Single	Infinite	Poisson	FCFS	Exponential	Unlimited	Drive-in teller at bank, one-lane toll bridge
2	Single channel	Single	Infinite	Poisson	FCFS	Constant	Unlimited	Roller coaster rides in amusement park
3	Single channel	Single	Infinite	Poisson	FCFS	Exponential	Limited	Ice cream stand, cashier in a restaurant
4	Single channel	Single	Infinite	Poisson	FCFS	Discrete distribution	Unlimited	Empirically derived distribution of flight time for a transcontinental flight
5	Single channel	Single	Infinite	Poisson	FCFS	Erlang	Unlimited	One-person barbershop
6	Multi-channel	Single	infinite	Poisson	FCFS	Exponential	Unlimited	Parts counter in auto agency, two-lane toll bridge

the service facility. This, of course, alters the characteristics of the waiting line under study and necessitates further analysis of the problem.

Waiting Line Equations

To underscore the importance and wide range of applications of waiting line analysis, we describe in this section six different waiting line systems and their characteristics (Exhibit 10.5), and present their respective steady-state equations (Exhibit 10.6). The definitions of the terms used in these equations are presented in Exhibit 10.7.

In addition to these equations, two additional formulas are important in understanding the relationships among the steady-state performance measures. First, the average total time in the system is equal to the average waiting time in the system plus the average service time, or

$$\bar{t}_s = \bar{t}_l + 1/\mu$$

In addition, the average total number of customers in the system is directly related to the total time in the system, or

$$\bar{n}_s = \lambda \bar{t}_s$$

This well-known relationship is known as Little's Law. This law is considered important in queuing theory because it is universally applicable, i.e., to any waiting-line situation. This is unlike most other queuing relationships which are situation-specific.

To illustrate how these models can be applied, we present two sample problems and their solutions for the first two models. There are more than six models, but the formulas and solutions become quite complicated, and those problems are generally solved using computer simulation. Also, in using these formulas, keep in mind that they are steady-state formulas, which assume that the process under study is ongoing. Thus, they may provide inaccurate results when applied to initial operations such as the manufacture of a new product or the start of a new business day by a service firm.

Exhibit 10.6

Equations for Solving Six Model Problems

Model 1
$$\bar{n}_l = \frac{\lambda^2}{\mu(\mu-\lambda)} \qquad \bar{t}_l = \frac{\lambda}{\mu(\mu-\lambda)} \qquad P_n = \left(1-\frac{\lambda}{\mu}\right)\left(\frac{\lambda}{\mu}\right)^n$$

$$\bar{n}_s = \frac{\lambda}{\mu(\mu-\lambda)} \qquad \bar{t}_s = \frac{1}{\mu-\lambda} \qquad \rho = \frac{\lambda}{\mu}$$

Model 2
$$\bar{n}_l = \frac{\lambda^2}{2\mu(\mu-\lambda)} \qquad \bar{t}_l = \frac{\lambda}{2\mu(\mu-\lambda)}$$

$$\bar{n}_s = \bar{n}_l + \frac{\lambda}{\mu} \qquad \bar{t}_s = \bar{t}_l + \frac{1}{\mu}$$

Model 3
$$\bar{n}_l = \left(\frac{\lambda}{\mu}\right)^2\left[\frac{1-Q\left(\frac{\lambda}{\mu}\right)^{-1}+(Q-1)\left(\frac{\lambda}{\mu}\right)^Q}{\left(1-\frac{\lambda}{\mu}\right)\left(1-\left(\frac{\lambda}{\mu}\right)^{Q+1}\right)}\right]$$

$$\bar{n}_s = \left(\frac{\lambda}{\mu}\right)\left[\frac{1-(Q+1)\left(\frac{\lambda}{\mu}\right)^Q+Q\left(\frac{\lambda}{\mu}\right)^{Q+1}}{\left(1-\frac{\lambda}{\mu}\right)\left(1-\left(\frac{\lambda}{\mu}\right)^{Q+1}\right)}\right] \qquad P_n = \left[\frac{1-\frac{\lambda}{\mu}}{1-\left(\frac{\lambda}{\mu}\right)^{Q+1}}\right]\left(\frac{\lambda}{\mu}\right)^n$$

Model 4
$$\bar{n}_l = \frac{\left(\frac{\lambda}{\mu}\right)^2+\lambda^2\sigma^2}{2\left(1-\frac{\lambda}{\mu}\right)} \qquad \bar{t}_l = \frac{\frac{\lambda}{\mu^2}+\lambda\sigma^2}{2\left(1-\frac{\lambda}{\mu}\right)}$$

$$\bar{n}_s = \bar{n}_l + \frac{\lambda}{\mu} \qquad \bar{t}_s = \bar{t}_l + \frac{1}{\mu}$$

Model 5
$$\bar{n}_l = \frac{K+1}{2K}\cdot\frac{\lambda^2}{\mu(\mu-\lambda)} \qquad \bar{t}_l = \frac{K+1}{2K}\cdot\frac{\lambda}{\mu(\mu-\lambda)}$$

$$\bar{n}_s = \bar{n}_l + \frac{\lambda}{\mu} \qquad \bar{t}_s = \bar{t}_l + \frac{1}{\mu}$$

Model 6
$$\bar{n}_l = \frac{\lambda\mu\left(\frac{\lambda}{\mu}\right)^M}{(M-1)!(M\mu-\lambda)^2}P_0 \qquad \bar{t}_l = \frac{P_0}{\mu M M!\left(1-\frac{\lambda}{\mu M}\right)^2}\left(\frac{\lambda}{\mu}\right)^M$$

$$\bar{n}_s = \bar{n}_l + \frac{\lambda}{\mu} \qquad \bar{t}_s = \bar{t}_l + \frac{1}{\mu}$$

$$P_0 = \frac{1}{\displaystyle\sum_{n=0}^{M-1}\frac{\left(\frac{\lambda}{\mu}\right)^n}{n!}+\frac{\left(\frac{\lambda}{\mu}\right)^M}{M!\left(1-\frac{\lambda}{\mu M}\right)}} \qquad P_w = \left(\frac{\lambda}{\mu}\right)^M\frac{P_0}{M!\left(1-\frac{\lambda}{\mu M}\right)}$$

Exhibit 10.7

Notations for Equations (Exhibit 10.6)

Infinite Queuing Notation

σ = Standard deviation
λ = Arrival rate
μ = Service rate
$\frac{1}{\mu}$ = Average service time

$\frac{1}{\lambda}$ = Average time between arrivals

ρ = Potential capacity utilization of the service facility (defined as λ/μ)

$\bar{n}_l$ = Average number waiting line
$\bar{n}_s$ = Average number in system (including any being served)
$\bar{t}_l$ = Average time waiting in line
$\bar{t}_s$ = Average total time in system (including time to be served)
Q = Maximum queue length
M = Number of channels

Arrival Rate	Service Rate	Capacity Utilization	Waiting Time (hr)	Waiting Time (min)
10	60	16.67%	0.003	0.20
20	60	33.33	0.008	0.50
30	60	50.00	0.017	1.00
40	60	66.67	0.033	2.00
45	60	75.00	0.050	3.00
50	60	83.33	0.083	5.00
55	60	91.67	0.183	11.00
56	60	93.33	0.233	14.00
57	60	95.00	0.317	19.00
58	60	96.67	0.483	29.00

Exhibit 10.8

Calculating the Relationship between Capacity Utilization and Waiting Time

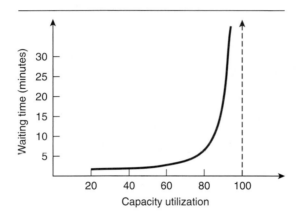

Exhibit 10.9

The Relationship between Capacity Utilization and Waiting Time

Capacity Utilization and Waiting Time

The capacity utilization of a service facility and the average waiting time for that facility are positively related. In other words, as capacity utilization increases, waiting time also increases. To illustrate this relationship, we use the formula for Model 1 (in Exhibit 10.6) to calculate the capacity utilization and average waiting time for a single-server facility. The results are shown in the table in Exhibit 10.8 and plotted in the graph in Exhibit 10.9. As a general rule of thumb, when the capacity utilization of the service facility is greater than 75 to 85 percent, the lines become unacceptably long to the majority of customers.

The Trade-Off between Balking and Reneging

Service managers, in designing their facilities, also need to recognize the trade-off that exists between having a large facility where customers can wait and the customer dissatisfaction that is associated with waiting too long prior to being served. In other words, the larger the waiting area, the less likely a customer will initially balk or not enter the facility at all. At the same time, for a given number of service stations, the larger the waiting area, the longer the average waiting time for the customer. This trade-off is shown in Exhibit 10.10.

If the wait is so long that the customer eventually reneges or leaves the line, then the customer, most likely, will be more dissatisfied than if he or she had balked or left in first place. For example, you are likely to be very dissatisfied if you call to make an airline reservation and have to wait on the phone for such a long period of time that you

Exhibit 10.10

The Trade-Off between Balking and Reneging

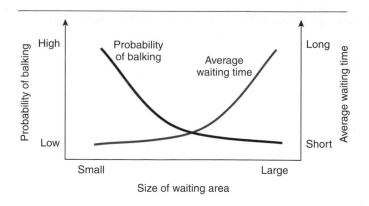

eventually hang up. However, you would probably be less dissatisfied if you call to make a reservation and get a busy signal, and then call back at a later time. Similarly, you will likely be more dissatisfied if you have to wait such a long time for a table in a restaurant that you finally leave before you are seated than you would be if you found the parking lot full and decided to come back at another time.

Two Typical Waiting Line Situations

Here is a quick preview of the two problems we have used to illustrate the first two waiting line models in Exhibits 10.5 and 10.6.

> *Problem 1: Customers in line.* A bank wants to know how many customers (or cars) are waiting for a drive-in teller, how long they have to wait, the utilization of the teller, and what the service rate would have to be so that 95 percent of the time there would be no more than three cars in the system at any one time.

> *Problem 2: Equipment selection.* A franchisee for Robot Car Wash must decide which equipment to purchase out of a choice of three. Larger units cost more, but wash cars faster. To make the decision, costs are related to revenue.

The two problems are solved using the equations in Exhibit 10.6 with the notations defined in Exhibit 10.7.

Problem 1: Customers in Line

Example

Nanaimo Bank wants to provide a drive-through window for its customers. Management estimates that customers will arrive in their cars at the rate of 15 per hour. The teller who will staff the window can service customers at the rate of 20 per hour.

Assuming Poisson arrivals and exponential service, find the

a. Capacity utilization of the teller.

b. Average number of cars in the waiting line.

c. Average number in the system.

d. Average waiting time in line.

e. Average waiting time in the system, including service.

a. The average capacity utilization of the teller is

$\mu = 20$ customers/hour

$\lambda = 15$ customers/hour

$$\rho = \frac{\lambda}{\mu} = \frac{15}{20} = 75 \text{ percent}$$

b. The average number of cars in the waiting line is

$$\bar{n}_l = \frac{\lambda^2}{\mu(\mu - \lambda)} = \frac{(15)^2}{20(20 - 15)} = 2.25 \text{ cars}$$

c. The average number in the system is

$$\bar{n}_s = \frac{\lambda}{\mu - \lambda} = \frac{15}{20 - 15} = 3 \text{ cars}$$

d. Average waiting time in line is

$$\bar{t}_l = \frac{\lambda}{\mu(\mu - \lambda)} = \frac{15}{20(20 - 15)} = 0.15 \text{ hour, or 9 minutes}$$

e. Average waiting time in the system is

$$\bar{t}_s = \frac{1}{\mu - \lambda} = \frac{1}{20 - 15} = 0.2 \text{ hour, or 12 minutes}$$

Because of limited space and a desire to provide an acceptable level of service, the bank manager would like to ensure, with 95 percent confidence, that not more than three cars will be in the system at any one time. What is the present level of service for the three-car limit? What level of teller use must be attained and what must be the service rate of the teller to assure the 95 percent level of service?

The present level of service for three cars or less is the probability that there are 0, 1, 2, or 3 cars in the system.

From Model 1, Exhibit 10.6:

$$P_n = \left(1 - \frac{\lambda}{\mu}\right)\left(\frac{\lambda}{\mu}\right)^n$$

at $n = 0$ $P_0 = (1 - 15/20)$ $(15/20)^0 = 0.250$

at $n = 1$ $P_1 = (1/4)$ $(15/20)^1 = 0.188$

at $n = 2$ $P_2 = (1/4)$ $(15/20)^2 = 0.141$

at $n = 3$ $P_3 = (1/4)$ $(15/20)^3 = \underline{0.105}$

$$\overline{0.684} \text{ or } 68.4 \text{ percent}$$

The probability of having more than three cars in the system is 1.0 minus the probability of three cars or less ($1.0 - 0.684 = 0.316$ or 31.6 percent).

For a 95 percent service level to three cars or less, this states that $P_0 + P_1 + P_2 + P_3 = 95$ percent.

$$0.95 = \left(1 - \frac{\lambda}{\mu}\right)\left(\frac{\lambda}{\mu}\right)^0 + \left(1 - \frac{\lambda}{\mu}\right)\left(\frac{\lambda}{\mu}\right)^1 + \left(1 - \frac{\lambda}{\mu}\right)\left(\frac{\lambda}{\mu}\right)^2 + \left(1 - \frac{\lambda}{\mu}\right)\left(\frac{\lambda}{\mu}\right)^3$$

$$0.95 = \left(1 - \frac{\lambda}{\mu}\right)\left[1 + \frac{\lambda}{\mu} + \left(\frac{\lambda}{\mu}\right)^2 + \left(\frac{\lambda}{\mu}\right)^3\right]$$

We can solve this by trial and error for values of λ/μ. If $\lambda/\mu = 0.50$,

$$0.95 \overset{?}{=} 0.5(1 + 0.05 + 0.25 + 0.125)$$
$$0.95 \neq 0.9375$$

With $\lambda/\mu = 0.45$

$$0.95 \overset{?}{=} (1 - 0.45)(1 + 0.45 + 0.203 + 0.091)$$
$$0.95 \neq 0.96$$

With $\lambda/\mu = 0.47$

$$0.95 \overset{?}{=} (1 - 0.47)(1 + 0.47 + 0.221 + 0.104) = 0.95135$$
$$0.95 \approx 0.95135$$

Therefore, with the utilization $\rho = \lambda/\mu$ of 47 percent, the probability of three cars or less in the system is 95 percent.

To find the rate of service required to attain this 95 percent service level, we simply solve the equation $\lambda/\mu = 0.47$ where λ = number of arrivals per hour. This gives μ = 31.92, or about 32 per hour.

That is, the teller must serve approximately 32 people per hour—a 60 percent increase over the original 20-per-hour capability—to be 95 percent confident that not more than three cars will be in the system. Perhaps service can be accelerated by modifying the method of service, adding another teller, or limiting the types of transactions available at the drive-in window. Note that with the condition of 95 percent confidence that three or fewer cars will be in the system, the teller will be idle 53 percent of the time.

Problem 2: Equipment Selection

Example

The Robot Car Wash Company franchises combination gas and car wash stations throughout Canada. Robot gives a free car wash with a gasoline fill-up or, for a wash alone, charges $5.00. Past experience shows that the number of customers that have car washes following fill-ups is about the same as for a wash alone. The average gross profit on a gasoline fill-up is about $7.00, and the cost of the car wash to Robot is $1.00. Robot Car Wash stations are open 14 hours a day.

Robot has three power units with drive assemblies, and a franchise must select the unit preferred. Unit I can wash cars at the rate of one every five minutes and is leased for $120 per day. Unit II, a larger unit, can wash cars at the rate of one every four minutes but costs $160 per day. Unit III, the largest, costs $220 per day and can wash a car in three minutes.

The franchisee estimates that customers will not wait in line more than five minutes for a car wash. A longer time will cause Robot to lose both gasoline sales and car wash sales.

If the estimate of customer arrivals resulting in washes is 10 per hour, which wash unit should be selected?

Using Unit I, calculate the average waiting time of customers in the wash line (μ for Unit I = per hour). From the Model 2 equations (Exhibit 10.6),

$$\bar{t}_l = \frac{\lambda}{2\mu(\mu - \lambda)} = \frac{10}{2(12)(12-10)} = 0.208 \text{ hour, or } 12\frac{1}{2} \text{ minutes}$$

For Unit II at 15 per hour,

$$\bar{t}_l = \frac{10}{2(15)(15-10)} = 0.067 \text{ hour, or 4 minutes}$$

If waiting time is the only criterion, Unit II should be purchased. However, before we make the final decision, we must look at the profit differential between both units.

With Unit I, some customers would balk or renege because of the $12\frac{1}{2}$-minute wait. And although this greatly complicates the mathematical analysis, we can gain some estimate of lost sales with Unit I by inserting $\bar{t}_l = 5$ minutes or 1/12 hour (the average length of time customers will wait) and solving for λ. This would be the effective arrival rate of customers:

$$\bar{t}_l = \frac{\lambda}{2\mu(\mu - \lambda)}$$

$$\lambda = \frac{2\bar{t}_l\mu^2}{1 + 2\bar{t}_l\mu}$$

$$\lambda = \frac{2(1/12)(12)^2}{1 + 2(1/12)(12)} = 8 \text{ per hour}$$

Therefore, since the original estimate of λ was 10 per hour, an estimated two customers per hour will be lost. Lost profit of two customers per hour × 14 hours × $\frac{1}{2}$ ($7.00 fill-up profit + $4.00 wash profit) = $154.00 per day.

Because the additional cost of Unit II over Unit I is only $40 per day, the loss of $154.00 profit obviously warrants the installation of Unit II.

The original constraint of a five-minute maximum wait is satisfied by Unit II. Therefore, Unit III should not be considered unless the arrival rate is expected to increase in the future.

Designing the Facility Using Waiting Line Characteristics

Once we know the characteristics of the current waiting system, using mathematical formulae similar to those described in Problems 1 and 2, we can calculate various performance measures such as average waiting time and average number of people in the line. These performance measures can help design or redesign a system. For example, if our current system is causing long lines because the arrival rates have increased, by using the formulae we can examine to what extent the waiting time might decrease if we increased the number of channels. This would help determine the number of channels we might need to add to our redesigned system to bring down our capacity utilization and maintain customer satisfaction.

Although waiting line formulae are quick to use, they depend on many simplifying assumptions and cannot give very detailed information. Thus, in practice there may be many situations for which waiting line formulae do not exist or for which more detailed measures than averages are needed. Computer simulation can be used to model such situations.

computer simulation

Mimicking or duplicating the operation of a real system using a computer-based model to study the systems's characteristics.

In **computer simulation**, a detailed model of the system is built on the computer. This provides the ability to track every customer as well as other elements of the system. It is much more flexible than mathematical formulae and can calculate more detailed performance measures under complex situations, such as waiting time for 90 percent of the arrivals, utilization of different parts of the system, or the effect on waiting times if the FCFS rule did not select the next customer. Powerful commercial packages with effective graphical interfaces and animation make simulation a powerful tool. Spreadsheet packages also allow for practical computer simulation of queues.[1] However, computer simulation is more expensive and slower than using mathematical formulae because it involves building customized models for the system. (See the opening vignette to this chapter for an example of a simulation of operations at Vancouver airport.)

---

[1]T. A. Grossman Jr., "Spreadsheet Modeling and Simulation Improves Understanding of Queues," *Interfaces*, 29, 3 (1999), pp. 88–103.

Conclusion

Waiting line problems present both a challenge and a frustration to those who try to solve them. One of the main concerns in dealing with waiting line problems is what procedure or priority rule to use in selecting the next product or customer to be served.

Many queuing problems appear simple until an attempt is made to solve them. This supplement has dealt with the simpler problems. When the situation becomes more complex, such as when there are multiple phases and/or where services are performed only in a particular sequence, computer simulation is usually necessary to obtain the optimal solution.

Key Terms

arrival rate p. 369   computer simulation p. 380

capacity utilization p. 372   service rate p. 371

Review and Discussion Questions

1. How many waiting lines did you encounter during your last airline flight?
2. Distinguish between a *channel* and a *phase*.
3. Which assumptions are necessary to employ the formulas given for Model 1?
4. In what way might the first-come, first-served rule be unfair to the customers waiting for service in a bank or hospital?
5. Identify the various types of waiting lines you encounter in a normal day.
6. Compare the queuing systems of McDonald's and Wendy's.
7. Why do you think doctors' and dentists' offices usually have such long waits?

Problem 1

Quick Lube, Inc., operates a fast lube and oil change garage. On a typical day, customers arrive at the rate of three per hour, and lube jobs are performed at an average rate of one every 15 minutes. The mechanics operate as a team on one car at a time.

Assuming Poisson arrivals and exponential service, determine the

a. Utilization of the lube team.
b. Average number of cars in line.
c. Average time a car waits before it is lubed.
d. Total time it takes a car to go through the system (i.e., waiting in line plus lube time).

Solution

$\lambda = 3, \mu = 4$

a. $\text{Utilization}(\rho) = \dfrac{\lambda}{\mu} = \dfrac{3}{4} = 75\%.$

b. $\bar{n}_l = \dfrac{\lambda^2}{\mu(\mu - \lambda)} = \dfrac{3^2}{4(4-3)} = \dfrac{9}{4} = 2.25$ cars in line.

c. $\bar{t}_l = \dfrac{\lambda}{\mu(\mu - \lambda)} = \dfrac{3}{4(4-3)} = \dfrac{3}{4} = 0.75$ hour $= 45$ minutes in line.

d. $\bar{t}_s = \dfrac{1}{\mu - \lambda} = \dfrac{1}{1} = 1$ hour total time in the system (waiting + lube).

Problem 2

Siobhan Vending Inc. (SVI) supplies vended food to a large university. Because students kick the machines out of anger and frustration, management has a constant repair problem. The machines break down on an average of three per hour, and the breakdowns are distributed in a Poisson manner. Downtime costs the company $25/hour per machine, and each maintenance worker gets $4 per hour. One worker can service machines at an average rate of five per hour, distributed exponentially; two workers, working together, can service seven per hour, distributed exponentially; and a team of three workers can do eight per hour, distributed exponentially.

What is the optimum maintenance crew size for servicing the machines?

Solution

Siobhan Vending Inc.

Case I: One worker.

$\lambda = 3/\text{hour}$ Poisson, $\mu = 5/\text{hour}$ exponential

The average number of machines (either broken down or being repaired) in the system is

$\bar{n}_s = \dfrac{\lambda}{\mu - \lambda} = \dfrac{3}{5-3} = \dfrac{3}{2} = 1\frac{1}{2}$ machines

Downtime cost is $25 \times 1.5 = $37.50 per hour; repair cost is $4.00 per hour; and total cost per hour for 1 worker is $37.50 + $4.00 = $41.50.

Downtime $(1.5 \times \$25)$ $= \$37.50$
Labour (1 worker $\times \$4$) = $\underline{\quad 4.00}$
$\underline{\$41.50}$

Case II: Two workers.

$\lambda = 3, \mu = 7$

$$\bar{n}_s = \frac{\lambda}{\mu - \lambda} = \frac{3}{7-3} = 0.75 \text{ machine}$$

Downtime $(0.75 \times \$25)$ $= \$18.75$
Labour (2 workers $\times \$4.00$) = $\underline{\quad 8.00}$
$\underline{\$26.75}$

Case III: Three workers.

$\lambda = 3, \mu = 8$

$$\bar{n}_s = \frac{\lambda}{\mu - \lambda} = \frac{3}{8-3} = \frac{3}{5} = 0.60 \text{ machine}$$

Downtime $(0.60 \times \$25)$ $= \$15.00$
Labour (3 workers $\times \$4.00$) = $\underline{\quad 12.00}$
$\underline{\$27.00}$

Comparing the costs for one, two, or three workers, we see that Case II with two workers is the best decision.

Problems

1. Widget Rajah is a manufacturer of different types of toys. Widget Rajah has been successful in automating production for its Cozmo toy. The Cozmo-Master 9000 requires a constant 45 seconds to produce a Cozmo. It has been estimated that components for Cozmo to be assembled by the Cozmo-Master 9000 will arrive at the Cozmo-Master 9000 machine in bins according to a Poisson distribution at an average of 1 every 50 seconds.
   a. What is the expected average time in the system for components to be assembled into Cozmos?
   b. To help determine the amount of space (in terms of number of parts) needed for the line at the machine, Widget Rajah would like to know the average line length (in parts) and the average number of parts in the system (both in line and at the machine).

2. Big Satvinder's drive-through kebab service is planning to build another store at a new location and must decide how much land to lease to optimize returns. Leased space for cars will cost $1000 per year per space. Big Jack is aware of the highly competitive nature of the quick-service food industry and knows that if his drive-through is full, customers will go elsewhere. The location under consideration has a potential customer arrival rate of 30 per hour (Poisson). Customers' orders are filled at the rate of 40 per hour (exponential) since Big Satvinder prepares food ahead of time. The average profit on each arrival is $0.60, and the store is open from noon to midnight every day. How many spaces for cars should be leased?

3. To support National Heart Week, the Heart Association plans to install a free blood pressure testing booth in Acadia Mall for the week. Previous experience indicates that, on the average, 10 persons per hour request a test. Assume arrivals are Poisson from an infinite population. Blood pressure measurements can be made at a constant time of five minutes each. Assume that the queue length can be infinite with FCFS discipline.

   a. What is the average number of persons that can be expected to be in line?

   b. What is the average number of persons that can be expected to be in the system?

   c. What is the average amount of time that a person can expect to spend in line?

   d. On average, how much time will it take to measure a person's blood pressure, including waiting time?

   e. On weekends, the arrival rate can be expected to increase to nearly 12 per hour. What effect will this have on the number in the waiting line?

4. The Ceecee company has a self-service coffee station for the convenience of its workers. Arrivals at the station follow a Poisson distribution at the rate of three per minute. In serving themselves, workers take about 15 seconds, which is exponentially distributed.

   a. How many workers would you expect to see, on the average, at the coffee station?

   b. How long would you expect it to take to get a cup of coffee?

   c. What percentage of time is the coffee station being used?

   d. What is the probability that there will be three or more people at the station?

   e. If an automatic coffee machine were installed that dispenses coffee at a constant time of 15 seconds, how would this change your answers to *a* and *b*?

5. Dr. L. Winston Cauchon is an allergist who has an excellent process in place for handling his regular patients who come in just for allergy injections. Patients arrive for an injection and fill out a name slip, which is then placed in an open slot that passes into another room staffed by one or two nurses. The specific injections for a patient are prepared and the patient is called through a speaker system into the room to receive the injection. At certain times during the day, the patient load drops and only one nurse is needed to administer the injections.

     Let's focus on the simpler case, when there is one nurse. Assume that patients arrive in a Poisson fashion and the service rate of the nurse is exponentially distributed. During this slower period, patients arrive with an interarrival time of approximately three minutes. It takes the nurse an average of two minutes to prepare the patients' serum and administer the injection.

   a. What is the average number of patients you would expect to see in Dr. Cauchon's facilities?

   b. How long would it take for a patient to wait, get an injection, and leave?

   c. What is the probability that there will be three or more patients on the premises?

   d. What is the utilization of the nurse?

6. The Yashin Income Tax Service is analyzing its customer service operations during the month prior to the April 30 filing deadline. On the basis of past data, it has been estimated that customers arrive according to a Poisson process with an average interarrival time of 12 minutes. The time to complete a return for a customer is exponentially distributed with a mean of 10 minutes. Based on this information, answer the following questions:

   a. If you went to Yashin, how much time would you allow for getting your return done?

   b. On average, how much room should be allowed for the waiting area?

   c. If the Yashin service were operating 12 hours per day, how many hours on average, per day, would the office be busy?

   d. What is the probability that the system is idle?

   e. If the arrival rate remains unchanged but the average time in the system must be 45 minutes or less, what needs to be changed?

   f. A robotic replacement has been developed for preparing the new "simplified" tax forms. If the service time became a constant nine minutes, what would total time in the system become?

7. The law firm of Larry, Ivana, and Joon (L, I, & J) specializes in the practice of waste disposal law and is interested in analyzing their caseload. Data were collected on the number of cases they received in a year and the times to complete each case. They consider themselves a dedicated firm and will only take on one case at a time. Calls for their services apparently follow a Poisson process, with a mean of one case every 30 days.

Given the fact that L, I, & J are outstanding in their field, clients will wait their turn and are served on a first-come, first-served basis. The data on the number of days to complete each case for the last 10 cases are 27, 26, 26, 25, 27, 24, 27, 23, 22, and 23.

Determine the average time for L, I, & J to complete a case, the average number of clients waiting, and the average wait for each client.

8. There is currently only one tollbooth at one of the smaller exits of a city parking lot. On average it takes about 40 seconds for the toll collector to take the money from the driver and, if necessary, return change. Cars arrive at the tollbooth at an average rate of 70 cars per hour.

   a. What is the average waiting time for a car before it pays the toll?
   b. What is the capacity utilization of the toll collector?
   c. The municipal authority has decided to install another toll collection station equipped with an electronic scanner to scan stickers on the windshields of cars that have signed up for this service. The scanning time is estimated to be 5 seconds, which is constant. Once the new electronic booth is installed, it is estimated that 40 percent of the cars will buy the stickers and use it. What will be the average waiting time for cars with stickers and for cars without stickers?

9. Independents.com is a startup dot-com company that provides a network for small independently owned inns and hotels. This network makes guest reservations and provides technical support for the managers of these properties. To begin operations, one customer service representative has been hired to answer telephone calls. (In other words, this is a one-person call centre.) It is estimated that the average call will take about three minutes to answer, and that initial demand is forecasted to be 50 calls per day over an eight-hour day.

   a. What will be the average waiting time before a call is answered?
   b. What is the capacity utilization of the customer service representative?
   c. After one week of operation, demand is exceeding the forecast, and is now averaging 80 calls per day. To provide better service, another customer service representative is hired. In addition, the calls are segmented by guest reservations and technical support, with each representative assigned to answer only one type of call. Based upon the first week's data, 75 percent of the calls are for reservations, while only 25 percent are for technical support. Additional data show that the average time to make a reservation is two minutes, while the time to answer a technical support question averages six minutes. With this additional information, determine the average waiting time for each type of call and the capacity utilization for each customer service representative.

10. An agricultural co-operative consists of a group of farmers that invest in a common business venture, often a processing facility for their farm products. Because a co-operative is owned by the farmers, they share in the costs and/or profits that the co-operative generates.

   A grape co-operative in British Columbia, which processes grapes for the making of wine, has one unloading dock at its facility. During the fall harvest, trucks arrive from the vineyards at an average rate of three per hour throughout the 12 hours that the facility is open every day. The growers rent these trucks with drivers at a cost of $75.00 per hour.

   Joe Newpol, the manager of the processing plant, is trying to decide how big a crew he should hire to unload the trucks. As a first step in determining this, he has estimated the following average times it will take to unload a truck for different crew sizes:

Crew Size	Average Unload Time (minutes)
4	18
5	15
6	12
7	10

He is currently paying workers $16.00 per hour, which includes benefits.

Based upon this information, how big a crew size should he hire in order to minimize total costs?

11. An automotive parts distributor delivers replacement parts to gas stations and garages in its area. On average, an order consists of 18 different items. Aspen Wang, the manager of the distribution centre, wants to know how many people she should assign to fill each order. The order filling times, based on the number of workers assigned to an order, are as follows:

Number of Workers	Order Filling Time
1	15
2	12
3	10
4	8

Workers are paid $12.00 per hour, including benefits. The cost of a delivery truck and driver is estimated to be $65.00 per hour.

If there is an average of 25 deliveries each day, and the facility is open 10 hours a day, how many workers should Aspen assign to fill an order to minimize total costs to the firm?

Case 1 The Cargo Pier at Dohar

Dohar, the main city and capital of a small island in the Caribbean, is the only cargo port on the island of Malysta. The island imports most of the products bought by its inhabitants, including clothing and food. The island also exports agricultural products, primarily sugar cane. To meet both its import and export requirements, Malysta has a ship arriving in port every two days, on average, but it can vary significantly due to weather.

Being a small island, it has awarded a contract for importing and exporting products to one shipping company. As part of the contract, the company has agreed to pay the costs of unloading the ships from the one cargo pier in Dohar.

The loading and unloading of a ship requires crews of individuals working together, although each crew often works independently of the others. The cost of a single crew is US$600 per hour, which includes the cost of their equipment. The time required to load or unload a ship depends on the number of crews that are hired, as shown in the following table:

Number of Crews	Order Filling Time (Hours)
1	24
2	16
3	12
4	10

The shipping company has estimated that the cost of owning and operating a ship is $10 000 per day.

How many crews should the shipping company employ to minimize its total costs?

11

Scheduling

Chapter Objectives

- Provide insight into the nature of scheduling and control of intermittent production systems.

- Emphasize the prevalence of job shop environments, notably in the service sector.

- Stress the interaction and interdependence of job shop planning and technology.

- Present examples showing the importance of worker scheduling in service sector job shops.

- Identify the major elements of scheduling workers in a service organization.

- Illustrate how technology can facilitate the scheduling of equipment and workers.

Matrikon—Software Solutions to Help You Be on Time Efficiently

In 1988, Nizar Somji and his wife Parviz launched Matrikon Inc. in Edmonton. Today it is on the list of Canada's fastest growing companies, with five Canadian and three U.S. offices. The list of clients listed on the company Web site reads like a *Who's Who* of North American business.

What does Matrikon do? It delivers software solutions for industrial IT, automation, and manufacturing collaboration that optimize and streamline plant operations for maximum agility and profitability. From a production scheduling perspective, Matrikon's advanced planning and scheduling (APS) system provides good solutions when changes in order priority, resource availability, operating conditions, and scheduling constraints are a daily issue.

For example, a common problem at Caterpillar Inc. is to cut customized parts out of a sheet of steel while at the same time ensuring that as little of the sheet as possible is wasted. Using Matrikon's APS, Caterpillar determines the best combinations of orders that need to be scheduled on the same machine and the sequence in which the orders have to be run to improve on-time delivery. Rolls-Royce Energy uses the system in the United States and in the United Kingdom to eliminate bottlenecks that could disrupt production. It provides them

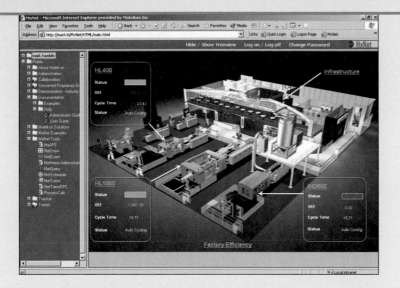

with better insight into conditions on the plant floor and in the supply chain so that they can provide realistic promise dates and thus improve customer satisfaction. At the same time the system reduces manufacturing costs due to better scheduling.

At Mercury Marine, the APS system is able to take the production requirements and generate a good schedule (assignment of jobs to machines and sequences, given worker availability and other constraints) in ninety minutes instead of days as it used to be when done manually. This allows Mercury Marine to do what-ifs quickly when the shop floor environment changes. At General Motor's medium-duty truck operation in Flint, Michigan, which makes cab-chassis combinations for garbage trucks, wreckers, snow ploughs, and dump trucks, Matrikon software was used to schedule the mind-boggling number of mixed (customized) models and addresses issues such as colour requirements, promised date, and so on. Based on this schedule, a computer communicates to the shop floor assembler which parts are to be picked for the next vehicle coming on the assembly line. Ford uses the system to optimize schedules for ten of its North American stamping plants and to perform what-if analysis and re-optimize in case of demand changes or stoppages of the stamping lines. One attractive feature is that the system can be integrated with the customer's existing planning and supply chain software, allowing users to maintain best practices.

In addition to scheduling software for job-shops and assembly lines described above, Matrikon also provides solutions for process industries and utilities. This includes processes such as control loop monitoring, process fault detection and alarm management, Web-based data viewing, and so on.

Sources:

Gyle Konotopetz, "Lessons of Lean Years Led to Leadership," *Business Edge* (January 2002).
Doug Bartholomew, "Scheduling for Complexity," *Industry Week* (April 2002), p. 81.
Jackie Mauriello, "Overcoming the Obstacles to APS," *Integrated Solutions* (August 2001).
Matrikon Inc., www.matrikon.com.

Managerial Issues

Scheduling is a critical element in both manufacturing and services. In manufacturing, scheduling is especially important in a job shop where orders or parts are typically processed in batches. Because each order requires a unique set of operations in a specified sequence, job shop scheduling can be very complicated. Consequently, management needs to look at the scheduling of both workers and equipment. To accomplish this task, some type of priority system is usually used to determine the order in which jobs are to be done.

Service managers, because labour is often a major cost element, focus almost exclusively on scheduling workers. Worker scheduling in services can be divided into two broad categories: (a) the scheduling of back-of-the-house workers and (b) the scheduling of front-of-the-house workers. For services that have sufficient buffer between their customers and the

back-of-the-house workers, scheduling issues are similar to those of a manufacturing operation. For both these types of operations, managers focus on high labour productivity and/or machine capacity utilization. At the same time they need to ensure that orders are completed on time.

The scheduling of front-of-the-house service workers is complicated by the fact that these workers must interact directly with the customers. In other words, these workers have to be available when customers want the service that their company provides. As a consequence, managers face a trade-off between providing high levels of customer service, in the form of short (or even no) customer waiting times, and obtaining high worker productivity. To obtain both high levels of worker productivity and fast customer service, service managers are increasingly turning to technology and scheduling software.

The Importance of Scheduling

scheduling

The short-term planning and control of the transformation process.

Scheduling, often used to mean short-term scheduling, involves the planning and control of the transformation process from a short-term or operational perspective, usually in a time frame of hours, days, or weeks. On the one hand, scheduling involves coordinating activities towards customer satisfaction. For example, if scheduling is not done properly an automobile body may arrive at the engine insertion point on the assembly line only to find that the engine has not arrived yet. Either the automobile has to come off the end of the line incomplete and wait for the engine to be inserted later, or the line has to stop until the engine arrives. In either case the customer (probably a car dealer) will be kept waiting. (Early arrival of the engine may also be problematic, since there may be no space to store it.) Similarly, imagine arriving at the airport only to find that your airline scheduled too few customer service agents. You probably would have to spend a long time in queue. On the other hand, scheduling also tries to ensure optimal use of resources. Unnecessary customer service agents in a particular shift would mean unnecessary labour costs for the airline. Optimal use of resources is critically important in health care because nurses, doctors, and equipment such as MRI machines are expensive and cannot be wasted or overworked. At the same time you have to ensure that patients do not wait too long to access these resources. You may have personally experienced the trade-off between customer service and use of resources at your college or university, where large classrooms often are a scarce commodity and therefore are used constantly from early morning to late evening (unlike smaller classrooms which may be less utilized). This may account for your large class at 8 a.m. or your exam on the last day of the Fall exam period.

Thus, scheduling is an important aspect of every organization, whether manufacturing or services, for profit or non-profit. Scheduling principles change, depending on whether the process is high volume, medium volume, or low volume. In this chapter we focus on low-volume or job shop scheduling. Some aspects of high-volume scheduling were discussed in assembly-line balancing in Chapter 8, and other aspects will be discussed under JIT in Chapter 13. Medium-volume scheduling is discussed in Chapters 15 and 16. We also discuss employee scheduling in services. Finally, we restrict ourselves to deterministic scheduling—where there is no uncertainty in the environment. Stochastic scheduling, used when there is uncertainty in processing times and availability of resources, is more complex and is left for advanced textbooks.

The Job Shop Defined

A **job shop** is a functional organization whose departments or work centres are organized around particular processes that consist of specific types of equipment and/or operations, such as drilling and assembly in a factory, or scanning and printing in a computer laboratory. A good example of a job shop in a service environment is a hospital, which has designated areas for blood tests, x-rays, and radiation treatments. In all these cases, the good produced or the service provided is based upon an individual order for a specific customer.

Like all aspects of operations management, job shops are affected by larger trends in the global economy. Jobs shops are becoming more specialized, and the training required of the workforce is becoming increasingly sophisticated. Furthermore, the use of automated processes and technologically advanced approaches to jobs will continue to increase. The information linkages between the job shop and the rest of the firm will be accessed more frequently by all involved parties. Costs (notably energy) will continue to rise, as will competitive pressures. The customer base will be better educated, more international in scope, and more socially aware, putting greater onus on the job shop to be socially responsible. Natural resources will become less available, and government regulation of the use of such resources may continue to rise. In short, job shop scheduling will remain a necessary part of the operation of the firm and, for the foreseeable future, will remain a difficult task.

> **job shop**
> Organization whose layout is process-oriented (vs. product-oriented) and that produces items in small, customized batches.

Scheduling in a Job Shop

A schedule is a timetable for performing activities, using resources, or allocating facilities. The purpose of operations scheduling in a job shop is to disaggregate the master production schedule (MPS) into time-phased weekly, daily, and/or hourly activities—in other words, to specify in precise terms the planned workload on the production process in the very short run. Operations control focuses on job-order progress and, when necessary, expediting orders and/or adjusting system capacity to make sure that the MPS is met.

In designing a scheduling and control system, provision must be made for efficient performance of the following functions:

1. Allocating or assigning orders, equipment, and personnel to work centres or other specified locations. This is also referred to as **loading**. Essentially, this is short-run capacity planning.

2. Determining the *sequence* of order performance; that is, establishing job priorities.

3. Initiating performance of the scheduled work. This is commonly termed the **dispatching of orders**.

4. Shop-floor control (or production activity control), which involves

    a. Reviewing the status and controlling the progress of orders as they are being worked on.

    b. **Expediting** late and critical orders.[1]

5. Revising the schedule to reflect recent changes in order status.

6. Assuring that quality control standards are being met.

> **loading**
> Allocating jobs to resources.

> **dispatching of orders**
> Releasing of orders to the factory floor.

> **expediting**
> Checking the progress of specific orders to ensure completion in a timely manner.

---

[1]Despite the fact that expediting is frowned on by production control specialists, it is nevertheless a reality of life. In fact, a typical entry-level job in production control is that of expediter or "stock-chaser." In some companies a good expediter—one who can negotiate a critical job through the system or who can scrounge up materials nobody thought were available—is a prized possession.

Exhibit 11.1

**Typical
Scheduling
Process**

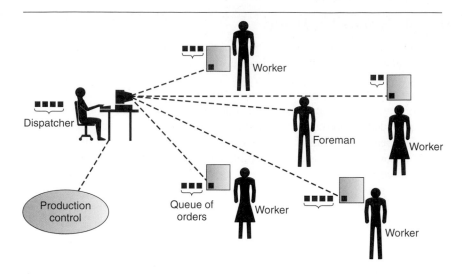

A simple job shop-scheduling process is shown in Exhibit 11.1. At the start of the day, the job dispatcher (in this case, a production control person assigned to this department) selects and sequences the available jobs to be run at individual workstations. The dispatcher's decisions are based on the operations and routing requirements of each job, status of existing jobs on the machines, the queue of work before each machine, job priorities, material availability, anticipated job orders to be released later in the day, and worker and machine capabilities. To help organize the schedule, the dispatcher draws on shop-floor information from the previous day and external information provided by central production control, process engineering, and so on. The dispatcher would also meet with the foreman or supervisor of the department to discuss the feasibility of the schedule, especially with respect to workforce considerations and identifying potential bottlenecks. Visual schedule boards provide an efficient and simple way to communicate the priority and status of work.

What makes scheduling each individual job so difficult? Consider the following factors:

- This good/service may never have been done before, so the estimates of the expected length of time for completion of the various components may be quite different from the actual time.

- The sequence of operations is extremely flexible and, with a cross-trained workforce, the number of possible sequences can be huge. Trying to assess the expected results of different sequences with the goal of finding the best sequence is usually very difficult.

- For different operations, the determination of the "best" sequence may vary—for one case it may be the minimization of waste, for another it may be the minimization of idle facilities, for a third it may be the maximization of throughput, and so on. Thus, even with extensive research into the job shop scheduling problem, it is hard to find quantitative or mechanical algorithms that are always appropriate to all situations.

Elements of the Job Shop Scheduling Problem

Job shops exist everywhere and, as a result, examples are plentiful. The emergency room at a hospital may be organized by function: The examination rooms are separate from the x-ray room, which is separate from the waiting room. Depending on the needs of the patient, different jobs are performed at different physical locations within the ER, and in some cases, at locations within the hospital other than the ER. A riding academy not only boards and exercises horses, but also provides lessons at different levels to different groups. A ski resort similarly may provide different levels of instruction to different students. The kitchen of a restaurant is also a job shop—different orders come in at different times and different meals may be prepared by different people.

But all these examples share some common elements:

- The "jobs"—whether they are riding students at an academy or orders for dinner at a restaurant—arrive at the job shop in some pattern.

- The ability of the job shop to complete these "jobs" in a given amount of time is dependent upon the capacity or "machinery" in the shop. For example, the number of students who may take riding lessons is limited by the number of horses present at the riding academy; the number of students who enroll in a given class may be limited by the number of seats available in the classroom.

- The ability of the job shop to complete these "jobs" is also dependent on the ratio of skilled workers to "machines." A riding academy may have lots of horses, but the number of riding students is also limited by the availability of skilled instructors. The number of meals that can be prepared in a timely fashion at a restaurant can be limited by the number of chefs working that evening (also by the number of ovens, stoves, and other cooking equipment available).

- The **flow pattern** of jobs through the shop varies from job to job. At a restaurant, one order might be for a sandwich and salad, another for a seven-course dinner. Consequently, the number and sequence of steps required to fill these two orders are dramatically different.

- Different jobs are often assigned different priorities. Some jobs are marked "rush" or "urgent" and may be from a preferred customer. Medical personnel at the ER in the hospital assign these priorities by performing triage so that the most serious patients are treated first.

- The criteria used to evaluate a given schedule differ from job shop to job shop. A restaurant may try to minimize wasted food or idle personnel.

flow pattern
Routes that materials follow through a factory to make a product.

Job Arrival Patterns

Jobs often arrive in a pattern that follows a known statistical distribution (for example, the Poisson distribution is relatively common), or they may arrive in batches (also called "lot" or "bulk" arrivals), or they may arrive such that the time between arrivals is constant. Furthermore, jobs may come with different priorities.

The "Machinery" in the Shop

The scheduling problem is also dependent on the number and variety of the equipment or "machines" in the shop. Furthermore, as these "machines" become smarter and are more capable of multitasking, the task of scheduling becomes more complicated.

machine-limited systems
Operations in which the capacity of the facility is determined by number of machines.

The Ratio of Skilled Workers to Machines

Job shops can be classified as either **machine-limited** or **labour-limited**, depending on whether workers outnumber machines or vice versa. In addition, jobs may be classified as *labour-intensive* or *machine-intensive*, depending on how much of the job may be performed using automated processes.

labour-limited systems
Operations in which the capacity of the facility is determined by number of workers.

The Flow Pattern of Jobs through the Shop

Exhibit 11.2 shows the various possible flows of jobs through a job shop. In some job shops, all jobs follow the same pattern; in others, the pattern is purely random. Most job shops fall somewhere in between these two extremes. Because of the apparent lack of organization, the flow of material through a job shop is often described as a *jumbled flow*.

Exhibit 11.2

Material Flows through a Job Shop

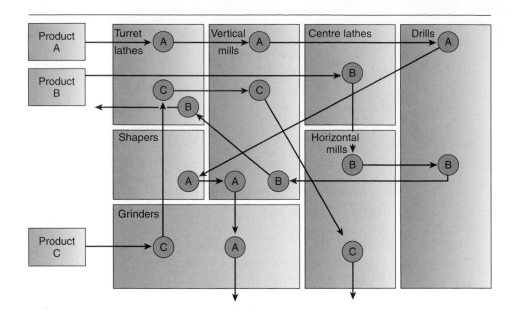

Priority Rules for Sequencing Jobs at Machines

priority rules

Criteria for determining the sequence or priority of jobs through a facility.

The process of determining which job is started first on a particular machine or work centre is known as sequencing or priority sequencing. **Priority rules** are the criteria by which the sequence of jobs is determined. These can be very simple, requiring only that jobs be sequenced according to one piece of data, such as processing time, due date, or order of arrival. Other rules, though equally simple, may require several pieces of information, typically to derive an index number such as in the *least slack rule* and the *critical ratio rule* (both defined later). Still others, such as Johnson's rule (also discussed later), apply to job scheduling on a sequence of machines and require a computational procedure to specify the order of performance. Ten of the more common priority rules for sequencing jobs are:

1. *FCFS—first come, first-served.* Orders are run in the order that they arrive in the department.

2. *SPT—shortest processing time.* Run the job with the shortest completion time first, next shortest second, and so on. This is identical to SOT—shortest operating time.

3. *Due date—earliest due date first.* Run the job with the earliest due date first. DDate—when referring to the entire job; OPNDD—when referring to the next operation.

4. *Start date—due date minus normal lead time.* Run the job with the earliest start date first.

5. *STR—slack time remaining.* This is calculated as the difference between the time remaining before the due date minus the processing time remaining. Orders with the shortest STR are run first.

6. *STR/OP—Slack time remaining per operation.* Orders with shortest STR/OP are run first, calculated as follows:

$$STR/OP = \frac{\text{Time remaining before due date} - \text{Remaining processing time}}{\text{Number of remaining operations}}$$

7. *CR—critical ratio.* This is calculated as the difference between the due date and the current date divided by the work remaining. Orders with the smallest CR are run first.

8. *QR—queue ratio.* This is calculated as the slack time remaining in the schedule divided by the planned remaining queue time. Orders with the smallest QR are run first.

9. *LCFS—last-come, first-served.* This rule occurs frequently by default. As orders arrive they are placed on the top of the stack and the operator usually picks up the order on top to run first.

10. *Random order—whim.* The supervisors or the operators select whichever job they feel like running.[2]

Schedule Evaluation Criteria

The following standard measures of schedule performance are used to evaluate priority rules:

1. Meeting due dates of customers or downstream operations.

2. Minimizing flow time (also known as cycle time or throughput time), which is the time a job spends in the shop.

3. Minimizing work in process.

4. Minimizing idle time of machines and workers.

Although we restrict ourselves to four criteria, other criteria are discussed in advanced textbooks on scheduling.

Priority Rules and Techniques

Scheduling n Jobs on One Machine

Let us compare some of these 10 priority rules in a static scheduling situation involving four jobs on one machine. (In scheduling terminology, this class of problems is referred to as an "*n* job—one-machine problem," or simply *n*/1.) The theoretical difficulty of this type of problem increases as more machines are considered; therefore, the only restriction on *n* is that it be a specified, finite integer.

Consider the following example: Ioannis Kyriakides is the supervisor of Legal Copy-Express, which provides copy services for Ottawa law firms in the downtown Ottawa area. Five customers submitted their orders at the beginning of the week. Specific scheduling data on these orders are as follows:

Job (in order of arrival)	Processing Time (days)	Due Date (days hence)
A	3	5
B	4	6
C	2	7
D	6	9
E	1	2

All orders require the use of the only colour copy machine that Legal Copy-Express has. Kyriakides therefore must decide on the processing sequence for the five orders.

[2]This list is modified from Donald W. Fogarty, John H. Blackstone Jr., and Thomas R. Hoffmann, *Production and Inventory Management* (Cincinnati: South-Western Publishing, 1991), pp. 452–453.

The evaluation criterion is to minimize flow time. Suppose that Kyriakides decides to use the FCFS rule in an attempt to make Legal Copy-Express appear fair to its customers. The FCFS rule results in the following flow times:

			FCFS Schedule			
				Flow Time (days)		
Job	Processing Time (days)	Due Date (days)	Start	Job Time		Finish
A	3	5	0	+ 3	=	3
B	4	6	3	+ 4	=	7
C	2	7	7	+ 2	=	9
D	6	9	9	+ 6	=	15
E	1	2	15	+ 1	=	16

Total flow time $= 3 + 7 + 9 + 15 + 16 = 50$ days

Mean flow time $\frac{50}{5} = 10$ days

Comparing the due date of each job with its flow time, we observe that only Job A will be on time. Jobs B, C, D, and E will be late by 1, 2, 6, and 14 days, respectively. On average, a job will be late by $(0 + 1 + 2 + 6 + 14)/5 = 4.6$ days.

Let's now consider the SPT rule. Here Kyriakides gives the highest priority to the order that has the shortest processing time. The resulting flow times are:

		SPT Schedule	
Job	Processing Time (days)	Due Date (days)	Flow Time (days)
E	1	2	$0 + 1 = 1$
C	2	7	$1 + 2 = 3$
A	3	5	$3 + 3 = 6$
B	4	6	$6 + 4 = 10$
D	6	9	$10 + 6 = 16$

Total flow time $= 1 + 3 + 6 + 10 + 16 = 36$ days

Mean flow time $= \frac{36}{5} = 7.2$ days

SPT results in lower average flow time. In addition, Jobs E and C will be ready before the due date, and Job A will be late by only one day. On average a job will be late by $(0 + 0 + 1 + 4 + 7)/5 = 2.4$ days.

If Kyriakides decides to use the DDate rule, the resulting schedule is:

		DDATE Schedule	
Job	Processing Time (days)	Due Date (days)	Flow Time (days)
E	1	2	$0 + 1 = 1$
A	3	5	$1 + 3 = 4$
B	4	6	$4 + 4 = 8$
C	2	7	$8 + 2 = 10$
D	6	9	$10 + 6 = 16$

Total completion time $= 1 + 4 + 8 + 10 + 16 = 39$ days

Mean flow time $= 7.8$ days

In this case Jobs B, C, and D will be late. On average, a job will be late by $(0 + 0 + 2 + 3 + 7)/5 = 2.4$ days.

In a similar manner, the flow times of the LCFS, random, and STR rules are as follows:

LCFS Schedule

Job	Processing Time (days)	Due Date (days)	Flow Time (days)
E	1	2	0 + 1 = 1
D	6	9	1 + 6 = 7
C	2	7	7 + 2 = 9
B	4	6	9 + 4 = 13
A	3	5	13 + 3 = 16

Total flow time = 46 days
Mean flow time = 9.2 days
Average days late/job = 4.0 days

Random Schedule

Job	Processing Time (days)	Due Date (days)	Flow Time (days)
D	6	9	0 + 6 = 6
C	2	7	6 + 2 = 8
A	3	5	8 + 3 = 11
E	1	2	11 + 1 = 12
B	4	6	12 + 4 = 16

Total flow time = 53 days
Mean flow time = 10.6 days
Average days late/job = 5.4 days

STR Schedule

Job	Processing Time (days)	Due Date (days)	Flow Time (days)
E	1	2	0 + 1 = 1
A	3	5	1 + 3 = 4
B	4	6	4 + 4 = 8
D	6	9	8 + 6 = 14
C	2	7	14 + 2 = 16

Total flow time = 43 days
Mean flow time = 8.6 days
Average days late/job = 3.2 days

These results are summarized below:

Scheduling Rule	Total Completion Time (days)	Average Completion Time (days)	Average Lateness (days)
FCFS	50	10.0	4.6
SPT	36	7.2	2.4
DDate	39	7.8	2.4
LCFS	46	9.2	4.0
Random	53	10.6	5.4
STR	43	8.6	3.2

In this example the SPT is better than the rest of the scheduling rules, but is this always the case? The answer is yes for some criteria and no for others. It can be shown mathematically that the SPT rule yields an optimum solution for the *n*/1 case with respect to evaluation criteria such as mean waiting time and mean completion time. In fact, this simple rule is so powerful that it has been termed "the most important concept in the entire subject of sequencing."[3] However, it is important to note that the SPT rule totally ignores the due dates of jobs. As a consequence, jobs with longer processing times often can be late.

Scheduling n Jobs on Two Machines

The next step up in complexity of job shop types is the *n*/2 case, where two or more jobs must be processed on two machines in a common sequence. As in the *n*/1 case, there is an approach that leads to an optimal solution according to certain criteria. Also, as in the *n*/1 case, we assume it is a static scheduling situation. The objective of this approach, termed *Johnson's rule* or *method* (after its developer), is to minimize the flow time, from the beginning of the first job until the completion of the last. Johnson's rule consists of the following steps:

1. List the operation time for each job on both machines.
2. Select the job with the shortest operation time.
3. If the shortest time is for the first machine, do that job first; if the shortest time is for the second machine, do that job last.
4. Repeat Steps 2 and 3 for each remaining job until the schedule is complete.

Example

The following example is based on a situation one of the authors has observed at an industrial laundry. This laundry cleans uniforms for organizations such as hospitals, restaurants, and hotels. Although all clothes can be washed and dried in the same machines, different uniforms have different requirements, just as different types of clothes that we use have different washing and drying requirements. For example, a certain type of hospital uniform may need a different type of detergent formula and wash cycle than a restaurant uniform or even other types of hospital uniforms. They also may have different drying times. Every day the facility receives batches of uniforms from different customers, all of which go through the same two steps—washing and drying. Johnson's rule is appropriate to use in this situation. Let's look at a hypothetical industrial laundry example.

Step 1: **List operation times (in minutes)**

Job	Operation Time on Machine 1 (Washing)	Operation Time on Machine 2 (Drying)
A	30	20
B	60	80
C	50	60
D	70	40

---

[3]R. W. Conway, William L. Maxwell, and Louis W. Miller, *Theory of Scheduling* (Reading, MA: Addison-Wesley Publishing, 1967), p. 26. A classic book on the subject.

Steps 2 and 3: **Select shortest operation time and assign**

Job A is shortest on Machine 2 and is assigned first and performed last. (Job A is now no longer available to be scheduled.)

Step 4: **Repeat Steps 2 and 3 until completion of schedule**

Select the shortest operation time among the remaining jobs. Job D is second shortest on Machine 2, thus it is performed second to last (remember Job A is last). Now, Jobs A and D are not available anymore for scheduling. Job C is the shortest on Machine 1 among the remaining jobs. Job C is performed first. Now, only Job B is left with the shortest operation time on Machine 1. Thus, according to Step 3, it is performed first among the remaining, or second overall (Job C was already scheduled first).

In summary, the solution sequence is C ! B ! D ! A, and the flow time is 250 minutes, which is a minimum. Also minimized are total idle time and mean idle time. The final schedule appears in Exhibit 11.3.

These steps result in scheduling the jobs having the shortest time in the beginning and ending of the schedule. As a result, the amount of concurrent operating time for the two machines is maximized, thus minimizing the total operating time required to complete the jobs.

Johnson's rule has been extended to yield an optimal solution for the $n/3$ case. When flow shop scheduling problems larger than $n/3$ arise (and they generally do), analytical solution procedures leading to optimality are not available. The reason for this is that even though the jobs may arrive in static fashion at the first machine, the scheduling problem becomes dynamic, and a series of waiting lines starts to form in front of machines downstream.

Scheduling n Jobs on m Machines—Complex Job Shops

Complex job shops are characterized by multiple machine centres processing a variety of different jobs arriving at the machine centres in an intermittent fashion throughout the day. If there are n jobs to be processed on m machines and all jobs are processed on all machines, then there are $(n!)^m$ alternative schedules for this job set. Because of the large number of schedules that exist for even small job shops, simulation is the only practical way to determine the relative merits of different priority rules in such situations. As in the n job on one machine case, the 10 priority rules (and more) have been compared relative to their performance on the evaluation criteria previously mentioned.

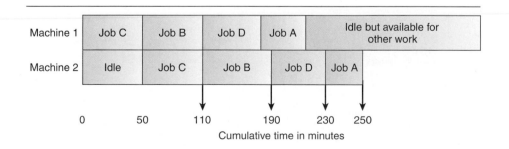

Exhibit 11.3

Optimal Schedule of Jobs Using Johnson's Rule

Which priority rule should be used? We believe that the needs of most manufacturers are reasonably satisfied by a relatively simple priority scheme that embodies the following principles:

1. It should be dynamic; that is, computed frequently during the course of a job to reflect changing conditions.

2. It should be based in one way or another on slack time (the difference between the work remaining to be done on a job and the time remaining to do it in). This is illustrated in the OM in Practice Box on the U.S. Air Force.

Theory of Constraints Scheduling

theory of constraints (TOC)

Philosophy that focuses on system constraints for continuous improvement.

Eliyahu Goldratt's **theory of constraints (TOC)** is a philosophy that focuses on continuous improvement by managing the *constraints* in a system.[4] TOC is sometimes called synchronous manufacturing. These constraints may be physical, such as machine capacity, or may relate to management policies such as pricing. TOC has five steps which imply continuous improvement:

● Step 1. Identify the system constraints. This is analogous to identifying the weakest link in the operations chain, the link which limits the system capability.

● Step 2. Decide how to exploit the system constraints, i.e., maximize the performance of the system given the constraints identified in Step 1.

● Step 3. Subordinate everything else to that decision. The rest of the system should be geared towards helping achieve Step 2, even if it means inefficiencies in the other parts.

● Step 4. Elevate the system constraints. That is, if performance is not satisfactory, acquire more of the constrained resource.

● Step 5. Go back to Step 1 for improvement if the previous steps result in new constraints.

This five-step process is followed by optimization algorithms which existed before TOC. Similarly, though TOC terms are used in this section, many of the principles discussed predate TOC under the term "management by constraints" (MBC), Just-In-Time (discussed in Chapter 13) and other practices.[5] However, Goldratt, with the help of APICS—the Educational Society for Resource Management (formerly the American Production and Inventory Control Society)—has been successful in providing a renewed focus on the importance of system constraints and presenting it in a manner easily understood by shop floor personnel.

drum-buffer-rope scheduling

A TOC scheduling method focusing on system constraints.

This discussion is restricted to the scheduling aspects of TOC. TOC advocates **drum-buffer-rope scheduling**. Exhibit 11.4 shows a production line where a product has to go through three steps sequentially to be completed. Each step is completed at different machine.

Exhibit 11.4

Traditional Production Line

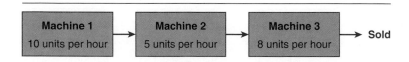

[4]Eliyahu Goldratt, *Theory of Constraints* (Great Barrington, MA: North River Press, 1990).
[5]D. Trietsch, "Balancing Resource Criticalities for Optimal Economic Performance and Growth," MSIS, University of Auckland, working paper no. 256 (2003).

A U.S. AIR FORCE MAINTENANCE DEPOT IMPROVES ON-TIME DELIVERY THROUGH BETTER SCHEDULING

Maintenance depots help overhaul and repair diverse equipment used by the U.S. Air Force worldwide. Poor management of shop-floor schedules can have a severe impact on the operations of the Air Force. One U.S. Air Force depot found that schedule performance for orders had become poor, leading to customer dissatisfaction. The depot was often operating on the "squeaky wheel" rule—the customer who complained the loudest got the quickest response.

Each job that came in had to be assigned to a machine first. Second, for any machine with multiple jobs waiting to be processed, the next job to be processed had to be determined (sequencing). The practice in the job shop was to assign a job to the least technologically capable machine capable of processing it, ignoring the queue in front of the machine. This meant that there was no attempt to distribute the workload across machines. If a machine had multiple jobs waiting to be processed, the job with the highest importance (in terms of severity of impact on

Air Force operations, if delayed) was selected, ignoring factors such as due dates and processing time.

Using historical data, researchers did a computer simulation of the operation of the depot. Different loading rules, such as ones that incorporated the job queues in front of machines and the average importance of jobs already waiting at machines, were considered in loading decisions. Similarly, different scheduling rules such as due date, shortest processing time, and modified slack-based rules (which incorporated job importance, processing time, and due dates) were simulated. The researchers found that the best results with respect to schedule performance came when queues in loading (distributing work more evenly), job importance, processing time, and dues dates were considered.

After implementing these rules and other scheduling recommendations made by the researchers, it was found that jobs completed on time almost *doubled*.

Source:
D. J. McFeely, W. P. Simpson, III, J. V. Simons Jr., "Scheduling to Achieve Multiple Criteria in an Air Force Depot CNC Machine Shop," *Production and Inventory Management Journal* (First Quarter, 1997), pp. 72–78.

What will happen if all machines run at their capacity? Machine 1 will process and send 10 units every hour to Machine 2. Machine 2 can process only 5 of those units each hour. The other 5 will not be processed and will form a queue and the queue will increase as the hours go by. So, at the end of 2 hours there will 10 units in queue waiting to be processed and so on. Machine 2 will, of course, send 5 units each hour to Machine 3. However, Machine 3 can produce 8 units per hour. Thus, it will process all 5 units coming in and still have some time left within the hour during which it will be idle.

In TOC, the slowest machine (or the lowest demand if it is less than the capacity of the slowest machine) constrains the system output and is called the drum. To prevent inventory from piling up, the system should run at the drumbeat (the rate of the slowest machine, or drum). In our example, the drumbeat is 5 units an hour, the rate of the slowest machine. Thus no inventory will pile up if the system produces at the rate of 5 units per hour (drumbeat) and 5 units will come out of Machine 3 every hour. This is the ideal situation. Since each unit of product is processed by all three machines, these machines are linked by a virtual rope. Machines linked by such a rope should all run at the drumbeat.

However, in systems there are uncertainties. For example, machines may break down, the supplier may not deliver on time, workers may be absent and so on. As shown in Exhibit 11.5, to avoid problems when the line runs at the drumbeat of 5 units per hour,

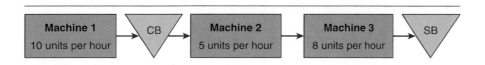

Exhibit 11.5

Drum-Buffer-Rope Scheduling

we maintain some inventory in front of the drum machine. This is called the constraint *buffer* (CB). The logic is as follows: If there is no inventory in front of Machine 2 and for whatever reason Machine 1 stops producing, Machine 2 will have to stop producing and we will lose output. To prevent this there is inventory so that Machine 2 (the bottleneck) will not be idled due to Machine 1. (In Chapter 13 we will see that with Just-In-Time systems the focus is on reducing these uncertainties, thus reducing the need for this buffer.)

With CB, if Machine 1 stops, Machine 2 continues working, using up the inventory. Why is there no inventory in front of Machine 1? Assume that Machine 1 has another machine feeding it and suppose that machine breaks down. Machine 1 will stop; however, Machine 2 can continue because of the CB. As soon as the feeder machine is up and running again, Machine 1 can start replenishing the CB because it can produce at the rate of 10 units per hour, whereas Machine 2 will consume only 5 units per hour. Once the CB is replenished, Machine 1 drops its production back to the drumbeat. So, even if Machine 1 stops for some time, it will not idle the system as long as the CB does not run out. In short, machines that have idle time need not have inventory because they can catch up. TOC also suggests a *shipping buffer* (SB) of finished products to respond to demand uncertainty. Both buffers could be in units of inventory or in units of time; that is, units are completed before they are needed (a time buffer) so that there is some slack.

Other rules in TOC scheduling are:

1. Balance the flow, not the capacity (drum-buffer-rope system).
2. Utilization of a non-bottleneck is determined by a constraint in the system (a bottleneck).
3. Utilization and activation of an input are not the same. Running a nonbottleneck machine at its capacity (activation) only produces unnecessary inventory.
4. Any loss in output at a bottleneck translates into a loss for the entire system.
5. Productivity gain attempts should first focus on bottlenecks because they constrain the system.
6. Bottlenecks determine the throughput (product completion rate) and inventory levels.
7. For optimization, transfer batches (from machine to machine) may not equal process batches (the preferred lot size to process a job at a machine). For example, if a process batch contains 100 units, it may be useful to transfer partial batches to speed throughput or to maintain the buffer.
8. The size of the process batches through the system should not be fixed.
9. Schedules should be established after evaluating all constraints simultaneously.

Control in the Job Shop

shop-floor control

Set of procedures for maintaining and communicating the status of orders and work centres.

Scheduling job priorities is just one aspect of **shop-floor control** (now often referred to as *production activity control*). The *APICS Dictionary* defines a *shop-floor control system* as A system for utilizing data from the shop floor as well as data processing files to maintain and communicate status information on shop orders and work centres.

The major functions of shop-floor control are:

1. Assigning priority to each shop order.
2. Maintaining work-in-process (WIP) quantity information.
3. Conveying shop-order status information to the office.

Exhibit 11.6

Shop-Floor Control

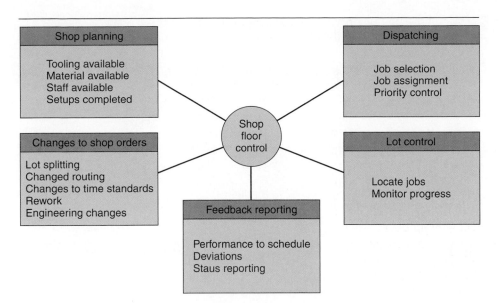

Source: "Shop Floor Control—Closing the Loop," *Inventory Management Newsletter,* August 1982. Centre for Inventory Management, Stone Mountain, Georgia 30087 USA.

4. Providing actual output data for capacity control purposes.

5. Providing quantity by location by shop order for WIP inventory and accounting purposes.

6. Providing measures of efficiency, utilization, and productivity of labour and machines.

Exhibit 11.6 illustrates more details related to shop-floor control. The relationship of shop floor control to other types of operational plans is shown in Exhibit 14.1 in Chapter 14.

Tools of Shop-Floor Control

There are a variety of written forms that can help the supervisor maintain control in the job shop; these are easily generated by the appropriate software and updated frequently through the normal interaction of supervisor and software.

●   The *dispatch list* (usually generated on a daily basis) tells the shop foreman what jobs need to be accomplished that day, what priority each has, and how long each will take. Exhibit 11.7A presents an example of a dispatch list.

●   *Exception reports* provide the supervisor with the information needed to handle special cases and problems. An example of this is the anticipated delay report shown in Exhibit 11.7B. Typically made out once or twice a week, these reports are reviewed to determine if any of the delays are serious enough to warrant revision of the master production schedule.

●   The *input/output control report*, or simply the I/O report, is used by the supervisor to monitor the relationship between the workload and the capacity of each work station. If these relationships are significantly out of balance, then the supervisor can identify where adjustments are needed. An example of such a report is shown in Exhibit 11.7C.

Exhibit 11.7

Some Basic Tools of Shop-Floor Control

A. Dispatch List

Work centre 1501—Day 205

Start date	Job #	Description	Run time
201	15131	Shaft	11.4
203	15143	Stud	20.6
205	15145	Spindle	4.3
205	15712	Spindle	8.6
207	15340	Metering rod	6.5
208	15312	Shaft	4.6

B. Anticipated Delay Report

Dept. 24 April 8

Part #	Sched. date	New date	Cause of delay	Action
17125	4/10	4/15	Fixture broke	Toolroom will return on 4/15
13044	4/11	5/1	Out for plating—plater on strike	New lot started
17653	4/11	4/14	New part-holes don't align	Engineering laying out new jig

C. Input/Output Control Report (B)

Work centre 0162

Week ending	5/05	5/12	5/19	5/26
Planned input	210	210	210	210
Actual input	110	150	140	130
Cumulative deviation	−100	−160	−230	−310
Planned output	210	210	210	210
Actual output	140	120	160	120
Cumulative deviation	−70	−160	−210	−300

Note: All figures are in standard hours.

- *Status reports* give the supervisor summaries of the performance of the operation, and usually include the number and percentage of jobs completed on time, the lateness of jobs not yet completed, the volume of output, and so forth. Two examples of status reports are the scrap report and the rework report.

input/output control

Assuring the amount of work accepted does not exceed the capacity of the facility.

Input/output control is a major feature of a control system. The major precept of I/O control is that the total workload accepted (the input) should never exceed the capacity to perform jobs (the output). When the input exceeds the output, then backlogs occur. This has several negative consequences: Jobs are completed late, making customers unhappy, and subsequent or related jobs incur a delay before they can be started. This delay also results in unsatisfied customers. Moreover, when jobs pile up at a work centre, congestion occurs, processing becomes inefficient, and the flow of work to downstream work centres becomes sporadic. An analogy of this phenomenon to the flow of water is shown in Exhibit 11.8.

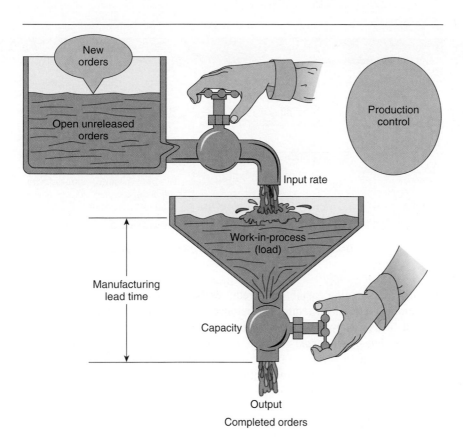

Exhibit 11.8

Shop Capacity Control Load Flow

Source: American Production and Inventory Control Society, "Training Aid—Shop Floor Control," undated. Reprinted with permission.

A simple but effective control device is the **Gantt chart**. It is used to help plan and track jobs, again using software. A Gantt chart is a type of bar chart that plots tasks to be done against time. It also helps show relationships between jobs. Exhibit 11.9 shows a small Gantt chart for a job shop attempting to complete three jobs (A, B, and C). This chart was prepared at the end of the day on Wednesday, and indicates that Job A is behind schedule, Job B is ahead of schedule, and Job C has been completed, but only after a delayed start for equipment maintenance. The Gantt chart shows how much ahead or behind schedule we are by comparing where we are now to where we planned to be. Other useful control devices include the PERT and CPM networks discussed in Chapter 4.

Shop-floor control systems in most modern plants are now computerized, with job status information entered directly into a computer as the job enters and leaves a work centre. Some plants have gone heavily into bar coding and optical scanners to speed up the reporting process and to cut down on data-entry errors.[6] As you might guess, the key problems in shop-floor control are data inaccuracy and lack of timeliness. When these occur, the information fed back to the overall planning system is wrong and incorrect production decisions are made. Typical results are excess inventory and/or stockout problems, missed due dates, and inaccuracies in job costing.

Gantt chart

Planning tool that plots activities on a time chart.

---

[6]Some companies also use "smartshelves"—inventory bins with weight sensors beneath each shelf. When an item is removed from inventory, a signal is sent to a central computer that notes the time, date, quantity, and location of the transaction.

Exhibit 11.9

	Chart Review Time		Current Time: 5 p.m. Wednesday				Gantt Chart Symbols	
Job	Monday	Tuesday	Wednesday	Thursday	Friday		⌐	Start of an activity
A							¬	End of an activity
							⌐ ¬	Schedule allowed activity time
B							▭	Actual work progress
C	Maintenance						✕	Time set aside for nonproduction activities; e.g., repairs, routine maintenance, material outages

Source: Professor Bob Parsons, Management Science Department, Northeastern University, Boston, MA. Used with permission.

Of course, maintaining data integrity requires that a sound data-gathering system be in place; but more important, it requires adherence to the system by everybody interacting with it. Most firms recognize this, but maintaining what is variously referred to as *shop discipline, data integrity,* or *data responsibility* is not always easy. And despite periodic drives to publicize the importance of careful shop-floor reporting by creating data-integrity task forces, inaccuracies still can creep into the system in many ways: A line worker drops a part under the workbench and pulls a replacement from stock without recording either transaction. An inventory clerk makes an error in a count. A manufacturing engineer fails to note a change in the routing of a part. A department supervisor decides to work jobs in a different order than specified in the dispatch list.

Scheduling Workers in Service Operations

Why Scheduling Is Important in Services

As discussed previously, one of the main distinctions between manufacturing and service operations is the customer's direct interaction with the service delivery process. Because of this interaction, the determination of the proper number of workers to schedule at any particular time is critical to the success of every service operation. On the one hand, scheduling too few workers results in unnecessarily long customer waiting times. On the other hand, scheduling too many workers results in overstaffing and the incurring of unnecessarily high labour costs, which negatively affect profits. The service manager, consequently, needs to schedule workers in a way that effectively satisfies customer demand while minimizing unnecessary labour costs.

The cost of labour in most services is a major cost component, often running 35 percent of sales and higher. For some services, in fact, virtually all of the direct costs can be considered as labour (examples of these types of services include consulting, legal work, home care nursing, and hair salons). Thus a small but unnecessary increase in labour can have a very significant impact on a firm's profits.

An important area in which scheduling is being applied is the delivery of health care (see OMP on health care and financial services). An aging population, combined with reduced funding, is putting pressure on the health care system in Canada. One way of releasing this pressure is by using resources more efficiently. Thus there has been increasing work done on scheduling in health care across Canada. For example, work has been done on the effective scheduling of doctors in emergency rooms in Montreal[7] and patients in a clinic in Calgary,[8] on using MRIs efficiently in Alberta,[9] and reducing wait times in the emergency department of a children's hospital in Ottawa.[10] Thus many aspects of heath care operations can be improved not only by serving patients faster, but also by reducing the waste of expensive resources such as doctors, nurses, and equipment, by analyzing the process and improving it through the use of better scheduling techniques.

A Framework for Scheduling Service Workers

Work schedules in service operations are usually developed on a weekly basis for several reasons. First, there are provincial and federal employment standards legislations that specify the maximum number of hours and/or days an employee can work in a given week, after which overtime premiums must be paid. This may differ from province to province.[11] Second, the distinction between full-time and part-time workers is often made on the basis of the number of hours worked in a calendar week. Full-time versus part-time status often determines the benefits paid by the employer, and may be related to union contracts that specify the minimum number of hours workers in each category may work. Finally, many workers, especially hourly workers, are paid on a weekly basis that is often mandated by legislation.

The procedure for developing a schedule for service workers can be divided into the following four major elements, as illustrated in Exhibit 11.10: (1) forecasting customer demand, (2) converting customer demand into worker requirements, (3) converting worker requirements into daily work schedules, and (4) converting daily work schedules into weekly work schedules.

Forecasting Demand

Since the delivery of most services takes place in the presence of the customer, the customer's arrival rate directly correlates with the demand level for the service operation. For example, the customer must be present at a restaurant to partake in the meal being served; the patient must be present in the hospital to receive treatment. In addition to the customer's presence at the point of service, the potential for high variability in the pattern of customer demand makes it extremely important for service managers to schedule workers efficiently. The first step, therefore, in developing a schedule that will permit the service operation to meet customer demand is to accurately forecast that demand.

There are several patterns of demand that need to be considered: variation in demand within days (or even hours), variation across days of the week, variations within a month, and seasonal variations. Because demand is often highly variable throughout a day, forecasting within-day variation is usually done in either hour or half-hour increments. Today, with the use of computers and more sophisticated point-of-sale (POS) equipment, the ability to record customer demand in even shorter time increments is possible (for example, 15-minute time intervals).

[7]Michael Carter and Sophie Lapierre, "Scheduling Emergency Room Physicians," *Health Care Management Science* 4, 2001, pp. 347–360.

[8]Kenneth J. Klassen and Thomas R. Rohleder, "Scheduling outpatient appointments in a dynamic environment," *Journal of Operations Management*, 14, no. 2, 1996, pp. 83–101.

[9]Sherry Oh, Erhan Erkut, Dan Haight, and Armann Ingolfsson, "Managing Line-ups for Alberta's MRIs: An Overview of the Issues Facing Edmonton and Calgary's Health Regions," *45th Annual Meeting of the Canadian Operation Research Society*, Vancouver, B.C., June 2003.

[10]John Blake, Michael Carter, and Susan Richardson, "An Analysis of Emergency Room Wait Time Issues via Computer Simulation." *INFOR*, 34, no. 4, November 1996, pp. 263–273.

[11]Loren E. Falkenberg, Thomas H. Stone and Noah M. Meltz, *Human Resource Management in Canada* (Toronto: Dryden, 1999), p. 57.

Exhibit 11.10

The Required Steps in a Worker Schedule

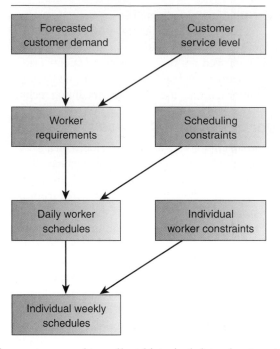

To develop a forecast we need to collect historical data about customer demand. The actual numbers of customers expecting service in a given time interval (that is, half hour or hour) are the preferred data. Fortunately, there is a wide range of POS equipment available that can capture these data, and, in many cases, even download them onto a computer for subsequent analysis.

Converting Customer Demand into Worker Requirements

Worker requirements in service operations can be divided into two major categories: front-of-the-house and back-of-the-house. Front-of-the-house workers are defined as those who have direct contact with the customer. Examples include a teller at a bank, a cashier at a discount department store, or the check-in personnel at an airline counter. Back-of-the-house workers are those who do not interact directly with customers. Examples include a cook in a restaurant or a baggage handler for an airline. (The scheduling of back-of-the-house workers is usually similar to scheduling workers in a manufacturing environment.)

A necessary element in the conversion of customer demand into front-of-the-house worker requirements is the establishment of a customer-service level. For example, many restaurants offer express lunches within a specified time period. As another example, the call centre of a certain Canadian bank requires that 80 percent of calls be answered within 20 seconds.

Knowing the average number of customers who require service in a given period of time and the average length of time it takes to provide service to each customer, a manager can determine how many workers to schedule for that time period to provide the desired level of service. Queuing theory, presented in the previous chapter, is a mathematically organized approach for establishing the relationship among the three following variables: (1) customer demand (for example, customers per hour); (2) available capacity, expressed in the number of workers on duty and the average time to service a customer; and (3) average customer waiting time.

To facilitate this process of converting customer demand into a specified number of workers, a service organization often will develop a labour requirements table. This table tells the manager how many workers are needed for different levels of demand. For some companies, these tables also will indicate where these workers should be assigned. With this type of table, the service manager only has to look up the forecasted demand in a given time period to determine how many workers to schedule and where they should be assigned. An example of a labour requirements table for a fast-food restaurant is shown in Exhibit 11.11.

Converting Worker Requirements into Daily Work Schedules

The next step in the scheduling process is the conversion of worker requirements for each time interval into a daily work or shift schedule. The basic goal here is to schedule a sufficient number of workers in a given time period to meet the expected demand at the

Scheduling lab tests and treatments for incoming patients requires balancing the urgency of the patient's problem with the availability of technicians and equipment.

target service level. However, there are usually additional factors that also need to be included, such as (*a*) the minimum length of a shift that might be prescribed by a union contract, (*b*) the maximum shift length permitted by legislation, and (*c*) the company's policies about rest and meal breaks. (See the OM in Practice Box on ambulances and financial services.) These factors can significantly affect how efficiently the organization can

Exhibit 11.11

An Example of a Labour Requirements Table for a Fast-Food Operation

Sales ($)/Hour Volume Guidelines	Total No. of Workers	Specific Worker Assignments						
		Grill	Windows	Drive-Thru	Bin	Fry	Floaters*	
$120	4	1	1	1	—	—	1	(Minimum staffing level)
150	5	1	1	1	—	—	2	
180	6	2	1	1	—	—	2	
210	7	2	2	1	—	—	2	
240	8	2	2	2	1	—	1	
275	9	2	2	2	1	—	2	
310	10	3	3	2	1	—	1	
345	11	3	3	2	1	1	1	
385	12	3	3	3	1	1	1	
425	13	4	3	3	1	1	1	
475	14	4	3	3	1	1	2	
525	15	4	4	3	1	1	2	
585	16	5	4	3	1	1	2	
645	17	5	5	3	1	1	2	(Full staffing level)

*Floaters help out: They patrol the lot, lobby, and restrooms; restock; and cover on breaks.

Source: Adapted from "McDonald's," Harvard Business School Case No. 681–044, 1980.

meet the target service level. These minimum shift constraints often result in a worker schedule in which the total number of labour hours needed to meet the minimum shift requirement(s) is greater than the actual number of labour hours required to satisfy customer demand.

In developing these schedules, many organizations use part-time rather than full-time workers to effectively meet customer-service goals while simultaneously controlling costs. Since part-time workers typically are paid less and also may be entitled to fewer (or even no) fringe benefits, the average hourly cost of the part-time worker is lower than that of the full-time worker. Part-time workers can be used to meet demand at peak periods (such as meal times in restaurants) or during periods when full-time workers would prefer not to work (such as weekends in hospitals).

Converting Daily Work Schedules into Weekly Work Schedules

The conversion of daily work schedules into weekly work schedules is more complicated than simply repeating the daily schedule procedure. In developing weekly schedules, managers need to take into consideration workers' days off for illness, holidays, and vacations. They also need to factor in the additional cost of paying workers to work on holidays if services are offered on those days. Workforce scheduling in a hospital, for example, can be particularly challenging on major holidays. In addition, these weekly schedules need to be assigned to specific individuals. Therefore, inputs into this module include individual worker constraints such as days off, hours available for work, and so forth.

The Use of Technology in Scheduling

As in most facets of business, information technology has had a significant impact on the ability of the manager to schedule workers. Early computer programs for scheduling workers were often cumbersome to use and limited in their applications. However, the advent of faster and more powerful computers coupled with newer software programs has resulted in worker scheduling programs that are both significantly more user friendly and, at the same time, more flexible in their applications.

The use of these automated scheduling programs has several advantages. First, it significantly reduces the amount of time a manager has to devote to developing a weekly work schedule. Previously, when manually scheduling workers, it was not uncommon for a manager in a complex service environment to devote one entire eight-hour day every week to developing a worker schedule for the following week. With an automated scheduling system, managers are no longer required to commit such a large amount of time to scheduling, allowing them more time to devote to actually managing the operation. This results in a more effectively managed business.

In addition, these software programs typically contain highly sophisticated mathematical formulas designed to minimize labour hours, subject to the constraints and conditions identified earlier in this chapter (such as the minimum number of hours per shift). Worker productivity is therefore also increased. Thus, as illustrated in the OM in Practice Box on scheduling ambulances, by using an automated scheduling system, a more efficient worker schedule can be generated in a fraction of the time previously required with a manual procedure.

Many of the automated systems available today are fully integrated systems that consist of several modules. Kronos, Inc., in Waltham, Massachusetts, one of the leading producers of automated workforce scheduling systems, offers a fully integrated service worker scheduling system.

Operations Management in Practice

SCHEDULING ALGORITHMS IMPROVE HEALTH CARE AND FINANCIAL SERVICES PLANNING

Urgences Santé is the public agency responsible for scheduling ambulances and crews in the Montreal area. The agency does not own any ambulances, but rather rents its ambulances and technicians from private companies. Traditionally, scheduling was done manually. The scheduling problem is quite complex because there are 80 ambulances and more than 150 crews. The agency decided to automate the scheduling process, so special mathematical algorithms for service scheduling were developed to determine schedules.

Many conditions have to be met in a feasible schedule, such as ensuring that the demand for ambulance services is always met, that rentals are distributed equally to the different companies, and that the distribution of shifts to the technician crews is fair. In addition, union contract conditions, such as gaps between shifts, the maximum number of consecutive working days, and so on, are also important considerations. Not only do the algorithms incorporate all these considerations, but they generate better schedules more quickly than can be done manually. As well, the number of renting hours per week was reduced by 45 percent.

Similarly, the Financial Services Group of Toronto had traditionally faced difficulties scheduling personnel to handle the RRSP rush early in the year. Ad hoc personnel planning had resulted in errors, rework, delays, overtime, undertime, and turnover. For the 1985 season they used service scheduling algorithms (similar to the ones in the Urgences Santé example) to improve planning. As a result, in spite of a 25 percent increase in volume compared to 1984, the costs of managing the RRSP rush decreased by 64 percent.

When scheduling employees it is important to balance efficiency and employee needs. For example, an efficient schedule that requires split shifts (because of variable customer demand during the day) may lead to employee dissatisfaction and be detrimental to the organization in the long run. For example, it is estimated that U.S. businesses are losing U.S.$206 billion in profit annually due to the hidden employee-related costs (such as lower productivity) of irregular schedules, night shifts, and extended hours.

Sources:

Jean Aubin, "Scheduling Ambulances," *Interfaces*, 22, no. 2 (1992), pp. 1–10.

Christoph von Lanzenauer, Ervin Harbauer, Brian Johnston, David Shuttleworth, "RRSP Flood: LP to the Rescue," *Interfaces* 17, no. 4 (1987), pp. 27–33.

Virginia Galt, "Night Shifts Ready for Wake-Up Call," *The Globe and Mail*, December 13, 2003, B1.

Examples of Scheduling in Services

As stated previously, the scheduling of service workers can be divided into two broad categories: "back-of-the-house" operations (where workers do not come into contact with customers) and "front-of-the-house" operations (where workers come into direct contact with the customers). Both types of service scheduling situations are presented here. The staffing requirements for the bank are an example of a back-of-the-house operation, whereas nurse staffing and scheduling are obviously a front-of-the-house operation.

Setting Staffing Levels in Banks

This example illustrates how central clearinghouses and back-office operations of large banks establish staffing plans. Basically, management wants to develop a staffing plan that (*a*) requires the least number of workers to accomplish the daily workload and (*b*) minimizes the variance between actual output and planned output.

In structuring the problem, bank management defines inputs (cheques, statements, investment documents, and so forth) as *products*, which are routed through different processes or *functions* (receiving, sorting, encoding, and so forth).

To solve the problem, first a monthly demand forecast is made by product for each function. This demand forecast for each product is then divided by the production rate (P/H) for those functions that the product requires. The result is the number of labour hours [H(std)] that are required to complete each function for that product. The labour hours are then converted into workers required per function. These figures are then tabled, summed,

Exhibit 11.12

Daily Staff Hours Required

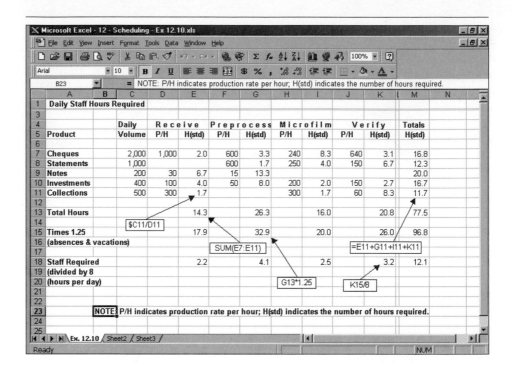

Product	Daily Volume	Receive P/H	Receive H(std)	Preprocess P/H	Preprocess H(std)	Microfilm P/H	Microfilm H(std)	Verify P/H	Verify H(std)	Totals H(std)
Cheques	2,000	1,000	2.0	600	3.3	240	8.3	640	3.1	16.8
Statements	1,000			600	1.7	250	4.0	150	6.7	12.3
Notes	200	30	6.7	15	13.3					20.0
Investments	400	100	4.0	50	8.0	200	2.0	150	2.7	16.7
Collections	500	300	1.7			300	1.7	60	8.3	11.7
Total Hours			14.3		26.3		16.0		20.8	77.5
			$C11/D11							
Times 1.25			17.9		32.9		20.0		26.0	96.8
(absences & vacations)				SUM(E7:E11)				=E11+G11+I11+K11		
Staff Required			2.2		4.1		2.5		3.2	12.1
(divided by 8										
(hours per day)					G13*1.25			K15/8		

NOTE: P/H indicates production rate per hour; H(std) indicates the number of hours required.

Exhibit 11.13

Staffing Plan

Function	Staff Required	Staff Available	Variance (±)	Management Actions
Receive	2.3	2.0	− 0.3	Use overtime
Preprocess	4.1	4.0	− 0.1	Use overtime
Microfilm	2.5	3.0	+ 0.5	Use excess to verify
Verify	3.3	3.0	− 0.3	Get 0.3 from microfilm

and adjusted by an absence and vacation factor to give planned hours, which are then divided by the number of hours in the workday to give us the number of workers required. This results in the daily staff hours required (see Exhibit 11.12), which becomes the basis for a departmental staffing plan that lists the workers required, workers available, variance, and managerial action in light of variance. (See Exhibit 11.13.)

In addition to their use in day-to-day planning, the hours required and the staffing plan provide information for scheduling individual workers, controlling operations, comparing capacity utilization with other branches, and starting up new branches.

Nurse Staffing and Scheduling

W. Abernathy, N. Baloff, and J. Hershey state, "The key element of effective nurse staffing is a well-conceived procedure for achieving an overall balance between the size of the nursing staff and the expected patient demand."[12] Their procedure, termed *aggregate budgeting*, is based upon a variety of interrelated activities and has a short-term schedule as a

---

[12]W. Abernathy, N. Baloff, and J. Hershey, "The Nurse Staffing Problem: Issues and Prospects," *Sloan Management Review* 13, no. 1 (Fall 1971), pp. 87–109.

Problem	Possible Solution
Accuracy of patient load forecast	Forecast frequently and rebudget monthly. Closely monitor seasonal demands, communicable diseases, and current occupancy
Forecasting nurse availability	Develop work standards for nurses for each level of possible demand (requires systematic data collection and analysis)
Complexity and time to rebudget	Use available computer programs
Flexibility in scheduling	Use variable staffing: Set regular staff levels slightly above minimum and absorb variation with broadskilled float nurses, part-time nurses, and overtime

Exhibit 11.14

General Problems in Nurse Scheduling

primary output. A number of severe, practical problems confront hospitals in deriving an effective yet low-cost aggregate budget. These difficulties, along with possible remedies, are listed in Exhibit 11.14.

Though most hospitals still use trial-and-error methods to develop worker schedules, management scientists have applied mathematical optimizing techniques to the problem with some success.

A major problem confronting health care managers today is the changing mix of patient needs and how it affects nurse staffing requirements. With the growing trend toward more outpatient treatment, patients who are hospitalized today are typically very ill, and thus require, on average, more individual attention. Under these conditions, the demands for nursing skills actually can increase, even though the number of patients in a designated area has remained unchanged.

Because of these increased patient needs, many hospitals are adapting a worker skill mix that incorporates lower-skilled technical support personnel to assist in the delivery of patient care, with the goal of reducing overall labour costs. This additional parameter of different worker skills has to be taken into consideration when determining personnel staffing requirements.

Of course, scheduling in services is not limited to workers. Eliashberg et al. discuss a scheduling method developed partly at the University of British Columbia that was used to schedule movie showings at theatres.[13]

Scheduling Consecutive Days Off

A practical problem encountered in many service organizations is setting schedules so that employees can have two consecutive days off even though the operation is open seven days a week. The importance of the problem stems from the fact that in most provinces, employment standards legislation[14] requires that overtime be paid for any hours worked (by hourly workers) in excess of 40 hours per week. Obviously, if two consecutive days off can't be scheduled each week for each employee, the likelihood of unnecessary overtime is quite high. In addition, most people probably prefer two consecutive days off per week.

---

[13]Jehoshua Eliashberg, Sanjeev Swami, Charles B. Weinberg, and Berend Wierenga, "Implementing and Evaluating SilverScreener: A Marketing Management Support System for Movie Exhibiters," *Interfaces* 31, no. 3 (May–June 2001), pp. S108–S127.

[14]Loren E. Falkenberg, Thomas H. Stone, and Noah M. Meltz, *Human Resource Management in Canada* (Toronto: Dryden, 1999), p. 59.

The following heuristic procedure was modified from that developed by James Browne and Rajen Tibrewala to deal with this problem:[15]

Objective. Find the weekly schedule that utilizes the fewest number of workers yet ensures that each has two consecutive days off, given the demands of the daily staffing schedule and assuming that the workers have no preference regarding which days they get off.

Procedure. Starting with the total number of workers required for each day of the week, create a schedule by adding one worker at a time. This is a two-step procedure:

Step 1   Circle the lowest pair of consecutive days off. The lowest pair is the one in which the highest number in the pair is equal to or lower than the highest number in any other pair. This ensures that the days with the highest requirements are covered by staff. (Monday and Sunday may be chosen even though they are at opposite ends of the array of days.) In case of ties choose the days-off pair with the lowest requirement on an adjacent day. This day may be before or after the pair. If a tie still remains, choose the first of the available tied pairs. (Do not bother using further tie-breaking rules, such as second-lowest adjacent days.)

Step 2   Subtract 1 from each of the remaining five days (i.e., the days not circled). This indicates that one less worker is required on these days, since the first worker has just been assigned to them.

Step 3   The two steps are repeated for the second worker, the third worker, and so forth, until no more workers are required to satisfy the schedule.

Example

	M	Tu	W	Th	F	S	Su
Requirement	**4**	**3**	**4**	**2**	**3**	**1**	**2**
Worker 1	4	3	4	2	3	(1	2)
Worker 2	3	2	3	1	(2	1)	2
Worker 3	2	1	2	0	2	(1	1)
Worker 4	1	(0	1)	0	1	1	1
Worker 5	0	0	1	0	0	0	0

Solution

This solution consists of five workers covering 19 worker days, although slightly different assignments may be equally satisfactory.

The schedule: Worker 1 is assigned S–Su off; Worker 2, F–S off; Worker 3, S–Su off; Worker 4, Tu–W off; and Worker 5 works only on Wednesday, since there are no further requirements for the other days.

---

[15]James J. Browne and Rajen K. Tibrewala, "Manpower Scheduling," *Industrial Engineering* 7, no. 8 (August 1975), pp. 22–23.

Job shops are prevalent throughout both the manufacturing and service sectors. Job shop scheduling has now become computer dependent and is inseparable from total manufacturing planning and control systems. In fact, the scheduling of the job shop is an integral part of this larger system.

Worker scheduling is especially important in service operations where labour is often a significant cost component. Here, too much labour negatively influences profits, but insufficient labour has a negative impact on customer service and, hence, adversely affects future sales.

Conclusion

Key Terms

dispatching of orders
    p. 389
drum-buffer-rope scheduling
    p. 398
expediting p. 389
flow pattern p. 391
Gantt chart p. 403

input/output control p. 402
job shop p. 389
labour-limited systems
    p. 391
loading p. 389
machine-limited systems
    p. 391

priority rules p. 392
scheduling p. 388
shop-floor control p. 400
theory of constraints (TOC)
    p. 398

Review and Discussion Questions

1. Identify the characteristics of a job shop. Why are job shops so prevalent, especially in the service sector?
2. What practical considerations are deterrents to using the SPT rule?
3. What priority rule do you use in scheduling your study time for midterm examinations? If you have five exams to study for, how many alternative schedules exist?
4. Why is it difficult to schedule workers in a service environment?
5. In Canada, there are certain assumptions made about the customer-service priority rules used in banks, restaurants, and retail stores. If you have the opportunity, ask an international student what rules are used in his or her country. To what factors might you attribute the differences, if any?
6. What job characteristics would lead you to schedule jobs according to "longest processing time first"?
7. In what way is the scheduling problem at the home office of a bank different from that of a branch?
8. Identify an example of a job shop where you are the scheduler/dispatcher. It might be your kitchen, your computer workstation, or something else. What priority rules would you use for this job shop, and why?
9. List some of the problems that a job shop scheduler faces when trying to estimate the personnel and machinery needed for a made-to-order job that has never been done before.
10. Assume you are the desk clerk at an upscale hotel and that you handle all registrations. You are dealing with your customers on a first-come, first-served basis when a professional football team arrives. They are playing a team from your city and will be staying at your hotel. How will you handle their registrations?
11. In many job shops, the percentage of work done by automated processes is increasing. For example, in a copy centre the copy machines now collate and staple automatically. In hospitals, more and more diagnoses are made by machines with remote sensors. Discuss how the capacity of machines to "do more" impacts the role of the job shop scheduler.
12. Examples of two-dimensional Gantt charts were presented in the chapter. Could a Gantt chart have three dimensions? Provide several examples.

13. What are some of the goods and services produced by a bottleneck system that you use? What characteristics do they have in common?

14. How does a bottleneck system affect the customer, the company, and the employees who work within the system?

15. In a service environment, can customer co-production be utilized to lessen the effects of a bottleneck? How?

Solved Problem

Problem

Joe's Auto Seat Cover and Paint Shop is bidding on a contract to do all the custom work for Smiling Ed's used car dealership. One of the main requirements for obtaining this contract is rapid delivery time, because Ed—for reasons we shall not go into here—wants the cars facelifted and back on his lot in a hurry. Ed says that if Joe can refit and repaint five cars that Ed has just received (from an unnamed source) in 24 hours or less, the contract will be his. The following is the time (in hours) required in the refitting shop and the paint shop for each of the five cars. Assuming that cars go through the refitting operations before they are repainted, can Joe meet the time requirements and get the contract?

Car	Refitting Time (hours)	Repairing Time (hours)
A	6	3
B	0	4
C	5	2
D	8	6
E	2	1

Solution

This problem can be viewed as a two-machine flow shop and can be solved easily using "Johnson's rule."

	Original Data		Johnson's Rule	
Car	Refitting Time (hours)	Repainting Time (hours)	Order of Selection	Position in Sequence
A	6	3	4th	3rd
B	0	4	1st	1st
C	5	2	3rd	4th
D	8	6	5th	2nd
E	2	1	2nd	5th

Graph of Johnson solution (not to scale):

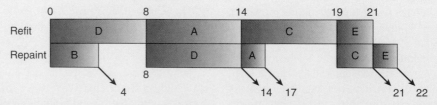

The total time for the five cars is 22 hours.

1. S. Chaudhary has three cars that must be overhauled by his ace mechanic, Jim. Given the following data about the cars, use the STR/OP priority rule (least slack remaining per operation) to determine Jim's scheduling priority for each.

Car	Customer Pick-Up Time (hours hence)	Remaining Overhaul Time (hours)	Remaining Operations
A	10	4	Painting
B	17	5	Wheel alignment, painting
C	15	1	Chrome plating, painting, seat repair

2. There are seven jobs that must be processed in two operations, A and B. All seven jobs must go through A and B in that sequence—A first, then B.

   a. Determine the optimal order in which the jobs should be sequenced through the process using these times:

Job	Process A Time	Process B Time
1	9	6
2	8	5
3	7	7
4	6	3
5	1	2
6	2	6
7	4	7

   b. Draw a graph similar to that for the solved problem showing the sequence of jobs.
   c. What is the total completion time for all seven jobs?

3. The following list of jobs in a critical department includes estimates of their required times:

Job	Required Time (days)	Days to Delivery Promise	Slack
A	8	12	4
B	3	9	6
C	7	8	1
D	1	11	10
E	10	−10	—
F	6	10	4
G	5	−8	—
H	4	6	2

   a. Use the shortest operation time rule to schedule these jobs. What is the schedule? What is the mean flow time?
   b. The boss doesn't like the schedule in (*a*). Jobs E and G must be done first, for obvious reasons (they are already late). Reschedule and do the best you can while scheduling Jobs E and G first and second, respectively. What is the new schedule? What is the new mean flow time?

4. The Walter-Russell manufacturing facility has five jobs to be scheduled into production. The following table gives the processing times plus the necessary wait times and other necessary delays for each of the jobs. Assume that today is April 3 and the jobs are due on the dates shown:

Job	Days of Actual Processing Time Required	Days of Necessary Delay Time	Total Time Required	Date Job Due
1	2	12	14	April 30
2	5	8	13	April 21
3	9	15	24	April 28
4	7	9	16	April 29
5	4	22	28	April 27

Determine two schedules, stating the order in which the jobs are to be done. Use the critical ratio priority rule for one. You may use any other rule for the second schedule as long as you state what it is.

5. An accounting firm, Debits R Us, would like to keep its auditing staff to a maximum of four people, yet satisfy the staffing needs and the policy of two days off per week. Given the following requirements, is this possible? What should the schedule be?

    Requirements (Monday through Sunday): 4, 3, 3, 2, 2, 4, 4.

6. Jobs A, B, C, D, and E must go through Processes I and II in that sequence (i.e., Process I first, then Process II).

    Use Johnson's rule to determine the optimal sequence to schedule the jobs to minimize the total required time.

Job	Required Processing Time on Process I	Required Processing Time on Process II
A	4	5
B	16	14
C	8	7
D	12	11
E	3	9

7. Joe was able to land a job as production scheduler in a brand-new custom refinishing auto service shop located near the border. This system is capable of handling 10 cars per day. The sequence now is customizing first, followed by repainting.

Car	Customizing Time (hours)	Painting (hours)	Car	Customizing Time (hours)	Painting (hours)
1	3.0	1.2	6	2.1	0.8
2	2.0	0.9	7	3.2	1.4
3	2.5	1.3	8	0.6	1.8
4	0.7	0.5	9	1.1	1.5
5	1.6	1.7	10	1.8	0.7

In what sequence should Joe schedule the cars?

8. The MedSports Clinic provides specialized medical care for sports-related injuries. A patient's visit to MedSports usually involves two separate stages. First, the patient meets with the doctor to explain the nature of his or her injury, and, if necessary, to have a physical examination by the doctor. Following the visit with the doctor, a set of x-rays is taken

of the injured part of the patient's body. The amount of time spent at each stage of the patient's visit can vary significantly, depending on the type of injury and whether or not this is the patient's first visit to the clinic. Because MedSports has just recently opened for business, there is currently only one doctor available at any one time, and only one x-ray technician and machine. On a given day, six patients have made appointments. It is estimated that each patient requires the following times (in minutes) for each of the two stages:

	Time (minutes)	
Patient	Examination	X-Ray
A	30	15
B	45	50
C	75	35
D	20	40
E	90	25
F	60	70

 a. Using Johnson's rule, determine the optimal order for scheduling these patients throughout the day.

 b. If the clinic opens at 9:00 a.m. with the first patient, what times should each of the patients be told to come into the clinic?

9. Mbeke Financial Services (MBFS) offers a wide variety of mutual funds to both corporate pension funds and individuals. Its customer service operation performs the following tasks relative to its customer accounts:

	Operations Required and Productivity (P/H)*			
Activity	Receiving	Scanning	Processing	Auditing
Change of address	125	75	100	
Change of beneficiary	125	75	50	
Transaction error	150	50	75	50
Deposit	200	100	75	150
Withdrawal	200	100	25	50

 *P/H = production rate per hour.

The daily volumes for each type of transaction for the following week are estimated to be as follows:

	Day of the Week				
	Mon	Tue	Wed	Thur	Fri
Change of address	2200	1600	1300	1000	1000
Change of beneficiary	1000	1200	800	600	500
Transaction error	400	300	500	400	300
Deposit	8500	7200	6800	6500	6500
Withdrawal	3000	3400	4000	3700	4200

Set up an Excel spreadsheet similar to that in Exhibit 11.12 and determine the number of workers needed for each function for each day of the week. (Assume that there is a 25 percent allowance factor for absences and vacations and that the normal workday is eight hours.)

10. The Wira Singha fast-food restaurant has forecasted hourly sales (in dollars) for next Monday to be the following:

Hour	Sales
11:00 a.m.	250
12:00 noon	625
1:00 p.m.	500
2:00 p.m.	375
3:00 p.m.	150
4:00 p.m.	100
5:00 p.m.	175
6:00 p.m.	400
7:00 p.m.	475
8:00 p.m.	300
9:00 p.m.	275
10:00 p.m.	125

Using the staffing table shown in Exhibit 11.11, determine the number of workers required for each hour of the day. (*Note*: The times stated above represent the beginning of each hour in which the sales are forecasted.)

12

Supply Chain Management

Chapter Objectives

- Introduce the concept of a firm's supply chain and show how it has evolved to its present status.

- Identify the issues involved in designing a supply chain.

- Present the requirements necessary for a successful supply chain.

- Discuss the impact of technology on a firm's supply chain.

Logistics Providers Are Providing More Value Added Services…

Not long ago all companies such as DHL, Federal Express (FedEx), UPS, and Canada Post's Purolator did was pick up an item from you and deliver it to the addressee. Now they do a lot more than that. They provide supply chain solutions. Purolator offers consulting services that help the customer comply with increased security regulations in this post-9/11 world. FedEx bought Kinko's, a chain of copy stores, in 2004 as a value-added service. Now, from your computer you can electronically deliver a document to Kinko's. Kinko's then will do the production of the documents, and FedEx will deliver the documents to your customer. For the same reason UPS bought Mail Boxes Etc. (now being rebranded as the UPS Store) in 2001. UPS also offers services in order fulfillment (picking, packing, and making required kits), repair and refurbishment, reverse logistics, and service parts logistics. DHL offers to take over management of customers' in-house logistics including distribution, transport, back-office, supply chain, and after sales. These value-added services are not unique. Most logistics service providers are moving in the same direction. They see this as a way to survive in the future.

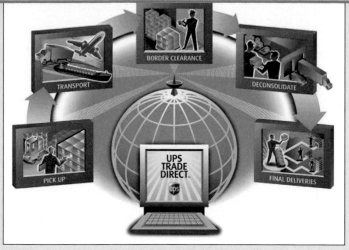

Source: http://pressroom.ups.com/multimedia/images/operations/

…While Others in the Supply Chain Are Shedding Non-Core Assets

This strategy of logistic providers to provide more services is taking place at the same time as high-tech communication products companies such as Nortel Networks of Toronto and U.S.-based Cisco and Lucent have been turning over some of their manufacturing plants to U.S.-based Solectron, Toronto-based Celestica, and others.

Companies such as Celestica are global electronics manufacturing service (EMS) providers. High-tech companies such as Nortel and Cisco have decided that their best strategy is to concentrate on the development of new products and leave the manufacturing to EMS experts.

This disvestiture of non-core assets is happening in many other industries too. This means that co-operative supply chain management will be a core competency in many industries because end-product supplier companies such as Nortel no longer control the supply chain. In addition, with global sourcing and marketing, logistics are more complicated. Issues such as quality, order status, on-time delivery, and design changes have to managed in co-operation with distant suppliers and third-party logistics providers such as Purolator.

Sources:

Jan Matthews, "More, better, faster: demand forces manufacturers to outsource," *Silicon Valley North*, 3, no. 9, June 2000.

Anonymous, "Celestica commences strategic outsourcing relationship with NEC," www.celestica.com, Newsrelease, April 1, 2002.

http://pressroom.ups.com/multimedia/images/operations/

www.ups.com

www.fedex.com

www.dhl.com

www.purolator.com

Managerial Issues

In recent years, managers have continued to focus their efforts on supply chain issues for several reasons. First, to be more responsive to the constantly changing needs of their customers, companies are concentrating their resources on their core competencies. With this narrower focus, firms are now buying a substantially greater proportion of the goods and services that go into their products than was previously the norm. In many cases, for example, the cost of the purchased raw materials and components is 60 percent (and often higher) of the cost of goods sold. As a result there is now greater dependency on suppliers and the need to develop long-term supplier relationships. In addition, the logistical costs (that is, the transportation and distribution costs) associated with the delivery of products have continued to increase, as firms are now able to extend their supply chains to the far corners of the world.

To further complicate matters, there is increasing pressure on managers to reduce their inventories, thereby placing further dependence on their suppliers. To address the need to reduce inventories, managers have introduced such concepts as *consignment inventories* and *vendor managed inventories* (*VMI*), which we will discuss in this chapter.

Advances in information technology have provided managers with a wide assortment of tools that allow them to better oversee their firms' supply chains. These include electronic data interchange (EDI) and business-to-business (B2B) marketplaces. This increased emphasis on a firm's supply chain has caused a dramatic shift in the role of the purchasing function. In the past, the purchasing function was typically viewed as being primarily a transactions-oriented function. Now it is seen by many firms as playing a more strategic role in determining the overall long-term success of the firm.

Definition of Supply Chain Management

supply chain

The steps and the firms that perform these steps in the transformation of raw material into finished products bought by customers.

inbound logistics

The delivery of goods and services that are purchased from suppliers and/or their distributors.

outbound logistics

The delivery of goods and services that are sold to a firm's customers and/or its distributors.

The goal of **supply chain** management is to apply a systems approach to managing the entire flow of information, materials, and services from raw material suppliers through factories and warehouses to the end customer. As Exhibit 12.1 shows, both manufacturing and service organizations have supply chains. The issues associated with the delivery of products to the firm from suppliers are referred to as **inbound logistics**. After the firm has added value by transforming the purchased goods and services, the finished products are localized through the firm's distributors or local service providers before delivery to the end customer (**outbound logistics**). Localization may involve only the delivery of the product or service to the customer or it may involve further transformation to tailor the product or service to the local market.

From a larger perspective, a supply chain can be defined as a group of organizations that perform the various processes that are required to make a finished product. Here the chain would begin with the actual raw materials and end with the finished product that is delivered to the end user or final customer. For example, if the finished product is a piece of wood furniture, then the supply chain, going backwards from the customer, would include (*a*) the retail operation where the furniture was purchased, (*b*) the shipping company that delivered it, (*c*) the furniture manufacturer, (*d*) the hardware manufacturer, and (*e*) the lumber companies that harvested the wood from the forests. If the end product is fresh fish fillets that are sold at a supermarket, then the supply chain would include (*a*) the supermarket, (*b*) the fresh fish supplier who delivered the fish, (*c*) the fish processor who filleted them, and (*d*) the fishermen who caught them.

Effective supply chain management can have many benefits for an organization. A study of firms in the U.S. computer industry[1] that had undergone supply chain transformation revealed the following:

- Cost reduction: Reductions of up to 30 percent each in transportation, warehousing, and inventory carrying costs.

[1]L. R. Kopczak, "Logistics Partnerships and Supply Chain Restructuring: Survey Results from the U.S. Computer Industry," *Production and Operations Management*, 6, no. 3 (1997).

Exhibit 12.1

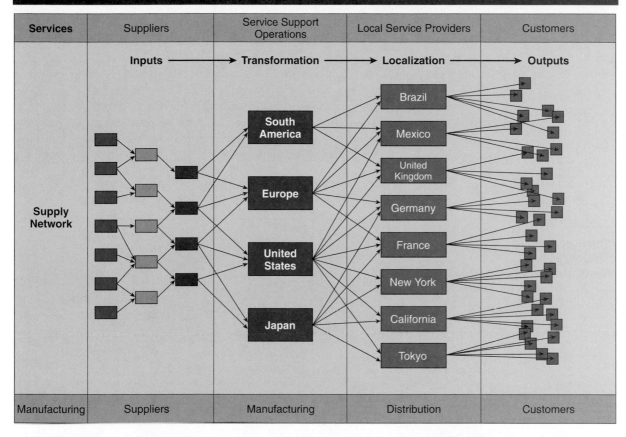

From: Richard B. Chase, F. Robert Jacobs, and Nicholas J. Aquilano, *Operations Management for Competitive Advantage*, 10th ed. (New York: Irwin McGraw-Hill, 2004), p. 365.

- Quality of service and information: Improvements of up to 50 percent in order cycle time and 10 to 20 percent for on-time delivery and product availability.
- Flexibility: Ability to focus on core competency.

Organizations in many different industries have profited from better supply chain management. By improving its supply chain management, Campbell Soup Company reduced its inventory level considerably while maintaining customer service, and Blockbuster Inc. has increased both the availability of movies and its profit through supplier partnerships.

Supply chain management, therefore, can be defined as the ability of a firm to work with its suppliers to provide high-quality material and components that are competitively priced. The degree of closeness of the relationship between vendor and customer, in many respects, differentiates one type of supply chain from another. The adoption of the term *supply chain management* in lieu of materials management or purchasing reflects top management's recognition of the strategic role of suppliers in contributing to the long-term success of the firm.

The Evolution of Supply Chain Management

Supply chain management is a relatively new concept in business. Previously, management theory suggested that the overall efficiency of the technical core or production function could be significantly improved if the core could be isolated or *buffered* to the greatest extent possible from an often erratic and uncertain external environment.

To isolate the technical core from suppliers (and also customers), companies established significant inventories of raw material and finished goods, as shown in Exhibit 12.2A. Although this approach produced highly efficient operations, it simultaneously made the core less responsive to changes in the marketplace. This inability to react quickly to changes in customer demand, preferences, and so forth was caused primarily by the significant amounts of raw material and finished goods inventories that were maintained, and that first had to be depleted before the firm could begin supplying customers with new product.

Exhibit 12.2

The Evolution of Supply Chain Management

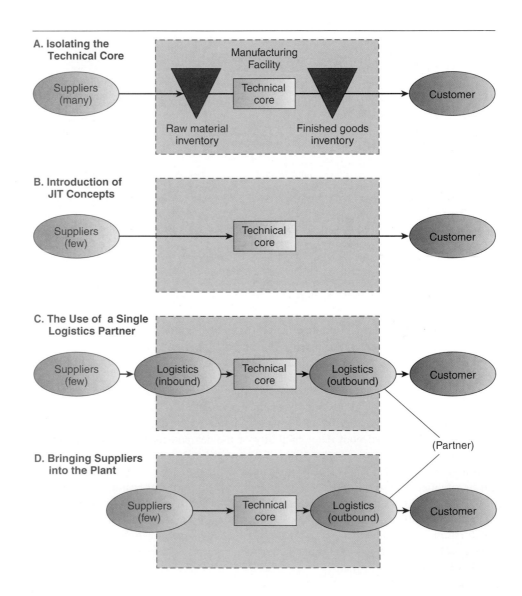

FIRE AT TOYOTA'S SUPPLIER STOPS PRODUCTION

Aisin Seiki provides 99 percent of the brake valves that Toyota uses in the assembly of its automobiles. Because Toyota uses a just-in-time (JIT) system with its vendors, it maintains only a four-hour supply of brake valves at each of its assembly plants. Consequently, when a fire destroyed Aisin Sekei's manufacturing facility on February 1, 1997, Toyota was forced to shut down its 20 automobile plants, which were producing 14 000 cars a day.

Although many experts predicted that it would take weeks before Aisin could begin producing valves, Toyota's plants were again turning out cars five days after the fire. This was accomplished through a concerted effort of all of Toyota's suppliers who worked together around the clock to provide an interim solution.

This example illustrates some of the risks in the supply chain model that Toyota follows and how it manages these risks. A company like Toyota that uses the JIT system (which has many advantages and is discussed in Chapter 13) tends to carry less inventory and thus is at greater risk of plant shutdowns when the supply chain is disrupted. Toyota manages these risks by being agile and also by close co-operation with its suppliers. This minimizes supply disruptions and allows Toyota to recover quickly if a disruption occurs.

Source:
Valerie Reitman, *The Wall Street Journal*, May 8, 1997, A1. Copyright © 1997 by Dow Jones & Co., Inc. Reproduced with permission.

Within this operating environment, companies often had antagonistic relationships with their suppliers. Every item that was purchased may have had several vendors. These vendors were played off against each other to obtain the lowest possible price, which was the primary criterion for being awarded a contract. Suppliers, recognizing that this relationship could very likely be terminated with the next contract, invested minimal time and money to address the specific needs of individual customers. Because of this short-term perspective, very little information was shared between these firms. Under such conditions the purchasing function within a manufacturing company often reported to the operations manager, and its primary objective was to purchase raw material and components at the lowest possible cost.

Today, companies are working more closely with their suppliers so that they can be more responsive to the changing needs of their customers. In so doing, they are significantly reducing, and in some cases eliminating, these previously established buffer inventories, as shown in Exhibit 12.2B.

Ryder System manages Saturn's supply chain that links suppliers, factories, and dealers. Saturn turns over its parts inventory quickly—over 300 times a year—so accurate information is essential. In the photo, drivers check the on-board computer that tells them where they should go, how to get there, and how long it should take.

Toyota is considered one of the pioneers in this area with its development of the *just-in-time* (*JIT*) concept, which virtually eliminates all raw material and work-in-process inventories. In adopting JIT, however, companies become more dependent on their suppliers. (See related OM in Practice, "Fire at Toyota's Supplier Stops Production.")

After JIT, the next stage in the supply chain management evolution was the use of a single logistics supplier to address all the transportation and distribution functions for the firm, as shown in Exhibit 12.2C, leading to the concept of *seamless logistics*. (Previously, firms dealt with many such transportation logistics vendors, again using cost as the primary criterion for selection.)

For example, Schneider Logistics of Green Bay, Wisconsin, was named, in January 1997, the logistics provider for General Motors' Canadian parts operation. In the fall of 1996, Schneider also established a long-term relationship with Case Corp., a manufacturer of construction and agricultural equipment. Under this agreement, Schneider handles all of Case's inbound shipments of parts from nearly 2000 suppliers worldwide, and outbound shipments of finished goods that total 40 000 pieces of equipment to some 150 countries around the world.[2]

A recent innovation in supply chain management is the incorporation of suppliers and their workers within the same manufacturing facility. Volkswagen's new automotive assembly plant in Brazil, discussed in an OMP box later in this chapter, provides a good example of this innovation, which is illustrated in Exhibit 12.2D.

Designing a Supply Chain

As seen in Exhibit 12.1, a supply chain includes suppliers, the transformation process, distributors, and customers. Thus a number of issues need to be addressed in designing a company's supply chain. These include:

- Vertical integration
- Facility location
- Procurement
- Inventory management
- Logistics
- Performance metrics
- Use of technology

Vertical Integration

Vertical integration refers to the proportion of the supply chain that the company owns. Henry Ford, to support his huge River Rouge automobile plant just outside of Detroit, Michigan, invested heavily in iron ore mines, forests, coal mines, and even cargo ships that transported raw material on the Great Lakes. His goal was to gain total control over his supply chain (which, in the end, he realized was not possible). Similarly, in 1896, the Nova Scotia Steel and Forge Company merged with the New Glasgow Iron, Coal and Railway Company (a company that owned iron ore deposits and railways), to obtain a secure supply of ore. The new company was called the Nova Scotia Steel Company. Because coal is required to run steel-producing furnaces, a few years later the merged company acquired the metallurgical coalfields owned by the General Mining Association of Sydney Mines, Cape Breton. In 1912 it formed the Eastern Car Company to build railway cars to use some of the steel that it produced.

The greater the degree or span of control that a firm has with respect to its supply chain, the more vertically integrated it is said to be. In other words, Nova Scotia Steel's operation could be described as being more vertically integrated in comparison to other steel manufacturers who focus solely on making steel from purchased ore. The Irving Group of New Brunswick is a current example of a vertically integrated company owning oil-and-gas refining facilities, petroleum trucking, and service stations.

As described in the opening vignette, the current trend in many industries is to become less vertically integrated. For example, telecommunications companies such as

---

[2]Michael Fabey, "Time Is Money: Seamless Logistics Are in Demand," *World Trade* (July 1997), pp. 53–54.

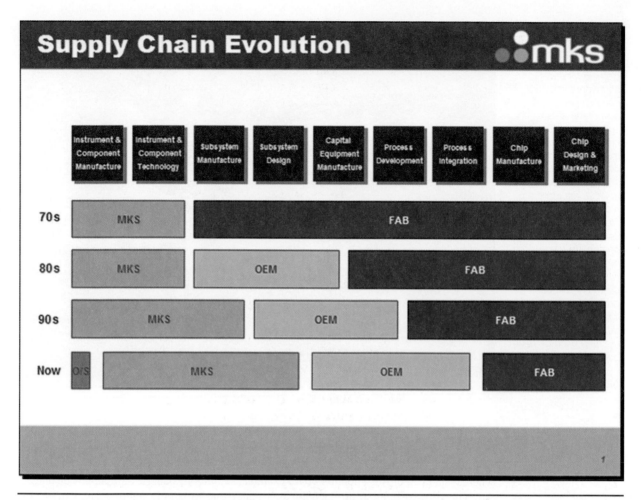

The supply chain for the computer-chip industry has changed dramatically, as computer chip manufacturers (FABs) have continued to focus on their core competencies of chip design and marketing, outsourcing many of the functions they previously did themselves to original equipment manufacturers (OEMs). Today, second-tier FAB suppliers such as MKS are outsourcing (O/S) major product components. Source: MKS Instruments, Inc.

Nortel and Cisco have outsourced their manufacturing to electronic EMS companies such as Solectron and Celestica. Proctor and Gamble (P&G) recently subcontracted all of its North American soap manufacturing to Newmarket, Ontario-based Trillium Health Care Products Inc. Similarly, Toronto-based Cott Corporation is the largest producer of carbonated soft drinks in the world, producing beverages that are sold under supermarket brand names. The idea is that companies such as Nortel, P&G, and supermarkets can then focus their scarce resources on strengthening their core competencies (such as new product development or marketing), while the suppliers can focus on their core competencies (such as manufacturing). In this way both companies will be better off.

On the other hand, clothing retailer Zara owns its own factories, which gives it more control over the supply chain and allows it to manufacture and deliver clothing quickly. Similarly, some the EMS companies have become more vertically integrated by doing some product design, producing more of their inputs, and providing after-sales product service for the ultimate customer.

Zara clothing store, an international retailer, sells trendy clothing for men and women. Its competitive advantage is its supply chain. Zara can design and manufacture its own clothing in less than 15 days and delivers to its stores twice a week. All its retail stores are linked by computer to the company's headquarters in Spain where sales data and customer feedback provide real-time information for decisions on fabric, cut, and price for new garments.

The outsourcing decision is also referred to as the *make-or-buy* decision. It is important to do a strategic analysis before outsourcing a component. Items that provide competitive advantage (such as designing and manufacturing engines at Honda) would not be outsourced, whereas standard off-the-shelf items (for example, automobile batteries) might be outsourced.

The vertical integration decision is a major one in supply chain management. On the one hand, becoming less vertically integrated means dealing with more partners in the supply chain, making procurement, co-operative product design, confidentiality and logistics more important. On the other hand, more vertical integration can mean the merging of companies with different cultures and incorporating the ability to manage a larger organization. Thus these decisions can have a major impact on the performance and competitiveness of an organization and should be taken only after a strategic and detailed analysis which considers multiple factors, not simply on cost considerations alone.

Facility Location

The number and locations of factories, warehouses, and retail stores are important decisions in any supply chain, since they are major decisions involving large expenditures. Thus they have to made after careful analysis. The considerations in facility location were discussed in detail in Chapter 7.

Procurement

Companies, as part of their supply chain programs, have significantly reduced the number of vendors they buy from. Managers currently believe in establishing long-term relationships with a few highly reliable, high-quality vendors rather than having multiple sources for every purchased item. For example, between 1991 and 1996, IBM reduced its number of suppliers from 1156 to 321, and Sony is planning to reduce the number of its suppliers from 4700 to 1000 within a few years. Other companies have also achieved reductions of this order. This is even more impressive in light of the fact that most of these companies are now offering a wider variety of products to their customers.

When selecting a supplier it is important to consider all of the costs involved, in other words, the "total cost of ownership." For example, the purchase price may only be the tip of the iceberg. One or more of the following costs may be added to the purchase price depending on the product or service that is being procured: transportation and installation, inventory management, administration and order processing, training employees to use the product, data acquisition and evaluation, operating and maintenance, and disposal.

Just as in facility location, there are a number of qualitative factors that have to be considered when selecting suppliers. These factors include the potential supplier's engineering capability, manufacturing strength, financial situation, information systems strength, management capabilities, research facilities, proximity, knowledge of sales personnel, labour relations, technical assistance capability, and so on. Other factors to examine may include the ability of the potential vendor to deliver consistently on time (reliability), to maintain consistent quality, and to react to unexpected increases in demand or a different product mix from the customer. As in location selection, sophisticated multifactor or multi-criteria decision models such as the Analytic Hierarchy Process (AHP) for handling complex decisions could be used. Chapter 13 discusses the long-term approach to supplier relationships followed by JIT companies.

With product life cycles becoming shorter and the cost of developing new products increasing, the risk associated with these new products also increases. To reduce their own financial exposure, many companies are requesting that vendors take on an increasing percentage of this risk. Volkswagen's new automotive plant in Brazil epitomizes this sharing of risk with vendors. (See the OM in Practice box.) Similarly, Boeing has many global partners in the development of its commercial airplanes.

One issue that is becoming increasingly important is that of fair trade practices. As discussed in the Chapter 2 under future sources of competitive advantage, companies are recognizing the importance of corporate responsibility within their supply chains. Thus it is important to ensure that supplier companies are environmentally conscious, provide acceptable working conditions, and respect human rights in issues such as use of child labour. For example, at some universities students have ensured that products sold on the campus through the university, such as clothing with the university logo, are purchased only from companies that follow fair trade practices.

Another emerging issue is that of fakes, or counterfeits and related to it, intellectual property theft. Some of you may have seen counterfeits of luxury goods such as watches, golf clubs, and handbags, but many other products are counterfeited as well. With the availability of better manufacturing and computer technology it is becoming easier to produce counterfeit products. Furthermore, with globalization there are now many more suppliers and they are widely dispersed geographically. Some are involved in dealing with counterfeit products which are often difficult to detect. Thus it is important to ensure the integrity not only of your suppliers but also of the suppliers upstream in the supply chain to ensure that counterfeit products do not enter your supply chain.

Suppliers of counterfeits may not follow fair trade or environmental practices in addition to violating copyright. In some cases suppliers contracted to produce authorized goods have become involved in counterfeiting by producing excess amounts not authorized by the customer (and selling them illegally) or by giving designs and equipment illegally to other suppliers to make counterfeits. The counterfeiting industry has even targeted automobile brakes, aircraft parts, and pharmaceutical drugs where the results of using counterfeits can be disastrous. Thus counterfeiting is an issue that is getting increasingly global attention because of the dangers it poses.

In addition to violating intellectual property rights, suppliers of counterfeit products may not follow fair trade or environmental practices. In some cases suppliers contracted to

VOLKSWAGEN BUILDS A DIFFERENT KIND OF ASSEMBLY PLANT IN BRAZIL

In November 1996, Volkswagen began operations at its new truck and bus assembly plant in Resende, Brazil. Unlike any other automotive assembly plant in the world, this facility has suppliers' personnel working side by side with VW's workers. This latest advancement in supply chain management is the concept of José Ignacio López de Arriortua, who is in charge of purchasing for VW. As a result, only 200 out of a total workforce of 1000 are VW employees. The remaining workers are employed by major subcontractors such as MWM-Cummins, which produces the engines and transmissions, and Rock well, which produces the suspension systems.

With this revolutionary approach to automotive assembly, VW hopes to increase both productivity and quality. At the same time, VW is sharing the risk of this new venture with its major suppliers, who have to shoulder a large percentage of the fixed operating costs of the plant. In exchange for this risk, these subcontractors hope to develop and maintain a long and profitable relationship with VW.

Sources:
Edvaldo Pereira Lima, "VW's Revolutionary Idea," *Industry Week,* March 17, 1997, and Diana J. Schemo, "Is VW's New Plant Lean, or Just Mean?" *New York Times,* November 19, 1996.

VW's Carmaking Co-op

Like Tom Sawyer and his fence-painting project, José Ignacio López de Arriortua designed Volkswagen's new truck plant in Resende, Brazil, around work done for Volkswagen's benefit by others. Major suppliers are assigned space in the plant and supply their own workers to add components to trucks rolling down the assembly line. Volkswagen's employees, a minority in the plant, supervise the work and inspect finished trucks; only when they pass are the suppliers paid.

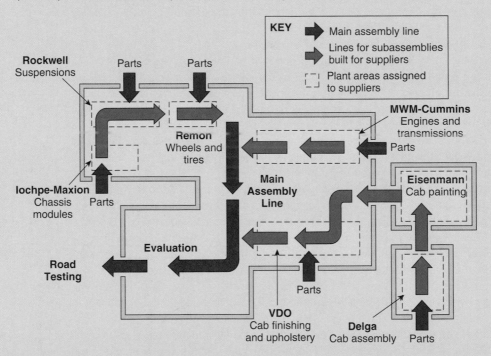

Source:
Graphic from Diana J. Schemo, "Is VW's New Plant Lean, or Just Mean?" *New York Times,* November 19, 1996. Reprinted with permission.

produce authorized goods produce excess amounts not authorized by the customer and sell them illegally or give designs and equipment illegally to other suppliers to make counterfeits. The counterfeiting industry has even targeted automobile brakes, aircraft parts, and pharmaceuticals, where the results can be disastrous. Thus counterfeiting is getting increasing global attention because of the dangers it poses.

Inventory Management

Supply chains convert raw material to finished products, which involves the storage and movement of different types of inventory. Therefore, organizations have to make decisions about how the inventory is controlled, such as how much to stock and when to order replenishments. Furthermore, organizations have to make decisions about how to co-ordinate these decisions among the supply chain partners. Inventory management is discussed in detail in Chapters 15 and 16. Just-in-time systems, the subject of Chapter 13, also relates to the management of inventory within supply chains. Managing inventory across the supply chain is sometimes called multi-echelon inventory management.

To reduce inventories without negatively affecting operations and customer deliveries, an increasing number of companies are using **consignment inventories** wherever possible. Consignment inventories are inventories that are physically in a company's facility but still owned by the supplier. Thus, they do not appear anywhere as an asset to the firm. Only when the components are actually used in the production of an end product does the ownership transfer to the firm, and then it transfers almost immediately to the customer upon shipment. Consignment inventories also are used in services, where the retailer doesn't pay the manufacturer for the product until it is actually sold to the end user.

consignment inventories
Inventories that are physically present in a firm's facility but that are still owned by the supplier.

Logistics

The continued emphasis on globalization with respect to both suppliers and customers has caused the supply chain to become longer in terms of time and distance. For example, in June 2003, the *Globe and Mail* reported that the Sudden Acute Respiratory Syndrome (SARS) outbreak in southern China, one of the top toy producing areas in the world, was threatening to affect the availability of toys in Canada for Christmas of 2003. The reasons were that the migrant production workers and the buyers who had to sample the toys would not or could not travel to the producing areas.[3] This was an issue in June because toys are made in China for the Christmas season months before the selling season starts in Canada (This production planning aspect is discussed in Chapter 14).

As a consequence of globalization and competition, the logistics associated with both the delivery of raw material and components to the company and the delivery of finished goods to its customers have taken on added importance. However, the lengthening of the supply chain runs counter to the firm's need for flexibility to provide customers with a wide variety of products that can be delivered quickly. Furthermore, increased security on inbound and outbound freight after 9/11 has added even more complexity to already-complex global supply chains.

Companies have therefore adopted various strategies to compensate for the longer supply chain. Some companies are locating distribution centres closer to customer markets so they can better serve these markets. For example, many computer manufacturers are producing components for the North American market in Guadalajara, Mexico, even though labour in China is cheaper, because it is closer and delivery is much quicker.[4] Important aspects of logistics are discussed below.

---

[3]Doug Young, "SARS Could Hurt Christmas," *The Globe and Mail*, June 25, 2003, B9.
[4]J. Friedland and G. McWilliams, "Guadalajara Builds Itself as a High-Tech Hub," *The Wall Street Journal*, March 2, 2000, B12.

Mode of Transportation

Different modes of transportation have their own advantages and disadvantages as seen in Exhibit 12.3. Thus a cost-benefit analysis should be undertaken before choosing the mode of transportation. Consider this example:[5] The Good Earth Vegetable Company was shipping produce to distant markets by train. The cost of shipping a ton of vegetables by train averaged less than half the cost of airfreight, so the company assumed that rail was the best method. But then Good Earth managers did a more complete analysis. To their surprise, they found that (as seen in Exhibit 12.4) the airfreight system was faster and cheaper.

Exhibit 12.3

Modes of Transportation

		Transporting features				
Mode	Cost	Delivery speed	No. of locations served	Ability to handle variety of goods	Frequency of shipments	Dependability in meeting schedules
Rail	Medium	Average	Extensive	High	Low	Medium
Water	Very low	Very slow	Limited	Very high	Very low	Medium
Truck	High	Fast	Very extensive	High	High	High
Air	Very high	Very fast	Extensive	Limited	High	High
Pipeline	Low	Slow	Very limited	Very limited	Medium	High

Source: Stanley Shapiro; Kenneth Wong; William Perreault, Jr.; Jerome McCarthy; *Basic Marketing* (Toronto, Ontario: McGraw-Hill Ryerson, 2002), p. 361.

Exhibit 12.4

Air versus Rail for Good Earth

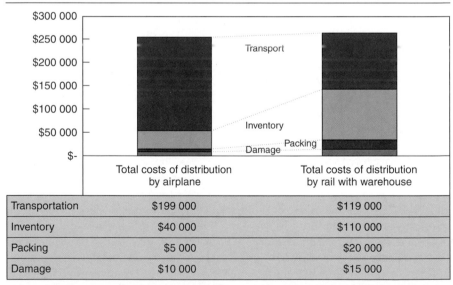

	Total costs of distribution by airplane	Total costs of distribution by rail with warehouse
Transportation	$199 000	$119 000
Inventory	$40 000	$110 000
Packing	$5 000	$20 000
Damage	$10 000	$15 000

Stanley Shapiro; Kenneth Wong; William Perreault, Jr.; E. Jerome McCarthy; *Basic Marketing* (Toronto, Ontario: McGraw-Hill Ryerson, 2002), p. 353.

[5]Stanley Shapiro, Kenneth Wong, William Perreault, Jr., Jerome McCarthy, *Basic Marketing* (Toronto: McGraw-Hill Ryerson, 2002).

Vendor-Managed Inventories

To decrease purchasing transaction costs and record-keeping costs, many firms use a concept known as **vendor-managed inventories (VMI)**, sometimes also called supplier-managed inventories (SMI). Under this concept, vendors manage the customer's inventory of the products they supply. For example, home improvement retailer RONA allows its suppliers to access its computer system to determine when they should replenish RONA's stock.[6] The supplier has oversight of the demand for its products, which helps its supply chain management, while RONA gets the advantage of decreased purchasing and record-keeping costs.

Third Party Logistics

Another approach to addressing the issue of a growing supply chain involves the establishment of a strategic alliance or partnership with a firm that specializes in transportation or logistics, called a **third party logistics (3PL)** provider. This is equivalent to outsourcing logistics and allows the company to focus on their core competencies while leaving the logistics function to outside specialists (See the OM in Practice Box on 3PL). An example is the logistics partnerships that Amazon.ca and Indigo.ca have with Canada Post. 3PL providers can perform a variety of services. Moreover, with their economies of scale they can invest in technologies that the customers may not be able to. For example, freight companies use satellite technology to pinpoint the location of trucks at any time or have other technologies that help track and deliver consignments on time.

As an example of one type of logistics service, L.L. Bean, the well-known mail-order firm specializing in outdoor equipment and clothing, has established such a partnership with FedEx. As a result, FedEx employees, who are physically located on a full-time basis at the L.L. Bean distribution facility in Freeport, Maine, handle all of the outbound shipments to L.L. Bean's customers (including the shipment of some packages by UPS).

Another approach to using a logistics partner is for a firm to store finished goods at the logistics partner's hub or distribution centre (warehouse outsourcing). Establishing an inventory at this point in the distribution channel will significantly reduce the delivery time of critical products. For example, both FedEx and UPS provide this service in Canada. Similarly, Metro Canada Logistics Inc., a 3PL provider, has warehouses in Vancouver, Calgary, Concord, Ontario, and Montreal to support its 3PL operations. In other cases the logistics provider will perform some assembly before delivery to the customer, as well as activities such as clearing customs, consolidation (combining loads coming from different sources but going to the same destination into one big load), and breaking bulk (breaking up a load coming from one source into multiple smaller loads meant for different destinations). In fact, UPS will even repair electronic products for manufacturers. These manufacturers in turn can promise quicker repair times for customers.

Disintermediation

Disintermediation is a term coined by futurist Stan Davis.[7] It refers to the growing trend of companies and organizations to try to get closer to both suppliers and customers by eliminating many of the intermediate steps or intermediaries that currently exist in the supply chain.

For example, Wal-Mart, as part of its strategy, built large regional distribution warehouses to store items for restocking its retail operations. As a result, significant capital was tied up in both facilities and inventory. Subsequently, Wal-Mart developed the concept of

vendor-managed inventories (VMI)
Inventories in a firm's facility that are the responsibility of the supplier to maintain and replenish as necessary.

3PL
When a company other than the customer or supplier provides logistics services.

disintermediation
Trend to reduce many of the steps in the supply chain.

[6]"Retailer to Suppliers: Track Inventory, Restock Shelves," *Information Week*, July 2, 2001, p. 24.
[7]Stanley Davis, *Future Perfect* (Reading, MA: Addison-Wesley, 1987).

THIRD PARTY LOGISTICS PROVIDERS HELP IN DIFFERENT WAYS

Third party logistics (3PL) is another trend in outsourcing that allows the outsourcing company to concentrate on what it does best. For example, Canadian Tire's warehouse in Calgary uses Genco Distribution System to manage the facility as a 3PL provider. "They have experience in cross-docking, flow through, and multi-channel processing," says Bruce Johnson, Canadian Tire VP of Distribution. Genco also handles product returns. Excel Logistics provides similar services for Wal-Mart in Canada.

Similarly, Peak Products Manufacturing Inc. of Vancouver uses PBB Global Logistics as its 3PL provider. Peak Products is a manufacturer and distributor of building and consumer products to wholesale and retail customers across North America, including Home Depot and Home Hardware.

How does PBB help? PBB ensures accurate and efficient customs clearance at key ports including Vancouver, Calgary, Montreal, and Toronto for goods shipped from Peak's manufacturing facilities in China. Goods are warehoused and orders are sent to individual stores, often on a next-day basis. Peak Products can use PBB's e-globallogistics.com tracing system to get full visibility of its shipments and inventories from manufacturing facilities in China to the shelves in North America. The system handles hundreds of products and thousands of individual transactions each month. As a result of Peak Product's alliance with PBB, Peak Products has experienced savings and a significant reduction in management and administrative involvement in logistics aspects. It has also allowed the company to focus on its core competencies—manufacturing and marketing.

Sources:

Candice Price, "Peak Performance for Peak Products," *World Trade* (December 2002), p. 38.

David Maloney, "Canadian Tire Rolls Out New DC," *Modern Materials Handling* (October 2002).

Peak Products Manufacturing, www.peakproducts.com.

Excel Logistics, www.excel.com.

---

cross-docking. By properly scheduling the arrival of vendor trucks at the receiving dock, Wal-Mart causes items to be unloaded from these trucks and immediately carried across to trucks on the shipping dock that are outbound for its retail operations. With the introduction of cross-docking, Wal-Mart was able to increase the number of its retail outlets without increasing the number or size of its distribution facilities. As seen in the OM in Practice Box on 3PL, Canadian Tire also practices cross-docking.

The next step in Wal-Mart's disintermediation process was to allow vendors direct, online access to their retail sales data (point of sale data) through a satellite network. With this system, vendors now decide how much to ship to Wal-Mart. This is basically a VMI system. In many cases, these products are shipped directly to retail stores, bypassing the distribution centres altogether.

Another example of disintermediation is in the airline industry. Here airlines are increasing their efforts to work directly with customers rather than through travel agents in order to save commission fees. This is being accomplished through airline Web sites that feature online ticketing instructions and through the increasing use of electronic ticketing. Similarly, the Dell model of direct sales removes retailers (intermediaries) such as Future Shop or Radio Shack from the supply chain.

When disintermediation does take place, there needs to be close coordination and planning among the different firms in the supply chain that are affected.

JIT II, developed in 1987 by Bose Corporation, which produces high-end stereo equipment, is a good example, of disintermediation and is now being adopted by a growing number of companies. The objective of JIT II is for the vendor and customer to work together much more closely, thereby eliminating many of the intermediate steps that now exist. To accomplish this, a vendor employee is provided with physical office space within the purchasing function of the customer. This approach eliminates the need for a buyer for the customer and a salesperson for the vendor.

As in VMI, the vendor representative has full access to the customer's database and therefore can translate the customer's purchase orders directly into orders for his or her company. This individual also participates in the customer's new product design process, offering suggestions for improving product performance and/or reducing costs.

Inventory Positioning

Inventory positioning involves deciding where and in what form to stock inventory in the supply chain. For example, if a company had only one warehouse in Canada, located in southwestern Ontario, the advantage would be that operating costs of the warehouse would be lower because of economies of scale. However, customer service might suffer. For example, if a retailer in Moose Jaw, Saskatchewan, ran out of stock it would take longer to replenish stock than if the company had a western warehouse in Calgary and thus positioned the inventory closer to the customer. However, if the item is easy to airfreight, such as electronic components, it might be better to have only one consolidated warehouse.

Companies can also use *drop shipping*, whereby the order-taking company gets the manufacturer or a logistics provider to deliver directly to the customer, bypassing the company's warehouse. This reduces distance and delivery time considerably. This practice is common among e-tailers. For example, orders placed through Indigo.ca are sent electronically to the Chapters/Indigo store nearest to the customer for fulfillment, bypassing the company's warehouse in Toronto. This reduces delivery time considerably.

Another aspect of positioning is the form in which inventory is stored in various locations. Many companies use **postponement**, which helps in mass customization. For example, Dell stocks only standardized computer parts, not the whole computer itself. Thus it postpones the assembly of the final product, assembling it only when it gets an actual order. Home improvement retailers use a similar strategy. The paint inventory consists of only standard colours. These standard colours are mixed to get the custom colour only after the customer requests it. Postponement is therefore a way for companies to carry inventory without having to worry about it not being consumed.

postponement
Strategy in which standard components are carried and quick final assembly of the finished product is done only after receipt of customer order.

Performance Metrics

Companies evaluate the performance of their supply chain with such measures as inventory turns, number of stockouts, lead times for order delivery, and overall costs. This allows the company to benchmark its performance against competitors and its own objectives. Kaplan and Norton suggest that a "balanced scorecard" approach including financial, customer, business process, and learning and growth measures be used at all levels of the supply chain.[8] For example, a company could set an objective of one stockout every 1000 orders versus of one every 100. Although this would improve the marketing objective of better service, from an operational standpoint the company might have to carry more inventory (unless it improves its process). This may be contrary to the operational objective of more inventory turns. It may also cost more. Supply chain measures have to balance different types of objectives.

Use of Technology

Technology continues to have a significant impact on the supply chain. **EDI (electronic data interchange)** provides a direct link between a manufacturer's database and that of its vendors. In addition, the increased use of personal computers allows customers to communicate directly with their vendors' systems. For example, Canada Post customers can track the delivery of their packages through their PCs.

Business-to-business (B2B) e-tailing has been one of the fastest growing segments on the Internet. One of the reasons for its high rate of growth has been the creation of electronic or B2B marketplaces. B2B marketplaces are virtual markets that bring buyers and sellers together. Usually these B2B marketplaces focus on a specific industry

EDI (electronic data interchange)
Direct link between a manufacturer's database and that of the vendor.

---

[8]R. S. Kaplan and D. P. Norton, *The Balanced Scorecard: Translating Strategy into Action* (Boston: Harvard Business School Press, 1996).

or product category, and the items being bought and sold are typically common, off-the-shelf products. Companies such as General Electric, who have embraced the Internet as a purchasing tool, have saved millions of dollars in purchased goods and services. Airlines have also started participating in virtual markets that allow them to reduce purchasing costs through processing efficiency and higher volumes. Another big advantage for airlines is that these electronic links enable them to locate a part quickly in an emergency repair situation and reduce the time that an aircraft is unable to fly because of a problem (it costs a lot of money when a plane is delayed).

Electronic marketplaces provide opportunities for different types of auctions, for companies to source hard-to-find components, and to unload excess inventory through brokers. One concern with auctions, however, is that they tend to be counterproductive in terms of creating long-term supplier relationships because they award contracts based on lowest bids. They also may not be appropriate for complex items for which close relationships with suppliers in terms of design and delivery are required.

At the same time, the use of technology, in many cases, can provide suppliers with a competitive barrier. A customer will typically establish an EDI link with only a few vendors. Potential new vendors have to demonstrate significant improvements in price and/or quality to warrant the additional costs of an added EDI link.

A number of other systems have been developed in addition to EDI, such as quick response (QR) and efficient consumer response (ECR). In all cases these terms refer to communication throughout a supply or distribution pipeline. These systems provide paperless communication between customers and vendors. Although there had already been some improvement in communication through the use of open computer systems using quick response UNIX or UNIX-type software, EDI, QR, and ECR go far beyond that.

quick response (QR) programs

Just-in-time replenishment system using bar-code scanning and EDI.

Quick response (QR) programs have grown rapidly. A survey by Deloitte & Touche showed that 68 percent of retailers either have implemented or plan to implement QR within their replenishment system within two years.[9] Quick response is based on bar-code scanning and EDI. Its intent is to create a just-in-time replenishment system between vendors and retailers.

Virtually all medium-sized and large retail stores use Universal Product Code (UPC) bar-code scanning. Point-of-sale (POS) scanning at the register also uses price-look-up (PLU), as reported by 90 percent of the respondents to the Deloitte & Touche survey. Increasingly, RFID technology (mentioned in Chapter 3 supplement) is being used to track and speed up shipments.

efficient consumer response (ECR)

Strategy for bringing distributors, suppliers, and grocers together using bar-code scanning and EDI.

Efficient consumer response (ECR) is a type of QR and EDI adopted by the supermarket industry as a business strategy. Distributors, suppliers, and grocers work together to bring products to consumers. The ECR systems often use bar-code scanning and EDI. Savings come from reduced supply chain costs and reduced inventory.

A study by Kurt Salmon Associates estimated that ECR could generate a potential savings of more than US$30 billion.[10] In the dry grocery segment this could cut supply-chain inventory from 104 days to 61 days. Another study by McKinsey estimated that dry grocery consumer prices could be reduced an average of 10.8 percent through industrywide adoption of ECR.[11] Without ECR, manufacturers push products on the markets by offering low prices on large quantities: A few times a year the manufacturer offers the grocer a low price on a large quantity of product. This is forward buying. The manufacturer then works with the supermarket to offer coupons and incentives to entice customers

---

[9]"Quick Response Grows," *Chain Store Age Executive* (May 1993), pp. 158–159.

[10]James Aaron Cooke, "The $30 Billion Promise," *Traffic Management* (December 1993), pp. 57–61.

[11]David B. Jenkins, "Jenkins Leads EDI Effort," *Chain Store Age Executive* (March 1993), p. 147.

Campbell uses a system they call Continuous Product Replenishment (CPR). At the food retailer's warehouse, Campbell product arrives from the plant to replenish inventory at the same steady rate as the consumer takes it off the shelf. CPR is driven by an electronic ordering system managed by Campbell, freeing the retailer from this task. Steady production that meets predetermined inventory levels results in cost efficiencies across the entire supply chain.

to buy the product during a promotion. Products not sold during the promotion are then stored in inventory to carry that supermarket until the next manufacturer's promotional deal.

ECR focuses on the customers to drive the system, not the manufacturers' deals. Customers pull goods through the store and through the pipeline by their purchases. This permits less inventory throughout the system.

Cooke cites a study that estimated that distributors purchase 80 percent of their merchandise during manufacturers' sales or "deals." They may buy four times per year and fill up their warehouses. Until the industry frees itself from this addiction to deal buying, all the great replenishment techniques will be worthless.[12]

The ability of suppliers to access a firm's sales data significantly reduces the *bullwhip* effect, which often occurs in a supply chain when there is no sharing of information.[13] The bullwhip effect occurs when a slight change in demand by the end user causes significant fluctuations in the quantities purchased by each of the firms in the supply chain, with the fluctuations increasing the further the firm is removed from the end user. Exhibit 12.5 shows a bullwhip effect similar to that experienced in many supply chains. In addition to lack of information sharing, ordering in volumes, also called forward buying (due to fixed costs of ordering or price discounts) and rationing and gaming (in case of shortages, customers tend to exaggerate orders to ensure that they get at least some amount), can cause the bullwhip effect. Lee et al. recommend (*a*) information sharing, (*b*) reducing the time in processing and receiving orders, (*c*) VMI, and (*d*) instituting an everyday price policy (i.e., getting rid of promotional pricing) in order to prevent the bullwhip effect.

---

[12]Cooke, "$30 Billion Promise," pp. 57–61.
[13]H. Lee, V. Padmanabhan, and S. Whang, "The Bullwhip Effect in Supply Chains," *Sloan Management Review* (Spring 1997), pp. 93–102.

Exhibit 12.5

Increasing Variability of Orders up the Supply Chain

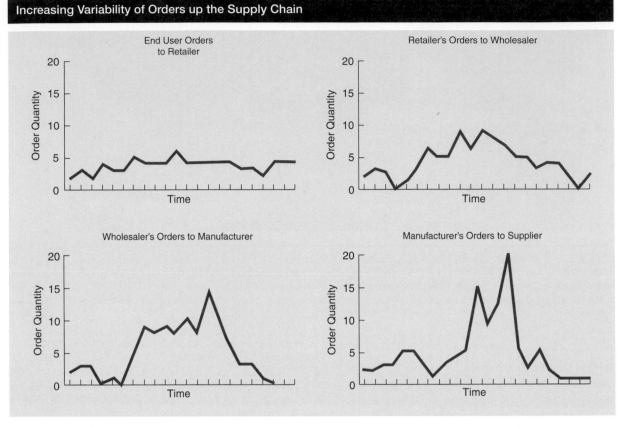

Source: R. B. Chase, F. R. Jacobs, and N. J. Aquilano, *Operations Management for Competitive Advantage*, 10th ed. (New York: Irwin McGraw-Hill, 2004), p. 102.

The bullwhip effect results in supply chains carrying excess inventory or experiencing shortages because of the fluctuations seen in Exhibit 12.5. Both these lead to unnecessary costs. For example, Proctor and Gamble found that due to forward buying and lack of information sharing, the orders for diapers at its factories were highly cyclical and unpredictable (even though babies use diapers at a constant rate and so demand really is constant). To improve the situation they began sharing information with customers and eliminated forward buying, which allowed them to produce and sell at a constant rate, avoiding shortages and excess inventories.[14]

The supply chain is also being affected by *m-business*. As the cost of mobile technology falls, it is becoming more economical for many firms to justify its adoption. For example, Pepsi Bottling Group's technicians previously used to phone in to find out where their next service calls were. They then faxed back billing information after the service call. Now this same information is sent directly to the technician's handheld device. By using this mobile technology, service response times have been reduced by 20 percent and the errors that occurred from using the old fax system have been eliminated.[15]

---

[14]James L. McKenney and Theodore H. Clark, *Procter & Gamble: Improving Consumer Value Through Process Redesign* (Harvard Business School Publishing, 1995).
[15]Heather Greene, "Winging into the Wireless," *BusinessWeek e.biz* (February 18, 2002), EB 8–EB 9.

Exhibit 12.6

Major SCM Software Packages		
Company	**Customers Include**	**Success Story**
i2 *www.i2.com*	Dell, Nike, CN Rail, 3M Canada	3M Canada increased its scheduling productivity by 20%, customer service from 92% to 98%, and reduced inventory by 23%.
Manugistics *www.manugistics.com*	Canadian Tire, Hewlett-Packard Mitsubishi	HP slashed its transportation budget by 25% and cut inventory at its top three Asia-Pacific resellers by more than half within just two months.
SAP *www.sap.com*	Carlsberg, Indigo, ASE Korea	In four months Carlsberg reduced inventories by 30% and increased order accuracy by 20%.
Peoplesoft *www.peoplesoft.com*	Bangkok General Hospital, Bausch & Lomb, Netergy Networks	Netergy Networks integrated manufacturing and engineering processes to slash new product development time by one-third.
SynQuest *www.synquest.com*	Titleist FootJoy Worldwide, Ford, Cara Operations	Titleist cut manufacturing lead times on custom golf balls by more than half, from 12 to 5 days.

Source: Kayte VanScoy, "Recession-Proof Your Business," *Smart Business*, December 2001/January 2002, pp. 84–88.

Exhibit 12.6 shows some of the major SCM software packages that are available, some of the companies that use the software, and how the software has impacted the supply chain. Further details on the available packages can be found in a 2003 survey of SCM packages by Aksoy and Derbez.[16]

Product Design to Facilitate Supply Chain Management

Companies have come to realize that product design can help or hinder supply chain management. Earlier we talked about the advantages of postponement, which involves carrying standardized components and assembling the final product only upon receipt of a customer order. Clearly, in order to do this the product must be modularly designed. In Chapter 3 we discussed life-cycle-based design, in which consideration is given to product disposal and recycling. Again, the product has to be designed in such a way as to ensure that the recycling or disposal can be done in a cost-effective manner.

A company that wishes to sell to global retailers such as French company Carrefour or Wal-Mart may have to design product to fit the shelf sizes or transportation equipment used by these customers. In Europe, many retailers have to take back packaging. Thus there is an incentive to design better packaging that is easier to handle from a supply chain perspective. These examples show that it is important to keep the supply chain in mind when designing products. This idea is explored further under reverse supply chain management, discussed later in this chapter.

Enterprise Resource Planning (ERP) Systems

In the last decade, there has emerged a new generation of software systems that links all of the various functional areas within an organization. The goal of these systems, which are

---

[16]Y. Aksoy and A. Derbez, "Software Survey: Supply Chain Management," *ORMS Today*, 30, no. 4 (June 2003), pp. 34–41.

enterprise resource planning system (ERP)

A fully integrated software system that links all of the major functional areas within an organization.

known as **enterprise resource planning (ERP) systems**, is to provide a company with a single, uniform software platform and database that will facilitate transactions among the different functional areas within a firm, and, in some cases, between firms and their customers and vendors.

Defining ERP Systems

Prior to the introduction of ERP systems, each functional area within an organization typically had its own software and database. These software packages were often incompatible with each other, which prevented transactions from taking place directly between systems. In addition, with more than one database, there were often multiple records for the same piece of data, which, in turn, caused delays and unnecessary errors throughout the firm. For example, an employee might be listed as John Smith in the Human Resources database, John S. Smith in the Accounting Department, and Dr. John Smith in the Engineering Department. From the computer systems' perspective, these were three different people. In such an environment, transactions between functions were often done manually, which was tedious, slow, and a source of additional errors. As a result, each of the functional areas within an organization was viewed as an independent operation, as illustrated in Exhibit 12.7A.

To address this issue of incompatibility and multiple databases, ERP systems were developed to provide an infrastructure with a common information technology platform that not only would link electronically all of the functional areas with a single database, but also address their individual needs, as shown in Exhibit 12.7B. Exhibit 12.8 illustrates how SAP, the leading ERP software firm, specifically provides this integration.

Evolution of ERP Systems

ERP systems didn't just happen overnight. They are an outgrowth of materials requirements planning (MRP) systems and manufacturing resources planning (MRP II), which were developed and introduced within the manufacturing function in the late 1960s and 1970s, and which are discussed in detail in Chapter 16.

Exhibit 12.7A

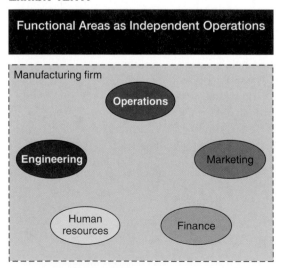

Exhibit 12.7B

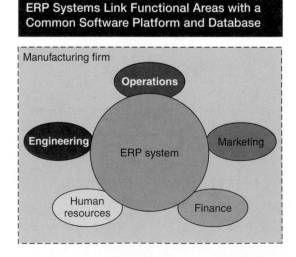

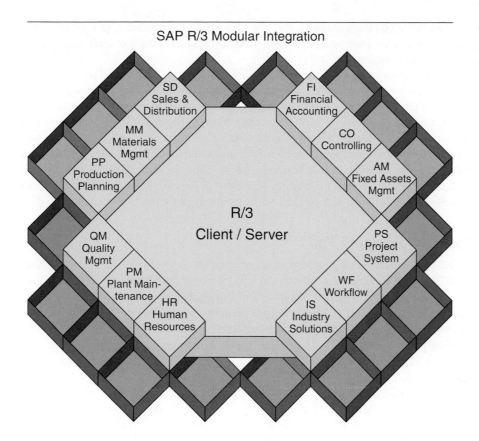

SAP R/3 Modular Integration

Exhibit 12.8

Example of How SAP's R/3 System Integrates an Organization

MRP systems provided the manufacturing function with a common database and software platform to link all of its areas, which included purchasing, planning, materials, and operations. Prior to the introduction of MRP systems, each of these individual areas was managed more or less as an independent operation, which often resulted in excessive inventories of materials and slow, inefficient, and often erroneous transactions. MRP II systems were a first attempt to integrate operations, marketing, finance, and engineering.

Just as MRP systems provided a common software platform and database for the manufacturing function, ERP systems, as mentioned previously, now link all of the functional areas within an organization by providing a common software platform and shared database.

The adoption of ERP systems by major corporations was accelerated in 1998 and 1999 by possible "Y2K problems" that existed in legacy computer systems dating back to the 1970s. For many firms, the cost of installing a new, state-of-the-art ERP system was comparable to fixing the old legacy systems. By choosing to install an ERP system, these firms were able to update their entire information technology infrastructure, instead of merely patching up their existing and much older systems. A survey in the June 2003 issue of *APICS—The Performance Advantage* magazine listed over 150 ERP vendors, with a wide ranges of costs and capabilities.

Benefits of ERP Systems

When properly installed and operating, an ERP system can provide a firm with a significant competitive advantage that can fully justify the investment of time and money. The benefits of using an ERP system can take many forms, including (*a*) reduction in the number of errors through the use of a common database, (*b*) faster customer response times, (*c*) faster order fulfillment times, and (*d*) better overall communication within the organization.

Hewlett-Packard Company provides a good example. One of Hewlett-Packard's manufacturing and distribution facilities, located in Geulstein, Germany, achieved significant improvements in operational performance after implementing SAP's ERP system, including on-time delivery exceeding 95 percent, cycle time reduced by 80 percent, inventories reduced by 30 percent, operating costs reduced by 30 percent, and distribution costs reduced by 70 percent. Pratt and Whitney Canada Corp. (P&WC), which manufactures and services aircraft engines, has locations in Nova Scotia, Quebec, Ontario, and Alberta. P&WC implemented its first SAP system in 1999 and has continued to upgrade successfully and plans to link all its locations using the ERP system.

Why ERP Systems Fail

The business landscape is littered with failed attempts at installing ERP systems. Hershey Foods Corporation, for example, incurred significant product distribution problems after it implemented SAP's R/3 system, resulting in its candy not being on retail shelves during its peak season between Halloween and Christmas. Sobeys pulled the plug on its SAP powered ERP system in 2001 because it felt that the system could not handle its ordering and data processing needs. (These difficulties in implementing ERP systems are not unique to SAP but exist with all ERP systems.) It is interesting to note that many of these causes of failure are the same as those identified as the reasons for MRP implementation failures 25 years ago.

The main reasons ERP systems fail are: (*a*) lack of top management commitment, (*b*) lack of adequate resources for selection and implementation, (*c*) lack of proper training of users and IT personnel, (*d*) lack of communication within the organization, and (*e*) lack of compatibility between the ERP and the organizational systems.

Issues in Selecting ERP Systems

Each ERP software package has its particular strengths and weaknesses. One may be very strong in the financial module, another in the human resources area. Still a third may be strong in the production or marketing area. In adopting a single system, a company must accept all the strengths and weaknesses of the system selected. By contrast, a firm using a best-of-breed approach selects software that has the best attributes for each functional area and then builds an interface that links all the various software packages together. (Obviously, this approach also has its drawbacks.)

Each ERP software package is designed around a specific business model with its own inherent business processes. These are usually based upon best business practices, which are determined by the software vendor. Consequently, in adopting a particular ERP system, a company must also adopt the built-in business model and its associated business processes. Although this represents an improvement for many firms, especially those that never had well-designed processes, firms that already have good businesses processes in place still will need to reconfigure them to be compatible with those in the ERP system. For example, scheduling software, installed by vendors such as Matrikon (described in the opening vignette of Chapter 11) needs to adapt to the ERP system. Similarly, certain ERP systems are designed to work best in process-oriented industries such as petroleum or chemicals, and consequently are not as readily applicable to discrete parts manufacturing.

The Reverse Supply Chain

Guide and Van Wassenhove define the reverse supply chain as the series of activities required to retrieve a used product or return from a customer and either dispose of it or reuse it.[17] Product returns are becoming an increasingly important issue for many reasons, including the existence of catalogue and Internet purchasing. In addition, regulatory authorities are increasingly mandating companies to pay more attention to reverse supply chains, and both consumers and regulations are encouraging companies to pay attention to the environment. For example, many European countries require vendors to take back transportation packaging.[18] Toxic materials such as mercury have to be recovered or disposed of properly.

Even where there are no regulations, companies are finding there are competitive advantages to being more proactive about reverse logistics. For example, Kodak has reduced its operating costs by remanufacturing its single use cameras after the film has been developed. Similarly, Noranda's new recycling facility in Brampton, Ontario, will process obsolete goods from electronics manufacturers and expects to make a profit after extracting metals and sending them to its refineries such as its copper smelter in Rouyn, Quebec. Other companies such as Bosch have created a new market by selling remanufactured power hand tools.

Guide and Van Wassenhove divide the reverse supply chain into five components, one or more of which might be done by a third party.

1. Product acquisition, which involves planning the quality, quantity, and timing of product returns. This is important, because reverse supply chain aspects such as product returns or used product repairs and recycling are unpredictable in nature with respect to timing and quantity.

2. Reverse logistics, which involves the transportation of the collected products to facilities that inspect, sort, and dispose of them.

3. Inspection and disposition involves determining what to do with the returned products. The returns might go to resellers, scrap merchants, or charities, for example.

4. Reconditioning involves capturing value from returned products by remanufacturing products for resale.

5. Distribution and sales involves distributing the returned, repaired, or recycled products through existing markets and creating new markets.

Companies successful in their reverse supply chains have often closely coordinated them with their forward supply chains, creating a closed-loop system. This implies that they design and manufacture products with eventual recycling in mind. Bosch, for example, places sensors in its power tool parts that indicate whether the parts are worth reconditioning. Other companies take steps to avoid unnecessary reverse supply chain occurrences by educating customers on product usage. For example, electronics giant Philips found that customers often returned items such as DVD players because they couldn't understand the instruction manual. These returns dropped significantly when Philips revised the product manual so that customers could understand it more easily.

---

[17]V. D. R. Guide Jr. and L.N. Van Wassenhove, "The Reverse Supply Chain," *Harvard Business Review* (February 2002), p. 25.

[18]R. S. Tibben-Lembke, "Life After Death: Reverse Logistics and the Product Life Cycle," *International Journal of Physical Distribution and Logistics Management*, 32, no. 3 (2002), pp. 223–244.

Requirements for a Successful Supply Chain

Several elements are necessary for the successful implementation of a supply chain management program. These elements often overlap and often are dependent on each other.

Trust

A primary ingredient in the establishment of a successful relationship between vendor and customer is the element of trust. Without trust, none of the other factors is possible. Trust allows vendors to participate and contribute in the new product development cycle.

Long-Term Relationships

With suppliers taking on a strategic role in a company, it is necessary to develop long-term relationships that permit the sharing of a strategic vision and even risk. The term often used in establishing these long-term relationships is *evergreen* contracts, implying they are automatically renewed as long as the vendors perform as agreed. There is also much more collaboration between the supplier and customer. For example, Cott Corp not only supplies store brand soft drinks to retail chains but also collaborates with them on packaging, promotions, and new product development of store-brand soft drinks. This aspect of long-term relationships is discussed in more detail in Chapter 13.

Information Sharing

Successful supply chain management requires the sharing of information between vendors and customers. This information can include everything from new product design specifications to capacity planning and scheduling, and even access to a customer's entire database. This also helps avoid the problems with bullwhip explained earlier. This is sometimes called collaborative planning, forecasting, and replenishment (CPFR). (See the Operations Management in Practice box.)

Individual Strengths of Organizations

If a firm enters into a long-term relationship with a vendor, it is in that firm's best interest that the vendor remain in business for a long period of time. Thus a good customer will work with a vendor to ensure it is profitable and remains financially strong. As mentioned in the section on procurement, the selection of proper vendors is also important.

The Right Type of Supply Chain

Fisher[19] points out that a supply chain has two primary functions: (1) physical—converting raw materials into components and eventually into finished goods and, (2) market mediation—ensuring that the variety of products reaching the marketplace matches what customers want to buy. The importance of each function depends on the type of products. Thus the best type of supply chain for a product depends on its characteristics.

At one extreme are companies such as Campbell Foods that make products such as soup, which have a long product life cycle and predictable demand but low profit margins. For these "functional products" the physical aspect of the supply chain is more important and the preferred supply chain is of an "efficient type," in which the primary objective is cost minimization. Market mediation is not complex because the product has predictable demand.

---

[19]M. L. Fisher, "What Is the Right Supply Chain for Your Product," *Harvard Business Review* (March–April 1997), pp. 105–116.

Operations Management in Practice

COLLABORATIVE FORECASTING AND PLANNING FOR SMOOTH SAILING

Ensuring that the right merchandise is in stock is a challenge for retailers selling seasonal products, as West Marine Inc. has found. The California-based company, the world's largest for boating supplies, has over US$500 million in annual sales. In Canada it has retail locations in Nanaimo, Sidney, Vancouver, and Victoria, all in British Columbia.

Recently it was unable to stock the right products at its stores due to poor supply chain management. The company realized that the key to improvement was to improve the front end of the supply chain—forecasting. They felt this would drive supply chain savings. The improvement process started with better forecasting and by linking store sales to warehouse replenishment. It also involved increased collaboration with its 200 top vendors, who accounted for over 90 percent of stocked items.

The process is called collaborative planning, forecasting, and replenishment (CPFR). CPFR involves collaboration between supply chain partners in forecasting, distribution, and production. For example, West Marine installed software that allowed it to track and analyze sales and shifts in consumer trends and then to make the necessary changes rapidly throughout the entire supply chain. As a result, the forecast accuracy increased to 85 percent. Other software improved supply chain visibility among its partners, linked point-of-sale forecasting to the order forecasts sent to suppliers, and provided electronic data interchange (EDI) capabilities with more than two-thirds of its suppliers.

Within the company, point-of-sale data are processed and forecasts are updated nightly. Merchandise and assortment planning as well as promotion decisions are based on these forecasts. Suppliers participate in building forecasts, and performance metrics are routinely reviewed with vendors, who keep West Marine informed of shortages.

Collaborative forecasting and planning allows a company to carry

- the right items (thus avoiding obsolescence—especially challenging in seasonal businesses)
- in the right amount (reducing buffer inventory due to more accurate sales predictions, which leads to lower inventory carrying costs)
- at the right location (saving unnecessary transportation costs)

As a result of their changes, West Marine increased its peak season in-stock rate to 96 percent while reducing costs at its distribution centres by US$3 million.

Sources:
"Accurate Forecasts Mean Smooth Sailing for West Marine," *Frontline Solutions* (October 2003), p. 39.
Walter McKaige, "Collaborating on the Supply Chain," *IIE Solutions* (March 2001), pp. 34–36.
West Marine Inc., www.westmarine.com.

At the other extreme are fashion merchandise or high-tech products such as computer components, which have very short life cycles and for which it is difficult to predict demand. These "innovative products" require a responsive supply chain. The primary function of such a supply chain is not to minimize cost but to ensure market mediation, so that the right product reaches the customer on time. Not doing so will result in high opportunity costs because profit margins are high. In such a chain one might use expensive but fast transportation methods such as airfreight as well as information technology to speed up production and delivery. For example, when Sony Playstations being transported by sea experienced delays at the Suez canal, the company chartered Russian cargo aircraft in order to deliver to customers on time.[20] Under these circumstances, suppliers are chosen for quick delivery and flexibility in responding to the changing market, not necessarily for their cost efficiency.

Even different models of the same product may have to be managed differently. For example, Dorel Industries of Westmount, Quebec, a global manufacturer of juvenile products such as strollers in all price ranges, sells some models through mass merchandisers and others through specialty boutiques. The market characteristics of the products sold through boutiques may be different than those sold through mass merchandisers.

---

[20]Alison Maitland, "Make sure you have your Christmas stock in," *Financial Times*, December 19, 2005, p. 12.

Within a product itself, some components may be of a commodity type while others are of a custom type. Commodity components may be purchased through the bidding process or through e-commerce sites. Batteries for cell phones are a good example of commodity components. Thus the company may switch suppliers frequently. For custom components that require considerable interaction between supplier and customer in design and manufacturing, such as proprietary circuitry in cell phones, the company may enter into long-term, close relationships with a few suppliers.

Thus a company may employ many different types of supply chains depending on the nature of the product or service and its components.

Conclusion

The importance of supply chain management continues to grow as companies become more dependent on their suppliers. The reasons for doing so include (*a*) increased emphasis on core competencies, (*b*) increased need for flexibility, and (*c*) a desire to share risk associated with new product development. As a consequence, the role of the supplier has shifted from being purely transactional, based on low cost, to being a partner that participates in strategic decisions of the firm. This dramatic shift in the role of the supplier has caused companies to establish long-term relationships with a smaller number of suppliers than was previously the case. Increased competition also has forced companies to look to the four corners of the globe for suppliers that can meet their needs as well as for possible locations of factories and warehouses.

However, although the use of international vendors has caused the supply chain to become longer in many cases, there is a trend toward disintermediation, which eliminates many of the intermediate stages in the overall supply chain. In addition, third party logistics providers are taking on responsibilities beyond simple transport of products.

Thus companies have realized the importance of designing the appropriate supply chain for their business as well as managing it effectively. Emerging issues in supply chain management include the use of technology and reverse supply chains.

Key Terms

3PL p. 433

consignment inventories
   p. 431

disintermediation p. 433

EDI (electronic data
interchange) p. 435

efficient consumer response
   (ECR) p. 436

enterprise resource planning
   system (ERP) p. 440

inbound logistics p. 422

outbound logistics p. 422

postponement p. 435

quick response (QR)
   programs p. 436

supply chain p. 422

vendor-managed inventories
   (VMI) p. 433

Review and Discussion Questions

1. What are the advantages and disadvantages to a firm of having a small number of suppliers?

2. Supply chain management as presented in this chapter pertains primarily to goods. What would be the different steps or elements in a supply chain for a service? Give an example.

3. How has technology impacted a firm's supply chain and the trend toward disintermediation?

4. What are the main differences between having a vendor's employees working in your manufacturing operation and hiring your own employees to do the same work?

5. Identify all of the steps in the supply chain for a hamburger that you buy at McDonald's. How might this supply chain differ for a McDonald's located in a developing country?

Visit the Web site of any of the supply chain management software vendors listed in Exhibit 12.5 and describe the firm's SCM software package in terms of price, size, and capabilities.

Case 1 | How a Quality Initiative Changed Whirlpool's Supply Chain

For over 30 years, Stanley Engineering Components (SEC), a division of the Stanley Works, had been manufacturing oven-door-latching mechanisms for the range-appliance industry. (The oven-door-latching mechanism locks an oven door during the self-cleaning cycle in both gas and electric ranges.) Its customers viewed SEC as a low-cost supplier of customer-designed stamped metal assemblies. In this capacity, SEC provided little input with respect to the designing, manufacturing, and marketing of their customers' end products. The largest of SEC's customers was the range-appliance division of the Whirlpool Corporation, the world's leading manufacturer and marketer of appliances. SEC has been a supplier of oven-door latches to Whirlpool for more than 20 years.

In early 1993, Whirlpool notified its existing and potential suppliers that it was instituting a new quality initiative, based on total quality management (TQM) principles, that directly affected its customer-supplier relationship. It now wanted its suppliers to be business partners, as compared to the existing customer-supplier arrangement in which price was the primary criterion for purchase. Whirlpool now asked potential suppliers to provide extra value-added services and encouraged them to (*a*) become partners who were to be experts in Whirlpool's business, (*b*) participate in customer-supplier teams, and (*c*) learn about the needs of Whirlpool's customers.

As business partners, Whirlpool wanted its suppliers to follow its strategy, which was to deliver world-class products that exceeded customer expectations. An important part of this strategy was Whirlpool's commitment to continuous quality improvement. Whirlpool was able to achieve this strategy by leveraging its suppliers' technical expertise. To accomplish this, its suppliers had to be flexible to

change and proactive to the continuous quality improvement of their products. In addition, Whirlpool's suppliers had to be able to produce consistently high-quality products at low cost, while providing additional services, which included free consulting, as well as other initiatives to decrease product cost and increase product quality.

Another of Whirlpool's goals was to decrease its number of suppliers. Therefore, in addition to the oven-door-latching mechanism, Whirlpool encouraged SEC to develop a program to manufacture oven-door hinges, because this additional product was viewed as a natural extension to SEC's product line because a hinge is also a stamped metal assembly. If SEC supplied both these products, Whirlpool could reduce its number of suppliers.

SEC had to make many changes within its organization to meet these new requirements. For example, SEC was now expected to initiate cost saving and quality improvement programs that extended far beyond SEC's own products. In addition, SEC had to assume significant risks. Its previous method of doing business, although far from risk-free, was in a stable environment, and SEC knew what was needed to compete successfully: low-cost products. On the other hand, supplying Whirlpool under its TQM principles meant competing in a highly uncertain environment that presented a significant risk of failure. If SEC was not able to meet Whirlpool's requirements, then Whirlpool would not consider it as a potential supplier. Losing Whirlpool's business would result in a 20 percent loss in sales along with high sunk costs, which could ultimately mean business failure for SEC.

As SEC considered changing its way of doing business with Whirlpool, it decided that all of its existing and future customers would also have to accept this new way of doing business, because SEC was not willing to operate two separate business structures. SEC consciously chose TQM as a competitive advantage and therefore assumed the risk of losing customers who did not endorse TQM principles. In this respect, SEC considered Whirlpool's demands an opportunity to force itself to change and to adopt TQM practices. SEC also realized that Whirlpool was not going to lead it through the TQM process; SEC would have to develop this on its own.

SEC also needed to change its business philosophy from being just a low-cost supplier to being a concerned business partner. To accomplish this, SEC began considering all aspects of the final product, not just those pertaining to the components it supplied. SEC showed its willingness to change in many ways. Perhaps the most striking example was SEC's using its own personnel to co-develop a latch and a hinge with Whirlpool, even though there was no guarantee that SEC would get Whirlpool's business. SEC personnel became free internal consultants to Whirlpool to demonstrate that they were committed to becoming a business partner.

Whirlpool expected its suppliers to provide a sustainable, competitive advantage that was consistent with its strategy, although Whirlpool did not provide any leadership to SEC. It simply imposed its demands. Developing a strategy for achieving Whirlpool's goals rested solely with the supplier. By not providing any detailed plans, Whirlpool left the strategic planning and implementation to SEC.

Whirlpool also wanted SEC to help predict consumer preferences. It therefore sought SEC's opinions, suggestions, and solutions to problems about many aspects of its products, most of which did not relate to SEC's components. Again SEC was expected to play the role of free consultant, even before it established formal agreements with Whirlpool.

One of Whirlpool's key strategic thrusts was to "effectively manage the selected technology base that emanates from the suppliers." To meet Whirlpool's objectives, SEC had to communicate Whirlpool's needs to all of SEC's employees and suppliers. Whirlpool demanded high-quality, low-cost, timely products, and SEC had to comply with these demands. Whirlpool stated that its chosen

suppliers would be the best in their class and their goals would be in line with Whirlpools' goals.

In early 1995, the buyers at Whirlpool accepted SEC's design proposals for the latch and hinge assemblies and awarded SEC the contract for these components. SEC started shipping small quantities of latches and hinges early in the spring of 1996. In mid-1996, Whirlpool awarded SEC a contract to supply smoke eliminators and venting tube assemblies. Since SEC first starting shipping components under its new supplier program, Whirlpool has awarded SEC $5 million in additional yearly business. At the same time, other suppliers lost this $5 million in business.

By adopting TQM, SEC became a successful competitor. Between 1993 and 1997, SEC sales to Whirlpool increased 125 percent, and its productivity increased by 76 percent. Over the same period, its sales to other customers (originally non-TQM customers) increased 25 percent. For SEC, implementing TQM, although risky and painful, was a success. SEC realized that it must solve problems immediately and provide the best possible design and quality at a competitive price. As a supplier, SEC needs to constantly initiate new technology ideas, because suppliers to organizations that use TQM principles must always be ready to change and be on the alert.

Questions

1. How did the customer-supplier relationship between SEC and Whirlpool change as a result of the TQM initiative?

2. How did Whirlpool help its suppliers to better understand Whirlpool's quality requirements? Should Whirlpool have helped more?

3. How has SEC made Whirlpool's products better?

4. What are the advantages and disadvantages when a new management initiative such as TQM is introduced into a firm's supply chain?

Source: Condensed from Christopher J. Roethlein and Paul M. Mangiameli, "The Realities of Becoming a Long-Term Supplier to a Large TQM Customer," *Interface* 29, no. 4 (1999), pp. 71–81.

Just-in-Time Systems

Chapter Objectives

- Introduce the underlying concepts of just-in-time (JIT) and the Japanese approach to improving productivity.

- Identify the differences between Japanese companies and North American firms with respect to implementing JIT, and explore why these differences exist.

- Identify the various elements that need to be included to successfully implement JIT within an organization.

- Illustrate how many JIT concepts have been implemented in services.

The 100 Yen Sushi House is no ordinary sushi restaurant. It is the ultimate showcase of Japanese productivity. The house featured an ellipsoid-shaped serving area in the middle of the room, where three or four cooks were busily preparing sushi. Perhaps 30 stools surrounded the serving area. As we took our seats at the counters, I noticed something special. There was a conveyor belt going around the ellipsoid service area, like a toy train track. On it I saw plates of sushi. There was every kind of sushi that you can think of—from the cheapest seaweed to the more expensive raw salmon or shrimp dishes. The price was uniform, however, 100 yen per plate. On closer examination, while my eyes were racing to keep up with the speed of the traveling plates, I found that a cheap seaweed plate had four pieces, while the more expensive raw salmon dish had only two pieces.

I saw a man with eight plates all stacked up neatly. As he got up to leave, the cashier looked over and said, "800 yen, please." The cashier had no cash register; she simply counted the number of plates and then multiplied by 100 yen.

The owner's daily operation is based on a careful analysis of information. The owner has a complete summary of demand information about the different types of sushi plates, and thus knows exactly how many of each type of sushi plate he should prepare and when. Furthermore, the whole operation is based on the repetitive manufacturing principle with appropriate just-in-time and quality control systems. For example, the store has a very limited refrigerator capacity. Thus, the store uses the just-in-time inventory control system. Instead of increasing the refrigeration capacity by purchasing additional refrigeration systems, the owner has an agreement with the fish vendor to deliver

fresh fish several times a day so that materials arrive just in time to be used for sushi making. The inventory cost is, therefore, minimal.

The available floor space is for workers and their necessary equipment but not for holding inventory. In the 100 Yen Sushi House, workers and their equipment are positioned so close together that sushi making is passed on hand to hand rather than as independent operations. The absence of walls of inventory allows the owner and workers to be involved in the total operation, from greeting the customer to serving what is ordered. Their tasks are tightly interrelated and everyone rushes to a problem spot to prevent the cascading effect of the problem throughout the work process.

The 100 Yen Sushi House is a labour-intensive operation, which is based mostly on simplicity and common sense rather than high technology, contrary to American perceptions. I was very impressed. As I finished my fifth plate, I saw the same octopus sushi plate going around for about the thirtieth time. Perhaps I had discovered the pitfall of the system. So I asked the owner how he takes care of the sanitary problems when a sushi plate goes around all day long, until an unfortunate customer eats it and perhaps gets food poisoning. He bowed with an apologetic smile and said, "Well, sir, we never let our sushi plates go unsold longer than about 30 minutes." Then he scratched his head and said, "Whenever one of our employees takes a break, he or she can take off unsold plates of sushi and either eat them or throw them away. We are very serious about our sushi quality."

Source:

Condensed from Sang M. Lee, "Japanese Management and the 100 Yen Sushi House," *Operations Management Review* 1, no. 2 (Winter 1983), pp. 45–48.

anagers can view just-in-time from two levels. From a strategic management perspective, JIT can be used as a management change tool, similar to total quality management or six sigma, not only to reduce waste and inventories on the factory floor, but also to increase quality and operational efficiency. At the day-to-day operating level, JIT provides management with a tool for controlling the flow of materials, identifying sources of error, and minimizing inventories.

JIT concepts are applicable to virtually all types of operational environments, including manufacturing and service operations. However, managers must recognize that the successful implementation of JIT is dependent on several factors, including strong supplier relationships and the concept of production linearity. (Production linearity means that over a given period of time, a constant quantity of products is produced every day, although the specific mix of the products can change within a broad range.)

The JIT Concept

JIT (just-in-time)

A coordinated approach that continuously reduces inventories while also improving quality.

JIT (just-in-time) is an integrated set of activities designed to continuously reduce waste in a system (called **muda** in Japanese) such as delays, and unnecessary inventory and labour. For example, in a JIT factory, parts arrive at a workstation "just in time" (when needed) and are completed and move through the operation quickly. Just-in-time is also based on the logic that nothing will be produced until it is needed. Exhibit 13.1 illustrates this process. Need is created by the product being pulled toward the user. When an item is sold, in theory, the market pulls a replacement from the last position in the system—final assembly in this case. This triggers an order to the factory production line, where a worker then pulls another unit from an upstream station in the flow to replace the unit taken. This upstream station then pulls from the next station further upstream and so on back to the release of the raw materials and components needed to make the product. To enable this pull process to work smoothly, JIT demands high levels of quality at each stage of the process, strong vendor relations, and a fairly predictable demand for the end product.

JIT can be viewed colloquially as "big JIT" and "little JIT." Big JIT (often termed lean manufacturing, lean operations, or lean production[1]) is the philosophy of operations management that seeks to eliminate waste in all aspects of a firm's activities: human relations, supplier relations, technology, and the management of materials and inventories. Little JIT

Exhibit 13.1

Pull System

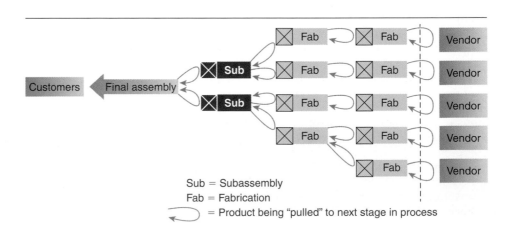

Sub = Subassembly
Fab = Fabrication
⟲ = Product being "pulled" to next stage in process

---

[1]Paul H. Zipkin, "Does Manufacturing Need a JIT Revolution?" *Harvard Business Review* (January–February, 1991), p. 41.

focuses more narrowly on scheduling goods inventories and providing service resources where and when needed. For example, companies such as Manpower Temporary Services and Pizza Hut essentially use pull signals to fill orders for replacement workers or pizzas, respectively. However, they do not necessarily integrate operations around other aspects of the JIT philosophy.

The JIT concept applies primarily to a repetitive manufacturing process. It does not necessarily require large volumes, but typically is restricted to those operations that produce the same parts over and over. Ideally, the finished product would be repetitive in nature. However, with customized products such as Dell's PCs, the repetitive segments of the business may only appear at the component and subcomponent level. Even so, applying JIT concepts to a portion of the business or applying some of the applicable JIT principles to the non-repetitive parts of the business still will produce significant improvements.

Two examples of the effect of JIT on productivity have been cited by the Ford Motor Company: The Escort automobile needed a transaxle, which was going to require a $300 million expansion at the Ford plant in Batavia, Ohio. Ford asked Japanese companies for an equivalent quotation, and Tokyo-Kogyo offered to construct a brand-new plant with the same rate of output at a competitive unit price for $100 million, a one-third ratio. A second example relates to Ford's Valencia engine plant, which produces two engines per employee per day, and requires 900 000 square feet of floor space. An almost identical engine is produced by the Toyota Motor Company in Japan, where they make nine engines per employee per day in a plant that has only 300 000 square feet of space. The issue is not only productivity per person, but also a much lower capital investment to achieve this manufacturing capability.

Finally, note that different companies use different terms to describe their JIT systems. IBM uses continuous flow manufacture, Hewlett-Packard Company uses "stockless production" at one plant and "repetitive manufacturing system" at another, while many other companies use "lean production." Synchronized material flow is still another term used. Exhibit 13.2 shows the JIT implementation plan at Hewlett Packard's Boise, Idaho plant which is a good overview of the different elements of JIT and how they relate to one another.

The Japanese Approach to Productivity

To fully appreciate the elements of Big JIT, it is useful to review the history and philosophy of its application in Japan.[2] The ability of Japanese manufacturers to compete in high-quality, low-cost production, which was widely publicized in the 1970s and early 1980s, still holds despite their current economic problems. Indeed, the good Japanese companies are still dominant or are strong competitors in automobiles, electronics, capital machinery, and shipbuilding, based on the capabilities they established over 20 years ago and kept improving upon. JIT is a major reason.

Many people believe these accomplishments are attributable to cultural differences. They envision Japanese employees dedicating their lives to their companies and working long hours for substandard wages which would be unthinkable in North America. The evidence, however, is contrary to these distorted notions. Consider the following: In 1977, a Japanese company named Matsushita (manufacturer of Panasonic, Quasar, and Technics brands) purchased a television plant in Chicago from a U.S. company. In the purchase contract, Matsushita agreed that all the hourly personnel would be retrained. Two years later,

[2]Adapted from Kenneth A. Wantuck, *The Japanese Approach to Productivity* (Southfield, MI: Bendix Corporation, 1983).

Exhibit 13.2

How to
Accomplish
Just-in-Time
Production

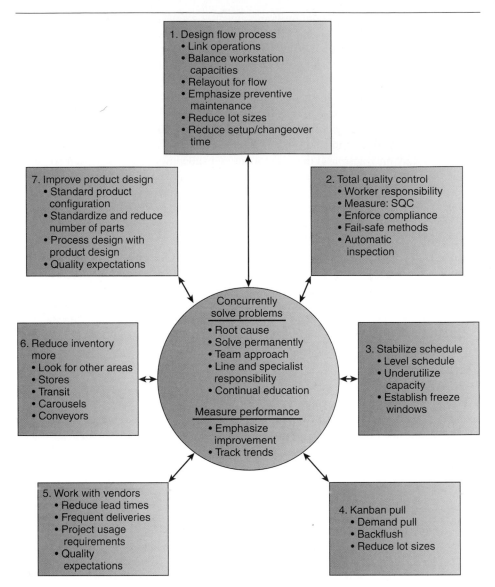

This diagram is modelled after the one used by Hewlett-Packard's Boise plant to accomplish its JIT program.

they still had essentially the same 1000 hourly employees and had managed to reduce the indirect staff by 50 percent (see Exhibit 13.3). Yet, during that period, daily production doubled. The quality, as measured by the number of defects per 100 TV sets built, improved 40-fold. Outside quality indicators also improved. Whereas the U.S. company (Motorola) had spent an average of US$16 million a year on warranty costs, Matsushita's expenditures were US$2 million. (That's for twice as many TV sets, so it's really a 16-to-1 ratio.) These are big differences—differences achieved in the United States with American workers. The issue is, how do the Japanese companies accomplish this and what can others learn from them? As JIT has spread across the world, companies in different countries have adapted it to their unique environments. Thus companies can learn from the experiences of other companies not only in Japan but around the world.

	Under Motorola	Under Matsushita*
Direct labour employees	1000	1000†
Indirect employees	600	300
Total employees	1600	1300
Daily production	1000	2000
Defect rate per 100 TV sets	160	4
Annual warranty cost ($ millions)	$16	$2

*2 years later.
†Same people.

Exhibit 13.3

Quasar Plant Productivity

What It Is	What It Does
• Management philosophy	• Attacks waste (time, inventory, scrap)
• "Pull" system through the plant	• Exposes problems and bottlenecks
• Quality products and services	• Achieves streamlined production
• Waste elimination	

What It Requires

- Employee participation
- Industrial engineering/basics
- Continuing improvement
- Focus on quality
- Small lot sizes
- Management support
- Long-term focus

Source: Adapted from Chris Gopal (of Price Waterhouse), "Notes on JIT."

Exhibit 13.4

Just-in-Time

Some aspects of JIT are not new. For example, the concept of continuous improvement and total quality management was made popular in Japan by Deming (see Chapter 6). Likewise, group technology is an old concept. You will see in Web Chapter 17 that Nova Scotian Samuel Cunard, founder of Cunard Lines, strongly believed in treating employees well. After World War II, certain Japanese companies integrated many of these concepts and successfully implemented JIT.

What the Japanese companies accomplished was to act on the principle that in every way, shape, and form you must eliminate waste. As the opening vignette and the OM in Practice Box on Toyota show, however, this does not mean that high-tech equipment or sophisticated software is necessary for JIT implementation. The focus is on improved management methods. Exhibit 13.4 highlights what just-in-time is, what it does, and what it requires.

Fundamentals of JIT

Taiichi Ohno, vice president of manufacturing at Toyota in the early 1950s, and Shigeo Shingo, head of industrial engineering and factory improvement training, developed a method of production called the Toyota Production System, which emphasized the

eliminate waste

Eliminate everything not essential to production, including safety stocks, waiting times, and extra labour.

minimization of all waste (**eliminate waste**) and focused on "doing it right the first time." Even after 50 years it is still being fine-tuned. Shingo recognized the importance of Ford's notion of nearly continuous production for achieving efficiency, but also wanted to enhance customer satisfaction (effectiveness) by modifying the system to facilitate the production of small batches. He recognized that high levels of inventory actually hindered a system's ability to make efficient, rapid changes in product mix. He focused his attention on reducing setup times so that the production system could be very responsive to changes in customer requirements while at the same time producing output nearly continuously with little or no waste. As a result of these efforts, Toyota over time identified what came to be known as the Seven Deadly Wastes:

1. Overproduction: producing more than is required by the market.
2. Waiting time: workers who are idle because they have completed their work or who watch machines but cannot prevent problems.
3. Transportation: moving materials between workstations without adding value.
4. Processing: downtime because machines need maintenance or repair.
5. Inventory: the costs associated with loss, obsolescence, and damage to inventories, as well as the cost of excess inventory itself. (Not all inventory is waste; some is required to prevent supply chain breakdown in case of uncertainties. The long-term objective is to reduce this inventory by reducing supply chain uncertainty.)
6. Motion: movement at the workstation that is not related to adding value to the product.
7. Waste from product defects: the costs of scrap and rework and, most important of all, the costs associated with defective output reaching the customer.

The definition of "waste" given by Fujio Cho, of the Toyota Motor Company, summarizes well the waste elimination philosophy. He calls waste "anything other than the minimum amount of equipment, materials, parts, and workers (working time) which are absolutely essential to production." That means no surplus, no safety stock. That means nothing is banked for future use. If you can't use it now, you don't make it now because it is considered waste. There are seven basic elements under this concept:

1. Just-in-time production.
2. Focus on quality.
3. Flexible process design and layout.
4. Involvement of workforce.
5. Close supplier relationships.
6. Innovative product design.
7. Focus on problem solving and continuous improvement.

Just-in-Time Production

JIT is based on a fundamental concept called just-in-time production. It requires the production of precisely the necessary units in the necessary quantities at the necessary time, with the objective of achieving plus or minus zero performance to schedule. It means that producing one extra piece is just as bad as being one piece short. In fact, anything over the minimum amount necessary is viewed as waste. This means that if production is not needed the machinery remains idle. This was a unique idea for North American managers,

JIT AT TOYOTA'S NORTH AMERICAN PLANTS

No discussion about JIT is complete without mentioning Toyota, the creator of the JIT manufacturing system and still one of its leading practitioners. However, Toyota will still tell you it has not mastered the art and views JIT as a process that can itself be continually improved upon. Different Toyota plants, such as the ones in Cambridge, Ontario, and Georgetown, Kentucky, employ JIT principles in a slightly different fashion depending on the plant attributes and supply base. Here are some of the features and results at those plants:

80 percent of materials used in Georgetown come from North America. The closer suppliers deliver more often than the farther ones. At Georgetown, most suppliers are within 300 km of the plant. At any given time at the Kentucky (or Cambridge) plant there is only three to four hours' worth of inventory; however, parts sourced from overseas may have up to five days worth of inventory. Between 1996 and 1997 Toyota was able to reduce the time it takes to produce an engine at Georgetown from 1.6 hours to 1.26 hours (21 percent). This was achieved through a kaizen (problem solving and continuous improvement) program.

In Cambridge, by working with TMM Canada, its logistics provider, Toyota has been able to cut in-house inventories by 28 percent, transportation lead time by 31 percent, and parts storage space by 37 percent. Only once has a parts shortage apparently hampered production. The Cambridge facility has about 200 suppliers. On average TMM Canada picks up material 7.8 times per day from each supplier. At the plant the parts bins are kept close to the line, eliminating five steps between workers and parts bins and gaining the equivalent of 6.25 workers in efficiency.

Toyota's production control process uses simple (though not simplistic) techniques such as the kanban system and co-operating with suppliers to ensure timely delivery and good quality.

Toyota does not inspect incoming inventory. As an example of simplicity and supplier co-operation, consider the following: With a US$12 dryer, a Toyota executive proved to engineers from Michigan's Summit Polymers Inc., a supplier, that their US$280 000 investment in robots and a paint oven to bake the dashboard vents they produce was actually causing quality problems and increasing costs. The equipment took up to 90 minutes to dry the paint and also caused quality flaws because parts gathered dust as they crept along a conveyor. The hair dryer did the job in less than three minutes. Summit's engineers replaced their paint system with some US$150 spray guns and a few light bulbs for drying and integrated the painting into the final assembly process. Along with some other changes using Toyota's help, Summit cut its defect rate to less than 60 per million parts from 3000 per million. As another example, Automotive Sunroof-Customcraft (ASC) Inc., of Kitchener, Ontario, which converts Solara coupe bodies to convertibles, developed many error-proofing techniques and process improvements with Toyota's help.

As part of its continuous improvement philosophy, Toyota is now moving beyond production management to improvement in the marketing area. Toyota plans to improve customer choice and satisfaction by allowing customers to pick the colour and options on some vehicle models and have the vehicle delivered in two weeks.

Sources:

Dave Zoia, "Toyota's Production System Comes to Logistics," *Ward's Auto World* (September 1999), pp. 77–78.

Tim Minahan, "JIT, A Process with Many Faces," *Purchasing* (September 4, 1997), pp. 42–43.

Norihiko Shirouzu, "Toyota Finds Success in Details," *The Globe and Mail*, March 15, 2001, B11.

Jeff Sabatini, "The Chop House," *Automotive Manufacturing and Production* (September 2000), pp. 68–71.

"Toyota Trumpets Quick Custom Delivery," *Calgary Herald*, August 8, 2003.

since a measure of good performance in North America had always been to meet or exceed the schedule and keep equipment running even though it meant building inventory that might not have been consumed. Moreover, it was contrary to the then-practice in many North American firms, which stocked extra material just in case something went wrong.

Underutilization of Capacity

Another feature of JIT alien to North American managers was underutilization of capacity. Underutilized (or excess) capacity is really the cost incurred by eliminating inventories as a buffer in the system. In traditional manufacturing, safety stocks (also called buffers which are additional inventories) and early deliveries are used as a hedge against shortfalls in production resulting from such things as poor quality, machine failures, and unanticipated bottlenecks. Under JIT, excess labour and machine capacity provide that hedge in lieu of inventory. Managers are now recognizing that excess capacity in the form of labour and equipment is generally far less expensive than carrying excess inventory. Moreover, excess labour can be put to work on other activities during slow periods when it is not needed for direct production. Furthermore, the low idle-time cost incurred by the relatively inexpensive machines favoured by JIT producers makes machine utilization a secondary issue for many firms. Finally, much of the excess capacity is by design—workers are expected to have time at the end of their shifts to meet with their work groups, clean up their workstations, and ponder potential improvements.

Small Lot Sizes

Under just-in-time, the ideal lot (batch) size is one piece. JIT companies view the manufacturing process as a giant network of interconnected work centres, in which the perfect arrangement would be to have each worker complete his or her task on a part and pass it directly to the next worker just as that person was ready for another piece. The idea is to drive all queues toward zero by reducing the lot size in order to:

- Minimize inventory investment (large lots mean making large quantities of items before they are needed and holding them as inventory)
- Shorten production lead times
- React faster to demand changes
- Uncover any quality problems

Exhibit 13.5 is an illustration that Japanese companies use to depict the last idea. They look on the water level in a river as inventory and the rocks as problems that might occur in a shop. A lot of water in the river hides the problems. Management assumes everything is fine. Invariably, the water level drops at the worst possible time, such as during an economic downturn. Management then must address the problems without the necessary resources to solve them. The Japanese say it is better to force the water level down on

Exhibit 13.5

Inventory Hides Problems

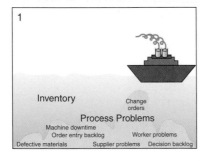
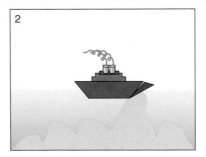
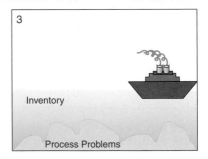
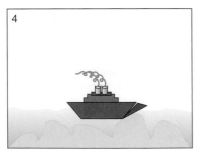

Operations Management in Practice

SMALL LOT PRINCIPLE APPLIES TO INFORMATION TOO!

Large-lot information processing problems are similar to those faced by manufacturing managers when producing in large batches (overtime, additional costs, transcription, identification, and calculation errors, as well as interruptions to production and costly rework of defects). Thus it is important that managers of information flow also recognize the advantages that small-lot information processing can provide.

For example, a large childcare agency was responsible for thousands of children daily. The integrity of its database of parent telephone numbers, children's known allergies, and other information was vital. However, the database never seemed to be current, making it unreliable.

Upon analysis, a consultant realized that the employees entering the data had other responsibilities. As a result they tended to accumulate database changes over long periods of time and then update the database in a large batch. When the method was changed so that updates were completed in small daily lots, the problem disappeared. Since the employees were at their computers anyway, setup was minimal, and entering a few records each day was easier than large-lot entry. The cost of the change was virtually nothing and it was very successful. In another instance in a government department, keying in information in small batches regularly (rather than in infrequent large batches) reduced the amount of correction needed.

Source:
Frank Gue, "Small Lot Principle Applies to Information," *APICS—The Performance Advantage* (August 1999), p. 56.

purpose (especially in good times), expose the problems, and fix them now, before they cause trouble.

The determination with which the Japanese companies work to reduce inventories is remarkable. To begin with, inventory is viewed as a negative, not as an asset. According to Toyota, "The value of inventory is disavowed." Auto air conditioner manufacturer Denso Corporation's attitude is even more severe: Inventory is "the root of all evil." Almost universally, the Japanese see inventory as a deterrent to product quality. Since the shop floor is designed to have very little inventory, the slightest aberration in the process resulting in extra parts is readily visible and serves as a red flag to which an immediate response is required.

Because it is impossible to have every worker in a complex manufacturing process adjacent to one another, and since the network also includes outside suppliers, Japanese companies recognize that the system must allow for some transit time between centres. However, transfer quantities are kept as small as possible. Vendors deliver their products several times a day to their customers, and constant pressure is exerted to reduce inventory in the system. However, if there is uncertainty in the system, JIT companies will hold some inventory.

Just-in-time production makes no allowances for contingencies. Every piece is expected to be correct when received. Every machine is expected to be available when needed to produce parts. Every delivery commitment is expected to be honoured at the precise time it is scheduled, not earlier, not later. Consequently, Japanese companies place heavy emphasis on quality, preventive maintenance, and mutual trust among all participants in the manufacturing enterprise. The process is given top priority and everyone conscientiously adheres to it.

Uniform Production in Small Lots

To effectively incorporate the just-in-time production concept, it is necessary that production flow as smoothly as possible in the shop. The starting point is what Japanese companies call uniform plant loading. Its objective is to dampen the reaction waves that normally occur in response to schedule variations. For example, when a significant change is made in final assembly, it creates changes in the requirements in the feeder operations, which are usually amplified because of lot sizing rules, setups, queues, and waiting time. By the time

Exhibit 13.6

Toyota Example of Mixed-Model Production Cycle in a Japanese Assembly Plant

Model	Monthly Quantity	Daily Quantity	Cycle (takt) Time (minutes)
Sedan	5000	250	2
Hardtop	2500	125	4
Wagon	2500	125	4
Sequence: Sedan, hardtop, sedan, wagon, sedan, hardtop, sedan, wagon, etc.			

the impact of the change is felt at the start of the supply chain, a 10 percent change at assembly could easily translate into a 100 percent change at the beginning of the operation.

Japanese companies say that the only way to eliminate that problem is to make the waves at the end as small as possible so that we only get ripples going through the shop, not shock waves. These companies accomplish this by setting up a firm monthly production plan during which the output rate is frozen. They also plan to build the same mix of products every day, even if the total quantities are small. For example, if they're only building a hundred pieces a month, they'll build five each day. Because they expect to build some quantity of everything that's on the schedule daily, they always have a total mix available to respond to variations in demand.

Going even further, they'll take those five units and intermix them on the assembly line. An example of how Toyota would do this is shown in Exhibit 13.6. Let us assume that three kinds of vehicles are being made in an assembly plant: sedans, hardtops, and station wagons. The monthly rates shown are then reduced to daily quantities (presuming a 20-day month) of 250, 125, and 125, respectively. From this, the necessary cycle times can be computed. Cycle time is the period of time between two identical units coming off the production line. The company uses this figure to adjust their resources to produce precisely the quantity that's needed—no more, no less. (This is identical to takt time, as presented in Chapter 8.)

Japanese companies do not concern themselves with achieving the rated speeds of their equipment. In North American shops, a given machine is rated at 1000 pieces per hour, so if 5000 pieces are needed the machine is run for five hours to obtain this month's requirement. The Japanese produce only the needed quantity each day, as required. To them, cycle time is the driver that defines how they assemble their resources to meet this month's production. If the rate for next month changes, the resources are reconfigured. These small lot sizes ensure that customers do not have to wait long for the next batch.

Kanban Production Control System

Most people view JIT as a pull system, where the material is drawn or sent for by the users as it is needed. The **Kanban** (kahn-bahn) **system** is a shop floor/vendor release and control system. The name comes from the Japanese word meaning card. It is a pull system because the authority to produce or supply comes from downstream operations. The signal sent is for a standard lot size conveyed in a standardized container, not just for a "bunch of parts." Some typical Kanban-type signals used to initiate production are:

Kanban pull system

Manual, self-regulating system for controlling the flow of material. Workers produce product only when the Kanban ahead of them is empty, thereby creating a "pull" system through the factory.

● Recycling travelling requisitions/cards

● "Hey Jane, make me another lot"

● A flashing light over a work centre, indicating the need for more parts

● A signal marker hanging on a post by the workstation(s) using the part(s)

● An empty slot or bin or floor space (see figure)

This system of material control replaces exactly what has been consumed and no more. Some systems use Kanban cards in a two-card system or a one-card system; some systems use no cards at all. The two-card system is actually one of the more complex control methods. Replenishment signals can be sent back electronically to the supplying operation to save time; however, care needs to be taken because much of the value of the Kanban system lies in its simplicity and its management visibility.

The majority of factories in Japan don't use Kanban cards per se. Kanban is a system used by the Toyota Motor Company system. However, many companies in both North America and Japan use pull systems with other types of signalling devices.

A pull system typically starts with the master production schedule specifying the final assembly schedule. By referring to the final assembly schedule, material schedulers and supervisors can see the days during the month when each part will be needed. They determine when to schedule supplier deliveries or internal parts manufacture by offsetting lead times from final assembly dates. The final assembly schedule therefore exerts the initial pull on the system, with Kanbans manually controlling the actual flow.

Between two operations within sight of each other, no cards are needed at all—only a strict restriction on the inventory between. This can be done by marking a space between operations called a Kanban square. If any of the squares are empty, workers fill them up, but cannot place inventory outside of the squares.

In a two card system, the flow of Kanban cards between two work centres is shown in Exhibit 13.7. The machining centre shown is making two parts, A and B, which are stored in standard containers in the machining centre storage area. When the assembly line needs more Part A from a full container, a worker takes the withdrawal Kanban from the empty container and travels to the machining centre storage area. He or she finds a full container of Part A, removes the production Kanban, and replaces it with the withdrawal Kanban card, which authorizes him or her to move the container. The freed production Kanban is then placed in a rack by the storage area as a work authorization for another lot of material. Parts are manufactured in the order in which cards are placed on the rack, which makes the set of cards in the rack a priority list for scheduling work on the factory floor. When enough parts are manufactured to fill the container, the production kanban is then attached to the full container, which is then sent to the storage area.

Many firms use withdrawal cards only. With the simplest one-card system, the worker at the assembly line (or more likely a material handler) walks to the machine centre with an empty container and a withdrawal Kanban. He or she then places the empty container at a designated spot, attaches the withdrawal card to a filled container, and carries it back to the assembly line. The worker at the machining centre would know that a refill is required because of the empty container. This type of system is appropriate where the same part is made by the same people every day. If it turns out that the demand for Part A is greater than planned and less than planned for Part B, the system self-regulates to these changes because there can be no more parts built than called for by the Kanban cards in circulation.

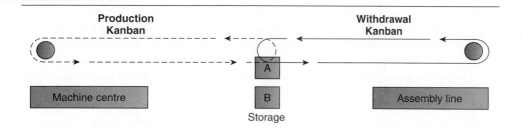

Exhibit 13.7

Flow of Two Kanbans

Production Kanban — Withdrawal Kanban

Machine centre — Storage (A, B) — Assembly line

At Bernard Welding Equipment, when part bins are emptied, a Kanban card is detached from the container, transferred to the appropriate work cell, and placed on a post to indicate the bin needs to be refilled. The card contains the part number, routing quantity, and bin number.

In a system where operations are within sight of each other, no cards are needed. Workers mark a square between operations. An empty Kanban square on this factory floor visually signals the need to be filled by a disk drive unit.

Mix changes of 10 to 20 percent can be accommodated easily because the shifts are gradual and the increments small. The ripple effect upstream is similarly dampened.

The number of pieces in a container never varies for a given part number. When production rates change, containers are added to or deleted from the system, according to a simple formula. The idea of safety stock is included in the basic calculation. In practice, efforts are made to reduce the lot sizes to keep inventories to a minimum and expose problems.

Reducing lot sizes in a pull system means removing interstage inventory. This is accomplished in a variety of ways: (*a*) by better balance of operations so that only two Kanban containers are used between two workstations rather than three, (*b*) by moving workstations closer together to cut transit time, (*c*) by automating processes that have high variability, and, of course, (*d*) by just-in-time deliveries.

The same approach is used to authorize vendor shipments. When both the customer and the vendor are using the Kanban system, the withdrawal Kanban serves as the authorization for the vendor to ship (reducing paperwork and administrative costs), while the production Kanban at the vendor's plant regulates production there.

The whole system hinges on everyone doing exactly what is authorized and following procedures explicitly. In fact, Japanese companies use no production coordinators on the shop floor, relying solely on supervisors to ensure compliance. Co-operative worker attitudes are essential to its success.

Results can be impressive. Jidosha Kiki (now Bosch Automotive Systems Corporation), a braking components affiliate company in Japan, installed a Kanban/just-in-time system with the help of its customer, Toyota. Within two years they had doubled productivity, tripled inventory turnover, and substantially reduced overtime and space requirements. Jidosha Kiki stated that the conversion was a slow and difficult learning process for its employees, even considering the Japanese culture, because all the old rules of thumb had to be tossed out the window and deep-rooted ideas had to be changed.

One of the advantages of the kanban system is that the signals are simple and visual (*visual management*). Another visual mechanism used with kanban in JIT environments is the *andon* board, which shows the status of production on a line. Exhibit 13.8 shows a number of andon boards. Workers and managers are able to see the status of the day's

Exhibit 13.8

Andon Boards

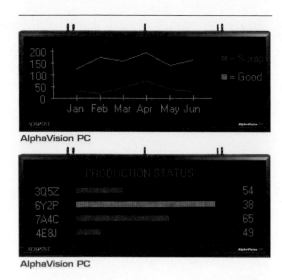

Source: www.adaptivedisplays.com. Used with permission.

production at a glance. Cycle times, number of rejects, actual production levels, and target levels are often depicted on andon boards.

Minimized Setup Times

Smaller lot sizes are closely related to setup/changeover time and are key to achieving a smooth flow (uniform production in small lots). Producing in small lots is impossible if machine setups take hours to accomplish. Imagine if you lived a two-hour drive from the nearest grocery store. You would not drive two hours just to buy one item. Most likely, to justify the long drive (and cost of driving) you would buy all items in bulk to make sure you would not run out for a long time. Also you would have to invest in a large refrigerator or freezer to store all the items you purchased in bulk. This will cost extra too. On the other hand, if you had a 24-hour grocery store in your apartment building you would need to buy only when you wanted to eat (just-in-time) and you could do with a small refrigerator. Also it would take you a lot less time each time to get your groceries. Thus Japanese companies realized that producing in small lots would be cheaper from an inventory perspective, and as an added bonus customers would not have to wait long to get their orders (because small lots can be completed and delivered more quickly than large lots). However, they also realized that, because large machines required many hours to set up, the only way small lots could be justified was by drastically reducing setup times. For example, if setup time on a machine were eight hours, you could not justify making only 10 units of an item that required 30 minutes to make and then setting up for another eight hours for another item. This would mean that your expensive machine would be idle most of the time. Rather, in order to justify the eight-hour setup you might make 1000 units each time the machine was set up, which would take 3000 minutes in total. However, if setup took only 5 minutes, running 10 units for 30 minutes and then setting up for another item would be perfectly feasible. Although this magnitude in setup time reduction might seem unlikely, in practice, as Exhibit 13.9 shows, many companies in different industries have indeed achieved such reductions (and reaped the benefits).

Japanese success in this area has received widespread acclaim. The Japanese aim for single-digit setup times (i.e., less than 10 minutes) for every machine in their factories. This is called SMED (single minute exchange of die). They've addressed not only big things, like presses, but small moulding machines and standard machine tools as well.

Exhibit 13.9

Setup Time Reduction Results

Industry	Equipment	Before	After	%
Assembly	Adhesive applicator	12:09:00	0:21:00	97%
Assembly	Air cleaner assembly	2:00:00	0:00:00	100%
Brake Manufacturing	Briquette press	1:05:00	0:12:00	82%
Cosmetics	Capper machine	0:09:36	0:03:21	65%
Electronics	PCB Insertion—radial	0:54:12	0:05:06	91%
Foundry	Moulding machine	0:10:00	0:06:12	38%
Metal Cutting	Casting drill	1:00:00	0:09:00	85%
Metal Fabrication	800-ton press	6:00:00	0:10:00	97%
Metal Fabrication	Aluminum extruder	1:09:00	0:02:12	97%
Packaging	Flex packaging line	3:00:00	0:10:00	94%
Paper	Sheeting	0:03:00	0:00:36	80%
Pharmaceutical	Centrifuge	0:12:00	0:02:12	82%
Plastics	250-ton injection molder	1:06:00	0:09:12	86%
Printing	Press make ready	9:30:00	4:20:00	54%
Wood	Router	0:09:00	0:01:18	86%

Source: www.strategosinc.com/setup_reduction3.htm, May 1, 2004. Reprinted with permission.

Again, this concept of faster setup is not new—compare the length of time you would need to replace a tire on your car with the time it takes in a Formula 1 race.

It is easy to achieve setup time reductions with a detailed analysis of the setup process. The Japanese separate setup time into two segments: **internal**—the part that must be done while a machine is stopped, and **external**—the part that can be done while the machine is operating. Simple things, such as the staging of replacement dies in anticipation of a change, fall into the external category, which, on the average, represents half of the usual setup time. For example, Spartan Plastics of London, Ontario, a manufacturer of plastic strips for the auto industry, reduced its setup time by preheating plastic extrusion dies. Previously the die was mounted on the extrusion machine and then heated to the correct temperature before plastic extrusion could begin, leading to long downtimes (all internal setup). By preheating the die to the correct temperature (external setup) before mounting it on the extrusion machine, plastic extrusion could begin immediately after the die was mounted (only the mounting of the die was now internal).[3]

internal setup

Setup that can be done only when machine is not operating.

external setup

Setup that can be done while the machine is in operation.

Another 50 percent reduction usually can be achieved by the application of time and motion studies and practice. (It is not unusual for a Japanese setup team to spend a full Saturday practising changeovers.) Time-saving devices such as hinged bolts, roller platforms, and folding brackets for temporary die staging are commonly used, all of which are low-cost items.

Only then is it necessary to spend larger sums of money on equipment such as automatic positioning of dies, rolling bolsters, and duplicate tool holders to reduce the last 15 percent or so. The result is that 90 percent or more of the setup time often can be eliminated.

The savings in setup time justify an increase in the number of lots produced, with a corresponding reduction in lot sizes. This makes the use of just-in-time production principles feasible, which in turn makes the Kanban control system practical. All the pieces fit together.

---

[3]Narendar Sumukadas and Chris Piper, *Spartan Plastics* (London: Ontario: University of Western Ontario, Ivey Management Services, 1997).

Focus on Quality

JIT and quality management have become linked in the minds of many managers—and for good reason. As stated in Chapter 6, total quality control refers to "building in" quality and not "inspecting it in." It also refers to all plant personnel taking responsibility for maintaining quality, not just "leaving it to the quality control department." When employees assume this responsibility, JIT is permitted to work at its optimal level, since only good products are pulled through the system. What results is having your cake and eating it too—high quality and high productivity. Exhibit 13.10 illustrates this relationship.

When items are produced in small lots, such as in the Kanban system, the inspection may be reduced to just two items: the first and the last. If they are perfect, assume that those produced in between are perfect as well.

When management demonstrates a high degree of confidence in people, it is possible to implement a quality concept that the Japanese called **Jidoka**. The word means "Stop everything when something goes wrong." It can be thought of as the Japanese concept of controlling quality at the source. Instead of using inspectors to find the problems that somebody else may have created, the worker in a Japanese factory becomes his or her own inspector. This concept was developed by Taiichi Ohno, who was vice president of manufacturing for Toyota Motor Company in the early 1950s.

Ohno was convinced that one of the big problems faced by Toyota was bringing quality levels up to the necessary standards that would permit Toyota to penetrate the world automotive market. He determined that the best thing to do was to give each person only one part to work on at a time so that under no circumstances would he or she be able to bury or hide problems by working on other parts. Jidoka push buttons were installed on the assembly lines. If anything went wrong—if a worker found a defective part, if he or she could not keep up with production, if production was going too fast according to the pace that was set for the day, or if he or she found a safety hazard—that worker was obligated to push the button. When the button was pushed, a light flashed, a bell rang, and the entire assembly line came to a grinding halt. People descended on the spot where the light

Jidoka

Japanese concept focusing on controlling the quality of a product at its source.

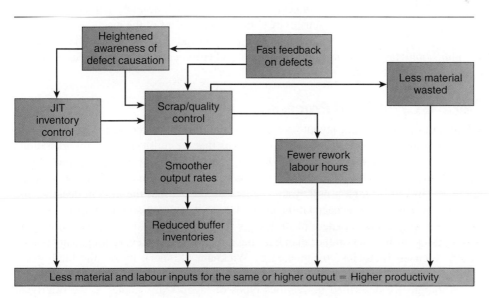

Exhibit 13.10

Relationship between JIT and Quality

Source: Richard J. Schonberger, "Some Observations on the Advantages and Implementation Issues of Just-in-Time Production Systems," *Journal of Operations Management* 3, no. 1 (November 1982), p. 5.

Toronto-based Cinram International, one of the world's largest manufacturers of recording media such as DVDs, CDs, and video and audio cassettes, uses Jidoka principles in its Toronto factory. When the production line is operating normally, the green light stays on. If the green switches to amber, it is a signal of a problem on the line and that help is needed. If it is red it indicates that the line is stopped due to problems that need to be fixed immediately.

Source: The Globe and Mail, July 19, 2003, B1.
Photo by Darryl James.

was flashing. It was something like a volunteer fire department: People came from the industrial engineering department, from management, from everywhere to respond to that particular alarm, and they fixed the problem on the spot.

Jidoka also encompasses automated inspection, sometimes called autonomation. Just like automation and robotics, Japanese companies believe that wherever possible inspection should be done by a machine because it's faster and more accurate. However, the inspection step is part of the production process. It therefore does not involve a separate location or person to perform it, and it automatically shuts off a machine when a problem arises. This prevents the mass production of defective parts. Line shutdowns in Japan are encouraged to protect quality and because management has confidence in the individual worker. No one likes to see a line stopped, but Ohno suggests that a day without a single Jidoka drill can mean people aren't being careful enough.

JIT companies also believe that prevention is better than inspection. So they use poke yokes (fail-safing) and statistical process control to prevent defects and to stop the process before defectives are produced. If a supplier workstation maintains a defect-free process, the customer workstation need not waste time inspecting the supplier's work.

Preventive maintenance is emphasized to ensure that a continuous workflow is not interrupted by machine downtime or as a result of poor quality from malfunctioning equipment. Much of this maintenance is carried out by the operators because they are responsible for the quality of products coming off the machines, and also because of their sensitivity to the idiosyncrasies of the machines as a result of working on them day in and day out. Finally, the fact that the JIT philosophy favours many simple machines rather than a few complex ones enables the operators to handle routine maintenance activities.

Flexible Layout and Processes

JIT requires that the plant layout be designed to ensure balanced and flexible workflow with a minimum of work in process. This means that we must view each workstation as an integral part of the overall production line, whether or not a physical line actually exists. Capacity balancing is done using the same logic as for an assembly line, and operations are linked through a pull system. This also means that the system designer must have a vision of how all aspects of the internal and external logistics system are related to the layout. In general, Japanese plant designs tend to be more focused, specializing on a narrow range of products rather than building a plant that does everything. This practice, called "**focused factories**" (originated by Wickham Skinner), makes the facility more manageable.

focused factories

Groups of small plants, each highly specialized in the products they manufacture.

Although we described the various types of layouts in Chapter 8, we briefly will describe a line flow operation, a job-shop layout, and group technology layouts to show how JIT can be applied.

Most people think of high-volume assembly lines when they think of JIT. This is because most of the literature and discussions on this topic have been about line layouts. However, job-shop environments, where functions are grouped together, offer perhaps the greatest benefits for JIT application.

JIT in a Line Flow or Product Layout

In assembly or fabrication lines, the focus is on product flow. Volumes may be high enough or tasks simple enough or costs low enough so that the required resources (people, machines, materials, etc.) can be arranged close together in a simple flow.

The cascading effect when JIT is applied between workstations is described in Exhibit 13.1 and the first paragraph of this chapter. The Kanban pull system is used to pull material between workstations with some inventory serving as a buffer between workstations. In theory, no one does any work until the product has been pulled from the end of the line, whether for final sale or for use somewhere else. In practice, since demand tends to be stable and continuous, a schedule is created for the completion of items based on demand forecasts. But note that overproduction will not be allowed because of the limit on inventory imposed by the Kanban system. Operating rules are straightforward: Always keep products that have been completed on the "completed" side of your workstation. If someone takes your completed work away, go upstream and get some more work to do. JIT companies often use flexible line layouts like the one shown in Exhibit 8.14 in Chapter 8 to have the ability to respond to changes in demand.

JIT in a Functional or Process (Job Shop) Layout

The majority of manufacturing plants are process-oriented, being organized by function (i.e., similar machines are grouped together as in Exhibit 8.2A). Many service facilities also are organized by function or process: hospitals, universities, department stores, etc. The main reason for this organization is that these machines or processes serve a variety of needs, none of which is large enough to justify a machine of its own. In this environment, the product or person requiring service must move longer distances.

To justify considering JIT as a valid way to produce goods, the basic requirement is that there be a continual need for the product, not that the product can be produced on an assembly line. The product does not have to be produced continuously in every phase of its creation. Items can be produced intermittently in batches throughout the majority of the sequence except for the final processing or final assembly, which may be continuous.

For example, a factory may have some of its products require a final assembly—that is, several parts and components produced in various parts of the firm are assembled together and then sold (Exhibit 13.1). Other products may require finish machining at a work centre before being ready for sale. In both cases, if demand is constant, these final steps are truly just-in-time as finished goods are pulled from the system.

The rest of the system preceding this final stage may not be just-in-time. Consider the machine centres, paint shops, foundries, heat treating areas, and the countless other locations that these parts and components go through before they reach the final stages. Can we operate these locations with the same Kanban and container logic we normally use for just-in-time? If the demand for parts is regular we can. However, if we are producing a one-time-only, customized batch of parts we may choose not to make any more than necessary because we do not know whether they will be needed again. Customers who require specialized parts recognize this and do not expect as quick service as they would for more standard parts. In any case, principles such as quality, preventive maintenance, setup reduction, workforce involvement, and many other JIT principles are always applicable.

Group Technology

group technology

Clustering dissimilar machines and operations in one cell to manufacture one family of products.

Chapter 8 discussed **group technology** and its advantages (see Exhibit 8.2B for the layout). JIT companies often employ group technology. Canon, a major electronic equipment maker, with 54 plants in 23 countries manufacturing cameras, printers, and copiers, recently implemented group technology in all of its assembly lines. As a result, work-in-process (WIP) inventory in its factories has been reduced from three days to six hours. Factory operating costs have been reduced by US$1.5 billion. Canon has decreased its real estate costs by $279 million because cells require less room, and because the reduced inventory level has resulted in fewer required warehouses (down from thirty-seven to eight).[4]

For group technology to work, people have to be flexible; to be flexible, people must identify with their companies, have a high degree of job security, and undergo continuous training. Another factor is how the machinery is configured. Sometimes it is set up to allow easy rearrangement as is the case at Spartan Plastics Canada Ltd. in London, Ontario, where equipment is placed on wheels to facilitate easy mixing and matching of equipment to product configurations.

5S

5S

A philosophy that aims for a clean and safe workplace

The **5S** philosophy is based on five Japanese words starting with S that imply a clean and safe workplace. 5S starts with sorting and discarding items that are not needed. For example, the Eaton Cutler Hammer factory in Calgary, which manufactures power supply equipment, has a designated area within the facility where all employees are expected to discard items, whether from the factory floor or offices, that have not been used for some time. This helps keep the workplace neat. 5S implies arranging the workplace and keeping it clean. Each tool used should have its place (there may be an outline of each tool drawn on the tool board so it's easy to locate and retrieve), and the equipment and workplace should be cleaned frequently. In addition, 5S requires a proper personal and work environment, which means wearing the right clothing and safety equipment. Furthermore, the physical layout should be designed to minimize stress and the equipment must be operated in a safe manner. Finally, like the PDCA model of Shewhart, 5S requires that process improvements be made permanent by including them in standard operating procedures. ICICI Bank Canada is an example of a pure service organization that has implemented 5S.

Involvement of the Workforce

For JIT to be successful, the workforce needs to be engaged in continuous improvement and involved in the process. It is management's responsibility to establish the culture that supports this kind of involvement.

The attitude of management toward the workers is critical. JIT managers listen to their workforce and encourage their suggestions for improvement. Employee involvement is a key element of JIT. In 1951, Kiichiro Toyoda learned about Ford's suggestion system and took it to a whole new level: Since the 1970s, Toyota plants have averaged 20 to 30 ideas per employee per year, and more than 80 percent of the suggestions are implemented.

Many JIT companies tap the knowledge of their employees to improve their operations. For example:

---

[4]Dreyfuss, J., "Profit Machine," *Bloomberg Markets*, October 2003, pp. 29–38.

- Milliken, a global fabric and specialty chemicals manufacturer, averages 110 ideas per employee each year.

- Dubal, an aluminum producer in the United Arab Emirates, averages more than nine ideas per employee per year.

- Dana Corporation, a global company with over 60 000 people, expects every employee to submit at least two ideas each month and implements 80 percent of them (see OMP on employee suggestions).[5]

Companies that do not seriously pursue improvement through employee ideas don't realize the full potential of JIT. For an employee suggestion program to be effective, the following factors have been found to be important:[6]

1. Top management commitment. Top management needs to understand and support the program and needs to make sure that resources and staffing are adequate to administer the program. Management should take the time to make sure that all front-line supervisors and low-level managers are on board.

2. Supervisor involvement. As an important communication channel between employees and management, direct supervisors should be involved in the management of the program. Management needs to be attuned to the risk that supervisors may initially resist suggestion programs out of fear that their employees' suggestions could make them look bad. To reduce that risk, supervisors should be recognized along with the award-winning employees.

3. Suggestion system administrator. Most successful programs are led by a suggestion system administrator who is responsible for the prompt and fair evaluation of suggestions.

4. Employee orientation and training. Employees need to be educated about the program, given examples of suggestions, and reassured that they won't lose their jobs if suggestions lead to productivity improvements.

5. Suggestion program committee. Successful suggestion programs generally are overseen by a suggestion program committee that does not administer the program, but meets regularly to review and update policies.

Other factors that have been found to be important are (*a*) clear policies about who can make suggestions, what types of suggestions will be considered, and how awards are determined and calculated; (*b*) clear procedures for submitting and processing suggestions; (*c*) a supportive cost system that enables the fair evaluation and reward of suggestions; (*d*) regular promotion and publicity for the program; (*e*) clear records that enable managers to track the program's success and compare outcomes to those of other companies; and (*f*) patience while the program becomes established.

Close Supplier Relationships

The specialized nature of Japanese factories has fostered the development of an enormous subcontractor network; many suppliers have fewer than 30 employees. More than 90 percent of all Japanese companies are part of supplier networks that are many layers deep, because there is so little vertical integration in Japanese factories.

---

[5]Alan Robinson and Dean Schroeder, *Ideas Are Free* (San Francisco: Berrett-Koehler Publishers, March 2004).
[6]Vincent G. Reuter, "Suggestion Systems: Utilization, Evaluation and Implementation," *California Management Review* 19, no. 3 (Spring 1977), pp. 78–89.

EMPLOYEE SUGGESTIONS PAY OFF AT CANADA POST AND THE DANA CORPORATION

Canada Post employee Craig Johnson earned a company reward of $10 000 (as well as the respect of his bosses and the admiration of his peers) for an innovation developed late one night in October 2004 on a Canada Post assembly line. He modified the sorting line machinery to generate mail barcodes on the fly. Previously, packages without barcodes had to be sorted manually by clerks such as Mr. Johnston and clogged up the machines. The time-saving idea, now being rolled out nationwide, has reduced the number of unmarked wayward parcels employees have to sort by 20 percent. The savings to Canada Post is expected to be significant.

The $10 000 came through the Canada Post employee involvement award program, an initiative designed to encourage and reward innovation on the job. This is an example of a culture of innovation at work, in which employees are encouraged to generate new ideas that benefit both themselves and their organization.

The Dana Corporation is a multibillion dollar conglomerate that produces truck and car parts and components for both automobile manufacturers and the after-purchase market. Two Canadian divisions of the company, the Spicer Driveshaft Division (in Thorold, Ontario) and The Structural Solutions Division (in Thorold, Virgil, and St. Mary's, all in Ontario) won Canada Awards of Excellence trophies in 2001. At Dana, all employees and management are encouraged to submit improvement ideas. This plays a very important role in Dana's endeavour not just to improve but to improve beyond expectations. In 1996, the employees of Dana Corp (worldwide) submitted a total of 666 120 suggestions, or 1.22 suggestions per employee per month. The result of employee input is a steady stream of improvements to the existing operation in the form of lower costs, less labour, and increased productivity, all of which directly affect the bottom line. Taking advantage of employee knowledge has become something of an obsession at Dana Corp. Says CEO Woody Morcott, "It's a core part of our value system." It begins in the classroom, where instructors at Dana University teach employees how to think about new ways of doing things. A major element in the success at Dana is their emphasis on the fact that workers are responsible for keeping the company competitive. Morcott admits he stole the idea when he visited a Japanese factory in the late 1980s. Each plant within Dana Corp. runs its own suggestion program, and it appears to be working. More than 70 percent of the suggestions submitted are adopted by the company.

Source:

Richard Teitelbaum, "How to Harness Gray Matter," *Fortune*, June 9, 1997, p. 168.

Anonymous, "Dana Corporation takes trophy in two divisions," *Excellence Magazine*, National Quality Institute, November 2002 (www.nqi.com/articles).

Rob Shaw, "Reward Employee Ideas—Literally," Globe and Mail, August 19, 2005, C1.

---

keiretsu

A Japanese term describing a network of companies that have close relationships with each other.

The company itself may be part of a close network of companies, not all of which may be suppliers, called a *keiretsu*. For example, a keiretsu may have a bank as one of the organizations in the network, which makes it easier for the companies in the network to obtain financing.

There are two kinds of suppliers: specialists in a narrow field who serve multiple customers (very much like North American suppliers) and captives, who usually make a small variety of parts for a single customer. The second kind is more prevalent in Japan. Sole-sourcing arrangements work in Japan because the relationships are based on a tremendous amount of mutual trust. They seek long-term partnerships between customer and supplier. North Americans who do business with Japanese companies know that the very first stages of negotiation involve an elaborate ceremony of getting to know one another to determine whether there is a potential long-term relationship in the picture. Japanese businesspeople are rarely interested in a one-time buy.

Suppliers in Japan consider themselves part of their customers' families. Often, key suppliers are invited to company functions such as picnics or parties. In return, suppliers deliver high-quality parts many times per day, often directly to the customer's assembly line. There is no receiving, no incoming inspection, no paperwork, no delays. It's an almost paper-free system, all built on mutual trust. Vendors are given a long-run picture of the demands that will be placed on their production and distribution systems. This permits them to develop level production schedules.

Trust is a two-way street. Because so many of the suppliers are small and undercapitalized, Japanese customers often advance money to finance them, if necessary. Customer process engineers and quality personnel help vendors improve their manufacturing systems to meet the rigid quality and delivery standards imposed. Efforts also are made to help vendors reduce their production process costs to help ensure their profitability. When there is an economic downturn, however, the customers will perform more of the work in-house instead of buying from vendors. They do this to protect their own workforces. Vendors are small and do not have the permanent, lifetime employment guarantees the major companies do. However, this is known in advance, and suppliers consider this an acceptable risk.

North American manufacturers have moved in the direction of closer co-operation with suppliers. For example, recently Intier Automotive Inc. of Newmarket, Ontario, got not only a contract to supply interiors for the next generation of small cars for General Motors, but also to manage the design and development of the interiors.[7] Intier's parent company, Aurora, Ontario-based Magna International, is a leading global supplier of technologically-advanced automotive systems, components, and complete modules to the major automobile manufacturers. Magna has not only 202 manufacturing divisions but also has 45 product development and engineering centres throughout North and South America, Europe, and Asia.[8] This allows them to move from being just a supplier to being a partner to the automobile companies. In fact, Magna has even moved one step further. It will be assembling the entire X3 sport utility vehicle for BMW at its factory in Graz, Austria. Despite these examples, it still appears that, compared to their North American competitors, Japanese automakers are more collaborative with their suppliers, and help improve their cost and quality, rather than just demanding lower prices.[9, 10]

Innovative Product and Process Design

Standard product configurations and fewer, standardized parts are important elements in good product designs for JIT. When the objective is to establish a simple routine process, anything that reduces variability in the end item or the materials that go into it is worth careful consideration. Thus JIT emphasizes concurrent engineering (Chapter 3) and modularization (Chapter 5).

Integrating process design with product design involves early consultation among product designers, process designers, and manufacturing personnel. Honda Motor Company is a good example of this type of innovative product and process design. Besides improving the producibility of the product, such interaction facilitates the processing of engineering changes orders (ECOs). ECOs can be extremely disruptive to the production process. They alter the specifications of the product, which in turn may call for new materials, new methods, and even new schedules. To minimize such disruptions, many JIT producers introduce their ECOs in batches, properly sequenced with the production schedule, rather than one by one, as is common in traditional manufacturing in North America. Although batching sounds obvious and simple, it requires a great deal of coordination and a willingness to delay what may be significant changes in a product design in exchange for maintaining production stability.

[7]Greg Keenan, "Intier Wins 'Huge' GM Small-Car Contract," *The Globe and Mail*, May 8, 2002, B7.
[8]Magna International Inc., www.magna.com.
[9]Greg Keenan, "Ford Yanks Contract from Decoma," *The Globe and Mail*, December 20, 2003, B1.
[10]Greg Keenan, "Big 3's Ties to Suppliers Are Eroding," *The Globe and Mail*, August 2, 2004, B1.

Focus on Problem Solving and Continuous Improvement

Kaizen

Kaizen is the Japanese term for continuous improvement.

A JIT application is not an overnight, turnkey installation. Rather, it is an evolutionary process that is continually seeking ways to improve production. This is called *Kaizen* in Japanese and is similar to the PDCA cycle in Chapter 6. (The case at the end of the supplement to Chapter 6 used kaizen to improve call waiting times.) Improvement is achieved by looking at problems as challenges rather than threats—problems that can be solved with common sense and detailed, rigorous analysis. In this respect, the keiretsu system is advantageous in that there is no pressure to make short-term profits at the expense of long-term benefit. In process improvement, as in most changes, there may a period of poorer performance before the benefits take effect. In North America, top managers are reluctant to implement changes that are counterproductive in the short run even though they may be beneficial in the long run. Many theorists attribute this to a focus on short-term share price and quarterly profit.

Problem-solving techniques are primarily continuous improvement methods. Evans Consoles Inc. of Calgary, a manufacturer of furniture and consoles for technology intensive work centres, is a company that has started using kaizen events (and lean manufacturing in general) as a continuous improvement tool. At a kaizen event, within the space of a few days, teams are trained in kaizen and implement improvements.

Effective problem solving means that the problem is solved permanently. Because JIT requires a team effort, problems are treated in a team context. Staff personnel are expected to be seen frequently on the shop floor, and in some companies are expected to arrive a half hour before production workers to ensure that everything is in order, thereby avoiding problems. The different quality improvement tools discussed in the supplement to Chapter 6 are also commonly used by JIT companies for problem solving.

Continual education is absolutely essential if the system is to avoid stagnation. Although JIT may cost little in the way of hardware, it requires a substantial investment in training so that people at all levels of the organization understand what the system demands and how they fit into it.

quality circles

Groups of workers who meet to discuss their common area of interest and problems they are encountering.

Another interesting technique is **quality circles**. The Japanese call them small group improvement activities (SGIA). A quality circle is a group of employees who volunteer to meet once a week on a scheduled basis to discuss their function and the problems they're encountering, to try to devise solutions to those problems, and to propose those solutions to management. The group may be led by a supervisor or a production worker. It usually includes people from a given discipline or a given production area. It also can be multidisciplinary, consisting, for instance, of all the material handlers who deliver materials to a department and the industrial engineers who work in that department. It does have to be led, though, by someone who is trained as a group leader. The employees who provide training to the group leaders are facilitators, and each one may coordinate the activities of a number of quality circles.

The quality circle works because it's an open forum. It takes some skill to prevent it from becoming a gripe session, but that's where the trained group leaders keep the members on target. Interestingly enough, only about one-third of the proposals generated turn out to be quality related. More than half are productivity oriented. It's amazing how many good ideas motivated employees can contribute toward the profitability and improved productivity of their companies. Quality circles are actually a manifestation of the consensus-driven, bottom-round management approach but are limited to these small groups.

Many performance measures emphasize the number of processes and practices changed to improve materials flow and reduce labour content, and the degree to which they do so. If the processes physically improve over time, lower costs follow. According to Hall, a department head in a Japanese JIT system is likely to be evaluated on the following factors:[11]

1. Improvement trends, including number of improvement projects undertaken, trends in costs, and productivity.

2. Quality trends, including reduction in defect rates, improvement in process capability, and improvement in quality procedures.

3. Running to a level schedule and providing parts when others need them.

4. Trends in departmental inventory levels (e.g., speed of flow).

5. Staying within budget for expenses.

6. Developing workforce skills, versatility, participation in changes, and morale.

JIT in North America

It makes sense to discuss JIT in a North American context rather than exclusively in the Canadian context. Once reason is that the automobile industry is a prime mover behind JIT and traditionally this industry has been located in Ontario and the Midwestern United States, and the different manufacturers in this industry are closely intertwined. In addition, the emergence of free trade has resulted in more bilateral trade. Thus, many U.S firms that have implemented JIT have Canadian suppliers and vice versa. For example, both Standard Aero (see opening vignette of Chapter 8) and Nortel Networks, who have implemented JIT, have plants in both Canada and the United States. Baron Colour Concentrates Ltd. of Kitchener, Ontario, has customers from Florida to British Columbia who have put a high value on JIT. The company tries to meet a goal of next day delivery by building plants across North America.[12]

JIT evolved in Japan in great part due to the unique characteristics of that country. Japan is a very small country in area. Distances between most of the major cities are, therefore, relatively short. In addition, a large proportion of its geographic area is mountainous. Consequently, most of Japan's population lives in a relatively small area, with space at a premium. So the majority of Japanese suppliers to the major companies are located close to the major firms' manufacturing facilities. In addition, most of the sales of these small firms tend to be to a single large customer, thereby making these small companies highly dependent. In contrast, North America has a very large geographic area. Suppliers, therefore, are often located thousands of kilometres away from production facilities. (As companies continue to extend their supply chains globally, their suppliers will become even more remotely located.) Finally, most North American firms have a much wider customer base, with any one customer representing only a small percentage of its sales. For these and various other reasons, JIT is practised somewhat differently in North America than it is in Japan, and has developed its own innovations.

"JIT in the United States often stands for Jumbo-Inventory-Transfer," said Peter Frasso, vice president and general manager of Varian Vacuum Products in Lexington, Massachusetts, at the April 1996 Annual Meeting of the Operations Management Association in Boston, Massachusetts. In other words, there are many large companies in North America that, instead of working with suppliers to synchronize operations, often try to

---

[11]Robert W. Hall, *Attaining Manufacturing Excellence* (Homewood, IL: Dow Jones-Irwin, 1987), pp. 254–255.

[12] "Compounders Define Goals," *Canadian Plastics* (October 1994), pp. 6–11.

force suppliers to maintain large stocks of inventory rather than keeping these inventories at their own facilities. Thus, although the large firms practice JIT within their own facilities, their suppliers deliver raw material and components from buffer inventories that are frequently located nearby. With this approach, transferring the inventory from the manufacturer to the supplier improves the performance of the large firm at the expense of the smaller supplier, which absorbs all of the risks and costs associated with these inventories. The long distances between suppliers and customers in North America also preclude the ability to provide products in small lot sizes at short time intervals (that is, several times a day, as is often the case in Japan).

Nevertheless, other aspects or elements of JIT, such as (*a*) reducing number of suppliers and working with suppliers in a partnership relationship, (*b*) reducing setup times, (*c*) encouraging worker participation, and (*d*) reducing inventories and waste, are being adopted by better companies, with recognizable benefits. A survey of U.S. manufacturers indicated that 86 percent of the respondents acknowledged some benefits from implementing JIT.[13] Even tire manufacturers, who normally produce in large batches, are building smaller plants with newer technology close to the automobile factories, which will allow them to reduce inventories and transportation time, and produce just-in-time. Other advantages of smaller lot sizes are expected to be better quality and safer tires.[14]

Because of these differences, many North American companies, in addition to having a JIT system, have adopted an MRP system (discussed in Chapter 16) in working with their suppliers. The MRP system provides suppliers with a forecast of the raw material and component requirements. Typically, these requirements are frozen for the immediate future, but can change the further out the requirements are. For example, the orders placed with a supplier might be fixed for the next six weeks, but the requirements may change beyond this six-week window. This approach allows suppliers to schedule work efficiently within their own facilities.

Company Experiences and Challenges with JIT Implementation

Companies all over the world have experienced significant performance improvements by implementing JIT. One study of 80 plants in Europe, for example, listed the following benefits from JIT:

1. Average reduction in inventory of about 50 percent.
2. Reduction in throughput time of 50 to 70 percent.
3. Reduction in setup times of as much as 50 percent without major investment in plant and equipment.
4. Increase in productivity of between 20 and 50 percent.
5. Payback time for investment in JIT averaging less than nine months.[15]

Additional success stories abound in production control journals. However, this does not mean that the implementation of JIT is trouble-free. JIT requires a long-term focus on

[13]Richard E. White, "An Empirical Assessment of JIT in U.S. Manufacturers," *Production and Inventory Management Journal* 34, no. 2 (1993), pp. 38–42.

[14]Timothy Aeppel, "Under the Glare of Recall, Tire Makers Are Giving New Technology a Spin," *The Wall Street Journal*, March 23, 2001, A1.

[15]Amrik Sohal and Keith Howard, "Trends in Materials Management," *International Journal of Production Distribution and Materials Management*, 17, no. 5 (1987), pp. 3–11.

continuous improvement because some of the major benefits may not appear in the short term. For some this might be stressful. It requires the co-operation of employees, management, and the supply chain. Adversarial relationships are detrimental to JIT implementation. The company management must also be prepared to manage in a less autocratic atmosphere, be prepared to focus on teamwork, and be willing to commit money and resources to employee and supplier training and education. All these efforts will help enhance flexibility within the system.

As seen the Toyota OM in Practice Box in Chapter 12, lack of inventory can result in operational disruptions, and companies must work to prevent disruptions, and be agile enough to respond to any disruptions. Companies have to realize that if there is uncertainty within the supply chain that cannot be eliminated, they may need to hold the appropriate amount of inventory within the supply chain to address this uncertainty (and modify JIT practice if necessary).

Other aspects that companies need to address when implementing JIT are managerial accounting and reward systems. For example, if employees are rewarded based on a piece rate, they might resist a kanban-type system that produces items only when required. Similarly, a managerial accounting system that encourages full utilization of machines also runs counter to the kanban system, which prefers idle machines to building excess inventory.

JIT in Services

Service organizations and service operations within manufacturing firms present interesting opportunities for the application of JIT concepts. Despite the many differences between service and manufacturing, both share the most basic attributes of production, because they employ processes that add value to the basic inputs with the objective of creating an end product or service.

JIT focuses on processes, not products and, therefore, it can be applied to any group of processes, including manufacturing and services. The JIT goal is approached by testing each step in the process to determine if it adds value to the product or service. If these steps do not add value, then the process is a candidate for reengineering. In this way, the process gradually and continually improves.

Both manufacturing and services can be improved with JIT because both involve processes, and JIT is essentially a process-oriented, waste-elimination philosophy. The themes of JIT process improvement should therefore apply equally in a service environment.

Application of JIT to Services

Duclos, Siha, and Lummus have suggested the following framework for describing the different ways in which JIT concepts have been applied to service organizations:[16]

- Synchronization and balance of information and workflow
- Total visibility of all components and processes
- Continuous improvement of the process
- Holistic approach to the elimination of waste
- Flexibility in the use of resources
- Respect for people

---

[16]Adapted from L. K. Duclos, S. M. Siha, and R. R. Lummus, "JIT in Services: A Review of Current Practices and Future Directions for Research," *International Journal of Service Industry Management* 6, no. 5 (1995), pp. 36–52.

Synchronization and Balance of Information and Workflow

Because services are intangible, it is important that there be synchronization between demand and capacity. In other words, capacity must be available when the customer demands it. From a workflow balance perspective, Feather and Cross report that the application of JIT techniques identified existing bottlenecks and eliminated unnecessary inventory buffers in the processing of contracts.[17] As as result, throughput time was reduced 60 percent and the backlog in the number of contracts to be processed was reduced 80 percent.

Canada Post is currently implementing "Lean Processing," the service version of lean manufacturing, in which they focus on one-piece flow. For example, in the past, packages collected from the sender would be received at the local processing facility, stored, and sorted many times before being shipped out. In the redesigned system, packages are received and sorted once and put on outbound trucks immediately (crossdocking), thus reducing delivery times and costs.

Total Visibility of All Components and Processes

A major element of JIT is that all operations that are required to complete a good or a service should be visible as widely as possible to all those involved in the process. Inasmuch as customers are usually an integral part of the service delivery process, they will often define value by what they can observe. As an example, many full-service restaurants now have open kitchens where the customers can actually see the food being prepared.

Continuous Improvement of the Process

Another critical element in successfully implementing JIT is the recognition of the need for continuous improvement. Service operations provide significant opportunities for achieving these incremental improvements. For example, using JIT techniques, a finance company was able to improve its credit evaluation process and reduce the processing time for a loan from twelve days to four.[18]

Holistic Approach to the Elimination of Waste

To be successful, JIT concepts must be adopted at all levels and in all functional areas within an organization. In addition, as discussed in the previous chapter, the application of JIT concepts should be expanded to include suppliers. In this respect, JIT concepts in this area have been applied successfully in the health care industry. Using JIT concepts and working closely with suppliers, hospital systems have reduced inventories at central stockrooms, with the ultimate goal of eliminating them altogether. The OM in Practice Box on JIT in Services illustrates JIT practices in services in diverse organizations.

Flexibility in the Use of Resources

Although the successful implementation of JIT requires that the level of units produced remain constant over a given period of time, the mix of these units can vary significantly. This requires a very flexible process that can accommodate a wide variety of products. Many services are highly customized, from the preparation of the food you order at a restaurant to the preparation of your tax return. Thus, a flexible process is necessary for these customized services. Wal-Mart provides a good example of process flexibility with its automated replenishment system, which can ship smaller quantities of goods to each store at frequent intervals. With this more flexible system, Wal-Mart has been able to lower

---

[17]J. J. Feather and K. F. Cross, "Workflow Analysis: Just-in-Time Techniques Simplify Administrative Process in Paperwork Operations," *Industrial Engineering* 20 (1988), pp. 32–40.
[18]J. Y. Lee, "JIT Works for Services Too," *CMA Magazine* 6 (1990), pp. 20–23.

Operations Management in Practice

JIT IS EFFECTIVE FOR SERVICE ENVIRONMENTS TOO

Consider the following cases in which JIT practices resulted in operational improvements within the service industry.

In one case, a large corporation whose principal products are telecommunication services, realized that poor inbound logistics was costing them money. For example, if shipments arrived too early compared to the installation date, the result was early payments that had an opportunity cost. Late shipments also resulted in additional costs (and probably irate customers).

The company reduced its vendor base, improved its relationships and communications with suppliers, formed multifunctional improvement teams, worked to reduce internal lead time for processing orders, improved its forecasting, and focused on potential "bottleneck" orders. As a result, vendor delivery performance improved and the number of warehouses was reduced from 40 to only 5.

In another case, a government warehousing contractor supplying products managed to save US$4.2 million in purchase price, US$720 000 in carrying costs, and US$2.3 million in labour costs through improved relationships with fewer suppliers. Additional benefits included better product quality, simplified ordering and receiving procedures, and quicker resolution of problems. In a third case, an overnight package company improved its service level from 79 percent to 99 percent and reduced its costs using JIT practices.

Similarly, when United Electric Controls (UEC) of Watertown, Massachusetts, implemented lean manufacturing methods, their efforts didn't end at the shop floor. UEC's accounting department also participated in continuous improvement and identified and eliminated wasteful practices.

Sources:

R. A. Inman and S. Mehra, "JIT Applications for Service Environments," *Production and Inventory Management Journal* (Third quarter 1991), pp. 16–20.

R. L. Jenson, J. W. Brackner, C. R. Skousen, "Low Fat Accounting," *CMA Magazine* (December–January 1997).

---

the average levels of inventory at each retail store without decreasing the level of customer service.[19]

Respect for People

Customers' direct involvement with the service delivery process often requires them to interact directly with employees. Within services, research has shown that the way in which management treats employees highly correlates with the way in which employees treat customers.[20] Thus, management must show respect for its employees if it wants them to similarly respect its customers.

---

[19]M. Ballou, "Wal-Mart Picks Progress Tools for Greater Flexibility," *Computerworld* 28, no. 9 (1994), p. 81; R. Halverson, "Logistical Supremacy Secures the Base—But Will It Translate Abroad?" *Discount Store News* 33, no. 23 (1994), pp. 107–108; G. Stalk Jr., "Competing on Capabilities: The New Rules of Corporate Strategy," *Harvard Business Review* 70, no. 2, pp. 57–69.

[20]B. Schneider and D. E. Bowen, *Winning the Service Game* (Cambridge, MA: Harvard Business School Press, 1995).

Conclusion

We have presented many of the potential benefits of just-in-time systems. At the same time, however, we need to caution that JIT applications are not universal. There are specific requirements for successful implementation, and we need to be careful not to be caught up in the excitement and promises.

In 1983, Hewlett-Packard created a videotape on JIT at its Boulder, Colorado, plant. It was an excellent video and fun to watch. Its purpose was to convince viewers that a

JIT pull system would produce significant benefits for most manufacturing plants. Although instructors still use this video in their classrooms, many of us caution against the message conveyed.

The video does not carry through a numerical analysis of the performance times, number of defects, work in process, and so on. This can lead to the wrong conclusions—which are that the JIT pull system was responsible for improved conditions.

In a journal article, Jerry Bowman presented the data.[21] After analyzing the data, he commented that the most significant benefits did not result from the pull system but from reducing lot sizes. The HP video showed that the best performance occurred when items were processed using a pull system in lots of one unit. Bowman commented, "If you manufacture in lot sizes of one in a 'flow' environment, you probably couldn't tell whether you were pushing or pulling nor would it matter." Consequently, students have difficulties distinguishing between an American automobile assembly line and a Japanese automobile assembly line.

JIT is becoming a principal manufacturing management concept and undoubtedly will continue to be so. But again, we caution you to be careful in its use.

Some of the concepts of JIT have been successfully introduced into service operations. Many of the characteristics that exist in JIT systems already are present in services, and, as a consequence, the benefits of implementing JIT in services have been readily apparent.

Key Terms

5S p. 468

eliminate waste p. 456

external setup p. 464

focused factory p. 466

group technology p. 468

internal setup p. 464

Jidoka p. 465

JIT (just-in-time) p. 452

Kaizen p. 472

Kanban pull system p. 460

keiretsu p. 470

quality circles p. 472

Review and Discussion Questions

1. Stopping waste is one of the most important parts of JIT. Identify some of the sources of waste and discuss how they may be eliminated.
2. Discuss JIT in a job-shop layout and in a line-flow layout.
3. Why is it important for JIT to have a stable schedule?
4. Are there any aspects of the Japanese approach that you could apply to your own current school activities? Explain.
5. Which objections might a marketing manager make about uniform plant loading?
6. What are the implications for cost accounting of JIT production?
7. Which questions would you want to ask the president of Toyota about his operations management?
8. Explain how cards are used in a Kanban system.
9. In which ways, if any, are the following systems analogous to Kanban: returning empty bottles to the supermarket and picking up filled ones; running a hot dog stand at lunchtime; withdrawing money from a chequing account; collecting eggs at a chicken ranch?
10. How does the old saying, "There's no such thing as a free lunch," pertain to the Japanese elimination of inventory?
11. Explain the relationship between quality and productivity under the JIT philosophy.
12. What are the differences between implementing JIT in a manufacturing facility and implementing it in a service operation?
13. Identify some of the ways JIT can be applied to a service operation.

---

[21]D. Jerry Bowman, "If You Don't Understand JIT, How Can You Implement It?" *Industrial Engineering* (February 1991), pp. 38–39.

Case 1 **Cheng Products Company**

Cheng Products Company is a supplier of gizmos for a large computer manufacturer located a few kilometres away. The company produces three different models of gizmos in production runs ranging from 100 to 300 units.

Case Exhibit 1

Gizmo Production Flow

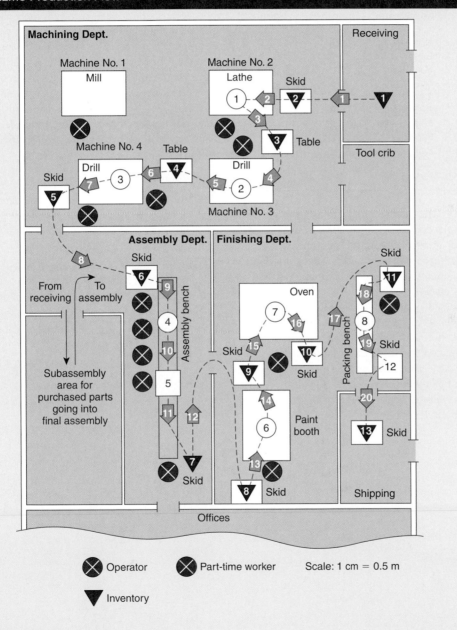

Operator   Part-time worker   Scale: 1 cm = 0.5 m

Inventory

The production flow of Models X and Y is shown in Case Exhibit 1. Model Z requires milling as its first step, but otherwise follows the same flow pattern as X and Y. Skids can hold up to 20 gizmos at a time. Approximate processing times per unit by operation number and equipment setup times are shown in the following table:

Operation Number and Name		Operation Times (minutes)	Setup Times (minutes)
–	Milling for Z	20	60
1	Lathe	50	30
2	Mod. 14 drill	15	5
3	Mod. 14 drill	40	5
4	Assembly step 1	50	
	Assembly step 2	45	
	Assembly step 3	50	
5	Inspection	30	
6	Paint	30	20
7	Oven	50	
8	Packing	5	

The demand for gizmos from the computer company ranges between 125 and 175 per month, equally divided among X, Y, and Z. Subassembly builds up inventory early in the month to make certain that a buffer stock is always available. Raw materials and purchased parts for subassemblies each constitutes 40 percent of the manufacturing cost of a gizmo. Both categories of parts are multiple sourced from about 80 vendors and are delivered at random times. (Gizmos have 40 different part numbers.)

Some other information: Scrap rates are about 10 percent each operation, inventory turns twice yearly, employees are paid on day rate, employee turnover is 25 percent per year, and net profit from operations is steady at 5 percent per year. Maintenance is performed as needed.

Nicholas Cheng, the manager, has been contemplating installing a new system to help control inventories and to "keep the skids filled." (It is his view that two days of work in front of a work station motivates the worker to produce at top speed.) He also is planning to add three inspectors to clean up the quality problem. Furthermore, he is thinking about setting up a rework line to speed up repairs. Although he is pleased with the high utilization of most of his equipment and labour, he is concerned about the idle time of his milling machine. Finally, he has asked his industrial engineering department to look into high-rise shelving to store parts coming off Machine 4.

Questions

1. Which of the changes being considered by Nicholas Cheng contradict the JIT philosophy?

2. Make recommendations for JIT improvements in such areas as scheduling, layout, Kanban, task groupings, and inventory. Use quantitative data as much as possible; state necessary assumptions.

3. Sketch the operation of a pull system for Cheng's current system.

4. Outline a plan for the introduction of JIT at Cheng.

14

Operations Planning: Overview and Aggregate Plans

Chapter Objectives

- Demonstrate how aggregate planning links long-range strategic planning and short-range scheduling.

- Present alternative strategies for matching supply and demand: adjusting supply (an operations function) or adjusting demand (a marketing function).

- Introduce strategies for developing aggregate plans and ways to identify their strengths and weaknesses.

- Define marginal costs and total costs as they pertain to aggregate planning.

- Introduce the concept of yield management as a tool for matching supply and demand in service operations.

Medium-Term Production and Inventory Planning at Kellogg's

The Kellogg Company is the world's largest producer of cereal and is also a leading producer of convenience foods. It operates four plants in the United States and one in London, Ontario. It has seven main distribution centres (DCs) and fifteen co-packers that contract to produce or pack some of Kellogg's products; that is, a total of 27 locations. In the cereal business alone the firm coordinates the production of about 80 products and the packaging, inventorying, and distribution of over 600 stock keeping units at the 27 locations. It has 90 production lines and 180 packaging lines. How do Kellogg's managers stay abreast of all these operations? They use a computerized planning system called the Kellogg Planning System (KPS) to manage the five plants in North America.

In the tactical version of the KPS, the company uses a mathematical technique called linear programming along with some rules of thumb (heuristics) to find the best long-term, cost-minimizing and integrated production, inventory, and distribution plan—keeping capacity constraints in mind. Time periods are four weeks long and the planning horizon is 18 months. Prior to the start of each fiscal year, planners estimate the plant costs and demands for the next

18 months. KPS then determines the best production allocation to the plants. This plan is then used to allocate the financial budgets within the plants, the inventory space requirements with the DC networks, and the equipment projection for transportation. The plan also ensures that items are never stocked more than five months to ensure freshness.

The system allows the company to do what-ifs with these allocations. For example, if the plan calls for an item to be produced at multiple locations (if no one plant is large enough to produce the forecasted demand), but some of the locations are poorly utilized, it can evaluate increasing the capacity at the lower-cost locations and fully or partially shutting down the higher-cost, poorly utilized lines. It can also answer questions such as how much inventory should be carried in general and how much extra inventory may be needed while shifting capacity from one plant to another. The KPS also helps determine the buffer inventory at various locations for different SKUs to protect against forecast errors. Presumably, the production allocation plans can then also be used to determine the employment plan at the different locations.

The KPS also has a detailed planning model (in the operational version) that determines the weekly production and packaging schedule for each quarter, subject to constraints of the 18-month plan determined by the KPS. This allows planners to adjust capacity to meet short-term demand through additional shifts, reallocation of production to a different facility, and so on. The detail planning is part of scheduling, a topic discussed in Chapter 11. The KPS therefore is a hierarchical planning system (doing both medium-term and short-term planning) similar to that seen in Exhibit 14.1.

The operational KPS reduced production, inventory, and distribution costs by $4.5 million in 1995. Tactical KPS was expected to yield savings between $35 and $40 million per year.

Source:
Gerald Brown, Joseph Keegan, Brian Vigus, and Kevin Wood, "The Kellogg Company Optimizes Production, Inventory, and Distribution," *Interfaces*, 31, no. 6 (2001), pp. 1–14.

Long-range strategic plans need to be translated into daily operational work schedules for the shop floor. To accomplish this, a series of steps, often referred to as hierarchical production planning, is required. In this process, units of production go from very broad definitions or product groups to specific items and models. For example, in the automobile industry, GM may look out five years and estimate the total number of cars it expects to sell. As the time horizon becomes closer, the number of cars is broken down into the number of Cadillacs, Buicks, Pontiacs, and so forth. In the short term, specific models within each car type are identified, such as the Cadillac DeVille or the Pontiac Aztek.

Aggregate planning, as an intermediate-range planning tool for management, provides the link between the long-range strategic plan and the short-range operational plan. It develops gross requirements for up to 12 to 18 months into the future, primarily for material and labour. As such, it presents a fairly broad perspective of the operation, addressing such issues as the number of workers needed in total, rather than the number of workers needed to do specific jobs.

The objective in developing an aggregate plan for a given time horizon is to match the demand for the firm's products with its ability to supply these products, and to do so at minimum cost. As part of the aggregate planning process, the operation manager identifies alternative methods for supplying the product, all of which are evaluated. Marketing management also plays a key role in this matching process, in terms of how it controls the demand for the product, using such marketing tools as pricing, advertising, and promotions. Both the marketing and operations functions need to work together to develop an aggregate plan that is both effective and efficient.

Overview of Operations Planning Activities

Every organization must plan its activities at several levels and operate these as a system. Exhibit 14.1 presents an overall view of planning and shows how aggregate planning relates to other activities of a manufacturing firm. The time dimension is shown as long, intermediate, and short range.

planning activities:

long-range planning

Focuses on strategic issues relating to capacity, process selection, and plant location.

intermediate-range planning

Focuses on tactical issues pertaining to aggregate workforce and material requirements for the coming year.

short-range planning

Addresses day-to-day issues of scheduling workers to specific jobs at assigned work stations.

Long-range or strategic planning is generally done once a year, focusing on a time horizon that is usually greater than a year. The length of the time horizon will vary from industry to industry. For those industries that require many years to plan and construct plants and facilities and to install specific processes (e.g., refineries), the time horizon may be 5 to 10 or more years. For other industries in which the ability to expand capacity is shorter (e.g., clothing manufacturing and many service industries), the time horizon may be two to five years or less.

Intermediate-range or tactical planning usually covers the period from 6 to 18 months in the future, with time increments or "buckets" that are monthly and/or quarterly. (The near-term time increments are often monthly, whereas those at the end of the time horizon tend to be quarterly, because these are usually less accurate.) Intermediate-range planning is typically reviewed and updated quarterly.

Short-range or operational planning covers the period from one day to six months, with the time increment usually being daily or weekly. As with long-range planning, the length of the time horizon for intermediate- and short-range planning will vary from industry to industry.

Long-Range Planning

Long-range planning begins with a statement of organizational objectives and goals for the next 2 to 10 years. *Corporate strategic planning* articulates how these objectives and goals are to be achieved in light of the company's capabilities and its economic and political environment as projected by its *business forecasting*. Elements of the strategic plan include product-line delineation, quality and pricing levels, and market penetration goals. *Product and market planning* translates these into individual market and product-line objectives, and includes a long-range production plan (basically a forecast of items to be manufactured for two years or more into the future). *Financial planning* analyzes the financial feasibility of

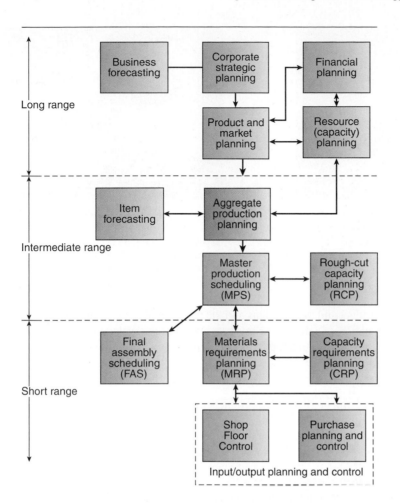

Exhibit 14.1

Overview of Operations Planning Activities

these objectives relative to capital requirements and return on investment goals. *Resource planning* identifies the facilities, equipment, and personnel needed to accomplish the long-range production plan, and thus is frequently referred to as *long-run capacity planning*.

The outsourcing (or *make-or-buy*) decision discussed in Chapter 12 is also a long range one. Outsourcing is different from subcontracting, which is used in medium-term planning. Outsourcing implies that a company makes a strategic decision not to make a part in-house and instead will purchase it from a supplier. Thus the decision is considered permanent. Subcontracting is used to describe the temporary contract to a subcontractor to produce parts for the company due to insufficient capacity. The company as well as the subcontractor may be making the same product to satisfy demand and the subcontracting will end when the company attains sufficient capacity.

Intermediate-Range Planning

Aggregate Planning

As noted in Exhibit 14.1, **aggregate planning** provides the primary link between the long-range strategic plans and the intermediate-range planning activities. Aggregate planning specifies monthly or quarterly output requirements by major product groups either in labour hours required or in units of production for up to 18 months into the future. Its main

aggregate planning
Process for determining most cost-effective way to match supply and demand over next 12–18 months.

Bombardier Aerospace of Montreal makes different types of aircraft such as regional jets, business jets, and amphibious aircraft.

The corporate plan specifies how many units to produce of each type of aircraft based on forecasts; the aggregate plan determines how to meet this requirement with available resources and how to acquire more resources if needed.

inputs are the product and market plans and the resource plan. Aggregate planning seeks to find that combination of monthly or quarterly workforce levels and inventory levels that minimizes total production-related costs over the planning period while meeting the forecasted demand for product.

Item Forecasting

This provides an estimate of specific products (and replacement parts), which, when integrated with the aggregate plan, becomes the output requirement for the master production schedule (MPS). The process of monitoring and integrating this information is termed *demand management*.

Master Production Scheduling (MPS)

master production schedule

Short-term schedule of specific end product requirements for the next several quarters.

The MPS generates the amounts and dates of specific end products. The **master production schedule** is usually fixed or "frozen" over the short run (six to eight weeks). Beyond six to eight weeks, various changes can be made, with essentially complete revisions possible after six months. As shown in Exhibit 14.1, the MPS depends on the product and market plans and resource plans outlined in the aggregate plan.

Rough-Cut or Resource Capacity Planning

rough-cut or resource capacity planning

Determination that adequate production capacity and warehousing are available to meet demand.

This reviews the MPS to make sure that no obvious capacity constraints would require changing the schedule. **Rough-cut or resource capacity planning** includes verifying that sufficient production and warehouse facilities, equipment, and labour are available and that key vendors have allocated adequate capacity to provide materials when needed.

Short-Range Planning

Materials Planning

Also known as *materials requirements planning (MRP)*, discussed in Chapter 16, this system takes the end product requirements from the MPS and breaks them down into their subassemblies and component parts. The materials plan specifies when production and purchase orders must be placed for each part and subassembly to complete the products on schedule.

Capacity Requirements Planning

Capacity requirements planning (CRP) should really be referred to as capacity requirements scheduling, because it provides a detailed schedule of when each operation is to run on each work centre or machine and how long it will take to process. The information it uses comes from planned (i.e., forecasted) and open (i.e., existing) orders that are generated by the materials plan. The CRP itself helps to validate the rough-cut capacity plan.

Final Assembly Scheduling

This activity identifies the various operations required to put the product in its final form. It is here that customized or final features of the product are scheduled. For example, a printer manufacturer would typically specify from various options a control panel configuration at this scheduling stage.

Input/Output Planning and Control

This refers to a variety of reports and procedures focusing on scheduled demands and capacity constraints derived from the materials plan.

Production Activity Control

Production activity control (PAC) is a relatively new term used to describe scheduling and shop-floor control activities. PAC involves the scheduling and controlling of day-to-day activities on the shop floor. At this point, the master production schedule is translated into the immediate priorities of daily work schedules.

Purchase Planning and Control

This activity deals with the acquisition and control of purchased items, again as specified by the materials plan. Input/output planning and control are necessary to make sure that purchasing not only is obtaining materials in time to meet the schedule, but is also aware of those orders that, for various reasons, call for rescheduling the delivery of purchased materials.

In summary, all of the planning approaches attempt to balance the capacity required with the capacity available, and then schedule and control production with respect to changes in the capacity balance. A good planning system is complete without being overwhelming, and has the confidence of its users up and down the organization structure.

Aggregate Planning

Again, aggregate planning is concerned with setting production rates by product group or other broad categories for the intermediate term (6 to 18 months). Note again in Exhibit 14.1 that the aggregate plan precedes the master schedule. *The main purpose of the aggregate plan is to specify that combination of production rate, workforce level, and the resulting inventory on hand or backlog that both minimizes costs (efficiency) and satisfies the forecasted demand (effectiveness).* **Production rate** refers to the quantity of product completed per unit of time (such as DVD players per hour or automobiles per day). **Workforce level** is the number of workers needed for production. When the number of units produced in any given period exceeds demand, the result is an **inventory on hand** of the product. When demand exceeds production, the result is a **backlog (or stockout)**, which represents the shortfall. Both inventories and backlogs are carried forward to the next time period. However, there can be situations when stockouts are not carried forward because the customer decided to purchase the product elsewhere rather than wait.

The process of aggregate planning varies from company to company. In some firms, it is a formalized report containing both planning objectives and the planning premises on

production rate
Capacity of output per unit of time (such as units per day or units per week).

workforce level
Number of workers required to provide a specified level of production.

inventory on hand
The surplus of units that results when production exceeds demand in a given time period.

backlog (or stockout)
The deficit in units that results when demand exceeds the number of units produced in a given time period.

which it is based. In other companies, particularly smaller ones, it may be more informal, e.g., in the form of verbal communications.

The process by which the plan itself is derived also varies. One common approach is to develop it from the corporate annual plan, as shown in Exhibit 14.1. A typical corporate plan contains a section on manufacturing that specifies how many units in each major product line need to be produced over the next 12 months to meet the sales forecast. The planner takes this information and attempts to determine how best to meet these requirements with available resources. Alternatively, some organizations combine output requirements into equivalent units and use this as the basis for aggregate planning. For example, a division of General Motors may be asked to produce a certain number of cars of all types at a particular facility. The production planner would then take the average labour hours required for all models as a basis for the overall aggregate plan. Refinements to this plan, specifically model types to be produced, would be reflected in shorter-term production plans. Another approach is to develop the aggregate plan by simulating various master production schedules and calculating corresponding capacity requirements to see if adequate labour and equipment exist at each work centre. If capacity is inadequate, additional requirements for overtime, subcontracting, extra workers, and so forth are specified for each product line and combined into a rough-cut capacity plan. This plan is then modified by trial-and-error or mathematical methods to derive a final and, one hopes, lower-cost plan.

Planning Environment

Exhibit 14.2 illustrates the internal and external factors that make up the production planning environment. In general, the factors in the external environment are outside the production planner's direct control. In some firms, demand for the product can be managed, but even so, the production planner must live with the sales projections and orders promised by the marketing function. This leaves the internal factors as the variables that can be adjusted to arrive at a feasible production plan.

The internal factors themselves differ in their degree of control. Current physical capacity (plant and equipment) is virtually fixed in the short run and, therefore, cannot be increased; union agreements often constrain what can be done in changing the workforce; and top management may set limits on the amount of money that can be tied up in inventories. Still, there is always some flexibility in managing these factors, and production planners can implement one or a combination of the **aggregate planning strategies** discussed here.

Exhibit 14.2

Required Inputs to the Production Planning System

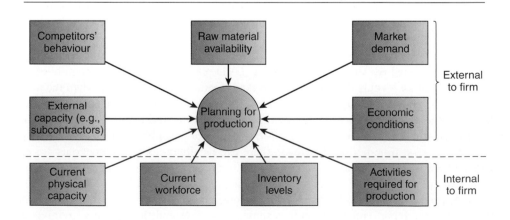

Aggregate Planning Strategies

There are essentially three aggregate planning strategies. These strategies involve trade-offs among workforce size, work hours, inventory, and order backlogs. When there is a need to adjust the workforce on a regular basis, many firms will maintain a nucleus of full-time employees, which is then increased as required with temporary workers, often hired through an employment agency. Temporary workers who perform well are then hired on a full-time basis, as the need arises. Working conditions are governed by various federal and provincial employment standards legislations as discussed in Chapter 11 and Web Chapter 17.

1. *Chase strategy.* Match the production rate to meet the order rate by hiring and laying off employees as the order rate varies. There are obvious motivational issues with this strategy. When order backlogs are low, employees may feel compelled to slow down out of fear of being laid off as soon as existing orders are completed.

    Some of the quantifiable costs of the layoff/hiring strategy are: (*a*) hiring/training costs, (*b*) reduced productivity and capacity due to the learning employees have to acquire after being hired, and (*c*) quality problems during ramp up due to untrained employees. Qualitative costs of the layoff/hiring strategy include: (*a*) loss of morale, (*b*) loss of knowledge through layoffs, and (*c*) poor customer service due to untrained employees.

2. *Stable workforce–variable work hours.* Vary the output by varying the number of hours worked through flexible work schedules or overtime. By varying the number of work hours, production quantities can be matched, within limits, to existing orders. This strategy provides workforce continuity and avoids many of the emotional and tangible costs of hiring and firing personnel associated with the chase strategy.

3. *Level strategy.* Maintain a stable workforce working at a constant output rate. Shortages and surpluses are absorbed by fluctuating inventory levels, order backlogs, and lost sales. Employees benefit from stable work hours, but inventory costs are increased. Another concern is the possibility of inventoried products becoming obsolete.

When just one of these variables is used to absorb demand fluctuations, it is termed a **pure strategy**; one or more used in combination is a **mixed strategy**. As you might suspect, mixed strategies are more widely used in industry. Companies can also help achieve stability by making complementary products or providing complementary services. For example, since air travel in Canada drops off during the winter, WestJet uses its aircraft (which would otherwise have been idle) to charter passengers to the Caribbean for Air Transat. Similarly, Bombardier Recreational Products makes snowmobiles for winter recreation and motorized watercraft and all-terrain vehicles for summer recreation.The complementary offerings help level demand, allowing for a level strategy without disadvantages such as reduced prices for national destinations during winter or fluctuations in the size of the workforce.

Exhibit 14.3A illustrates a pure chase strategy. Here production is in lockstep with demand. In other words, the number of units required in each time interval equals the number of units that production will make. Exhibit 14.3B, on the other hand, demonstrates a pure level strategy. Here production is held constant, regardless of the demand. The difference between demand and production is accounted for in a "buffer" inventory of finished goods. When demand exceeds production, the difference is taken out of finished goods inventory (−I); when demand is less than production, the difference is placed back into inventory (+I). (It is assumed that when demand exceeds production in the initial cycle, as shown in Exhibit 14.3B, there is sufficient inventory on hand at the beginning of the aggregate planning period to supply the required number of units.) When there is insufficient inventory on hand to meet demand, a backlog occurs.

---

aggregate planning strategies:

pure strategy
Either a chase strategy when production exactly matches demand or a level strategy when production remains constant over a specified number of time periods.

mixed strategy
Combination of chase and level strategies to match supply and demand.

Exhibit 14.3

**Examples of
Pure Chase and
Pure Level
Strategies**

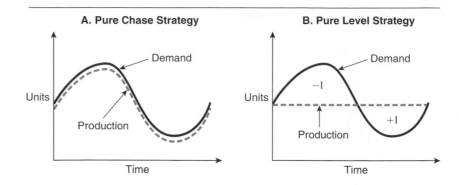

Certain industries, due to their inherent operating characteristics, favour one type of strategy over the other. For example, services tend to follow a chase strategy because the customer is involved in the service delivery process. (If your restaurant is too crowded on a Saturday night, customers will not wait until Monday morning when you have more than enough capacity available to serve them!) Process-oriented facilities, on the other hand, such as breweries and refineries, tend to follow a level strategy because their high fixed costs require that they operate at a high level of capacity utilization.

Subcontracting

In addition to these strategies, managers may choose to subcontract some portion of production. This strategy is similar to the chase strategy, but hiring and laying off are translated into subcontracting and not subcontracting. Some level of subcontracting can be desirable to accommodate demand fluctuations. However, unless the relationship with the supplier is particularly strong, a manufacturer can lose some control over schedule and quality. For this reason, extensive subcontracting may be viewed as a high-risk strategy.

Relevant Costs

There are four primary costs that are relevant to aggregate production planning. These are:

1. *Basic production costs*. These are the fixed and variable costs incurred in producing a given product type in a given time period. Included are material costs, direct and indirect labour costs, and regular as well as overtime compensation.

2. *Costs associated with changes in the production rate*. Typical costs in this category are those involved in hiring, training, and laying off personnel. Additional one-time costs also might be associated with adding another shift.

3. *Inventory holding costs*. A major component is the cost of capital tied up in inventory. Other components include storage, insurance, taxes, spoilage, and obsolescence.

4. *Backlog (a stockout) costs*. Usually these costs are very difficult to measure and include costs of expediting, loss of customer goodwill, and loss of sales revenues resulting from cancelled orders because the product is not available.

(For a more detailed explanation of inventory carrying costs and backlog costs, see Chapter 15.)

Budgets

To receive funding, operations managers are generally required to submit annual, and sometimes quarterly, budget requests. Aggregate planning activities are key to the success of the budgeting process. Recall that the goal of aggregate planning is to meet forecasted product demand while minimizing the total production-related costs over the planning horizon by determining the optimal combination of workforce levels and inventory levels. Thus, aggregate planning provides justification for the requested budget amount. Accurate intermediate-range planning increases both the likelihood of receiving the requested budget and of operating within the limits of the budget.

In the next section, we provide examples of intermediate-range planning in both a manufacturing and a service setting. These examples illustrate the trade-offs associated with different production planning strategies.

Aggregate Planning Techniques

Companies still use simple trial-and-error charting and graphic methods to develop their aggregate plans. Computer spreadsheets and graphics packages are now available to facilitate the process. A trial-and-error approach involves costing out various production planning alternatives and selecting the one with the lowest cost. In addition to the trial-and-error method (used in this chapter), there are more sophisticated approaches, including linear programming, the linear decision rule, and various heuristic methods. Of these, only linear programming has seen broad application.

To properly develop and evaluate an aggregate plan, we need first to divide it into two stages. The first stage is the development of a feasible plan that provides the required number of products under the conditions stated. After this aggregate plan has been developed, the next step is to determine the costs associated with the plan.

Some of the costs included in an aggregate plan are presented in a form that is typically not found in the accounting records of a firm. For example, there is usually no cost of carrying inventory. Instead, the individual component costs associated with carrying inventory are listed in separate categories (e.g., the cost of storage is rent, insurance, taxes, etc.; the cost of obsolescence is reflected in higher material and labour costs, etc.).

Full Costs versus Marginal Costs

Before we can begin to solve the aggregate planning problem, we need first to recognize the difference between full costs and marginal or incremental costs. Full costs are all the actual, out-of-pocket costs associated with a particular aggregate plan. Included in full costs are the costs of material, labour, and other direct, variable costs. Full costs are often used for developing a projected labour and material budget that will be needed to support an aggregate plan.

Marginal or incremental costs are only those unique costs that are attributable to a particular aggregate plan. With this approach, we assume that the total number of products forecasted over the time horizon need to be built, regardless of the alternative selected. The incremental costs are, therefore, only those costs that are above and beyond those required to build the product by the most economical means (which is usually on the first shift in-house). Included in marginal costs are hiring and firing costs, inventory carrying costs, and overtime and/or second- and third-shift premium costs. To demonstrate the difference, we will use both the full-cost and marginal-cost methods to solve the aggregate planning problem for the D&H Company. You will note that both methods result in selecting the same alternative plan, based on lowest cost. The different alternatives also are ranked in the same order with both methods of costing. The advantage of using the marginal-cost approach is that we do not have to include a lot of numerical figures that have no impact on the final decision.

A Simple Example of Aggregate Planning

Matt Koslow is the operations manager for the Pham Shirt Company. In this capacity he is required to develop an aggregate plan for the next six months with the goal of meeting demand during this period while minimizing costs. As a first step in developing this plan, he obtained from the marketing department the following forecast for shirts:

January	February	March	April	May	June
2400	1200	2800	3600	3200	3600

Matt has estimated the following production data:

Inventory carrying cost	$1.50 per shirt per month
Stockout cost	$3.00 per shirt per month
Hiring cost	$200 per employee
Firing cost	$300 per employee
Labour per shirt	2 hours
Hourly wage	$8.00 per hour
Beginning employment level	30 employees
Beginning inventory level	0 shirts
Hours per employee per day	8 hours
Work days per month	20 days

Using marginal costs, develop both a chase strategy and a level strategy to determine which is the more economical.

a.   See the spreadsheet for marginal cost of chase strategy.

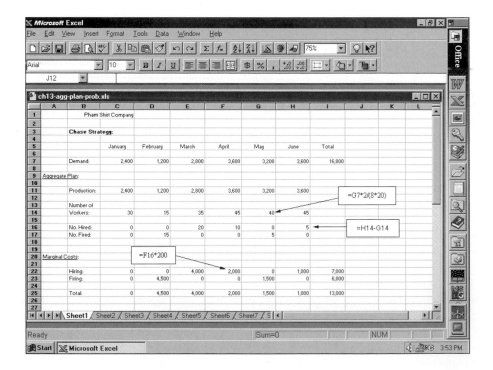

b.   See the spreadsheet for marginal cost of level strategy.

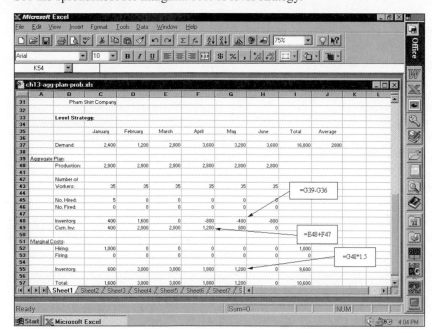

In summary, the costs of each of the strategies are:

Chase strategy	$13 000
Level strategy	$10 600

Therefore, Matt should elect to go with the level strategy.

A More In-Depth Example: The D&H Company

A firm with pronounced seasonal variation normally plans production with a 12-month time horizon to capture the extremes in demand during the busiest and slowest months.

We present here an in-depth example using a six-month horizon to more clearly illustrate the general concepts that are involved in aggregate planning. We are given specific information about the D&H Company in Exhibit 14.4. Each alternative plan that is developed and presented is accompanied by both its full and marginal cost calculations to provide a comparison of these two approaches.

The first step in evaluating each alternative plan is to convert the demand forecast into production requirements. This is accomplished by subtracting the amount of inventory on hand at the beginning of the forecast period. In the D&H example, the beginning inventory on hand is 400 units.

We are now ready to formulate and evaluate alternative aggregate or production plans for the D&H Company. Although one could develop a large number of alternative aggregate plans, we present four plans that we will evaluate with the objective of selecting that one with the lowest costs.

Plan 1. Pure chase strategy. Produce to exact monthly production requirements using a regular eight-hour day by varying workforce size.

Exhibit 14.4

Forecasted Demand and Workdays for the D&H Company

	Jan.	Feb.	Mar.	Apr.	May	June	Total
Demand forecast (units)	2200	1500	1100	900	1100	1600	8400
Working days (per month)	22	19	21	21	22	20	125
Costs							
Material cost	$100/unit						
Inventory holding cost	$1.50/unit-month (based on ending inventory level)						
Stockout cost	$5/unit/month (based on ending stockout level)						
Subcontracting cost	$125/unit						
Hiring and training cost	$200/worker						
Layoff cost	$250/worker						
Labour required per unit	5 hours						
Labour cost (first 8 hours each day)	$4/hour						
Overtime cost (time and a half)	$6/hour						
Inventory							
Beginning inventory	400 units						
Workforce							
Number of workers currently employed	30						

Plan 2. Pure level strategy. Produce to meet expected average demand over the next six months by maintaining a constant workforce. This constant number of workers is calculated by *averaging* the demand forecast over the horizon. Take the total production requirements for all six months and determine how many workers would be needed if each month's requirements were the same [(8,400 − 400) units × 5 hours per unit ÷ (125 days × 8 hours per day) = 40 workers]. Inventory is allowed to accumulate, and backlogs, when they occur, are carried forward and filled from the next month's production.

Plan 3. Minimum workforce with subcontracting strategy. Produce to meet the minimum expected demand (April) using a constant workforce on regular time. Subcontract to meet additional output requirements. The number of workers is calculated by identifying the minimum monthly production requirement and determining how many workers would be needed for that month [(900 units × 6 months × 5 hours per unit) ÷ (125 days × 8 hours per day) = 27 workers] and subcontracting any monthly difference between requirements and production.

Plan 4. Constant workforce with overtime strategy. Produce to meet expected demand for all but the first two months using a constant workforce on regular time. Use overtime to meet additional output requirements.

The number of workers needed in this alternative is determined as follows:

1100 + 900 + 1100 + 1600 = 4700 units (March–June)

4700 units × 5 labour hours per unit = 23 500 worker-hours

23 500 worker-hours/8 hours per day = 2938 worker-days

2938 worker-days/84 days (March–June) ≅ 35 workers

Having identified each of the four alternatives, the next step is to develop an aggregate plan for each alternative, showing all of the detailed calculations. These are presented in Exhibits 14.5, 14.6, 14.7, and 14.8. Once the details of each production plan have been developed, we then can determine the costs associated with each plan. These costs (both

	Jan.	Feb.	March	April	May	June	Total
Demand forecast	2 200	1 500	1 100	900	1 100	1 600	8 400
Initial inventory	400						
Production requirements	1 800	1 500	1 100	900	1 100	1 600	8 000
Aggregate plan							
Workers required	51	49	33	27	31	50	
Workers hired	21	0	0	0	4	19	
Workers fired	0	2	16	6	0	0	
Units produced	1 800	1 500	1 100	900	1 100	1 600	8 000
Costs—full							
Regular production	36 000	30 000	22 000	18 000	22 000	32 000	160 000
Material costs	180 000	150 000	110 000	90 000	110 000	160 000	800 000
Hiring costs	4 200	0	0	0	800	3 800	8 800
Firing costs	0	500	4 000	1 500	0	0	6 000
Total full costs	220 200	180 500	136 000	109 500	132 800	195 800	974 800
Costs—incremental							
Hiring costs	4 200	0	0	0	800	3 800	8 800
Firing costs	0	500	4 000	1 500	0	0	6 000
Total incremental costs	4 200	500	4 000	1 500	800	3 800	14 800

Exhibit 14.5

First Alternative: Pure Chase Strategy

	Jan.	Feb.	March	April	May	June	Total
Demand forecast	2 200	1 500	1 100	900	1 100	1 600	8 400
Initial inventory	400						
Production requirements	1 800	1 500	1 100	900	1 100	1 600	8 000
Aggregate plan							
Workers required	40	40	40	40	40	40	
Workers hired	10	0	0	0	0	0	
Workers fired	0	0	0	0	0	0	
Units produced	1 408	1 216	1 344	1 344	1 408	1 280	8 000
Monthly inventory buildup	(392)	(284)	244	444	308	(320)	
Ending inventory	(392)	(676)	(432)	12	320	0	
Costs—full							
Regular production	28 160	24 320	26 880	26 880	28 160	25 600	160 000
Material costs	140 800	121 600	134 400	134 400	140 800	128 000	800 000
Hiring costs	2 000	0	0	0	0	0	2 000
Firing costs	0	0	0	0	0	0	0
Inventory carrying costs	0	0	0	18	480	0	498
Stockout costs	1 960	3 380	2 160	0	0	0	7 500
Total full costs	172 920	149 300	163 440	161 298	169 440	153 600	969 998
Costs—incremental							
Hiring costs	2 000	0	0	0	0	0	2 000
Firing costs	0	0	0	0	0	0	0
Inventory carrying costs	0	0	0	18	480	0	498
Stockout costs	1 960	3 380	2 160	0	0	0	7 500
Total incremental costs	3 960	3 380	2 160	18	480	0	9 998

Exhibit 14.6

Second Alternative: Pure Level Strategy

Exhibit 14.7

Third Alternative: Minimum Workforce with Subcontracting Strategy

	Jan.	Feb.	March	April	May	June	Total
Demand forecast	2 200	1 500	1 100	900	1 100	1 600	8 400
Initial inventory	400						
Production requirements	1 800	1 500	1 100	900	1 100	1 600	8 000
Aggregate plan							
Workers required	27	27	27	27	27	27	
Workers hired	0	0	0	0	0	0	
Workers fired	3	0	0	0	0	0	
Units produced	950	821	907	907	950	864	5 399
Monthly inventory buildup	0	0	0	7	0	0	
Units subcontracted	850	679	193	0	143	736	2 601
Costs—full							
Regular production	19 000	16 420	18 140	18 140	19 000	17 280	107 980
Material costs	95 000	82 100	90 700	90 700	95 000	86 400	539 900
Hiring costs	0	0	0	0	0	0	0
Firing costs	750	0	0	0	0	0	750
Inventory carrying costs	0	0	0	11	0	0	11
Subcontracting costs	106 250	84 875	24 125	0	17 875	92 000	325 125
Total full costs	221 000	183 395	132 965	108 851	131 875	195 680	973 766
Costs—incremental							
Hiring costs	0	0	0	0	0	0	0
Firing costs	750	0	0	0	0	0	750
Inventory carrying costs	0	0	0	11	0	0	11
Subcontracting costs	4 250	3 395	965	0	715	3 680	13 005
Total incremental costs	5 000	3 395	965	11	715	3 680	13 766

Exhibit 14.8

Fourth Alternative: Constant Workforce with Overtime Strategy

	Jan.	Feb.	March	April	May	June	Total
Demand forecast	2 200	1 500	1 100	900	1 100	1 600	8 400
Initial inventory	400						
Production requirements	1 800	1 500	1 100	900	1 100	1 600	8 000
Aggregate plan							
Workers required	35	35	35	35	35	35	
Workers hired	5	0	0	0	0	0	
Workers fired	0	0	0	0	0	0	
Units produced—regular	1 232	1 064	1 176	1 176	1 232	1 120	7 000
Units produced—overtime	568	436					1 004
Monthly inventory buildup	0	0	76	276	132	(480)	
Ending inventory	0	0	76	352	484	4	
Costs—full							
Regular production	24 640	21 280	23 520	23 520	24 640	22 400	140 000
Overtime production	17 040	13 080	0	0	0	0	30 120
Material costs	180 000	150 000	117 600	117 600	123 200	112 000	800 400
Hiring costs	1 000	0	0	0	0	0	1 000
Firing costs	0	0	0	0	0	0	0
Inventory carrying costs	0	0	114	528	726	6	1 374
Total full costs	222 680	184 360	141 234	141 648	148 566	134 406	972 894
Costs—incremental							
Overtime production	5 680	4 360	0	0	0	0	10 040
Hiring costs	1 000	0	0	0	0	0	1 000
Firing costs	0	0	0	0	0	0	0
Inventory carrying costs			114	528	726	6	1 374
Total incremental costs	6 680	4 360	114	528	726	6	12 414

full costs and marginal costs) also are included in their respective exhibits. A summary of these costs is presented in Exhibit 14.9, showing that the pure level strategy is the lowest cost alternative.

Exhibit 14.10A gives a graphical picture of production in plan 2 (pure level strategy). It is seen that backlogs exist in January, February, and March, but by April inventories start to build up, and ending inventory for the plan is zero. No graph for Plan 1 (chase) is shown because production requirements and planned production are identical with no backlogs and inventory.

Exhibits 14.10B for plan 3 (minimum workforce with subcontracting strategy) and 14.10C for plan 4 (constant workforce with overtime strategy) are similar to 14.10A

Alternative	Full Costs	Marginal Costs
Pure chase	$974 800	$14 800
Pure level	$969 998	$ 9 998
Minimum workforce with subcontracting	$973 766	$13 766
Constant workforce with overtime	$972 894	$12 414

Exhibit 14.9

Summary of Costs for Alternative Aggregate Plans

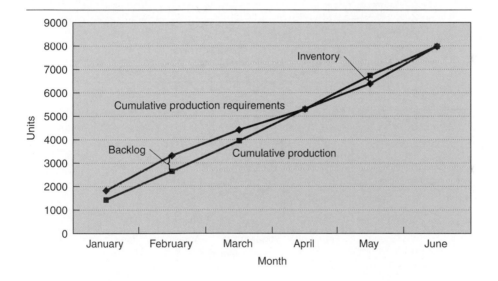

Exhibit 14.10A

D&H Company— Production Plan 2

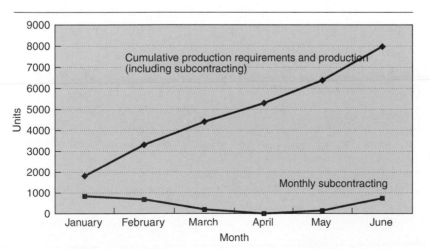

Exhibit 14.10B

D&H Company— Production Plan 3

Exhibit 14.10C

D&H Company—
Production
Plan 4

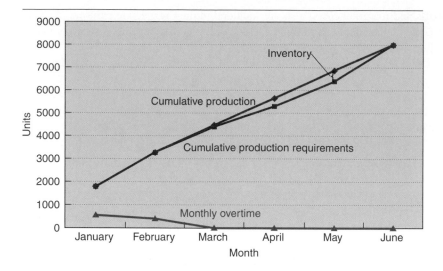

Exhibit 14.10D

Monthly
Employment
Levels—Different
Plans

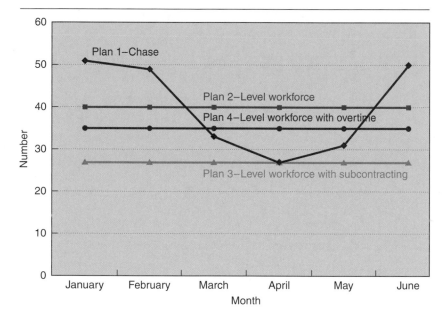

except that they also show the monthly subcontracted production and overtime production respectively. Exhibit 14.10D shows the monthly employment for each plan.

Aggregate Planning Applied to Services: Victoria Parks and Recreation Department

Charting and graphic techniques are also very useful for aggregate planning in service applications. The following example shows how a city's parks and recreation department used the alternatives of full-time employees, part-time employees, and subcontracting to meet its commitment to provide service to the city.

The Victoria Parks and Recreation Department is responsible for developing and maintaining open space, all public recreational programs, adult sports leagues, golf courses, tennis courts, pools, and so forth. There are 336 full-time-equivalent employees (FTEs). Of these, 216 are full-time permanent personnel who provide the administration and year-round maintenance to all areas. The remaining 120 year-long FTE positions are part time, with about 75 percent of them being used during the summer and the remaining 25 percent being used in the fall, winter, and spring seasons. The 75 percent (or 90 FTE positions) show up as approximately 800 part-time summer jobs—lifeguards, baseball umpires, and instructors in summer programs for children. The 800 part-time jobs are derived from 90 FTEs because many of these positions last only for a month or two, while the FTEs are based on employment for an entire year. Although we have not shown it, the demand for employees will be based on the projected monthly demand in customer hours (number of customers × hours per customer) for the upcoming planning horizon.

Currently, the parks and recreation work that is subcontracted amounts to less than $100 000. This is for the golf and tennis pros and for grounds maintenance at the libraries and veterans cemetery.

Because of the nature of city employment, the probable bad public image, and civil service rules, the option to hire and fire full-time help daily and/or weekly to meet seasonal demand is pretty much out of the question. However, temporary part-time help is authorized and traditional. Also, it is virtually impossible to have regular (full-time) staff for all of the summer jobs. During the summer months, the approximately 800 part-time employees are staffing many programs that occur simultaneously, prohibiting level scheduling over a normal 40-hour week. Also, a wider variety of skills is required than can be expected from full-time employees (e.g., umpires; coaches; lifeguards; teachers of ceramics, guitar, karate, belly dancing, and yoga).

Under these conditions, the following three options are open to the department in its aggregate planning:

1. The present method, which is to maintain a medium-level full-time staff and schedule work during off seasons (such as rebuilding baseball fields during the winter months) and use part-time help during peak demands.

2. Maintain a lower level of staff over the year and subcontract all additional work presently done by full-time staff (still using part-time help).

3. Maintain an administrative staff only and subcontract all work, including part-time help. (This would entail contracts to landscaping firms, pool-maintenance companies, and newly created private firms to employ and supply part-time help.)

The common unit of measure of work across all areas is full-time-equivalent jobs or employees (referred to as FTEs). For example, assume in the same week that 30 lifeguards worked 20 hours each, 40 instructors worked 15 hours each, and 35 baseball umpires worked 10 hours each. This is equivalent to $(30 \times 20) + (40 \times 15) + (35 + 10) = 1550 \div 40 = 38.75$ FTE positions for that week. Although a considerable amount of workload can be shifted to the off season, most of the work must be done when required.

Full-time employees consist of three groups: (1) the skeleton group of key department personnel coordinating with the city, setting policy, determining budgets, measuring performance, and so forth; (2) the administrative group of supervisory and office personnel who are responsible for or whose jobs are directly linked to the direct-labour workers; and (3) the direct-labour workforce of 116 full-time positions. These workers physically maintain the department's areas of responsibility, such as cleaning up, mowing golf greens and ballfields, trimming trees, and watering grass.

Cost information needed to determine the best alternative strategy is:

Full-Time Direct-Labour Employees	
Average wage rate	$8.90 per hour
Fringe benefits	17% of wage rate
Administrative costs	20% of wage rate
Part-Time Employees	
Average wage rate	$8.06 per hour
Fringe benefits	11% of wage rate
Administrative costs	25% of wage rate
Subcontracting all full-time jobs	$3.2 million
Subcontracting all part-time jobs	$3.7 million

June and July are the peak demand seasons in Victoria. Exhibits 14.11 and 14.12 show the high seasonal requirements for June and July personnel. The part-time help reaches 576 full-time-equivalent positions (although in actual numbers, this is approximately 800 different employees). After a low fall and winter staffing level, the demand shown as "full-time direct" reaches 130 in March, when grounds are reseeded and fertilized, and then increases to a high of 325 in July. The present method levels this uneven demand over the year to an average of 116 full-time, year-round employees by early scheduling of work. As previously mentioned, no attempt is made to hire and lay off full-time workers to meet this uneven demand.

Exhibit 14.13 shows the cost calculations for all three alternatives. Exhibit 14.14 compares the total costs for each alternative. From this analysis, it appears that the department is already using the lowest-cost alternative (Alternative 1).

Exhibit 14.11

Actual Demand Requirement for Full-Time Direct Employees and Full-Time-Equivalent (FTE) Part-Time Employees

	Jan.	Feb.	March	April	May	June	July	Aug.	Sept.	Oct.	Nov.	Dec.	Total
Days	22	20	21	22	21	20	21	21	21	23	18	22	252
Full-time employees	66	28	130	90	195	290	325	92	45	32	29	60	
Full-time days*	1452	560	2730	1980	4095	5800	6825	1932	945	736	522	1320	28 897
Full-time-equivalent part-time employees	41	75	72	68	72	302	576	72	0	68	84	27	
FTE days	902	1500	1512	1496	1512	6040	12 096	1512	0	1564	1512	594	30 240

Note: Some workweFeks are staggered to include weekdays, but this does not affect the number of workdays per employee.
*Full-time days are derived by multiplying the number of days in each month by the number of workers.

Exhibit 14.12

Monthly Requirement for Full-Time Direct-Labour Employees (Other than Key Personnel) and Full-Time Equivalent Part-Time Employees

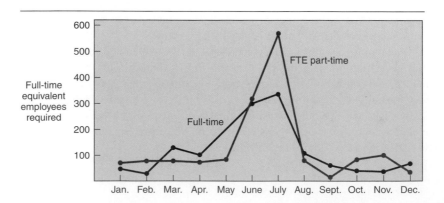

Exhibit 14.13

Three Possible Plans for the Parks and Recreation Department

Alternative 1: Maintain 116 full-time regular direct workers. Schedule work during off seasons to level workload throughout the year. Continue to use 120 full-time-equivalent (FTE) part-time employees to meet high demand periods.

Costs	Days per Year (Exhibit 14.11)	Hours (employees × days × 8 hours)	Wages (full-time, $8.90; part-time, $8.06)	Fringe Benefits (full-time, 17%; part-time, 11%)	Administrative Cost (full-time, 20%; part-time, 25%)
116 full-time regular employees	252	233 856	$2 081 318	$353 824	$416 264
120 part-time employees	252	241 920	1 949 875	214 486	487 469
Total cost = $5 503 236			$4 031 193	$568 310	$903 733

Alternative 2: Maintain 50 full-time regular direct workers and the present 120 FTE part-time employees. Subcontract jobs, releasing 66 full-time regular employees. Subcontract cost, $2 200 000.

Costs	Days per Year (Exhibit 14.11)	Hours (employees × days × 8 hours)	Wages (full-time, $8.90; part-time, $8.06)	Fringe Benefits (full-time, 17%; part-time, 11%)	Administrative Cost (full-time, 20%; part-time, 25%)	Subcontract Cost
50 full-time employees	252	100 800	$ 897 120	$152 510	$179 424	
120 FTE part-time employees	252	241 920	1 949 875	214 486	487 469	
Subcontracting cost						$2 200 000
Total cost = $6 080 884			$2 846 995	$366 996	$666 893	$2 200 000

Alternative 3: Subcontract all jobs previously performed by 116 full-time regular employees. Subcontract cost, $3 700 000. Subcontract all jobs previously performed by 120 full-time-equivalent part-time employees. Subcontract cost, $3 200 000.

Cost	Subcontract Cost
0 full-time employees	
0 part-time employees	
Subcontract full-time jobs	$3 200 000
Subcontract part-time jobs	3 700 000
Total cost	$6 900 000

Exhibit 14.14

Comparison of Costs for All Three Alternatives			
	Alternative 1: 116 Full-time Direct Labour Employees, 120 FTE Part-Time Employees	Alternative 2: 50 Full-Time Direct Labour Employees, 120 FTE Part-Time Employees, Subcontracting	Alternative 3: Subcontracting Jobs Formerly Performed by 116 Direct Labour Full-time Employees and 120 FTE Part-Time Employees
Wages	$4 031 193	$2 846 995	—
Fringe benefits	568 310	366 996	—
Administrative costs	903 733	666 893	—
Subcontracting, full-time jobs		2 200 000	$3 200 000
Subcontracting, part-time jobs			3 700 000
Total	$5 503 236	$6 080 884	$6 900 000

Yield Management in Aggregate Planning

Aggregate planning in services is very different from that in manufacturing. This is due, in large part, to the fact that the capacity of service operations is often viewed as highly perishable because it cannot be saved or inventoried for future use. For example, the empty seats at a hockey game early in the season cannot be saved for use during the playoffs. Thus, services do not have the luxury of choosing between chase and level strategies, as do manufacturing firms, but rather always must use the chase strategy. In other words, capacity must be available when the customer wants it.

yield management

Concept used in certain service operations that attempts to match supply and demand.

However, even within this constraint, the service manager has considerable latitude in planning. For those services that have high fixed costs and low variable costs, it is important to maximize capacity utilization even if it means reducing prices to attract additional customers during slow periods of demand. This method, known as **yield management** or *revenue management*, attempts to simultaneously integrate demand management (by changing prices) and supply management (by controlling availability). The goal of yield management is to sell all available capacity, even at discount prices, but, at the same time, not to turn away a full-paying customer because the capacity has previously been sold to a bargain hunter. Examples of industries that apply yield management concepts include airlines that offer discounts for advanced reservations and car rental agencies and hotels that offer discounts on weekends. (See the OM in Practice Box on National Car Rental.) The concept of yield management is introduced in this chapter; quantitative solutions for yield management are explained in the next chapter which discusses inventory management (yield management is analogous to inventory management in services). Yield management also is mentioned in the forecasting chapter.

After yield management has been applied to a service operation, the service manager then determines the aggregate workforce requirements in a manner similar to that described previously for a manufacturing company.

To take maximum advantage of yield management, a service should have the following characteristics: (*a*) the ability to segment its markets, (*b*) high fixed and low variable costs, (*c*) product perishability, and (*d*) the ability to presell capacity.[1]

---

[1]Sheryl E. Kimes, "Yield-Management: A Tool for Capacity-Constrained Service Firms," *Journal of Operations Management* 8, no. 4 (October 1989), pp. 348–363.

YIELD MANAGEMENT AT NATIONAL CAR RENTAL

National Car Rental, faced with possible liquidation in 1993 by General Motors, its parent company, was under significant pressure to produce both a substantial and sustainable profit. To accomplish this, management decided to adopt a comprehensive revenue management system. Instead of a constant car rental price, the revenue management system demonstrated that a variable pricing policy that fluctuated with demand would result in significantly higher profits.

The revenue management system was implemented in two phases. The first phase was introduced in July 1993, with the goal of showing immediate profits, which it did. The second phase focused on developing a state-of-the-art revenue management system for the car rental industry. This phase was successfully implemented in July 1994.

As a result of this revenue management system, profits significantly increased, and General Motors was able to sell National Car Rental in 1995 for an amount in excess of $1 billion.

Sources:

Ernest Johnson, "1994 Trophy Award: National Car Rental Systems, Inc." *Scorecard: The Revenue Management Quarterly,* First Quarter 1995; M. K. Geraghty and Ernest Johnson, "Revenue Management Saves National Car Rental," *Interfaces* 27, no. 1 (January–February 1997), pp. 107–127.

Market Segmentation

A major issue in the successful implementation of yield management is the ability of the firm to segment its markets. Proper segmentation will prevent all of the firm's customers from taking advantage of price reductions when they are offered to fill available capacity.

Market segmentation can be done in several ways. The first is to impose significant restrictions on customers who use the lower prices. For example, airlines require customers to stay over a Saturday night or to purchase their tickets from 7 to 30 days in advance to qualify for lower airfares. These very same conditions, however, prevent the business traveller, who usually travels midweek on short notice, from taking advantage of the lower fares.

Another method of segmentation is to offer lower prices on only specific days of the week or times of the day. Movie theatres offer reduced ticket prices for matinees, which senior citizens can take advantage of during weekdays. Similarly, downtown hotels typically offer discounts on weekends when business travellers are home, as an incentive for tourists.

High Fixed and Low Variable Costs

High fixed and low variable costs allow a firm to offer significant discounts while still being able to cover variable costs. When a service firm has this type of cost profile, profits are directly related to sales. In other words, the more sales generated, the more profits are made.

For example, if the variable cost associated with having a hotel room cleaned is estimated at $25 (which would include the labour to clean the room and the replacement of any material that was consumed, such as soap and shampoo, as well as fresh sheets and towels), then any price that the hotel could get for the room above the $25 variable cost would be financially beneficial (as opposed to leaving the room empty for the night).

Product Perishability

The underlying reason that yield management can be applied to many types of services is the perishability of service capacity. In other words, service capacity cannot be saved for future use. (Wouldn't it be great if all-inclusive resorts could save all of their empty rooms during the year for use during the Christmas holiday periods and March break!) Given that capacity in a service operation is perishable, the service manager should try to maximize capacity utilization whenever possible, even if it means offering large discounts to attract customers—provided that the discounted prices exceed the variable cost.

Presold Capacity

A final requirement for the successful implementation of yield management is that the lower-priced capacity can be sold in advance. This limits the availability of capacity to the higher-priced market segments. As an illustration, hotels usually work with conference planners several years in advance of a conference, offering a given number of rooms at the lowest room rates. Travel groups usually plan tours within a year before they need them and therefore also receive a discount. Finally, the last-minute customer, or "walk-in," will pay top dollar or the "rack rate" for a hotel room.

Aggregate Planning in Practice

Buxey[2] surveyed 42 Australian manufacturers in different industries to examine the type of aggregate plans they used. He found that almost three-quarters of the companies used chase or modified chase plans (similar to a mixed plan, but very close to chase). Primarily these were companies with high product variety and/or high seasonality in demand. They did not want to carry excess inventory because they could not be sure it would be sold. Also, if the product is perishable or bulky, carrying inventory is expensive. Thus the chase strategy reduced the financial exposure. Furthermore, many of the companies operated on a JIT basis that discouraged inventory buildup.

Recall, however, that the chase strategy has disadvantages in terms of loss of worker morale and excessive training costs if workers are laid off frequently. Thus, most companies following a chase or modified chase plan did not lay off permanent employees. Another reason why companies avoided layoffs is that in some industries, it is difficult to find and train skilled employees; thus it was important to retain them. Companies were even willing to let employees be idle for part of the time rather than lay them off. Companies also developed complementary products (such as cooling fans and heaters) so that employees could be switched from one product to another when seasons changed. The study also indicated that overtime usually is not planned, but is left for emergency situations such as an unexpected sales order or machine breakdown. Some of the strategies used by companies following a chase plan are shown in Exhibit 14.15.

Exhibit 14.15

Strategies used by firms using chase and modified chase aggregate planning to avoid laying off full-time employees

When demand is low	When demand is high
• Idle time	• Additional shifts
• Employees are assigned to complementary products	• Part-time employees (especially for simpler work)
• Employees are assigned to activities such as quality and productivity improvement or retooling the line	• Overtime
• Vacations	• Subcontracting out work
• Subcontract work from other firms (even in related industries)	• Producing some customer orders earlier (acceptable to carry inventory that is guaranteed to be sold)
• Employee attrition	

[2]Geoff Buxey, "Strategy not tactics drives aggregate planning," *International Journal of Production Economics*, 85, 2003, pp. 331–346.

The study also indicated that a level strategy was followed by companies manufacturing a small variety of stable products with little seasonality. Thus, sales forecasts were quite reliable and, because of the stability in demand, not much buildup of inventory was needed. In some cases items were made to order (backorders), but usually were delivered within 24 hours. So backordering did not seem to be a common strategy. Some companies used modularization in their product line to ensure a fairly stable demand for components. Customer orders are assembled from standard components.

Yet other companies used mixed strategies because they did not have enough flexibility to follow a chase plan. At the same time, issues such as perishability or limited warehouse capacity did not allow them to build the amount of inventory a level plan might require. Others employed "demand management" by changing prices to reduce or increase demand.

The companies in the survey did not use mathematical algorithms to develop aggregate plans; they tended to use trial-and-error-type methods. The production plans for periods in the immediate future were considered "firm" or "frozen" (changes were discouraged); periods further in the future were considered more flexible or "open."

Conclusion

Aggregate planning provides the link between the corporate strategic and capacity plans and workforce size, inventory quantity, and production levels. It does not involve detailed planning. There are some practical considerations in aggregate planning.

First, demand variations are a fact of life, so the planning system must include sufficient flexibility to cope with such variations. Flexibility can be achieved by developing alternative sources of supply, cross-training workers to handle a wide variety of orders, and engaging in more frequent replanning during high-demand periods.

Second, decision rules for production planning should be adhered to once they have been selected. However, they should be carefully analyzed prior to implementation by such checks as using simulation of historical data to see what really would have happened if these rules had been in operation in the past.

Services typically require a chase strategy due to the customer's direct involvement with the service delivery system. However, services, under certain conditions, can successfully apply the concept of yield management, which simultaneously adjusts customer demand and the operation's capacity, with the goal of maximizing the firm's profit.

Key Terms

aggregate planning p. 485
aggregate planning strategies p. 489
   mixed strategy p. 489
   pure strategy p. 489
backlog (or stockout) p. 487
inventory on hand p. 487

master production schedule p. 486
planning activities p. 484
   intermediate-range planning p. 484
   long-range planning p. 484

short-range planning p. 484
production rate p. 487
rough-cut or resource capacity planning p. 486
workforce level p. 487
yield management p. 502

Review and Discussion Questions

1. What are the basic controllable variables of a production planning problem? What are the four major costs?
2. Distinguish between pure and mixed strategies in production planning.
3. Compare the best plans in the D&H Company and the Victoria Parks and Recreation Department. What do they have in common?
4. How does forecast accuracy relate, in general, to the practical application of the aggregate planning models discussed in the chapter?
5. In which way does the time horizon chosen for an aggregate plan determine whether or not it is the best plan for the firm?
6. Under what conditions is the concept of yield management most appropriate for service operations?

Solved Problem

Problem

Jason Enterprises (JE) is producing video telephones for the home market. Quality is not quite as good as it could be at this point, but the selling price is low and Jason has the opportunity to study market response while spending more time in additional R&D work.

At this stage, however, JE needs to develop an aggregate production plan for the six months from January through June. As you can guess, you have been commissioned to create the plan. The following information is available to help you:

	Jan.	Feb.	March	April	May	June
Demand data						
Beginning inventory	200					
Forecast demand	500	600	650	800	900	800
Cost data						
Holding cost	$10/unit/month					
Stockout cost	$20/unit/month					
Subcontracting cost/unit	$100					
Hiring cost/worker	$50					
Layoff cost/worker	$100					
Labour cost/hour—straight time	$12.50					
Labour cost/hour—overtime	$18.75					
Production data						
Labour hours/unit	4					
Workdays/month	22					
Current workforce	10					

What is the cost of each of the following production strategies?

a. Chase strategy; vary workforce (assuming a starting workforce of 10 and hiring and layoff).
b. Constant workforce; vary inventory and stockout only (assuming a starting workforce of 10 and hiring).
c. Level workforce of 10; vary overtime only; inventory carryover permitted.
d. Level workforce of 10; vary overtime only; inventory carryover not permitted.

Also compare the monthly employment levels.

Solution

a. Plan 1: Chase strategy; vary workforce (assume 10 in workforce to start).

	(1) Production Requirement	(2) Production Hours Required (1) × 4	(3) Hours/Month per Worker 22 × 8	(4) Workers Required (2) ÷ (3)	(5) Workers Hired	(6) Workers Fired
Month						
January	300	1200	176	7	0	3
February	600	2400	176	14	7	0
March	650	2600	176	15	1	0
April	800	3200	176	18	3	0
May	900	3600	176	20	2	0
June	800	3200	176	18	0	2

Month	(7) Hiring Cost (5) × $50	(8) Layoff Cost (6) × $100	(9) Straight-Time Cost (2) × $12.50
January	0	$300	$ 15 000
February	350	0	30 000
March	50	0	32 500
April	150	0	40 000
May	100	0	45 000
June	0	200	40 000
	$650	$500	$202 500

Total cost for plan:

Hiring cost	$ 650
Layoff cost	500
Straight-time cost	202 500
Total	$ 203 650

b. Plan 2: Constant workforce; vary inventory and stockout only. (Hire 5 more employees.)

Month	(1) Cumulative Production Requirement	(2) Production Hours Available 22 × 8 × 15	(3) Units Produced (2) ÷ 4	(4) Cumulative Production
January	300	2640	675	675
February	900	2640	675	1350
March	1550	2640	675	2025
April	2350	2640	675	2700
May	3250	2640	675	3375
June	4050	2640	675	4050

Total cost for plan:

Hiring cost	$ 250
Inventory cost	17 750
Straight-time cost	202 500
Total	$220 500

Month	(5) Units Short (1) − (4)	(6) Shortage Cost (5) × $20	(7) Units in Excess (4) − (1)	(8) Inventory Cost (7) × $10	(9) Straight-Time Cost (3) × 4 × 12.5
January	$0	0	375	3750	$ 33 750
February	0	0	450	4500	33 750
March	0	0	475	4750	33 750
April	0	0	350	3500	33 750
May	0	0	125	1250	33 750
June	0	0	0	0	33 750
				$17 750	$202 500

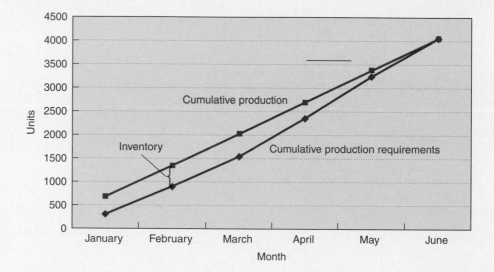

c. Plan 3: Level workforce of 10; vary overtime only; inventory carryover permitted.

Month	(1) Production Requirement	(2) Standard Time Hours Available 22 × 8 × 10	(3) Standard Time Units Produced (2) ÷ 4	(4) Overtime Required in Units (1) − (3)
January	300	1760	440	0
February	460*	1760	440	20
March	650	1760	440	210
April	800	1760	440	360
May	900	1760	440	460
June	800	1760	440	360
				1410

*600 − 140 units of beginning inventory in February.

Month	(5) Overtime Required in Hours (4) × 4	(6) Overtime Cost (5) × \$18.75	(7) Straight- Time Cost (2) × \$12.50	(8) Excess Inventory Costs [(3) − (1)] × \$10
January	0	\$ 0	\$ 22 000	\$1400
February	80	1 500	22 000	
March	840	15 750	22 000	
April	1440	27 000	22 000	
May	1840	34 500	22 000	
June	1440	27 000	22 000	
		\$105 750	\$132 000	\$1400

Total cost for plan:

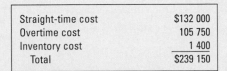

Straight-time cost	\$132 000
Overtime cost	105 750
Inventory cost	1 400
Total	\$239 150

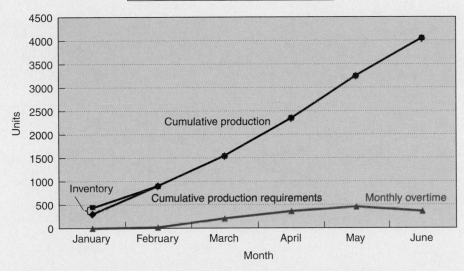

d. Plan 4: Constant workforce of 10; vary overtime only; inventory carryover not permitted.

Month	(1) Production Requirement	(2) Standard-Time Hours Available 22 × 8 × 10	(3) Standard-Time Units Produced Min. [(2) ÷ 4; (1)]	(4) Overtime Required in Units (1) − (3)
January	300	1760	300	0
February	600	1760	440	160
March	650	1760	440	210
April	800	1760	440	360
May	900	1760	440	460
June	800	1760	440	360

Month	(5) Overtime Required in Hours (4) × 4	(6) Overtime Cost (5) × $18.75	(7) Standard-Time Cost (2) × $12.50	(8) Excess Inventory Costs [(3) − (1)] × $10
January	0	$ 0	$ 22 000	$1400
February	640	12 000	22 000	
March	840	15 750	22 000	
April	1440	27 000	22 000	
May	1840	34 500	22 000	
June	1440	27 000	22 000	
		$116 250	$132 000	$1400

Total cost for plan:

Straight-time cost	$132 000
Overtime cost	116 250
Excess inventory cost	1400
Total	$249 650

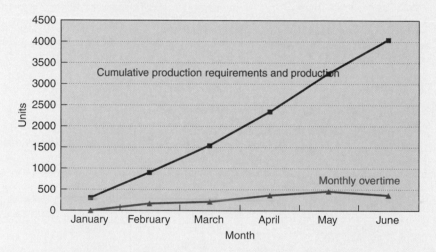

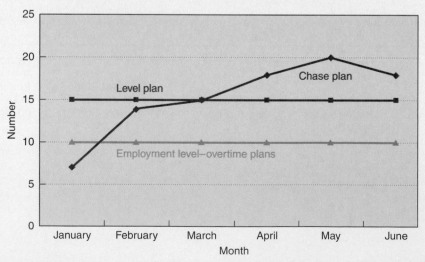

1. Develop a production plan and calculate the annual cost for the E. Rohleder Company whose unit demand forecast is fall, 10 000; winter, 8000; spring, 7000; summer, 12 000. Inventory at the beginning of fall is 500 units. At the beginning of fall you have 30 workers, but you plan to hire temporary workers at the beginning of summer and lay them off at the end of summer. In addition, you have negotiated with the union an option to use the regular workforce on overtime during winter or spring if overtime is necessary to prevent stockouts at the end of those quarters. Overtime is *not* available during the fall. Relevant costs are: hiring, $100 for each temp; layoff, $200 for each regular worker laid off; inventory holding, $5 per unit per quarter; back order, $10 per unit per quarter; straight time, $5 per hour; overtime, $8 per hour. Assume that worker productivity is two hours per unit, with eight hours per day and 60 days per season.

2. Develop an aggregate production plan for the D & J Bischak Company for a four-month period: February through May. For February and March, you should produce to exactly meet the demand forecast. For April and May, you should use overtime and inventory with a stable workforce. However, government constraints put a maximum of 5000 hours of overtime labour per month in April and May (zero overtime in February and March). If demand exceeds supply, then back orders occur. There are 100 workers on January 31. You are given the following unit demand forecast: February, 80 000; March, 64 000; April, 100 000; May, 40 000. Worker productivity is four units per hour. Assume eight hours per day, 20 days per month and zero inventory on February 1. Costs are: hiring, $50 per new worker; layoff, $70 per worker laid off; inventory holding, $10 per unit per month; straight-time labour, $10 per hour; overtime, $15 per hour; back order, $20 per unit per month. Find the total cost of this plan.

3. Develop an aggregate production plan for the next year for the SBV Menon Company. The unit demand forecast is spring, 20 000; summer, 10 000; fall, 15 000; winter, 18 000. At the beginning of spring you have 70 workers and 1000 units in inventory. The union contract specifies that you may lay off workers only once a year, at the beginning of summer. Also, you may hire new workers only at the end of summer to begin regular work in the fall. The number of workers laid off at the beginning of summer and the number hired at the end of summer should result in planned production levels for summer and fall that equal the demand forecasts for summer and fall respectively. If demand exceeds supply, use overtime in spring only, which means that back orders could occur in winter. You are given these costs: hiring, $100 per new worker; layoff, $200 per worker laid off; holding, $20 per unit per quarter; back order costs, $8 per unit per quarter; straight-time labour, $10 per hour; overtime, $15 per hour. Worker productivity is two hours per unit. Assume eight hours per day and 50 days per quarter. Find the total cost.

4. Souza, Inc. needs to develop an aggregate plan for its product line. Relevant data are:

Production time	1 hour per unit
Average labour cost	$10 per hour
Work-week	5 days, 8 hours each day
Days per month	Assume 20 workdays per month
Beginning inventory	500 units
Safety stock	One-half of monthly forecast
Shortage cost	$20 per unit per month
Inventory carrying cost	$5 per unit per month

The forecast for January to December 1998 is:

Jan.	Feb.	March	April	May	June	July	Aug.	Sept.	Oct.	Nov.	Dec.
2500	3000	4000	3500	3500	3000	3000	4000	4000	4000	3000	3000

Management prefers to keep a constant workforce and production level, absorbing variations in demand through inventory excesses and shortages. Demand that is not met is carried over to the following month.

Develop an aggregate plan that will meet the demand and other conditions of the problem. Do not try to find the optimal solution; just find a good solution and state the procedure you might use to test for a better solution. Make any necessary assumptions.

5. Erkut Video Concepts produces a line of CD players to be linked to personal computers for video games. With such a computer/CD link, the game becomes a very realistic experience. In a simple driving game where the joystick steers the vehicle, for example, rather than seeing computer graphics on the screen, the player is actually viewing a segment of a CD shot from a real moving vehicle. Depending on the action of the player (hitting a guard rail, for example) the disc moves virtually instantaneously to that segment and the player becomes part of an actual accident of real vehicles (staged, of course).

Erkut is trying to determine a production plan for the next 12 months. The main criterion for this plan is that the employment level be held constant over the period. Erkut is continuing in its R&D efforts to develop new applications and prefers not to cause any adverse feeling with the local workforce. For the same reasons, all employees should put in full work weeks, even if this is not the lowest-cost alternative. The number of CD players forecast for the next 12 months is:

Month	Forecast Demand	Month	Forecast Demand
January	600	July	200
February	800	August	200
March	900	September	300
April	600	October	700
May	400	November	800
June	300	December	900

Manufacturing cost is $200 per player, equally divided between materials and labour. Inventory storage costs are $5 per CD player per month. A shortage results in lost sales and is estimated to cost an overall $20 per unit short. (Shortages are not carried forward since the sales are lost.)

The inventory on hand at the beginning of the planning period is 200 units. Ten labour hours are required per CD player. The workday is eight hours.

Develop an aggregate production schedule for the year using a constant workforce. For simplicity, assume 22 working days each month except July, when the plant closes down for three weeks' vacation (leaving seven working days). Make any assumptions you need.

6. The Bebehani Chemical Company (BCC) is vitally concerned about generating a production schedule for their products for the coming fiscal year (July–June). The operations manager at BCC, Mr. Perspa Cassidy, has been charged with generating an aggregate plan for this time period so that BCC can meet its demand with the minimum utilization of resources.

Mr. Cassidy first aggregates the various products that BCC sells into a single aggregate production unit and forecasts the demand for the following four quarters:

Quarter	Quarter #1 Jul/Aug/Sept	Quarter #2 Oct/Nov/Dec	Quarter #3 Jan/Feb/Mar	Quarter #4 Apr/May/June
Demand forecast	10 000	9800	9400	10 200

On March 1 (prior to quarter #1) there are 1200 units in BCC's inventory, and the forecast demand for the fourth quarter of the previous year is 9900 units. Mr. Cassidy knows that to keep one unit in inventory for one month costs $5; furthermore, BCC uses average inventory when computing inventory costs. The workforce on March 1 consists of 40 employees, each of whom produces exactly four (4) units in an 8-hour day. For the coming four quarters, Mr. Cassidy has determined the number of productive days for each quarter to be as follows:

Quarter	Quarter #1 Jul/Aug/Sept	Quarter #2 Oct/Nov/Dec	Quarter #3 Jan/Feb/Mar	Quarter #4 Apr/May/June
Number of productive days	56	60	61	63

Each of the regular employees is paid at the rate of $53 per day; however, overtime is available at the rate of $80 per day. BCC has a very strict quality control policy and does not allow subcontracting. In addition, BCC wishes to maintain their reputation with their customers and has adopted a policy that *all* demand must be met on time.

Mr. Cassidy recognizes that meeting all demand can be difficult. He is faced with two limitations: (1) he is using aggregate units and (2) he has only his forecasts as a basis for his aggregate plan. However, he believes that his forecasts are quite good and decides to use his figures objectively (i.e., he decides not to keep any safety stock).

The workforce can be increased or decreased at the discretion of Mr. Cassidy, but no more than a 25 percent increase or decrease (using integer values) is allowed in any given quarter due to union regulations. Mr. Cassidy knows that should he wish to hire and/or fire, the total increase/decrease in the workforce (when using whole people) cannot exceed the 25 percent mark. Fortunately, BCC is located in an area where there is no shortage of skilled labour.

To hire a new individual and train him/her requires exactly one quarter and costs $1200. All new employees start on the first day of a given quarter. Hence, they cannot be considered part of the productive labour force until after their first quarter. To fire an individual costs $1000, and when an individual is fired, he or she remains part of the productive workforce until the end of the quarter in which he or she was fired.

Mr. Cassidy believes that he has all the data he needs; hence, he starts to determine the aggregate capacity plan. He selects a strategy of trying to maintain a relatively stable workforce, while letting inventory levels fluctuate.

a. Perform the initial calculations Mr. Cassidy would need prior to completing the grid that follows.

b. Develop an aggregate plan for Mr. Cassidy by filling in the grid.

c. What is the total cost of Mr. Cassidy's plan?

(1) Qtr.	(2) Demand	(3) Prod. Hours Req. (2) × 2	(4) Prod. Days per Qtr.	(5) Prod. hrs per Qtr. per Worker (4) × 8	(6) No. of Empls.	(7) Total Prod. hrs Avail. per Qtr. (5) × (6)	(8) Straight-Time Cost (4) × (6) × $53	(9) No. of Units Short	(10) Short Cost	(11) No. of OT Units Req.	(12) No. of OT Days Req. (11)/4
NOW	9 900	19 800	63	504	40	20 160	$133 560	0	$0	0	0
1	10 000		56						0		
2	9 800		60						0		
3	9 400		61						0		
4	10 200		63						0		

(13) Overtime Cost (12) × $80	(14) No. of Unit Sub.	(15) Sub. Cost.	(16) No. of Empls. Hired	(17) Hiring Cost (16) × $1200	(18) No. of Empls. Fired	(19) Firing Cost (18) × $1000	(20) Begin. Inv.	(21) End. Inv.	(22) Ave. Inv. (20) + (21) 2	(23) Inv. Cost (22) × $15
$0	0	$0	0	$0	0	$ 0	1200	1380	1290	$19 350
							1380			

7. Osakwe's Marina at Peggy's Cove, as part of the service it offers to its customers, stores boats during the winter months. In addition, the marina, at the request of the customer, will paint the hull of the boat, which must be done every year to prevent barnacles from attaching to the hull.

Dave Osakwe, the owner of the marina, has received orders for the following sizes of boats to be stored and painted, and also has estimated the number of hours required to paint each size boat:

Boat Size	Number of Boats	Number of Labour Hours to Paint
Small (12′–19′)	38	6
Medium (20′–34′)	31	12
Large (35′ and larger)	14	25

Dave currently employs one handyman during the summer months who does a wide variety of tasks. As one option, Dave can continue to employ this person during the six winter months (November–April) and have him paint the boat hulls. With this option the person would work 160 hours per month for each of the six months. Dave estimates the cost of painting the boats to be $30.00 per hour, which includes both labour and materials ($20.00 for labour and $10.00 for materials). Because the boat owners will not pay Dave until the spring when their boats go in the water, Dave will have to borrow money from his bank for the labour and materials at an annual rate of 18 percent, or 1.5 percent per month.

As a second alternative, Dave can let the handyman go at the end of the season and then hire the necessary number of workers to get all of the boats painted in April, just before they go into the water. At the end of the month, he would let all but the handyman go. The cost of hiring a worker for this kind of work is estimated to be $100.00 per person and the layoff cost is estimated at $75.00 per person.

A third option would be to hire fewer workers in April and have them all work overtime. In this case, each worker would work 60 hours a week, or 240 hours for the month. The overtime premium is 50 percent of the cost of labour, or $10.00 per hour.

Develop an aggregate plan for each of these alternatives. Which one would you recommend?

Case 1 Laurier Brokerage Firm

Consider the national operations group of the Laurier brokerage firm. The group, housed in an office building located in the Bay Street area, handles the transactions generated by registered representatives in 12 branch offices throughout Canada. As with all firms in the brokerage industry, Laurier's transactions must be settled within five trading days. This five-day period allows operations managers to smooth out the daily volume fluctuations.

Fundamental shifts in the stock market's volume and mix can occur overnight, so the operations manager must be prepared to handle extremely wide swings in volume. For example, on the strength of an international peace rumour, the number of transactions of Laurier rose from 5600 one day to 12 200 the next.

Managers of Laurier, not unlike their counterparts in other firms, have trouble predicting volume. In fact, a random number generator can predict volume a month or even a week into the future almost as well as the managers can.

How do the operations managers in Laurier manage capacity when there are such wide swings? The answer differs according to the tasks and constraints facing each manager. Here's what two managers in the same firm might say:

Manager A: The capacity in our operation is currently 12 000 transactions per day. Of course, what we should gear up for is always a problem. For example, our volume this year ranged from 4000 to 15000 transactions per day. It's a good thing we have a turnover rate, because in periods of low volume it helps us reduce our personnel without the morale problems caused by layoffs. [The labour turnover rate in this department is over 100 percent per year.]

Manager B: For any valid budgeting procedure, one needs to estimate volume within 15 percent. Correlations between actual and expected volume in the brokerage industry have been so poor that I question the value of budgeting at all. I maintain our capacity at a level of 17 000 transactions per day.

Why the big difference in capacity management in the same firm? Manager A is in charge of the cashiering operation—the handling of certificates, cheques, and cash. The personnel in cashiering are messengers, clerks, and supervisors. The equipment—file cabinets, vaults, calculators—is uncomplicated.

Manager B, however, is in charge of handling orders, an information-processing function. The personnel are data-entry clerks, EDP specialists, and systems analysts. The equipment is complex—computers, LANs, file servers, and communication devices that link national operations with the branches. The employees under B's control had performed their tasks manually until increased volume and a standardization of the information needs made it worthwhile to install computers.

Because the lead times required to increase the capacity of the information processing operations are long and the incremental cost of the capacity to handle the last 5000 transactions is low (only some extra peripheral equipment is needed), Manager B maintains the capacity to handle 17 000 transactions per day. He holds to this level even though the average number of daily transactions for any month has never been higher than 11 000 and the number of transactions for any one day has never been higher than 16 000.

Because of the great uncertainty about the future status of the stock certificate, the situation is completely different in cashiering. Attempts to automate the cashiering function to the degree reached by the order-processing group have been thwarted because of the high risk of selecting a system not compatible with the future format of the stock certificate.

In other words, Manager A is tied to the chase demand strategy, and his counterpart, Manager B in the adjacent office, is locked into the level capacity strategy. However, each desires to incorporate more of the other's strategy into his own. A is developing a computerized system to handle the information-processing requirements of cashiering; B is searching for some variable costs in the order-processing operation that can be deleted in periods of low volume.

Questions

1. What appear to be the primary differences between these two departments?

2. Do these differences eliminate certain strategy choices for either manager?

3. Which factors cause the current strategy to be desirable for each manager?

4. What are the mixed or subcontracting possibilities?

5. What are the problems associated with low standardization?

Source: Management of Service Operations, 1/e, by Sasser/Olsen/ Wykoff, © 1978. Reprinted by permission of Prentice Hall, Inc., Upper Saddle River, NJ.

Case 2 | La Buena Compañía de España, S.A.

La Buena Compañía de España, S.A. (LBC), located just outside of Barcelona, Spain, produces kitchen tables that it sells throughout Western Europe. Sales have been increasing steadily over the past several years, due in large part to the free trade among Western European countries that has resulted from the formation of the European Union (EU).

Jordi Garolera, the operations manager at LBC, is currently developing an aggregate plan for the next six months. In order to be able to evaluate alternative plans, Jordi has collected the following information:

Production Data

20 workdays per month
7.5 hours per workday
2.5 labour-hours per table (average)
On-hand inventory: 300 tables
Current workforce: 25 workers

Cost Data

Hourly wages: 8 euros per hour
Hiring costs: 200 euros per employee
Firing costs: 700 euros per employee
Material cost per table: 100 euros
Overtime costs: 50 percent premium
Inventory carrying costs: 2 euros per unit per month
Stockout costs: 10 euros per unit per month

Jordi has just returned from a meeting with the marketing manager who provided him with a sales forecast for the next six months of 13 260 tables, which is broken down as follows by month:

Month	Jan.	Feb.	Mar.	Apr.	May	June
Forecast (Tables)	1740	1740	2460	3240	2220	1860

Questions

1. Using Excel or a similar spreadsheet, compare the costs of a pure chase strategy and a pure level strategy. Which type of strategy would you recommend?

2. As another alternative, Jordi was considering using a level workforce of 30 employees and working overtime to eliminate any stockouts. Evaluate this alternative and compare it to the pure strategies.

3. What alternative aggregate plans could you suggest to Jordi? What are the relative strengths and weaknesses of these plan(s)?

Source: © 1997 by Mark M. Davis.

15

Inventory Systems for Independent Demand

Chapter Objectives

- Introduce the different types of inventories that can exist in an organization and provide a rationale for companies to maintain inventories.

- Identify the various costs associated with carrying and maintaining inventories.

- Define the classical inventory models and the conditions necessary for them to be applicable.

- Show how the economic order quantity is calculated for each of the different inventory models.

- Introduce the single-period inventory model and the concept of yield management with respect to service operations.

- Present some of the current inventory management trends and issues that exist in companies.

The senior executives of Alpha Numerics were having their annual retreat to review accomplishments of the past year and to discuss major policy issues for the coming year.* As was the norm, the retreat was held at a small hotel in Cape Breton, well removed from the company's actual manufacturing facility in Halifax.

The first day's meeting had gone well, but in the early evening, after dinner, the subject of inventory control and the number of shortages that had occurred over the past year came up for discussion. The vice president of engineering, Moshe Goldberg, suggested that, as a solution to the shortage problem, purchasing should order all of the projected material requirements at the beginning of the year.

The vice president of manufacturing, Sid Stonechild, was so taken back by this suggestion that, to the amazement of the others in the room, he leaped onto the conference table and shouted out, "Inventory is evil!" He turned to the president, Patricia Brown, and said, "If we were to follow this suggestion, Madam President, do you have an extra 2500 square metres of

*This meeting of senior corporate executives actually took place, although the names of the firm, locations, and persons have been disguised.

"Something's got to go, Fenton. You, me or this inventory—and it's not going to be me."

warehouse space where we can store the material?" The president shook her head no. "And do you, Mr. Vice President of Finance, have an extra $5 million to buy all this material?" Raj Brar similarly shook his head.

"And are you, Mr. Vice President of Marketing, going to provide me with a perfect forecast of the products we expect to sell for the next year?" Jin Yu said, "No, of course not. That would be impossible." And turning to the VP of engineering who had made the initial proposal, he said, "And you'll keep the same designs in the coming year without making any changes, won't you?" The VP of engineering said, "That would be very unrealistic." All of the individuals in the room then looked up to the VP of manufacturing still standing on the conference table and said, "We see what you mean. Inventory is indeed evil!"

Managerial Issues

Management's view towards inventory has changed significantly over the past several years. Previously, managers perceived inventory as an asset because it appears as an asset in the firm's financial reports. However, as seen in the opening vignette, this is no longer the case.

As we have seen, product life cycles are becoming ever shorter, increasing the likelihood of product obsolescence, as seen in the accompanying OM in Practice box. As we also have seen, excessive inventories on the manufacturing floor tend to conceal a wide variety of problems. Moreover, inventory storage costs are typically very expensive, averaging 30 to 35 percent annually of the value of the inventory—and in some cases much higher.

For all these reasons, managers now look at inventory as a liability to the firm, something to be reduced or eliminated wherever possible, as illustrated in the GE advertisement.

Consequently, no topic in operations is more often discussed by managers or perceived to be more important than inventory. There is a continuous effort among managers to reduce inventories in all categories, beginning with raw materials and purchased parts, through to work-in-process, and ultimately to finished goods. (See the OM in Practice Box on inventories in Canada).

Definition of Inventory

Inventory is defined as the stock of any item or resource used in an organization. An *inventory management system* is the set of policies and controls that monitors levels of inventory and determines (*a*) what levels should be maintained, (*b*) when stock should be replenished, and (*c*) how large orders should be.

types of inventory:

raw material

Vendor-supplied items that have not had any labour added.

finished goods

Completed products still in the possession of the firm.

work-in-process (WIP)

Items that have been partially processed but are still incomplete.

In a broader context, inventory can include inputs such as human, financial, energy, equipment, and physical items such as **raw materials**; outputs such as parts, components, and **finished goods**; and interim stages of the process, such as partially finished goods or **work-in-process (WIP)**. The choice of which items to include in inventory depends on the organization. A manufacturing operation can have an inventory of personnel, machines, and working capital, as well as raw materials and finished goods. An airline can have an inventory of seats; a modern drugstore, an inventory of medicines, batteries, and toys; and an engineering firm, an inventory of engineering talent.

By convention, manufacturing inventory generally refers to materials that contribute to or become part of a firm's product output. In services, inventory generally refers to the tangible goods that are sold and the supplies necessary to administer the service. Customers waiting in line at a service operation also can be viewed as inventory similar to parts waiting to be processed in a factory.

The basic purpose of inventory analysis in manufacturing and stockkeeping services is to specify (*a*) when items should be ordered and (*b*) how large the order should be. Recent trends have modified the simple questions of "when" and "how many." As we saw in Chapter 12 on supply chain management, many firms are entering into longer-term relationships with vendors to supply their needs for perhaps the entire year. This changes the "when" and "how many to order" to "when" and "how many to deliver."

Reasons for Maintaining Inventory

Organizations maintain inventories for several reasons. These include:

1. **To protect against uncertainty.** For purposes of inventory management, we examine uncertainty in three areas. First, there is uncertainty with respect to raw materials, which necessitates raw material inventory. Here, uncertainty pertains both to the lead time that can vary due to unexpected delays and to the amount of raw material received.

   Uncertainty also occurs in the transformation process. Here work-in-process (WIP) inventories absorb the variability that exists between the stages of the process, thereby providing independence between operations and improving efficiency. In addition, this WIP inventory can be used to decouple the stages in a process.

Finally, uncertainty exists with respect to the demand for a firm's finished products. If the demand for a product were known precisely, it could be possible to manufacture products so that demand would be exactly met. However, more often demand is not totally known, and a safety stock of finished goods inventory is therefore maintained to absorb variations.

2. *To support a strategic plan.* As we learned in the previous chapter on aggregate planning, when a firm adopts a level strategy, an inventory of finished goods is required to buffer the cyclic demand for product from the level output generated by the transformation process. Under these circumstances, when demand exceeds production, the difference is withdrawn from inventory; when demand is less than production, the difference is placed back into inventory.

3. *To take advantage of economies of scale.* Each time we place an order or do a setup to perform an operation, we incur a fixed cost, regardless of the quantity involved. Thus, the larger the quantity ordered or produced, the lower the average total cost per unit. However, as we shall see shortly, there are trade-offs to be considered in determining the proper lot size.

In addition, companies often offer discounts for larger-quantity orders, as an incentive to customers to buy more than they normally would. This results in accumulations of items that otherwise would not exist. Firms offer quantity discounts for several reasons, including the need to reduce excessive stockpiles and to generate positive cash flow. In addition, there are economies of scale with respect to transportation costs, especially when products are shipped in either full trailer loads or full car loads.

Inventory Costs

In making any decision with respect to inventories, the following costs should be taken into consideration:

Holding or Carrying Costs

This broad category is usually subdivided into three segments: storage costs, capital costs, and obsolescence/shrinkage costs. *Storage costs* include the cost of the storage facility in the form of rent or depreciation, insurance, taxes, utilities, security, and facility personnel.

Capital costs can vary, depending on the firm's financial situation. For example, if the firm has an excess of cash, then the capital cost is the interest lost by putting the money into inventory instead of short-term notes. If the firm has an alternative project to invest in, then the capital cost is the opportunity cost of the anticipated return of that project. If the firm has to borrow funds to maintain an inventory, then the capital cost is the interest paid on those funds.

Obsolescence costs recognize that products tend to depreciate in value over time. This is especially true in high-technology industries where newer and better (and often cheaper) products are constantly being introduced. In this category, we also include spoilage costs associated with products that have a short shelf life, such as perishable food products and some types of prescription drugs. *Shrinkage costs* track pilferage and breakage.

Operations Management in Practice

COMPANIES WRITE OFF MILLIONS OF DOLLARS IN OBSOLETE INVENTORIES

It seemed for a while as if high tech or so called "New Economy" companies were exempt from business cycles and would not be burdened with excess inventories. However, during the economic slowdown of 2000–2001 (also referred to by some as a recession), many high-technology companies had to write off significant amounts of obsolete inventories. These inventories were the result of the inability of these firms' managers to anticipate the economic downturn and the associated decrease in sales. These excessive inventories occurred at all levels of the supply chain, including semiconductor manufacturers, electronic contract manufacturers, and PC makers. Although "old economy" companies such as Proctor & Gamble can stock excess products such as diapers for sale another day, high-tech inventory becomes obsolete very quickly. According to Steve Ward, general manager for IBM's Global sector, "Lean inventories are absolutely critical. In parts of our business, the value of components drops about 1.5 percent a month." IBM survived better than many other companies because of better inventory and supply chain management practices. During the slowdown, the overall level of IBM inventories was at its lowest level since 1988. Listed below are some high-tech companies and the amounts of inventory they wrote off.

Company	Amount of Inventory Written Off*
Cisco Systems	$2.25 billion
Nortel Networks	950 million
Agere Systems	270 million
Micron Technology	260 million
Altera Corp.	115 million
Vitesse Semiconductor	50.6 million
Alliance Semiconductor	50 million
Xilinx	32 million

*All in U.S. dollars.

Sources:
Edward Teach, "The Great Inventory Correction," *CFO* (September 2001), pp. 58–62.
Mark Heinzl, "Nortel Expects $19.2 Billion Quarterly Loss—Major Restructuring Is Set, Signaling a Turnaround for Telecoms Isn't Near," *The Wall Street Journal*, June 18, 2001, A3.
Brian Milner, "Tech Firms Fumble Through Great Inventory Screwup," *The Globe and Mail*, April 27, 2001, B15.

Setup or Order Preparation or Ordering Costs

These are usually associated with the production of a lot internally or the placing of an order externally with a vendor. Unlike holding costs, these costs are independent of the number of units requested. Setup costs are related to the amount of time needed to adjust the equipment to perform a specific task, including the alignment of special tooling such as jigs and fixtures. Order preparation costs (also called ordering costs) pertain to the costs involved in placing an order with a vendor. These may include telephone charges, a delivery fee, expediting costs, and the time required to process a purchase order.

Shortage (or Stockout) Costs

When the stock of an item is depleted and a customer orders that product, a stockout cost is incurred. This is usually the sum of the lost profit and any "ill-will" generated. There is a trade-off between carrying stock to satisfy demand and the costs resulting from stockout. This balance is sometimes difficult to obtain, since it may not be possible to accurately estimate lost profits, the effects of lost customers, or late penalties.

Purchase Costs

These are the actual costs of the material purchased. Purchase costs per unit tend to remain constant unless quantity discounts (discussed later in this chapter) are offered.

In addition to these traditional inventory costs, transportation costs also affect the lot size. (In determining the proper lot size, transportation costs often are included in the purchase cost of the material.)

Independent versus Dependent Demand

Briefly, the distinction between **independent** and **dependent demand** is this: With independent demand, the demands for various items are unrelated to each other and

types of demand:

independent demand
Pertains to the requirements for end products.

dependent demand
Requirements for components and subassemblies that are directly dependent on the demand for the end products in which they are used.

522

therefore the required quantities of each must be determined separately or independently. With dependent demand (addressed in detail in the next chapter), the requirement for any one item is a direct result of the need for some other item, usually a higher-level item of which it is a component or subassembly.

In concept, dependent demand is a relatively straightforward computational problem. The required quantities of a dependent-demand item are simply computed, based on the number needed in each higher-level item in which it is used. For example, if an automobile company plans on producing 500 automobiles per day, it will need 2000 wheels and tires (plus spares). The number of wheels and tires needed is *dependent* on the production level for automobiles and not derived separately. The demand for auto-mobiles, on the other hand, is *independent*—it comes from many sources external to the automobile firm and is not a part of other products, and so is unrelated to the demand for other products.

To determine the quantities of independent items that must be produced, firms usually turn to their sales and market research departments. They use a variety of techniques, including customer surveys, forecasting techniques, and economic and sociological trends.Because independent demand is uncertain, extra units must be carried in inventory.

Types of Inventory Systems

An inventory system provides the organizational structure and operating policies for maintaining and controlling the products to be stocked. The system is responsible for the ordering and receipt of goods—timing the order placement and keeping track of what has been ordered, how much, and from whom. The system must also provide follow-up to answer such questions as: Has the vendor received the order? Has it been shipped? Are the dates correct? Are the procedures established for reordering or returning undesirable merchandise?

Fixed-Order-Quantity and Fixed-Time-Period Systems

There are two general types of inventory systems: **fixed-order-quantity** (also called the Q-system) and **fixed-time-period** (also referred to as the P-system).

The basic distinction between the two is that the fixed-order-quantity model is "event triggered" and the fixed-time-period model is "time triggered." That is, the fixed-order-quantity model initiates an order when the event of reaching a specified reorder level occurs. This event may take place at any time, depending on the demand for the items. By contrast, the fixed-time-period model is limited to placing orders at the end of a predetermined time period; only the passage of time triggers the model. Advances in information technology, including the bar coding of products, bar code scanners, and point-of-sale (POS) computers, have greatly reduced the cost and facilitated the use of the fixed-order quantity model. As a result, there has been an increasing trend towards the fixed-order quantity model, and away from the fixed-time period model.

To use the fixed-order-quantity model, which places an order when the remaining inventory drops to a predetermined order point, R, the inventory remaining must be continually monitored. Thus, the fixed-order-quantity model is a *perpetual* inventory system, which requires that every time a withdrawal from or an addition to inventory is made, records must be updated to ensure that the reorder point has or has not been reached. For the fixed-time-period model, inventory is counted only at the end of the review period. No counting takes place in the interim (although some firms have

types of inventory systems:

fixed-order-quantity
System in which the order quantity remains constant but the time between orders varies.

fixed-time-period
System in which the time period between orders remains constant but the order quantity varies.

created variations of systems that combine features of both). Some additional differences that tend to influence the choice of systems are:

- The fixed-time-period model typically has a larger average inventory because it also must protect against stockout during the review period, T; the fixed-quantity model has no review period.

- The fixed-time-period model is preferred when several different items are purchased from the same vendor, and there are potential economies of scale savings from ordering all these items at the same time.

- The fixed-order-quantity model is preferred for more expensive items because average inventory is lower.

- The fixed-order-quantity model is more appropriate for important items such as critical repair parts because there is closer monitoring and therefore quicker response to a potential stockout.

- The fixed-order-quantity model requires more time and resources to maintain because every addition or withdrawal is recorded.

Exhibit 15.1 illustrates the different events that occur when each of the two models is put into use and becomes an operating system. As we can see, the fixed-order-quantity system focuses on order quantities and reorder points. Procedurally, each time a unit is taken out of stock, the withdrawal is recorded and the amount remaining in inventory is immediately compared to the reorder point. If it has dropped to this point or below, an order for Q items is placed. If it has not, the system remains in an idle state until the next withdrawal.

Exhibit 15.1

Comparison of Fixed-Order-Quantity and Fixed-Time-Period Reordering Inventory Systems

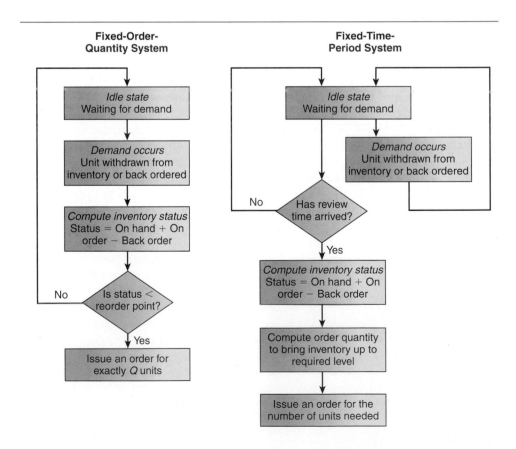

In the fixed-time-period system, a decision to place an order is made at a predetermined time interval (for example, each week or month), when the stock is counted or reviewed. Whether an order is actually placed depends on the inventory status at that time.

Basic Inventory Models
Basic Fixed-Order-Quantity Model

The simplest model in this category is appropriate when all aspects of the situation are known with certainty. If the annual demand for a product is 1000 units, it is precisely 1000—not 1000 plus or minus 10 percent. In addition, the setup costs and holding costs are known and constant. Although the assumption of complete certainty is rarely valid, it provides a good starting point for our coverage of inventory models.

The fixed-order-quantity model attempts to determine both the specific point, R, at which an order will be placed and the size of that order, Q. The order (or reorder) point, R, is always a specified number of units actually in inventory. The solution to a fixed-order-quantity model may stipulate something like this: When the number of units of inventory on hand drops to 36, place an order for 57 more units.

Exhibit 15.2 and the discussion about deriving the optimal order quantity are based on the following assumptions of the model:

● Demand for the product is known, constant, and uniform throughout the period

● Lead time (L), which is the time from ordering to receipt, is constant

● Price per unit of product is constant (no quantity discounts)

● Order preparation or setup costs are constant

● All demands for the product are known with certainty; thus, there are no back orders or stockouts

● There is no interaction with other products

The "sawtooth effect" relating Q and R in Exhibit 15.2 shows that when inventory drops to point R, an order is placed. This order is received at the end of the lead time period L, which, as stated above, remains constant.

In constructing any inventory model, the first step is to develop a functional relationship between the variables of interest and the measure of effectiveness. In this case, since we are concerned with cost, the following equation would pertain:

$$\begin{matrix} \text{Total} \\ \text{annual cost} \end{matrix} = \begin{matrix} \text{Annual} \\ \text{purchase cost} \end{matrix} + \begin{matrix} \text{Annual} \\ \text{order preparation cost} \end{matrix} + \begin{matrix} \text{Annual} \\ \text{holding cost} \end{matrix}$$

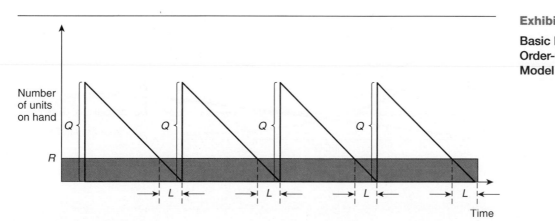

Exhibit 15.2

Basic Fixed-Order-Quantity Model

or

$$TC = DC + \frac{D}{Q}S + \frac{Q}{2}H \qquad (15.1)$$

where

TC = Total annual cost

D = Annual demand in units

C = Cost per unit

Q = Quantity to be ordered (the optimum amount is termed the **economic order quantity—EOQ)**

economic order quantity (EOQ)

Optimal quantity to order, taking into consideration both the cost to carry inventory and the cost to order the item.

S = Setup or order preparation cost (per setup or order)

H = Annual holding cost per unit
(*Note:* The holding cost often is defined as an annual percentage of the cost of the item. In these instances, $H = iC$, where i is the annual percentage carrying cost.)

On the right side of the equation, DC is the annual purchase cost for the units, *(D/Q)S* is the annual order preparation cost (which is the actual number of orders placed, D/Q, times the cost of each order, S), and $(Q/2)H$ is the annual holding cost (which is the average inventory, $Q/2$, times the cost per unit for holding and storage, H). These cost relationships are shown graphically in Exhibit 15.3.

The next step is to find that order quantity, Q, for which total cost is a minimum. In Exhibit 15.3, the total cost is at minimum at the point where the slope of the total cost curve is zero. Using calculus, the appropriate procedure involves taking the first derivative of total cost with respect to Q (which is the slope) and setting this equal to zero. For the basic model considered here, the calculations to obtain the economic order quantity (EOQ) would be as follows:

$$TC = DC + \frac{D}{Q}S + \frac{Q}{2}H$$

$$\text{First derivative} = \frac{dTC}{dQ} = 0 + \left(\frac{-DS}{Q^2}\right) + \frac{H}{2} = 0$$

Solving for Q gives us the economic order quantity, or EOQ,

$$EOQ = \sqrt{\frac{2DS}{H}} \qquad (15.2)$$

Exhibit 15.3

Annual Product Costs, Based on Size of the Order

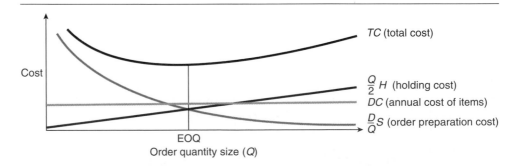

Because this simple model assumes both constant demand and lead time, no safety stock is necessary, and the **reorder point (ROP)**, R, is simply

$$R = \bar{d}\bar{L} \qquad (15.3)$$

where

R = Reorder point

$\bar{d}$ = Average demand per time period [constant in this model]

$\bar{L}$ = Average number of time periods between placing an order and its delivery [constant in this model]

reorder point (ROP)

The inventory level in units that, when reached, triggers a new order for the item.

Example

Find the economic order quantity and the reorder point, given the following data:

Annual demand $(D) = 1000$ units

Order preparation cost $(S) = \$5.00$ per order

Holding cost $(H) = \$1.25$ per unit per year

Cost per unit $(C) = \$12.50$

Lead time $(\bar{L}) = 5$ days (constant)

Daily demand $(\bar{d}) = 1000/365$ (constant)

What quantity should be ordered, and when?

Solution

The optimal order quantity is

$$EOQ = \sqrt{\frac{2DS}{H}} = \sqrt{\frac{2(1000)5}{1.25}} = \sqrt{8000} = 89.4 \text{ units}$$

The reorder point is

$$R = \bar{d}\bar{L} = \frac{1000}{365}(5) = 13.7 \text{ units}$$

Rounding to the nearest unit, the inventory policy is as follows: When the number of units in inventory drops to 14, place an order for 89 more units.

The total annual cost will be

$$TC = DC + \frac{D}{Q}S + \frac{Q}{2}H$$

$$= 1000(12.50) + \frac{1000}{89}(5) + \frac{89}{2}(1.25)$$

$$= \$12611.81$$

Note that in this example, the annual purchase cost of the units was not required to determine the order quantity and the reorder point. Also note that in Exhibit 15.3, the total cost curve is relatively flat around the EOQ, which is the norm, indicating that only minor increases in total cost will occur on either side of the EOQ. Thus, in the above example, we might order 90 units about once a month for the sake of simplicity and convenience without fear of incurring excessive costs.

Fixed-Order-Quantity Model with Usage

fixed-order-quantity model with usage

Considers a supplier that will provide an order quantity over a period of time rather than all at once.

The basic fixed-order-quantity model assumes that the quantity ordered is received in one lot, but frequently this is not the case. In many situations, the production of an inventory item and the usage of that item take place simultaneously (which is referred to as a **fixed-order-quantity model with usage**). This is particularly true when one part of a production system acts as a supplier to another part. For example, while aluminum extrusions are being made to fill an order for aluminum windows, the extrusions are cut and the windows assembled before the entire extrusion order is completed. Also, companies are beginning to enter into longer-term arrangements with vendors. Under such contracts, a single order or *blanket* contract may cover product or material requirements over a six-month or one-year period with the vendor making deliveries weekly or even more frequently. Often with blanket contracts, the amount to be delivered each time period will be determined at a future date. This model differs from our previous discussion of batch sizes because it includes a continual usage rate d. If we let d denote a constant demand rate (or usage rate) for an item in production and p is the production rate of the process that produces the item, we may develop the following total cost equation (obviously, the production rate must exceed the demand or usage rate; otherwise Q would be infinite, resulting in continual production):

$$TC = DC + (D/Q)S + (Q/2)H$$

However, with this model, as seen in Exhibit 15.4, Q is not the maximum inventory on hand, because we are consuming the product as it is being delivered over time. Thus, the above equation is rewritten as follows:

$$TC = DC + (D/Q)S + (I_{max}/2)H \tag{15.4}$$

and

$$I_{max} = (p - d)(Q/p) \tag{15.5}$$

where $(p - d)$ is the amount of inventory that accumulates each time period and (Q/p) is the number of time periods required to fill the order. Substituting, we have

$$TC = DC + \frac{D}{Q}S + \frac{(p-d)QH}{2p}$$

Again differentiating with respect to Q and setting the equation equal to zero, we obtain

$$EOQ = \sqrt{\frac{2DS}{H} \cdot \frac{p}{(p-d)}} \tag{15.6}$$

This model is shown in Exhibit 15.4. We can see that the maximum number of units on hand is always less than the order quantity, Q. Note in Equation 15.6, that as p becomes very large, the right-hand term $(p/(p - d))$ approaches one and we have our original EOQ formula.

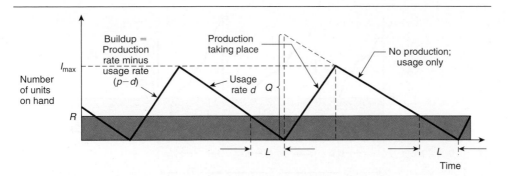

Exhibit 15.4

Fixed-Order-Quantity Model with Usage during Production Time

Example

Product X is a standard item in a firm's inventory. Final assembly of the product is performed on an assembly line that is in operation every weekday. One of the components of product X (call it component X_1) is produced in another department. This department, when it produces X_1, does so at the rate of 100 units per day. The assembly line uses component X_1 at the rate of 40 units per day.

Given the following data, what is the optimal production lot size of component X_1? What is the reorder point?

$$\text{Daily usage rate } (\bar{d}) = 40 \text{ units per day (constant)}$$
$$\text{Annual demand } (D) = 10\ 000\ (40 \text{ units per day} \times 250 \text{ working days})$$
$$\text{Daily production } (p) = 100 \text{ units per day}$$
$$\text{Cost of production setup } (S) = \$50$$
$$\text{Annual holding cost } (H) = \$0.50 \text{ per unit per year}$$
$$\text{Cost of component } X_1\ (C) = \$7 \text{ each}$$
$$\text{Lead time } (\bar{L}) = 7 \text{ days (constant)}$$

Solution

The optimal order quantity and the reorder point for component X_1 arc calculated as follows:

$$\text{EOQ} = \sqrt{\frac{2DS}{H} \cdot \frac{p}{p-d}} = \sqrt{\frac{2(10\ 000)50}{0.50} \cdot \frac{100}{100-40}} = 1826 \text{ units}$$

$$R = \bar{d}\bar{L} = 40(7) = 280 \text{ units}$$

This states that an order for 1826 units of component X_1 should be placed when the level of inventory of X_1 stock drops to 280 units.

At 100 units per day, this run would take 18.26 days to complete and provide a 45.65-day supply for the assembly line (1826/40). Theoretically, the producing department would be occupied with other work during the 27.39 days when component X_1 is not being produced.

Incorporating Demand Uncertainty in Fixed-Order-Quantity Models

Recall that in the fixed-order-quantity models discussed thus far, the inventory is adjusted every time a sale or withdrawal is made, and when the ROP, R, is reached an order for a

Exhibit 15.5

Fixed-Order-Quantity Model With Uncertain Demand

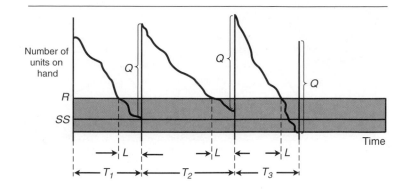

fixed quantity, Q, is placed. However, in practice, the demand is not known with certainty (hence our use of the general term $\bar{d}$ for daily demand). As a result, the demand line will not be straight, as in Exhibits 15.2 or 15.4, but be crooked as in Exhibit 15.5. Thus, exactly when (on the time axis in Exhibit 15.5) a new order will be placed is not known. For example, because sales were slower in the second time interval (T_2), the reorder point was reached later than during T_1; i.e., $T_2 > T_1$. Note that, regardless of the inventory level, when an order is placed it will be for a fixed quantity, Q. Although in Figure 15.5 the lead time L is shown as constant, it too can vary, hence our use of the general term $\bar{L}$ for length of the lead time.

safety stock (SS)

Additional inventory carried in excess of expected demand to prevent stockouts.

Companies thus add some **safety stock (SS)** to account for this uncertainty. For example, note that in time interval T_3, the sales level was higher than normal. As a result, some of the safety stock had to be used to satisfy demand. In fact, had there been no safety stock, a shortage would have occurred. As seen in Exhibit 15.5, R is higher than in the case in which there is no uncertainty (Exhibit 5.2) because it has to incorporate not only the expected or average demand during lead time ($\bar{d}\bar{L}$), but also the safety stock. (Safety stock will discussed in more detail later.) Therefore, under uncertainty, the basic fixed-order-quantity model can be described as an "order quantity remains fixed, but the time interval (between orders) varies" model.

Fixed-Time-Period Model

When demand and/or lead time is uncertain, an alternative model to the basic fixed-order-quantity model is the fixed-time-period model in which inventory is counted and produced at fixed intervals, such as every week or every month. Counting inventory and placing orders on a periodic basis are desirable for situations in which vendors make routine visits to customers (such as when snack distributors make daily visits to corner grocery stores or to snack machines on your college campus) and take orders for their complete line of products, or when buyers want to combine orders to save on transportation costs. Other firms operate on a fixed time period to facilitate planning their inventory count; for example, Distributor X calls every two weeks, and employees therefore know that all of Distributor X's products must be counted at that time.

With a fixed-time-period model, there is usually a ceiling or *par* inventory that is established for each item. As seen in Exhibit 15.6, where a fixed-time-period model under demand uncertainty is shown, the difference between the par value and the quantity on hand when the count is taken is the amount ordered, which will vary from period to period, depending on the actual usage (e.g., Q_1, Q_2, and Q_3 in Exhibit 15.6). Here, negative inventory, as seen in the third cycle in Exhibit 15.6, is treated as a back order, which must be filled (even with safety stock backorders can occur, though, hopefully, rarely). Thus, in

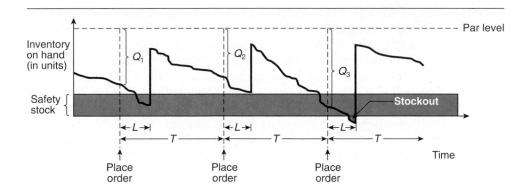

Exhibit 15.6

Fixed-Time-Period Inventory Model with Uncertain Demand

this model the time interval between orders remains fixed, but the quantity ordered varies, as compared to the fixed-order-quantity model, in which just the reverse is true: the order quantity remains fixed, but the time interval varies.

Thumbs Up Foods Inc. of Calgary, a small manufacturer of packaged Indian food, follows a fixed-time-period production model, in which an item such as a samosa would be made only once a week. Orders have to be placed by the day before the samosas are made (although extra quantities are made to cater to drop-in customers). One reason Thumbs Up follows the fixed-time-period model is that they don't have the physical space to setup a separate line for each product they manufacture (where it is easy to start production if the reorder point is reached). Thus they use the same line with different fixtures. Changing fixtures entails a significant setup activity, which makes it difficult to respond when a reorder point is reached randomly (as is usually the case in practice in a fixed-order-quantity model).

From the planning perspective of both their customers and themselves, it is better for Thumbs Up to use the fixed-time-period model. Customers know that orders have to be placed on a fixed day of the week; Thumbs Up can plan ahead knowing that they make certain items only on certain days. The disadvantage of the fixed-time-period model is that, because the inventory is replenished only after a fixed time interval, there is a greater chance of running out of stock than with a fixed-order-quantity model. For example, if Thumbs Up runs out of samosas midweek, customers might have to wait for the next run of samosas to be done at the end of the week. If they had used the fixed-order-quantity model, they would have started a new batch of samosas as soon as the reorder point was reached before midweek, thus preventing a stockout.

Quantity-Discount Model

The **quantity-discount model** takes into consideration the fact that the purchase cost of an item can vary with the order size. There are two types of quantity discounts: those given on an incremental basis and those given for all units. With the incremental approach, the quantity discount only applies to those units above a certain level. For example, the cost of a product is $65.00 per unit for quantities between 1 and 100 and $60.00 per unit for quantities over 100 units. We determine that we want to buy this product in quantities of 250 units at a time. With the incremental approach, we would pay $65.00 for the first 100 units and $60.00 for the remaining 150 units. With the all-units approach, which is presented here in detail, we would pay $60.00 apiece for all 250 units. Thus, the unit cost is determined by the size of the purchase order.

To determine the optimal quantity to order with this model, we first calculate the EOQ for each unit cost. (*Note:* If using H as a holding cost instead of i, then H will vary along with C.) If the resulting EOQs are all feasible, that is, the EOQs fall within their respective

quantity-discount model

Addresses price discounts associated with minimum order quantities.

quantity ranges, then we select the EOQ that is associated with the lowest unit cost. However, as is more often the case, some of the EOQs may not be feasible (i.e., the quantity does not fall within the feasible unit-cost range). In these situations, we first calculate the total cost for each unit cost at the EOQ or EOQs where it is feasible. Where it is not feasible, we calculate the total cost at the minimum quantity where the respective unit cost is first applicable. These total costs are then compared and the quantity or EOQ associated with the lowest total cost is the order quantity that is selected.

Procedurally, the largest order quantity (lowest unit price) is solved first; if the resulting Q is valid or feasible, that is the answer. If not, the next largest order quantity (second lowest price) is derived. If that is feasible, the total cost of this Q is compared to the total cost of using the order quantity at the price break above, and the lowest total cost determines the optimal Q.

Example

Consider the following case, where

> D = 10 000 units (annual demand)
>
> S = \$20 to place each order
>
> i = 20 percent of cost (annual carrying costs, storage, interest, obsolescence, etc.)
>
> C = Cost per unit:

Order Size (units)	Cost per Unit
0–499	C_1 = \$5.00
500–999	C_2 = 4.50
1000 and over	C_3 = 3.90

What quantity should be ordered?

Solution

The appropriate equations from the basic fixed-quantity model are:

$$TC = DC + \frac{D}{Q}S + \frac{Q}{2}H$$

and

$$Q = \sqrt{\frac{2DS}{iC}}$$

Solving for the economic order size at each price, we obtain the following:

Range	Unit Cost	EOQ	Feasible
0–499	\$5.00	632	No
500–999	4.50	667	Yes
Over 1000	3.90	716	No

These results are shown in Exhibit 15.7, which depicts the relationship between the total cost and the order quantity for each of the unit costs. Using the procedure described above, we now calculate the total cost for 666 units at \$4.50 per unit and 1000 units at \$3.90 per unit. These calculations are shown in Exhibit 15.8. Comparing these two total costs, we conclude that the economic order quantity is 1000 units.

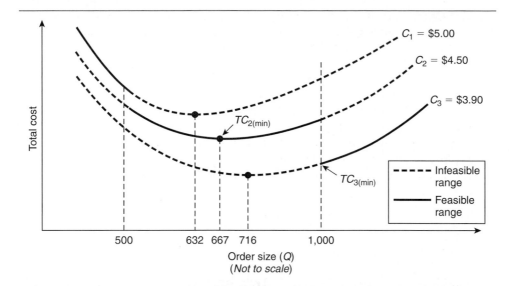

Exhibit 15.7

Total Cost Curves for a Quantity-Discount Model

Exhibit 15.8

Total Cost Calculations in a Quantity-Discount Model

	Q = 667 where C = $4.50	**Price Break 1000**
Holding cost $\left(\dfrac{Q}{2}iC\right)$	$\dfrac{667}{2}(0.20)4.50 = \$300$	$\dfrac{1000}{2}(0.20)3.90 = \$390$
Ordering cost $\left(\dfrac{D}{Q}S\right)$	$\dfrac{10\,000(20)}{667} = \$300$	$\dfrac{10\,000(20)}{1000} = \$200$
Holding and ordering cost	$600	$590
Purchase cost (DC)	10 000(4.50)	10 000(3.90)
Total cost	$TC_{2(min)} = \$45\,600$	$TC_{3(min)} = \$39\,590$

One practical consideration in quantity-discount problems is that the cost reduction from volume purchases frequently makes it seemingly economical to order amounts larger than the EOQ. Thus, when applying the model we must be particularly careful to obtain a valid estimate of product obsolescence and warehousing costs.

In-Transit Inventory Model

The stretching of the supply chain to all corners of the globe has caused managers to take a closer look at the various costs associated with the delivery of products. These costs are often referred to as **in-transit inventory costs** and are usually associated with delivery of raw material and components that are inbound to the plant. The reason for this is that most products are sold FOB at the vendor's plant. (FOB stands for free-on-board, which is the point at which ownership and title to the goods are transferred from the supplier to the customer.)

When deciding which is the most economical mode of transportation to use, a manager needs to take into consideration two cost elements: the actual costs of transportation and the in-transit inventory carrying costs of product while in transit. These carrying costs consist primarily of the cost of the capital tied up when items are purchased at the vendor's plant, but are not available for use until they arrive at the firm's plant. Typically, the slower the mode of transportation, the lower the

in-transit inventory costs

Combination of transportation costs and carrying costs associated with delivery of products.

Exhibit 15.9

The Trade-Off between Transportation Costs and the Cost of Capital with Respect to the Shipment of Products

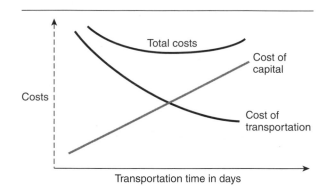

transportation costs, the longer the shipment time, and thus the higher the in-transit carrying cost. The trade-off between these two costs is shown in Exhibit 15.9.

Total costs = Transportation costs + In-transit inventory carrying costs + Purchase costs

$$TC \quad = \quad DM \quad + \quad \left(\frac{X}{365}\right)iDC \quad + DC \qquad (15.7)$$

where

D = Annual demand

M = Transportation cost per unit

X = Transportation time in days

i = Annual cost of capital

C = Unit cost per item

Example

A company located in Hartford, Connecticut, has agreed to purchase an item from a manufacturer in Vancouver, British Columbia. The purchasing agent in Hartford has identified two alternative methods for shipping the item: truck or cargo ship (via the Panama Canal).

A summary of the relevant costs for each mode of transportation is as follows:

		Mode 1 (truck)	Mode 2 (ship)
	Number of days in-transit (X):	14	45
	Transportation cost per unit (M):	$3.00	$1.50
Additional data:	In-transit carrying cost (i):	20% per annum	
	Annual demand (D):	2000 units	
	Unit cost (C):	$150.00	

Which mode of transportation should the purchasing agent select?

Solution

$TC_1 = DM_1 + (X_1/365)iDC \neq TC_1 = (2000)(3.00) + (14/365)(0.20)(2000)(150)$

$TC_1 = 6000 + 2301.37 \neq \$8301.37$

$TC_2 = (2000)(1.50) + (45/365)(0.20)(2000)(150)$

$TC_2 = 3000 + 7397.26 \neq \$10\ 397.26$

Based on this analysis, the more economical mode of transportation is by truck, even though the actual transportation cost per unit is twice that of sending the items by ship. Note that when evaluating alternative modes of transportation from the same vendor, the purchase cost remains the same and, for simplicity, is not included in the analysis.

Inventories and Service Levels

We have already briefly discussed the issue of demand uncertainty in both the fixed-order-quantity and fixed-time-period-models. In these situations it is necessary to build in a safety stock that takes into consideration the variation in demand and lead time (thus far we have not discussed lead time uncertainty). This safety stock is in addition to the average demand that is forecasted during the lead time.

The amount of safety stock (SS) that a firm should have for any given item is dependent on three factors: (1) the variation in demand, (2) the variability in the lead time required to replenish the item, and (3) the desired level of service that the company wants to provide its customers. Here, service level refers to the probability that all customer orders placed during the lead time will be filled from inventory and that customers will not have to wait because of a stockout. (Recall from Exhibit (15.5 that in a fixed-order-quantity model, the lead time starts when the inventory level falls to R and the company places a replenishment order with its supplier. The lead time ends when the order is received. It is during this time that the company is subject to stockouts due to customer demand.) Thus, a 95 percent service level can be interpreted as a 95 percent probability that all customer orders placed during the lead time will be filled from on-hand inventory.

Exhibit 15.10 illustrates the concept of safety stock in the fixed-order-quantity model with various distributions of demand and/or lead times. R corresponds to the required reorder point (ROP) for a certain service level. For example, assume that R is the ROP for a desired service level of 95 percent. This implies that 95 percent of total demand during the lead time will be less than R, leaving only a 5 percent (the tail) probability that demand during lead time will be greater than R resulting in a stockout. Naturally, if the desired service level is increased to 99 percent, the value of R will have to increase to R_1 to ensure that 99 percent of all demand

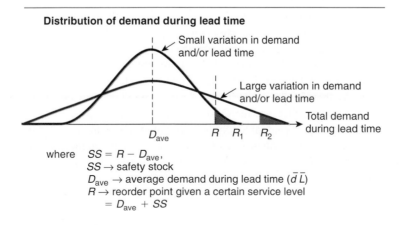

Exhibit 15.10

The Impact of Variation and Service Level on the Amount of Safety Stock (SS) Required

In this chapter we have discussed inventory models based primarily on the EOQ model. Historically, EOQ-based models have been popular because of their simplicity and because they give good approximations even when some of the assumptions are violated to some extent. However, most practitioners would caution against using the EOQ or any other model blindly (which is what companies have often done, to the detriment of their costs and customer service).

There are many inventory models for managers to choose from. It is important to choose the inventory model that fits the situation of the item or items under consideration. Sometimes a simple modification to the EOQ can produce good results, as was the case with a Big 3 automaker and its service parts supply chain in the U.S. Furthermore, with improvements in computing power in recent years, many supply chain management and ERP software programs incorporate sophisticated methods for determining optimal order quantities in today's complex and fast-changing operational environment. These methods may be very different from EOQ-type models. Computer simulation is another method used for determining order quantities. 3M is a company that has started institutionalizing the use of sophisticated inventory modelling and computer simulation to improve its inventory management across its diverse product lines. So far it has saved millions of dollars without compromising customer service levels.

Sources:
Dan Strike, "Reducing Inventory through Safety Stock and Lot-Size Optimization," 2003 *APICS International Conference Proceedings,* F10, pp. 1–9.
Alan R. Cannon and Richard E. Crandall, "The Way Things Never Were," *APICS—The Performance Advantage,* January 2004, pp. 32–36.
Chuck LaMacchia, "A New Take," *APICS—The Performance Advantage,* January 2003, pp. 20–23.

during lead time is less than or equal to the stock on hand. The amount of the required SS also will increase correspondingly since $SS = R_1 - D_{ave}$ and D_{ave} has not changed.

Similarly, if the variation in demand and/or lead time increases, the variance in the distribution of demand during lead time will also increase (as shown in Exhibit 15.10), leading to a corresponding decrease in service level (given the original ROP, R), since the tail is now larger. So the value of R will have to increase to R_2 to maintain the same service level.

In a fixed-time-period model, in addition to the three factors (demand variability, variability in lead time, and service level), the length of the interval is also a factor. So, if a firm such as Thumbs Up made samosas only once weekly, it would have to carry more safety stock than if it made samosas daily. An example of the calculation of safety stock is illustrated in the section on safety stock in the single period model.

Economic Order Quantity Models in Relation to the Real World

Criticizing classical inventory models is currently fashionable with some members of industry and consulting groups. Proportionately, there is much less open criticism from academia. In a manufacturing environment, the major weaknesses associated with the classical EOQ models focus on the numbers. These numbers are the values assigned to setup costs, holding costs, and demands used in the equations. These costs are often very difficult to measure and, therefore, are error prone. Also, demand is rarely constant, but instead is usually a fluctuating number (see the OMP box on lot sizing in practice).

Elliott Weiss states the problem nicely by explaining that many users of the equations focus on optimizing a set of numbers that often are taken as a given fact.[1] Rather, he states, we should be managing lot sizing and inventory control. The current moves toward reduced inventory costs and quantities, such as just-in-time systems, stress the importance of reducing lot sizes. The means of reducing lot sizes is to reduce setup time and cost.

---

[1]Elliot N. Weiss, "Lot Sizing Is Dead: Long Live Lot Sizing," *Production and Inventory Management Journal* (First Quarter 1990), pp. 76–78.

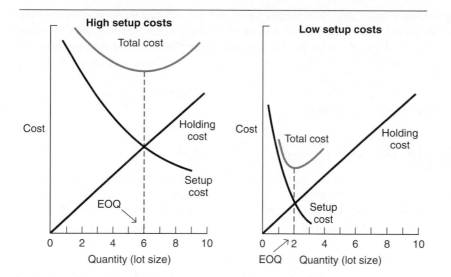

Exhibit 15.11

The Impact of
Lower Setup
Costs

Effect of Reduced Setup Costs on Lot Sizes

In Chapter 13 we emphasized that JIT focuses on reducing setup times in order to reduce lot sizes (order quantities). In that chapter we discussed JIT conceptually; here we discuss it using a quantitative example (since you are now familiar with the EOQ). In the problem we solved under the basic fixed-order-order-quantity model, with an order (setup) cost of $5, we arrived at an EOQ of 89.4 units and a total annual cost of $12 611.81. If we ignore the purchase cost of the items, the total of the inventory carrying (holding) and order preparation costs is $111.81.

Suppose the company and its supplier set up an electronic ordering system that reduces the order preparation cost to $1. The updated EOQ and the total annual cost are as follows:

$$\text{Updated EOQ} = \sqrt{\frac{2(1000)1}{1.25}} = \sqrt{1600} = 40 \text{ units}$$

Updated total annual cost (TC) =

$$DC + \frac{D}{Q}S + \frac{Q}{2}H = 1000(12.5) + \frac{1000}{40}(1) + \frac{40}{2}(1.25) = \$12\,550.00$$

Actually, if we ignore the purchase cost of the items, the total of the inventory carrying and order preparation costs is $50. So, by reducing the ordering (setup) cost per order by 80% we have decreased both the EOQ (optimal lot size) and annual carrying and ordering costs (individually and in total) by over 50%. The general relationship between setup costs and other costs (carrying costs, ordering costs, and total annual costs) and between setup costs and the EOQ is shown in Exhibit 15.11.

For a firm with thousands of items in its inventory, reducing setup costs by using electronic ordering with its suppliers (or simplifying the process in other ways discussed under JIT) and making machine changeovers easier can yield significant inventory costs savings, in addition to the customer service benefits discussed under JIT. As a result, many companies are putting a lot of effort into reducing setup cost.

Perishable Inventory

Although all inventories are subject to obsolescence, some products are considered highly perishable because they are only viable for a very short time period. After that period has elapsed, their value decreases significantly, and the reduced value is often only their salvage or scrap value. Examples of such products include newspapers and Christmas trees. In each case, the value of the product drops dramatically from one time period to the next. (In the case of newspapers, the time period is a day; in the case of Christmas trees, it is the month or so before Christmas.) The determination of the proper or "optimum" inventory level to establish for this group of products is often referred to as the **single-period inventory (newsboy) model.**

single-period inventory (newsboy) model
Addresses items that are highly perishable from one period to the next.

Single-Period Inventory Model

Certain characteristics are associated with products that fall into the single-period inventory model. These include (*a*) the product is only viable for sale during a single time period; (*b*) the demand for the product is highly variable, but follows a known probability distribution; and (*c*) the scrap value of the product or the value of the product after the time period has elapsed is less than the initial cost of the product. This model is also called the newsboy model.

The goal in determining the proper level of inventory for these products is to balance the gross profit generated by the sale of each unit with the cost incurred for each unit that is unsold after the time period has elapsed. Since the demand in these problems follows a probability distribution, we want to pick that level of inventory that maximizes our expected profit. When the probability distribution is discrete, we can solve the problem using an expected value matrix.

Example

Dick Moore sells Christmas trees, which he grows on his farm in northern Ontario. Because bad weather and heavy snow are common in the month of December, Dick always harvests by December 1 the trees he intends to sell in a given year. Dick has been selling trees for many years and has kept detailed records of sales in previous years. From these data, he has determined that the probability of selling various quantities of trees in a given year is as follows:

Demand (trees)	Probability
500	0.15
550	0.20
600	0.25
650	0.30
700	0.10

For the coming year, Dick will sell his trees for an average price of $25 each. His cost to grow and cut each tree is estimated to be $10. Any unsold trees at the end of the season can be sold for kindling wood at a price of $5 apiece. What is the optimal number of trees that Dick should harvest?

Solution

Using the above information, we develop the following payoff table to determine the net profit that will be generated for every combination of trees that are cut and customer demand (*Note:* Profit, as defined here, also takes into account the opportunity cost associated with lost sales, which is not a strict definition of profit by accounting standards):

Probability	0.15	0.20	0.25	0.30	0.10	
Customer Demand	500	550	600	650	700	
Number of Trees Cut						**Expected Profit**
500	7500	6750	6000	5250	4500	$6000
550	7250	8250	7500	6750	6000	7238
600	7000	8000	9000	8250	7500	8125
650	6750	7750	8750	9750	9000	8575
700	6500	7500	8500	9500	10500	8500

The values in the payoff table can be divided into three groups. In the first group, the number of trees cut exactly equals demand. The profit generated when this happens is

$$\text{Profit} = D(SP - C)$$

where

D = Demand

SP = Selling price per tree

C = Cost per tree

Thus, if we have a demand for 550 trees and we cut 550 trees, then the profit generated is

$$\text{Profit} = 550(25 - 10) = 550(15) = \$8250$$

The second group consists of those combinations where demand exceeds the number of trees cut. Here we have to take into consideration the opportunity cost associated with the lost revenues resulting from unsatisfied demand. The profit generated in these cases is as follows:

$$\text{Profit} = Q(SP - C) - (D - Q)(SP - C)$$

where

Q = Number of trees cut down

If we have a demand for 650 trees and we have harvested only 500 trees, then the resulting profit is

$$\text{Profit} = 500(25 - 10) - (650 - 500)(25 - 10)$$
$$= 500(15) - 150(15)$$
$$= 7500 - 2250 = \$5250$$

The third case occurs when the quantity of trees we have harvested exceeds the demand. Here we have to sell off the excessive inventory at a loss. The net profit calculated is as follows:

$$\text{Profit} = D(SP - C) - (Q - D)(C - SV)$$

where

SV = scrap value

If we harvested 700 trees and demand is only for 550 trees, then the profit generated is

$$\text{Profit} = 550(25 - 10) - (700 - 550)(10 - 5)$$
$$= 550(15) - (150)(5)$$
$$= 8250 - 750 = \$7500$$

After we have determined all of the values in the payoff table, we next calculate the expected profit associated with each of the quantities of trees we decide to harvest. This is done by multiplying the probability of each demand occurring by the profit generated by that demand. For example, if we decide to harvest 600 trees, the expected profit is:

$$\text{Expected profit (600)} = (0.15)(7000) + (0.20)(8000) + (0.25)(9000)$$
$$+ (0.30)(8250) + (0.10)(7500)$$
$$\text{EP(600)} = 1050 + 1600 + 2250 + 2475 + 750$$
$$\text{EP(600)} = \$8125$$

Finally, we select that quantity of trees to harvest that yields the maximum expected profit. In this case, Dick Moore should harvest 650 trees, because the expected profit from that decision is $8575, as shown in the table above.

Safety Stock in the Single-Period Inventory Model

In the Christmas tree example, the optimal stocking level was 650 trees. What service level does this provide and what is the implied safety stock (SS)? To determine these levels Dick has to determine the cumulative probability of tree demand as shown in Exhibit 15.12. The cumulative probability of a demand level is the probability that demand will be equal to or less than that level. For example, the cumulative probability of demand being less than or equal to 650 trees is 0.9, which is the sum of the probabilities of demands of 650, 600, 550, and 500 trees. This implies that the service level if Dick stocked 650 units would be 0.9 or 90 percent because 90 percent of the customers would expect to get a tree from his inventory. Only 10 percent would have to return without a tree.

What would be the SS in this case? Similar to the logic used in Exhibit 15.10, SS = *planned stocking level* − D_{ave}, where *planned stocking level* = 650 (note that the only variation of concern is in demand, because Dick plans to place only one order during the Christmas season. Thus lead time is not relevant here). D_{ave} is the average or expected demand which is given by $[(500 \times 0.15) + (550 \times 0.20) + (600 \times 0.25) + (650 \times 0.30) + (700 \times 0.10)] = 600$ trees. Thus the implied SS is 650 − 600 = 50 trees.

Now assume that for customer service reasons, Dick wishes to have a 95 percent service level, regardless of profit. What would be his optimal stock level and implied SS? From Exhibit 15.12, we see that Dick would increase his stocking level to 700 trees (in fact he would actually have a 100 percent service level) to achieve the 95 percent service level. The implied SS would increase to (700 − 600) or 100 trees.

Inventory Management in Services

In service operations, the "product" sold is considered highly perishable. As discussed in previous chapters, hotel rooms that are unoccupied for one night cannot be saved for

Exhibit 15.12

Cumulative Probability for Christmas Tree Problem

Demand	Probability	Cumulative Probability
500	0.15	0.15
550	0.2	0.35
600	0.25	0.6
650	0.3	0.9
700	0.1	1.0

INVENTORIES FALL IN CANADA

The latest available study by the Bank of Canada on inventory management at a macro level reveals inventory levels in Canada in most business sectors have been decreasing due to better management practices and information technology (one exception is the department store sector). The table below gives the decreases or increases by sector in the stock-to-sales ratio. This ratio is defined as the number of months of current dollar sales held in inventory. For example, if a firm has a $100 000 in sales every month and the average inventory level is $150 000, the stock-to-sales ration is 1.5. The lower this ratio, the lower the amount of inventory carried.

Sector	Improvement in percentage in the stock-to-sales ratio between 1981 and 1995
Manufacturing	30 percent
Wholesale*	15 percent
Department store	(40 percent)

*Wholesale includes general wholesale distributors, export merchants, import merchants, and mail order wholesalers. Their functions include breaking bulk, delivery service to customers, and assembly of primary products from farmers, fishermen, loggers, and trappers.

Why have the manufacturing and the wholesale sectors been able to reduce inventories while department stores have increased their inventories? Here are some of the reasons.

The Manufacturing Sector
Powered by the automobile sector, inventories were reduced as a result of JIT practices, information technology such as ERP, bar coding, electronic data interchange (EDI), and innovative product design such as modularization.

The Wholesale Trade Sector
The improvement here is a reflection of the widespread adoption of information processing technology in inventory management to reduce the amount of capital tied up in inventory. The use of bar codes that speed up and reduce errors in tracking inventories is an example. There is also the widespread use of EDI and other modes of business-to-business (B2B) electronic communication in orders, shipping, billing, and other inventory requests. The accuracy of these communications reduces inventory in the supply chain. ERPs are also becoming popular in reducing inventory to an appropriate level. Companies such as Canadian Tire and Wal-Mart are using logistics practices such as cross-docking to reduce transportation time and inventories. For example, through the use of the techniques mentioned above, Canadian Tire has reduced inventory at its warehouses by $50 million, while increasing the stock turns and inventory accuracy.

Department Store Sector
The surprising contrary trend in increased inventory in the department store sector is seen in spite of information technology improvements. For example, scanners that read bar codes give instant information on pricing, inventory, and sales history. Other market response systems keep track of what shoppers buy. ERP, EDI, VMI, and other innovations then help retailers communicate rapidly with suppliers or distribution centres, enabling retailers to restock popular items rapidly and eliminate oversupplies of less popular items. Thus they have also been managing their inventory better.

However, increased competition and the proliferation of products have resulted in retailers carrying more inventory to ensure that stockouts, which force customers to go elsewhere, do not occur. For example, the arrival of "big box" stores such as Toys "Я" Us, Home Depot, and Costco has increased competition and contributed to the proliferation of products (the tendency of manufacturers to design different products to cater to different customers). However, the data from 1994 and 1995 indicate that technological innovations may have begun to reduce retail inventory.

Sources:
Hung-Hay Lau, "The Role of Inventory Management in Canadian Economic Fluctuations," *Bank of Canada Review* (Spring 1996), pp. 31–44.
David Maloney, "Canadian Tire Rolls Out New DC," *Modern Materials Handling* (October 2002), pp. 15–21.

---

another night. Similarly, airline seats on a plane that are not used on a given date cannot be saved for use at a future time. Because the product sold in service operations is so perishable, the approach to managing the sale of the product is similar to that for the single-period inventory problem.

Yield Management or Revenue Management

As discussed in Chapter 14, a service should have certain characteristics to take full advantage of yield management, including a cost structure that consists of high fixed and low variable costs. Examples of such services, mentioned earlier, include airlines, hotels, and car rental companies. For these types of services, profits are directly related to sales because variable costs, as a percentage of sales, are very low. Consequently, the goal for these firms is to maximize sales or revenues by maximizing capacity utilization, even if it means selling some of the available capacity at reduced prices—as long as these prices are greater than the variable cost. For example, if the variable cost to clean and restock a hotel room with towels, soap, shampoo, and so forth is $25, then any room rate greater than $25 will contribute to profit. Thus, it would be better to let a hotel guest have the room for $50 for a night than to let the room remain empty, even if the regular or "rack" rate is $135 per night.

The challenge for managers of these types of services is to determine what percentage of available capacity to allocate to different prices. On the one hand, substantial amounts of capacity can usually be sold in advance at rates that are significantly discounted. For example, airlines usually require a 21-day advance purchase for their super-saver fares, which offer the lowest prices; similarly, organizations holding conferences usually reserve hotel rooms years in advance of their meeting, again at substantially reduced rates.

At the same time, however, the service manager does not want to turn away a last-minute customer (who usually pays the full rate) because the capacity has been previously sold at a discounted rate. When this happens, opportunity costs are incurred. The methodology for determining the percentage of capacity to allocate to each market segment or price is referred to as yield management or revenue management. By using yield management, the service manager is simultaneously managing both the supply and demand for the firm's capacity. Demand is controlled by the different price structures: Lower prices increase demand; higher prices decrease demand. Supply is controlled by limiting the capacity available at each of the different price structures.

Yield management principles can be used to manage the pricing of perishable or seasonal goods; they are similar to services in that they lose their value within a short period of time. For example, a retailer carrying a particular style of winter sweaters may use yield management software to periodically reset prices or markdowns on the sweaters so that the total profits by the end of the selling season are maximized.

As an illustration of how a service firm will use pricing to manage demand, consider the following example. A search on travelocity.ca on December 20, 2005, for travel on December 21, 2005, and returning on December 23, 2005, from Vancouver, British Columbia, to Miami, Florida, yielded the cheapest fare of $928.39. By paying this high fare the passenger is able to leave soon and return in two days with a choice of three outgoing flights. A cheaper fare of $508.20 was available, but with many restrictions. The passenger could not leave before December 24, 2005. The only flight available was at 10.20 p.m. on Christmas Eve! If the passenger did leave on December 24, she would have to return on December 25 or on December 29 or later to avail herself of the cheap fare. It is important to note that although the level of service is significantly different for first class and business class passengers, the passengers receive the same level of service for all other fares. (In addition to the fares listed, there are special fares from time to time when demand is lower than forecasted.)

Example

Jacob and Evan Raser own a small hotel with 65 rooms in Banff, Alberta. During the summer, there are many cultural and recreational activities going on in this region. The maximum room rate they charge during this time is $150 per night. However, although the hotel is usually sold out on weekends, it is never sold out during the week. From historical data, the two brothers have developed the following probability table with respect to the number of rooms occupied during a weeknight (i.e., Sunday through Thursday nights):

Number of Rooms Occupied	Probability
45	0.15
50	0.30
55	0.20
60	0.35

The variable cost to clean an occupied room is estimated to be $25. The two brothers have recently been approached by a group representing retired people on limited incomes. The group is doing a special promotion for their spring newsletter and want to include a hotel that would offer reduced room rates during the week if retirees made reservations at least one month in advance. The group assures Jacob and Evan that if the rate were $95 per night, they could sell all the rooms available on a weekday night. How many rooms should Jacob and Evan allocate to this lower rate for weeknights?

Solution

As with the Christmas tree problem, we construct the following payoff table:

Probability	0.15	0.30	0.20	0.35	
Customer Demand	45	50	55	60	
Number of Rooms Available at $150	—	—	—	—	Expected Profit
45	7025	6750	6475	6200	$6543.75
50	6325	7300	7025	6750	6906.25
55	5625	6600	7575	7300	6893.75
60	4925	5900	6875	7850	6640.00

Similarly, as with the Christmas tree problem, the values in the payoff table can be divided into three groups. In the first group, the number of rooms reserved for full rate (i.e., $150/night) exactly equals demand. The profit generated when this happens is

$$\text{Profit} = D(SP - C) + (N - D)(DP - C)$$

where

D = Demand

SP = Standard room rate per night

DP = Discounted room rate per night

C = Variable cost to clean a room per night

N = Total number of rooms in the hotel

Thus, if we have a demand for 50 rooms and we allocate 50 rooms at the standard rate, then the profit generated is

$$\text{Profit} = 50(150 - 25) + (65 - 50)(95 - 25)$$
$$= 6250 + 1050 = \$7300$$

The second group consists of those combinations where demand for the standard room rate exceeds the number of rooms allocated for this rate. Here we have to take into consideration the opportunity cost associated with the lost revenues resulting from unsatisfied demand at the standard rate, because the rooms were sold to the retirees at the discounted rate. Thus the opportunity cost is the difference between the standard rate and the discounted rate. The profit generated in these cases is as follows:

$$\text{Profit} = Q(SP - C) + (N - Q)(DP - C) - (D - Q)(SP - DP)$$

where

Q = Number of rooms allocated at the standard rate

If we have a demand for 60 rooms per night at the standard rate and we have allocated only 50 rooms, then the resulting profit is

$$\text{Profit} = 50(150 - 25) + (65 - 50)(95 - 25) - (60 - 50)(150 - 95)$$
$$= 6250 + 1050 - 550 = \$6750$$

The third case occurs when the number of rooms allocated at the standard rate exceeds the demand. Here we have to take into account the opportunity cost of not selling the rooms earlier to the retirees. The net profit calculated is therefore as follows:

$$\text{Profit} = D(SP - C) + (N - Q)(DP - C) - (Q - D)(DP - C)$$

If we have reserved 60 rooms per night for the standard room rate and demand is only for 50 rooms, then the profit generated is

$$\text{Profit} = 50(150 - 25) + (65 - 60)(95 - 25) - (60 - 50)(95 - 25)$$
$$= 6250 + 350 - 700 = \$5900$$

After we have determined all of the values in the payoff table, we next have to calculate the expected profit associated with the number of rooms reserved at the standard rate. This is calculated by multiplying the probability associated with each level of demand by the profit generated by that demand. For example, if we decide to allocate 55 rooms at the standard rate, then the expected profit from this decision is

$$\text{Expected profit (55)} = (0.15)(5625) + (0.30)(6600) + (0.20)(7575)$$
$$+ (0.35)(7300)$$
$$\text{EP(55)} = 843.75 + 1980 + 1515 + 2555$$
$$= \$6893.75$$

Finally, we select that number of rooms to allocate at the standard rate that yields the maximum expected profit. In this case, Jacob and Evan should allocate 50 rooms a night during the week at the standard rate and provide the retiree group with 15 rooms a night, because this decision provides the maximum expected profit of $6906.25, as shown in the table above. Below is the Excel spreadsheet solution.

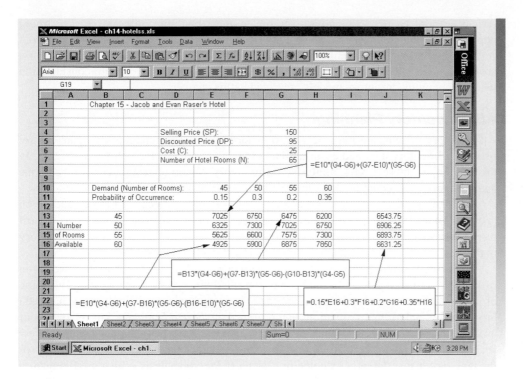

Additional Issues in Inventory Management

Determining Realistic Costs

Most inventory models give optimal solutions so long as the conditions of the system meet the constraints and/or assumptions of the model. Although this is easy to state, it is difficult to implement. Obtaining actual order, setup, carrying, and shortage costs is often difficult—sometimes impossible. Part of the problem occurs because accounting data are usually averages, whereas to determine the proper lot sizes we need the marginal costs. Exhibit 15.13 compares the assumed smoothly ascending cost to the more realistic actual cost. For example, a corporate buyer is a salaried person. The marginal cost for the buyer's labour to place additional orders up to a full workload is zero. When another buyer is hired, it is a step function. (In theory, the marginal cost of the order that caused hiring the new buyer is the cost for the additional buyer.)

The same problem occurs in determining carrying costs. Warehouse costs, for example, may be close to zero if empty storage areas are available. Also, most companies can only estimate actual carrying costs, since they include obsolescence (a guess, at best),

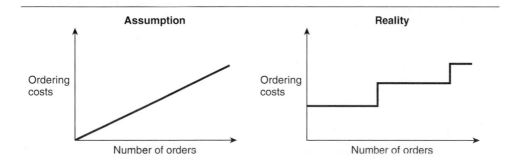

Exhibit 15.13

Cost to Place Orders versus the Number of Orders Placed: Linear Assumption and Normal Reality

cost of capital (which depends on internal money available, alternative investment opportunities, and sources of new capital), and insurance costs (which may range from zero, if current insurance premiums cover more than the assets on hand, to the cost of a new policy). It is therefore important that we take these circumstances into consideration when applying the inventory models presented in this chapter.

ABC Inventory Planning

ABC analysis

Method for grouping inventory items by dollar volume to identify those items to be monitored closely.

All inventory systems are plagued by two major problems: maintaining adequate control over each inventory item and ensuring that accurate records of stock on hand are kept. In this section, we present **ABC analysis**—an inventory system offering a control technique and inventory cycle counting that can improve record accuracy.

Maintaining inventory through counting, placing orders, receiving stock, and so on takes personnel time and costs money. When there are limits on these resources, as is most often the case, the logical move is to try to use the available resources to control inventory in the best way. In other words, focus on the most important items in inventory.

In the eighteenth century, Villefredo Pareto, in a study of the distribution of wealth in Milan, found that 20 percent of the people controlled 80 percent of the wealth. This logic of the few having the greatest importance and the many having little importance has been broadened to include many situations and is termed the *Pareto Principle.* This is true in our everyday lives, where most of the decisions we make are relatively unimportant but a few shape our future, and is certainly true in inventory systems, where a few items account for the bulk of our investment. (As noted in Chapter 6, Pareto analysis is also used in quality management to identify the most frequent types of errors.) In addition, companies use this principle to focus on a few important aspects of business such as customer accounts, sales territories, operating costs, accounts receivables, and so on.

Any inventory system must specify when an order is to be placed for an item and how many units to order. In most situations involving inventory control, there are so many items involved that it is not practical to model and give thorough treatment to each and every item. To get around this problem, the ABC classification scheme divides inventory items into three groupings: high dollar usage (A), moderate dollar usage (B), and low dollar usage (C). Dollar usage (unit cost × volume sold) is a measure of importance; an item low in cost but high in volume can be more important than a high-cost item with low volume.

We explain ABC analysis using the example below which shows the unit values and annual usage (volume) of an inventory with ten items. The ABC analysis is done using the following four steps:

Example

Item No.	Unit Value ($)	Annual Usage
3	5	3000
19	100	8
22	1000	95
23	4.25	100
27	25	10000
36	0.15	10000
41	2.25	100
54	0.75	10000
68	500	150
82	26	500

Step 1: Calculate the annual dollar usage.

The annual dollar usage for each item is the value of the units of the item sold on an annual basis. This is arrived at by multiplying the unit value by the annual usage as shown. This can be done quickly using a spreadsheet.

Arial		10	B I U ≡ ≡ ≡ ▦ $ % , .0 .00
E23		fx	

	A	B	C	D
3				
4		ABC Analysis		
5				Annual Dollar Usage ($)
6		Unit	Annual	(Unit value ×
7	Item No.	Value ($)	Usage	Annual usage)
8	3	5	3500	17500
9	19	100	8	800
10	22	1000	95	95000
11	23	4.25	100	B9×C9 425
12	27	2.5	8000	20000
13	36	0.15	10000	1500
14	41	2.25	100	225
15	54	0.75	5000	3750
16	68	500	150	75000
17	82	26	700	18200
18				
19		Total Annual Dollar Usage		232400
20				

Step 2: Sort the items based on annual dollar usage.

Using the sorting capabilities of spreadsheets, it is easy to sort the inventory items according to the annual dollar usage, from highest to lowest.

Arial		10	B I U ≡ ≡ ≡ ▦ $ % , .0 .00
D26		fx	

	A	B	C	D
3				
4		ABC Analysis		
5				Annual Dollar Usage ($)
6		Unit	Annual	(Unit value ×
7	Item No.	Value ($)	Usage	Annual usage)
8	22	1000	95	95000
9	68	500	150	75000
10	27	2.5	8000	20000
11	82	26	700	B9×C9 18200
12	3	5	3500	17500
13	54	0.75	5000	3750
14	36	0.15	10000	1500
15	19	100	8	800
16	23	4.25	100	425
17	41	2.25	100	225
18				
19		Total Annual Dollar Usage		232400
20				

Step 3: Calculate the individual and cumulative dollar usage percentages.

In this step we calculate the annual dollar usage for each item as a percentage of total annual dollar usage and then calculate the corresponding cumulative values.

	A	B	C	D	E	F	G	H	I
	Arial		10	B I U ≡ ≡ ≡ 国 $ % , ⁺.⁰⁸ .⁰⁰₈ 拝 拝 □ ▾ ◈ ▾ A ▾ ▾					
	F27		ƒₓ						
3									
4		**ABC Analysis**							
5				Annual Dollar Usage ($)		Percentage			
6		Unit	Annual	(Unit value ×)		of total Annual	Cumulative		
7	Item No.	Value ($)	Usage	Annual usage)		Dollar Usage	Percentage		
8	22	1000	95	95000		40.88	40.88		
9	68	500	150	75000		32.27	73.15		
10	27	2.5	8000	20000		8.61	81.76	G8+F9	
11	82	26	700	18200		7.83	89.59		
12	3	5	3500	17500		7.53	97.12		
13	54	0.75	5000	3750		1.61	98.73		
14	36	0.15	10000	1500		0.65	99.38		
15	19	100	8	800		0.34	99.72		
16	23	4.25	100	425		0.18	99.90		
17	41	2.25	100	225		0.10	100.00		
18									
19		**Total Annual Dollar Usage**		232400					

(B9×C9 labels cell D9; D9/D19 labels cell F9)

Step 4: Classify each item into A, B, and C categories.

The ABC approach divides this list into three groupings by value: A items constitute roughly the top 15 percent of the items, B items the next 35 percent, and C items the last 50 percent. From observation, it appears that the list in the spreadsheet above may be meaningfully grouped with A including 20 percent (2 of the 10), B including 30 percent, and C including 50 percent. These points show clear delineations between sections. The result of this segmentation is shown below. In this example, 20 percent of the items account for 73.15 percent of the value of the inventory. The analysis is also shown in graphic form created by using a spreadsheet. This format is useful in communicating your analysis to others visually. It clearly shows that two items of the ten account for a large percentage of the value, whereas five of the ten items account for very little. This analysis indicates which items the company should focus its efforts on in order to manage the inventory effectively.

Classification	Item Number	Annual Dollar Usage	Percentage of Total Value	Percentage of Total Items
A	22, 68	$170 000	73.15	20%
B	27, 82, 03,	55 700	23.97	30
C	54, 36, 19, 23, 41	6 700	2.88	50
		$232 400	100.0%	100%

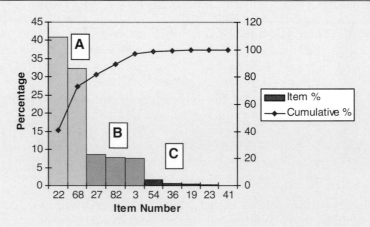

Segmentation may not always occur so neatly. The objective, though, is to try to separate the important from the unimportant. Where the lines actually break depends on the particular inventory under question and on how much personnel time is available (with more time a firm could define larger A or B categories).

The purpose of classifying items into groups is to establish the appropriate degree of control for each item. On a periodic basis, for example, Class A items may be more clearly controlled with weekly ordering, B items may be ordered biweekly, and C items may be ordered monthly or bimonthly. Note that the unit cost of items is not related to their classification. An A item may have a high dollar volume through a combination of either low cost and high usage or high cost and low usage. Similarly, C items may have a low dollar volume either because of low demand or low cost. In an automobile service station, for example, gasoline would be an A item with daily tabulation; tires, batteries, oil, grease, and transmission fluid may be B items and ordered every two to four weeks; and C items would consist of valve stems, windshield wiper blades, radiator caps, hoses, fan belts, oil and gas additives, car wax, and so forth. C items may be ordered every two or three months or even be allowed to run out before reordering since the penalty for stockout is not serious. We may also spend more effort on forecasting, vendor development, and inventory counting for A items than for B and C items.

Sometimes, an item may be critical to a system if its absence creates a sizable loss. In this case, regardless of the item's classification, sufficiently large stocks should be kept on hand to prevent runout. One way to ensure closer control is to designate this item as an A or a B item, forcing it into the category even if its dollar volume does not warrant such inclusion.

Inventory Accuracy

Every production system must have agreement, within some specified range, between what the record says is in inventory and what actually is in inventory. There are many reasons records and inventory may not agree. For example, having an open stockroom area allows items to be removed for both legitimate and unauthorized purposes. The legitimate removal may have been done in a hurry and simply not recorded. Sometimes parts are misplaced, turning up months later. Parts often are stored in several locations, but records may be lost or the location recorded incorrectly. Sometimes stock replenishment orders are recorded as received, when in fact they never were. Occasionally, a group of parts is recorded as having been removed from inventory, but the customer order is cancelled and the parts are replaced in inventory without cancelling the record. To keep the production system flowing smoothly without parts shortages and efficiently without excess balances, it is important that inventory records be accurate.

Backflush is a term used to designate how component parts are accounted for in a pull system. Rather than keeping track of each individual part on a daily basis by job, pull systems periodically (such as once a month) develop detailed lists of all the components contained in a product and calculate how many of each part must have gone into the final product(s) completed. This eliminates a major shop-floor data collection activity, thereby further simplifying the production management job. Bar-code technology allows Philips' Medical Products Group in Andover, Massachusetts, to backflush on a continuous, ongoing basis. For example, when a printed circuit board is completed with all of its components in place, that board's bar code is scanned into the system. As a result of the scanning, all of the board's components are removed from inventory while, at the same time, the completed board is placed into inventory.

Cycle counting is used to continuously reconcile inventory with inventory records, usually in association with ABC analysis. Rather than shutting down the business for a full

backflush
Calculating the consumption of component parts inventory periodically based on final product completion.

cycle counting
A method of counting inventory in which different items are counted at different times.

inventory count, items within each classification are counted on a regular basis but at different times. A items would be counted more frequently than C items because of their importance.

Current Trends in Inventory Management

As noted in the opening vignette, managers in leading-edge companies recognize that inventory really isn't an asset, but rather a liability. Consequently, the average amount of inventory that these firms have on hand relative to their annual sales has been going down in recent years, even though in many cases the number of products they make has increased.

Firms have been able to reduce their inventories for several reasons. First, companies have focused their efforts on reducing setup or order costs. The lower these costs, the smaller the economic order quantities. In addition, companies are now working much more closely with their vendors. Through these relationships, product throughput times and thus lead times have been reduced significantly, again reducing the need to carry inventory. Finally, through advances in technology, many companies, such as Dell Computer, are now building to order rather than to stock, thereby totally eliminating finished goods inventories.

Conclusion

This chapter introduces the two main categories of inventory demand: independent (referring to the external demand for a firm's end product) dependent (usually referring to the demand within the firm for items created because of the demand for more complex items of which they are a part). Most industries have items in both categories. In manufacturing, for example, independent demand is common for finished products, service and repair parts, and operating supplies; dependent demand is common for those parts and materials needed to produce the end product. In wholesale and retail sales of consumer goods, most demand is independent—each item is an end item, with the wholesaler or retailer doing no further assembly or fabrication.

We also introduce the single-period inventory model for those products that are highly perishable. We then extend this model to discuss yield management, which provides service operations with a methodology to maximize their revenues.

In this chapter we also emphasize that inventory reduction requires a knowledge of the operating system. It is not simply a case of selecting an inventory model off the shelf and plugging in some numbers. In the first place, the model might not be appropriate. In the second place, the numbers might not be relevant. It is also important to understand that inventory management is no longer a trade-off or compromise. (Very often determining order quantities is referred to as a trade-off problem; that is, trading off holding costs for setup costs. Today companies want to reduce both.)

The simple fact is that firms typically have very large investments in inventory, and the cost to carry this inventory runs from 30 to 35 percent and more of the inventory's worth annually. Therefore, a major goal of most firms today is to reduce inventory; they expect this also to lead to improved quality and performance, and to greatly reduced costs.

Key Terms

Key Formulas

Q model

Total annual cost for an order quantity Q, an annual demand D, a per-unit cost C, setup cost S, and an annual per-unit holding cost H.

$$TC = DC + \frac{D}{Q}S + \frac{Q}{2}H \qquad (15.1)$$

Q model

Optimum or economic order quantity.

$$EOQ = \sqrt{\frac{2DS}{H}} \qquad (15.2)$$

Q model

Reorder point is based upon an average demand of $\bar{d}$ units per time period (e.g., days, weeks) and lead time L (stated in the same units of time as the demand).

$$R = \bar{d}L \qquad (15.3)$$

Q model with usage

Total annual cost for an order quantity Q, an annual demand D, with a maximum inventory on hand of I_{max}, a per-unit cost C, setup cost S, and an annual per-unit holding cost H.

$$TC = DC + (D/Q)S + (I_{max}/2)H \qquad (15.4)$$

Q model with usage

Maximum inventory on hand for an order quantity Q, production rate of p units per time period, and usage rate of d units per time period.

$$I_{max} = (p - d)(Q/p) \qquad (15.5)$$

Q model with usage

Optimum or economic order quantity when items are produced at a rate of p units per time period and are used at a rate of d units per time period.

$$EOQ = \sqrt{\frac{2DS}{H} \cdot \frac{p}{(p-d)}} \qquad (15.6)$$

In-transit Inventory Model

$$TC = DM + \left(\frac{X}{365}\right)iDC + DC \qquad (15.7)$$

Review and Discussion Questions

1. Distinguish between dependent and independent demand in a McDonald's, in an integrated manufacturer of personal copiers, and in a pharmaceutical supply house.
2. Distinguish between work-in-process inventory, safety-stock inventory, and seasonal inventory.
3. Discuss the nature of the costs that affect inventory size.
4. Under which conditions would a plant manager elect to use a fixed-order-quantity model as opposed to a fixed-time-period model? What are the disadvantages of using a fixed-time-period ordering system?
5. There is a current trend to reduce inventories. How is this being accomplished and what is the impact of lower inventories to the firm, its suppliers, and its customers?
6. Discuss the general procedure for determining the order quantity when quantity discounts are involved. Would there be any differences in the procedure if holding costs were a fixed percentage of item cost rather than a constant amount?
7. What two basic questions must be answered by an inventory-control decision rule?
8. Discuss the assumptions that are inherent in production setup cost, ordering cost, and carrying costs. How valid are they?
9. "The nice thing about inventory models is that you can pull one off the shelf and apply it so long as your cost estimates are accurate." Comment.
10. Which type of inventory system would you use in the following situations?
    a. Supplying your kitchen with fresh food.
    b. Obtaining a daily newspaper.
    c. Buying gasoline for your car.
11. Why is it desirable to classify items into groups, as the ABC classification scheme does?
12. In addition to airlines, hotels, and car rental firms, what other types of services would be appropriate for yield management?
13. Call up a hotel and ask about their room rates for weekdays, weekends, high season, and low season. Explain the logic for these prices.

Solved Problems

Problem 1

Items purchased from a vendor cost $20 each, and the forecast for next year's demand is 1000 units. If it costs $5 every time an order is placed for more units and the carrying cost is $4 per unit per year, what quantity should be ordered each time?

a. What is the total ordering cost for a year?

b. What is the total carrying cost for a year?

Solution

The quantity to be ordered each time is

$$\text{EOP} = \sqrt{\frac{2DS}{H}} = \sqrt{\frac{2(100)5}{4}} = 50 \text{ units}$$

a. The total ordering cost for a year is

$$\frac{D}{Q}S = \frac{1000}{50}(\$5) = \$100$$

b. The carrying cost for a year is

$$\frac{Q}{2}H = \frac{50}{2}(\$4) = \$100$$

Problem 2

A department store sells (among other things) sports shirts for casual wear. Mr. Koste is in charge of the men's department, and knows that the annual demand for one of these shirts is fairly constant at 250 shirts per year. These shirts are obtained only from the manufacturer, who charges a delivery fee of $65, regardless of the number of shirts delivered with that order. In addition, in-house costs associated with each order total $6.

The manufacturer charges $16.25 per shirt, but is willing to lower the price by 3 percent per shirt if the department store will order at least 2 gross (288) each time. Of course, this means that some shirts must be kept in inventory, and the holding costs have been estimated at 8.5 percent per year.

Should Mr. Koste recommend that the department store accept the offer of the quantity discount?

Solution

$$D = 250$$
$$S = 65 + 6 = \$71$$
$$H = iC$$
$$i = 0.085$$
$$C = \$16.25$$

$$Q = \sqrt{\frac{2DS}{iC}} = \sqrt{\frac{(2)(250)(71)}{(0.085)(16.25)}} \approx 160$$

As $160 < 288$, compute

$$TC(160) = (16.25)(250) + \left(\frac{250}{160}\right)(71) + \left(\frac{160}{2}\right)(0.085)(16.25)$$
$$= \$4283.94$$

and

$$TC(288) = \left[(0.97)(16.25)(250)\right] + \left(\frac{250}{288}\right)(71) + \left(\frac{288}{2}\right)(0.085)\left[(0.97)(16.25)\right]$$
$$= \$4195.19$$

Since the total cost at 288 is lower than that at 160, accept the discount.

Problem 3

Elkin Shoes, Inc. (ESI), is a manufacturing firm that produces a variety of shoes and boots. They have recently started operation of a factory in Alberta and have opened a factory outlet store adjacent to the factory. The production manager at the factory is trying to ascertain the optimal number of sheepskin boots to produce with each production run. After careful analysis, he believes that the following data are correct:

Annual demand for the boots: 12 000 pairs

Days/year the outlet store is open: 240

Daily production capacity of the factory: 200 pairs

Setup cost incurred to start boot production: $800

Annual storage cost per pair of boots: $60

What should the production manager recommend as the optimal production lot size?

Solution

D = Annual demand = 12 000

d = Daily demand = 12 000/240 = 50

p = Daily production = 200

S = Setup cost = $800

H = Holding cost = $60

$$Q = \sqrt{\frac{2DS}{H} \cdot \left(\frac{p}{p-d}\right)} = \sqrt{\frac{(2)(12\ 000)(800)}{60} \cdot \left(\frac{200}{200-50}\right)} \approx 653$$

Problem 4

DAT, Inc. produces digital audiotapes to be used in the consumer audio division. DAT doesn't have sufficient personnel in its inventory supply section to closely control each item stocked, so you have been asked to determine an ABC classification. The following shows a sample from the inventory records:

Item	Average Monthly Demand	Price per Unit
1	700	$ 6.00
2	200	4.00
3	2000	12.00
4	1100	20.00
5	4000	21.00
6	100	10.00
7	3000	2.00
8	2500	1.00
9	500	10.00
10	1000	2.00

Solution

1. Calculate monthly usage.

Item number	Average monthly demand (1)	Price per unit (2)	Monthly usage (1) x (2)
1	700	6	4 200
2	200	4	800
3	2000	12	24 000
4	1100	20	22 000
5	4000	21	84 000
6	100	10	1 000
7	3000	2	6 000
8	2500	1	2 500
9	500	10	5 000
10	1000	2	2 000

2. Sort according to monthly usage.

Item number	Average monthly demand	Price per unit	Monthly usage
5	4000	21	84 000
3	2000	12	24 000
4	1100	20	22 000
7	3000	2	6 000
9	500	10	5 000
1	700	6	4 200
8	2500	1	2 500
10	1000	2	2 000
6	100	10	1 000
2	200	4	800
Total Monthly Usage			151 500

3. Calculate cumulative percentages and classify.

Monthly usage	% of Total Monthly Usage	Cumulative %	Class
84 000	55.4	55.4	A
24 000	15.8	71.3	B
22 000	14.5	85.8	B
6 000	4.0	89.8	C
5 000	3.3	93.1	C
4 200	2.8	95.8	C
2 500	1.7	97.5	C
2 000	1.3	98.8	C
1 000	0.7	99.5	C
800	0.5	100.0	C
Total 151 500			

Problems

1. Annual demand for an item is 2500 units. The cost to place an order is $5, and holding cost is 20 percent per annum of the cost of the item. Items have the following cost schedule:

1 to 99	$10.00 each
100 to 199	$ 9.80 each
200 and over	$ 9.60 each

What is the economic order quantity (EOQ)?

2. Demand for an item is 2000 units per year. Each order placed costs $25; the annual cost to carry items in inventory is $0.50 each.

   a. In what quantities should the item be ordered?

   b. What is the total cost of carrying and ordering inventory?

3. Item X is a standard item stocked in a company's inventory of component parts. Each year, the firm, on a random basis, uses about 2000 of Item X, which costs $25 each. Annual storage costs, which include insurance and cost of capital, amount to $5 per unit of average inventory. Every time an order is placed, it costs $10.

a. Whenever Item X is ordered, what should the order size be?

b. What is the annual cost for ordering Item X?

c. What is the annual cost for storing Item X?

4. Ray Kanjian's Satellite Emporium wishes to determine the best order size for its best-selling satellite dish (model TS111). Ray has estimated the annual demand for this model at 1000 units. His cost to carry one unit is $100 per year per unit, and he has estimated that each order costs $25 to place.

a. Using the EOQ model, how many should Ray order each time?

b. How often will orders be placed?

c. If the emporium is open 250 days per year and it takes two working days to get a replenishment after the order is placed (lead time), what is the reorder point?

5. Demand for an item is 1000 units per year. Each order placed costs $10; the annual cost to carry items in inventory is $2 each.

a. In what quantities should the item be ordered and how often?

b. Supposing a $100 discount on each order is given if orders are placed in quantities of 500 or more. Should orders be placed in quantities of 500, or should you stick to the decision you made in a?

c. If the business works 52 weeks per year and the lead time is 3 weeks, what is the reorder point?

6. A particular raw material is available to the Angkor company at three different prices, depending on the size of the orders, as follows:

Less than 100 kg	$20 per kg
100 kg to 999 kg	$19 per kg
1000 kg and more	$18 per kg

The cost to place an order is $40. Annual demand is 3000 units. Holding (or carrying) cost is 25 percent per annum.

What is the economic order quantity to buy each time?

7. In the past, Obote Industries has used a fixed-time inventory system that involved taking a complete inventory count of all items each month. However, increasing labour costs are forcing Obote Industries to examine ways to reduce the amount of labour involved in inventory stockrooms without increasing other costs, such as shortage costs.

The following table is a random sample of 20 of Obote's items.

Item Number	Annual Usage	Item Number	Annual Usage
1	$ 1 500	11	$13 000
2	12 000	12	600
3	2 200	13	42 000
4	50 000	14	9 900
5	9 600	15	1 200
6	750	16	10 200
7	2 000	17	4 000
8	11 000	18	61 000
9	800	19	3 500
10	15 000	20	2 900

a. What would you recommend Obote do to cut back its labour cost? (Illustrate using an ABC plan.)

b. Item 15 is critical to continued operations. How would you recommend it be classified?

8. Magnetron, Inc., manufactures microwave ovens for the commercial market. Currently, Magnetron is producing part 2104 in its fabrication shop for use in the adjacent unit assembly area. Next year's requirement for part 2104 is estimated at 20 000 units. Part 2104 is valued at $50 per unit, and the combined storage and handling cost is $8 per unit per year. The cost of preparing the order and making the production setup is $200. The plant operates 250 days per year. The assembly area completes 80 units per day, every working day, and the fabrication shop produces 160 units per day when it is producing part 2104.

   a. Compute the economic order quantity.

   b. How many orders will be placed each year?

   c. If part 2104 could be purchased from another firm with the same costs as described, what would the order quantity be? (The order is received all at once.)

   d. If the average lead time to order from another firm is 10 working days and a safety stock level is set at 500 units, what is the reorder point?

9. Garrett Corporation, a turbine manufacturer, operates its plants on an 18-hour day, 300 days a year. Titanium blades can be produced on its turbine blade machine number 1 (TBM1) at a rate of 500 per hour, and the average usage rate is 5000 per day. The blades cost $15 apiece, and carrying costs are $0.10 per day per blade because of insurance, interest on investments, and space allocation. TBM1 costs $250 to set up for each run. Lead time requires production to begin after stock drops to 500 blades. What is the optimal production run for TBM1?

10. C. Simmons Products, Inc., is having a problem trying to control inventory. There is insufficient time to devote to all its items equally. The following is a sample of some items stocked, along with the annual usage of each item expressed in dollar volume.

Item	Annual Dollar	Item	Annual Dollar
a	$ 7 000	k	$80 000
b	1 000	l	400
c	14 000	m	1 100
d	2 000	n	30 000
e	24 000	o	1 900
f	68 000	p	800
g	17 000	q	90 000
h	900	r	12 000
i	1 700	s	3 000
j	2 300	t	32 000

Can you suggest a system for allocating inventory control time? Specify where each item from the list would be placed.

11. The Sum and Yang Company, Incorporated (SY), produces copper contacts that it uses in switches and relays. SY needs to determine the order quantity Q to meet the annual demand at the lowest cost.

   The price of copper depends on the quantity ordered. The following are the price-break data and other relevant data for the problem:

Price of copper	$0.82 per kg up to 2499 kg
	$0.81 per kg for orders between 2500 and 4999 kg
	$0.80 per kg for orders greater than 5000 kg
Annual demand	50 000 kg per year
Holding cost	20 percent per year
Ordering cost	$30

Which quantity should be ordered?

12. Mike Delgado, owner of Bagel Maker bakery, is trying to decide how many bagels he should make each morning. He currently sells fresh bagels for $5.25 per dozen. Any bagels that are left over at the end of the day are sold the next day as "yesterday's bagels" for $3.00 per dozen. Mike estimates that the material and labour to make a dozen bagels is $3.75. To help him decide how many bagels to make each morning, he has collected the following information based on historical data:

	Dozens of Bagels Sold						
	12	14	16	18	20	22	24
	Probability						
Weekdays (Monday–Friday)	.15	.25	.25	.20	.15	.00	.00
Weekends (Saturday–Sunday)	.05	.15	.15	.25	.20	.15	.05

a. How many dozens of bagels should Mike make weekday mornings? What is the implied service level and SS?

b. How many dozens of bagels should Mike make on weekend mornings? What is the implied service level and SS?

13. Anju Groves owns a parking lot in downtown Peterborough with 100 spaces. She can offer an "early bird" special for $12.00 a day and knows she can attract as many customers who work in downtown Peterborough as she is willing to allocate parking spaces at this low daily rate. The hourly rate that she charges is $6.00 and the average customer stays for about $3\frac{1}{2}$ hours. Anju has collected the following data on how many parking spaces a day she has had occupied at the hourly rate:

Parking spaces	65	70	75	80	85
Probability	.15	.20	.25	.30	.10

If we assume that only one hourly customer per day occupies a given parking space, how many spaces should Anju allocate for the early bird special to maximize her profits?

14. An automobile company in Ontario currently purchases 100 000 tires a year from a manufacturer located 50 km from its assembly plant. The price per tire is $40. Because of the close proximity of the two plants, the vendor delivers these tires free of charge. The purchasing agent recently has been approached by a tire manufacturer in Asia who has agreed to provide these tires for $35 each. Through inquiries, the purchasing agent has determined that it will cost an additional $4.50 per tire to ship the tires from Asia to the plant in Ontario. In addition, it will take approximately six weeks for a shipment to arrive. Currently the cost of capital for the automobile company is 20 percent per year. From which vendor should the purchasing agent buy tires?

15. Varughese Computer Company in the greater Kitchener-Waterloo area currently buys electronic modules at a price of $26 per unit from a vendor located in Tijuana, Mexico. The firm's buyer is currently evaluating two alternative modes for transporting these modules. The first way is overland on a trailer truck. The cost with this method is $2.50 per module and transport takes approximately two weeks. The second way is to ship the modules air freight, which takes only two days to deliver at a cost of $3 per unit. Currently the computer maker is buying 25 000 modules per year. The cost of

capital for the firm is estimated at 18 percent per year. Which mode of transportation do you recommend?

16. As the purchasing agent for a small company located in central France, Laurence Garreau has recently sent out a request for proposal for a small motor used in a subassembly that her firm manufactures for the automobile industry. The annual requirement for this motor is 25 000 units, and she has estimated the cost of in-transit inventory to be 25 percent per year.

    The first quotation she receives is from a company in Southeast Asia. The unit price per motor from this firm is 45 euros. In addition, the transportation cost per unit is 4 euros. The transit time from Southeast Asia, using an ocean freighter, is estimated to be 50 days in total. The second quotation she receives is from a company in Mexico that is very anxious to do business in Europe. The unit price per motor from this company is 43 euros, and the transportation cost per unit is 6.5 euros, but it will take only 10 days in total to deliver the motors because the company will be using air freight.

    a. Evaluate each of these proposals to determine which is the most economical alternative. What is your recommendation? (Be specific and show all your calculations.)

    b. What factors, in addition to cost, need to be taken into consideration in arriving at a final decision as to which supplier to use?

Merdeka Gas Grills: Inventory and Supply Chain Management

Merdeka manufactures premium gas grills for the North American market. Its gas grills require over 30 separate components, ranging from the relatively expensive bowl, lid, and burner (unit costs greater than $50), down to the many low unit cost (less than $1) items such as grill clips and screws. All Merdeka models use common low unit cost components which can be purchased from any industrial supply company.

Merdeka uses an integrated business system (ERP) software package to manage its purchasing, sales, inventory and production management, and accounting functions. Excited by the information and control the software can provide, Merdeka entered into the computer system as an item every single component required for its gas grills. Furthermore, by having shop floor staff enter into the system the quantity consumed of every component used during the assembly process, the computer system keeps constant track of on-hand inventory of every component. Purchasing staff then print inventory reordering reports each morning and compare on-hand inventory to previously calculated reorder points to determine if a purchase order needs to be prepared.

In an effort to keep material costs down, Merdeka's purchasing department has identified multiple suppliers for each component. When an order for a component is required, a buyer contacts potential suppliers requesting a quote, then orders from the supplier that quoted the lowest unit cost. By using various suppliers for each component, with each supplier having various delivery lead times, Merdeka maintains a significant safety stock on each component to buffer this delivery variability.

Once a year, production shuts down for a two-day inventory count of all components. After the year-end count is entered, discrepancies between the actual physical inventory and the on-hand quantity in the computer system are corrected (they typically range from a 10% to 15% quantity loss for each individual component). Recognizing this

Case Exhibit 1

Item No.	Unit Value ($)	Annual Usage (units)
1013	68.13	105
2691	0.54	4368
2862	11.67	298
3846	0.77	3067
4456	23.43	564
5066	2.43	1264
6392	6.12	1994
6547	0.8	2476
7675	1.65	656
8725	99.84	297

pattern over the years, Merdeka's purchasing staff "mentally adjust down" the on-hand quantities that appear on their daily inventory reordering reports. This uncertainty regarding on-hand inventory quantities also causes purchasing staff to bump up their required order quantities throughout the year, typically by at least 20%.

Recently, increased competition has forced Merdeka to review its operations for potential efficiency improvements. One manager suggested starting with an ABC analysis of the inventory. A study was initiated to do this. Case Exhibit 1 shows a representative sample from this study.

Questions

1. Classify the 10 items shown into A, B, and C categories. Do the sample data indicate that Merdeka's inventory could be classified into more than three categories?

2. How might your inventory management policies differ for the A versus the C categories? For example, how would the frequency of ordering, using fixed-order-quantity versus fixed time-period models, computerization, vendor development, inventory counting, and other management aspects differ conceptually?

3. Are there other potential improvements for Merdeka that you can think of?

Source:
This case was written by Brent Snider and Jaydeep Balakrishnan of the Haskayne School of Business at the University of Calgary. It is based on a real situation.

16

Materials Planning for Dependent Demand

Chapter Objectives

- Explain the changing role of materials requirements planning (MRP) within a manufacturing organization.

- Discuss the role of MRP within an enterprise resource planning (ERP) system.

- Introduce the fundamental concepts and calculations that drive an MRP system.

- Define the various elements that make up an MRP system.

- Demonstrate how MRP-related systems are applied in service operations.

- Recognize that MRP and JIT can be used together within an organization.

- Introduce distribution requirement planning (DRP).

Merck Frosst Canada & Co., a division of Merck and Company, produces a wide variety of high-quality pharmaceutical products. The company's history goes back to 1899 when Frosst and Co. was established in Montreal. It has focused on research and development ever since. For example, in the 1940s it pioneered the field of nuclear medicine with the development and commercialization of the first radioactive pharmaceutical products for sale both domestically and internationally. The company merged with Merck & Co in 1965. Shortly after implementing an MRP II software system, management recognized the need to focus on becoming a Class A manufacturing company to achieve manufacturing excellence. To accomplish this, managers began in 1998 to work closely with the Oliver Wight Company, an MRP consulting firm. As a result of this effort, Merck Frosst Canada & Co. was able

to achieve Class A excellence very quickly, and with very impressive results, some of which included

- On-time delivery increased over a three-year period from 75 percent to 98 percent
- Supplier delivery performance increased from 75 percent to 85 percent
- Manufacturing cycle time was dramatically reduced
- Inventories were reduced from an average of 5.3 months to 3.9 months

Source:

Provided courtesy of the Oliver Wight Companies, New London, NH.
http://collections.ic.gc.ca/heirloom_series/volume4

In Chapter 15 we discussed the inventory management of items that are considered to have independent demand, generally end items such as appliances or automobiles. In this chapter we discuss the inventory management of components that go into the manufacturing of these end items. Although some of the models used in Chapter 15 can be used for managing some components, others cannot. This chapter introduces new methods for managing the inventory and production schedule of components and subassemblies. Furthermore, because each end item may have thousands of components, the use of a computerized system is necessary. Thus, not only do we have inventory management issues, we also have data processing and system implementation and management issues.

Independent versus Dependent Demand MRP Systems

dependent demand

Demand for components that depend on end item demand.

When we are dealing with end products, such as automobiles, refrigerators, and personal computers, the inventory models presented in the previous chapter are often applicable. This is especially true when the demand for these types of products is considered to be *independent* and relatively constant throughout the year. However, there is another category of products: the subassemblies and components that go into these end products. For this group of products, the demand is not independent, but rather, is *dependent* on the demand for the end products in which they are used. For example, the demand for automobile tires is dependent on the demand for cars. Similarly, the demand for keyboards is dependent on the demand for personal computers. In both cases, once the demand for the end product has been established, be it cars or PCs, the demand for the components used in these products can be determined easily. To address the inventory issues associated with these types of products, a concept known as materials requirements planning (MRP) is used.

As mentioned in the Evolution of ERP systems section in Chapter 12, MRP was originally designed as a stand-alone system that operated almost exclusively within the manufacturing or operations function of a company. Today, an MRP system is often integrated into an enterprise resource planning (ERP) system, which is typically organizationwide. In essence, as shown in the comparison between Exhibits 16.1 and 16.2, what MRP initially did for manufacturing, in terms of integrating all of the various operational elements, ERP is now doing across all of the functions within an organization.

Exhibit 16.1

The Role of MRP within the Manufacturing Function

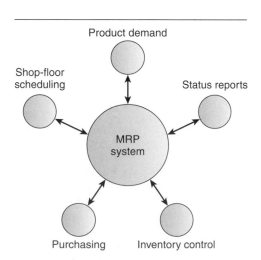

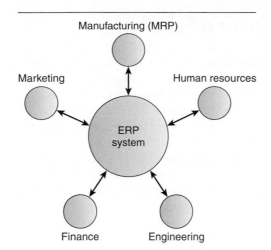

Exhibit 16.2

The Role of MRP within an ERP System

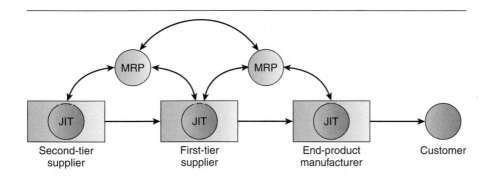

Exhibit 16.3

Integrating MRP and JIT into the Supply Chain

Over the years, the role of MRP has changed significantly. Initially, MRP was used primarily for shop-floor control within the company. Today, many of the leading-edge manufacturing firms, however, use JIT for shop-floor control and utilize MRP to determine the subassembly and component requirements that are supplied by vendors, as shown in Exhibit 16.3. With continuous emphasis on reducing both inventories and lead times, the need for accurate information, in terms of the quantities of individual items required and their respective due dates, is more important today than ever before. And this type of information is readily provided with MRP. MRP systems, in part or in whole, are used in manufacturing firms both large and small. As discussed in the managerial issues section, manufacturing often involves dependent demand. The reason is that MRP provides a logical and readily understandable approach to the problem of determining the number of parts, components, and raw materials needed to produce each end item. MRP also provides the time schedule specifying when each of these materials, parts, and components should be ordered or produced.

The original MRP planned only materials. However, as computer power and speed increased over the past 20 or so years and applications expanded, so did the breadth of MRP. Soon it considered resources as well as materials; now MRP also stands for *manufacturing resource planning (MRP II)*, which will be discussed later in this chapter.

Since MRP and MRP II are information systems similar to ERP, the same implementation issues as discussed in Chapter 12 exist.

Master Production Schedule

The aggregate production plan, as presented in Chapter 14, specifies product groups. It does not specify exact items. The next level down in the planning process after the development of the aggregate plan is the master production schedule. The **master production schedule (MPS)** is the time-phased plan specifying how many and when the firm plans to build each specific end item. For example, the aggregate plan for a furniture company may specify the total volume of mattresses it plans to produce over the next month or next quarter. The MPS then goes to the next step down in the process and identifies the specific models and sizes of the mattresses. All the mattresses sold by the company would be specified by the MPS. The MPS also states period by period (which is usually weekly) how many and when each of these mattress types is needed.

Still further down the disaggregation process is the MRP program, which calculates the requirements and schedules for all of the raw materials, parts, and supplies needed to make each of the different mattresses identified in the MPS.

master production schedule (MPS)

Production plan that specifies how many of, and when to build, each end item.

Time Fences

Flexibility within an MPS depends on several factors, including production lead time, the commitment of parts and components to a specific end item, the relationship between the customer and supplier, the amount of excess capacity, and the reluctance or willingness of management to make changes.

Exhibit 16.4 shows an example of a master production schedule time fence. Management defines *time fences* as periods of time, with each period having some specified level of opportunity for the customer to make changes. (The customer may be the firm's own marketing department, which may be considering product promotions, broadening variety, etc.) Note in the exhibit that for the next eight weeks the MPS for this particular firm is frozen. Each firm has its own time fences and operating rules. Under these rules, *frozen* could be defined as anything from absolutely no changes in one firm to only the most minor of changes in another. *Moderately firm* may allow changes in specific products within a product group, so long as parts are available. *Flexible* may allow almost any variations in products, with the provision that capacity remain about the same and that there be no long lead-time items involved.

The purpose of time fences is to maintain a reasonably controlled flow through the production system. Unless some operating rules are established and adhered to, the system could be chaotic and filled with overdue orders and constant expediting.

Exhibit 16.4

Master Production Schedule Time Fences

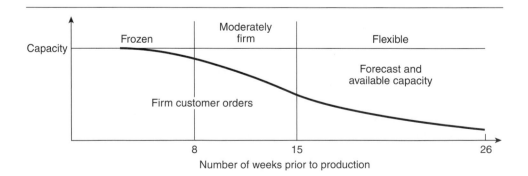

With the trend towards reducing lead times and increasing product choices, companies are continuously trying to reduce the time period within which the MPS is frozen without wreaking havoc on the factory floor. This allows firms to react more quickly to changes in customer demand. To accomplish this, the overall quantity of products within a product group or family is typically frozen while the mix of products, within the group or family, in terms of specific models, remains flexible up until the last minute.

Materials Requirements Planning (MRP) Systems

Using an MPS that is derived from an aggregate plan, a **materials requirements planning (MRP)** system then creates the requirements and schedules for identifying the specific parts, components, and materials that are necessary to produce the end products that have been ordered. Included here are the exact number of each item that is needed and the dates when orders for these items should be released and be received or completed within the production cycle. Today's MRP systems use a computer program to carry out these operations. Most firms have used computerized inventory systems for years, but they were independent of the scheduling system; MRP now links these two elements.

Materials requirements planning is not new in concept. Logic dictates that the Romans probably used it in their construction projects, the Venetians in their shipbuilding, and the Chinese in building the Great Wall. Building contractors have always been forced into planning for material to be delivered when needed and not before, because of space limitations. What is new is the larger scale and the more rapid changes that can be made through the use of computers. Now firms that produce many products involving thousands of parts and materials can take advantage of MRP.

materials requirements planning (MRP) Determines the number of subassemblies, components, and raw materials required and their build dates to complete a given number of end products by a specific date.

Purposes, Objectives, and Philosophy of MRP

The main purposes of an MRP system are to control inventory levels, assign operating priorities to items, and plan capacity to load the production system. These may be briefly expanded as follows:

Inventory

> Order the right part
>
> Order the right quantity
>
> Order at the right time

Priorities

> Order with the right due date
>
> Keep the due date valid

Capacity

> Plan for a complete load
>
> Plan an accurate load
>
> Plan for an adequate time to view future load

> The *theme* of MRP is "getting the right materials to the right place at the right time."

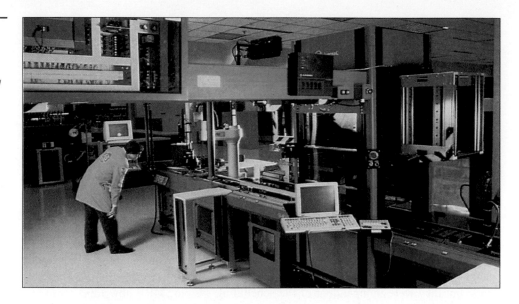

The MRP system at Allen-Bradley, a manufacturer of circuit boards, receives an order and schedules appropriate production. Board panels are automatically routed to the required process, such as this robotic cell that inserts nonstandard components.

The *objectives* of inventory management under an MRP system are to improve customer service, minimize inventory investment, and maximize production operating efficiency.

The *philosophy* of materials requirements planning is that materials should be expedited (hurried) when their lack would delay the overall production schedule and de-expedited (delayed) when the schedule falls behind and postpones their need. Traditionally, and perhaps still typically, when an order is behind schedule, significant effort is spent trying to get it back on schedule. However, the opposite is not always true; when an order, for whatever reason, has its completion date delayed, the appropriate adjustments are not made in the schedule. This results in a one-sided effort—late orders are expedited, but early orders are not de-expedited or delayed. Aside from perhaps using scarce capacity, it is preferable not to have raw materials and work in process before they are actually needed, because inventories tie up capital, clutter up stockrooms, delay the introduction of design changes, and prevent the cancellation or delay of existing orders.

The relationship of MRP to other types of operational planning is shown in Exhibit 14.1 in Chapter 14.

Benefits of an MRP System

Manufacturing companies with more than $15 million in annual sales are most likely to have some form of a computerized MRP system. A computerized system is necessary because of the sheer volume of materials, supplies, and components that are part of expanding product lines, and the speed that firms need to react to constant changes in the system. When firms switch from manual or computerized systems to an MRP system, they realize many benefits, including:

- More competitive pricing
- Lower selling price
- Lower inventory levels
- Improved customer service
- Faster response to market demands

Operations Management in Practice

CLASS A PERFORMANCE COMPANIES REAP SIGNIFICANT BENEFITS FROM MRP

Firms that have achieved excellence in implementing MRP are designated Class A companies. Listed below are several Class A companies and the benefits they have achieved.

Company	Product	Benefits from MRP
Allergan America Puerto Rico	Pharmaceuticals	Inventory reduced from 87 to 49 days Supplier on-time delivery up from 43 percent to 99 percent On-time customer deliveries up from 40 percent to 100 percent
The Clarkson Company Sparks, Nevada	Industrial valves	Reduced inventories 30 percent for a US$500 000 savings Improved forecast accuracy to more than 90 percent Reduced lead time from 6–8 weeks to 2 weeks
Kraft Food Limited Melbourne, Australia	Foods	Inventories reduced from US$9 million to US$6 million On-time deliveries improved from 40 percent to 100 percent Finished goods inventories reduced by 18 percent

Source: Provided courtesy of the Oliver Wight Companies, New London, NH.

- Increased flexibility to change the master schedule
- Reduced setup and tear-down costs
- Reduced idle time

In addition, the MRP system

- Gives advanced notice so managers can see the planned schedule before the orders are actually released
- Tells when to de-expedite as well as expedite
- Delays or cancels orders
- Changes order quantities
- Advances or delays order due dates
- Aids capacity planning

After converting to an MRP system, many firms claim as much as a 40 percent reduction in inventory investment. (See the OM in Practice Box.)

Where MRP Can Be Used

MRP is being used in a variety of industries with a job-shop environment (meaning that a number of products are made in batches using the same production equipment). The list in Exhibit 16.5 includes process industries, but note that the processes mentioned are confined to job runs that alternate output products and do not include continuous processes such as petroleum or steel.

As you can see in the exhibit, MRP is most valuable to companies involved in assembly operations and least valuable to those in fabrication. Another factor that affects the degree of benefit gained from an MRP system is the number of levels in the product. The greater the number of levels, the greater the benefit of MRP.

One more point to note: MRP typically does not work well in companies that produce a low number of units annually. This is especially true for companies producing complex, expensive products requiring advanced research and design. Under such circumstances,

Exhibit 16.5

Industry
Applications
and Expected
Benefits

Industry Type	Examples	Expected Benefits
Assemble-to-stock	Combines multiple component parts into a finished product, which is then stocked in inventory to satisfy customer demand. Examples: watches, tools, appliances.	High
Fabricate-to-stock	Items are manufactured by machine rather than assembled from parts. These are standard stock items carried in anticipation of customer demand. Examples: piston rings, electrical switches.	Low
Assemble-to-order	A final assembly is made from standard options that the customer chooses. Examples: trucks, generators, motors.	High
Fabricate-to-order	Items manufactured by machine to customer order. These are generally industrial orders. Examples: bearings, gears, fasteners.	Low
Manufacture-to-order	Items fabricated or assembled completely to customer specification. Examples: turbine generators, heavy machine tools.	High
Process	Industries such as foundries, rubber and plastics, specialty paper, chemicals, paint, drug, food processors.	Medium

experience has shown that lead times tend to be too long and too uncertain, and the product configuration too complex for MRP to handle. These types of companies need the control features that network scheduling techniques offer, and thus would be better off using project scheduling methods (covered previously in Chapter 4).

MRP System Structure

The MRP system most closely interacts with the MPS schedule, the bill of materials file, the inventory records file, and the output reports. Exhibit 16.6 shows a portion of Exhibit 14.1 in Chapter 14 with several additions. Note that capacity is not addressed here, nor are there any feedback loops to higher levels. We discuss these elements later in this chapter under MRP II and capacity requirements planning.

Each facet of Exhibit 16.6 is subsequently explained in more detail, but essentially the MRP system works as follows: Forecasted sales and firm orders for products are used to create an MPS, which states the number of items to be produced during specific time periods. A bill of materials file identifies the specific materials used to make each item and the correct quantities of each. The inventory records file contains data such as the number of units on hand and on order. These three sources—(1) the MPS, (2) the bill of materials file, and (3) the inventory records file—become the data sources for the MRP program, which essentially expands or "explodes" the MPS into a detailed order scheduling plan for the entire production sequence.

Demand for Products

As stated earlier, the demand for end items is primarily derived from two sources: known customers and forecast demand. Known customers are those who have placed specific orders, such as those generated by sales personnel or from interdependent transactions. These orders usually carry promised delivery dates. There is no forecasting involved in these orders—we simply add them up. The second source is forecasted demand. These are the normal, independent-demand orders; the forecasting models presented in Chapter 9

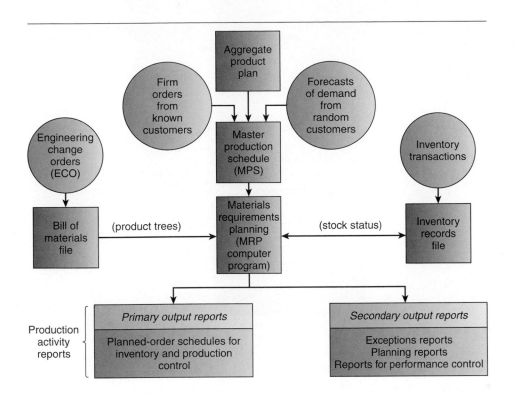

Exhibit 16.6

**Overall View
of the Inputs to
a Standard
Materials
Requirements
Planning
Program and the
Reports
Generated by
the Program**

can be used to predict the quantities. The demand from both the known customers and the forecast demand are used as inputs for developing the MPS.

Available-to-Promise

When a firm manufactures products to meet a projected sales forecast, the MPS can also provide information on the quantities and dates when specific products and models will be available for delivery. The quantities and delivery dates of these products that have not been previously committed are often referred to as *available-to-promise*. As an illustration, a firm has scheduled to build 100 units of a given product during the first week of February, of which 35 are to meet specific customer orders and the remaining 65 are to meet forecasted customer orders. However, at a given point in time, for example, the third week in January, the marketing department has already taken orders for 40 of the 65 that are to be built to forecast. This leaves 25 units that are available-to-promise for delivery during that week.

Demand for Spare Parts and Supplies

In addition to the demand for end products, customers also order specific parts and components as spare parts to provide for service and repair. This demand for items less complex than the end product is not usually part of the MPS; instead, it is fed directly into the MRP program at the appropriate levels. That is, it is added in as a gross requirement for that part or component.

Bill of Materials File

The **bill of materials (BOM)** file contains the complete product description, listing not only the materials, parts, and components, but also the sequences in which the product is created.

**bill of materials
(BOM)**

A list of subassemblies, components, and raw materials, and their respective quantities, required to produce specific end items.

Exhibit 16.7

Exploded View of End Item

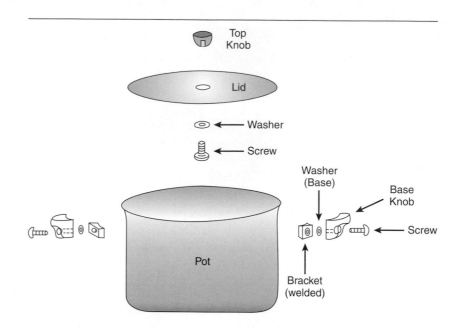

The BOM file is often referred to as the *product structure* or *product tree file* because it shows how a product is put together. It identifies each item and the quantity used per unit of the item in which it is used.

To illustrate this, consider the manufacture of a saucepan (end item) that is shown in an exploded view in Exhibit 16.7. The saucepan consists of a top and a base. The top is assembled using a lid and top handle. The top handle consists of the knob, screw, and washer. Similarly, the base can be broken down into its constituent components, as shown in the exhibit. Some of the components may be manufactured, others purchased.

The product structure tree for the product is shown in Exhibit 16.8A with the part (component) names and part numbers. The number in brackets beside the part name shows the number of units required for each parent. For example, two base handles and brackets are required for each saucepan. Each part has a unique part number to identify it throughout the supply chain. You have probably experienced this when you called in to order a replacement part for a product such as a household appliance or electronic equipment, and the customer service agent asked you for the item part number (or had you describe it so that the part number could be identified). Note that both the top and base use the same type of screw and washer (same part numbers). This follows the design-or-manufacture principle. In addition to the advantages of this principle mentioned in Chapter 3, by using common parts, the company has less stockkeeping units to manage, and this will help better control the inventory as well as reduce the database resources required. In addition, the company may get a price discount from its supplier for larger volumes. In practice, when the BOM is printed out it is in an indented format as shown in Exhibit 16.8B. This is more efficient for computer processing. A data element (called a *pointer* or *locator*) also is contained in each file to identify the parent of each part and allows retracing upward through the process. For complex products the number of components may be too large to present in a tree format. Note there is only one level of indent in the format.

Low-Level Coding

If all identical parts occur at the same level for each end product, the total number of parts and materials needed for a product can be easily computed. However, consider Product

Exhibit 16.8A

BOM in Tree and Indented Format

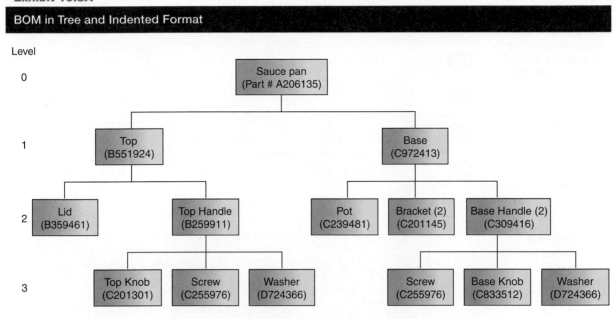

Exhibit 16.8B

Part Name (Part No.)	Subcomponents	Number per Parent
Saucepan (A206135)	Top (B551924)	1
	Base (C972413)	1
Top (B551924)	Lid (B359461)	1
	Top Handle (B259911)	1
Top Handle (B259911)	Top Knob (C201301)	1
	Screw (C255976)	1
	Washer (D724366)	1
Base (C972413)	Pot (C239481)	1
	Bracket (C201145)	2
	Base Handle (C309416)	2
Base Handle (C309416)	Screw (C255976)	1
	Base Knob (C833512)	1
	Washer (D724366)	1

L shown in Exhibit 16.9A. Notice that Item N in Product L, for example, occurs both as an input to L and as an input to M. Item N therefore needs to be lowered to level 2 (Exhibit 16.9B) to bring all the Ns down to their lowest common level. This is referred to as *low-level coding*. When all identical items are placed at the same level, it becomes a simple matter for the computer to scan across each level and summarize the number of units of each item required. Similarly, Items S and T are lowered to level 4. The low level code may be included in the BOM file shown in Exhibit 16.8B (though it is not shown here).

Inventory Records File

The **inventory records file** in a computerized system can be quite lengthy. Each item in inventory is carried as a separate file, and the range of details carried about an item is

inventory records file

Computerized record-keeping system for the inventory status of all subassemblies, components, and raw materials.

Exhibit 16.9

Product L Hierarchy in (A) Expanded to the Lowest Level of Each Item in (B)

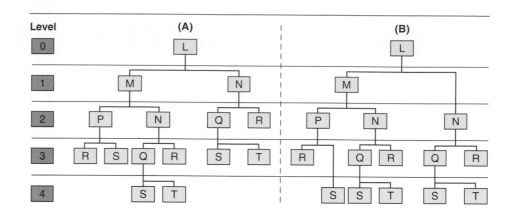

Exhibit 16.10

The Inventory Status Record for an Item in Inventory

almost limitless. Although Exhibit 16.10 is from an earlier version of MRP, it shows the variety of information contained in the inventory records files. The MRP program accesses the *status* segment of the file according to specific time periods (called *time buckets* in MRP slang). These files are accessed as needed during the program run.

The MRP program performs its analysis from the top of the product structure downward, exploding requirements level by level. There are times, however, when it is desirable to identify the parent item that caused the materials requirement. The MRP program allows the creation of a *peg record* file either separately or as part of the inventory record file. Pegging requirements allows us to retrace a materials requirement upward in the product structure through each level, identifying each parent item that created the demand.

Inventory Transactions File

The inventory status file is kept up to date by posting inventory transactions as they occur. These changes are a result of stock receipts and disbursements, scrap and obsolescence losses, wrong parts, cancelled orders, and so forth.

MRP Computer Program

The MRP program operates on the inventory file, the MPS, and the BOM file. It works as follows: A list of end items needed by time periods (or time "buckets") is specified by the MPS. A description of the materials and parts needed to make each item is specified in the BOM file. The number of units of each item and material currently on hand and on order are contained in the inventory file. The MRP program "works" on the inventory file (which is segmented into time periods), while continually referring to the BOM file to compute the quantities of each item needed. The number of units of each item required is then adjusted for on-hand amounts and amounts previously ordered; the net requirements are then "offset" (set back in time) to allow for the lead time needed to obtain the material and/or to make the items.

If the MRP program being used does not consider capacity constraints, the master scheduler must manually perform some capacity balancing. Through an iterative process, the master scheduler feeds a tentative MPS into the MRP program (along with other items requiring the same resources) and the output is examined for production feasibility. The MPS is then adjusted to try to correct any imbalances, and the program is executed again. This process is repeated until the output is acceptable. Although it would seem to be a simple matter to have the computer simulate various schedules that take into consideration resource limitations, in reality it is usually a large and time-consuming problem.

To further complicate the problem, there is often not one MPS, but a number of them. Firms will frequently divide the scheduling work among the schedulers by assigning one master scheduler to each major product line. As a result, each master scheduler must compete for limited resources for his or her own product line. As a group, however, they are trying to balance resource usage and due dates for the production system as a whole.

Output Reports

Because the MRP program has access to the BOM file, the MPS, and the inventory records file, outputs or reports can take on an almost unlimited range of format and content. These reports are usually classified as *primary* and *secondary* output reports. (With the expansion of MRP into MRP II, many additional reports are available.)

Primary Reports

Primary reports are the main or normal reports used for inventory and production control. These reports include:

1. Planned order releases: give the date and quantity of orders that are planned to be released (for production or for purchase), giving planners forward visibility.

2. Order release notices: give instructions to release orders that need to be placed in the current period, either in production or with suppliers.

3. Change notices: indicate modifications to the due dates of planned orders.

4. Cancellations or suspensions: indicate planned orders on the MPS that are cancelled or suspended.

5. Inventory Status Data: give the current on-hand inventory for each item.

Secondary Reports

Additional reports, which are optional in an MRP program, fall into the following main categories:

1. Planning reports: to be used, for example, in forecasting inventory and specifying requirements over some future time horizon.

Exhibit 16.11

Lot-for-Lot
Method of
Determining
Production
Quantities

Period	1	2	3	4	5	6
Net Requirements	50	60	70	60	95	75
Production Quantity	50	60	70	60	95	75

2. Performance reports: for purposes of pointing out inactive items and determining the agreement between actual and programmed item lead times and between actual and programmed quantity usage and costs.

3. Exceptions reports: point out serious discrepancies, such as errors, out-of-range situations, late or overdue orders, excessive scrap, or nonexistent parts.

Lot Sizing in MRP Systems

The determination of lot sizes in an MRP system is a complicated and difficult problem. Lot sizes are the part quantities isssued in the planned order release sections of an MRP schedule. For parts produced in-house, lot sizes are the production quantities or batch sizes. For purchased parts, they are the quantities ordered from the supplier. Lot sizes generally meet part requirements for one or more periods.

Most lot-sizing techniques deal with how to balance the setup or order costs and holding costs associated with meeting the net requirements generated by the MRP planning process. Many MRP systems have options for computing lot sizes based on some of the more commonly used techniques. It should be obvious, though, that the use of lot-sizing techniques increases the complexity in generating MRP schedules. When fully exploded, the numbers of parts scheduled can be enormous.

There are various lot-sizing techniques that can be used with MRP systems such as: (*a*) lot-for-lot (L4L or LFL), (*b*) economic order quantity (EOQ), (*c*) least period cost (LPC), also called the Silver–Meal method,[1] (*d*) least unit cost (LUC), and (*e*) part period balancing. Different lot sizing techniques may work better with different problems.

Lot-for-lot (L4L) is a common technique; it

- Sets planned orders to exactly match the net requirements

- Produces exactly what is needed each period with none carried over into future periods

- Minimizes carrying cost

- Does not take into account setup costs or capacity limitations

Exhibit 16.11 illustrates the lot-for-lot method, with the production lot sizes in each period equalling the net requirements in each respective period. The other methods mentioned are more sophisticated techniques. Details may be found in more advanced textbooks on production planning.

A Simple MRP Example

To demonstrate how the various elements of an MRP system are integrated, we present a simple problem to demonstrate how quantities are calculated, lead times are offset, and order releases and receipts are established.

---

[1]E. A. Silver and H. Meal, "A Simple Modification to the EOQ for the Case of a Time Varying Demand," *Production and Inventory Management Journal*, 10, no. 4 (1969), pp. 52–65.

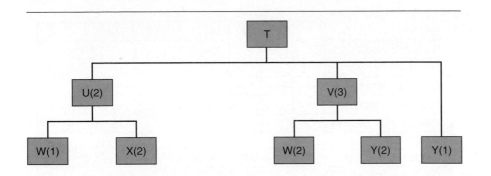

Exhibit 16.12

Product
Structure Tree
for Product T

Bill of Materials (Product Structure Tree) File

Suppose that we want to produce Product T, which consists of two parts U, three parts V, and one part Y. Part U, in turn, is made of one part W and two parts X. Part V is made of two parts W and two parts Y. Exhibit 16.12 shows the product structure tree for Product T.

Inventory Records File

Next, we need to consider the lead times needed to obtain these items, that is, either to produce the parts internally or to obtain them from an outside vendor. Assume that the lead times to make the parts and their respective on-hand inventories and scheduled receipts are as follows:

Part	Lead Time (weeks)	On-Hand Inventory	Scheduled Receipts*
T	1	25	–
U	2	5	5
V	2	15	–
W	3	30	–
X	2	20	–
Y	1	10	–

*Subassemblies or parts that have been previously ordered but are not scheduled for delivery until a future date (week three for subassembly U in this example).

Lot Sizes

For all parts except X and Y, by using JIT principles and reducing setup times, L4L reordering has become feasible and is being used. For parts X and Y, however, high setup costs are still incurred and this results in larger quantities determined by one of the other lot-sizing rules being used. For X the lot size is 300, and for Y the lot size is 450.

Running the MRP Program

If we know when Product T is required (this information comes from the MPS; in this case assume that 100 completed units are required in week 8), we can create a time schedule chart specifying when all the material necessary to build T must be ordered and received to meet this requirement. Exhibit 16.13 shows which items are needed and when. We thus have created a materials requirements plan based on the demand for Product T and the knowledge of how T is made, current inventories on hand from the prior period, and the time needed to obtain each part.

Exhibit 16.13

Materials
Requirements
Plan for
Completing 100
units of Product
T in Period 8

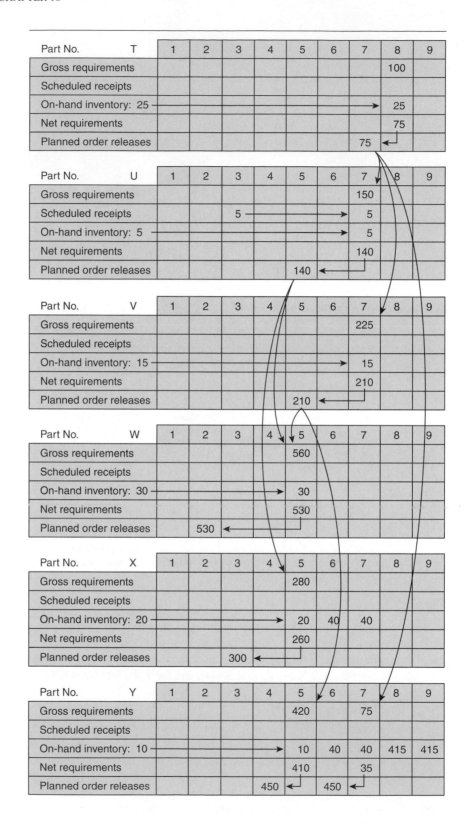

Part No. T	1	2	3	4	5	6	7	8	9
Gross requirements								100	
Scheduled receipts									
On-hand inventory: 25								25	
Net requirements								75	
Planned order releases							75		

Part No. U	1	2	3	4	5	6	7	8	9
Gross requirements							150		
Scheduled receipts			5				5		
On-hand inventory: 5							5		
Net requirements							140		
Planned order releases					140				

Part No. V	1	2	3	4	5	6	7	8	9
Gross requirements							225		
Scheduled receipts									
On-hand inventory: 15							15		
Net requirements							210		
Planned order releases					210				

Part No. W	1	2	3	4	5	6	7	8	9
Gross requirements					560				
Scheduled receipts									
On-hand inventory: 30					30				
Net requirements					530				
Planned order releases		530							

Part No. X	1	2	3	4	5	6	7	8	9
Gross requirements					280				
Scheduled receipts									
On-hand inventory: 20					20	40	40		
Net requirements					260				
Planned order releases			300						

Part No. Y	1	2	3	4	5	6	7	8	9
Gross requirements					420		75		
Scheduled receipts									
On-hand inventory: 10					10	40	40	415	415
Net requirements					410		35		
Planned order releases				450		450			

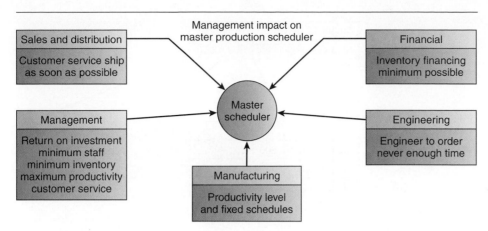

Exhibit 16.14

The Environment of the Master Scheduler

Source: Romeyn C. Everdell and Woodrow W. Chamberlain, "Master Scheduling in a Multi-Plant Environment," *Proceedings of the American Production and Inventory Control Society* (1980), p. 421. Reprinted with permission.

From this simple illustration, it should be obvious that manually developing a materials requirements plan for thousands or even hundreds of items would be impractical—a great deal of computation is needed, and a tremendous amount of data must be available about the inventory status (number of units on hand, on order, and so forth) and about the product structure (how the product is made and how many units of each material are required). A computer is an integral part of every MRP system. However, our emphasis in this chapter is on understanding the general structure of the system and on the supporting computer files that are required because the underlying logic of the program is essentially the same as that for our simple example.

Generally, the MPS, which is the primary driver of the MRP system, deals with finished products or end items. If the end item is quite large and/or quite expensive, the MPS may schedule major subassemblies or components instead.

All production systems have limited capacity and limited resources. This presents a challenge for the master scheduler. Exhibit 16.14 shows the environment in which the master scheduler works. Although the aggregate plan provides the general range of operation, the master scheduler must massage the aggregate plan into an MPS that specifies exactly what is to be produced. These decisions are made while responding to pressures from various functional areas.

To determine an acceptable schedule that is feasible for the shop, trial master production schedules are run through the MRP program in an iterative process. The resulting planned order releases (the detailed production schedules) are reviewed to ensure that resources are available and completion times are reasonable. What may appear to be a feasible MPS may, in fact, require excessive resources once the resource requirements for the materials, parts, and components for the lower levels are determined. If this occurs (which is usually the case), the MPS is adjusted to reflect these limitations and the MRP program is run again. To ensure good master scheduling, the master scheduler (i.e., the human being) must:

- Include all demands from product sales, warehouse replenishment, spares, and interplant requirements
- Never lose sight of the aggregate plan

Exhibit 16.15

The Aggregate Plan and the Master Production Schedule for Mattresses

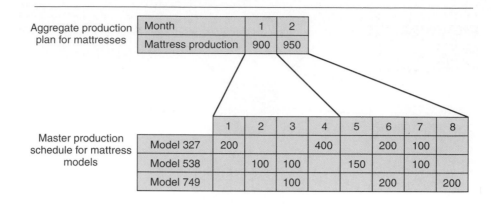

- Be involved with customer order promising

- Be visible to all levels of management

- Objectively trade off manufacturing, marketing, and engineering conflicts

- Identify and communicate all problems

Exhibit 16.15 illustrates the relationship between an aggregate plan and its master production schedule. The upper portion of the exhibit shows an aggregate plan for the total number of mattresses planned per month for a furniture manufacturer, without regard to mattress type. The lower portion of the exhibit shows an MPS specifying the exact type of mattress and the quantity planned for production by week. The next level down (not shown) would be the MRP program that develops detailed schedules showing when cotton batting, springs, and hardwood are needed to make the mattresses.

Capacity Requirements Planning (CRP)

In the previous sections of this chapter that focused on the MPS and running the MRP program, we mentioned that production capacity is usually some finite amount and obviously has limits. We also cited the interaction between the scheduler and rerunning the MRP program to obtain feasible schedules in light of this limited capacity. In this section we explicitly point out how capacity is computed and what the usual procedure is for addressing capacity constraints. Exhibit 16.18 shows the role of CRP within an MRP environment.

Computing Work Centre Load

Each work centre is generally a functionally defined centre where jobs routed to it require the same type of work, on the same type of equipment. From the work centre view, if there is adequate capacity, the problem is one of priorities: which job to do first. If there is insufficient capacity, however, the problem must be resolved by the master scheduler.

Exhibit 16.16 shows a work centre that has various jobs assigned to it. Note that the capacity per week was computed at the bottom of the exhibit as 161.5 hours. The jobs scheduled for the three weeks result in two weeks with undercapacity and one week requiring overcapacity.

Exhibit 16.16 uses the terms *utilization* and *efficiency*. Both have been defined and used in a variety of ways, some conflicting. In this exhibit, *utilization* refers to the actual time the machines are used. *Efficiency* refers to how well the machine is performing while it is

Week	Job No.	Units	Setup Time	Run Time per Unit	Total Job Time	Total for Week
10	145	100	3.5	0.23	26.5	
	167	160	2.4	0.26	44.0	
	158	70	1.2	0.13	10.3	
	193	300	6.0	0.17	57.0	137.8
11	132	80	5.0	0.36	33.8	
	126	150	3.0	0.22	36.0	
	180	180	2.5	0.30	56.5	
	178	120	4.0	0.50	64.0	190.3
12	147	90	3.0	0.18	19.2	
	156	200	3.5	0.14	31.5	
	198	250	1.5	0.16	41.5	
	172	100	2.0	0.12	14.0	
	139	120	2.2	0.17	22.6	128.8

Exhibit 16.16

Workload for Work Centre A

Computing Work Centre Capacity

The available capacity in standard hours is 161.5 hours per five-day week, calculated as (2 machines) (2 shifts) (10 hours/shift) (85% machine utilization) (95% efficiency).

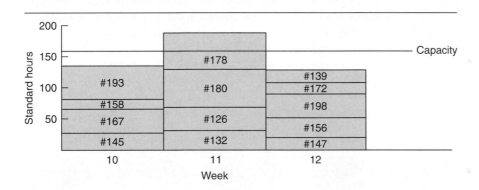

Exhibit 16.17

Scheduled Workload for Work Centre A

being used. Efficiency is usually defined as a comparison of actual performance to a defined standard output or an engineering design rate. For instance, a machine used for six hours of an eight-hour shift was utilized 6/8 or 75 percent. If the standard output for that machine is established as 200 parts per hour and an average of 250 parts per hour were actually produced, then the efficiency of that machine is 125 percent. Note that in these definitions efficiency can be more than 100 percent, but utilization can never exceed 100 percent.

Exhibit 16.17 shows a loading representation of Work Centre A for the three weeks. The scheduled work exceeds capacity for Week 11. There are several options available:

1. Work overtime.

2. Select an alternate work centre that could perform the task.

3. Subcontract to an outside shop.

4. Try to schedule part of the work of Week 11 earlier into Week 10, and delay part of the work into Week 12.

5. Renegotiate the due date and reschedule.

An MRP program with a capacity requirements planning module allows rescheduling to try to level capacity. Two techniques used are backward scheduling and forward scheduling—the fourth option on the preceding list. The objective of the master scheduler is to try to level out the load in Exhibit 16.17 so that the requirements for the work centre remain within the available capacity.

Manufacturing Resource Planning (MRP II)

Earlier in this chapter our discussion of MRP focused only on the *materials* requirements that resulted from an explosion of the master schedule. We did not include the needs of all the other types of resources, such as staffing, facilities, and tools. In addition, although we discussed *capacity requirements planning*, we did this somewhat externally to the MRP system. In this section we discuss the logic of more advanced versions of MRP that include a wider range of resources and outputs. Exhibit 16.18 shows an MRP II system.

MRP II

manufacturing resource planning (MRP II)

Advanced MRP system that takes into consideration the equipment capacities and other resources associated with a manufacturing facility.

An expansion of the materials requirements planning program to include other portions of the production system was natural and to be expected. One of the first to be included was the purchasing function. At the same time, there was a more detailed inclusion of the production system itself—on the shop floor, in dispatching, and in the detailed scheduling control. MRP already had included work centre capacity limitations, so it was obvious the name *materials requirements planning* no longer adequately described the expanded system. Someone (probably MRP pioneer Ollie Wight) introduced the name **manufacturing resource planning (MRP II)** to reflect the idea that more and more of the firm was becoming involved in the program. To quote Wight,

> The fundamental manufacturing equation is:
> What are we going to make?
> What does it take to make it?

Exhibit 16.18

An Overview of MRP II

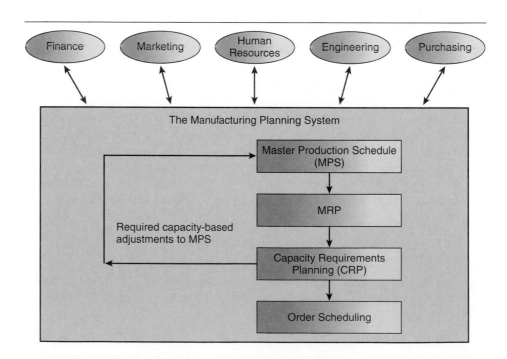

What do we have?

What do we have to get?[2]

The initial intent for MRP II was to plan and monitor all the resources of a manufacturing firm—manufacturing, marketing, finance, human resources, and engineering—through a closed-loop system generating financial figures. The second important intent of the MRP II concept was that it simulate the manufacturing system. It is generally conceived now as being a total, companywide system that allows everyone (buyers, marketing staff, production, accounting) to work with the same game plan and use the same numbers. It is capable of simulation to plan and test alternative strategies. Kodak Canada and Merck Frosst Canada & Co. are examples of Canadian companies that have Class A MRP II systems.

Sales and Operations Planning

Sales and operations planning (S&OP) is an extension of MRP II that goes outside of the manufacturing function,[3] aligning customer demand with both in-house and supplier resources. The S&OP review process is typically performed on a monthly basis, with a rolling planning horizon of 18 to 24 months. The outputs of the S&OP process include (*a*) revised sales plan, (*b*) production plan, (*c*) inventory levels, and (*d*) customer lead times or backlogs.

A key goal of the S&OP process is to balance the firm's resources with customer demand, which frequently involves the decoupling of demand from supply. As we learned in the chapter on aggregate planning, a firm can manufacture products in different volumes and time periods than that requested by the customer in order to maximize the overall efficiency of the process. Therefore, in decoupling supply from demand, some of the decisions to be made include (*a*) producing to order or to inventory, (*b*) adjusting customer lead times or backlogs, and (*c*) changing capacity, such as working overtime or adding another shift.

Distribution Requirements Planning (DRP)

As shown in the OM in Practice Box on ERPs, companies can use technology to link to their suppliers or other facilities within the same company. These links can help plan distribution inventories in addition to within-facility scheduling.

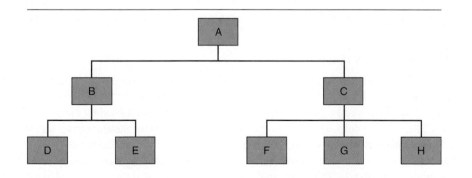

Exhibit 16.19

Distribution Requirements Planning

---

[2]Oliver Wight, *The Executive's Guide to Successful MRP II* (Williston, VT: Oliver Wight Limited Publications, 1982), pp. 6, 17.

[3]Adapted from George Palmatier, "Sales and Operations Planning—An Executive Level Synopsis" (New London, NH: The Oliver Wight Companies).

ERP POWERS EXHAUST SYSTEMS PRODUCER

Wescast Industries Inc. of Brantford, Ontario, manufactures exhaust systems and other niche components for the auto industry. It has manufacturing and/or design facilities in Canada, the United States, the United Kingdom, Germany, and Hungary. Until a few years ago it had a Unix-based ERP system that could process orders, but had no MRP or CRP capability, making planning difficult. As a result, operations were inefficient. Financial closing took two weeks to complete and inventory levels were higher than desirable. Data were entered in multiple systems and multiple spreadsheets.

In the mid- to late-1990s Wescast implemented an ERP called TRANS4M from Agilisys, in a phased fashion, module by module. A phased approach is an incremental approach that allows the user to manage the changes more easily. Although slower than replacing the entire system all at once, it is less risky. The software included fully integrated modules for manufacturing, financials, release control management, planning and scheduling, inventory management, and EDI. It has helped Wescast transform itself from being just an executor of designs from the auto manufacturers to being a collaborator on design and in cost and material control.

Since the ERP implementation, better EDI links have resulted in inventory levels being reduced by more than 60 percent. Manufacturing efficiency and information processing have improved. Inventory accuracy and shipping efficiency are higher as a result of bar-coding. The bar-code information can be used to transmit shipping data to the customer via EDI, and the receiving process at the customer's facility is expedited.

Wescast is considering implementing SupplyWEB software from Agilisys. This will allow smaller suppliers to communicate with Wescast over the Internet. They can also access Wescast item requirements and plan accordingly, and in form Wescast of shipments through the Internet. This avoids the suppliers having to set up expensive and dedicated EDI systems.

Sources:
"Supplier Slashes Inventory," *www.manufacturingsystems.com*, (October 1999).
Wescast Industries Inc., www.wescast.com.
Agilisys Inc., www.agilisys.com.

---

distribution requirements planning (DRP)
The use of MRP logic in the planning of distribution inventories.

The use of MRP logic in the planning of distribution inventories is called **distribution requirements planning (DRP)**. Consider the product structure in Exhibit 16.19. Let A represent the factory, let B and C represent distribution centres (DCs), and let D, E, F, G and H represent retail outlets. If we know the lead times for shipping from the retail outlets to the DCs and from the DCs to the factory, the DRP problem becomes very similar to a MRP problem.

Starting from the retail outlets and moving up to the DC and the factory, given the gross requirements, the available inventories, and lot sizes, we can calculate the scheduled receipts, net requirements, and the planned shipping releases just as we would do in MRP. Thus DRP is an MRP-like tool for planning shipments and production in a supply chain. At the factory, the DRP shipping plan would become the input for the gross requirements in the MRP.

MRP in Services

In general, MRP systems have not made significant inroads in service operations. This is due, in part, to the belief that MRP is strictly a manufacturing tool. However, modified versions of MRP are used in service operations in which an actual product is manufactured as part of the service delivery process. Examples of these quasi-manufacturing services, as stated in an earlier chapter, include restaurants and bakeries where food is prepared on-site. In these types of service operations, the inventory management system usually consists of one or more point-of-sale (POS) terminals (or cash registers) that are connected to a central computer. This computer can be located either on-site at the retail operation or at a remote regional or headquarters location.

The POS terminals are designed for *single-item pricing*, in which the cashier simply pushes a single key on the terminal that represents a specific item on the menu. The computer system then automatically posts the price of that item. At the same time, within the central computer system, is the bill-of-materials (or recipe) for the item that has just been sold. All of the ingredients that go into that item are subtracted out from the inventory records file. The computer inventory files are then compared to the actual physical inventories on a periodic basis. Typically these systems have reorder points built into them that will automatically signal when a specific item is running low.

Some of these service operations also use this modified MRP system to order raw ingredients to meet future sales, in a manner similar to that of an MRP system in a manufacturing environment. First, a forecast of end items to be sold is generated (for example, hamburgers). The forecasted demand for these items is then "exploded" against the bills of materials (or recipes) for the end items to determine the gross requirements. Finally, these requirements are compared to on-hand inventories to determine the actual amounts of raw ingredients to be ordered and the delivery dates when they are needed.

The MRP approach would appear to be valuable in producing services because service scheduling consists of identifying the final service and then tracing back to the resources needed, such as equipment, space, and personnel. Consider, for example, a hospital operating room planning an open-heart surgery. The master schedule can establish a time for the surgery (or surgeries, if several are scheduled). The BOM could specify all required equipment and personnel—MDs, nurses, anesthesiologist, operating room, heart/lung machine, defibrillator, and so forth. The inventory status file would show the availability of the resources and commit them to the project. The MRP program then could produce a schedule showing when various parts of the operation are to be started, expected completion times, required materials, and so forth. Checking this schedule would allow "capacity planning" in answering such questions as "Are all the materials and personnel available?" and "Does the system produce a feasible schedule?"

We still believe that MRP systems eventually will find their way into a greater variety of service applications. One reason for the delay is that even service managers who are aware of it believe that MRP is just a manufacturing tool. Also, service managers tend to be people-oriented and skeptical of tools from outside their industry.

Conclusion

Since the 1970s, MRP has grown from its initial purpose of determining simple time schedules, to its present role that ties together all major functions of an organization. During its growth and its application, MRP's disadvantages as a scheduling mechanism have been well recognized and are due largely to the fact that MRP tries to do too much given the dynamic, often jumpy environment in which it is trying to operate.

However, MRP is recognized for its excellent databases and linkages within the firm. MRP also does a good job generating master schedules. Many firms in repetitive manufacturing are installing JIT systems that are linked with their MRP systems. JIT takes the master production schedule as its pulling force, but does not use MRP's generated schedule. Results indicate that this combined approach is working very well.

MRP's service applications have not fared as well as in manufacturing, although they are making inroads in various forms in quasi-manufacturing service operations such as restaurants and bakeries.

Key Terms

bill of materials (BOM)
  p. 571

dependent demand p. 564

distribution requirements
  planning (DRP) p. 584

inventory records file p. 573

manufacturing resource
  planning (MRP II) p. 582

master production schedule
  (MPS) p. 566

materials requirements
  planning (MRP) p. 567

Review and Discussion Questions

1. Although MRP appears reasonable, it did not become popular until recently. Discuss the reasons why.
2. Discuss the meaning of MRP terms such as *planned order releases* and *scheduled order receipts*.
3. Most practitioners currently update MRP weekly or biweekly. Would it be more valuable if it were updated daily? Discuss.
4. What is the role of safety stock in an MRP system?
5. Contrast the significance of the term *lead time* in the traditional EOQ context and in an MRP system.
6. Discuss the importance of the MPS in an MRP system.

7. "MRP just prepares shopping lists—it doesn't do the shopping or cook the dinner." Comment.
8. What are the sources of demand in an MRP system? Are these dependent or independent, and how are they used as inputs to the system?
9. State the types of data that would be carried in the bill of materials file and the inventory record file.
10. How does MRP II differ from MRP?
11. Why isn't MRP more widespread in services?
12. MRP often is referred to as a "push" system, whereas JIT often is said to be a "pull" system. Comment.
13. How does MRP relate to an ERP system?

Solved Problems

Problem 1

Product X, manufactured by the JBE company, is made of two units of Y and three units of Z. Y is made up of one unit of A and two units of B. Z is made up of two units of A and three units of C.

The table below shows the lead times (LT), inventory remaining from prior period, scheduled receipts, and lot sizes for the various products.

Part	LT (weeks)	On-hand Inventory (Units)	Scheduled Receipts (Units)	Lot Size*(Units)
X	1	5		L4L
Y	1	7		210
Z	2	21		L4L
A	1	10	124 in week 4	400
B	3	28		L4L
C	3	367		700

*For the non-L4L lot sizes, if more than one lot is required, multiples of the lot size can be used.

a. Draw the product structure tree.
b. If 100 units of X are required in both weeks 8 and 10, develop a planning schedule showing when each item should be ordered and in what quantity.

Solution

a.

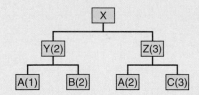

b.

	Period	1	2	3	4	5	6	7	8	9	10
Item X	Gross requirements								100		100
LT = 1	Scheduled receipts										
Q = L4L	On hand (from prior period)	5	5	5	5	5	5	5	5	0	0
	Net requirements								95		100
	Planned order receipts								95		100
	Planned order releases							95		100	

	Period	1	2	3	4	5	6	7	8	9	10
Item Y	Gross requirements							190		200	
LT = 1	Scheduled receipts										
Q = 210	On hand (from prior period)	7	7	7	7	7	7	7	27	27	64
	Net requirements							183		173	
	Planned order receipts							210		210	
	Planned order releases						210		210		

	Period	1	2	3	4	5	6	7	8	9	10
Item Z	Gross requirements							285		300	
LT = 2	Scheduled receipts										
Q = L4L	On hand (from prior period)	21	21	21	21	21	21	21	0	0	0
	Net requirements							264		300	
	Planned order receipts							264		300	
	Planned order releases					264		300			

	Period	1	2	3	4	5	6	7	8	9	10
Item A	Gross requirements					528	210	600	210		
LT = 1	Scheduled receipts				124						
Q = 400	On hand (from prior period)	10	10	10	10	134	6	196	396	186	186
	Net requirements					394	204	404	0		
	Planned order receipts					400	400	800			
	Planned order releases				400	400	800				

Period		1	2	3	4	5	6	7	8	9	10
Item B	Gross requirements						420		420		
LT = 3	Scheduled receipts										
Q = L4L	On hand (from prior period)	28	28	28	28	28	28	0	0	0	0
	Net requirements						392		420		
	Planned order receipts						392		420		
	Planned order releases			392		420					

Period		1	2	3	4	5	6	7	8	9	10
Item C	Gross requirements					792		900			
LT = 3	Scheduled receipts										
Q = 700	On hand (from prior period)	367	367	367	367	367	275	275	75	75	75
	Net requirements					425		625			
	Planned order receipts					700		700			
	Planned order releases		700		700						

Problem 2

Product M is made of two units of N and three of P. N is made of two units of R and four units of S. R is made of one unit of S and three units of T. P is made of two units of T and four units of U.

a. Show the product structure tree.

b. If 100 Ms are required, how many units of each component are needed?

c. Show both a single-level bill of material and an indented bill of material.

Solution

a.

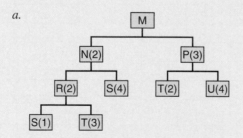

b. $M = 100$ 　　$S = 800 + 400 = 1200$
　　$N = 200$ 　　$T = 600 + 1200 = 1800$
　　$P = 300$ 　　$U = 1200$
　　$R = 400$

c.

Single-level BOM

M	N
	P
N	
	R
	S
R	
	S
	T
P	
	T
	U

Indented BOM

M			
	N		
		R	
			S
			T
		S	
	P		
		T	
		U	

Problems

1. In the following MRP planning schedule for Item J, indicate the correct net requirements, planned order receipts, and planned order releases to meet the gross requirements. Lead time is one week.

Week Number

Item J	0	1	2	3	4	5
Gross requirements			75		50	70
On-hand inventory: 40						
Net requirements						
Planned order receipt						
Planned order releases						

2. Assume that Product Z is made of two units of A and four units of B. A is made of three units of C and four of D. D is made of two units of E.

    The lead time for purchase or fabrication of each unit to final assembly: Z takes two weeks; A, B, C, and D take one week each; and E takes three weeks.

    Fifty units are required in Period 10. (Assume that there is currently no inventory on hand of any of these items.)

    a. Draw a product structure tree.

    b. Using a lot-for-lot ordering policy develop an MRP planning schedule showing gross and net requirements and order release and order receipt dates.

    Note: For Problems 3 through 6, to simplify data handling to include the receipt of orders that have actually been placed in previous periods, the six-level scheme shown below can be used. (There are a number of different techniques used in practice, but the important issue is to keep track of what is on hand, what is expected to arrive, what is needed, and what size orders should be placed.) One way to calculate the numbers is as follows:

Week

Gross requirements									
Scheduled receipts									
On-hand inventory:									
Net requirements									
Planned order receipt									
Planned order release									

3. One unit of A is made of three units of B, one unit of C, and two units of D. B is composed of two units of E and one unit of D. C is made of one unit of B and two units of E. E is made of one unit of F.

   Items B, C, E, and F have one-week lead times; A and D have lead times of two weeks.

   Assume that lot-for-lot (L4L) lot sizing is used for items A, B, and F; lots of size 50, 50, and 200 are used for items C, D, and E, respectively. Items C, E, and F have on-hand (beginning) inventories of 10, 50, and 150, respectively; all other items have zero beginning inventory. We are scheduled to receive 10 units of A in Week 5, 50 units of E in Week 4, and also 50 units of F in Week 4. There are no other scheduled receipts. If 30 units of A are required in Week 8, use the low-level-coded product structure tree to find the necessary planned order releases for all components.

4. One unit of A is made of two units of B, three units of C, and two units of D. B is composed of one unit of E and two units of F. C is made of two units of F and one unit of D. E is made of two units of D. Items A, C, D, and F have one-week lead times; B and E have lead times of two weeks. Lot-for-lot (L4L) lot sizing is used for items A, B, C, and D; lots of size 50 and 180 are used for items E and F, respectively. Item C has an on-hand (beginning) inventory of 15; D has an on-hand inventory of 50; all other items have zero beginning inventory. We are scheduled to receive 20 units of item E in Week 4; there are no other scheduled receipts.

   Construct simple and low-level-coded product structure trees and indented and summarized bills of materials.

   If 20 units of A are required in Week 8, use the low-level-coded product structure tree to find the necessary planned order releases for all components. (See note prior to Problem 3.)

5. One unit of A is made of one unit of B and one unit of C. B is made of four units of C and one unit each of E and F. C is made of two units of D and one unit of E. E is made of three units of F. Item C has a lead time of one week; items A, B, E, and F have two-week lead times; and item D has a lead time of three weeks. Lot-for-lot (L4L) lot sizing is used for items A, D, and E; lots of size 50, 100, and 50 are used for items B, C, and F, respectively. Items A, C, D, and E have on-hand (beginning) inventories of 20, 50, 100, and 10, respectively; all other items have zero beginning inventory. We are scheduled to receive 10 units of A in Week 5, 100 units of C in Week 6, and 100 units of D in Week 4; there are no other scheduled receipts. If 50 units of A are required in Week 10, use the low-level-coded product structure tree to find the necessary planned order releases for all components. (See note prior to Problem 3.)

6. One unit of A is made of two units of B and one unit of C. B is made of three units of D and one unit of F. C is composed of three units of B, one unit of D, and four units of E. D is made of one unit of E. Item C has a lead time of one week; items A, B, E, and F have two-week lead times; and item D has a lead time of three weeks. Lot-for-lot (L4L) lot sizing is used for items C, E, and F; lots of size 20, 40, and 160 are used for items A, B, and D, respectively. Items A, B, D, and E have on-hand (beginning) inventories of 5, 10, 100, and 100, respectively; all other items have zero begin ning inventories. We are scheduled to receive 10 units of A in Week 3, 20 units of B in Week 7, 60 units of E in Week 2, and 40 units of F in Week 5; there are no other scheduled receipts. If 20 units of A are required in Week 10, use the low-level-coded product structure tree to find the necessary planned order releases for all components. (See note prior to Problem 3.)

7. (This problem is intended as a very simple exercise to go from the aggregate plan to the master schedule to the MRP.) Gigamemory Storage Devices, Inc., produces CD-ROMs (Read Only Memory) and WORMs (Write Once Read Many) for the computer market. Aggregate demand for the WORMs for the next two quarters are 2100 units and 2700 units. Assume that the demand is distributed evenly for each month of the quarter.

There are two models of the WORM: an internal model and an external model. The drive assemblies in both are the same but the electronics and housing are different. Demand is higher for the external model and currently is 70 percent of the aggregate demand.

The bill of materials and the lead times follow. One drive assembly and one electronic and housing unit go into each WORM.

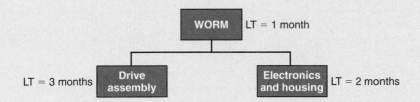

The MRP system is run monthly. Currently, 200 external WORMs and 100 internal WORMs are in stock. Also in stock are 250 drive assemblies, 50 internal electronic and housing units, and 125 external electronic and housing units.

Problem: Show the aggregate plan, the master production schedule, and the full MRP with the gross and net requirements and planned order releases. (Assume a lot-for-lot ordering policy.)

8. Product A is an end item and is made from two units of B and four of C. B is made of three units of D and two of E. C is made of two units of F and two of E.

A has a lead time of one week. B, C, and E have lead times of two weeks, and D and F have lead times of three weeks. Currently, there are no units of inventory on hand.

   a. Draw the product structure tree.

   b. If 100 units of A are required in Week 10, develop the MRP planning schedule, specifying when items are to be ordered and received. (Assume a lot-for-lot ordering policy.)

9. Product A consists of two units of subassembly B, three units of C, and one unit of D. B is composed of four units of E and three units of F. C is made of two units of H and three units of D. H is made of five units of E and two units of G.

   a. Construct a simple product structure tree.

   b. Construct a product structure tree using low-level coding.

   c. Construct an indented bill of materials.

   d. To produce 100 units of A, determine the numbers of units of B, C, D, E, F, G, and H are required. (Assume a lot-for-lot ordering policy.)

10. Teepee Products, Inc. produces two AM/FM cassette players for automobiles. Both radio/cassette units are identical, but the mounting hardware and finish trim differ. The standard model fits intermediate- and full-size cars, and the sports model fits small sports cars.

Teepee Products handles its production in the following way. The chassis (radio/ cassette unit) is assembled in Mexico and has a manufacturing lead time of two weeks. The mounting hardware is purchased from a sheet steel company and has a three-week lead time. The finish trim is purchased from a Taiwan electronics company with offices in Los Angeles as prepackaged units consisting of knobs and various trim pieces. Trim packages have a two-week lead time. Final assembly time may be disregarded, since adding the trim package and mounting are performed by the customer.

Teepee Products supplies wholesalers and retailers, who place specific orders for both models up to eight weeks in advance. These orders, together with enough additional units to satisfy the small number of individual sales, are summarized in the following demand schedule:

	Week							
	1	2	3	4	5	6	7	8
Standard model				300				400
Sports model					200			100

There are currently 50 radio/cassette units on hand but no trim packages or mounting hardware.

Prepare a material requirements plan to meet the demand schedule exactly. Specify the gross and net requirements, on-hand amounts, and the planned order releases and receipts for each period for the cassette/radio chassis, the standard trim and sports car model trim, and the standard mounting hardware and the sports car mounting hardware.

11. Brown and Brown Electronics manufactures a line of digital audiotape players. Although there are differences among the various products, there are a number of common parts within each player. The product structure, showing the number of each item required, lead times, and the current inventory on hand for the parts and components, follows:

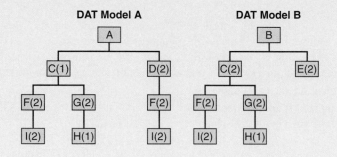

	Number Currently in Stock	Lead Time (weeks)
DAT Model A	30	1
DAT Model B	50	2
Subassembly C	75	1
Subassembly D	80	2
Subassembly E	100	1
Part F	150	1
Part G	40	1
Raw material H	200	2
Raw material I	300	2

Brown and Brown created a forecast that it plans to use as its master production schedule, producing exactly to schedule. Part of the MPS shows a demand for 700 units of Model A and 1200 units of Model B in Week 10.

Develop an MRP schedule to meet that demand.

Case 1   Nichols Company

This particular December day seemed bleak to Joe Williams, president of Nichols Company (NCO). He sat in his office watching the dying embers of his fireplace, hoping to clear his mind. Suddenly there came a tapping by someone gently rapping, rapping at his office door. "Another headache," he muttered, "tapping at my office door. Only that and nothing more."*

The intruder was Barney Thompson, director of marketing. "A major account has just cancelled a large purchase of A units because we are back ordered on tubing. This can't continue. My sales force is out beating the bushes for customers and our production manager can't provide the product."

For the past several months, operations at NCO have been unsteady. Inventory levels have been too high, while at the same time there have been stockouts. This resulted in many late deliveries, complaints, and cancellations. To compound the problem, overtime was excessive.

History

Nichols Company was started by Joe Williams and Peter Schaap, both with MBAs from the University of Lloydminster. Much has happened since Williams and Schaap formed the company. Schaap has left the company and is working in real estate development in Queensland, Australia. Under the direction of Williams, NCO has diversified to include a number of other products.

*With apologies to E.A.P

NCO currently has 355 full-time employees directly involved in manufacturing its three primary products, A, B, and C. Final assembly takes place in a converted warehouse adjacent to NCO's main plant.

The Meeting

Williams called a meeting the next day to get input into the problems facing NCO and to lay the groundwork for some solutions. Attending the meeting, besides himself and Barney Thompson, were Yuri Volkov of production and inventory control, Trevor Hansen of purchasing, and Nadia Jergeas of accounting.

The meeting lasted all morning. Participation was vocal and intense.

Volkov said, "The forecasts that marketing sends us are always way off. We are constantly having to expedite one product or another to meet current demand. This runs up our overtime."

Thompson said, "Production tries to run too lean. We need a larger inventory of finished goods. If I had the merchandise, my salespeople could sell 20 percent more product."

Jergeas said, "No way! Our inventory is already uncomfortably high. We can't afford the holding costs, not to mention how fast technology changes around here causing even more inventory, much of it obsolete."

Case Exhibit 1

Bills of Materials for Products A, B, and C

Product A		Product B		Product C		
.A		.B		.C		
.D(4)		.F(2)		.G(2)		
	.I(3)	.G(3)				.I(2)
.E(1)		.I(2)		.H(1)		
.F(4)						

Case Exhibit 2

Work Centre Routings for Products and Components

Item	Work Centre Number	Standard Time (hours per unit)
Product A	1	0.20
	4	0.10
Product B	2	0.30
	4	0.08
Product C	3	0.10
	4	0.05
Component D	1	0.15
	4	0.10
Component E	2	0.15
	4	0.05
Component F	2	0.15
	3	0.20
Component G	1	0.30
	2	0.10
Component H	1	0.05
	3	0.10

Case Exhibit 3

Inventory Levels and Lead Times for Each Item on the Bill of Material at the Beginning of Week 1

Product/Component	On Hand (units)	Lead Time (weeks)
Product A	100	1
Product B	200	1
Product C	175	1
Component D	200	1
Component E	195	1
Component F	120	1
Component G	200	1
Component H	200	1
I (raw material)	300	1

Hansen said, "The only way I can meet our stringent cost requirements is to buy in volume."

At the end of the meeting, Williams had lots of input but no specific plan. What do you think he should do?

Use Case Exhibits 1–4 showing relevant data to answer the specific questions at the end of the case.

Case Exhibit 4

Forecasted Demand for Weeks 4–27			
Week	Product A	Product B	Product C
1			
2			
3			
4	1500	2200	1200
5	1700	2100	1400
6	1150	1900	1000
7	1100	1800	1500
8	1000	1800	1400
9	1100	1600	1100
10	1400	1600	1800
11	1400	1700	1700
12	1700	1700	1300
13	1700	1700	1700
14	1800	1700	1700
15	1900	1900	1500
16	2200	2300	2300
17	2000	2300	2300
18	1700	2100	2000
19	1600	1900	1700
20	1400	1800	1800
21	1100	1800	2200
22	1000	1900	1900
23	1400	1700	2400
24	1400	1700	2400
25	1500	1700	2600
26	1600	1800	2400
27	1500	1900	2500

Questions

Use Excel (or another spreadsheet if you prefer) to solve the Nichols Company case.

Simplifying assumption: To get the program started, some time is needed at the beginning because MRP backloads the system. For simplicity, assume that the forecasts (and therefore demands) are zero for Periods 1 through 3. Also assume that the starting inventory specified in Case Exhibit 3 is available from Week 1. For the master production schedule, use only the end Items A, B, and C.

To modify production quantities, adjust only Products A, B, and C. Do not adjust the quantities of D, E, F, G, H, and I. These should be linked so that changes in A, B, and C automatically adjust them.

	Capacity	Cost
Work centre 1	6000 hours available	$20 per hour
Work centre 2	4500 hours available	$25 per hour
Work centre 3	2400 hours available	$35 per hour
Work centre 4	1200 hours available	$65 per hour

Inventory carrying cost

End items A, B, and C	$2.00 per unit
Components D, E, F, G, and H	$1.50 per unit
Raw material I	$1.00 per unit

Back-order cost

End items A, B, and C	$20 per unit per week
Components D, E, F, G, and H	$14 per unit per week
Raw material I	$8 per unit per week

1. Disregarding machine-centre limitations, develop an MRP schedule and also capacity profiles for the four machine centres.

2. Work centre capacities and costs follow. Repeat Question 1 creating a *feasible* schedule (within the capacities of the machine centres) and compute the relevant costs. Do this by adjusting the MPS only. Try to minimize the total cost of operation for the 27 weeks.

3. Suppose end items had to be ordered in multiples of 100 units, components in multiples of 500 units, and raw materials in multiples of 1000 units. How would this change your schedule?

Case 2 — Merdeka Gas Grills: Implementing MRP

In the case at the end of Chapter 15 (Case 1), you were introduced to the Merdeka company. As mentioned, they manufacture premium gas grills for the North American market. Each of these gas grills requires over 30 separate components. You may also recall that Merdeka used an integrated business system (ERP) software package to manage their purchasing, sales, inventory and production management, and accounting functions. Assume that the ERP software has MRP embedded in it.

Question:

1. Should every item be controlled using an MRP system? What types of items might you want to manage using the MRP system? Why? What type of items might you not want to manage using the MRP system? Why not?

2. Would you keep safety stock separately for each part? For example, if subassembly C consisted of components A and B, would you have safety stocks for A, B, and C?

3. What characteristics of an item used by Merdeka would make it ideal for a JIT system? For an EOQ system?

This case was written for classroom discussion by Brent Snider and Jaydeep Balakrishnan of the Haskayne School of Business at the University of Calgary. It is based on a real situation.

Appendix A: Areas of the Standard Normal Distribution

z	.00	.01	.02	.03	.04	.05	.06	.07	.08	.09
0.0	.0000	.0040	.0080	.0120	.0160	.0199	.0239	.0279	.0319	.0359
0.1	.0398	.0438	.0478	.0517	.0557	.0596	.0636	.0675	.0714	.0753
0.2	.0793	.0832	.0871	.0910	.0948	.0987	.1026	.1064	.1103	.1141
0.3	.1179	.1217	.1255	.1293	.1331	.1368	.1406	.1443	.1480	.1517
0.4	.1554	.1591	.1628	.1664	.1700	.1736	.1772	.1808	.1844	.1879
0.5	.1915	.1950	.1985	.2019	.2054	.2088	.2123	.2157	.2190	.2224
0.6	.2257	.2291	.2324	.2357	.2389	.2422	.2454	.2486	.2517	.2549
0.7	.2580	.2611	.2642	.2673	.2703	.2734	.2764	.2794	.2823	.2852
0.8	.2881	.2910	.2939	.2967	.2995	.3023	.3051	.3078	.3106	.3133
0.9	.3159	.3186	.3212	.3238	.3264	.3289	.3315	.3340	.3365	.3389
1.0	.3413	.3438	.3461	.3485	.3508	.3531	.3554	.3577	.3599	.3621
1.1	.3643	.3665	.3686	.3708	.3729	.3749	.3770	.3790	.3810	.3830
1.2	.3849	.3869	.3888	.3907	.3925	.3944	.3962	.3980	.3997	.4015
1.3	.4032	.4049	.4066	.4082	.4099	.4115	.4131	.4147	.4162	.4177
1.4	.4192	.4207	.4222	.4236	.4251	.4265	.4279	.4292	.4306	.4319
1.5	.4332	.4345	.4357	.4370	.4382	.4394	.4406	.4418	.4429	.4441
1.6	.4452	.4463	.4474	.4484	.4495	.4505	.4515	.4525	.4535	.4545
1.7	.4554	.4564	.4573	.4582	.4591	.4599	.4608	.4616	.4625	.4633
1.8	.4641	.4649	.4656	.4664	.4671	.4678	.4686	.4693	.4699	.4706
1.9	.4713	.4719	.4726	.4732	.4738	.4744	.4750	.4756	.4761	.4767
2.0	.4772	.4778	.4783	.4788	.4793	.4798	.4803	.4808	.4812	.4817
2.1	.4821	.4826	.4830	.4834	.4838	.4842	.4846	.4850	.4854	.4857
2.2	.4861	.4864	.4868	.4871	.4875	.4878	.4881	.4884	.4887	.4890
2.3	.4893	.4896	.4898	.4901	.4904	.4906	.4909	.4911	.4913	.4916
2.4	.4918	.4920	.4922	.4925	.4927	.4929	.4931	.4932	.4934	.4936
2.5	.4938	.4940	.4941	.4943	.4945	.4946	.4948	.4949	.4951	.4952
2.6	.4953	.4955	.4956	.4957	.4959	.4960	.4961	.4962	.4963	.4964
2.7	.4965	.4966	.4967	.4968	.4969	.4970	.4971	.4972	.4973	.4974
2.8	.4974	.4975	.4976	.4977	.4977	.4978	.4979	.4979	.4980	.4981
2.9	.4981	.4982	.4982	.4983	.4984	.4984	.4985	.4985	.4986	.4986
3.0	.4987	.4987	.4987	.4988	.4988	.4989	.4989	.4989	.4990	.4990

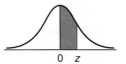

An entry in the table represents the proportion under the shaded curve that is between $z = 0$ and a positive value of z. Areas for negative values of z are obtained by symmetry.

Source: Paul G. Hoel, *Elementary Statistics* (New York: John Wiley & Sons, 1960), p. 240.

Appendix B: Areas of the Cumulative Standard Normal Distribution

Table 1

Areas under the Standardized Normal Curve from $-\infty$ to $-z$

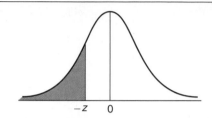

.09	.08	.07	.06	.05	.04	.03	.02	.01	.00	z
.0002	.0003	.0003	.0003	.0003	.0003	.0003	.0003	.0003	.0003	−3.4
.0003	.0004	.0004	.0004	.0004	.0004	.0004	.0005	.0005	.0005	−3.3
.0005	.0005	.0005	.0006	.0006	.0006	.0006	.0006	.0007	.0007	−3.2
.0007	.0007	.0008	.0008	.0008	.0008	.0009	.0009	.0009	.0010	−3.1
.0010	.0010	.0011	.0011	.0011	.0012	.0012	.0013	.0013	.0013	−3.0
.0014	.0014	.0015	.0015	.0016	.0016	.0017	.0018	.0018	.0019	−2.9
.0019	.0020	.0021	.0021	.0022	.0023	.0023	.0024	.0025	.0026	−2.8
.0026	.0027	.0028	.0029	.0030	.0031	.0032	.0033	.0034	.0035	−2.7
.0036	.0037	.0038	.0039	.0040	.0041	.0043	.0044	.0045	.0047	−2.6
.0048	.0049	.0051	.0052	.0054	.0055	.0057	.0059	.0060	.0062	−2.5
.0064	.0066	.0068	.0069	.0071	.0073	.0075	.0078	.0080	.0082	−2.4
.0084	.0087	.0089	.0091	.0094	.0096	.0099	.0102	.0104	.0107	−2.3
.0110	.0113	.0116	.0119	.0122	.0125	.0129	.0132	.0136	.0139	−2.2
.0143	.0146	.0150	.0154	.0158	.0162	.0166	.0170	.0174	.0179	−2.1
.0183	.0188	.0192	.0197	.0202	.0207	.0212	.0217	.0222	.0228	−2.0
.0233	.0239	.0244	.0250	.0256	.0262	.0268	.0274	.0281	.0287	−1.9
.0294	.0301	.0307	.0314	.0322	.0329	.0336	.0344	.0351	.0359	−1.8
.0367	.0375	.0384	.0392	.0401	.0409	.0418	.0427	.0436	.0446	−1.7
.0455	.0465	.0475	.0485	.0495	.0505	.0516	.0526	.0537	.0548	−1.6
.0559	.0571	.0582	.0594	.0606	.0618	.0630	.0643	.0655	.0668	−1.5
.0681	.0694	.0708	.0721	.0735	.0749	.0764	.0778	.0793	.0808	−1.4
.0823	.0838	.0853	.0869	.0885	.0901	.0918	.0934	.0951	.0968	−1.3
.0985	.1003	.1020	.1038	.1056	.1075	.1093	.1112	.1131	.1151	−1.2
.1170	.1190	.1210	.1230	.1251	.1271	.1292	.1314	.1335	.1357	−1.1
.1379	.1401	.1423	.1446	.1469	.1492	.1515	.1539	.1562	.1587	−1.0
.1611	.1635	.1660	.1685	.1711	.1736	.1762	.1788	.1814	.1841	−0.9
.1867	.1894	.1922	.1949	.1977	.2005	.2033	.2061	.2090	.2119	−0.8
.2148	.2177	.2206	.2236	.2266	.2296	.2327	.2358	.2389	.2420	−0.7
.2451	.2483	.2514	.2546	.2578	.2611	.2643	.2676	.2709	.2743	−0.6
.2776	.2810	.2843	.2877	.2912	.2946	.2981	.3015	.3050	.3085	−0.5
.3121	.3156	.3192	.3228	.3264	.3300	.3336	.3372	.3409	.3446	−0.4
.3483	.3520	.3557	.3594	.3632	.3669	.3707	.3745	.3783	.3821	−0.3
.3859	.3897	.3936	.3974	.4013	.4052	.4090	.4129	.4168	.4207	−0.2
.4247	.4286	.4325	.4364	.4404	.4443	.4483	.4522	.4562	.4602	−0.1
.4641	.4681	.4721	.4761	.4801	.4840	.4880	.4920	.4960	.5000	−0.0

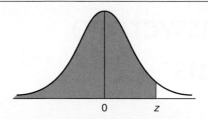

Table 2

Areas under the Standardized Normal Curve from −∞ to +z

z	.00	.01	.02	.03	.04	.05	.06	.07	.08	.09
.0	.5000	.5040	.5080	.5120	.5160	.5199	.5239	.5279	.5319	.5359
.1	.5398	.5438	.5478	.5517	.5557	.5596	.5636	.5675	.5714	.5753
.2	.5793	.5832	.5871	.5910	.5948	.5987	.6026	.6064	.6103	.6141
.3	.6179	.6217	.6255	.6293	.6331	.6368	.6406	.6443	.6480	.6517
.4	.6554	.6591	.6628	.6664	.6700	.6736	.6772	.6808	.6844	.6879
.5	.6915	.6950	.6985	.7019	.7054	.7088	.7123	.7157	.7190	.7224
.6	.7257	.7291	.7324	.7357	.7389	.7422	.7454	.7486	.7517	.7549
.7	.7580	.7611	.7642	.7673	.7703	.7734	.7764	.7794	.7823	.7852
.8	.7881	.7910	.7939	.7967	.7995	.8023	.8051	.8078	.8106	.8133
.9	.8159	.8186	.8212	.8238	.8264	.8289	.8315	.8340	.8365	.8389
1.0	.8413	.8438	.8461	.8485	.8508	.8531	.8554	.8577	.8599	.8621
1.1	.8643	.8665	.8686	.8708	.8729	.8749	.8770	.8790	.8810	.8830
1.2	.8849	.8869	.8888	.8907	.8925	.8944	.8962	.8980	.8997	.9015
1.3	.9032	.9049	.9066	.9082	.9099	.9115	.9131	.9147	.9162	.9177
1.4	.9192	.9207	.9222	.9236	.9251	.9265	.9279	.9292	.9306	.9319
1.5	.9332	.9345	.9357	.9370	.9382	.9394	.9406	.9418	.9429	.9441
1.6	.9452	.9463	.9474	.9484	.9495	.9505	.9515	.9525	.9535	.9545
1.7	.9554	.9564	.9573	.9582	.9591	.9599	.9608	.9616	.9625	.9633
1.8	.9641	.9649	.9656	.9664	.9671	.9678	.9686	.9693	.9699	.9706
1.9	.9713	.9719	.9726	.9732	.9738	.9744	.9750	.9756	.9761	.9767
2.0	.9772	.9778	.9783	.9788	.9793	.9798	.9803	.9808	.9812	.9817
2.1	.9821	.9826	.9830	.9834	.9838	.9842	.9846	.9850	.9854	.9857
2.2	.9861	.9864	.9868	.9871	.9875	.9878	.9881	.9884	.9887	.9890
2.3	.9893	.9896	.9898	.9901	.9904	.9906	.9909	.9911	.9913	.9916
2.4	.9918	.9920	.9922	.9925	.9927	.9929	.9931	.9932	.9934	.9936
2.5	.9938	.9940	.9941	.9943	.9945	.9946	.9948	.9949	.9951	.9952
2.6	.9953	.9955	.9956	.9957	.9959	.9960	.9961	.9962	.9963	.9964
2.7	.9965	.9966	.9967	.9968	.9969	.9970	.9971	.9972	.9973	.9974
2.8	.9974	.9975	.9976	.9977	.9977	.9978	.9979	.9979	.9980	.9981
2.9	.9981	.9982	.9982	.9983	.9984	.9984	.9985	.9985	.9986	.9986
3.0	.9987	.9987	.9987	.9988	.9988	.9989	.9989	.9989	.9990	.9990
3.1	.9990	.9991	.9991	.9991	.9991	.9992	.9992	.9992	.9993	.9993
3.2	.9993	.9993	.9994	.9994	.9994	.9994	.9994	.9995	.9995	.9995
3.3	.9995	.9995	.9995	.9996	.9996	.9996	.9996	.9996	.9996	.9997
3.4	.9997	.9997	.9997	.9997	.9997	.9997	.9997	.9997	.9997	.9998

Appendix C: Answers to Selected Problems

Chapter 4

1. *b.* A–C–D–E–G.

    c. 26 weeks.

    d. 6 weeks (15 – 9).

8. *a.* Critical path is A–C–D–F–G.

    b.

Day	Cost	Activity
First	$1,000	A
Second	1,200	C
Third	1,500	D (or F)
Fourth	1,500	F (or D)
	$5,200	

Supplement 5

1. *a.* 1.65 minutes.

    b. 1.90 (minutes rounded).

    c. $94.86.

5. *a.* $NT = .9286$ minute/part.

    b. $ST = 1.0679$ minute/part.

    c. Daily output = 449.50.
    Day's wages = $44.49.

Web Supplement 5

2. *a.*

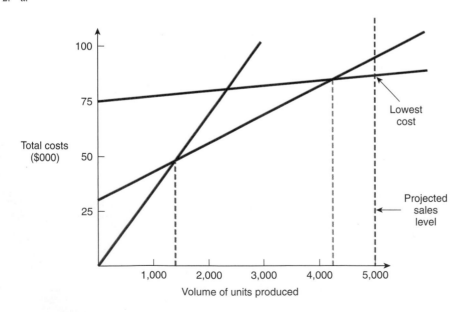

b. Break-even between Alternatives 1 and 2:

$$32x = 30,000 + 12x$$
$$20x = 30,000$$
$$x = 1,500 \text{ units}$$

Break-even between Alternatives 2 and 3:

$$30,000 + 12x = 75,000 + 2x$$
$$10x = 45,000$$
$$x = 4,500 \text{ units}$$

c. Based on lowest total costs, the company should choose Alternative 3, which is to invest the $75,000 in fixed costs and use unskilled labor.

7. The straight-line depreciation method yields a 15.9 percent return. The sum-of-the-years' digits yields a 17.1 percent return. Thus, neither method of depreciation will provide the minimum 20 percent return.

Supplement 6

1. *a.* $C_{pk} = .889$.

    b. $C_{pk} = 1.11$.

    The process is capable but needs to adjust mean downward to achieve 100 percent perfect quality.

2. *a.* $p = .067$.
    UCL = .194.
    LCL = 0.

b. Stop the process. There is wide variation and two are out of limits.

Chapter 8

1. Output/day: 24B + 24D.
   Process times: 12 min./B and 8 min./D.
   BB/DDD BB BB/DDD repetitively.

2. *a.* 27 seconds.

   b. 7 stations.

   c. 78.3 percent.

   d. Reduce cycle time to 25 seconds and work 8½ minutes overtime.

4. $44,500.

Chapter 9

2. *a.* 15.

   b. 14.3.

   c. 13.4.

   d. $Y = a + bX = 10.8 + .77X.$

   e. $Y = 10.8 + .77(7) = 16.2.$

9. MAD = 58.3
   TS = −6
   Model is poor at giving a good forecast.

Supplement 10

1. $\bar{t}_s$ = 4.125 minutes.
   $\bar{n}_j$ = 4.05 cars.
   $\bar{n}_s$ = 4.95 cars.

2. *4 spaces:* Stand busy 67.2 percent
   5 spaces: Stand busy 69.6 percent
   6 spaces: Stand busy 71.15 percent
   7 spaces: Stand busy 72.22 percent
   8 spaces: Net loss = $160;
   7 spaces should be leased.

Chapter 11

1.

Car	Priority
C	First
A	Tie for second
B	Tie for second

6. Johnson's method: E, A, B, D, C.

Chapter 14

1. Total cost = $413,600.

4. Ending inventory = safety stock.
   Inventory cost includes forecast and safety stock.
   Shortage cost is only based on the forecast.
   Total cost = $413,750.

Chapter 15

1. TC = $24,254.50.
   Q at 200 is the optimum order size.

6. TC = $56,370.
   1,000 at a time.

7. *a.* A (4, 13, 18), B (2, 5, 8, 10, 11, 14, 16), C (remainder).

   b. Classify as A.

14.

Transportation Costs	Carrying Costs
TC = $450,000.00 = $530,547.95	$80,547.95
Cost per tire: $5.305479	
Total cost: $40.30548	

Continue buying from current supplier at $40.00 per tire delivered.

Chapter 16

2.

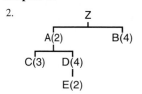

9. *c.* .A

   .B(2)

   .E(4)

   .F(3)

   .C(3)

   .D(3)

   .H(2)

   .E(5)

   .G(2)

   .D(1)

   d.

Level 0	100 units of A
Level 1	200 units of B
	300 units of C
Level 2	600 units of F
	600 units of H
	1000 units of D
Level 3	3800 units of E
	1200 units of G

Photo Credits

Bibliography

Chapter 1

Ammeson, Jane. "When in Rome." *Northwest Airlines World Traveler* (March 1993).

Canfor Corporation. www.canfor.com

Chase, Richard B., and David A. Garvin. "The Service Factory." *Harvard Business Review* 67, no. 4 (July–August 1989): 61–69.

Chase, Richard B., F. Robert Jacobs, and Nicholas J. Aquilano. *Operations Management for Competitive Advantage*, 10th ed. New York: Irwin McGraw Hill, 2004.

Chase, Richard B., and Eric L. Prentis: "Operations Management: A Field Rediscovered." *Journal of Management* 13, no. 2 (October 1987): 351–366.

"Consultant News." cited in *The Economist* (March 22, 1997): 40.

Demers, Julie. "NAFTA: Free Trade or Trade Dispute." *The New Canadian Magazine* (May/June 2003): 37–41.

Domtar Inc. www.domtar.com

Duclos, Leslie K., Samia M. Siha, and Rhonda R. Lummus. "JIT in Services: A Review of Current Practices and Future Directions for Research." *International Journal of Service Industry Management* 6, no. 5 (1995): 36–52.

Epcor. www.epcor.com

Finning International Inc. www.finning.com

Flaherty, M. Therese. *Global Operations Management*. New York: McGraw-Hill, 1996.

Fleming, Charles and Thomas Kamm. "AXA's CEO Set to Push Synergies." *The Wall Street Journal*, May 3, 2000.

"Fortis Buys Belize Stake." *The Globe and Mail,* January 29, 2001, B13.

Fortis Inc. www.fortis.ca

Greene, Constance. *Eli Whitney and the Birth of American Technology*. Boston: Little, Brown and Company, 1956.

Hammonds, K. H., and M. Roman. "Itching to Get onto the Factory Floor." *Business Week* (October 14, 1991).

Holusha, John. "Ford Thinks Green for Historic River Rouge Plant," *The New York Times*, November 26, 2000, p. 11. 7.

Kanavi, Shivanand. "New Steel in an Old Bottle." *Business India* (July 23, 2001): 54–60.

Levitt, Theodore. "Production-Line Approach to Service." *Harvard Business Review* 50, no. 5 (September–October 1972): 41–52.

Levitt, Theodore. "The Industrialization of Service." *Harvard Business Review* 54, no. 5 (September–October 1976): 63–74.

McMillan, Charles J. "Production Planning in Japan." *Journal of General Management* 8, no. 4 (1984): 44–71.

Narayandas, Das and V. Kasturi Rangan, "Dell Computer Corporation," Harvard Business School case No. 9-596-058, revised September, 1996.

Peters, Tom, and KQED Golden Gate Productions. *The Power of Excellence: The Forgotten Customer*. Jack Hilton Productions, Video Publishing House, Inc., 1987.

Pomfret, Richard. *The Economic Development of Canada*. Toronto, Ontario: Methuen, 1981.

Porter, Michael E. and the Monitor Company. *Canada at the Crossroads: The New Reality of a New Competitive Environment. A Report to the Business Council on National Issues and the Minister of Supply and Services.* Ottawa: Business Council on National Issues, 1991, pg. 4.

Potash Corp. www.potashcorp.com

"Potash Corp. Acquires 26% of Arab Potash." *The Globe and Mail*, October 17, 2003, B16.

Robertson, Heather. *Driving Force: The McLaughlin Family and the Age of the Car.* Toronto, Ontario: McClelland and Stewart, 1995.

Serwer, Andy. "Dell Does Domination," *Fortune* (January 21, 2002): 71–75.

Shah, Jennifer Baljko. "Dell Writes the Book On Efficiency—Processes Focus On Understanding Where Supply, Demand Diverge," *Ebn* (December 17, 2001): 32.

Skinner, Wickham. "Manufacturing— Missing Link in Corporate Strategy." *Harvard Business Review* (May–June 1969) 136–145.

Skinner, Wickham. "The Focused Factory." *Harvard Business Review* (May–June 1974): 113–121.

Balakrishnan, Jaydeep; Janice Eliasson and Timothy R.C. Sweet. "Factors Affecting the Evolution of Manufacturing in Canada: An Historical Perspective" forthcoming in the Journal of Operations Management.

Wylie, Peter. "Indigenous Technological Adaptation in Canadian Manufacturing, 1900–1929." *Canadian Journal of Economics*, 23, no. 4 (1990): 856–872.

Chapter 2

Anderson, M. "Case Study: Sobeys Inc." *National Post Business* (September 2003): 30–36.

Cara Operations Limited. www.cara.com

Chase, R.B., and D.A. Garvin. "The Service Factory." *Harvard Business Review*, 67, no. 4 (July–August 1989): 61–69.

Chase, Richard B., F. Robert Jacobs, and Nicholas J. Aquilano. *Operations Management for Competitive Advantage*, 10th ed. New York: Irwin McGraw Hill, 2004.

Davidow, W.H., and B. Uttal. "Service Companies: Focus or Falter." *Harvard Business Review* 67, no. 4 (July–August 1989): 77–85.

Davis, Stan, and Christopher Meyer. *Blur: The Speed of Change in the Connected Economy*. New York: Ernst & Young Center for Business Innovation, Warner Books, 1998.

DiGiacomo, Gordon. Case Study: *Dofasco's Healthy Lifestyles Program*. Canadian Labour and Business Centre, 2002. www.clbc.ca

Dofasco Inc. www.dofasco.com

Echikson, William, "The Mark of Zara." *Business Week* (May 29, 2000): 98–100.

English, Bob. "Canada Sales Set Record in '02." *Automotive News* (January 20, 2003): 42.

Folpe, Jane M. "Zara Has a Made-to-Order Plan for Success." *Fortune* (September 4, 2000): 80.

Garvin, D.A. *Operations Strategy: Text and Cases*. Englewood Cliffs, NJ: Prentice Hall, 1992.

Guilford, Dave. "GM's Smith Says Asia Is Key to Future." *Automotive News* (March 31, 2003): 26.

Hart, C.W.L. "The Power of the Unconditional Service Guarantees."

Harvard Business Review 66, no. 4 (July–August 1988): 56–62.

Hayes, Robert, and Gary Pisano. "Beyond World Class: The New Manufacturing Strategy." *Harvard Business Review* 72, no. 1 (January–February 1994): 77–86.

Hax, Arnaldo C., and Nicolas S. Majluf. *The Strategy Concept and Process.* Upper Saddle River, NJ: Prentice Hall, 1996.

Heller, Richard. "Galician Beauty." *Forbes* (May 28, 2001): 98.

Henkoff, Ronald. "Keeping Motorola on a Roll." *Fortune* (April 18, 1994): 67–78.

Higgins, James M. *The Management Challenge.* New York: MacMillan Publishing Company, 1994.

Hill, T. *Manufacturing Strategy: Text and Cases*, 3rd ed. Burr Ridge, IL: Irwin/McGraw-Hill, 2000.

Marchal, Laurent. *Space* (Winter 2003): 4.

Martin, Justin. "Give 'Em Exactly What They Want." *Fortune* (November 10, 1997): 238–285.

McGuire, Stryker. "Fast Fashion: How a Secretive Spanish Tycoon has Defied the PostWar Tide of Globalization, Bringing Factory Jobs from Latin America back to Europe." *Newsweek*, International Edition (September 17, 2001): 36.

Mintzberg, Henry, and J.B. Quinn. *The Strategy Process: Concepts and Contexts.* Englewood Cliffs, New Jersey: Prentice Hall, 1992.

Naisbitt, J., and P. Aburdene. *Megatrends 2000.* New York: William Morrow Co., 1990.

National Quality Institute. www.nqi.com

Nikiforuk, A. "Saint or Sinner." *Canadian Business* (May 13, 2002).

Normann, Richard, and Rafael Ramirez. "From Value Chain to Value Constellation: Designing Interactive Strategy." *Harvard Business Review* 71, no. 3 (July–August 1993): 65–77.

Porter, Michael. *Competitive Advantage: Creating and Sustaining Superior Performance.* New York: The Free Press, 1985.

Porter, Michael E., and Claas van der Linde. "Green and Competitive: Ending the Stalemate." *Harvard Business Review* 73, no. 5 (September–October 1995): 120–134.

Ramu, Priya. "Report on Canada's Steel Industry." *World at Six.* CBC Radio, August 6, 2003.

Skinner, C. Wickham. "Manufacturing—The Missing Link in Corporate Strategy." *Harvard Business Review* 47, no. 3 (May–June 1969): 136–145.

Skinner, C. Wickham. "The Focused Factory." *Harvard Business Review* 52, no. 3 (May–June 1974): 113–122.

Stalk Jr., George. "Time and Innovation." *Canadian Business Review* 20, no. 3 (Autumn 1993): 15–18.

Vandermerwe, S. *From Tin Soldiers to Russian Dolls: Creating Added Value Through Services.* Oxford, England: Butterworth-Heinemann, 1993.

Wise, Richard, and Peter Baumgartner. (1999). "Go Downstream: The New Profit Imperative in Manufacturing." *Harvard Business Review* 77, no. 5 (September–October 1999): 133–141.

"Zellers Is Stretched in Apparel-Rack War. Analysts Suggest Strategies for Battling Wal-Mart." *Winnipeg Free Press*, August 19, 2002, B6.

Chapter 3

Adler, Paul S., A. Mandelbaum, V. Nguyen, and E. Schwerer. "Getting the Most Out of Your Product Development Process." *Harvard Business Review* 74 (1996).

Albrecht, Karl, and Ron Zemke. *Service America! Doing Business in the New Economy.* Homewood, IL: Dow-Jones Irwin, 1985.

Blackburn, J.D. *Time-Based Competition: The Next Battleground in American Manufacturing.* Homewood, IL: Business One Irwin, 1991.

CAE, www.cae.com

Chase, Richard B. "The Customer Contact Approach to Services: Theoretical Bases and Practical Extensions." *Operations Research* 21, no. 4 (1981): 698–705.

Clark, Kim B. "Project Scope and Project Performance: The Effect of Parts Strategy and Supplier Involvement on Product Development." *Management Science* 35 (1989): 1247–1263.

Clark, Kim B., and Steven C. Wheelwright. *Managing New Product and Process Development: Text and Cases.* New York: The Free Press, 1993.

Cohen, Morris A., J. Eliashberg, and T. Ho. "New Product Development: The Performance and Time-to-Market Tradeoff." *Management Science* 42 (1996): 173–186.

Cooper, R.G. and E.J. Kleinschmidt, *Formal Processes for Managing New Products: The Industry Experience.* Hamilton, Ontario: McMaster University, 1991.

Davis, D.B. "Beating the Clock." *Electronic Business* (May 29, 1989): 21–29.

Dvorak, Phred. "Sony to Slash 20000 Jobs." *The Globe and Mail.* October 29, 2003, B8.

Ettlie, John E. "Integrated Design and New Product Success." *Journal of Operations Management* 15 (1997): 33–55.

EXFO Electro-Optical Engineering Inc. www.exfo.com

Fitzsimmons, James A., P. Kouvelis, and D.N. Mallick. "Design Strategy and Its Interface with Manufacturing and Marketing: A Conceptual Framework." *Journal of Operations Management* 10 (1991): 398–415.

Griffin, A. "Metrics for Measuring Product Development Cycle Time." *Journal of Product Innovation Management* 10 (1993): 112–125.

Gupta, A.K., and D.L. Wilemon. "Accelerating the Development of Technology-Based New Products." *California Management Review* 32 (1990): 24–44.

Hamilton, S. "New-Product Development and Manufacturing Competitiveness: A Hewlett-Packard Perspective." In *Time-Based Competition: The Next Battleground in American Manufacturing.* Ed. J. D. Blackburn. Chap. 8. Homewood, IL: Business One Irwin, 1991.

Heskett, James L. "Lessons from the Service Sector." *Harvard Business Review* (March–April 1987): 118–126.

Heskett, James L. *Managing in the Service Economy.* Cambridge, MA: Harvard University Press, 1986.

Johnson, Susan, Larry Menor, Aleta Roth, and Richard Chase. "Critical Evaluation of the New Service Development Process: Integrating Service Innovation and Service Design." In *New Service Development: Creating Memorable Experiences.* Chap. 1. Sage Publications, Thousand Oaks, CA 2000.

Judge, Paul C. "Customer Service EMC Corp." *Fast Company* (June 2001): 138–145.

Krishnan, V., S.D. Eppinger, and D.E. Whitnewy. "A Model-Based Framework to Overlap Product Development Activities." *Management Science* 43, no. 4 (1997): 437–451.

Kurawarwala, A.A., and H. Matsuo. "Cost of Delay in Time to Market and Capacity Restriction." Working Paper 93-01-02, University of Texas at Austin, April 15, 1993.

Kurawarwala, A.A., and H. Matsuo. "Forecasting and Inventory Management of Short Life-Cycle Products." *Operations Research* 44 (1996): 131–150.

Levitt, Theodore. "Production-Line Approach to Service." *Harvard Business Review* 50, no. 5 (September–October 1972): 41–52.

Lovelock, C.H. and R.F. Young. "Look to Customers to Increase Productivity."

Harvard Business Review 57, no. 2 (May–June 1979): 168–178.

O'Brian, James. "Survival of the Fittest." *Canadian Business* (September 2, 2003): 46–49.

Peters, Tom. *Quality!* Palo Alta, CA: TPG Communications, 1986.

Port, Otis. "The Best-Engineered Part Is No Part at All." *Business Week* (May 8, 1989): 150.

Schmenner, Roger W. "How Can Service Businesses Survive and Prosper?" *Sloan Management Review* 27, no. 3 (Spring 1986): 21–32.

Scott, Karyl. "EMC Shores Up Its Offense." *Information Week* (October 2, 2000): 72–82.

Stalk, G., Jr., and T.M. Hout. *Competing Against Time: How Time-Based Competition Is Reshaping Global Markets.* New York: The Free Press, 1990.

Swink, M., J. Sandvig, and V.A. Mabert. "Customizing Concurrent Engineering Processes: Five Case Studies." *Journal of Product Innovation Management* 13 (1996): 229–244.

Terwiesch, C., and C.H. Loch. "Measuring the Effectiveness of Overlapping Development Activities." *Management Science* 45 (1999): 455–465.

"UPS To Use Ballard Fuel Cell in Fleet." *The Globe and Mail,* May 20, 2003, B2.

Urban, G.L., T. Carter, S. Gaskin, and Z. Mucha. "Market Share Rewards to Pioneering Brands: An Empirical Analysis and Strategic Implications." *Management Science* 32 (1986): 645–659.

Visions (January 2001). www.pdma.org/visions/jan01

Wheelwright, S.C., and K.B. Clark. "Creating Project Plans to Focus Product Development." *Harvard Business Review* 70 (1992).

Wheelwright, S.C., and K.B. Clark. *Revolutionizing Product Development: Quantum Leaps in Speed, Efficiency and Quality.* New York: The Free Press, 1992.

Supplement 3

Brin, Dinah W. "Check it Out!" *The Middlesex News* (Framingham, MA), August 11, 1996.

Buckler, Grant. "Radio Frequency ID Is Key to Auto Industry." *The Globe and Mail*, October 9, 2003, B14.

Clemons J., and K. Unger. "Product Lifecycle Management: The Key Link Between the Internal and External Supply Chains." *MESA International Conference and Exposition* (June 2002).

Collier, David A. *Service Management: The Automation of Services.* Reston, VA: Reston Publishing, 1986.

Davis, Stan. *Future Perfect.* Reading, MA: Addison-Wesler, 1987.

Hackett, Gregory P. "Investing in Technology: The Service Sector Sinkhole?" *Sloan Management Review* (Winter 1990): 97–103.

Krell, E., "From Design to Destruction" (September 1, 2003). www.the manufacturer.com

Optimal Robotics Corp. www.opmr.com

Quinn, J.B. "Technology in Services: Past Myths and Future Challenges." In *Technology in Services: Policies for Growth, Trade and Employment.* Washington, DC: National Academy Press, 1988.

Quinn, J.B., and M.N. Bailey. "Information Technology: Increasing Productivity in Services." *Academy of Management Executive* 8, no. 3 (1994).

Roach, S.S. "Services Under Siege—The Restructuring Imperative." *Harvard Business Review* (September–October 1991).

Sequin, D. "Hawking Hogtown." *Canadian Business* (May 26, 2003).

Simpson, J., "The Truth About Atlantic Canada's Economy." *The Globe and Mail*, June 2, 2001, A17.

Zellner, Wendy. "Where the Net Delivers: Travel." *Business Week* (June 11, 2001): 142–144.

Chapter 4

Billows, Richard. "A Buyer's Guide to Selecting Project Management Software." Denver, CO: The Hampton Group, 2001. www.4pm.com/articles/selpmsw.html

Carrillo, Karen M. "Is It All a Project?" *InformationWeek* (February 23, 1998): 100–104.

Cleland, David (ed.). *Field Guide to Project Management.* New York: John Wiley & Sons, 1997.

Devaux, Stephen A. *Total Project Control: A Manager's Guide to Integrated Project Planning, Measuring, and Tracking.* New York: John Wiley & Sons, 1999.

EllisDon Corporation. www.ellisdon.com

Fox, Terry L., and J. Wayne Spence. "Tools of the Trade: A Survey of Project Management Tools." *Project Management Journal* (September 1998): 20–29.

Gay, Clifford F., and Erik W. Larson. *Project Management,* Burr Ridge, IL, Irwin/McGraw-Hill, 2000.

Gibb-Clark, M. "Ellis Don Rebuilds How It Does Business." *The Globe and Mail*, May 1, 2000, M1.

Gray, C.F. and E.W. Larson. *Project Management: The Managerial Process.* New York, NY: McGraw-Hill, 2000.

Holland, R.G. "The XV Olympic Winter Games: A Case Study in Project Management." *PM Network* (November 1989): 8–12.

Hughes, Michael William. "Why Projects Fail: The Effects of Ignoring the Obvious." *Industrial Engineering* 18, no. 4 (April 1986): 14–18.

Kerzner, Harold. *Applied Project Management: Best Practices on Implementation.* New York: John Wiley & Sons, 1999.

Meredith, Jack, and Samuel J. Mantel. *Project Management: A Managerial Approach.* New York: John Wiley & Sons, 1999.

Martin, Paula, and Karen Tate. *Getting Started in Project Management.* New York: John Wiley & Sons, 2001.

Shtub, A., J.F. Bard, and S. Globerson. *Project Management: Engineering, Technology and Implementation.* Englewood Cliffs, NJ: Prentice Hall, 1994.

Stevenson, William J., and Mehran Hojati. *Operations Management.* 2nd ed. Toronto: McGraw-Hill Ryerson, 2004.

Thamhain, Hans J. "Effective Leadership Style for Managing Project Teams." In *Handbook of Program and Project Management*, ed. P. C. Dinsmore. New York: AMACOM, 1992.

Thamhain, Hans J. "Managing Technologically Innovative Team Efforts Towards New Product Success." *Journal of Production Innovation Management* 7, no. 1 (March 1990).

Chapter 5

Albrecht, Karl, and Ron Zemke. *Service America! Doing Business in the New Economy.* Homewood, IL: Dow Jones-Irwin, 1985.

Anupindi, Ravi; Sunil Chopra; Sudhakar D. Deshmukh; Jan A. Van Mieghem; and Eitan Zemel. *Managing Business Process Flows.* Upper Saddle River, NJ: Prentice Hall, 1999.

Baglole, J. "How Canada Gets Jets Across the Sea—Satellite Cops Control Trans-Atlantic Air Traffic, Including U.S. Carriers." *Wall Street Journal,* May 9, 2002, A12.

Bernstein, A. "Quality Is Becoming Job One in the Office, Too." *Business Week* (April 29, 1991).

Bitran, Gabriel R., and Johannes Hoech. "The Humanization of Service: Respect at the Moment of Truth." *Sloan Management Review* (Winter 1990): 89–96.

Camp, Robert C. *Benchmarking: The Search for Industry Best Practices That Lead to Superior Performance.* Milwaukee, WI: American Society for Quality Control, Quality Press, 1989.

Camp, Robert C. *Business Process Benchmarking: Findings and Implementing Best Practices.* Milwaukee, WI: ASQC Quality Press, 1995.

Canadian Business. www.canadianbusiness.com

Chase, R.B. "The Customer Contact Approach to Services: Theoretical Bases and Practical Extensions." *Operations Research* 21, no. 4 (1981): 698–705.

Davenport, Thomas H. "Reengineering a Business Process." Harvard Business School Note 9-396-054. Harvard Business School Publishing, November 13, 1995.

Fitzsimmons, James A., and Mona J. Fitzsimmons. *Service Management: Operations, Strategy, and Information Technology.* 3rd ed. New York: McGraw-Hill/Irwin, 2000.

Hall, Gene; Jim Rosenthal; and Judy Wade. "How to Make Reengineering Really Work." *Harvard Business Review* (November–December 1993).

Hammer, Michael. "Reengineering Work: Don't Automate, Obliterate." *Harvard Business Review* (July–August 1990): 104–112.

Hammer, Michael, and James Champy. *Reengineering the Corporation: A Manifesto for Business Revolution.* New York: HarperCollins Books, 1993.

Harrington, H. James; Erik K.C. Esseling; and Harm Van Nimwegen. *Business Process Improvement Workbook.* New York: McGraw-Hill, 1997.

Levitt, Theodore. "Production-Line Approach to Service." *Harvard Business Review* 50, no. 5 (September–October 1972): 41–52.

Main, Jeremy. "How to Steal the Best Ideas Around." *Fortune* (October 19, 1992).

Manganelli, Raymond L., and Steven P. Raspa. "Why Reengineering Has Failed." *Management Review* (July 1995): 39–43.

National Quality Institute. www.nqi.ca

Ordonez, Jennifer. "Next! An Efficiency Drive: Fast-Food Lanes Are Getting Even Faster—Big Chains, Vying for Traffic, Use High-Tech Timers, 'Kitchen Choreography'—Mesclun in a Milkshake Cup?" *Wall Street Journal*, May 18, 2000, A1.

Port, Otis, and Geoffrey Smith. "Beg, Borrow and Benchmark." *Business Week* (November 30, 1992).

Roehm, Harper A., Donald Klein, and Joseph F. Castellano. "Springing to World-Class Manufacturing." *Management Accounting* (March 1991): 40–44.

Shostack, G. Lynn. "Designing Services That Deliver." *Harvard Business Review* 62, no. 1 (January–February 1984): 133–139.

Silent Witness Enterprises Ltd. www.silent witness.com

Smith, Fred, Letter to FedEx Management. October 7, 1996.

Stoddard, Donna, B. Sirkka, L. Jarvenpaa; and Michael Littlejohn. "The Reality of Business Reengineering: Pacific Bell's Centrex Provisioning Process." *California Management Review* 38, no. 3 (Spring 1996): 57–76.

Rikert, David C. *Burger King.* Harvard Business School Case No. 681–045. Boston: Harvard Business School, 1980.

Rikert, David C. *McDonald's Corporation.* Harvard Business School Case No. 681–044. Boston: Harvard Business School, 1980.

Womack, James P., and Daniel T. Jones. *Lean Thinking: Banish Waste and Create Wealth in Your Corporation.* New York: Simon and Shuster, 1996, p. 43.

Supplement 5

Adler, Paul S. "The Return of the Stopwatch." *The Economist* (January 23, 1993): 69.

Barnes, Frank C. "Principles of Motion Economy: Revisited, Reviewed and Restored." *Proceedings of the Southern Management Association Annual Meeting.* Atlanta, GA, 1983. 298.

Barnes, Ralph M. *Motion and Time Study: Design and Measurement of Work.* 8th ed. New York: John Wiley & Sons, 1980.

Bélanger, J. "Job Control and Productivity: New Evidence From Canada." *British Journal of Industrial Relations,* 27, no. 3 (1989): 347–364.

Joel-Cohen, S. *Abdominal and Vaginal Hysterectomy: New Techniques Based on Time and Motion Studies.* London: William Heinemann Medical Books, 1977.

Niebel, Benjamin W. *Motion and Time Study.* 7th ed. Homewood, IL: Richard D. Irwin, 1982.

Niles, John L. "To Increase Productivity, Audit the Old Incentive Plan." *Industrial Engineering* (January 1980): 20–23.

"The Promise of Reengineering." *Fortune* (May 3, 1993): 96.

Smalley, Harold E., and John Freeman. *Hospital Industrial Engineering.* New York: Reinhold, 1966. p. 409.

Chapter 6

Aeppel, Timothy. "Ex-Firestone Workers to Testify in Suit—Retired Decatur Employees Are Expected to Call Tire Inspection Rushed," *The Wall Street Journal*, August 23, 2000, p. A3.

Berry, L.L., V.A. Zeithaml, and A. Parasuraman. "Five Imperatives for Improving Service Quality." *Sloan Management Review*, no. 29 (Summer 1990): 29–38.

Bombardier Inc. www.bombardier.com.

Bounds, Greg, Lyle Yorks, Mel Adams, and Gipsie Rannet. *Total Quality Management: Towards the Emerging Paradigm.* New York: McGraw-Hill, 1994.

Brethour, Patrick. "Human Error Costs TransAlta $24-Million on Contract Bids." *The Globe and Mail*, June 4, 2003, B11.

Canadian Framework for Business Excellence. Toronto, Ontario: National Quality Institute, 2000.

Canadian Standards Association. www.csa.ca

"Compounders Define Goals." *Canadian Plastics* (October 1994): 6–11.

Corbett, Dan. "PEP in the City." *Excellence Magazine.* National Quality Institute. November 29, 2002.

Cox, Kevin. "High Liner Charts a Sea Change." *The Globe and Mail*, February 5, 1999, B25.

Crosby, Philip B. *Quality Is Free.* New York: New American Library, 1979.

Crosby, Philip B. *Quality Without Tears.* New York: McGraw-Hill, 1984.

DeFeo, Joseph A. "The Tip of the Iceberg." *Quality Progress* (May 2001): 29–37.

The Deming Prize Guide. Union of Japanese Scientists and Engineers (JUSE). Tokyo, Japan, 1999.

Deming, W. Edwards. *Quality, Productivity and Competitive Position.* Cambridge, MA: MIT Center for Advanced Engineering Study, 1982.

Demone, Henry. Address to Shareholders, May 1, 2003. www.highlinerfoods.com

Department of Trade and Industry, U.K. Government. http://www.dti.gov.uk

Dofasco Inc. www.dofasco.com

Eldridge, Earle, and Sara Nathan. "Data Point to Firestone Tires Made at Illinois Factory—Ford Analysis Shows High Rate of Warranty Claims from Decatur Plant," *USA Today*, August 14, 2000, p. B1.

Feigenbaum, A.V. *Total Quality Control.* 3rd ed. New York: McGraw-Hill, 1983.

Fogarty, Thomas A. "Retirees Cite Production Practices—Depositions in '92 Case May Shed Light on Recent Problems, but Company, Unions Dispute Claims," *USA Today*, August 24, 2000, p. B3.

Ford, Royal. "Ford Lightens Up on Explorer for Safety's Sake," *Boston Globe*, December 16, 2000, p. D1.

Fuchs, Edward. "Total Quality Management from the Future." *Quality Management Journal* (October 1993): 26–34.

Garvin, David. "Competing on the Eight Dimensions of Quality." *Harvard Business Review* (November–December 1987): 101–109.

Geyelin, Milo. "Theories Mount Regarding Root of Tire Defects," *The Wall Street Journal*, Aug. 23, 2000, p. B9.

Gitlow, Howard, Allan Oppenheim, and Rosa Oppenheim. *Quality Management: Tools and Methods for Improvement.* 2nd ed. Burr Ridge, IL: Irwin/McGraw-Hill, 1995.

Goetsch, David L., and Stanley B. Davis. *Introduction to Total Quality: Quality Management for Production, Processes and Services.* 2nd ed. Upper Saddle River, NJ: Prentice Hall, 1997.

Grant, N.G. and L.J. Taylor. "Case Study: Canada Awards for Excellence Trophy Recipient." *Excellence Magazine* (Winter 2001) www.nqi.com

Greenwald, John. "Tired of Each Other," *Time* (June 4, 2001): 51–52.

Harrold, Dave. "Designing for Six Sigma Capability." *Control Engineering,* January 1999.

Harry, Mikel J. "Abatement of Business Risk Is Key to Six Sigma: A Closer Link to Executive Thinking." *Quality Progress* (July 2000): 72–76.

Hart, Christopher W.L. "The Power of Unconditional Service Guarantees." *Harvard Business Review* (July–August 1988): 54–62.

Healey, James R., and Sara Nathan. "Could $1 Worth of Nylon Have Saved People's Lives? Experts: Caps on Steel Belts May Help Stop Shredded Tires," *USA Today*, August 9, 2000, p. B1.

Helwig, David. "City of Sault Ste. Marie on PEP Journey." *SooToday.com*, April 9, 2003.

Hoyer, R.W. and Brooke B.Y. Hoyer. "What Is Quality?" *Quality Progress* (July 2001): 53–62.

Huyink, David S., and Craig Westover. *ISO 9000: Motivating the People; Mastering the Process; Achieving Registration!* Burr Ridge, IL: Irwin Professional Publishing, 1994.

IMC Global Inc. www.imcglobal.com

Ishikawa, Kaoru. Translated by David J. Lu. *What Is Total Quality Control?—The Japanese Way.* Englewood Cliffs, NJ: Prentice Hall, 1985.

Jenkins, Holman W., Jr. "Tires and Torts: Parsing Out the Firestone Blame," *Asian Wall Street Journal*, May 31, 2001, p. 6.

Juran, Joseph M. *Juran on Quality by Design: The New Steps for Planning Quality in Goods and Services.* New York: The Free Press, 1992.

Kiley, David. "Ford Bites $3B Bullet to Replace Tires Firestone Viewed as Risk," *USA Today*, May 23, 2001, p. B1.

Legault, Michael. "Achieving Perfection." *Canadian Plastics* (November 1998): 35–37.

Lilly, Wayne. "Where Do CEOs Come from, Who Hired Them—and How Do They Stay at the Top? The Elusive Grail: Six Sigma Is But the Latest Twist in the Search for Management Excellence." *National Post*, November 1, 2001.

Lucas, James M. "The Essential Six Sigma," *Quality Progress* (January, 2002): 27–30.

Mahood, Casey. "National Sea Stock Hits 52-Week High, CEO Suggest Investors Eyeing Its New Product and Strategic Success." *The Globe and Mail*, April 29, 1997, B17.

Management Systems Standards: The Story So Far. Canada's Experience with ISO 9000, ISO 14000 and QS-9000. Ottawa, Ontario: Standards Council of Canada, 2000. 1.

March, A. "A Note on Quality: The Views of Deming, Juran and Crosby." Note No. 9-687-011. ICCH, Harvard Business School, Cambridge, MA, 1986.

"Mining Company Accelerates Return on Six Sigma with Action Workout." *Quality Digest* (March 2002). www.qualitydigest.com/mar02/html/apps1.html

National Quality Institute. www.nqi.com

Parasuraman, A., L.L. Berry, and V.A. Zeithaml. "SERVQUAL: A Multiple-Item Scale for Measuring Consumer Perceptions of Service Quality." Marketing Science Institute, Cambridge, MA, 1986.

Parasuraman, A., L.L. Berry, and V.A. Zeithaml. "Understanding, Measuring, and Improving Service Quality: Findings from a Multiphase Research Program." *Service Breakthroughs: Changing the Rules of the Game.* New York: The Free Press, 1989.

Peter, Joseph and Katie Davidman. "Aeronautical and Technical Services—Natural Resources Canada." Discussion Paper No. W/08, Canadian Policy Research Networks, 1999. www.cprn.org/cprn.html

Peters, Tom. *Thriving on Chaos.* New York: Knopf, 1987.

Peters, Tom and Robert H. Waterman Jr. *In Search of Excellence.* New York: Harper and Row, 1982.

Picard, André. "A Tiny Pinprick, a Deadly Outcome." *The Globe and Mail*, December 1, 2003, A1.

Powers, Stephen, and Timothy Aeppel. "Firestone Ties Accidents to Weight of Explorer—Ford Denies that Load Increased Significantly," *Asian Wall Street Journal*, December 23, 2000, p. 1.

QMI. www.qmi.com

Quality Imperative. VHS. Ottawa, Ontario: Stonehaven Productions, 1991.

Rabbitt, John T., and Peter A. Bergh. *The ISO 9000 Book: A Global Competitor's Guide to Compliance and Certification.* 2nd ed. White Plains, NY: Quality Resources, a division of the Kraus Organization Limited, 1994.

Rao, Ashok; L.P. Carr et al. *Total Quality Management: A Cross Functional Perspective.* New York: John Wiley & Sons, 1996.

Reichhold, F.F., and W.E. Sasser. "Zero Defections: Quality Comes to Services." *Harvard Business Review* 68, no. 5 (September–October 1990): 105–111.

Ross, Joel E. *Total Quality Management: Text, Cases and Readings.* Delray Beach, FL: St. Lucie Press, 1993.

Salegna, Gary, and Farzaneh Fazel. "Obstacles to Implementing Quality." *Quality Progress* (July 2000): 53–57.

"Six Sigma, Bombardier Style." *The Globe and Mail*, September 26, 1997, P64.

Standards Council of Canada. www.scc.ca

Stevenson, William J., and Mehran Hojati. *Operations Management*, 2nd Cdn ed. Toronto, Ontario: McGraw Hill Ryerson, 2004.

Stewart, John. "Quality Marks Life at St. Luke." *Mississauga News*, March 3, 2003.

Suncor Energy Inc. www.suncor.com

Swift, Allan. "Blackbelts in Problem Solving: Bombardier and Noranda Profit from the Six Sigma Management Technique." *The Ottawa Citizen*, March 2, 2000, B3.

Taguchi, G. *On-Line Quality Control During Production*. Tokyo: Japanese Standards Association, 1987.

Tanikawa, Miki. "Bridgestone President Admits Tire Quality-Control Problems," *The New York Times*, September 10, 2000, p. C12.

Tenner, A.R., and I.J. DeToro. *Total Quality Management*. Reading, MA: Addison-Wesley, 1992.

Turner, Joseph. "Is an Out-of-Spec Product Really Out of Spec?" *Quality Progress* (December 1990): 57–59.

Walton, Mary. *Deming Management at Work*. New York: Perigree Books, 1991.

West, John E. "Implementing ISO 9001:2000." *Quality Progress* (May 2001): 65–70.

Willis, Andrew. "High-Tech Broker Hurt by Misrouted Order." *The Globe and Mail*, June 5, 2003, B1.

Zaun, Todd. "Bridgestone's Net Fell 80% Last Year—Results Reflect Huge Loss at U.S. Unit After Firestone Recall—Outlook for Subsidiary's Sales and Bottom Line Remains Grim," *Asian Wall Street Journal*, February 23, 2001, p. 4.

Zeithaml, V.A.; L.L. Berry; and A. Parasuraman. "Communication and Control Processes in the Delivery of Service Quality." *Journal of Marketing* 52 (April 1988): 35–48.

Supplement 6

Aslup, Fred, and Ricky M. Watson. *Practical Statistical Process Control: A Tool for Quality Manufacturing*. New York: Van Nostrand Reinhold, 1993.

Dodge, H.F., and H.G. Romig. *Sampling Inspection Tables—Single and Double Sampling*. New York: John Wiley & Sons, 1959.

Grant, E.L., and R. Leavenworth. *Statistical Quality Control*. New York: McGraw-Hill, 1964.

Hradesky, John L. *Productivity and Quality Improvement: A Practical Guide to Implementing Statistical Process Control*. New York: McGraw-Hill, 1988.

Imai, Masaaki. *Kaizen: The Key to Japan's Competitive Success*. New York: McGraw-Hill, 1986. pp. 54–58.

Juran, J.M., and F.M. Gryna. *Quality Planning and Analysis*. 2nd ed. New York: McGraw-Hill, 1980.

Military Standard Sampling Procedures and Tables for Inspection by Attributes. MIL-STD-105D. Washington, DC: U.S. Government Printing Office, 1983.

Taguchi, G. *On-Line Quality Control during Production*. Tokyo: Japanese Standards Association, 1987.

Thompson, James R., and Jacek Koronacki. *Statistical Process Control for Quality Improvement*. New York: Chapman & Hall, 1993.

Turner, Joseph. "Is an Out-of-Spec Product Really Out of Spec?" *Quality Progress* (December 1990): 57–59.

Walker, Sharron. "Special Report: Quality in Education on the Move. Using Statistical Control to Improve Attendance." *Quality Digest* (1995). www.qualitydigest.com/rep/control.html

Wetherill, G. Barrie, and Don W. Brown. *Statistical Process Control: Theory and Practice*. New York: Chapman & Hall, 1991.

Wheeler, Donald J. *Understanding Variation: The Key to Managing Chaos*. Knoxville, TN: SPC Press, Inc., 1993.

Chapter 7

Blackburn, Joseph D. *Time-Based Competition: The Next Battle Ground in American Manufacturing*. Homewood, IL: Richard D. Irwin, 1991.

Chazin, Michael. "The New Global Reality." *Upholstery Design and Management* (December 2002): 12–16.

Exter, Thomas G. "The Next Step Is Called GIS." *American Demographics* 14, no. 5 (May 1992).

Francis, R.L.; L.F. McGinnis; and J.A. White. *Facility Layout and Location: An Analytical Approach*. 2nd ed. Englewood Cliffs, NJ: Prentice Hall, 1992.

Garrison, Sue. "After Push Came to Shove." *Business Geographics* (February 2000): 11.

Goerzen, Anthony. *Palliser Furniture*. London, Ontario: University of Western Ontario, Ivey Management Services, 1998.

Hayes, Robert H., and Steven C. Wheelwright. *Restoring Our Competitive Edge*. New York: John Wiley & Sons, 1984.

Heskitt, James L., W. Earl Sasser, Christopher W.L. Hart. *Service Breakthroughs*. New York: The Free Press, 1990.

Joerger, Albert; Stephen D. DeGloria; and Malcolm A. Noden. "Applying Geographic Information Systems." *Cornell Hotel and Restaurant Administration Quarterly* (August 1999).

Kirbyson, Geoff. "Winnipeg Furniture Maker Sets Up Shops in Asia, Europe." *Winnipeg Free Press*, August 11, 2000, B5.

Krajewski, L.J. and L.P Ritzman. *Operations Management*. Upper Saddle River, NJ: Prentice Hall, 2002. p. 336.

Lovelock, Christopher. "Strategies for Managing Capacity-Constrained Services." *Managing Services: Marketing, Operations Management and Human Resources*. 2nd ed. Englewood Cliffs, NJ: Prentice Hall, 1992.

MacCormack, Alan D.; Lawrence J. Newman III; and Donald B. Rosenfeld. "The New Dynamics of Global Manufacturing Site Location." *Sloan Management Review* (Summer 1994): 69–80.

Mackinnon, Mark. "Prayers Answered for Cape Bretoners: 900 to 1500 new Jobs." *The Globe and Mail,* March 31, 2000, A7.

Manivannan, S., and Dipak Chudhuri. "Computer-Aided Facility Layout Algorithm Generates Alternatives to Increase Firm's Productivity." *Industrial Engineering* (May 1984).

Maruca, Regina F.; Raymond Burke; Sir Richard Greenbury; and Robert A. Smith, "Retailing: Confronting the Challenges that Face Brick-and-Mortar Stores." *Harvard Business Review* (July–August 1999): 3–12.

Mason, Mark. "United States Direct Investment in Japan: Trends and Prospects." *California Management Review* (Fall 1992): 98–115.

McDonalds Corporation. www.mcdonalds.ca

Moon, Youngeme and Kerry Herman. *McDonald's in Russia: Managing a Crisis*. Cambridge, MA: Harvard Business School Publishing, 2003.

Moutinho, Luiz; Bruce Curry; and Fiona Davies. "Comparative Computer Approaches to Multi-Outlet Retail Site Location Decisions." *The Service Industries Journal* 13, no. 4 (October 1993): 201–220.

Oliver, S. "A Canadian Hospital Does Brisk Business in Rupture Repairs." *The Wall Street Journal*, February 7, 1978.

Palliser Furniture. www.palliser.com

"Palliser Looks for 400-M in Canadian Sales." *Winnipeg Free Press*, March 5, 1999, B12.

Reid, Hal. "Retailers Seek the Unique." *Business Geographics* 5, no. 2 (February 1997): 32–35.

Schonberger, R.J. "The Rationalization of Production." *Proceedings of the 50th Anniversary of the Academy of*

Management. Chicago: Academy of Management, 1986, pp. 64–70.

"Shouldice Hospital Limited." Harvard Business School Case 5-686-120. Boston: Harvard Business School, 1986.

Shouldice Hospital. http://www.shouldice.com/

Strazewski, Len. "Silicon Valley Holds Fertile Kids' Market." *Franchise Times* (February 1997).

Tayman, Jeff, and Louis Pol. "Retail Site Selection and Geographic Information Systems." *Journal of Applied Business Research* 11, no. 2, pp. 46–54.

Tuck, Simon. "Ottawa, Ontario Rev Up Interest in Auto Industry." *The Globe and Mail,* April 21, 2003, B1.

Wheelwright, Steven C., ed. *Capacity Planning and Facilities Choice: Course Module.* Boston: Harvard Business School, 1979.

York, Geoffrey. "Golden Arches Stretching over Russia." *The Globe and Mail,* December 3, 1998, B10

Chapter 8

Barbee, Gene. "The Best Laid Plans: Part II." *Bobbin,* 37, no. 12 (1996): 107–110.

Bitner, Mary Jo. "Servicescapes: The Impact of Physical Surroundings on Customers and Employees." *The Journal of Marketing* (April 1992): 57–71.

Buffa, E.S., G.C. Armour, and T.E. Vollmann. "Allocating Facilities with CRAFT." *Harvard Business Review,* 42, no. 2 (1964): 136–158.

Choobinch, F. "A Framework for the Design of Cellular Manufacturing Systems." *International Journal of Production Research* 26, no. 7 (1988): 1116–1172.

Dobyns, Lloyd, and Reuven Frank. *If Japan Can, Why Can't We?* New York: NBC-TV News Presentation, June 24, 1980.

Dodd, Leon, Jr. "The Team Approach to ISO 9000:2000 at Standard Aero Alliance." *The Journal for Quality and Participation* (Spring 2002): 41–44.

Fernberg, Patricia. "Focus on Facilities: Wood Gundy BCE Place." *Modern Office Technology* (March 1991): 53–54.

Francis, R.L.; L.F. McGinnis; and J.A. White. *Facility Layout and Location: An Analytical Approach.* 2nd ed. Englewood Cliffs, NJ: Prentice Hall, 1992.

Green, Timothy J., and Randall P. Sadowski. "A Review of Cellular Manufacturing Assumptions, Advantages and Design Techniques." *Journal of Operations Management* 4, no. 2 (February 1984): 85–97.

Hall, Robert W. "Time Prints and Takt Times." *Target: Innovation at Work* 14, no. 3 (1998): 6–13.

Hayes, Robert H., and Steven C. Wheelwright. *Restoring Our Competitive Edge.* New York: John Wiley & Sons, 1984.

Heskett, J.L.; W.E. Sasser Jr.; and C.W.L. Hart. *Service Breakthroughs: Changing the Rules of the Game.* New York: Free Press, 1990.

Hyer, Nancy Lea. "The Potential of Group Technology for U.S. Manufacturing." *Journal of Operations Management* 4, no. 3 (May 1984): 183–202.

Manivannan, S., and Dipak Chudhuri. "Computer-Aided Facility Layout Algorithm Generates Alternatives to Increase Firm's Productivity." *Industrial Engineering* (May 1984).

Mondon, Yasuhiro. *Toyota Production System: Practical Approach to Production Management.* Atlanta, GA: Industrial Engineering and Management Press, 1983.

Schonberger, Richard J. "The Rationalization of Production." *Proceedings of the 50th Anniversary of the Academy of Management.* Chicago: Academy of Management, 1986, pp. 64–70.

Soubry, Paul. Presentation by the President of Standard Aero to the APICS Winnipeg Chapter. April 18, 2002.

Standard Aero Limited. www.standard aero.com

Sumukadas, Narendar and Chris Piper, *Spartan Plastics.* London, Ontario: University of Western Ontario, Ivey Management Services, 1997.

Vannelli, Anthony, and K. Ravi Kumar. "A Method for Finding Minimal Bottleneck Cells for Grouping Part-Machine Families." *International Journal of Production Research* 24, no. 2 (1986): 387–400.

Chapter 9

Burruss, Jim, and Dorothy Kuettner. "Forecasting for Short-Lived Products: Hewlett Packard's Journey. *Journal of Business Forecasting* (Winter 2002–2003): 9–14.

Carlberg, Ralph. "BioComp Systems on Demand Forecasting." Biocomp Systems, Inc., Redmond, WA, 1996.

Davis, Mark M., and Paul D. Berger. "Sales Forecasting in a Retail Service Environment." *The Journal of Business Forecasting* (Winter 1989): 8–17.

DeLurgio, Stephen A. *Forecasting Principals and Applications.* Burr Ridge, IL: Irwin/McGraw-Hill, 1998.

Diebold, Francis X. *Elements of Forecasting.* Cincinnati, OH: Southwestern College Publishing, 1998.

Hample, Scott. "R U Ready for AI?" *Marketing Tools* (May 1, 1996): 60.

Hanke, John E., and Arthur G. Reitsch. *Business Forecasting.* 6th ed. Upper Saddle River, NJ: Prentice Hall,

Hueter, Jackie, and William Swart. "An Integrated Labor-Management System for Taco Bell." *Interfaces* 28, no. 1 (January–February 1998): 75–91.

Jain, Chaman L. "Explosion in the Forecasting Function in Corporate America." *The Journal of Business Forecasting* (Summer 1999): 2, 28.

Makridakis, Spyros; Steven C. Wheelwright; and Rob J. Hyndman. *Forecasting: Methods and Applications.* 3rd ed. New York: John Wiley & Sons, 1998.

McKaige, Walter. "Collaborating on the Supply Chain." *IIE Solutions* (March 2001): 34–36.

Moore, Karl; Robert Burbach; and Roger Heeler. "Using Neural Networks to Analyze Qualitative Data." *Marketing Research* 7 (January 1, 1995): 34.

Newbold, Paul, and Theodore Bos. *Introductory Business Forecasting.* Cincinnati, OH: South-Western Publishing Co., 1990.

Wilson, J. Holton, and Barry Keating. *Business Forecasting.* Burr Ridge, IL: Irwin/McGraw-Hill, 1998.

Xu, Weidong. "Long Range Planning for Call Centers at FedEx." *The Journal of Business Forecasting* (Winter 1999–2000): 6–11.

Yurkiewicz, Jack. "Forecasting Software Survey." *ORMS Today* (February 2003): 44–51. www.orms-today.com

Chapter 10

Bartfai, P., and J. Tomko. *Point Processes Queuing Problems.* New York: Elsevier-North Holland Publishing, 1981.

Bruell, Steven C. *Computational Algorithms for Closed Queuing Networks.* New York: Elsevier-North Holland Publishing, 1980.

Decter, Michael. "Now the Hard Part Begins: From Romanow to a Deal." *Winnipeg Free Press,* December 8, 2002, B4.

Katz, K.L.; B.M. Larson; and R.C. Larson. "Prescription for the Waiting Time Blues: Entertain, Enlighten, and Engage." *Sloan Management Review* 32, no. 2 (Winter 1991): 44–53.

"The Kirby Solution." *Winnipeg Free Press,* October 26, 2002, A16.

Gorney, Leonard. *Queuing Theory: A Solving Approach.* Princeton, NJ: Petrocelli, 1981.

Hillier, Frederick S., et al. *Queuing Tables and Graphs.* New York: Elsevier-North Holland Publishing, 1981.

Newell, Gordon F. *Applications of Queuing Theory.* New York: Chapman and Hall, 1982.

Oh, Sherry; Erhan Erkut; Dan Haight; and Armann Ingolfsson. "Managing Line-ups for Alberta's MRIs: An Overview of the Issues Facing Edmonton and Calgary's Health Regions." *45th Annual Meeting of the Canadian Operation Research Society*, Vancouver, B.C., June 2003.

Picard, André. "Patients Hail Proposals on Drug Costs, Waiting Lists." *The Globe and Mail*, October 26, 2002, A4.

Solomon, Susan L. *Simulation of Waiting Lines.* Englewood Cliffs, NJ: Prentice Hall, 1983.

Srivastava, H.M., and B.R. Kashyap. *Special Functions in Queuing Theory: And Related Stochastic Processes.* New York: Academic Press, 1982.

Vinrod, B., and T. Altiok. "Approximating Unreliable Queuing Networks under the Assumption of Exponentiality." *Journal of the Operational Research Society* (March 1986): 309–316.

Chapter 11

Abernathy, W.; N. Baloff; and J. Hershey. "The Nurse Staffing Problem: Issues and Prospects." *Sloan Management Review* 13, no. 1 (Fall 1971): 87–109.

Aubin, Jean. "Scheduling Ambulances." *Interfaces*, 22, no. 2 (1992): 1–10.

Baker, K.R. "The Effects of Input Control in a Simple Scheduling Model." *Journal of Operations Management* 4, no. 2 (February 1984): 99–112.

Barthlomew, Doug. "Scheduling for Complexity." *Industry Week* (April 2002): 81.

Conway, Richard W.; William L. Maxwell; and Louis W. Miller. *Theory of Scheduling.* Reading, MA: Addison-Wesley Publishing, 1967.

Eliashberg, Jehoshua, Sanjeev Swami, Charles B. Weinberg, and Berend Wierenga. "Implementing and Evaluating SilverScreener: A Marketing Management Support System for Movie Exhibitors." *Interfaces* 31, no. 3 (May–June 2001): S108–S127.

Falkenberg, Loren E., Thomas H. Stone, and Noa M. Meltz. *Human Resource Management in Canada.* Toronto, Ontario: Dryden, 1999.

Fogarty, Donald W.; John H. Blackstone Jr.; and Thomas R. Hoffmann. *Production and Inventory Management.* Cincinnati: South-Western Publishing, 1991.

Galt, Virginia. "Night Shifts Ready for Wake-Up Call," *The Globe and Mail*, December 13, 2003, B1.

Gershkoff, I. "Optimizing Flight Crew Schedules." *Interfaces* 19, no. 4 (July–August 1989): 29–43.

Goldratt, Eliyahu. *Theory of Constraints.* Great Barrington, MA: North River Press, 1990.

Johnson, S. M. "Optimal Two Stage and Three Stage Production Schedules with Setup Times Included." *Naval Logistics Quarterly* 1, no. 1 (March 1954): 61–68.

Konotopetz, Gyle. "Lessons of Lean Years Led to Leadership." *Business Edge* (January 2002).

Lanzenauer, Christoph von, Ervin Harbauer, Brian Johnston, David Shuttleworth. "RRSP Flood: LP to the Rescue." *Interfaces*, 17, no. 4 (1987): 27–33.

Matrikon Inc., www.matrikon.com

Mauriello, Jackie. "Overcoming the Obstacles to APS." *Integrated Solutions* (August 2001).

McFeely, D.J.; W.W. Simpson, III; J.C. Simons, Jr. "Scheduling to Achieve Multiple Criteria in an Air Force Depot CNC Machine Shop." *Production and Inventory Management Journal* (First Quarter, 1997): 72–78.

Moody, P.E. *Strategic Manufacturing: Dynamic New Directions for the 1990s.* Homewood, IL: Richard D. Irwin, 1990.

Morton and Pentico. *Heuristic Scheduling Systems.* New York: John Wiley & Sons, 1993, p. 28.

Richter, H. "Thirty Years of Airline Operations Research." *Interfaces* 19, no. 4 (July–August 1989): 3–9.

Trietsch, D. "Balancing Resource Criticalities for Optimal Economic Performance and Growth." MSIS, University of Auckland. Working paper no. 256 (2003).

Vollman, Thomas E.; William L. Berry; and D. Clay Whybark. *Manufacturing Planning and Control.* 4th ed. Burr Ridge, IL: Irwin, 1997.

Chapter 12

"Accurate Forecasts Mean Smooth Sailing for West Marine." *Frontline Solutions* (October 2003): 39.

APICS—The Educational Society for Resource Management. www.apics.org

Bowersox, Donald J., and David J. Closs. *Logistical Management: The Integrated Supply Chain Process.* New York: McGraw-Hill, 1996.

Careless, James. "Airlines Going On-line with 'Virtual Marketplace'", *The Globe and Mail*, July 31, 2003, B8.

"Celestica Commences Strategic Outsourcing Relationship with NEC." Newsrelease. www.celestica.com April 1, 2002.

Cinram International, Inc. www.cinram.com

Cooke, James Aaron. "The $30 Billion Promise." *Traffic Management* (December 1993): 57–61.

Coyle, J.J.; E.J. Bardi; and C. John Langley Jr. *The Management of Business Logistics.* 6th ed. Minneapolis/ St. Paul, MN: West, 1996.

Davis, Stanley M. *Future Perfect.* Reading, MA: Addison-Wesley, 1987.

Dixon, Lance E. *JITII®.* Bose Corporation.

Dorel Industries. www.dorel.com

Dvorak, Phred, "Sony to Slash 20000 jobs," *The Globe and Mail*, October 29, 2003, B8.

Fabey, Michael. "Time Is Money: Seamless Logistics Are in Demand." *World Trade* (July 1997): 53–54.

Fisher, M.L. "What Is the Right Supply Chain for Your Product." *Harvard Business Review* (March–April 1997): 105–116.

Friedland, J. and G. McWilliams. "Guadalajara Builds Itself as a High-Tech Hub." *The Wall Street Journal.* March 2, 2000, B12.

Greene, Heather. "Winging into the Wireless." *BusinessWeek e.biz* (February 18, 2002): EB 8–EB 9.

Guide, V.D.R., Jr. and L.N. Van Wassenhove. "The Reverse Supply Chain." *Harvard Business Review* (February 2002): 25.

Handfield, R.B. and E.L. Nichols, Jr. *Introduction to Supply Chain Management.* Upper Saddle River: NJ, Prentice Hall, 1999.

Heath-Rawlings, Jordan. "Cott Celebrates Record Growth." *The Globe and Mail.* July 21, 2003, B9.

Jenkins, David B. "Jenkins Leads EDI Effort." *Chain Store Age Executive* (March 1993): 147.

Johnson, M.E., and D.F. Pyke. "A Framework for Teaching Supply Chain Management." *Production and Operations Management*, 9, no. 1 (Spring 2000): 2–17.

Kaplan, R.S., and D.P. Norton. *The Balanced Scorecard: Translating Strategy into Action.* Boston: MA, Harvard Business School Press, 1996.

Kopczak, L.R. "Logistics Partnerships and Supply Chain Restructuring: Survey

Results from the U.S. Computer Industry." *Production and Operations Management*, 6, 3 (1997).

Lee, H.; V. Padmanabhan; and S. Whang. "The Bullwhip Effect in Supply Chains." *Sloan Management Review* (Spring 1997): 93–102.

Leenders, Michiel R., and Harold E. Fearon. *Purchasing and Supply Management.* 11th ed. Burr Ridge, IL: Irwin/McGraw-Hill, 1997.

Lima, Edvaldo Pereira. "VW's Revolutionary Idea." *Industry Week,* March 17, 1997.

Maloney, David. "Canadian Tire Rolls Out New DC." *Modern Materials Handling* (October 2002).

Matthews, Jan. "More, Better, Faster: Demand Forces Manufacturers to Outsource." *Silicon Valley North*, 3, no. 9 (June 2000).

McKaige, Walter. "Collaborating on the Supply Chain." *IIE Solutions* (March 2001): 34–36.

Peak Products Manufacturing. www.peakproducts.com

Pitts, Gordon. "Cott President Steering Firm to New Phase." *The Globe and Mail.* September 8, 2003, B3.

Pitts, Gordon. "Small Producer Cleans Up Making Soap." *The Globe and Mail.* July 28, 2003, B1.

Price, Candice. "Peak Performance for Peak Products." *World Trade* (December 2002): 38.

"Quick Response Grows." *Chain Store Age Executive* (May 1993): 158–159.

Reitman, Valerie. *The Wall Street Journal,* May 8, 1997, p. A1.

"Retailer to Suppliers: Track Inventory, Restock Shelves." *Information Week.* (July 2, 2001): 24.

Schemo, Diana J. "Is VW's New Plant Lean, or Just Mean?" *New York Times,* November 19, 1996.

Shapiro, Stanley; Wong, Kenneth; Perreault, William D. Jr.; McCarthy, E. Jerome; *Basic Marketing.* Toronto, Ontario: McGraw Hill Ryerson, 2002.

Supply Chain and Logistics Canada. www.infochain.org

Tibben-Lembke, R.S. "Life After Death: Reverse Logistics and the Product Life Cycle." *International Journal of Physical Distribution and Logistics Management,* 32, no. 3 (2002): 223–244.

Ticoll, David. "Electronics Recycling Needs Cleaning Up." *The Globe and Mail*, November 13, 2003, B13.

VanScoy, Kayte, "Recession-Proof Your Business," *Smart Business* (December 2001/January 2002): 84–88.

Warson, Albert. "More Firms Outsource Warehouses." *The Globe and Mail.* October 28, 2003, B13.

West Marine Inc. www.westmarine.com

Young, Doug. "SARS Could Hurt Christmas." *The Globe and Mail.* June 25, 2003, B9.

Chapter 13

Aeppel, Timothy. "Under the Glare of Recall, Tire Makers Are Giving New Technology a Spin." *The Wall Street Journal*, March 23, 2001, A1.

Ballou, M. "Wal-Mart Picks Progress Tools for Greater Flexibility." *Computerworld* 28, no. 9 (1994): 81.

Boudette, Neal. "BMW Steers Magna's Way." *The Wall Street Journal*, September 10, 2003.

Bowman, D. Jerry. "If You Don't Understand JIT, How Can You Implement It?" *Industrial Engineering* (February 1991): 38–39.

"Compounders Define Goals." *Canadian Plastics* (October 1994): 6–11.

Duclos, L.K.; S.M. Siha; and R.R. Lummus. "JIT in Services: A Review of Current Practices and Future Directions for Research." *International Journal of Service Industry Management* 6, no. 5 (1995): 36–52.

Feather, J.J., and K.F. Cross. "Workflow Analysis, Just-in-Time Techniques Simplify Administrative Process in Paperwork Operations." *Industrial Engineering* 20 (1988): 32–40.

Fucini, Joseph J., and Suzy Fucini. *Working for the Japanese.* New York: Free Press, 1990.

George, Michael, Dave Rowlands, Bill Kautle. *What Is Lean Six Sigma?* New York: McGraw Hill, 2004.

Gue, Frank. "Small Lot Principle Applies to Information." *APICS— The Performance Advantage* (August 1999): 56.

Hall, Robert. *Zero Inventories.* Homewood, IL: Dow Jones-Irwin, 1983.

Hall, Robert. *Attaining Manufacturing Excellence.* Homewood, IL: Dow Jones-Irwin, 1987.

Halverson, R. "Logistical Supremacy Secures the Base—But Will It Translate Abroad?" *Discount Store News* 33, no. 23 (1994): 107–108.

Inman, R. Anthony, and Satish Mehra. "The Transferability of Just-in-Time Concepts to American Small Business." *Interfaces* 20, no. 2 (March–April 1990): 30–37.

Jenson, R.L., J.W. Brackner, C.R. Skousen, "Low Fat Accounting," *CMA Magazine* (December–January 1997).

Keenan, Greg. "Ford Yanks Contract from Decoma." *The Globe and Mail*, December 20, 2003, B1.

Keenan, Greg. "Intier Wins 'Huge' GM Small-Car Contract." *The Globe and Mail*, May 8, 2002, B7.

Klein, Janice. "A Re-examination of Autonomy in Light of New Manufacturing Practices." *Human Relations* 43 (1990).

Lee, J. Y. "JIT Works for Services Too." *CMA Magazine* 6 (1990): 20–23.

Lee, Sang M. "Japanese Management and the 100 Yen Sushi House." *Operations Management Review* 1, no. 2 (Winter 1983): 45–48.

Liker, Jeffrey. *The Toyota Way: 14 Management Principles from the World's Greatest Manufacturer.* New York: McGraw Hill, 2003.

Magna International Inc. www.magna.com

Minahan, Tim. "JIT, A Process with Many Faces." *Purchasing* (September 4, 1997): 42–43.

Ohno, Taiichi. *Toyota Production System: Beyond Large-Scale Production.* Cambridge, MA: Productivity Press, 1988.

Ohno, Taiichi, and Setsuo Mito. *Just-in-Time for Today and Tomorrow.* Cambridge, MA: Productivity Press, 1988.

Rata, Ernest. "Saturn: Rising Star." *Purchasing* (September 9, 1993): 44–47.

Sabatini, Jeff. "The Chop House," *Automotive Manufacturing and Production* (September 2000): 68–71.

Schneider, B., and D.E. Bowen. *Winning the Service Game.* Cambridge, MA: Harvard Business School Press, 1995.

Schonberger, Richard J. *Japanese Productivity Techniques.* New York: Free Press, 1982.

Schonberger, Richard J. *World Class Manufacturing: The Lessons of Simplicity Applied.* New York: Free Press, 1986.

Schonberger, Richard J. *Building a Chain of Customers: Linking Business Functions to Create a World-Class Company.* New York: Free Press, 1989.

Shingo, Shigeo. *A Study of the Toyota Production System from an Industrial Engineering Viewpoint.* Cambridge, MA: Productivity Press, 1989.

Shirouzu, Norihiko. "Toyota Finds Success in Details." *The Globe and Mail*, March 15, 2001, B11.

Sohal, Amrik, and Keith Howard. "Trends in Materials Management." *International Journal of Production Distribution and Materials Management* 17, no. 5 (1987): 3–41.

Stalk, G., Jr. "Competing on Capabilities: The New Rules of Corporate Strategy."

Harvard Business Review 70, no. 2, pp. 57–69.

Suzaki, Kiyoshi. *The New Manufacturing Challenge: Techniques for Continuous Improvement.* New York: Free Press, 1987.

"Toyota Trumpets Quick Custom Delivery," *Calgary Herald*, August 8, 2003.

Wantuck, Kenneth A. "The Japanese Approach to Productivity." Southfield, MI: Bendix Corporation, 1983.

White, Richard E. "An Empirical Assessment of JIT in U.S. Manufacturers." *Production and Inventory Management Journal* 34, no. 2 (1993): 38–42.

Zipkin, Paul H. "Does Manufacturing Need a JIT Revolution?" *Harvard Business Review* (January–February 1991): 40–50.

Zoia, Dave. "Toyota's Production System Comes to Logistics." *Ward's Auto World* (September 1999): 77–78.

Chapter 14

Brown, Gerald, Joseph Keegan, Brian Vigus, and Kevin Wood. "The Kellogg Company Optimizes Production, Inventory, and Distribution." *Interfaces*, 31, no. 6 (2001): 1–14.

Geraghty, M.K., and Ernest Johnson. "Revenue Management Saves National Car Rental." *Interfaces* 27, no. 1 (January–February 1997): 107–127.

Johnson, Ernest. "1994 Trophy Award: National Car Rental Systems, Inc." *Scorecard: The Revenue Management Quarterly*, First Quarter 1995.

Kimes, Sheryl E. "Yield-Management: A Tool for Capacity-Constrained Service Firms." *Journal of Operations Management* 8, no. 4 (October 1989): 348–363.

McArthur, Keith. "WestJet Expanding into Charters." *The Globe and Mail*, August 21, 2003, B18.

Plossl, G.W. *Production and Inventory Control: Principles and Techniques.* 2nd ed. Englewood Cliffs, NJ: Prentice Hall, 1985.

Sasser, W.E.; R.P. Olsen; and D.D. Wyckoff. *Management of Service Operations.* Boston: Allyn & Bacon, 1978.

Silver, E.A., and R. Peterson. *Decision Systems for Inventory Management and Production Planning.* 2nd ed. New York: John Wiley & Sons, 1985.

Vollmann, T.E.; W.L. Berry; and D.C. Whybark. *Manufacturing Planning and Control Systems.* 3rd ed. Homewood, IL: Richard D. Irwin, 1992.

Chapter 15

Anderson, Edward J. "Testing Feasibility in a Lot Scheduling Problem." *Operations Research* (November–December 1990): 1079–1089.

Bernhard, Paul. "The Carrying Cost Paradox: How Do You Manage It?" *Industrial Engineering* (November 1989): 40–46.

Davis, Samuel G. "Scheduling Economic Lot Size Production Runs." *Management Science* (August 1990): 985–999.

Fitzsimmons, James, and Mona Fitzsimmons. *Service Management: Operations, Strategy, and Information Technology.* New York: McGraw-Hill, 1998.

Fogarty, Donald W.; John H. Blackstone; and Thomas R. Hoffmann. *Production and Inventory Management.* 2nd ed. Cincinnati, OH: South-Western Publishing, 1991.

Freeland, James R.; John P. Leschke; and Elliott N. Weiss. "Guidelines for Setup Reduction Programs to Achieve Zero Inventory." *Journal of Operations Management* (January 1990): 75–80.

Harris, Ford Whitman. "How Many Parts to Make at Once." *Operations Research* (November–December 1990): 947–951.

Heinzl, Mark. "Nortel Expects $19.2 Billion Quarterly Loss—Major Restructuring Is Set, Signaling a Turnaround for Telecoms Isn't Near." *The Wall Street Journal*, June 18, 2001, A3.

Kimes, Sheryl E. "Yield-Management: A Tool for Capacity-Constrained Service Firms." *Journal of Operations Management* 8, no. 4 (1989).

Lau, Hung-Hay. "The Role of Inventory Management in Canadian Economic Fluctuations." *Bank of Canada Review* (Spring 1996): 31–44.

Maloney, David. "Canadian Tire Rolls Out New DC." *Modern Materials Handling* (October 2002): 15–21.

Milner, Brian. "Tech Firms Fumble Through Great Inventory Screwup." *The Globe and Mail*, April 27, 2001, B15.

Silver, Edward A.; David F. Pyke, and Rien Peterson. *Inventory Management and Production Planning and Scheduling.* New York, NY: Wiley, 1998.

Teach, Edward. "The Great Inventory Correction." *CFO* (September 2001): 58–62.

Tersine, Richard J. *Principles of Inventory and Materials Management.* 3rd ed. New York: North-Holland, 1988.

Vollmann, T.E.; W.L. Berry; and D.C. Whybark. *Manufacturing Planning and Control Systems.* 3rd ed. Homewood, IL: Richard D. Irwin, 1992.

Weiss, Elliott N. "Lot Sizing Is Dead: Long Live Lot Sizing." *Production and Inventory Management Journal* (First Quarter 1990): 76–78.

Young, Jan B. *Modern Inventory Operations: Methods for Accuracy and Productivity.* New York: Van Nostrand Reinhold, 1991.

Chapter 16

Agilisys Inc. www.agilisys.com

Biggs, Joseph R., and Ellen J. Long. "Gaining the Competitive Edge with MRP/MRP II." *Management Accounting* (May 1988): 27–32.

Flapper, S.D.P.; G.J. Miltenburg; and J. Wijngaard. "Embedding JIT into MRP." *International Journal of Production Research* 29, no. 2 (1991): 329–341.

Goodrich, Thomas. "JIT & MRP Can Work Together." *Automation* (April 1989): 46–47.

Knight, Robert M. "Furniture Maker Uses MRP II to Cut Lead Time." *Computerworld* (June 8, 1992): 80.

Orlicky, Joseph. *Materials Requirements Planning.* New York: McGraw-Hill, 1975. (This is the classic book on MRP.)

Palmatier, George. *Sales and Operations Planning—An Executive Level Synopsis.* New London, NH: The Oliver Wight Companies.

Production and Inventory Management Journal and *APICS: The Performance Advantage.* Practitioner journals with numerous articles on MRP and MRP II. Many of these cite the difficulties and experiences of practitioners.

Silver, E.A. and H. Meal. "A Simple Modification to the EOQ for the Case of a Time Varying Demand." *Production and Inventory Management Journal* 10, no. 4 (1969): 52–65.

Sipper, Daniel, and Robert Bulfin. *Production Planning, Control and Integration.* New York: McGraw-Hill, 1997.

Staiti, Chris. "Customers Drive New Manufacturing Software." *Datamation* (November 15, 1993): 72.

"Supplier Slashes Inventory." www.manufacturingsystems.com. (October 1999).

Turbide, David A. *MRP+: The Adaptation, Enhancement and Application of MRP II.* New York: Industrial Press, 1993, p. 11.

Vollmann, Thomas E.; William L. Berry; and D. Clay Whybark. *Manufacturing Planning and Control Systems.* 4th ed. Burr Ridge, IL: Irwin, 1997.

Wescast Industries Inc. www.wescast.com

Wight, Oliver. *The Executive's Guide to Successful MRP II.* Williston, VT: Oliver Wight Limited Publications, 1982. pp. 6, 17.

Glossary

3PL (p. 433) When a company other than the customer or supplier provides logistics services.

5S (p. 468) A philosophy that aims for a clean and safe workplace.

ABC analysis (p. 546) Method for grouping inventory items by dollar volume to identify those items to be monitored closely.

acceptable quality level (AQL) (p. 228) Maximum percentage of defects that a company is willing to accept.

aggregate planning (p. 485) Process for determining most cost-effective way to match supply and demand over next 12–18 months.

aggregate planning strategies: (p. 489)

   pure strategy Either a chase strategy when production exactly matches demand or a level strategy when production remains constant over a specified number of time periods.

   mixed strategy Combination of chase and level strategies to match supply and demand.

agile manufacturing (p. 140) Ability of a manufacturing process to respond quickly to the demands of the customer.

agile manufacturing (p. 278) Ability of a manufacturing process to respond quickly to changes in the marketplace.

arrival rate (p. 369) Rate at which customers arrive into a service delivery system, usually expressed in terms of customers per hour.

assembly line balancing (p. 306) Assignment of tasks to workstations within a given cycle time and with minimum idle worker time.

asynchronous transactions (p. 82) Transactions in which there is a delay in time with respect to the communication between the parties involved.

backflush (p. 549) Calculating the consumption of component parts inventory periodically based on final product completion.

backlog (or stockout) (p. 487) The deficit in units that results when demand exceeds the number of units produced in a given time period.

back-of-the-house (p. 270) A service facility, or that part of the service

process, that does not come in contact with the customer.

benchmarking (p. 152) Comparision of a company's measures of performances with those of firms considered to be world class.

bill of materials (BOM) (p. 571) A list of subassemblies, components, and raw materials, and their respective quantities, required to produce specific end items.

bottleneck (p. 145) Stage or stages that limit the total output of a process.

bricks-and-mortar operation (p. 269) A front-of-the-house service that requires a physical structure to interact directly with the customer.

business process (p. 149) A set of sequential tasks or activities that cross functional boundaries and recognize their interdependence with other processes or business processes.

CAE criteria (p. 204) Criteria for assessing overall quality of an organization and determining the winner(s) of the CAE awards.

capacity (p. 138) Output of a process in a given time period.

capacity flexibility (p. 278) Ability to provide a wide range of products and volumes with short lead times.

capacity planning (p. 280) Determination of which level of capacity to operate at to meet customer demand in a cost-efficient manner.

capacity utilization (p. 139) Percentage of available capacity that is actually used.

capacity utilization (p. 372) Percentage of time a service station is busy serving a customer.

causal relationship forecasting (p. 331) Relating demand to an underlying factor other than time.

centre-of-gravity method (p. 273) A quantitative approach for determining the optimal location for a facility based upon minimizing total distribution costs.

competitive priorities (p. 30) How the operations function provides a firm with a specific competitive advantage.

competitive priorities (p. 32)

   cost Providing low-cost products.

   quality Providing high-quality products.

   delivery Providing products quickly.

   flexibility Providing a wide variety of products.

   service How products are delivered and supported.

computer-aided (or -assisted) design (CAD) (p. 78) Designing a product using a specially equipped computer.

computer-aided design and manufacturing system (CAD/CAM) (p. 78) Integration of design and production of a product through use of a computer.

computer-integrated manufacturing (CIM) (p. 78) Integration of all aspects of manufacturing through computer.

computer simulation (p. 380) Mimicking or duplicating the operation of a real system using a computer-based model to study the systems's characteristics.

concurrent engineering (p. 54) The simultaneous and coordinated efforts of all functional areas, which accelerates the time to market for new products.

conformance quality (p. 200) Defines how well the product is made with respect to its design specifications.

consignment inventories (p. 431) Inventories that are physically present in a firm's facility but that are still owned by the supplier.

content requirements (p. 263) Requirement that a percentage of a product must be made within a country for it to be sold there.

continuous improvement (p. 199) Concept that recognizes that quality improvement is a journey with no end and that there is a need to look continuously for new approaches for improving quality.

control limits (p. 231) Points on an acceptance sampling chart that distinguish between the accept and reject region(s). Also, points on a process control chart that distinguish between a process being in and out of control.

corporate strategy (p. 28) Overall strategy adopted by the parent corporation.

cost leadership (p. 29) Producing the lowest-cost products.

cost of detection/ appraisal (p. 196) Costs associated with the test and inspection of subassemblies and products after they have been made.

cost of failure (p. 196) Costs associated with the failure of a defective product.

cost of prevention (p. 196) Costs associated with the development of programs to prevent defectives from occurring in the first place.

cost of quality (p. 195) Framework for identifying quality components that are related to producing both high-quality products and low-quality products, with the goal of minimizing the total cost of quality.

CPM (critical path method) (p. 100) Project scheduling technique using deterministic activity times.

CRAFT (p. 301) Computerized relative allocation of facilities technique (CRAFT) performs intelligent pairwise exchanges of departments and locations.

crash costs (p. 113) Additional costs of an activity when time to complete it is shortened.

critical path (p. 103) Longest sequence of activities that determines the overall length of the project.

critical success factors (p. 40) The activities, conditions, or other deliverables that are necessary for the firm to achieve its business goals.

cycle counting (p. 549) A method of counting inventory in which different items are counted at different times.

dependent demand (p. 564) Demand for components that depend on end item demand.

design quality (p. 200) Specific characteristics of the product that determine its value in the marketplace.

differentiation (p. 29) Offering products that differ significantly from the competition.

disintermediation (p. 82) The elimination of intermediate steps or organizations.

disintermediation (p. 433) Trend to reduce many of the steps in the supply chain.

dispatching of orders (p. 389) Releasing of orders to the factory floor.

distinctive (core) competency (p. 40) An exceptional capability that creates a preference for a firm and its products or services in the market-place, enabling it to achieve a leadership position over time.

distribution requirements planning (DRP) (p. 584) The use of MRP logic in the planning of distribution inventories.

drum-buffer-rope scheduling (p. 398) A TOC scheduling method focusing on system constraints.

economic order quantity (EOQ) (p. 526) Optimal quantity to order, taking into consideration both the cost to carry inventory and the cost to order the item.

EDI (electronic data interchange) (p. 435) Direct link between a manufacturer's database and that of the vendor.

efficient consumer response (ECR) (p. 436) Strategy for bringing distributors, suppliers, and grocers together using bar-code scanning and EDI.

eliminate waste (p. 456) Eliminate everything not essential to production, including safety stocks, waiting times, and extra labour.

enterprise resource planning system (ERP) (p. 440) A fully integrated software system that links all of the major functional areas within an organization.

expediting (p. 389) Checking the progress of specific orders to ensure completion in a timely manner.

exponential smoothing (p. 338) Time-series forecasting technique that does not require large amounts of historical data.

exponential smoothing constant alpha (α) (p. 339) Value between 0 and 1 used in exponential smoothing to minimize the error between historical demand and respective forecasts.

external failure costs (p. 196) Costs associated with producing defective products that are delivered to the customer.

external setup (p. 464) Setup that can be done while the machine is in operation.

factor-rating systems (p. 271) A qualitative approach for evaluating alternative site locations.

fail-safing (p. 149) Designing a service process so as to make it error free or foolproof.

fixed-order-quantity model with usage (p. 528) Considers a supplier that will provide an order quantity over a period of time rather than all at once.

fixed-position layout (p. 301) The product, because of its size and/or weight, remains in one location and processes are brought to it.

flexible manufacturing system (FMS) (p. 78) Manufacturing facility that is automated to some extent and produces a wide variety of products.

flow pattern (p. 391) Routes that materials follow through a factory to make a product.

focused factories (p. 466) Groups of small plants, each highly specialized in the products they manufacture.

front-of-the-house (p. 271) A service facility, or that part of the service process, that interacts directly with the customer.

functional strategies (p. 30) Strategy developed by a function within an organization to support the business strategy.

Gantt Chart (p. 98) Graphical technique that shows the amount of time required for each activity and the sequence in which activities are to be performed.

Gantt chart (p. 403) Planning tool that plots activities on a time chart.

geographic information systems (GIS) (p. 266) Computer tool that assesses alternative locations for service operations.

global economy, global village, global landscape (p. 14) Terms used to describe how the world is becoming smaller and countries are becoming more dependent on each other.

granularity (p. 151) A term used to describe the level of detail that is used in analyzing a process.

group technology (p. 468) Clustering dissimilar machines and operations in one cell to manufacture one family of products.

group technology (G/T) or cellular layout (p. 300) Groups of dissimilar machines brought together in a work cell to perform tasks on a family of products that share common attributes.

high degree of customer contact (p. 66) Service operations that require a high percentage of customer contact time.

house of quality (p. 56) Part of the quality function deployment process that uses customer feedback for product design criteria.

hybrid process (p. 144) Multistage process that consists of more than one type of process.

inbound logistics (p. 422) The delivery of goods and services that are purchased from suppliers and/or their distributors.

industrial robots (p. 78) Programmable machines that can perform multiple functions.

input/output control (p. 402) Assuring the amount of work accepted does not exceed the capacity of the facility.

intermittent process (p. 61) Process that produces products in small lot sizes.

internal failure costs (p. 196) Costs associated with producing defective products that are identified prior to shipment.

internal setup (p. 464) Setup that can be done only when machine is not operating.

in-transit inventory costs (p. 533) Combination of transportation costs and carrying costs associated with delivery of products.

inventory on hand (p. 487) The surplus of units that results when production exceeds demand in a given time period.

inventory records file (p. 573) Computerized record-keeping system for the inventory status of all subassemblies, components, and raw materials.

islands of automation (p. 79) Automated factories or portions that include NC equipment, automated storage/retrieval systems, robots, and machining centres.

ISO 9000 series quality standards (p. 209) International set of standards for managing the processes that an organization uses to produce its goods and services.

ISO 14000 (p. 210) International set of standards for managing processes that an organization uses for environmental management.

Jidoka (p. 465) Japanese concept focusing on controlling the quality of a product at its source.

JIT (just-in-time) (p. 452) A coordinated approach that continuously reduces inventories while also improving quality.

job shop (p. 389) Organization whose layout is process-oriented (vs. product-oriented) and that produces items in small, customized batches.

Kaizen (p. 472) Kaizen is the Japanese term for continuous improvement.

Kanban pull system (p. 460) Manual, self-regulating system for controlling the flow of material. Workers produce product only when the Kanban ahead of them is empty, thereby creating a "pull" system through the factory.

keiretsu (p. 470) A Japanese term describing a network of companies that have close relationships with each other.

labour-limited systems (p. 391) Operations in which the capacity of the facility is determined by number of workers.

linear regression analysis (p. 349) Type of forecasting technique that assumes that the relationship between the dependent and independent variables is a straight line.

line-flow process (p. 61) Continuous process that produces high-volume, highly standardized products.

loading (p. 389) Allocating jobs to resources.

low degree of customer contact (p. 66) Service operations that require a low percentage of customer contact time.

machine-limited systems (p. 391) Operations in which the capacity of the facility is determined by number of machines.

machining centres (p. 77) Operations where machine tools are changed automatically as part of the process.

make-to-order system (p. 142) Process for making customized products to meet individual customer requirements.

make-to-stock system (p. 142) Process for making highly standardized products for finished goods inventory.

manufacturing resource planning (MRP II) (p. 582) Advanced MRP system that takes into consideration the equipment capacities and other resources associated with a manufacturing facility.

market segmentation (p. 30) Satisfying the needs of a particular market niche.

mass customization (p. 34) Providing high volume products that are individually customized to meet the specific needs of each customer.

master production schedule (p. 486) Short-term schedule of specific end product requirements for the next several quarters.

master production schedule (MPS) (p. 566) Production plan that specifies how many of, and when to build, each end item.

materials requirements planning (MRP) (p. 567) Determines the number of subassemblies, components, and raw materials required and their build dates to complete a given number of end products by a specific date.

mean absolute deviation (MAD) (p. 345) Average forecasting error based upon the absolute difference between the actual and forecast demands.

mean absolute percentage error (MAPE) (p. 348) The average absolute difference between the actual and forecast demands expressed as a percentage of the actual demand.

milestones (p. 94) Specific major events to be completed at certain times in the project.

mission (p. 28) A statement about the organization's business scope and methods of competing.

modular design (p. 58) Designing a product using standard components and subassemblies to produce customized products.

modularization (p. 142) Use of standard components and subassemblies to produce customized products.

moving assembly line (p. 21) A mass production line in which the product moves along the line while workers at sequential locations add value to the product.

multistage process (p. 144) Process that consists of more than one step.

neural networks (p. 349) A forecasting technique simulating human learning that develops complex relationships between model inputs and outputs.

new product development (NPD) process (p. 54) The method by which new products evolve from conceptualization through engineering to manufacturing and marketing.

new service development (NSD) process (p. 65) The method by which new services evolve from conceptualization through to marketing and delivery to the customer.

numerically controlled (NC) machines (p. 77) Manufacturing equipment that is directly controlled by a computer.

operating characteristic (OC) curves (p. 230) Curves that show the probability of accepting lots that contain different percentages of defectives.

operations management (p. 4) Management of the conversion process that transforms inputs such as raw material and labour into outputs in the form of finished goods and services.

operations strategy (p. 30) How the operations function contributes to competitive advantage.

order-qualifiers (p. 39) Minimum characteristics of a firm or its products to be considered as a source of purchase.

order-winners (p. 39) Characteristics of a firm that distinguish it from its competition so that it is selected as the source of purchase.

outbound logistics (p. 422) The delivery of goods and services that are sold to a firm's customers and/or its distributors.

PERT (program evaluation and review technique) (p. 100) Project scheduling technique using probabilistic activity times.

planning activities: (p. 484)

long-range planning Focuses on strategic issues relating to capacity, process selection, and plant location.

intermediate-range planning Focuses on tactical issues pertaining to aggregate workforce and material requirements for the coming year.

short-range planning Addresses day-to-day issues of scheduling workers to specific jobs at assigned work stations.

poka-yoke (p. 200) Simple devices, such as automatic shutoff valves or fixtures to orient parts, that prevent defects from being produced.

postponement (p. 435) Strategy in which standard components are carried and quick final assembly of the finished product is done only after receipt of customer order.

priority rules (p. 392) Criteria for determining the sequence or priority of jobs through a facility.

process (p. 136) Actual conversion of inputs to output.

process flow chart (p. 136) Schematic diagram describing a process.

process layout (p. 299) Similar operations are performed in a common or functional area, regardless of the product in which the parts are used.

process velocity (p. 141) Ratio of total throughput time for a product to the value-added time.

product layout (p. 300) Equipment/operations are located according to the progressive steps required to make the product.

product's specifications (p. 58) Output from the design activity that states all criteria for building a product.

production rate (p. 487) Capacity of output per unit of time (such as units per day or units per week).

productivity (p. 137) Efficiency of a process.

program (p. 94) Synonym for a project, although it also can consist of several interrelated projects.

project (p. 93) Series of related jobs or tasks focused on the completion of an overall objective.

project process (p. 60) Process that focuses on making one-of-a-kind products.

qualitative techniques (p. 331) Nonquantitative forecasting techniques based upon expert opinions and intuition. Typically used when there are no data available.

quality circles (p. 472) Groups of workers who meet to discuss their common area of interest and problems they are encountering.

quality dimensions (p. 189) Recognition that quality can be defined in many ways and that companies can use quality as a competitive advantage.

quality function deployment (QFD) (p. 56) Process for translating customer requirements into a product's design.

quality gurus (p. 192) Individuals who have been identified as making a significant contribution to improving the quality of goods and services.

quantity-discount model (p. 531) Addresses price discounts associated with minimum order quantities.

quasi-manufacturing operation (p. 271) A service firm's dedicated production and distribution facility that supplies its retail operations.

quick response (QR) programs (p. 436) Just-in-time replenishment system using bar-code scanning and EDI.

radio frequency identification (RFID) (p. 79) A system that uses radio waves to identify and track inventory.

reengineering (p. 155) Process of rethinking and restructuring an organization.

reorder point (ROP) (p. 527) The inventory level in units that, when reached, triggers a new order for the item.

rough-cut or resource capacity planning (p. 486) Determination that adequate production capacity and warehousing are available to meet demand.

safety stock (SS) (p. 530) Additional inventory carried in excess of expected demand to prevent stock outs.

scheduling (p. 388) The short-term planning and control of the transformation process.

scientific management (p. 20) Systematic approach to increasing worker productivity introduced by Fredrick W. Taylor.

service blueprint (p. 147) Process flow chart for services that includes the customer.

service rate (p. 371) Capacity of a service station, usually expressed in terms of customers per hour. The reciprocal of the service rate is the average time to serve a customer.

servicescape (p. 316) Describes the physical surroundings in a service operation that can affect a customer's perception of the service received.

shop-floor control (p. 400) Set of procedures for maintaining and communicating the status of orders and work centres.

simple moving average (p. 335) Average over a given number of time periods that is updated by replacing the date in the oldest period with those in the most recent period.

single-period inventory (newsboy) model (p. 538) Addresses items that are highly perishable from one period to the next.

Six Sigma (p. 202) A statistically based, structured methodology for identifying and eliminating causes of errors in a process.

slack time (p. 103) Amount of time an activity can be delayed without affecting the completion date of the overall project.

special economic zones (SEZ) (p. 265) Duty-free areas in a country established to attract foreign investment in the form of manufacturing facilities.

statistical process control (SPC) (p. 192) Methods, such as control charts, that signal shifts in a process that will likely lead to products and/or services not meeting customer requirements.

statistical process control (SPC) (p. 233) Statistical method for determining whether a particular process is in or out of control.

strategic business unit (SBU) (p. 28) Stand-alone business within a conglomerate that operates like an independent company.

supply chain (p. 422) The steps and the firms that perform these steps in the transformation of raw material into finished products bought by customers.

synchronous transactions (p. 82) Transactions that take place in real time without any time delays, usually between individuals.

Taguchi methods (p. 246) Statistical technique for identifying the cause(s) of process variation that reduces the number of tests that are necessary.

takt time (p. 306) The time interval between stations on an assembly line.

theory of constraints (TOC) (p. 398) Philosophy that focuses on system constraints for continuous improvement.

therbligs (p. 169) Basic units of measurement used in micromotion analysis.

throughput time (p. 306) The overall elapsed time from when the manufacture of a product is first begun to when that specific product is completed.

time–cost trade-off models (p. 113) Models that develop the relationship between direct project costs, indirect costs, and time to complete the project.

time-series analysis (p. 331) Analyzing data by time periods (for example, hours, days, weeks) to determine if trends or patterns occur.

time standard (p. 175) Established time for completing a job, used in determining labour costs associated with making a product.

time study (p. 173) Determination, with use of a stopwatch, of how long it takes to complete a task or set of tasks.

total quality management (TQM) (p. 198) Approach to integrating quality at all levels of an organization.

tracking signal (p. 346) Measure of error to determine if the forecast is staying within specified limits of the actual demand.

transformation process (p. 6) Actual conversion of inputs into outputs.

trend smoothing constant delta (δ) (p. 342) Value between 0 and 1 that is used in exponential smoothing when there is a trend.

types of data: (p. 227)
  attribute data Data that count items, such as the number of defective items on a sample.
  variable data Data that measure a particular product characteristic such as length or weight.

types of demand: (p. 522)
  independent demand Pertains to the requirements for end products.
  dependent demand Requirements for components and subassemblies that are directly dependent on the demand for the end products in which they are used.

types of inventory: (p. 520)
  raw material Vendor-supplied items that have not had any labour added.
  finished goods Completed products still in the possession of the firm.
  work-in-process (WIP) Items that have been partially processed but are still incomplete.

types of inventory systems: (p. 523)
  fixed-order-quantity System in which the order quantity remains constant but the time between orders varies.
  fixed-time-period System in which the time period between orders remains constant but the order quantity varies.

types of sampling errors: (p. 228)
  α error, Type I error, or producer's risk Occurs when a sample says parts are bad or the process is out of control when the opposite is true.
  β error, Type II error, or consumer's risk Occurs when a sample says parts are good or the process is in control when just the reverse is true.

unit life cycle costs (p. 59) The cost of each unit of the product over its entire life.

value chain (p. 17) Steps an organization requires to produce a good or a service regardless of where they are performed.

value stream mapping (VSM) (p. 145) Developing a flow chart to eliminate wasteful activities and improve the process.

vendor-managed inventories (VMI) (p. 433) Inventories in a firm's facility that are the responsibility of the supplier to maintain and replenish as necessary.

virtual enterprise (p. 18) Company whose boundaries are not clearly defined due to the integration of customers and suppliers.

vision (p. 28) A statement that provides long-term direction and motivation for the organization.

voice of the customer (p. 54) Customer feedback used in quality functional deployment process to determine product specifications.

weighted moving average (p. 337) Simple moving average in which weights are assigned to each time period in the average. The sum of all of the weights must equal one.

work breakdown structure (WBS) (p. 94) Method by which a project is divided into tasks and subtasks.

workforce level (p. 487) Number of workers required to provide a specified level of production.

work measurement (p. 172) Methodology used for establishing time standards.

work sampling (p. 175) Technique for estimating how workers allocate their time among various activities throughout a workday.

yield management (p. 502) Concept used in certain service operations that attempts to match supply and demand.

Name Index

Subject Index